COUNTRY, PARK, & CITY

The Architecture and Life of Calvert Vaux

FRANCIS R. KOWSKY

New York • Oxford

Oxford University Press

1998

Oxford University Press

Oxford   New York

Athens   Auckland   Bangkok   Bogota   Bombay   Buenos Aires
Calcutta   Cape Town   Dar es Salaam   Delhi   Florence   Hong Kong
Istanbul   Karachi   Kuala Lumpur   Madras   Madrid   Melbourne
Mexico City   Nairobi   Paris   Singapore   Taipei   Tokyo   Toronto   Warsaw

and associated companies in
Berlin   Ibadan

Published by Oxford University Press, Inc.
198 Madison Avenue, New York, New York 10016

Oxford is a registered trademark of Oxford University Press

Library of Congress Cataloging-in-Publication Data
Kowsky, Francis R., 1943–
Country, park, and city : the architecture and life
of Calvert Vaux / Francis R. Kowsky
p.   cm.
Includes bibliographical references and index.
ISBN 0-19-511495-7
1. Vaux, Calvert, 1824–1895.
2. Architects—United States—Biography.   I. Title.
NA737.V4K68   1997
720'.92—dc21   97-3780
[B]

Title page photograph: Calvert Vaux.
Courtesy of National Park Service,
Frederick Law Olmsted National Historic Site.

2 3 4 5 6 7 8 9

Printed in the United States of America
on acid-free paper

To Dennis Steadman Francis

PREFACE

I undertook to write this book because I admire the architecture and landscape designs of Calvert Vaux. Like many others, I have been especially grateful to him for the lovely bridges and other structures that grace the Central Park landscape. Beyond the borders of this extraordinary park, Vaux designed many fine High Victorian structures that fuse a spirit of Romanticism with functional organization of space. Indeed, his intellectual approach to design—his way of looking at a problem "comprehensively," paying attention to the larger context of a building or park—is an enduring lesson from his career. Vaux also endears himself to us as an idealist who believed that buildings and parks foremost were products of art. In the spirit of this conviction, he devoted himself to advancing the standing of the disciplines of architecture and landscape architecture when these professions were in their infancy. One must esteem a man who always stood ready to do battle in defense of his high ideals.

I have also enjoyed writing this book because I share Vaux's love for New York City and the magnificent landscape of the Hudson Valley. Truly, Vaux has guided me through a significant portion of the physical and cultural history of the metropolis and introduced me close-up to individuals who shaped the later phase of the so-called Hudson River School of American landscape painting. Furthermore, as a man with an active mind, Vaux took genuine interest in the best in the world around him. With considerable enthusiasm, he enjoyed many aspects of the abundant intellectual and cultural life that New York, for the first time in its history, had to offer.

A great deal has been written about Vaux's rightfully famous partner and friend, Frederick Law Olmsted, but comparatively little has appeared on Vaux. For this reason, I have endeavored to make this book an inclusive study of Vaux's career, life, and thought. Because no diaries or significant collections of personal papers survive, this task has led me to reconstruct much of his history from various sources, especially the Olmsted Papers at the Library of Congress and the diary of artist Jervis McEntee, Vaux's brother-in-law, in the Smithsonian

Institution's Archives of American Art. The diary of Alfred Janson Bloor, an assistant to Vaux, also provided valuable information about projects of the late 1850s and early 1860s, and the diary of Vaux's friend James H. Morse, an educator and writer, yielded insights into Vaux's later life. Both of these items are preserved in the New-York Historical Society, where Margaret Heilbrun, library director, offered special help with interpreting these texts. The society was one of several institutions where I conducted significant portions of my research. Others include the Library of Congress; the New York Public Library, which possesses in its Rare Books and Manuscripts Division a small collection of Vaux's papers; and the Buffalo and Erie County Public Library, an institution with a remarkable collection of nineteenth-century architectural journals.

Many individuals have generously helped me with this undertaking. I wish to acknowledge especially those whose contributions have aided me in the largest measure. These are Charles Beveridge, series editor of the Olmsted Papers, whose help with issues of fact and interpretation has been invaluable to me; David Schuyler, assistant editor of the Olmsted Papers, who has been especially helpful with Vaux's relation to A. J. Downing; Joy Kestenbaum, who has shared many items of importance from her wide knowledge of Vaux's career; Charles McLaughlin, editor in chief of the Olmsted Papers, who provided many useful research suggestions; Tiny Himmel, who helped especially with Vaux's early days in London; Elizabeth Blackmar, coauthor of the most thorough history of Central Park, who shared aspects of her research with me; Sarah Bradford Landau, who generously shared her wide knowledge of New York City's nineteenth-century architecture with me; Herbert Mitchell, who has kindly let me reproduce many images of Central Park from his extensive collection of stereo views; Paul Pasquarello, who has done much fine copy photography; William Loos, rare book librarian, Buffalo and Erie County Public Library, who helped me locate many useful items in that splendid institution; the late R. Steven Janke, who offered many valuable editorial suggestions; Marjorie Lord of the Inter-Library Loan Office at State University of New York (SUNY) College at Buffalo's Butler Library, who diligently searched out and obtained many items for me; Stephen Mangione, who provided excellent photographic services; and my wife, Hélène, whose many perceptive criticisms have improved the manuscript at every stage of its existence and whose constant attentiveness has been a great source of encouragement.

Others have shared with me their knowledge of particular Vaux projects or helped greatly to aid my research. These include J. Winthrop Aldrich, deputy commissioner for historic preservation, New York Office of Parks, Recreation and Historic Preservation (NYOPRHP); Mary Beth Betts, curator of architecture, New-York Historical Society; Kenneth R. Cobb, director, Municipal Archives, City of New York; Meg Crawford; Peter Dwyer; Russell A. Grills, director, Lorenzo Historic Site, NYOPRHP; Kenneth Hawkins; H. Morrison Heckscher, curator, American Decorative Arts, Metropolitan Museum of Art; Thomas Hubka; the late Thomas Kyle; Nancy W. Lacolla, director, Downing Park Planning Committee; Arlyn Levee; Arnold Lewis; Michael Lewis; Kenneth Lutter, landscape architect, Taconic Region, NYOPRHP; Margaret MacDonald, library clerk, SUNY College at Buffalo; Edyth McKitrick, archivist, Grace Church; Jacqueline R. McSwiggan, vice president and secretary, Bank of New York; W. Berkeley Mann, archivist, Sheppard Pratt Health System; Allen Marquart; Melodye Moore, director, Mills Mansion State Historic Site,

NYOPRHP; Louis V. Mills; Janet Myles; R. E. Niederer, superintendent, Hillside Cemetery, Middletown, New York; Austin O'Brien, NYOPRHP; Patricia M. O'Donnell; Kitty Oliver; Amelia Peck, assistant curator, American Decorative Arts, Metropolitan Museum of Art; Peter Pennoyer; Elizabeth Plewniak, library clerk, SUNY College at Buffalo; Carolyn Pitts, historian, National Park Service; Victor Remer, archivist, Children's Aid Society; Angela Reynolds, manuscripts researcher, Morris Library, Southern Illinois University; James Ryan, director, Olana State Historic Site, NYOPRHP; Janet St. Louis; Lilly Sent, librarian, SUNY College at Buffalo; Constantine Sidamon-Eristoff; Albert B. Southwick; Judith Doolin Spikes; Dorothy Lee Tatum; Sally S. Taylor; Lowell Thing; Tupper Thomas, Prospect Park administrator; the late Rex Wasserman, Prospect Park historian; and Karen Zukowski, Olana archivist. I wish also to acknowledge the National Endowment for the Humanities for awarding me a Fellowship for College Teachers and the State University of New York College at Buffalo for granting me a sabbatical leave to work on this book and for providing me with many other forms of support.

Finally, writing this book has stirred many fond memories of enjoyable visits to Vaux's works and lively discussions about the architect and his circle with the late Dennis Francis. Dennis, to whom this book is dedicated, was one of architectural history's most resourceful researchers and the first person to delve deeply into Vaux's career. Together, we covered a lot of ground.

Buffalo, New York　　　　　　　　　　　　　　　　　　　　　F. R. K.
October 1996

CONTENTS

COUNTRY, PARK, & CITY

INTRODUCTION

Calvert Vaux (1824–1895) fervently advocated the power of art to refine and elevate the human spirit. An accomplished architect and landscape architect, he believed that well-planned, picturesque buildings and naturalistically laid-out parks and grounds enhanced the lives of all who used them. After a six-year period in Newburgh, New York, where he settled in 1850 following his training as an architect in his native England, Vaux established himself in New York City. He would practice there for the next 40 years. During this long career, he designed houses for men of wealth as well as for artists and writers and middle-class clients. He also laid out parks and cemeteries, drew plans for some of the largest public edifices America had yet seen, erected model tenements and other buildings intended to improve the conditions of the urban poor, called for intelligently planned apartment houses at an early date, and, not least of all, built many charming structures in the nation's new public parks. His name, however, has been overshadowed by the reputations of his more well-known associates, Andrew Jackson Downing (1815–1852), the man who brought him to America, and Frederick Law Olmsted (1822–1903), the man whom Vaux introduced to the profession of landscape architecture.

Vaux's friendship with Olmsted, who was two years his senior, began in the autumn of 1857. At that time, the commissioners of Central Park announced a competition to determine a plan for the new park. Vaux, who had been living in New York for about a year, appealed to Olmsted to join him in the preparation of a design to be entered in the competition. The result of their collaboration was the famous Greensward plan, which the commissioners adopted in April 1858 and which Olmsted and Vaux were hired to implement. Their association at Central Park formed the basis of a professional partnership and placed them at the vanguard of the nascent American park movement. Interrupted by the Civil War, Olmsted and Vaux's partnership endured until 1872; thereafter, they cooperated from time to time on special projects, notably the laying out of the Niagara Reservation in the mid-1880s. By that time, Olmsted had discovered and advanced his surpassing genius for park and city planning. He gained wide recognition in America and abroad as a master of these new disciplines. Ambitious, successful, and allied with many political and cultural leaders of his time, Olmsted became a national public figure who succeeded in placing parks, parkways, and residential suburbs on the agenda of American social reform. Although Vaux shared and even helped form Olmsted's notions of the social purposes of art, he never attained the wide reputation that Olmsted earned.

Though he was by no means prone to shrink from a fight or to shy away from using the press as a forum to advance his ideas when he thought principles were at stake, Vaux was reluctant to become too seriously involved in issues that would take him far beyond the limits of his profession. Less suited by background and temperament to be a magnetic, pragmatic man of affairs than was Olmsted, Vaux "brooded over his problems of landscape architecture, studied and drew plans, tested them on the ground for hours and days by wandering over the terrain he was considering," said one person who knew him well. He could have become so absorbed in this work that "time and place seemed nothing to him."[1] More than once, Vaux, who could be irascible and strong-willed, expressed his impatience with Olmsted for paying more attention to managing the park and its workers than to perfecting its design. And perhaps because Vaux always remained committed to solving esthetic and planning problems—devoted to artistic purposes, as he would have said—than to park management, social theorizing, and political action, he was doomed to be cast into a secondary position as far as public perception of the two men was concerned.

Nonetheless, the fact that Olmsted was often given sole or primary responsibility for the design of Central Park—in which Vaux did some of his best work—put a strain on the two men's friendship. Vaux, with justification, saw his role as initiator and equal partner in the historic design being forgotten, and the prospect troubled him deeply. For his part, Olmsted, whenever asked, took pains to acknowledge Vaux as cocreator of the plan. But sometimes, it appears, he let others assume the impression of his predominance. Olmsted biographer Melvin Kalfus is probably correct in his contention that Olmsted's overriding desire to be a success led him at times to forget the role of Vaux in the Central Park design.[2] The issue first came to a head in correspondence that Vaux wrote to Olmsted during the Civil War, when Olmsted was managing the Mariposa Mining Estate in California. In his earnest letters—which reveal how well Vaux understood Olmsted the man as well as how highly he valued his talents and comradeship—Vaux gave frank expression to his frustration with Olmsted's egotism. "I brought as much as you to the park," he asserted. His contributions had included "education, special fitness to take up new problems, a love of the race, a love of the park and all it meant intellectually," Vaux maintained. He had "worked faithfully and fraternally" with Olmsted, but, he protested, his friend "did not believe in" his right to "joint title."[3] The issue surfaced publicly in 1878 when E. L. Godkin, editor of the *Nation*, published a letter in the *Tribune* protesting Olmsted's dismissal from his Central Park post that failed to mention Vaux as codesigner of the park. The omission sparked an angry reply from Vaux. "I am the author in every respect equally with Mr. Olmsted" of the Central Park plan, Vaux asserted.[4] The matter attracted public attention again in 1887, when Mariana Van Rensselaer published in the *American Architect and Building News* a series of essays on landscape gardening. In her writings she created the impression that Vaux had played a secondary role in the Central Park design. Olmsted himself promptly corrected the mistake with a precisely worded letter to the journal's editor.[5]

Yet despite Olmsted's repeated assertions to the contrary, the impression endured that Vaux occupied a lesser place to Olmsted at Central Park and elsewhere. This was a particularly ironic injustice of history because when the two men created the Greensward plan in 1857, Vaux, who had just published a book on domestic architecture, possessed far more professional knowledge than did Olmsted. "A widening interest in examples of beautiful art, not only in buildings proper but in the layout of cities that included great open spaces in their arrangement and design," said Vaux's son Bowyer, had prompted his father in the 1840s to tour Continental cities.[6] This experience, coupled with Vaux's professional architectural training—to say nothing of his work with Andrew Jackson Downing, a pioneer of landscape architecture in America—gave Vaux a command of the Romantic tradition of design that in the early 1850s surpassed that of any of his contemporaries on this side of the Atlantic.

WHILE IT MIGHT BE impossible to separate the work of Olmsted and Vaux in passages of landscape they jointly designed, the many park structures that were erected in Central Park and in other parks planned by the partners were Vaux's responsibility. These buildings, bridges, and pavilions constituted a significant contribution to the architecture of his times. They form a fascinating part of Vaux's career. "The popular taste can never incline to horticultural subjects, if confined to dry, practical details, with slow, unimpressive occupations," wrote Henry T. Williams, editor, 18 years after Downing, of the *Horticulturist*, "but throw in rural ornament and tasty embellishments, and neat rustic architecture, and horticulture is elevated from a lower to a higher range of life subjects, fit or people to love and patronize."[7] He was referring to that special class of buildings that had developed in conjunction with the art of landscape architecture. Downing, Vaux's American mentor, had himself periodically discussed the subject of garden architecture in his articles and books. But the rise of the urban public park movement, which can be said to have begun in earnest with Olmsted and Vaux's 1857 plan for Central Park, called forth the creation of many such structures, frequently on a large scale. For in addition to artfully crafted landscape, park designers had to provide for the public's comfort in a variety of pleasurable circumstances. Boathouses, refectories, dairies, belvederes, summerhouses, shelters, and bridges, as well as many different sorts of outdoor furniture, came into being to serve the simple pastimes that people hoped to enjoy in their new parks.

To furnish the park landscape with incidents of appropriate decoration was as much a function of these structures as the actual uses they served. This was architecture in which the element of delight clearly outweighed all other considerations. "And garden architecture," wrote Vaux's contemporary, Edward Kemp, a landscape architect, "has liniments of its own so decidedly removed from house architecture, and so seldom studied, that the ordinary practitioner is at sea the moment he enters the region of the garden." The success of these buildings, said Kemp, was "less a matter of rule and measurement" than a question of "the eye." The special challenge of park and garden architecture, asserted Kemp, "requires a man to be as much an artist (at least in feeling) as an architect."

Moreover, the garden architect, said Kemp, had "to make a general picture, and not simply to set a work of art, as it were, on a solitary pedestal."[8]

The notion that the landscape architect was a composer of pictures and that he used architecture as an element of composition, was, of course, familiar knowledge by the middle of the nineteenth century. "He is bound to create views, if we may here use a word of so much weight of meaning," wrote Charles H. J. Smith, the British landscape architect whose book *Parks and Pleasure Grounds* appeared in an American edition in 1853. "In short," said Smith, "his business is what is technically called composition," and he compared the modern landscape architect to the landscape painter who creates "pictures by the combination of the finest objects which the artist has copied into his sketch-book, or can recall by his memory, or can embody by his imagination."[9] Earlier British writers, especially Richard Payne Knight and Uvedale Price, had spoken of landscape in painterly terms. The idyllic views of the seventeenth-century French landscape artist Claude Lorraine had inspired an enduring attitude toward picturesque nature in the English-speaking world. Many British gardeners, like Humphrey Repton, whom Vaux revered as the man who "established the true art of gardening on a firm basis,"[10] had sought to emulate Claude's poetic vision. The ordained role of architecture in this scheme of things was to enhance the mood created by the landscape architect in his passages of scenery. Style, historical as well as exotic, became a language used to evoke a host of sensations and associations, from the melancholy of Gothic ruins to the noble sentiments of Classical temples. Foremost, garden architecture was an architecture of fantasy. It made its appeal to the imagination, while, secondarily, perhaps serving as shelter from an unexpected shower in a far part of a capacious park.

Public parks in Europe and America brought this aristocratic tradition to a broader audience. In these large new municipal pleasure grounds, architecture complemented the great theme of nature, which, in the paradise contrived by art, provided release from the tensions of everyday life in the modern city. Moorish kiosks, medieval belvederes, and Swiss chalets put to flight thoughts of the trying world pressing the boundaries of the park. They invited the visitor to cultivate the way of leisure, that delicate new pleasure that was the gift of nineteenth-century urban life to the expanding middle class.

Calvert Vaux, who had grown up in England and traveled on the Continent, was well aware of the venerable history of garden architecture. Yet in addition to his professional knowledge of the special genre of park architecture, Vaux clearly possessed the "eye" that Kemp pronounced necessary to the successful designer of landscape structures. As a young man, Vaux responded to the charms of scenery and displayed considerable talent as a renderer of buildings and places. On his trip on the Continent in the 1840s, undertaken with the architect George Truefitt, he made numerous sketches. In later years, Samuel Parsons Jr., a pupil and associate of Vaux, testified that Vaux commanded great facility in sketching, both in black and white and in color. He "made many notes of Nature's ways in field and forest," Parsons recalled.[11] For a time in 1863, Vaux even took drawing lessons from Thomas Farrar, whose striking watercolors exemplified Pre-Raphaelite realism in America. Vaux's son Downing treasured the memory of his father as an artist in the Ruskinian mold. He recalled that the architect frequently timed his vacations to be with his artist friends in the woods and mountains. There, said Downing, Vaux greatly enjoyed "planting his umbrella and camp-stool in some commanding position where he could 'daub' along all day in a faithful and painstaking effort to reproduce on canvas, with unfamiliar brush, the rugged mountain slope or moss-covered rock, the dark pool reflecting overhanging trees, or the intricate interlacing of the foliage of some old monarch of the forest standing alone like a sentinel of nature on guard."[12]

Clearly, Vaux shared the esthetic point of view of many American landscape painters of his day. Indeed, among his close friends he numbered such artists as Worthington Whittredge, Eastman Johnson, R. Sanford Gifford, Frederic Edwin Church, and Jervis McEntee. A frequent visitor to the Tenth Street Studio building, he often participated in the intellectual and social life of that unique art haven. Vaux enjoyed an especially close friendship with the landscape painter Jervis McEntee, the brother of his wife Mary, whom he married in 1856. Shortly before then, Vaux had designed a studio and an adjoining house for McEntee at Rondout, New York. Over the years, Vaux and his family stayed regularly at McEntee's Hudson Valley home. The artist recorded in his diary many walks and sketching trips that he and Vaux made into the nearby Catskills.

It is a pity that Vaux's sketchbook from his first European journey, as well as nearly all of his American nature studies, are lost. We can, however, enjoy through the medium of reproductions in nineteenth-century publications passages of sensitively observed scenery from Vaux's hand. Among these are sketches that he made at the time of Downing's death showing Highland Garden, Downing's Hudson Valley home. *Restawhile on the Palisades*, a pen-and-ink drawing that Vaux made in the summer of 1879 of the cliffs bordering the Hudson north of New York City (Fig. 8.9), is another instance of Vaux's skillful depiction of landscape. Vaux must have gone often to sketch there, for in addition to the *Restawhile* drawing he wrote a perceptive analysis of Palisades scenery. It more fully than any other document reveals how he looked at the natural world with the eye of a painter, seeking to discern the variety and unity of a picture:

> We have first the sky which will have its own individual color and character; then the cliff which usually contrasts boldly with it, light against dark or dark against light;—the space between the horizon and shore line next fills the eye, and it is always sufficiently far off to have a hue of its own, dependent on the day, gradated, of course, within itself, but so different from the sky or the cliffs that it makes the impression on the eye, of a distant strip of delicate half tint. The water again no matter what the general effect may be, is sure to take the light in its own individual way and to be a unit of color so far as the most distant portion, which contrasts with the cliff, is concerned.[13]

In *Restawhile*, the idyllic mood holds sway, weaving architecture and nature into an image strongly evocative of place and atmosphere. Dominating all, a rustic gazebo offers itself to the viewer's attention as a place from which to look upon this splendid scene. Standing where a classical or medieval ruin might have stood in a painting by Claude or by his latter-day American imitator, Thomas Doughty, this fragile temple to Romantic sensibility brings the vast scenery within the realm of human comprehension. It persuades us that nature is to be viewed as we would view a picture, from a well-chosen and quiet vantage point. This charming piece of garden architecture suggests the pleasures of contemplation awaiting the receptive observer who will linger beneath its roof. Representing humankind and its capacity to appreciate beauty in the natural world, the gazebo humanizes the landscape, as the buildings in Olmsted and Vaux's urban parks were meant to do. With such graphic evidence before us, we can safely assume that Vaux possessed that gift of artistic feeling of which Kemp spoke. It is also evident from his parks that Vaux could marshall that sensibility to create structures that served both the demands of public use and the pleasures of visual delight.

ALTHOUGH NO SUCCINCT testimony from Vaux himself exists that might be regarded as a statement of his esthetic philosophy, the memoirs of Samuel Parsons Jr. hold a plausible facsimile. "Mr. Vaux was profoundly in love with Nature," wrote Parsons, "and endeavored to study and comprehend her in all her moods." But beyond that, Vaux believed in "transforming her by the magical power of the imagination and endeavored so to dress his thought, or design his ideal, as to heighten her beauty and at the same time leave her essential features, her soul, unprofaned." Parsons went on to characterize Vaux as a "romanticist," a man who valued sensibility and the translation of feeling as the motive forces of art. He recollected that Vaux himself had said that "the artist is he who is able through the medium of his work to create in those who study it emotions akin to those in him which inspired the work. Not only does he see the vision himself, but he opens our eyes, so that we can see it too."[14] For Vaux, nature spoke to the heart through the eyes.

In his professional work, Vaux sought to apply this Romantic and pictorial sensibility to his landscape designs. "But as what is well designed to nourish the body and enliven the spirits through the stomach," wrote he and Olmsted in 1872, "makes a dinner a dinner, so what is well designed to recreate the mind from urban oppressions through the eye, makes the Park the Park."[15] Like a painter before his easel struggling to transform nature into art, Vaux, said Parsons, "endeavored to divine the secret of a particular bit of Nature's design and use the idea in his own composition so that one would feel the scene to be thoroughly natural, familiar even, and yet transfigured and elevated by higher emotions."[16] This attitude was surely one of the reasons why Vaux found Downing so congenial. Downing had said that "landscape gardening, as an art, does not consist, as many seem to suppose, in producing a counterfeit of nature, but in idealizing natural beauty in a lawn, park, or garden."[17] In his supplement to the sixth edition (1859) of Downing's *A Treatise on the Theory and Practice of Landscape Gardening*, Henry Winthrop Sargent, a client of Vaux's, included two views of the Terrace area in Central Park that nicely illustrate Parsons's contention. The lower woodcut shows the site as Vaux and Olmsted encountered it when making their preliminary designs. The upper view shows the landscape "transfigured and elevated by higher emotions." Here the architect has suppressed some things, accentuated others, added a lake where a natural depression suggested it, and enriched the land with trees and shrubs. Bareness has given way to lushness, baldness to texture, flatness to depth, and uniformity to the play of light and shade, and the salient elements of the former landscape—the rock outcroppings in the foreground and the undulating rise and fall of surfaces—more strongly assert themselves.

In his landscape designs, Vaux sought, as did his partner Olmsted, to express pastoral sentiments. To Parsons, however, Vaux possessed a more introverted spirit. "There was an intimate and subtle quality in Mr. Vaux's work at its best that we scarcely find elsewhere, not in Repton, Puckler or Olmsted," he wrote. These men had "conceived large schemes and produced great results," but none of them "was the poet and painter in their art that Vaux was."[18] And one suspects that the intimate vignettes drawn by A. F. Bellows for Clarence Cook's 1869 book on Central Park more faithfully reflect the park as Vaux would have wished us to experience it—as a series of close, sheltered spaces—than perhaps Olmsted, who favored broad passages of nature, would have preferred. This complementary difference of approaches to landscape architecture may have been the reason why the two men worked so well together.

IT WAS TRULY A fateful event for American art when in 1857 Calvert Vaux, a young man with considerable experience in architecture and landscape architecture, invited Olmsted, a lover of natural beauty who had no professional training of any sort—nor, apparently, possessed any artistic abilities—to join him in the preparation of the Greensward entry for the Central Park competition. And during the years of the Civil War, when Olmsted went off to California to manage the ill-fated Mariposa Mining Estate, it was Vaux who was responsible for calling him back to the East and to the fledgling discipline of landscape architecture that Vaux hoped to make strong. The work they did together laid the foundations for the American park movement. Parsons, and perhaps others of his time, believed that the esthetic contributions of Vaux to their heroic endeavor outweighed those of Olmsted. It is not, however, my intention to lift Vaux at the expense of Olmsted. Rather, I wish to show that Calvert Vaux, a tireless idealist who designed buildings that wedded picturesque expression to the demands of use and who laid out parks and private grounds that celebrated nature's ways, was one of American art's most intelligent and sympathetic partisans.

WHAT IS A YOUNG ARCHITECT TO DO, AND HOW IS HE TO GET ON?
1824–1850

Calvert Vaux made the decision to leave his native England and to emigrate to the United States the day that he met Andrew Jackson Downing, a man whom many in America regarded as the supreme authority on matters of cultivated living. The encounter took place in London late in the summer of 1850, near the end of the European tour that Downing had been making since July of that year. "I was in a settled position and surrounded by friends," said Vaux, "but I liked him so much, his foresight and observation were so apparent in the conversations we had and above all his style was so calculated to win confidence, that without a fear I relinquished all and accompanied him."[1] After supplying references to Downing, Vaux made arrangements for his departure. In the meantime, Downing took off on a hasty trip to Paris. Perhaps he went armed with advice from Vaux on what to see. Five years before, the young architect's keen interest in the nascent urban park movement had led him to travel to the Continent to see royal parks and public gardens there.[2] In early September, after Downing had returned to England, he and Vaux sailed together from Liverpool to New York. Within three weeks of having met Downing, Vaux was hard at work with him in Newburgh at the office that Downing had created in his home, the Tudor villa that many knew as Highland Garden. Initially, Vaux, who was one of a number of professionally trained English architects to emigrate to the United States before the Civil War, had agreed to accept the post of assistant; by the end of the year Downing had made him his partner.[3] This whirlwind sequence of events bears out a friend's appraisal of Downing as a man who possessed "an almost intuitive perception of character" and in whom were combined the qualities of "keen perception, great energy, decision, and boldness."[4]

By midcentury, Downing was riding the crest of a wave of fame that had lifted him to prominence as America's foremost authority on horticulture and domestic architecture. He had successfully brought about the wedding of these two disciplines before a large audience of well-to-do and middle-class readers of his earnestly written books and articles. His *Treatise on the Theory and Practice of*

Landscape Gardening of 1841, *Cottage Residences* of 1842 (with other editions throughout the 1840s), and essays in the *Horticulturist*, which he began editing in 1846, instructed the growing class of American homeowners in how best to arrange their dwellings and to lay out the grounds around them. Having begun his adult life as a nurseryman in the Hudson River town of Newburgh, he had become the oracle of picturesque architecture and naturalistic garden design to a generation of home-building Americans whose imagination had been captivated by the Hudson River School landscape painters. His popular works exemplified "the advantages of a studied irregularity and broadly conceived picturesqueness in arranging country houses that may be intended for naturally irregular and picturesque sites," said Vaux, and in the estimation of historian David Schuyler, they made him America's "Apostle of Taste."[5] In England, whence Downing derived many of his ideas, his name was also respected. John Claudius Loudon, the dean of British horticulturists and a man with whom Downing has often been compared, called him "a man of taste" and recommended his books to his countrymen.

Downing undertook his trip to Europe at a significant turning point in his career. Having just finished his third book, *The Architecture of Country Houses*, Downing had formed a plan to go into the business of furnishing designs for houses and grounds. Up to this time, he had been content to accept gentlemanly remuneration for advice, much of it informal and even verbal, that he gave to persons landscaping the grounds around existing dwellings. As for buildings themselves, Downing, although an articulate critic and theorist of architecture, lacked sufficient practical knowledge to plan and execute designs on his own. This inadequacy had led him to rely on the knowledge and example of professionals like John Notman, Richard Upjohn, and Gervase Wheeler, men whose works often appeared as exemplars in Downing's books and articles. But his strongest tie to the profession was with Alexander Jackson Davis, with whom Downing formed an informal association in the early 1840s. For a modest fee, Davis prepared drawings for buildings after sketches that Downing had furnished him. Many of these projects, as well as full-blown works by Davis himself, illustrated Downing's writings, and in *Cottage Residences* Downing recommended Davis as the architect his readers should consult if they desired professional services.

Now, having both sold his nursery business and concluded litigation that had tied up his assets for some considerable time, Downing hoped to capitalize on the demand for well-designed homes and gardens that his writings had stimulated. Before he left for Europe—the first and only such trip he was to make—Downing suggested to Davis that they regularize their partnership. As Downing scholar George B. Tatum has pointed out, precedents for such alliances between landscape architects and architects existed in the collaborations of Capability Brown with Henry Holland and that of Humphrey Repton with John Nash and John Adey Repton. Davis, however, declined to pursue the matter with Downing.

In going abroad, Downing intended as much to hire an assistant as to visit the great gardens and public grounds that he had known only through books. (After his trip, he published in the *Horticulturist* vivid descriptions of the places he had seen.) Shortly before his departure in early July he breezily informed Davis that he had "taken it into [his] head to run over to London on a little business." It must have come as a surprise to Davis to learn from Downing upon his return that "finding a clever young architect in London I persuaded him to come out with me & work at architecture and landscape gardening with me." Despite Downing's protestations to Davis of continued "pleasant intercourse & joint partnership of feeling," the older men's relationship came to an abrupt end with the arrival of Vaux. In his 1852 revised edition of *Cottage Residences*, Downing deleted Davis's name from the discussion of architectural services. And while Vaux himself never directly criticized the influence that his predecessor had had on the formation of Downing's architectural notions, he later referred to Downing's books as deficient in the area of architectural expression. Clarence Cook (1828–1900), who served as assistant to Downing and Vaux, was less generous toward Davis: "What heaps of money he has wasted and worse," complained Cook, "what numbers he has disgusted with architecture! Yet, for a long time, Downing treated this person with great respect and consideration, acknowledged his indebtedness to him, put his designs into his books and recommended him to his friends."[6] What Cook's caustic remarks indicate is that for America, as well as for Downing, the arrival of Vaux and others like him heralded a new direction in architectural taste. Sadly, Davis became a victim of the times; his influential career had virtually ended by the start of the Civil War, although he lived on until 1892. Given the evasive tone of Downing's letters to Davis before and after his European trip, one wonders if a dawning awareness of the increasingly passé character of Davis's designs, which Davis had conceived without the benefit of formal architectural training, could have motivated Downing to hitch his fortunes to a younger, more modern talent from abroad.

In his search for an assistant, Downing proceeded to London's Architectural Association, a fledgling organization whose 150 members were largely young draftsmen, architects, and students. The association had come into being in the fall of 1847 with the goal of improving the level of architectural education and discourse while seeking to raise the public's estimation of the profession. "The business of the Association," stated its organizers, "is to consist of the production of designs for previously determined subjects; the reading of papers on the several branches of science and art, comprehended under the term Architecture; free and open discussion; and contribution to the Society's portfolio of subjects, displaying either originality of design, examples of construction and decoration, or modes of representation."[7] On alternate Fridays, members of the association read papers that became the focus of debate. Vaux delivered at least one such lecture, a paper on the subject of "the supply and discharge of water to buildings," with special reference to "the details of arrangement in which the responsibility of the architect is more especially involved."[8] On intermediate Fridays, members displayed sketches produced in response to a given theme.

In addition to these charettes, the association sponsored an annual exhibition of architectural drawings and models that it opened to all free of charge. This event was a forum especially for new talent, whose work was unlikely to be shown in the Royal Academy exhibitions. The association maintained an equal distance from the Royal Institute of British Architects (RIBA), where many younger men felt unwelcome. Undoubtedly, the *Builder* spoke for many aspiring architects, including Vaux, when it called on the institute to "open its arms wider, increase the number of its allies, objurgate narrowness, and maintain its position, not by keeping back others, but by advancing itself."[9] Each year, the association's exhibition had attracted a wider audience. In February 1850, the association announced its intention to hold its next exhibition during August and September in rooms loaned to it by the New Society of Water-Color Painters. The exhibition that opened on August 12 contained 190 drawings and was a great success, in spite of the summer schedule. It was a fateful event for Vaux. Explaining his purpose to the secretary of the association (probably the architect John P. Seddon), Downing was introduced to Vaux, whom he immediately asked to join him in looking over the drawings on display. Vaux must have proudly directed Downing to his own work, two drawings for a baptistery that the *Builder* praised for the way "a lantern light is made to rise from the octagonal intersection of groining, cleverly devised."[10] Downing too must have found the baptistery design, as well as its creator, to his liking, for he promptly made Vaux an offer of employment. Without hesitation, Vaux accepted. By the following evening, the two men had concluded the formalities and were prepared to begin promising new phases in both of their careers.

WHAT LITTLE WE KNOW about Vaux before he met Downing suggests that circumstances would have disposed Vaux to take a bold step that moment in his life. The son of a surgeon, Vaux, who was born on December 20, 1824, had spent his earliest years together with his younger brother, Alfred (born 1828), and sisters, Emily (born 1823) and Julia (dates unknown), in comfortable circumstances in a house at 36 Pudding Lane, not far from London Bridge. We can only speculate on what effect the death of Vaux's father at the age of 42, in September 1833, had on the young Vaux, who was then only eight years old.[11] Three months after his father's funeral, Vaux entered the nearby Merchant Taylors' School. Having learned to "read and write pretty well" and having mastered "the 'Accidence' in King Edward the Sixth's *Latin Grammar,*" Vaux took his place among the venerable institution's 250 students, who came from the ranks of prosperous families.[12] His classmates were the sons of solicitors, merchants, attorneys, and clergymen. Housed in the red brick building that Sir Christopher Wren had designed after the Great Fire, the school in Vaux's day retained its original seventeenth-century furniture. It is unlikely, however, that these surroundings activated young Calvert's curiosity in architecture. One of his contemporaries remarked that the school "possessed few features of architectural interest or beauty."[13] Nonetheless, Vaux was one day to draw lessons about modern street planning from Wren's thwarted scheme for the rebuilding of the Pudding Lane neighborhood, where the Great Fire had begun.

As a young pupil at the Merchant Taylors' School Vaux received a classical education. Here he learned the Latin that would spice his adult writings and acquired an enduring interest in literature, art, and history. (In adulthood Vaux would write a perceptive essay on Marcus Aurelius.) We also can assume that Vaux took away from the Merchant Taylors' School, where the curriculum paid special attention to Anglican ideals of religious training, that devotion to "higher and noble principles of action" which Matthew Arnold regarded as the chief legacy of English public school education and which was to be a conspicuous trait of Vaux's character in his later professional life.

Young Calvert remained at the Merchant Taylors' School for four years, until 1838, after which the family seems to have moved from Pudding Lane.[14] City directories give no clue to the Vauxes' address in the late 1830s and early 1840s, but it is likely that they resided on Kennington Place, across from Kennington Common, in South London, where Vaux was documented as living in

1848.[15] At least one biography states that he attended a private school on nearby Harleyford Place run by one Francis Adolphus Reynell. Reynell's academy must have been one of the many private schools for boys that flourished in London before the advent of municipal education. Unfortunately, nothing is known of the curriculum Reynell followed.[16]

Vaux's new neighborhood was less distinguished than the family's former address. A contemporary described Kennington Common as "a small, graceless square, surrounded with houses and poisoned by the stench of vitriol works and by black open sluggish ditches."[17] The common had long been favored by evangelical preachers for outdoor sermonizing and by dissenting political groups for public demonstrations. The most historic political gathering to take place on the common occurred on April 10, 1848, when the radically minded Chartists—a populist movement so-called from the People's Charter, which sought universal suffrage, annual parliaments, vote by ballot, rejection of property qualifications for the right to vote, and equalized electoral districts—assembled over 15,000 people there. The demonstration threw respectable London into a panic. Police surrounded public buildings, soldiers guarded all bridges, and 170,000 special constables, among whom was Louis Napoleon, the future emperor of France, were enlisted to maintain order. Vaux was also sworn in as a special constable. Armed with a baton and wearing a white badge, he would have watched the historic proceedings take place without incident. Considering the strong republican sentiments that Vaux would express later in his life, as well as his distaste for the despotic Second Empire, one wonders if his sympathies did not lie more with the protestors than with his fellow constables. But the days of the common as Vaux had known it were numbered. Already in 1841, the area had been proposed for upgrading by the creation there of an ornamental lake surrounded by villas. While nothing came of this scheme, shortly after Vaux left for America, the notorious square became one of London's earliest landscaped public parks. The transformation solved a pressing aesthetic and health problem but at the same time foreclosed the use of the space by working-class political movements.

LONG BEFORE HE SERVED the queen as special constable, Vaux had begun his architectural studies. At the relatively late age of 19, Vaux became, in 1843, an articled pupil of Lewis Nockalls Cottingham. Cottingham, who was one of the elders of the English Gothic Revival, had supervised the sometimes overzealous restoration of a number of important medieval churches. These included the Chapel of Magdalene College (1829), Oxford; Rochester Cathedral (1825); St. Alban's Abbey (1833); and the Temple Church (1840), London. During the time that Vaux spent in his office, Cottingham, who was proud that ancestors in his family had been artists and craftsmen in the Middle Ages, would have been devoting much of his staff's attention to the effort to return Hereford Cathedral to its Romanesque appearance. This work included removing later vaulting, rebuilding the famous stone crossing lantern, re-creating Norman-style moldings, and erecting a new timber roof over the nave.[18] The work at Hereford remained unfinished at Cottingham's death in October 1847 but went forward under his son, Nockalls Johnson Cottingham, who had started as a pupil in the office several years before Vaux.

As a fresh apprentice, Vaux must have thought himself fortunate to have begun his architectural studies under Cottingham's knowledgeable tutelage. For in addition to his many restorations and new buildings, Cottingham was well-known for the drawings that he had published in the 1820s of Westminster Hall and the Chapel of Henry VII, as well as for books on Gothic ornament and historic iron and brass. Furthermore, Cottingham had built country houses (notably Snelston Hall and estate village [1822–1830] in Derbyshire, where he also laid out the grounds in the informal style); planned new streets and designed many urban dwellings in the Waterloo Bridge Road area on the Surrey side of London (where he built his own house); erected banks (the one in Bury St. Edmund's of 1844–1846 was most admired), hotels, and other commercial buildings; and published a book on Greek and Roman architecture. Generous and affectionate by nature, Cottingham enjoyed a special reputation for "sound and able instruction" of the young. Among the resources he provided to eager pupils like Vaux was not only a large library but an extensive collection of medieval furniture and architectural fragments. These objects he housed in underground rooms of his design at his home in Waterloo Bridge Road. The collection, noted a contemporary, "may justly be considered as unique, comprising as it does specimens and casts of all the rarest examples in the different styles of architecture, arranged in chronological order, in numerous apartments appropriately furnished."[19] One assumes that Vaux became intimately familiar with the bas reliefs from the north transept of Westminster Abbey, the "roof of carved oak, painted and gilt, from an old council chamber of a City corporation," several fourteenth-century windows from the Church of St. Catherine in London, the fragment of a fireplace from the Star Chamber at Westminster, the facsimile of the tomb of William de Valence, the processional cross from Glastonbury Abbey, the hanging silver lantern from Seville, the numerous examples of stamped leather and carved furniture, and the many other splendid objects that were in Cottingham's unusual house. Between his employer's museum, library, and office, Vaux had a superb opportunity, even in the days before institutionalized architecture training, to acquire a broad and deep knowledge of architecture, both its practice and its history.

Vaux also took away from Cottingham's office an enduring friendship with fellow architect George Truefitt. Truefitt studied with Cottingham as an apprentice from 1839 to 1844, after which he worked briefly for two other members of the profession. Truefitt was especially adept at rendering and may have encouraged Vaux to perfect his skill with the pencil. (Vaux imitated Truefitt's lettering in his two-character monogram.) In the summer of 1846, Truefitt and Vaux went together on a walking tour of France, Germany, and Belgium.[20] During the trip, Truefitt made many sketches of historic buildings, architectural details, and panoramic views. The following year, he published 60 examples as *Architectural Sketches on the Continent*, a book that won the praise of the influential Ecclesiological Society and others who saw it. "We have a very agreeable book of plates," noted a reviewer in the *Ecclesiologist*, "for which we thank the author, and which we hope may be profitable to him."[21] In the preface to the little volume, Truefitt told the reader that in addition to stopping at principal sites, he had sought out villages and byways that were "seldom visited by Architectural tourists." Therefore, most of the subjects in the portfolio were new to most readers. Truefitt advanced his perspective views and vignettes as "hints to the artist," images that he hoped would be more suggestive of the esthetic character of a detail or building than merely descriptive of its dimensions and appearance. From the list of plates, we learn that, among other places, Truefitt and Vaux had rambled through Normandy, Picardy, and the Rhine Valley, as well as visited Paris, Cologne, Strassburg, Liege, Antwerp, and Louvain. Unfortunately, none of the sketches that Vaux must have made along the way have survived, but we can surmise that he often sat alongside his friend taking his own views of Truefitt's subjects. Vaux also may have brought away other vital lessons from his tour. In the opinion of modern British architect David Matzdorf, Vaux's Continental journey "cemented firmly his concern with the rural and urban contexts of buildings, their relationships to the land and to other buildings, in a way that was essential to his later role in the urban parks movement."[22] Coming on the heels of Truefitt and Vaux's formal education and apprenticeship, this footloose summer abroad was an adventure of liberation and discovery that neither man ever forgot. In articles written at the time of Truefitt's retirement and later when he died, the friends' tour featured as one of the significant events of his life.

Back in London, Truefitt began to advance his career. In the spring of 1847, his competition entry for the Army and Navy Club earned him much praise, especially when a full-page illustration (Fig. 1.1) of it appeared in the *Builder*. The architect obviously had drawn on his memories of the late medieval guild-halls of Flanders that he and Vaux had recently admired. The design (which did not win the competition) exhibited airy elevations, with ranges of mullioned windows and a wealth of figural and ornamental carving. As one of only two Gothic designs entered in the competition, the drawing, said one critic, displayed "great care and knowledge of forms."[23] Indeed, the evident attention to detail and studied historicism bore the impress of Truefitt's years with the antiquarian Cottingham. Truefitt exhibited the drawing the following year at the Royal Academy along with a design for an unidentified residence that he was erecting in Pall Mall and a drawing for a marble baptismal font recently completed in Manchester Cathedral. In 1848, Truefitt won first prize in the competition for a Tudor-style savings bank at Newbury, Berkshire. And in the 1850 Architectural Association exhibition that Downing had visited with Vaux, Truefitt displayed his *Design for Rebuilding the Church of St. Thomas at Newport* and a drawing for a picturesque wrought iron lamp standard in Manchester, where he had struck up a long-term professional relationship with the vestry of the cathedral.

Truefitt's reputation with churchmen was bolstered further by the publication of his second book, *Designs for Country Churches*, which appeared in 1850. The folio volume contained twenty perspective views of hypothetical churches "generally conceived with reference to specific though imaginary varieties of site: they merely profess to the attempts to think in 'Gothic,' exclusive of actual authority." The *Ecclesiologist*, despite serious reservations, conceded that the designs "indicate vigour and spirit."[24] The quaint Decorated-style church that the *Builder* chose to illustrate demonstrated Truefitt's special sensitivity to the relation between rural buildings and their settings. Discerning the emotive potential of a certain creekside site, Truefitt nestled his church into the sloping stream bank. Moreover, the only access to the chapel's portal was by means of an arched bridge crossing from the opposite shore. With grace and imagination, Truefitt showed how to develop the potential of a site so that "advantage is taken to give individuality to the design." One of those who must have appreciated the picturesque conception was Vaux. The sense of intimacy between building and site, as well as the whimsical device of the bridge, anticipated the spirit that would animate many of his later park structures.

FIGURE 1.1. George Truefitt, design for the Army and Navy Club, London, 1847. From *Builder* 5 (May 5, 1847). Courtesy of Buffalo and Erie County Public Library.

At midcentury, George Truefitt could be counted one of the bright lights of the rising generation. In the decades following his friend's departure for America, Truefitt secured for himself a comfortable niche in the British architectural profession. By 1890, he had erected buildings in 25 counties in England and Scotland—many of these commissions having come to him as a result of winning competitions—and he lived in a picturesque dwelling at Shelsley Lodge, Worthing, where, in the manner of his old mentor Cottingham, he surrounded himself with architectural curiosities that he had collected since his student days with Vaux. One can only wonder, however, what Vaux might have thought, at the outset of his career in London, about the success that his friend was achieving in their chosen profession—success considerably greater than Vaux's own. Clearly, Truefitt, who was the same age as Vaux, was the more successful of the two men. This obvious fact, as well as what we may infer was Truefitt's more dominant role in the friendship, may have given rise to Vaux's son's mistaken impression that his father had apprenticed to Truefitt.[25] And although Bowyer Vaux misread the relationship that existed between his father and his father's friend, he was correct to assume that Vaux learned a good deal from Truefitt. In any event, we can count the friendship with George Truefitt as the first of three close attachments that Vaux made in his lifetime with others who possessed status superior to his. From Truefitt, Vaux would have acquired a love for sketching, a sharpened appreciation of the picturesque, and the resolve to pursue an architectural career.

ANOTHER ARCHITECT FRIEND in London was George Godwin. By the early 1840s, Godwin, who was nine years Vaux's senior, had attained a position of respect and influence in the London architectural profession. As an expert on the history of Gothic ecclesiastical architecture, he had restored a number of medieval buildings and, in 1838, had published *The Churches of London*. Of his own designs with which Vaux would have been familiar, St. Mary's, West Brompton, Middlesex, of 1849, represents the scholarly, restrained expression Godwin sought. But Godwin was best-known as the editor of the *Builder*, a position that he held from 1842 until his death in 1888. Godwin's devotion to the journal and the profession it represented was legendary; "it was war to the knife with any one who menaced the interests of the *Builder* in any way," wrote his successor.[26] As editor, he became an eloquent and influential spokesman for the improvement of architectural education and for the professionalization of architectural practice. Because of these concerns, he took special interest in the new Architectural Association, whose meetings the *Builder* often chronicled. "We should find that in upholding the dignity and high character of the profession," he once told the association's members, "we were best advancing our own individual interests."[27] And as a public spokesman for all architects, he sought to smooth any feathers that the maverick organization might have ruffled among the members of the architectural and art establishment. Shortly before the opening of the association's exhibition that Downing saw, Godwin had called upon the RIBA to give its support to the "young members of the profession who had spiritedly and at much personal cost" organized the event. As for the Royal Academy, Godwin succeeded in winning the goodwill of Charles Robert Cockerell for the success of the exhibit. The esteemed architect to the Bank of England, who held the post of professor of architecture at the

Royal Academy, assured Godwin that he need not fear that the exhibition would be "looked at with other than friendly feelings."[28] No letters survive to shed light on the depth and nature of Vaux's friendship with Godwin, although we can assume that Vaux benefited from the counsel and influence of his successful friend. It is probable, for example, that Godwin, whom friends remembered as an enthusiastic companion, gave Vaux and Truefitt advice on where to go and what to see on their 1846 tour, for Godwin had visited the Low Countries before them and had kept a detailed journal of his travels.[29] It is also intriguing to speculate that Vaux might have picked up his interest in the theater from Godwin, who attended performances regularly and even wrote plays. Perhaps, too, Godwin's dedication to the cause of improved housing for the poor spurred a similar interest in Vaux, who in later life would serve as architect to the Children's Aid Society in New York. Godwin had also seen a need for architects to study landscape architecture. "We should be glad to see architects paying some little attention to landscape gardening," he exhorted the readers of the *Builder* in 1849. Asserting that "both they and proprietors may take our word for the fact that skill in it does not come by intuition," he noted that "at the present moment we know scarcely any persons who may pretend to be masters in the art." He continued with words that were prophetic of sentiments that Vaux would utter as champion of the American park movement: "To the flagging spirit of the hard worker in towns, the mere mention of quiet fields induces a refreshing and soothing vision," said Godwin. And surely Vaux would have smiled to read, in later life, Godwin's affirmation that "the study of landscape gardening lends additional interest to every country ramble . . . and brings a healthful as well as profitable result." Godwin made these remarks in an 1849 review of the fourth edition of Downing's *A Treatise on Landscape Gardening*, which he ranked among the best books on the subject.[30] It is highly likely that a year later, Godwin, along with Truefitt, received a hurried request from Vaux to furnish the references that Downing had requested.

AT THE TIME OF HIS meeting with Downing, Vaux remarked that he "was in a settled position." The statement implies that Vaux was well situated in London when he made the decision to join Downing in America. In the absence of any papers or personal documents from this period of Vaux's life, one is at a loss to affirm this spirited assertion. However, a number of clues suggest that Vaux did not enjoy the standing he claimed but stood ready to seize any opportunity that would improve his professional circumstances. Vaux had entered Cottingham's office at the period when his mentor was becoming less and less active due to a lingering illness that eventually claimed his life. According to the obituary of Cottingham in the *Art Journal*, his elder son Nockalls had "been long actively engaged in almost solely carrying on" his father's wide practice. This included the restoration of Hereford Cathedral, where the new reredos was from the son's designs. Another project was the completion of a church near Lincoln which had been begun before the elder Cottingham's death in 1847 but which the *Builder* confided was "exclusively from the younger Mr. Cottingham's designs, though not hitherto so stated."[31] Behind the scenes, life in the Cottingham office must not have been what Vaux had hoped for when he apprenticed there. Apparently Vaux entered the Cottingham office in 1843; he left in 1846, probably just before he and Truefitt went on their summer tour of the Continent. This was a short apprenticeship, the normal term being at least five years. Was Vaux's early departure occasioned by the ascendency of the younger Cottingham in the affairs of the office? It may have been that Vaux became dissatisfied with his situation as apprentice not to an eminent master but to a favored son who was only a year older than Vaux and who appears to have had little talent for architecture or for business.

As it turned out, Vaux was wise to have distanced himself from the younger Cottingham, for the son's reputation and fortunes declined steadily after his father's death in 1847. Entirely on his own, Nockalls Cottingham was unable to maintain the high standards of design that had come to be expected of the office. His plans for a village school erected in 1848 at Great Chesterford, Essex, were "much injured by the enormous size of some of the details," said a critic (probably George Godwin) in the *Builder*, which had the same to say about his designs for a large corn exchange at Saffron Walden in Essex. "Indeed, the great calibre of some of the details," complained the *Builder*, "makes the building almost a caricature of Gothic architecture."[32] This was especially harsh criticism for the son of a man who had been revered as a scholar of Gothic detail and ornament. The *Ecclesiologist* was equally unkind to Cottingham. It cited the village school design as "full of pretension," called the Saffron Walden building "a kind of nightmare recollection of Flemish Hotels de Ville," and took exception to the restoration at Hereford.[33] An unctuous man who affected a "stylish and much-bescented" manner, Cottingham seems to have gotten little work after these commissions. Moreover, his underhanded treatment of William Holman Hunt and other Pre-Raphaelite painters whom Cottingham sought to engage as decorators ruined his reputation with the budding avant-garde artistic community.[34] By 1851, deteriorating finances forced Cottingham to put his father's famous architectural collection up for sale. Nevertheless, the income from the auction did little to improve Cottingham's circumstances; in May 1854, listing himself as a surveyor, he filed for bankruptcy.[35] In the early fall of the same year, possibly heartened by the success of Vaux and other English architects who had gone abroad, Cottingham set sail for New York. A passenger on the ill-fated *Arctic*, he met his death on September 27, when the ship, navigating in dense fog off Cape Race, was struck by another vessel and went down. Cottingham's tragic end scarcely attracted the attention of the British architectural press.[36]

But even if Vaux had been right to dissociate himself from Nockalls Cottingham, what was he doing between the autumn of 1846, when he came back to London after his trip with Truefitt, and August 1850, when he met Downing? The answer seems to be not very much, at least in the field of architecture. His son Bowyer related that as a young man, his father had earned money by lettering maps. Vaux was well paid for this work, which he did on a part-time basis, because he had developed the ability to write backward rapidly. This unusual skill saved lithographers considerable time in the preparation of maps for printing. This tedious work had paid for Vaux's travels with Truefitt, and undoubtedly it continued to provide income after he returned. No evidence has come to light of any architectural commission, and the baptistery designs that Vaux exhibited in 1850 were the sole drawings that were even remarked upon in the architectural press. Vaux, who by 1848 was living in the far suburb of Newington, may have helped his friend Truefitt from time to time and certainly participated in the stimulating talk and sketching exercises at the rooms of the

Architectural Association. But from the perspective of our own time, it appears that Vaux, whose apprenticeship was abnormally brief, spent the years between 1846 and 1850 continuing to sharpen his architectural skills while earning a living as a letterer.

The period of the later 1840s proved a difficult time for many young men trying to establish themselves in the British architectural profession. In addition to the conspicuous failure of young Cottingham, many others found success an elusive prize. The establishment of the Architectural Association was, in part, an outgrowth of the frustration that many idealistic young men had felt at being locked out of a profession that they dearly wanted to practice. Among the many ills they perceived holding them back were the tyranny of established talents, loose professional standards, unregulated competitions, education that was left to the vagaries of a medieval system of apprenticeship, and the low esteem architects possessed in the public eye. In words that could have been penned by Vaux, an anonymous correspondent to the *Builder* in 1847 asked: "What is a young architect to do, and how is he to get on? Suppose he is out of his time; he has been on the continent . . . for improvement; has no end of sketches and drawings; a love for the profession; and a very great desire to be doing something." If he did not care to do hack work, there was little chance for employment; if he entered competitions, he wasted great time and effort, for the job invariably went to a local favorite who proceeded to steal ideas from his unreturned entry; if he established his own office, few employed his services, for "gentlemen do not run after an architect as they do after a doctor"; and, finally, if out of desperation he sought the counsel of his seniors at the RIBA, he was told: "Young man, you must not expect everything at first. . . . Get your friends to give you a job."[37] It seems to me that the picture drawn by the *Builder's* correspondent reflected Vaux's situation as much as that of many of his aspiring colleagues.

For Vaux, therefore, the appearance of Downing at the doors of the Architectural Association in the late summer of 1850 was a fortunate event. Judging from the lament of the *Builder* correspondent, few of Vaux's fellows could have hoped for so promising an offer as the one Downing extended to him that fateful day. The author suspects that Vaux, close witness to his friend Truefitt's distancing success, fully realized his good fortune. After spending an agreeable afternoon with the well-known American visitor, Vaux dared not hesitate to accept the position that he knew others would eagerly seize. In Downing, Vaux had found an employer who shared the idealism of the young members of the Architectural Association. At the same time, the American's substantial reputation promised to attract important and challenging commissions to the new business venture he was inviting Vaux to share. And on the personal level, Vaux would have realized that Downing was a man old enough to guide him, yet young enough for friendship. His prospects for success must have seemed remarkably brighter to Vaux the day after he had met Downing than they had appeared before this encounter. Fortune had smiled on an earnest young architect who, like the correspondent to the *Builder*, must have had "a very great desire to be doing something." In the New World, Vaux would be given the chance to prove to himself and to others the worth of the training, knowledge, and sensibility he had cultivated in the Old.

2

IL BUONO
E IL BELLO
1850–1852

Within two weeks of Downing and Vaux's departure from Liverpool on the *Canada*, the two men were at work in the office Downing had created in his home. On the 50-mile steamer journey northward from New York City, Vaux would have seen for the first time the magnificent panorama of Hudson River scenery that had made this ride famous. The celebrated landscape of cliffs and highlands was destined to become the backdrop of Vaux's long life in America. The valley's Romantic beauty—which Vaux would come to know intimately as a resident, as a walker frequenting its picturesque byways, as an artist sketching its forest and natural wonders, and as an architect designing buildings attentive to its compelling loveliness—would deeply impress itself on his imagination. And he could have had no better companion to introduce him to its charms than Downing, a man whom many identified as the region's preeminent citizen.

Downing's own home, Highland Garden, overlooked the river above the flourishing town of Newburgh. Comprising several acres of carefully landscaped grounds, Highland Garden was to many of Downing's contemporaries his finest achievement, a monument to his Italian motto, *il buono e il bello*. "It was a palace and a garden in one," runs a typical description, "all care and trouble were shut out, all joy and pleasure shut in. . . . Like unto heaven it was!"[1] Taking inspiration from a plate in English architect Francis Goodwin's *Rural Architecture* (1835), Downing had erected an Elizabethan or Tudor-style villa in 1838. At the age of 24, he was just beginning his life as a serious thinker on the topics of domestic architecture and horticulture. Here Downing and his wife Caroline lived with the fullest regard for Victorian ideals of domesticity and liberality. Downing enjoyed nothing so much as filling his house with interesting and congenial guests, many of whom were also his clients. "It would be overleaping the bounds of literary decorum were we to mention other than public names whose presence made this place glad," wrote an associate of Downing's. "Suffice it that nowhere, we believe, in America has hospitality been more genuinely dispensed to guests worthy of all that the lordliest hospitality could offer."[2] Typical of the good times that Vaux must have shared here was the first Christmas that he celebrated in America, three months after his arrival. "We all danced to a fiddle upon the marble pavement of the hall," remembered a guest—the writer George William Curtis—"by the light of rustic candles wreathed with Christmas green, and under the antlers, pikes, helmets, and breastplates, and plumed hats of cavaliers, that hung upon the walls." It was as if, said Curtis, "the very genius of English Christmas ruled the revel."[3] Curtis also treasured memories of days devoted to "books, conversation, driving, working, lying on the lawn, excursions into the mountains, across the river, visits to beautiful neighboring places, boating, botanizing, painting," and evenings given over to fine music. Vaux himself cherished long discussions with Downing on Emerson, whom Downing believed to be "an accurate anatomist of the human mind," and Hazlitt, on whose works Downing based his own literary style.[4] "Knowing how wide awake and keen for intellectual cultivation and knowledge Mr. Calvert Vaux was, and having listened to innumerable conversations of his," recalled a later acquaintance of Vaux's, "I can imagine the profound influence upon the younger man of his intellectual discourse with his well read and thoughtful partner."[5]

The dwelling itself has long since disappeared, so we must reconstruct our knowledge of this special place from historic photographs, nineteenth-century engravings, and written descriptions. A picture taken in the 1920s (Fig. 2.1) at the time of demolition shows the villa, the brick walls of which were covered with sepia-toned stucco ruled to resemble courses of stone, and gives poignant testimony to the life that once was lived there. At first Downing continued to use a room above the parlor on the south side of the house (labeled "P" in Fig. 2.2) for his office. (This room was behind the blocked-up window visible on the second floor in Fig. 2.1.) For the fastidious Downing, however, such an arrangement, which confused domestic life with occupation, could not long be tolerated. In 1851, he and Vaux added a one-story brick extension to the back of the dwelling to accommodate better the demands of their expanding business. The addition, approached by a special path and carefully concealed from the house by judiciously planted shrubbery, provided more space than the former bedroom and avoided the necessity of clients entering the living quarters. Visible behind the house at the left in Figure 2.1, this wing held a small office (labeled "S" in Fig. 2.2) for Downing's personal use immediately adjacent to the dwelling and, beyond that, the workroom proper (labeled "O" on the plan in Fig. 2.2). The photograph also shows the double window that lighted Downing's private study, as well as the projecting vestibule that sheltered the clients' entrance. A tall chimney stack at the rear vented the fireplace that warmed the comfortable work space and, as Vaux would later explain, was well placed to prevent the occurrence of drafts.[6] "No place could be more delightful than this room to work in," stated Clarence Cook, who joined Downing and Vaux as an assistant in the winter of 1852. "On one side the southern windows let in warm and cheerful sunlight," recounts Cook, "on another the rows of books give a grace and charm to the apartment, and opposite them the bright wood fire warms body and soul with its crackling flames."[7] Downing himself could enter and leave his study through a revolving bookcase that opened into the southwest corner of the library (labeled "L" on the plan in Fig. 2.2). This method of internal communication, which had not appeared in plans in Downing's books, could have been suggested by Vaux, for he favored it in later houses

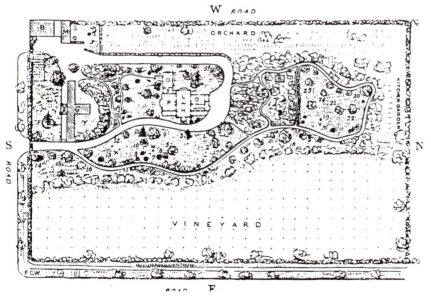

FIGURE 2.1. *(above)*
A. J. Downing,
Highland Garden,
Newburgh, N.Y.,
1838. Courtesy
of Thomas Kyle.

FIGURE 2.2. *(at left)*
Highland Garden,
house and grounds
plan. From
Horticulturist 8, n.s.
(January 1853).
Courtesy of
Buffalo and Erie
County Public
Library.

of his design.[8] Linking the study to the library was especially apt, for in winter, the library, which was smaller than the south parlor, became the focus of family life. Thus, Downing could move easily between the worlds of work and pleasure. Such commonsense planning also distinguished the dwellings that Downing and Vaux designed for their clients.

But all who knew Highland Garden agreed that the grounds were its chief delight. In a space of five acres, Downing had laid out a miniature paradise of naturalistic beauty. Sandwiched between an orchard on the west and a large vineyard on the east, the ornamental grounds of the property enclosed the area around the villa and stretched to the northern boundary of the property (Fig. 2.2). Within this zone, which Downing had planted with lawns, trees, shrubs, and flowers, several pathways led visitors along a gently winding circuit. Here and there, one took glimpses of the distant river and far-off mountains through openings that Downing had carefully placed in the screen of plantings that hid the vineyard and orchard from view. Vaux drew one of these vistas, including in it the large bronze replica of a vase from the Borghese gardens that Downing had placed on the lawn the year after Vaux arrived. In the farther parts of the grounds, Downing had built two rustic structures. The Hermitage (Fig. 2.3), a deeply embowered log and bark shelter, stood in the secluded northern part of the property, near a small rockwork garden of moss, thyme, and ferns. Elsewhere, the Arbor, also made of unfinished logs, provided a covered place from which to view the river. In addition, secluded rustic seats enticed the stroller to linger and quietly communicate with the genius of the place. To be sure, the house and grounds at Highland Garden epitomized what Walter Creese

FIGURE 2.3. A. J. Downing, the Hermitage at Highland Garden, 1840s. From *Horticulturist* 8, n.s. (January 1853). Courtesy of Buffalo and Erie County Public Library.

has so aptly characterized as Downing's ability "to manufacture integrated environments that held warmth, intimacy, and amenity."[9] Here, Vaux came to know firsthand one of the masterpieces of American Romantic landscape architecture. In the coming decades, he would make enjoyment of this tradition accessible to a wide public in the cities and suburbs of his adopted country.

Downing presided over his idyllic domain with an air of genial proprietorship. In 1838, he had married Caroline DeWint, the eldest daughter of a prominent Dutch family who lived across the river from Newburgh at Fishkill Landing. Reflective by nature and prone to dress in dark colors, Downing seemed to enjoy fulfilling the role of gentleman that he had mapped out for himself. Largely self-taught, he had succeeded in creating a persona that partook of the best aspects of high breeding, apparently without elitist overtones. Downing himself appeared friendly but reserved in his manner—what some perceived as stiffness or hauteur was probably his deliberate attempt to project an impression of self-confidence and correct deportment, tinged with a nuance of Romantic introspection. The Swedish feminist and novelist Fredrika Bremer, like other women, responded to Downing's poetical nature and gentle demeanor. When they met for the first time in the fall of 1849, at the beginning of her two-year American tour, Fredrika described him as a "gentleman dressed in black, with a refined, gentlemanly appearance, and manner, and a pair of the handsomest brown eyes I ever saw."[10] Thereafter, she showed no reluctance in expressing the deep admiration she felt for him. She even praised his choice of a mate, finding the nimble Caroline "a delicate, pretty little woman . . . of a bird-like nature"; she was, thought Bremer, the perfect hostess to the many friends and guests who frequented her husband's genial home. For his part, Downing seems to have responded to his visitor's ardor, expressing his feelings with gifts of flowers and, within the bounds of Victorian propriety, encouraging a warm friendship.

Perhaps because of her infatuation with Downing, when Fredrika returned to Highland Garden in September 1850, after her national tour, she barely mentioned Vaux. Yet since the Swedish writer was on her way to England in a few days to compare social conditions there with what she had learned in America, it seems likely that she would have talked to the bright young man whom her beloved Downing had recently brought back with him from London. One can easily imagine the three of them in lively conversation in her host's "dusky parlor," which she found so agreeable. Downing, who had read Ruskin and admired the Pre-Raphaelites, might have reiterated his reflection that while the English had no want of genius, they had need of "spirituality." And Vaux, the recent immigrant, would surely have listened avidly as the widely traveled visitor gave her candid appraisal of the problems that industrialization had brought about in his homeland. It was Fredrika Bremer's view that the English state was sitting on a social volcano that might explode at any moment. The only remedy that she foresaw for the widespread poverty there was "a great system of national education" like the one already established in the United States. "How fortunate you are, here," she declared to Downing, "who have been able to begin anew, and make a firm foundation before the building is overcrowded."[11]

All who knew Downing well, including Vaux—who left an especially poignant tribute to his friend in the form of a sepia portrait[12]—spoke of the lofty standards he set for himself in all areas of life. He was a perfectionist in everything he did. This included even the lighter pastimes he so fondly cultivated at Highland Garden. Remembering an impersonation of a trouble-some English traveler that Downing had once acted out, Clarence Cook remarked that Downing was "a man who attempted nothing that he did not feel confident he could perform in the most complete manner."[13] The civilized tone of life that Downing set at Highland Garden was undoubtedly as high-minded and affable as his many friends and associates described it. The ambiance was one that Vaux, himself an idealist, must have found congenial. He would, however, have quickly realized how distant it was from the run of everyday life in his new country. The only shadow that hung over Highland Garden seems to have been the worry for money. Yet even that unpleasantness was on the way to disap-pearing, given the rapid advance of the firm's affairs.

THE YEAR AND 11 months that Vaux spent with Downing, from September 1850 until July 1852, when a senseless steamboat accident claimed Downing's life, was a time of enormous activity for both men. During this period, Downing devoted much of his attention to revising his books, including a new edition of *Cottage Residences*, and preparing monthly numbers of the *Horticulturist*, the journal of suburban and rural living published in Albany by Luther Tucker. Downing's editorials give us a fair idea of the issues that concerned him during this time. Essays on country churches, the establishment of an agricultural college, the need for public parks in America's cities, the state of American architecture, the choice of the best shade trees for city streets, and the character of English rural life as described by Frederick Law Olmsted in *Walks and Talks of an American Farmer* (1852) suggest topics that Downing must have discussed with Vaux as well as with his readers. And although we have none of Downing's professional papers or office records, we are told that Downing and Vaux attracted clients from many parts of the East. The main sources of our knowl-edge of their architectural work are the fourth edition of *Cottage Residences*, which appeared in May 1852, and Vaux's own book, *Villas and Cottages*, which came out five years later and illustrated several houses that were designed dur-ing Vaux's time with Downing. Vaux presented these buildings as his own work, allowing that Downing had only cast his "genial influence" over their creation.[14] From this statement, as well as from the evidence of the designs themselves, which both show the influence of new modes of Gothic, French, and Palladian design and possess more tightly organized plans and a sense of larger scale, I conclude that soon after his arrival Vaux took major responsibility for architec-tural work in the office. This work arrangement would certainly have been in keeping with Downing's original purpose in seeking an architect associate. By the end of 1850, Vaux had so won Downing's confidence that he made him his partner.

Undoubtedly, the first undertaking to which Vaux turned his attention after arriving in Newburgh was the estate of Matthew Vassar at Poughkeepsie, New York. In early July 1850, Vassar, who had amassed a fortune in the brewery busi-ness, had purchased a large tract of land near the Hudson which he hoped would become a rural cemetery. It appears, however, that Vassar proceeded to improve the grounds from the beginning with the idea in mind that the land might be turned to his personal use. Eventually, when the cemetery association deter-mined to locate elsewhere, Vassar took up a residence here, giving the place the name Springside.[15] Probably soon after Downing's return from England, Vassar contacted him for advice on laying out the 100-acre property. In the fall of 1850, local newspapers reported that Downing had been engaged to guide the work. A topographical map of the grounds was made by an engineer, and work progressed quickly. By early July 1852, a visitor hailed the grounds, which by then possessed over two miles of drives and walks, several fountains, and numerous small buildings as well as a working farm, as the "realization of a painter's dream, the embodiment of the poet's glowing thought."[16] Vaux described the estate as "being full of easy sweeps and gentle undulations, . . . somewhat secluded and parklike in character, [with] fine healthy trees being scattered in groups and masses over the whole extent." Roads and other designed elements, he said, were "adapted to the peculiar features of the situation."[17] Springside was the first occasion that Vaux had to see how Downing conceived and executed a comprehensive landscape scheme.

In addition to ordering the natural setting, Downing and Vaux were responsible for erecting a number of buildings at Springside. The board-and-batten carriage barn must have been the first architectural project on which Vaux worked as Downing's assistant. At this early stage in their relationship, Downing probably followed the routine he was accustomed to with Davis and presented Vaux with a rough sketch which he expected to see worked up into architectural renderings.[18] One drawing for the coach house, lettered in script "AJD" and dated 1850, shows an elevation in halting perspective at the top of a page with an elevation and two ground plans in freehand beneath it. This sheet probably originated with Downing. Other, much larger drawings for the barn resemble plans from the Cottingham office. These surely were by Vaux. The comparison suggests that the hand that executed the small version could only imitate the conventions that the larger drawings fully embodied.[19]

What role Vaux may have played in the evolution of the design of the carriage house is difficult to assess. The ground plans on the drawings and on the sketch are the same. The elevation drawing, however, reveals that a number of subtle changes were made to Downing's initial suggestion. In the full-blown presentation drawing, the proportions of roof to walls are nearly equal; windows are raised to just beneath the roof; piecrust ornament along the roof crest is deleted; the hayloft door in the gable is changed, and a curved roof hood shades the barn door. All of these adjustments have the effect of clarifying the original conception, tightening and balancing its proportions, and imparting more vertical emphasis to the structure. Downing published a perspective view of the handsome stable in the February 1851 issue of the *Horticulturist*,[20] where he drew special attention to the ventilator tower, the first elaborate example of this feature to appear in his architectural illustrations. Could this element, which does so much to impart the mood of festive picturesqueness lacking in earlier designs for stables that Downing had published, have been suggested by Vaux? He was often to employ it in his later designs for houses; there, as here, it focuses and accentuates the tall proportions of the design.[21] Perhaps because it held a special place in his memory, Vaux later singled out the barn as one of the significant additions to the fourth edition of *Cottage Residences*.

Other board-and-batten buildings erected on the grounds of Springside by Downing and Vaux included an entrance lodge and a summer cottage. The latter structure, now in ruins, became Vassar's permanent residence, for the anticipated principal dwelling never materialized. Both of these dependencies echoed designs for small dwellings in the Bracketed style that Downing had published in the 1840s and, like the carriage barn, owed their conception to him. The gate lodge alone survives intact to give us a good idea of the charm that Springside's architecture once possessed. (It is, in fact, the second version of the design for the entrance building. The first scheme, showing a stucco-covered gatehouse, survives as a drawing by Vaux.) Vaux surely would have found these buildings reminiscent of Davis and hopelessly quaint and out-of-date. One assumes that he held his tongue while they got built. Nonetheless, the lodge and cottage showed Vaux how with "studied irregularity and broadly conceived picturesqueness" Downing gave even a modest dwelling the sense of belonging to its setting. There was nothing Downing disliked more, said Vaux, than "the square boxes," as he called the usual houses of his countrymen, that one encountered outside the charmed grounds of properties like Springside.[22]

The fate of the original designs for the porter's lodge may have been tied to the unexecuted design for a large brick residence planned for a terraced hilltop site near the northern edge of the Vassar property (Fig. 2.4). This grand dwelling, which Vaux included in his book *Villas and Cottages*, survives in a series of splendid architectural renderings dated 1851 and drawn by Vaux, who by this time was taking responsibility for conceiving and developing the firm's architectural designs. Distinguished by Flemish gables, tall, clustered chimneys, and massive wooden porches, the brick and stone exterior bears the impress of Vaux's influence. He would have been thoroughly familiar with the taste for Elizabethan architecture that asserted itself in England in the 1830s and 1840s. To the leading examples of Victorian country houses in this manner, notably Edward Blore's Pull Court (1834–1846) and Anthony Salvin's renowned Harlaxton

FIGURE 2.4. "Design for a Residence for Matthew Vassar, Esq., Principal Elevation," Poughkeepsie, N.Y., 1851. Courtesy of Special Collections, Vassar College Libraries.

DESIGN FOR A RESIDENCE FOR MATTHEW VASSAR ESQ
PRINCIPAL ELEVATION ¼ SCALE

Manor (1837), can be added work Cottingham did in 1833–1834 for the Earl Craven at Coombe Abbey. Herbert Williams's Public Dispensary at Brighton, an illustration of which appeared in the *Builder* in January 1850, exemplified the enduring popularity of this style. From such sources, Vaux produced a design whose scale and authority exceeded anything that had appeared in the pages of Downing's books.

In addition to Vaux's elevation drawings and plans, a detailed list of specifications exists for Vassar's mansion.[23] The only such document to survive for a work by the firm, it reveals how valuable to Downing was Vaux's practical knowledge of building practices. From it, as well as from *Villas and Cottages*, we also learn that the walls were to have been of a "soft reddish" brick, with brownstone of a "gray tint" for windows and openings; the roofs were to be covered with greenish gray slates; and the woodwork of the veranda was to be painted a "warm oak color." Mixed materials, asserted Vaux, would impart "sufficient variety of color to accord with the irregular outline, and the red would have a refreshing effect in a situation secluded and sheltered among rich green trees."[24] It is a pity that he and Matthew Vassar never got the chance to see the building constructed. (Vaux, however, would have been highly amused to see how in 1868 the Miller Iron Company of Providence mimicked Vassar's commodious dwelling in its design for a cast iron birdhouse.)

ANOTHER IMPORTANT COMMISSION on the Hudson came from Warren Delano II, a wealthy importer and trader, who in 1851 engaged Downing and Vaux to enlarge the two-story brick house that he had bought on land two miles north of Newburgh. The alterations to the house and grounds, which Delano called Algonac, were completed by August 1852.[25] The work expanded a rather modest Bracketed cottage into an impressive country seat in the Italian style (Fig. 2.5), a mode of design that Downing had done much to popularize in his books. In order to reconcile the old and new portions of the house and to ensure harmony between building and grounds, Downing and Vaux covered exterior walls with the fawn-colored stucco that Downing favored over traditional white paint.[26] The predominant features of Downing and Vaux's remodeling was a three-story tower added to the east side of the older building. Here they located the new entrance, sheltering it beneath a large porte cochere. From the spacious balcony above, as well as from the handsome Palladian window that graced the third-floor level of the tower, family and guests could enjoy views of the grounds in front of the house. Likewise, to a person looking toward the river from windows in the southern side of the mansion it seemed "as though the green lawns might almost reach into the water."[27]

While no plans have survived for Algonac, written descriptions give some idea of the interior arrangements. The most striking space was the square entrance hall in which Warren Delano proudly arrayed many fine objets d'art that he had brought back from the Far East, where, in the 1840s, he had made his fortune. At one side, screened by three large round arches, the main staircase rose through the tower to the second floor, where numerous bedrooms overlooked the spacious grounds. In one of these rooms on September 21, 1854, was born Sara Delano, mother of Franklin Delano Roosevelt.

Certainly, Vaux's influence informed the design of Algonac. The proportions of the tower, for example, embody a certain High Victorian amplitude and

monumentality lacking in those that graced most of the Tuscan villas in Downing's books. And nowhere in his publications did Downing illustrate a porte
cochere of such substantial proportions as that at Algonac. Evidence of Vaux's
hand in the design also comes from his book *Villas and Cottages*. In his introduction, Vaux illustrated the triple arches that stood between the entrance hall
and the staircase hall (illustrated on page 76), an arrangement that linked the
two areas into one grand space. "In this plan," stated Vaux, "the upper flight
of the principal stairs is supported on the arcade, and the two halls being thus
connected together, a light, airy effect is produced." Historic photographs of
the staircase hall at Algonac—surely one of the early instances of this feature in
mid-nineteenth-century domestic architecture—confirm Vaux's assertion. The
introduction to *Villas and Cottages* also contains a design for a bay window that
followed the one that filled the narrow end of Algonac's drawing room, where
it seemed to extend the room into the landscape. For Downing, who on his
recent trip to England had seen "spacious Italian villas, more Italian than in
Italy,"[28] it must have been a pleasure to work directly with so up-to-date an
architect as Vaux on such a grand realization of this popular mode of British
domestic architecture.

From old photographs and written accounts, one gathers that the grounds of
Algonac were as splendid as the house. Since Warren Delano counted Downing
as a friend with whom he shared an interest in horticulture, it seems likely that
the two men together took up the pleasant labor of planning the roads and des-
ignating the location of trees and shrubs. One description of Algonac in its days
of brilliance indicates that "on the lawns Mr. Delano and Mr. Downing had
planted spruces and hemlocks and pines for the winter, oaks and beeches and
maples and exotic trees and flowering shrubs from China for the other seasons."[29] Lovely Algonac remained one of the Hudson Valley's enchanted places
until 1916, when fire destroyed the magnificent house. In a later time, the
grounds were subdivided for modern residences. Today, virtually nothing
remains of the Victorian idyll of well-to-do rural life that Downing and Vaux
had created there.[30]

THE FREE OR IRREGULAR Italian style, as Vaux termed it, stood equal in his view to the so-called Rural Gothic, a mode of architectural expression that Downing, following the lead of European thinkers, had identified with the picturesque. Many Gothic dwellings had appeared in Downing's publications, and as his associate, Vaux made plans for a number of such houses, many of which were erected in the Newburgh area. These buildings, however, differed in form from those made popular by Downing and Davis. The Tudor villa, of which Highland Garden was a notable example, as well as the wooden Bracketed cottage gave way to a new interpretation of Gothic that surely owed its appearance to Vaux.[31] These houses represent an updating of the picturesque Gothic tradition that was in line with developments in England and on the Continent. Compared with the houses that Downing had created with Davis, these dwellings are more vertical in expression and more compact in plan and outline. Their "Gothic" character resides in steep proportions, rising and falling lines of saddleback and jerkin head roofs, architectural details such as brackets, vergeboards, and trusses, and pronounced patterns of light and shade produced by projecting elements such as eaves, balconies, and bay windows. By midcentury, this sort of exaltation of rural vernacular forms had become widely identified with England. In this respect, Anglophile architect Jacques-Louis Brocher's 1858 remodeling of the Villa Lammermoor for Sir Robert Peel near Geneva, Switzerland (Fig 2.6), exemplifies, like Vaux's American dwellings, the wide popularity of this "style des cottages anglais."[32]

FIGURE 2.6. J.-L. Brocher, Villa Lammermoor, the Sir Robert Peel house, Geneva, 1858. Courtesy of Musée du Vieux Geneve.

The brick house for William L. Findlay (Fig. 2.7), which the firm constructed on a site near Newburgh, excelled all of the Gothic dwellings that Vaux designed while with Downing. A series of projecting and receding volumes corresponding to the major divisions of the plan created full-bodied masses in light and shade. Porches and oriole and bay windows modulated the surface of the building and extended interior space into the out-of-doors. And tall roofs, fronted by decorative bargeboards and gently curved at the eaves, molded chimney stacks, and a large wooden turret (intended to collect ventilation flues) all directed the eye upward.

The picturesque elevations of the Findlay house developed from an unusual cruciform plan (Fig. 2.8) in which all of the ground-floor rooms communicate with the entrance hall by means of double sliding doors. The layout, Vaux tells us, grew out of the client's desire to use the home primarily for summertime entertaining. "It would hardly be possible to have a more airy and open arrangement for summer," he stated, "for, standing in the hall when the rooms are thrown open, one can see clear through the house, north, south, east, and west; and the porch, hall vestibule, library, dining-room, drawing-room, and veranda, are converted, as it were, into one connected apartment."[33] Responding to Findlay's desire for gracious summer living, Vaux developed a plan that anticipated the easy flow of space and internal vistas of late-nineteenth-century Shingle-style dwellings.

In addition, the Findlay house, which possessed extensive grounds, was carefully attuned to its highland location overlooking the Hudson. Vaux took special note of the "vista effect" obtained from the hall through the lateral bay windows at the ends of the dining room and drawing room. But the most engaging picture was the one that the Findlays enjoyed from the library looking back toward the entrance. On a summer evening, explained Vaux, "when the doors are open, anyone sitting in the library bay can see the river view framed, as it were, in the outer arch of the porch." This was Vaux's clearest assertion of the commitment he shared with Downing to reconcile the client's domestic life with the emotive potential of his dwelling's natural setting. The Findlay house epitomizes a type of dwelling that Vaux would design for the next two decades.

Seeking to express sympathy with its picturesque surroundings was also a controlling factor in the design of other Gothic houses that the firm designed. Joel T. Headley, the author of many popular travel and historical books, commissioned a house for a site at nearby New Windsor, New York. "Its steep roof lines harmonize admirably with the bold hills of the Hudson Highlands," said Downing when he illustrated the two-story brick dwelling as the frontispiece of the 1852 edition of *Cottage Residences*. Downing described the house, which Vaux claimed as his own creation,[34] as in the "Rhine style." He was referring primarily to the slender entrance tower crowned by a steeply curved, spirelike roof. Such bowed profiles, Downing asserted, were a distinguishing feature of Rhenish buildings and represented a sort of sublimation into architecture of the characteristics of the landscape. "It is, in fact," he wrote, "a repetition of the grand hollow or mountain curve formed by the sides of almost all great hills rising from the water's edge, and forms the connecting link that unites and brings into harmony the opposite lines, perpendicular and horizontal, which are found, the one in the tower and the other in the water or landscape level at its base."[35] The tower, nonetheless, was a costly gesture of Romantic association for Headley, who had told Downing and Vaux that he did not want to pay for fanciful

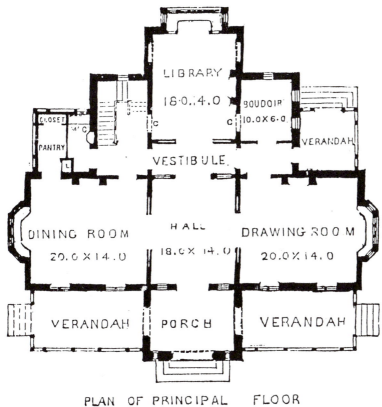

FIGURE 2.7. *(above)* William L. Findlay house, Newburgh, N.Y., 1851–1852. Courtesy of Buffalo and Erie County Public Library.

FIGURE 2.8. *(at left)* Findlay house, plan. From C. Vaux, *Villas and Cottages* (1857). Courtesy of Buffalo and Erie County Public Library.

decoration. Nonetheless, Headley came to feel much at home in his fictive Rhineland solitude. His still existing house must have given him a pleasant sense of detachment from the demands of publishers, who, despite his often pompous style, found a sustained market for his 30 books. Here too, beneath his princely tower, his ego must have been out of range of harsh attacks by critics such as Edgar Allan Poe, who called Headley "The Autocrat of all the Quacks."[36]

For David Moore, a lumber dealer, the partnership built a square house of brick that from its Newburgh city lot enjoyed good views of the river. The dwelling's numerous dormer windows and projecting hoods, as well as a covered balcony over the ground-floor bay window, imparted "individuality and completeness to the design," said Vaux.[37] As in the case of the Findlay house, the Moore house capitalized on the possibilities of the site. With the river in mind, Vaux designed the major feature of the interior, a drawing room, across the full width of the back of the house. "From this drawing-room," he wrote, "the windows open on to a wide, spacious veranda, commanding an extensive view of the Hudson."

With the scenery equally in mind, the firm prepared plans for a brick Gothic residence for Frederick J. Betts, a prominent figure in the New York State legal profession and a friend who had once helped Downing out of a difficult financial situation. On the flat central portion of the roof of the Betts house, Vaux proposed to create a viewing platform. The location of Betts's property endowed the novel stage, which was surrounded by a low railing, with an exceptional panorama of beautiful highland scenery. "Such a view," said Vaux, who was to design many park structures with provisions for the pleasure of looking, "would differ very much from the more circumscribed landscapes to be obtained from the windows at a lower level, and would have a marked character and interest of its own."[38]

MUCH MORE URBAN IN spirit than these Gothic residences was the house that Vaux designed while with Downing for Dr. William A. M. Culbert (Fig. 2.9), a homeopathic physician who over his long career in Newburgh earned the love and respect of many of his fellow citizens for his good judgment and fatherly counsel. A native of New York City, Culbert was a protege of Valentine Mott, the noted surgeon, and a graduate of New York University, where he had pursued graduate studies in the liberal arts before medical school. In 1847, at the age of 25, the cultivated young doctor set up practice in Newburgh, where his patients represented many leading families of the vicinity. Several years later, anticipating marriage to Henrietta Powell, a granddaughter of steamboat magnate Thomas Powell, Culbert commissioned Downing and Vaux to design for him a handsome brick and brownstone residence and office. The lot he had selected was on Grand Street, a thoroughfare that was becoming the principal residential address in Newburgh. Vaux predicted that eventually the street would rank as one of the grand American avenues. Running parallel to the Hudson, which could be glimpsed in the distance below, the wide roadway shaded by maturing elms and maples promised, said Vaux, "to produce an effect that may equal the far-famed Hill-house Avenue in New Haven." And at every corner one enjoyed a picture of the river "framed in the foliage of the trees on the side streets."[39] At one of these intersections, Dr. Culbert chose to erect his new house.

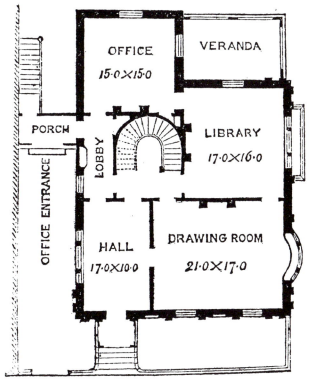

FIGURE 2.9. *(above)* William A. M. Culbert house, Newburgh, N.Y., 1851–1852. From *Harper's New Monthly Magazine*, November 1855.

FIGURE 2.10. *(at left)* Culbert house, plan. From C. Vaux, *Villas and Cottages* (1857). Courtesy of Buffalo and Erie County Public Library.

A desire for dignified elegance guided Vaux in the design of the dwelling's exterior and interior. Brownstone Tuscan pilasters and recessed panels articulated the two main elevations, which were divided into two slightly unequal layers by a wide architrave molding. The arrangement, together with the transomed casement windows and fanciful stone gables, echoed Sebastiano Serlio's famous Chateau of Ancy-le-Franc, and one assumes that Vaux had brought with him from England a copy of the sixteenth-century Italian architect's *L'Architectura*, a standard work that had gone through many editions by Vaux's day. Above the carved stone cornice, Vaux enlivened the design with a high concave curved roof carrying a crown of filigree iron railing. Delicate ironwork also supported the entrance porch on Grand Street, as well as a small veranda overlooking the side street. Both the drawing room facing Grand Street and the bedrooms above received abundant light from the tall casement windows.

Inside the house, Vaux also introduced elements redolent of French design. "In Paris and other Continental cities," he said, "the circular, or elliptical, staircase is in great demand," and he introduced one here running from the basement to the chamber floor. But Vaux did not let elegance of detail distract his attention from the practical need to devise a plan (Fig. 2.10) that would equally accommodate the client's professional and private life. Perhaps with his own youth as a doctor's son in mind, Vaux arranged the ground plan so that the consultation office on the principal floor stood isolated from the family living quarters. Patients were expected to enter by a special side doorway that opened into a small lobby adjacent to the rear office. Even those rare visitors who might call at the front door could be ushered directly into this side lobby from the hall without disturbing the doctor's family. Displaying a skillful sense of planning, a serious knowledge of the style of Francis I, and an awareness of modern-day Parisian suburban domestic architecture, Vaux created a dwelling for Dr. Culbert that brought a remarkable degree of sophistication to Newburgh's most handsome thoroughfare.[40]

A very different type of client was James Hall, an eminent geologist and promoter of many scientific endeavors, including the mapping of the State of New York. Since the 1840s, Hall had sought advice on horticultural matters from Downing and his brother Charles. In 1852, Hall engaged Downing and Vaux to plan his estate on Beaverkill Creek on the outskirts of Albany, New York. The partners made a design for a wooden house that may not have been constructed. The building was to have been sided with clapboard, a method of covering that Vaux considered superior to the board-and-batten system that Downing had done so much to popularize in the 1840s. "It is well suited for barns or small buildings, where the battens are relatively large enough to form part of the design," Vaux conceded, "but when used on a larger scale, it is apt to give a striped, liney appearance to a house that injures its broad, general effect, and to draw particular attention to the fact that it is built of wood." For this reason, he thought that "the ordinary mode of horizontal siding seems preferable in most situations."[41] In addition to providing a design for the main house, Downing and Vaux also apparently advised Hall on the Italian-style brick office, which Hall's biographer, John M. Clarke, reported contained "one large room and galleries for his collections assembled in some thousands of drawers, with a study framed in books."[42] Unfortunately, the Hall property, which today comprises Albany's Lincoln Park, bears scarce witness to the home and grounds that once existed there.

WHEN DOWNING MET HIS death in a steamboat accident in the summer of 1852, he had been on his way to Newport. There he intended to discuss plans that he and Vaux had made for a large summer home for Daniel Parish, a nephew of Downing's wealthy Newburgh neighbor Thomas Powell. Parish and his brother Henry were among the richest men in New York City. They had made their money, said a biographer, in "one of the most remarkable commercial houses that ever existed in the city," a clothing business with branches in several southern cities.[43] In 1838, having secured a fortune, Daniel Parish retired from trade to devote himself to financial speculations. At midcentury, Parish set his sights on Newport as an elegant summer address, as other New Yorkers of his class were doing. Perhaps at his uncle's suggestion, Daniel and his wife Mary Ann chose Downing to realize their opulent dream. After Downing's death, Vaux saw the Parish house through to completion. The *Horticulturist* reported in May 1853 that the seaside villa on Bellevue Avenue (Fig. 2.11) was nearly finished and that the grounds were being laid out and planted.

Taking his cue from the character of the site, a piece of level ground some 20 feet above the Atlantic, Vaux deliberately created a design of unusual severity and simplicity. The location, stated the *Horticulturist* with Vaux's prompting, "was suggestive of the dignified repose of the ocean as a whole rather than of its restless excitement in detail; it was therefore thought desirable in the design for the house, to avoid irregularities and smallness of parts as much as possible, and to give more prominence to the horizontal than to the vertical lines of the composition." The result was a dwelling of two parts: a square, symmetrical two-story main section and, on the north, a lower, T-shaped service wing. A continuous stringcourse molding tied the two portions together into a unified composition

FIGURE 2.11. Daniel Parish house, Newport, R.I., 1851–1852. Courtesy of Newport Historical Society.

that signaled the prominence of the living quarters over the lesser rooms that served them. Classical elements increased the monumental effect, including a rusticated stone porte cochere (which recalls the ground floor of Gottfried Semper's 1847 Gemäldegalerie in Dresden) and a two-story loggia set into the back wall between curved bay windows of the dining room and drawing room. Often referred to as "ombras" in the literature of the time, recessed arcades such as this, said Vaux, imparted contrasts of light and shade to a building while affording its inhabitants a place of leisure more secluded from observation and the elements than a veranda. (With this feature, the ocean side of the Parish villa anticipated Richard Morris Hunt's more famous Breakers of the 1890s.) From the ground floor of the loggia of the Parish house, one could stroll onto the lawn that stretched to the sea cliffs at the end of the property. On the south side of the mansion (away from the sea), visitors could enjoy the grounds from the protection of a deep veranda that extended far into the garden.[44]

The exterior of the Parish house was unlike anything Downing had published in his books and articles. Crystalline and Classical, as Vincent Scully long ago pointed out, its blocklike mass and severe detailing harked back to Palladio, whose plainer sixteenth-century villas—the Villa Godi rather than Maser or La Rotunda—continued to inspire certain nineteenth-century designers of smaller country houses in England and on the Continent.[45] Repton's design for Langley house is one example. In fact, the Parish house finds a close parallel in the work of Swiss architect Jacques-Louis Brocher. Brocher studied briefly at the Ecole des Beaux-Arts in Paris and spent considerable time in England. Back in Geneva, he became one of a number of architects who since the mid-1830s had been catering to families of wealth who, smitten with Rousseau and the Romantic notion of Nature *idyllique sauvage*, were erecting on the shores of Lake Léman comfortable villas that took full advantage of Byronic views of the lake and mountains. As art historian Leila El-Wakil has pointed out, this simple but elegant "*classicisme libéré*" appealed to the restrained taste of the haute bourgeoisie in the tiny republic whose scenery Ruskin found so compellingly beautiful. Especially Brocher's villa Petit Malagny (1844; Fig. 2.12), with its cubic volumes, central broken pediment, low hipped roof, bare surfaces, and flanking verandas, shares the Palladian spirit of Vaux's Parish house. Although it is unlikely that Vaux was aware of Brocher's architecture, the Swiss villa serves to illustrate the international Palladian tradition from which Vaux and Downing derived the design of the Parish house. One can be sure that the appearance of this type of architecture in the partners' work was due to the knowledge of this mode of design that Vaux brought with him from England.

For the clarity of spatial arrangement and the liberal dimensions of rooms, the plan of the principal floor (Fig. 2.13) of the Parish villa surpassed anything that had appeared in Downing's publications. Surely taking responsibility for the design, Vaux developed the dining room and drawing room (each 19' × 29') together with a plant cabinet and the ground floor of the arcade into an interconnected suite. The three equidistant doorways connecting these spaces lined up enfilade fashion and framed the lateral windows looking from the drawing room onto the pavilion. Openness was thus wedded to a certain degree of formality in a way that forecast many later Newport "cottages" and marked a radical departure from the kind of planning embodied in Richard Upjohn's nearby Gothic Revival masterpiece, Kingscote, the house he designed in 1839 for southern plantation owner George Noble Jones.

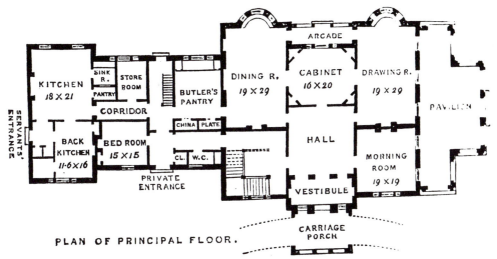

PLAN OF PRINCIPAL FLOOR.

FIGURE 2.12. (above) J.-L. Brocher, Petit Malagny,
Geneva, 1844. Photograph by the author.

FIGURE 2.13. (below) Parish house, plan. From
C. Vaux, *Villas and Cottages* (1857). Courtesy of
Buffalo and Erie County Public Library.

Downing was particularly anxious that the Parish house be successful. "Mr. Downing knew that Newport was the great social exchange of the country," wrote his friend George Curtis, "and that a fine house of his designing erected there would be of the greatest service to his art"[46] Tragically, the explosion of the *Henry Clay* at Yonkers doomed Downing's plans to meet Curtis at Newport and, with Caroline, to be received by fashionable society. If he had lived, Downing would have been heartened by the appreciative notice the resort community took of his and Vaux's efforts. In 1853, a local newspaper wrote that "Mr. Parish's villa claims, with Redwood Library, the distinction of being Newport's chief architectural beauty."[47] Daniel Parish himself was apparently immensely pleased with the design of his new house; after fire destroyed it in 1855, he engaged Vaux the following year to rebuild the original design, although on a spot somewhat closer to the water.[48]

THE PARISH VILLA WAS an example of the more expensive commissions that Downing and Vaux were increasingly attracting. Of even grander scale was an unbuilt project for a stone villa for Samuel D. Dakin, a Manhattan attorney. The ungainly-looking structure, which awkwardly combined elements of Tudor, Moorish, and Gothic architecture, was begun but never finished on a site overlooking the Hudson, possibly at Dobbs Ferry.[49] More successful was the design that Downing and Vaux prepared for the biggest house of their partnership years (Fig. 2.14). The client's name is not recorded, but Vaux indicated that detailed plans existed by the time of Downing's death. The patron apparently had a large collection of paintings that he wished to display in two corridors opening off a central hall. Here a fountain would have added the murmur of splashing water to the pleasure of viewing works of art. Simply termed a "Villa on a Large Scale" when Vaux included the house as the last design in *Villas and Cottages*, it had carved Moorish-style verandas on the side and back and a curious tower that bid to focus the many projecting and receding volumes and the rising and falling lines of gables and dormers.

FIGURE 2.14. Gardiner G. Howland house, location unknown, 1851–1852. From *Harper's New Monthly Magazine,* November 1855.

The extensive mansion, acknowledged a British critic, "might rank with the best class of the Elizabethan manor-houses of England."[50] He probably had in mind such works as Anthony Salvin's Harlaxton Manor (1831–1837) and William Burn's Dartrey (1843), outstanding representatives of a class of country seat to which Vaux knew few in America could aspire. The extended plan pointed up what Vaux identified as a chief difference between American and English country houses. Most American dwellings, said Vaux, required compact plans because of the need to conserve heat and the difficulty in obtaining servants. This house, however, more closely resembled British mansions, which delighted "in halls and passages, long corridors and wide vestibules, galleries, and staircases."[51] Be that as it may, aspects of the plan bore resemblance to the Parish house. Symmetry governed the arrangement of spaces in the main part of the dwelling, where the dining room and drawing room (each 30' × 20') were joined by a square parlor (20' × 20') and connected to the library (34' × 20') to form a unified suite opening onto a terrace that commanded fine views. (A formidable array of large Gothic windows on this side of the house would also have scanned the unidentified locale.) And like the Parish house, this villa imitated current English fashion in having a morning room, here labeled "boudoir," at one corner of the principal floor. One assumes that Vaux would have explained to Downing and their wealthy clients that such rooms were intended to be used, as Jill Franklin says of British examples, "as the feminine equivalent of the study, but less gloomy."[52] A more universal space was the deep pavilion in the Moorish style that projected from the side of the boudoir and library, recalling the broad arcaded porch on the side of the Newport villa. On the other end of the house, the extensive service wing stretched along a corridor leading from the dining room to the kitchen. Unfortunately, reported Vaux, the unnamed man of wealth and culture for whom this palatial country residence was planned— I believe the client to have been Gardiner G. Howland, a retired New York merchant who had been a prominent director of the Bank of New York and the moving force behind the creation of the Hudson River Railroad—died suddenly before he could begin construction.[53]

Whatever judgment we may level at these two upscale dwellings, they demonstrate the growing success of Downing's enterprise. Indeed, his business had grown so much since Vaux's arrival in September 1850 that it had become necessary to hire another architectural assistant. In February 1852, Downing and Vaux brought from London Frederick Clarke Withers (1828–1901), a young architect who in later years would become Vaux's partner and have a distinguished career as a Gothic Revival church architect.[54] Withers was joined about the same time by Clarence Cook, a recent Harvard graduate with apparently no architectural experience. For the last six months of Downing's life, Withers and Cook assisted Downing and Vaux on their ever widening architectural and landscape design practice.

IN ADDITION TO commissions for private houses, Downing and Vaux devoted their efforts to other types of work. For Milton J. Stone, the partners erected a "range of stores" in Boston. Commercial Block, as Stone called the waterfront building, still stands at 126–144 Commercial Street, at the corner of Richmond Street (Fig. 2.15).[55] The five-story structure was designed to house rows of shops at ground level and offices in the four stories above. This type of speculative building has been identified with the beginnings of the department store and office building, but for its construction Vaux had acquainted himself with what historian John M. Bryan has called "the Boston granite style."[56] Like earlier local dockside structures, Commercial Block employs Quincy granite throughout, with piers of solid stone framing ground-level windows and entrances. But in the design of his building, Vaux refined the esthetic character of this vernacular architecture, while remaining true to the special properties of its adamantine material. Drastically simplifying such academic decorative features as molded stringcourses and quoins and carefully varying the spacing and size of windows (their pattern of diminishing height as well as the motif of squareish windows resting directly on the upper stringcourse recall Lewis N. Cottingham's 1826 Duke of York Hotel), Vaux imparted a sense of pleasing proportion to the uniformly rusticated facade, which before the modern addition of another floor terminated with the cornice that echoes the ground-floor architrave. One wonders if Vaux had taken lessons from Karl Friedrich Schinkel's functionalist exterior of the Bauakademie (1836) in Berlin, substituting for the Prussian architect's many-colored bricks and tiles monochromatic gray granite. In the rationalist spirit of Schinkel (whose work Cottingham had liked), Vaux emphasized mass and texture and ranked historicism second to the forceful expression of his building's native material.

FIGURE 2.15. Commercial Block, Boston, 1851–1852. Photograph by the author.

The elegance and straightforward character of the Commercial Block's granite exterior drew the attention of Sigfried Giedion, the early historian of modern architecture. In his seminal *Space, Time and Architecture*, he singled out the building, without knowing its architect, as a prime example of Boston's midcentury granite architecture and suggested that it might have exerted a formative influence on H. H. Richardson.[57] Richardson entered Harvard shortly after Commercial Block was completed and could have looked at it and other recent stone structures that lined the Boston waterfront, such as Gridley James Fox Bryant's Mercantile Wharf building of 1857, which unequivocally emulates Vaux's handsome design. It is also likely that after 1865, when Richardson returned from five years of architectural study in Paris and started to practice in New York City, as an acquaintance of Vaux he became aware of Vaux's association with this building. Together with certain of Vaux's constructions in Central Park, it may have both stimulated the younger man's awareness of the expressive potential of rusticated masonry and influenced the clarity and simplicity of his buildings. As Giedion suggested, the "well-proportioned and logical" Commercial Block bears a distant resemblance to the great master's Marshall Field Store of 1885 in Chicago.

In addition to creating a forward-looking treatment for the facade of the Commercial Block, Vaux attempted to make the building more secure from damage by fire than older granite buildings: despite the durability of their material, these structures were susceptible to destruction during a conflagration, when burning joists exerted outward pressure on the walls and toppled them over. In order to prevent this from happening, Vaux introduced a new method of internal construction. Rather than build the wooden floor joists directly into the walls, as was the usual practice, he had them rest on stone corbels projecting inward from the wall surface. By this novel system Vaux hoped to exempt the Commercial Block from the greatest threat that owners of such properties faced. Undoubtedly, he and Downing were aware of the important role that this commission could play in their future business prospects, and they must have wanted to make the Commercial Block, inside and out, as emblematic of modernity as possible. It would not have been lost upon them that the building's prominent location in the heart of Boston's bustling waterfront district might attract attention to the firm and help them to cultivate a clientele other than suburban homeowners.

ALREADY, EVEN BEFORE the construction of the Commercial Block, Downing had been given the historic opportunity to extend his practice of landscape architecture beyond the limits of private life. In the months immediately after Vaux's arrival in America, Downing was greatly occupied with plans for a public park at Washington. It was a project that he hoped might educate all urban Americans to the benefits that large parks could bestow upon their cities. "He intended to have made the Public Grounds at Washington as nearly perfect as his taste and Experience would allow him," remembered Vaux, "and trusted that they might act favorably toward the accomplishment of his great desire— Public Pleasure grounds everywhere."[58] Initially, Joseph Henry, secretary of the Smithsonian Institution, recommended Downing to President Fillmore as the man who could create a park worthy of the nation on the land between the Capitol and the White House. On November 25, 1851, Downing visited

Washington to meet with Henry and fellow New Yorker Fillmore, who shared Downing's interest in parks and horticulture.

Congress too was eager to make improvements to the federal city. Having just passed the Compromise Act, which outlawed slave trading in the city (until 1850 a notorious slave pen stood within view of Henry's Smithsonian office), it was in the mood, as Therese O'Malley has pointed out, to encourage non-partisan civic projects. In those divisive times, many believed it imperative to strengthen in the minds of both southerners and northerners the city's image as the vital center of the Union.[59] Together with Ignatius Mudd, commissioner of public buildings, and several prominent individuals, Downing surveyed the area. After his inspection, Downing returned to Newburgh armed with plats and profiles that Mudd furnished him to develop his plan. And surely the prospect of such an important commission must have contributed to the jubilation of the 1850 Christmas celebrations at Highland Garden. By the beginning of the new year, recalled Vaux, Downing had formulated his ideas.

By early March of 1851, he had sent a plan and descriptive statement to the Regents of the Smithsonian. With their blessing, Henry approached Fillmore with the scheme and easily won the president's approval. On April 12, Fillmore gave the go-ahead to begin construction of the eastern portion of the 150-acre park. Work began soon thereafter, and Downing traveled to Washington each month for a week or more to monitor its progress. But soon Downing found himself having to deal with troublesome clients—legislators who considered his fee unearned and the cost of the project too great. Back at Newburgh, Vaux surely commiserated with him over the bickering and unsympathetic treatment he was forced to endure in Washington—a predicament that Vaux must later have looked upon as prophetic of the problems that he and Olmsted faced in their dealings with politicians and park commissioners.

Undoubtedly prompted by the difficulties in Washington, Vaux wrote a long essay entitled "Should a Republic Encourage the Arts?" Downing published it in the February 1852 issue of the *Horticulturist*. In dense prose, Vaux sought to answer those whom Downing criticized for believing "that a government like ours should necessarily confine its duties to making and executing laws" and should not spend money "for that species of higher education which grows out of a direct encouragement of the arts."[60] Defining architecture as "the art of the beautiful in building . . . the whole art of giving to a building all the beauties or perfections of which it is capable; perfection of plan and perfection of execution," Vaux argued that if the government did not set high standards for the nation's public buildings, then the people would be denied their greatest opportunity to exercise "one of the noblest gifts of the Creator." Good public architecture, asserted Vaux, was a right, for it was clear that "providing suitable national buildings . . . is a necessary part of the business of government." Perhaps buoyed by his partner's philosophical support, Downing brought matters to a head in February 1852 when he met with Fillmore and members of his cabinet to defend his position and to demand authority to act without interference. His effort proved successful, and from March 1852, when Congress gave its approval for the western portion of the project, Downing was in control of the situation and work progressed smoothly. Indeed, Downing's mandate expanded to include Lafayette Square, the area in front of the White House. A few months later, Downing undertook the last trip of his life, in part, to attend to his duties in Washington.

Downing proposed a six-part scheme for the long and narrow L-shaped piece of land that linked the White House to the Capitol. The major gateway to the park was to have been a marble arch facing Pennsylvania Avenue near the White House. "From this entrance," wrote Downing's good friend Anne Lynch, the hostess to New York's literati who was in Washington while work on the park was in progress, "a series of carriage drives, forty feet wide . . . will lead, in graceful curved lines, beneath lofty shade trees, through the whole park," a distance of five miles.[61] Immediately after passing under the arch, the public proceeded through either of two gates leading to the President's Park and the Parade. (A third gate, guarded by a porter's lodge, gave access to the private grounds around the White House.) This area to the south of the White House consisted of a broad lawn (suitable for military parades) encircled by a border of trees and shrubs, beneath which wound the walks and drives. From the President's Park, a suspension bridge carried carriages and pedestrians across Tiber Creek to Monument Park, the name Downing gave to the precinct around the as yet unfinished Washington Monument. Here Downing proposed to plant native trees in scattered clusters to frame views of the Potomac. From Monument Park, one moved eastward toward the Capitol through a series of varied landscapes. The major divisions were formed by the streets that crossed the parkland. Downing sought to minimize the interruption these straight thoroughfares caused to the landscape by planting their edges, like the outer borders of the park, with trees. In this way, he sought to protect park users from the sights and sounds of the city. As a further protection, iron fences engulfed in hedges were to line these streets, with gates at the entrance to each park path or carriage drive crossing.[62]

It is impossible to say exactly what Vaux's role was in this historic project. The plan of February 1851 and "Explanatory Notes" that are dated March 3 bear Downing's name only; however, Vaux, who had probably drawn the ground plan, may have had a hand in the design as well. Specifically, one can assume that the two notable architectural features, the suspension bridge and the arch, owe much to Vaux's inspiration. It is also likely that Vaux played a role in suggesting modifications to Robert Mill's Washington Monument. Vaux reported that Downing had "entirely objected" to the design drawn by Mills and had prepared "a study of what he thought (if an obelisk must be the design to be chosen) would be the most appropriate finish."[63] Given Vaux's role as Downing's architectural associate, it is likely that he contributed ideas to this now lost proposal.

The foremost architectural feature that Downing planned for Washington was the triumphal arch that was to stand at the White House entrance to the park. This monumental portal, Downing predicted, would become one of the city's outstanding architectural attractions. In the margin of the text of the "Explanatory Notes" that he sent to Washington on March 3, he included a rough sketch of the Roman-style arch. A few days before, Vaux had delivered a drawing of the archway to Anne Lynch for an article she had prepared on Washington that appeared in *Harper's* the following December.[64] The published engraving (Fig. 2.16) is, in fact, the best record of the arch design to survive. Slightly different from the sketch version, the published design features an allegorical figure above the attic story on which are carved the words "E Pluribus Unum," a notion that was being sorely tested in Washington during the 1850s.

Surely this sophisticated piece of Classicism, which generally resembles Percier and Fontaine's Arc du Carrousel (1806) at the entrance to the Tuileries

FIGURE 2.16.
Design for a
triumphal arch,
Washington,
D.C., 1851–1852.
From *Harper's
New Monthly
Magazine*,
December 1852.
Courtesy of
Buffalo and Erie
County Public
Library.

in Paris, was a product of Vaux's superior architectural training. Vaux also must have been able to tell Downing of the lively debate that had taken place in London architectural circles over moving Marble Arch from the front of Buckingham Palace to the entrance of Hyde Park, a transformation that was completed in 1851. A thorough Anglophile, Downing would have found compelling the idea of employing a majestic arch under circumstances similar to those of the London example, even though others might have felt such hyperbolic symbolism undemocratic. In any event, like the rest of Downing's dream for a magnificent national park in the nation's capital, the arch was forgotten after his death.

MORE CHALLENGING AS A work of practical engineering was the competition entry submitted in the spring of 1852 under the Downing and Vaux firm name for a structure to house the Exhibition of the Industry of All Nations, planned for the following year in New York City (Fig. 2.17). Passed over in favor of Carstensen and Gildermeister's Crystal Palace, the scheme, for which Vaux undoubtedly should be given credit, consisted of a colossal dome intended to extend the full width of Reservoir Square (the present Bryant Park) on Sixth Avenue. Undoubtedly, Vaux intended the design to meet the reproach that had been leveled at Joseph Paxton's Crystal Palace, which had held London's Great Exhibition of 1851. Critics had faulted that vast iron and glass structure for its lack of any strong architectural centerpoint. They had also reproved the immense nave and transept plan because it had prevented visitors from obtaining an overall impression of the many national displays. Although the idea

FIGURE 2.17.
Design for a temporary building to house the Exhibition of the Industry of All Nations, New York City, 1852. From Benjamin Silliman and Charles R. Goodrich, *The World of Science, Art, and Industry Illustrated from Examples in the New-York Exhibition, 1853–54* (New York, 1854). Courtesy of Buffalo and Erie County Public Library.

of housing the New York exhibition in a great domed space could have been inspired by Thomas H. Lewis's 1852 design for the metal and glass Royal Panopticon in London, Vaux proposed to build his dome of wood and canvas and to support it on four concentric rings of iron columns. This inexpensive method of construction, which shared similarities with John Benson's 1852 Dublin Exhibition building, bore comparison, noted science writers Benjamin Silliman and Charles Goodrich, with an eggshell, "whose double dome of lime is furnished with an uninterrupted tie in the interior by its tough membranous lining." This lining was to be held in place "with thin curved ribs, placed at short distances, secured with angle iron, and notched into circular ties made of several firmly bolted thicknesses of two-inch plank." In theory, the stability of the dome depended on these ties, which did away with "the difficulty of thrust" and left only the weight of the materials to be sustained.[65] The impression of lightness was to have been evoked on the outside by encasing the ribs in tin and glass tile so that in sunlight they would shimmer like silver. On the interior, Vaux sought to achieve a vast and buoyant space. Abundant light entered from many ranges of windows that diminished in size toward the top. To enhance the sense of skyward distance, the internal canvas lining would have been painted a "pearl-gray color at the springing line, gradually deepening into an intense blue at the crown." The sense of wonder that this great canopy would have inspired would have been worthy of such visionary schemes as those of Boullée in the previous century.

Even though Vaux's design required no centering to erect, the judges found the entry unacceptable because of its wood and canvas materials.[66] All expectations were geared to a structure employing the new iron and glass technology immortalized by Paxton in his great Crystal Palace. Downing and Vaux may have been basing their hopes for success on the judges' sober realization that metal construction on such a scale had never been attempted in the United States. The utilization of readily available materials in an innovative way, however, was not enough of an attraction to dissuade the exhibit organizers, who had actually approached Paxton for a design, apparently from their desire to rival or outdo London. Disappointment over losing the competition must have been tinged with an element of irony, for Downing had often touted the virtues of modern iron and glass conservatories. For Vaux, the New York exposition building was the first of several such structures that he would contrive. Sadly, none of them was ever erected.

THE LAST COMMISSION ON which Vaux collaborated with Downing was the Dudley Observatory in Albany, New York (Fig. 2.18). Vaux forwarded plans and specifications to the observatory's building committee on July 23, 1852, shortly after Downing had boarded the ill-fated *Henry Clay*. Yet neither the drawings nor any documents from the early history of the observatory, which has been demolished, exist to tell in detail the story of Downing and Vaux's involvement with this fascinating building.[67] The brainchild of Dr. James H. Armsby, a civic-minded Albany physician, the observatory was to form part of a new university that Armsby hoped would be established in Albany. In June 1851, Armsby got the celebrated astronomer O. M. Mitchel of Cincinnati to agree to advise the building committee, if money could be found to erect the formidable structure. Within a short time, the widow of Charles Dudley, an Albany mayor and United States senator, had pledged a large donation to the trustees, and in March 1852, the observatory's board of directors won approval from the state legislature to

FIGURE 2.18. Dudley Observatory, Albany, N.Y., 1852. Courtesy of the collection of the McKinney Library, Albany Institute of History and Art.

incorporate. Mitchel then selected a hilltop building site that overlooked the Hudson and commanded views in every direction, including an uninterrupted 12-mile prospect to the south.

Mitchel's involvement with the observatory from the start gave him control over every aspect of its gestation. This included the layout of the new building, which followed the three-part division common to many early nineteenth-century observatories. Exactly when Downing and Vaux became involved with the undertaking, which was completed in 1854, is unknown. Perhaps Armsby approached Downing because he knew that he shared his interest in scientific education, for since 1849 Downing had been working with others in Albany to establish an agricultural college there. One must assume that to Vaux fell the task of creating an architectural program from Mitchel's requirements, while Downing took charge of devising a plan for the grounds. These, we know, were laid out with curving walks and planted with sturdy trees that protected the elevated building from the wind.

Sited above Albany, like the Juvarra's eighteenth-century church La Superga above Turin, the Dudley Observatory responded to its dramatic spot with a baroque composition of projecting and receding volumes. A Tuscan Doric portico came forward from the impressive red brick and brownstone facade to mark the entrance. Above the pediment loomed the revolving viewing dome, which was made of wood and, like the Culbert house, decorated with Tuscan Doric pilasters. The windowless ground floor had two 40-foot wings whose walls bowed forward, echoing the curve of the Ledoux-like cylinder above. Recessed vertical channels, defined by large quoins and seeming to have split the walls in two, marked the so-called collimeter piers that astronomers used in conjunction with meridian instruments. On the back of the building, a rectangular north wing contained space for a library and work rooms. Sharing the spirit of monumentality with the Parish house—as well as specific features such as quoins, stringcourse moldings, and the Orders—the observatory design interpreted Mitchel's plan with weight and dignity. Its general ecclesiastical appearance imparted a vague sanctity to contemporary science's quest for celestial knowledge.

THE FINAL TASK THAT Downing performed in his Highland Garden office on the sunny morning of July 28, 1852, was to pen a postscript to a letter to accompany the Dudley Observatory plans to Albany. Young Clarence Cook recalled how "he came into the office to bid us good-bye and departed with his fine face clad in smiles of glad anticipation, leaving us regretful that for two weeks we should be without the pleasure of his daily presence."[68] A short time later, Downing, his wife, and members of her family boarded the steamer *Henry Clay* for New York and the first leg of a journey that would take him to Washington, Boston, and Newport. About 16 miles above New York, the boiler of the *Henry Clay*, which had been racing another vessel, exploded, setting fire to the boat and causing panic among the passengers. Many jumped overboard to save themselves, including Downing, who was a fine swimmer. Unfortunately, he was pulled under and drowned in a heroic attempt to save a woman whom he had once swum the river to visit.

Receiving news of the disaster, Vaux immediately left Newburgh for the scene of the wreck. He stood watch there through the night as bodies were retrieved from the river. Poor Caroline, who had survived by clinging to one of the wooden chairs that her husband and other men had tossed overboard to aid those in the water, returned home to await news of her spouse's fate. To Vaux fell the grim task of identifying the body. "I reside at Newburgh; I have known Mr. Downing; I am his partner in business; I have just seen his body; it was taken out from near the wreck," read his terse statement to the coroner.[69]

The afternoon of July 29, Vaux, whom Downing had called "one of my family,"[70] accompanied the body back to Highland Garden, where Downing was laid out in his library. "A terrific storm burst over the river and crashed among the hills," recalled George Curtis, "and the wild sympathy of nature surrounded that blasted home." The next morning, which dawned bright and clear, Downing was buried, "not yet thirty-seven years old," noted Curtis, "but with great duties done in this world."[71] Beyond the circle of family and friends, many in the nation sincerely mourned Downing's death. Among them was Frederick Law Olmsted, who had briefly visited Downing and Vaux at Newburgh in the summer of 1851 and who regarded Downing as "a great benefactor of our race."[72] Legions of Americans shared his sentiment. "It is not saying too much that Mr. Downing was doing more to cultivate and elevate the tastes of our people than all others," wrote James Hall to Vaux on learning the news of Downing's death. He added that "if we regard advancement in civilization and refinement as our highest aim, he was greatly aiding in its accomplishment."[73] Downing's personal quest for what historian Adam Sweeting calls "genteel romanticism" had ended, but through the medium of his books his uplifting message would long outlive him.

For Vaux, Downing's death provoked a professional as well as a personal crisis. Although he had enjoyed a close relationship with Downing and had earned the respect of many influential clients, Vaux was hardly in the position to be regarded as Downing's successor by those who read his books and articles. Vaux was not ready or able to carry on Downing's public campaigns to improve horticulture, architecture, and landscape gardening. In the months following his partner's death, however, Vaux continued to run the office in Highland Garden. By the following June, Vaux and fellow Englishman Withers moved the practice, which still used Downing's name, to Water Street in Newburgh.

Vaux carried many benefits away from his extraordinary two years with Downing. Within a short time, he had exchanged obscurity in London for membership in a circle of American literati, artists, and sympathetic clients who had money to spend on fine homes. He had also worked on notable architectural and landscape design projects. His immediate future as an architect would be taken up with completing works he and Downing had begun together; beyond that, he was in a good position to build on his reputation as the man whom the beatified Downing had chosen for his partner. In the next few years, Vaux lived up to these expectations and established a significant place for himself in the fledgling American architectural profession.

THE INEXHAUSTIBLE
DEMAND FOR RURAL
RESIDENCES
1853–1856

3

For four years following Downing's death, Vaux remained in Newburgh, where he continued to enjoy success as a designer of country houses. With Withers, who apparently graduated from assistant to partner in the firm some time in 1853, Vaux prepared designs for houses along the Hudson and elsewhere that continued to embody the values he had espoused during his days with Downing. Eventually the greater attractions and opportunities of New York City induced him to move there. In 1856, Vaux, married and with a young family, left Newburgh as a resident, but his ties to the Hudson Valley never loosened.

Indicative of his state of mind as he set his new course in his profession was his essay "American Architecture," which appeared in the April 1853 issue of the *Horticulturist*.[1] Taking a broad view of the subject and writing in a far more readable style than his earlier piece in the same journal, Vaux revealed himself to be a thoughtful, sympathetic critic of the state of architecture in his adopted country. Generally, he realized, the level of achievement in America, with some notable exceptions, left much to be desired; "there are the buildings," he said, "but where is the architecture?" Undoubtedly mindful of his sketching tour of the Continent with George Truefitt, Vaux lamented that here one does not "linger with pleasure over the reminiscences of a provincial tour." In particular, the mass of American houses "are unsatisfactory in form, proportion, color, and light and shade." But Vaux dwelt less on the negative picture than on analyzing the reasons why Americans seemed to have so little interest in good architecture. For one thing, he believed, most people confused ornament and display with high art. Instead, real beauty, said Vaux, came from functional plans and those abstract factors that he enumerated as form, proportion, color, and light and shade. It does not depend, he said, "on any ornament that may be superadded to the useful and necessary forms of which it is composed, but on the arrangement of those forms themselves, so that they may balance each other and suggest the pleasant idea of harmonious proportion, fitness, and agreeable variety to the eye, and through the eye to the mind." This architectonic theory of the picturesque was inherent in the buildings that Vaux had designed with Downing. It would be the philosophy that guided him for the rest of his career.

Vaux saw America's weak architectural tradition as stemming from a number of causes. Among them was the spirit of Puritanism that "was ever in opposition to any advance in the fine arts." Also to blame were the lack of esthetic education in public schools and the indifferent standards of workmanship in the building trades. But most of all, Vaux believed that architecture suffered from the absence of a true professional class of architects and an informed public. The solution to these problems lay in education and the spread of knowledge. Echoing the demands of the Chartists, whose demonstration he had watched at Kennington Common, Vaux stated that "education must be liberal and comprehensive as well as universal and cheap." Once the nation had "professors of ability, workmen of ability and an appreciative able public," the architectural profession would grow and prosper, and one day, Vaux predicted, the discipline would be included in the American college curriculum. Furthermore, Vaux believed that the press could play a powerful role in educating public taste. Extolling the memory of Downing, Vaux called for the publication of inexpensive books on architecture that would teach the general public to "see clearly and thus be led to criticize freely, prefer wisely, and act judiciously." (Perhaps he already had in mind the publication of his own book.) Moreover, the building profession itself was in sore need of a national journal "that should diffuse sound theoretical and practical information." Imbued with the spirit of reform that Vaux had shared with his earnest young colleagues at the Architectural Association, "American Architecture" cogently analyzed the current state of its subject and accurately predicted its future. Especially after his move to New York, Vaux would join with others seeking to establish the profession on a firm foundation as well as to advance its place in the realm of American culture.

ONE OF THE FIRST CLIENTS to visit the ill-fated office at Highland Garden after Downing's death must have been Nathaniel Parker Willis. "Idlewild," the "many gabled cottage" that Willis commissioned from Vaux in 1852, kept vigil over the river from a lofty plateau near Storm King Mountain at Cornwall, New York (Fig. 3.1). "You see its front-porch from the thronged thoroughfare of the Hudson," wrote Willis, a prolific poet, playwright, journalist, and editor of the popular *Home Journal*.[2] Vaux called the wild, pine-girt post "exactly such a one as a medieval knight would have selected for his strong-hold."[3] Vaux acknowledged that people loved the sight of castles on the Rhine but that Americans would find little sympathy with the feudal way of life that had sustained them. Yet Vaux held that the esthetic appeal of those romantic piles could be distilled and used in modern ways to produce the same emotive effects. He asserted that "beauty of outline and color and a picturesque grouping fully equal to that which was realized by the barons of yore . . . may undoubtedly be reproduced in the rural architecture needed by Americans of the 19th century." There is no better evocation of the poetic spirit of these remarks than Jasper Cropsey's famous painting *Autumn—On the Hudson* (c. 1869), a panoramic scene that features Willis's Idlewild in the middle distance. Likewise, T. A. Richards's more modest sketches of Idlewild that appeared in *Harper's Monthly* in 1858 (Fig. 3.2) emphasize the expressive alliance of house and place about which Vaux wrote.[4] For Vaux, Willis's Gothic-style cottage demonstrated that this type of

FIGURE 3.1. *(above)*
Idlewild, the N. P. Willis house, Cornwall-
on-Hudson, N.Y., 1852. Courtesy of
Cornwall Public Library.

FIGURE 3.2. *(at left)*
T. A. Richards, "View of Idlewild from
the River." From *Harper's New Monthly
Magazine,* January 1858. Courtesy of
Buffalo and Erie County Public Library.

picturesque beauty could be created by middle-class homeowners as well as by families of great and enduring wealth.

At age 53, Willis decided to take up residence in the country to improve his failing health. In the spring of 1852, he embarked on an extended trip to the South and Bermuda hoping to regain his strength and was thus away when his friend Downing met his tragic end. When Willis returned home, he heeded his physician's advice to move out of the city. By autumn, he had obtained plans from Vaux for a brick house on 70 acres of land near Moodna Creek. On July 26, 1853, he moved his family into Idlewild, where he would count among his neighbors Joel Headley and Clarence Cook. Leaving behind New York, where for many years he had been "a colorful part of the daily Broadway scene,"[5] this stalwart of American letters made Idlewild a celebrated place where visits from famous writers of the day were commonplace. Here, too, Willis penned a series of ruminating essays that he published as *Outdoors at Idlewild* (1854). Indicative of their tone is the passage he wrote about Idlewild itself, which he saw as metaphor for well-balanced existence. Referring to the wild and secluded ravine that stood near the house, as well as to the Hudson River vista his property enjoyed, Willis reflected that his beloved cottage "is a pretty type of the two lives which they live who are wise—the life in full view, which the world thinks all; and the life out of sight, of which the world knows nothing."[6]

Once Vaux had made the plans for the brick house, Willis took them in hand. So concerned was he to have the dwelling fit the site that, Vaux tells us, Willis outlined the building on the ground before any work began. The results repaid the labor, for, said Vaux, the new house "was made to look not new, points of view were not sacrificed, and time was not lost in waiting for young trees to grow in place of old ones that would have had to be removed for the sake of a prospect." Painted a soft yellow and set among hemlocks and other evergreens, the house—like Wodenethe, which was visible in the distance—was a sort of gallery of river and mountain scenery. The various windows, said Vaux, held "a separate picture set in a frame of unfading foliage."[7] Although, as Walter Creese has observed, Vaux perceived that "Idlewild was a major expression of an amateur personality," he also saw Willis as the embodiment of the new category of rural resident that Downing had introduced to nature's friendship.[8]

Enamored of his romantic site, the poetic-minded Willis seemed less interested in the interior arrangements of his house, which he apparently left entirely in Vaux's hands. His one requirement was simple interior finish. Recently remarried and with a growing family, he wished to keep costs down. With children in mind, Vaux planned a well-lit and spacious hall in the attic story where youngsters might play without disturbing life in the rest of the house. Probably also for the children's amusement as well as for esthetic effect, he proposed that Willis erect a bell turret on the roof, with the rope descending to the ground-floor pantry. To his later regret, Willis chose to ignore this and other suggestions Vaux had made. In a letter he wrote to Vaux two years after moving into Idlewild, Willis expressed sorrow that, for reasons of economy, he had not built a bay window in the library, a porte cochere at the door, and the fanciful bell turret on the roof, as Vaux had recommended. Perhaps because of his delicate health, he also lamented not having put a door connecting his library with the bedroom Vaux had provided next to it. Nonetheless, Willis thoroughly enjoyed living in the house and found special pleasure in the 13' × 23' entrance hall, which he used, in the manner of other nineteenth-century homeowners, for an informal drawing room and picture gallery. Willis concluded his letter by telling Vaux that "we have felicitated ourselves on having fallen into such skillful and tasteful hands as your own."[9] Surely wishing to capitalize on the celebrity that Willis had conferred on Idlewild in his writings, Vaux chose to illustrate the author's home as the frontispiece to the first edition of *Villas and Cottages*.

Jeremiah Robins was another client who came to Vaux within months of Downing's death.[10] He, however, heeded the advice Vaux had given Willis and constructed a picturesque turret on the roof of the house he built at Yonkers, New York.[11] Robins, who owned a meatpacking business in New York City, told Vaux that he and his family especially appreciated the roomy and open feeling of the interior. Contributing significantly to the informal quality of the plan was the fact that Vaux developed the rooms around a spacious entrance hall into which descended an open staircase. "A staircase of this sort may be made quite an agreeable feature in an open front hall," said Vaux, who again anticipated the more relaxed mood of late-nineteenth-century American country house planning.

COMMISSIONS LIKE THOSE FROM Willis, an internationally known writer, and Robins, a member of the New York business community, were encouraging for Vaux, who hoped to be seen as carrying the mantel of Downing. Even more important was the decision of Downing's old friend Henry Winthrop Sargent to engage Vaux to add a new wing to Wodenethe, his mansion at Fishkill Landing (present Beacon), New York. Sargent, a man of means in a position to indulge his avid interest in horticulture, had come to the area after growing up in Boston, where he graduated from Harvard in 1830, and serving as a partner in the New York office of the Paris bank owned by his uncle, Samuel Welles. In 1840, the year after his marriage, Sargent purchased a house and 20 acres of ground overlooking the Hudson across from Newburgh and abandoned the business world to devote all of his energies to transforming his property into one of the foremost country seats in America. During this period, Sargent became a close friend of Downing, who undoubtedly advised him on improving his grounds. Sargent cut existing trees and planted many new ones to frame vistas of the Hudson, which although half a mile away seemed to border the grounds. Sargent also took pains to conceal the boundary of his property behind a screen of plantings in order to increase the impression of its extent. In 1849, Downing called Wodenethe (which no longer exists) "a bijou full of interest for the lover of rural beauty."[12]

To Vaux, Sargent would have represented the best example of how sons of a rich family should pass their lives. Rather than enter business, Vaux believed that they "ought to be in every department of literature, science, and art, not as dilettanti connoisseurs, but as earnest laborers, striving boldly for a higher national excellence than has yet been achieved." Men such as Sargent, by advancing knowledge in a chosen field, would be benefiting all of the nation. "The rich should study to be practical theorists, so that the less rich may be theoretical practitioners," thought Vaux. The true worth of the class of men to which Sargent belonged, in Vaux's eyes, was to breed individuals "one step in advance of the rest of creation." With the blessings of wealth at their disposal, these heroes of culture and science could "give ample, unembarrassed study to any subject that suits [their] powers, and to work out its resources quietly and steadily."[13] Sargent, the aristocratic horticulturist, was in a position to implement and advance theories and practices that Downing had been only able to write about.

Wodenethe was frequently cited as one of the strongest proofs of Downing's salubrious influence on American gardening. In the 30 years after Downing's death, Sargent, who often wrote on horticultural topics, helped keep alive the memory of his departed friend by contributing addendums to reprints of his books. To Vaux, who must have been introduced to Sargent by Downing in the early days of his residence at Newburgh, Wodenethe would have held a special place in the preservation of Downing's legacy. He would have given particular attention to the manner in which the old house could be enlarged without disturbing the exceptional ambience. The plans that Vaux furnished Sargent for a large brick addition in the Italian style grouped sympathetically with the existing sedate Federal dwelling.[14] In expanding the house that Downing had known, Vaux added new elements to balance with the old in an overall composition of architectural forms that historic prints and photographs reveal as gracious rather than picturesque.

Viewing the house from the river side, as shown in the handsome engraving that Sargent published as the frontispiece to his "Supplement" to the 1859 edition of Downing's *Treatise on the Theory and Practice of Landscape Gardening* (Fig. 3.3), one sees the three-level addition of porch, projecting bay, and tower that Vaux designed to stand adjacent to the older house, which was distinguished by a two-story curved central bay. On the north side of Vaux's addition, greenhouses are visible; behind them stands a smaller two-story wing that may have been moved from elsewhere on the property to adjoin Vaux's new central section. According to Vaux's plans (which have survived), the rear of the ground floor of his addition held a new dining room with a large polygonal bay that extended into the grounds beneath a deep veranda. On the front or east side of the house, the addition was developed into a three-story tower (Fig. 3.4) with a bedroom on the ground floor and two other bedrooms on each floor above. Stairs from the third level led to an external octagonal viewing platform from which the roof sloped away in gentle curves. (Citing Wodenethe as an example, Vaux stated his preference for curved rooflines, which he said "will always have an easy, agreeable effect, if well managed.")[15] From the fanciful open-air platform, one would have enjoyed breathtaking views in all directions, and the artist who drew the engraved view alluded to this fact by including figures there. The Romantic notion of the house as belvedere had also informed Sargent's own thinking about the planting of the grounds. From the house, he said, each window framed "one distinct and separate view . . . making, as it were, a series of cabinet pictures."[16]

On the interior, Vaux lavished much attention on making the dining room a warm and inviting space. A large bay window extended the room onto a polygonal veranda that overlooked the lawns and the distant Hudson. The paneled walls of this room gained richness from the liberal use of black walnut, oak, and yellow pine. These woods were merely oiled to reveal their natural beauty, for Vaux championed the "pleasant and harmonious result that may always be obtained by a judicious treatment of unpainted materials in the interior of a house."[17] The wall panels, including the moveable one that hid a dumbwaiter to the basement kitchen, Vaux filled with "richly-embroidered material." The ceiling bore a grid design in plaster tinted in harmony with the walls, and

FIGURE 3.3. *(above)* Wodenethe, the Henry W. Sargent house, Beacon, N.Y., 1853. From A. J. Downing, *Treatise*. Courtesy of Buffalo and Erie County Public Library.

FIGURE 3.4. *(below)* Wodenethe, entrance facade. Courtesy of Beacon Historical Society.

a massive oak chimneypiece centered on the north wall stood guard against the cold. Vaux designed this oak mantelpiece, as well as permanent sideboards incorporating the three woods of the room, with uncomplicated lines so that local artisans could make them. In so doing, he was putting into practice an observation he had made in "American Architecture" concerning native craftsmanship. "To ensure workmen of ability," he had written, "a reasonable chance to improve is alone wanted. So long as the general demand is for monotonous, common-place, stereotyped work, the average of ability will necessarily be low." Like Ruskin, whose ideas must have shaped his thinking on this subject, Vaux believed in the innate goodness of handicraft and displayed a longtime concern for promoting the development of the building trades in America. Vaux took pride in the success of this handsome room and featured elements of it in his book *Villas and Cottages*.

PERHAPS AS EARLY AS 1853, Vaux undertook another important project on the Hudson, the house and grounds for Lydig Munson Hoyt and his wife, Blanche Geraldine Livingston, at Staatsburg, New York (Fig. 3.5). Although the plans for this Gothic stone dwelling are dated 1855, Vaux must have consulted with Hoyt about charting the 92-acre farm and pleasure grounds somewhat earlier. The delay in determining the plans may have been related to the time it took the Hoyts to acquire their land. In August 1852, Lydig Hoyt, the heir of a wealthy New York City merchant, had purchased 62 acres, but it was another two years before his wife, a descendent of Governor Morgan Lewis, received a portion of the adjacent Lewis-Livingston property from her mother. Furthermore, Vaux himself testified that it took a while for him and the owners to agree on the best location for the house. Featured as Design 26 in *Villas and Cottages*, the building was finished by the time the book appeared in February 1857.

The Hoyts had acquired a wooded promontory jutting into a broad bend in the Hudson a few miles south of Montgomery Place. It aptly bore the name its owners gave it: the Point. To the west and north, the property enjoyed expansive river views. It was also far enough removed from the tracks of the Hudson River Railroad that the noise of passing trains, which marred the solitude of Washington Irving at Sunnyside and many other riparian homeowners on the

FIGURE 3.5.
L. M. Hoyt house,
Staatsburg, N.Y.,
1853–1855.
Courtesy of New
York Office of
Parks, Recreation
and Historic
Preservation.

east side of the valley, did not reach the Point. The Hoyts' gently undulating land supported many fine trees and offered numerous opportunities for Vaux to try out the landscape design skills he must have sharpened under Downing's tutelage. With his guiding principle in mind that the "great charm in the forms of natural landscape lies in its well-balanced irregularity,"[18] Vaux proceeded to lay out roads and to site the house and other buildings with the aim of preserving and enhancing the rich treasure of scenery that nature had stored up at the Point.

Continuing an existing farm road that entered the property from the Albany Post Road, Vaux conducted the visitor to the house along a winding course that offered many charming vignettes of country life. Rounding an upland marsh, the drive hugged the base of a forested ridge while offering the traveler bucolic glimpses of cattle grazing in open meadowland across the way. Where the road rose to the top of a small ridge, Vaux located a brick stable (replaced in the early twentieth century by a larger structure). Here the road forked, one branch turning northward to a farm cottage and vegetable garden and the other veering south through a shallow ravine and up again to the site of the house.[19] (A third road led from the stable to a deepwater dock, the ownership of which the Livingston family retained.) Following this three-quarter-mile approach road today, one can still appreciate the care with which Vaux adapted its twistings and turnings to the singularity of the ground. Along this shady lane, we can almost hear Vaux reciting the words that he wrote on planning rural drives: "A single existing tree," he said, "ought often to be all-sufficient reason of slightly diverting the line of a road, so as to take advantage of its shade, instead of cutting it down and grubbing up its roots."[20] The accumulated influences of study, travel, sketching, and life with Downing that had formed Vaux's attitude toward landscape design had reached maturity by the time he laid out the drives and otherwise arranged the Hoyt property. And although the landscape stands in need of restoration, it is still poignantly evocative of its past beauty.

The most difficult problem Vaux encountered was that of finding the right location for the house. After much deliberation, he fixed upon the spot that commanded the best views of the river. This elevated area, however, was uneven and had many handsome trees that merited preservation, factors that came to play a role in the design of the house itself. Rather than fill in the land around

the site to make level lawns, like those that stretched behind the Parish villa, Vaux chose to keep "a varied outline and picturesque effect in the immediate vicinity of the house" by retaining the naturally sloping land on all sides of the dwelling.[21] On this god-given pedestal, Vaux erected a grand building using bluestone quarried on the property. This granite-hard rock, once it weathered, assumed a soft gray tonality that in this particular situation Vaux thought was far more beautiful "than any brownstone, marble or brick." He set it off with brownstone trim and dark red mortar joints. From the road, one's first view of this profoundly site-specific house is the animated east facade, above which a large overhanging dormer holds genial vigil over the approach (Fig. 3.6). As one rounds the bend, the more sedate main facade on the south, with its powerfully projected twin gables, comes into view.

The centerpiece of this symmetrical facade is the boldly protruding brownstone porch. Manifesting and sheltering the front door, this arched and buttressed gateway to the interior bestows a certain drama on the action of entry. Indeed, the porch, maintained Vaux, was the part of the house that first "appeals to the attention of the visitor," and he used the Hoyt house example in *Villas and Cottages* to demonstrate how this feature could be treated on the most liberal scale. In the warmer months, the emphatic architectural statement of welcome was to be enhanced by abundant plants. For as Vaux remarked about a similar porch on the Alexander Wright house (c. 1853) in Goshen, New York, the balcony served the women of the family as a place to cultivate potted flowers.[22] The porch also gave access to the wooden verandas on either side of it, joining them together. On the occasion of summer parties, Vaux suggested hanging calico curtains behind the veranda posts, over which vines should be trained to grow. The enchanting effect of such a "leafy gallery," he reflected, was especially "cool and elegant" when set off by lamplight at night. Used in this way, the porch and verandas became festive outdoor rooms.

After the site was fixed, said Vaux, "it then became a question how to suit the design of the house to the formation of the ground." To meet the challenge, Vaux planned a compact, square building and avoided wasting pretty views on a service wing (a usual feature on a house of this size) by putting the kitchen in the basement. The rooms of the principal floor (Fig. 3.7) were spacious and thoughtfully adapted to the special outlook the house enjoyed.[23] From the entrance hall, one had access on the west to a 24' × 18' drawing room and an equally large billiard room, a feature that marked this as the home of a man of leisure. (Lydig Hoyt, whom George Templeton Strong remembered as a man fond of poetic expression, also took pride in his library, for which Vaux designed the bookcases, an oak fireplace, and an ornamental plaster ceiling.)[24] The dining room of nearly the same dimensions on the north expanded into a large bay window that called one's attention to the beautiful water and mountain scenery upriver. These three living rooms opened onto a large terrace that allowed guests to view the river in the open air beneath the cover of a large hood. This novel canopy was sustained by overhead chains rather than by supporting posts, which would have obstructed the views from inside the house. This magnificent dwelling now stands boarded up and silently communing with the river in a setting uncommonly lovely and remote. Fortunately, the State of New York (the present owner) is committed to restoring this masterpiece of High Victorian discourse between architecture and nature.[25]

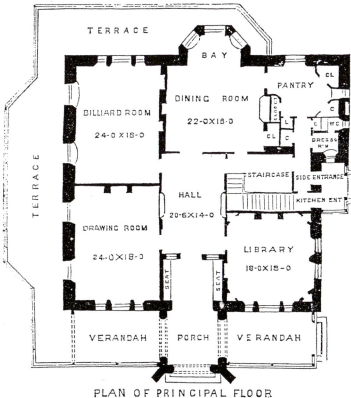

FIGURE 3.6. *(above)* Hoyt house, entrance facade. Courtesy of New York Office of Parks, Recreation and Historic Preservation.

FIGURE 3.7. *(at left)* Hoyt house, plan. From C. Vaux, *Villas and Cottages* (1857). Courtesy of Buffalo and Erie County Public Library.

THERE WAS PERHAPS no truer expression of the Romantic attachment to the poetry of landscape that characterized the high culture of the age than the little board-and-batten studio and cottage that Vaux designed in 1853 or early 1854 for the painter Jervis McEntee at Rondout, New York. McEntee, who shared Irish and Huguenot ancestry, was a native of this small riverside community, which was located about 30 miles north of Newburgh and is now part of Kingston. He was the eldest son of James Swan McEntee, a prominent engineer and canal builder who owned a large property on Weinbergh Hill above the town. As a youngster, Jervis had had his imagination awakened to the beauties of nature by a family friend, the minor nature poet Henry Pickering. In 1850, at the age of 22, McEntee determined on a career as a painter. His decision may have been encouraged by Frederic E. Church, "a brisk, energetic young fellow" two years his senior whom McEntee had known since 1848. During the winter of 1850–1851, McEntee studied with Church, occupying a small studio in New York adjacent to that of the rising artist. By 1852, Jervis was back in Rondout supporting himself with a flour and seed business and exhibiting paintings at the National Academy of Design. He must have spent his free time walking the nearby Catskills seeking subjects for pictures. Love for the mountains, especially their quiet, out-of-the-way locales that he knew intimately, would endure his whole life, and he would often take Vaux along on his wanderings, for they became the closest of friends.

On November 1, 1854, McEntee busied himself around his "new little house"—a cottage attached to the studio that Vaux tells us was begun sometime after the studio—before taking the boat for New York to marry Gertrude Sawyer. She was the daughter of his schoolmaster, the Reverend Thomas J. Sawyer, a well-known Universalist minister whose wife, Caroline, enjoyed a wide reputation as a writer and editor. Jervis and Gertrude, whose life together seems to have been wonderfully happy, returned the next day to the idyllic home that was to be nearly as much a part of Vaux's life as it was of the McEntees'.[26] For the next four decades Vaux, who had married McEntee's younger sister Mary on May 5, 1854, would visit here so frequently that it virtually became his family's second home. Over these years, McEntee devoted himself heart and soul to his introspective, often melancholy scenes of fields and woods that are so unlike the grandiose creations of his teacher Church. Rather than Church, it was to the poet William Cullen Bryant that McEntee, a poet in his own right, turned for inspiration. Never fully appreciated for his genius, the shy but warm-hearted McEntee nonetheless merited a respectable place among the second generation of American landscape painters.

The studio that according to a family tradition Vaux designed in exchange for a painting was built of wood in the board-and-batten style. (Clapboard was used for the rest of the house.) Certainly, McEntee helped Vaux with siting the building, which Vaux noted "is finely placed on an elevated site, and commands an extended view of the Kaatskills and the Hudson."[27] A hooded bench attached to the northwest wall of the studio, its position emphasized by a steep gable and a tall chimney stack, provided an ideal spot from which the artist could survey the far extending view, although he seldom painted it, preferring more intimate scenes in nature. Instead of sketching, one could imagine him here reading Bryant, whose poems often stirred his imagination to picture making. Vaux himself must have sat gazing at the wonderful panorama that the cozy studio commanded. "The scenery in the neighborhood of this cottage is of

the most striking and varied description," he declared, "and the eye looks over a range of country extending from the North and South Beacons at Fishkill, on one side, to the lofty Round Top and Woodstock Peak on the other. A white, isolated speck, visible in the gray distance, marks the situation of the Kattskill Mountain House." Vaux gave graphic expression to these words in the sketch he rendered to illustrate the studio and its surroundings in *Villas and Cottages* (Fig. 3.8). And perhaps it was appreciation of the splendid little studio and cottage that Vaux built for his pupil that influenced Frederic Church many years later to consult Vaux when he constructed his far grander hilltop home and studio at Hudson, New York.

Inside, the McEntee studio and cottage were simply finished. In order to make the 22' × 16' studio seem bigger, the space rose to the rafters. A large fireplace warmed the room, which had its own entrance on the southern side, and a large round-headed window on the north admitted abundant light. Attached to the studio, McEntee had built only part of the projected cottage, including a dining room and small bedroom on the ground floor and three bedrooms on the second level. The kitchen was in the basement. These modest accommodations were to remain fixed throughout the artist's life; he never added the parlor and veranda that Vaux included in his plan. Apparently the studio itself did double duty as living room, a fact recalled by the artist's painting *Solitaire*, which shows Gertrude playing cards beside the large north window. Indeed, many were the occasions when the McEntees and Vauxes enjoyed the cheery atmosphere of this snug belvedere.

FOR VAUX, NEWBURGH continued to be fertile ground for commissions in the years immediately after Downing's death. The house he designed in 1853 or early in 1854 for William E. Warren masterfully embodies his ideal of the middle-class suburban dwelling conceived to harmonize in elevation and plan with its picturesque surroundings (Fig. 3.9).[28] Located on a steeply sloping lot on Montgomery Street, the brick and brownstone house, which still stands, again demonstrated Vaux's maxim that in "country houses the design has to be adapted to the location, and not the location to the design."[29] To carry out this requirement, Vaux treated the front and back in distinctly different ways. On the side facing the street, which is on level ground, Vaux emphasized verticality by means

FIGURE 3.8. Jervis McEntee studio, Rondout, N.Y., 1853–1854. From C. Vaux, *Villas and Cottages* (1857). Courtesy of Buffalo and Erie County Public Library.

FIGURE 3.9.
William Warren
house, New-
burgh, N.Y.,
1853–1855.
Courtesy of
National Park
Service, Historic
American
Buildings
Survey.

of a steep gable projecting from the center. Slender buttresses at the angles and pointed arches framing the openings of the entrance added to the steep effect. Vaux also indulged his taste for picturesque details in order to give the street facade a certain richness and chiaroscuro. Window hoods shelter the ground-floor windows, cusped vergeboards define the central gable, and a hooded wooden balcony hangs above the entrance porch, lending a festive air to the entire facade. (The enchanting balcony frames a window that lighted a small bedroom that one would like to imagine belonged to the Warrens' only daughter, Mary.) The compact proportions and well-integrated ornamental features of this charming facade epitomized the sense of delight and intimacy that characterize so much of Vaux's domestic architecture.

On the rear, horizontality prevailed (Fig. 3.10). The reason for this, Vaux said, was that this side of the house would be seen from a steep angle from below and, therefore, would appear ungainly tall if steps were not taken to mitigate its height. Instead of introducing conspicuous gables, Vaux kept the skyline flat by means of a simple hipped roof with dormers to light attic rooms. Since splendid views of the Hudson were to be enjoyed on this side of the dwelling, Vaux erected a 12-foot-deep veranda across the 33-foot width of the house, its straight lines adding another element of horizontality to the design and its airy appearance softening the relative plainness of this elevation. For those who occupied the two rear bedrooms, the balustraded veranda roof served as a spacious balcony from which they could see as far as West Point.

Relation to the landscape also governed the disposition of the main rooms of the interior (Fig. 3.11). On the street side of the symmetrical plan, which bore a resemblance to the David Moore house, were concentrated the hall, stairs, and

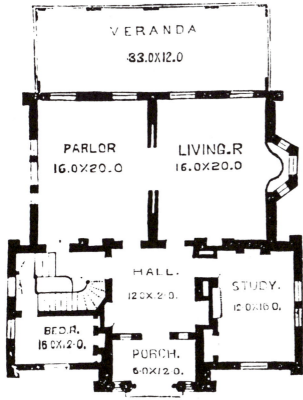

VERANDA
33.0X12.0

PARLOR
16.0X20.0

LIVING.R
16.0X20.0

HALL.
12.0X.2.0.

STUDY.
12.0X16.0.

BED.R.
16.0X12.0.

PORCH.
6.0X12.0.

FIGURE 3.10. *(above)*
Warren house, rear view. Courtesy
of National Park Service, Historic
American Buildings Survey.

FIGURE 3.11. *(at left)*
Warren house, plan. From C. Vaux,
Villas and Cottages (1857). Courtesy
of Buffalo and Erie County Public
Library.

two small rooms, one of which served as a study. Here, one presumes, Warren, a self-made man "indebted almost entirely to his natural force of character for his elevation from obscurity" in Connecticut to prominence in New York City and in Newburgh,[30] must have hoped to escape from time to time from the pressures of his many duties. These included his duties as treasurer of the Delaware, Lackawanna and Western Railroad, deputy comptroller of New York City, and president of the International Life Insurance Company. The back half of the house, with its fine river views, held two 16' × 20' parlors that opened into each other by means of sliding doors and communicated with the veranda through floor-length windows. The veranda assumed special importance in the plan because, said Vaux, the grounds offered little opportunity to develop an adequate garden. Therefore, the porch was sure to become the favorite outdoor space in summertime, hence its ample dimensions. Exceptionally, Vaux relegated the dining room and kitchen to the basement. Vaux's evident intention in his plan was to subordinate all of its chief elements to the primary importance of the back parlors and veranda. Developing these spaces at the expense of others, he gave the Warrens the opportunity to enjoy most fully the airy prospect that their home commanded. Working within the restrictions of a city lot, Vaux orchestrated major themes in his work: orientation to the landscape; picturesque variety in elevations disciplined by the nature of the site; manipulation of architectural elements with an eye to imparting a sense of movement and texture; concern for physical comfort and convenience (an ingenious water closet was included); and details that lent an easy, light-hearted air to the notion of home.

DURING 1853, VAUX gained the confidence of many other clients in the Newburgh area and elsewhere, and eventually he formed a partnership with F. C. Withers to handle the trade. This partnership probably came about in the early part of 1854, for in his book *Villas and Cottages*, which would have been in press late in 1856, Vaux mentioned that the partnership with Withers had lasted three years. *Villas and Cottages* also contains a record of a number of projects that Vaux undertook as the sole head of the firm (in which Withers continued the status of assistant he had occupied with Downing); these, such as the Warren and Sargent commissions, would have come to the office, therefore, from the late summer of 1852 to the beginning of 1854.

In addition to William Warren, at least three other individuals in prosperous Newburgh became Vaux's clients during this period. One of these was John J. Monell, a man who was to become a life-long friend of Vaux and the second husband of Caroline Downing. A lawyer known for his "fine presence . . . sonorous voice . . . and ready command of language," Monell was a congenial man who, despite the fact that he served only one brief term on the bench, liked being called "Judge." As legal adviser to James Gordon Bennett and William Cullen Bryant, he occupied an important behind-the-scenes position in New York political and cultural life during the last part of the century. Little, however, is known about the house that Vaux designed for him in 1853–1854 other than the facts that it overlooked a glen and that Vaux erected a beautiful trellis to screen the kitchen veranda from the garden.[31]

Elderly Thomas Powell, the wealthy merchant and steamboat operator who had given his nephew Daniel Parish his start in business, sought Vaux's services to remodel his existing Newburgh residence. The Powell homestead was a large, five-bay Federal-style house with twin end chimneys and a nondescript rectangular addition at one side (Fig. 3.12). Such houses, with their trim lines and flush eaves, were the "square boxes" that Downing and Vaux thought so unworthy of the beauties of the American countryside. Nonetheless, Vaux conceded that in cases like this, where the structure was sound and the residence had been in the same family for many years, it was best for both financial and sentimental reasons to preserve the dwelling and remodel. Tokens of family history, observed Vaux from the perspective of a European immigrant, "are so valuable, and so little fostered by the ordinary course of events in American families, that they deserve to be cherished in every possible way."[32] Long before the dawning of the modern preservation notion of historic integrity, Vaux took the matter in hand and proceeded to reshape the building according to his principles of picturesque design. Rooflines were raised, eaves were brought out beyond the walls on brackets, hoods were placed over certain openings, bay windows were introduced to enlarge the fenestration of major rooms, new verandas were built, chimney flues were redirected to massive stacks, and a pretty ventilation turret appeared above the new wing that broke up the flatness of the original facade where it joined the old side wing. The resulting transformation disclosed how different Vaux's dynamic and pictorial High Victorian design esthetic was from the chaste Classicism of the epoch that had formed the house. Remade, the Powell residence gave form to Vaux's theory that "the eye will be more likely to take pleasure in a rural composition that consists of a group of forms well-connected and massed together into one individual whole, than in a study characterized by symmetrical uniformity, . . . for the former suggests . . . a freedom from effort, and offers the opportunity for a gradual examination, if preferred; whereas the latter must be grasped in all its completeness at once, and can only be truly enjoyed as a whole."[33]

FIGURE 3.12. Thomas Powell house, New-burgh, N.Y., 1853–1855. From John J. Nutt, *Newburgh, Her Institutions, Industries, and Leading Citizens* (Newburgh, NY, 1891). Courtesy of Buffalo and Erie County Public Library.

Little remained of the exterior appearance of the first house, although Vaux had counseled that in these circumstances the "best way is to do as little as possible beyond obtaining the leading features of arrangement and appearance that the alteration or addition is designed to procure." Perhaps Vaux's advice fell victim to both the generous budget that was at his disposal and to the social aspirations of his true client, the longtime administrator of Powell's affairs— his son-in-law, Homer Ramsdell. A foremost citizen of Newburgh who was sometimes referred to as "Captain," Ramsdell had in the summer of 1853 assumed the presidency of the Erie Railroad, which he was to manage with great acuity through four stormy years. To renovate the unpretentious home where his father-in-law had lived for half a century was Ramsdell's idea, and he was pleased with the results. Writing to Vaux from his office in New York, Ramsdell brushed aside the question of cost, saying that he had not even kept records of the expenses. He went on to express his admiration for the way Vaux had commuted the life of the old house. "We have now an agreeable arrange-ment of rooms, with all the minor conveniences that so materially help to make a country house enjoyable," he said, "[yet] with all its alterations, it is still the old homestead of the family."[34]

Robert L. Case, president of the Security Life Insurance Company, took an especially close interest in the practical aspects of the house he employed Vaux to build for him on a hilltop site. For example, Case dictated that the walls of his dwelling be built of brick faced with clapboard, a method of construction traditional in the Hudson Valley but one that Vaux thought faulty. While it made for a snug, dry interior, "it seems undesirable," reasoned Vaux, "to have a brick house, and to give it the appearance of a wooden one, as brick is the superior and more durable-looking material." Vaux concentrated his attention on creat-ing varied elevations and a functional plan that he later said others might imi-tate.[35] The building could be adapted, he said, "to almost any situation by a proper arrangement of the roofs." Because in this particular case the house stood on elevated, open land, he drew roofs of moderate pitch, whereas, he advised, if it were erected on flat terrain or in a valley he would have chosen a high-pitched roof.

THE EXAMPLE OF THE Powell house may have induced William Kent to hire Vaux in 1853 to remodel the house he had purchased across the river from New-burgh at Fishkill Landing. Kent, whose renowned father, Chancellor James Kent, had fostered the career of Downing's friend Frederick Betts, was a distinguished jurist who had taught law at Harvard and had been one of the organizers of the law department at New York University. His chief requirement in the renovation of the dwelling, which Vaux described as "a fairly-proportioned, square country residence, with a kitchen wing," was to add a library for the 12,000 volumes he owned. Vaux proceeded by condemning the old kitchen wing, which had been built in such a way as to block the best views of the river. It was a relic of a time that paid little heed to the charms of natural scenery that captivated Vaux. Demolishing the kitchen, Vaux erected a new wing in its place that held the library on the ground floor and bedrooms above. A large polygo-nal bay window in the center of the long rectangular room extended the library into the landscape beneath the protection of a large wooden veranda, which, said Vaux, enjoyed a splendid view that before could not be seen. Seeking to mitigate the long, narrow proportions of the 50' × 19' bookcase-lined space, the architect divided it into three areas by means of short projecting walls. Overhead, Vaux devised an elaborate plaster ceiling with pronounced transverse ribs to mitigate the disproportionate length of the room. With the kitchen wing now relegated to the north side of the library, where it would protect the unusually large room from winter weather, the remodeled dwelling, which cost $11,000, greatly pleased its owner.

Also for a site in Fishkill Landing, Vaux planned a wooden cottage for Dr. John de la Montagnie, a homeopathic physician and promoter of improved medical education. The doctor's picturesque cottage was one of the finest embodiments of the mood of rural intimacy in Vaux's early career. The property, which is adjacent to Sargent's Wodenethe, commanded "several beautiful views," Vaux said, "both of the Hudson and of the noble hills that rise up at this point from its eastern shore."[36] Applying the full measure of his genius to the problem of adapting the house to its site, Vaux marshaled a picturesque composition of masses, broad roofs eloquent of shelter, and a subtle color scheme to bring into being what he proudly described as "an unpretending, but really rural house."

The cottage (which has since been altered and enlarged) was sited in a small hollow. From the high public road, one approached the entrance along a curving drive. Soon the visitor gained an oblique view of the house perched on a little mound that seemed natural but had been formed with soil excavated for the basement. Roofs appeared deliberately large in proportion to the walls in order to make the building seem low, an effect, said Vaux, that shadows cast by the widely overhanging eaves enhanced. One entered the house through a wooden porch that also served as a small veranda. Above, at the eaveline, a Bracketed dormer reminiscent of a similar feature on the side of the Hoyt house provided a recess at the top of the stairs "for a chair and a table at a window that looks out on a cheerful view." On the rear of the house, inhabitants enjoyed a veranda from which they might look at a pleasant prospect of tree-bordered greensward.

Vaux especially relied on color to help assimilate the de la Montagnie cottage to its natural surroundings. Condemning, as had Downing before him, the prevailing American taste for white paint on country houses, Vaux called for the use of quiet, subtle tones that would make the dwelling less noticeable in the landscape. His description of the paint scheme for the De la Montagnie house demonstrates this premise as well as his injunction to use four shades of paint on a dwelling. The clapboards, Vaux tells us, were painted "a rather warm gray," while the trim was picked out in a considerably darker "grayish tint," with some brown added to increase the contrast. "The stiles of the Venetian blinds," said Vaux, "are rather lighter than the window-dressings, while the slats and the panels of the verge-boards are of a cool dark brown." As the roof was covered with wooden shingles that would soon weather to a silvery grey, the overall appearance of the house was "free from either startling contrast or wearisome monotony." This scheme, declared Vaux, who had obviously thought much about the appeal of color in architecture, had the added advantage of imparting an appearance of coolness in the summer and of warmth in the winter; "when choosing the tints for a house," he professed, one should "select a happy medium that shall be suited to more seasons than one." The doctor, who believed in the power of nature to heal, must have felt perfectly at home in his new surroundings.

During or soon after 1853, Vaux received commissions for houses from several individuals farther afield than the mid-Hudson region. For Charles H. Rogers, a lead manufacturer with offices on Wall Street, Vaux designed and supervised the construction of an extensive wooden villa located across the East River from Manhattan at Ravenswood. The pleasant Long Island residential community had been attracting a small colony of affluent home builders since the mid-1830s, when A. J. Davis proposed to erect a stunning row of 10 shore-line villas there.[37] In 1852, a steamboat began crossing to Manhattan. To provide the Rogers family with the opportunity to enjoy an interesting view of the busy river, Vaux raised a four-story tower above the entrance to the house. From beneath its octagonal observatory, Vaux said, one could obtain a prospect that trees and buildings interrupted from the lower windows of the house.

The Rogerses' property extended down to the water's edge, where Vaux located a handsome little polygonal boathouse. Vaux took care, however, that the structure remained invisible from the house. To insinuate quietly such secondary structures into the landscape was a tenet of Vaux's design philosophy. "It is always disagreeable to see such a building . . . where it will be in the way of the view from the house, or have an awkward appearance from the road, . . . or be so prominent that it attracts an undue share of attention," wrote Vaux in reference to a stable he designed around this time for James Chambers in Westchester County, New York. "But, on the other hand," Vaux believed, "it is very agreeable to catch a view of the inferior buildings belonging to a rural home whenever they happen to be picturesquely designed, and grouped with a due regard to retirement among the trees surrounding the house."[38] Such thinking also would guide Vaux when he designed buildings in public parks, especially those in Central Park.

For E. S. Hall of Millville, Massachusetts, Vaux planned a brick villa at Middletown, Connecticut, a place which Vaux praised as "unquestionably one of the most pleasant and attractive neighborhoods in which to build a country seat to be found in the Eastern States."[39] Hall, whose property overlooked the beautiful Connecticut River, began in 1853 to lay out the lawns and drives around the building site. This work was still in progress when Vaux illustrated the house in his November 1855 article, "Hints for Country House Builders." Like the Parish villa at Newport, the Hall residence, with its lengthening lines, pedimentlike gables, and low-pitched hipped roof, embodied the sedate Palladian tradition which Vaux had brought with him from England and which also manifested itself in another country house that he designed around this time for an unnamed client in Orange County, New York.[40] Unfortunately, Hall never got around to erecting the dwelling, for which Vaux prepared a complete set of plans; others, however, were to be inspired by its example.[41]

By May 1854, Vaux had every reason to believe that a growing and successful career lay ahead of him. Acting on this confident assumption, he took a major step in his personal life, marrying Mary Swan McEntee, the younger sister of Jervis McEntee. For the next two years they made their home in Newburgh, where two children were born to them, Bowyer in 1855 and Downing in 1856.[42] During this period, Vaux's architectural practice continued to expand, and he completed his book *Villas and Cottages*, which he started in 1854. The book memorialized his busy professional life in America until the time he left Newburgh for New York City.

Written at the moment when Vaux commenced life as a father, the book contains a number of passages that reflect his enlightened attitudes toward child rearing. Of central importance to him was the wholesome influence of home life on the growing child. "And it is not for ourselves alone," he asserted, "but for the sake of our children, that we should love to build our homes, whether they be villas, cottages, or log-houses, beautifully and well."[43] It was in the home that the child first experienced his god-given desire for beauty. If his earliest surroundings provided no means of gratifying this "unspoiled instinct," Vaux feared, the youngster would grow up an arid individual. "It is frequently from this cause, and from this cause alone," he admonished, "that an impulsive, high-spirited, light-hearted boy will dwindle by degrees into a sharp, shrewd, narrow-minded, and selfish youth; from thence again into a prudent, hard, and horny manhood, and at last into a covetous, unloving, and unloved old age."

Of nearly equal importance with the home was the influence of education. Vaux believed that the American public school system "lies at the root of every healthy idea of reform now at work in the world." But he faulted schools for not providing art education, for failing to "urge the unspoiled, pliable young minds of the rising generation to the study of the beautiful as well as to the acquirement of reading, writing, and arithmetic." Why not, he suggested, incorporate study of art history and "the leading principles of good taste" into the daily grammar school curriculum?[44] One assumes that he often talked to his own children about these subjects.

Vaux's enthusiasm for American free schools encouraged him to hope that someday the country would extend this principle to include other cultural institutions. He looked forward to the day when Americans would see the need to establish in their cities educational and recreational facilities from which all children could derive benefit. Articulating a high-minded philosophy of social democracy that he espoused all his life, Vaux affirmed that "public baths, gymnasiums, theaters, music-halls, libraries, lecture-rooms, parks, gardens, picture-galleries, museums, schools, and every thing that is needed for the liberal education of an intelligent freeman's children, can easily be obtained by the genuine republican if he will only take the trouble to want them."[45] His words were prophetic, and in later years Vaux would design buildings for pioneering cultural institutions.

Concerning religion, which Vaux recognized exercised powerful influence over society, he lamented the want of broad-mindedness in America. "Meagre sectarianism and private intolerance," he ventured, "under the names of religious freedom and universal toleration, have been serious drawbacks."[46] He especially disliked the entrenched Protestant bias against art and beauty. By the time Vaux had moved his family to New York, he had abandoned any allegiance to Anglicanism that he may have brought with him from England and had begun to espouse liberal Unitarianism.

IN ADDITION TO opinions about modern life, *Villas and Cottages*, as we have seen, reveals the names and locations of many of the clients for whom Vaux worked in the years immediately after Downing's death. During his partnership with Withers, which must have lasted for approximately the three years from early 1854 to the end of 1856, Vaux continued to obtain desirable commissions for country houses from an ever widening circle of home builders. These projects are distinguished in *Villas and Cottages* by the initials "V&W." One assumes that Withers's role in these designs was secondary, for, as the narrator of *Villas and Cottages*, Vaux represented all the buildings as his own creations. Indeed, Vaux had illustrated and discussed many of the houses in "Hints for Country House Builders" in the November 1855 issue of *Harper's New Monthly Magazine*, where he made no mention of Withers.[47] And in some cases, drawings that survive for projects labeled "V&W" in the book bear Vaux's name alone.

By the end of 1854, Vaux had made a second proposal for Matthew Vassar's mansion at Springside.[48] Vaux's design survives in a perspective drawing dated 1854 as well as in plans for the first and second floors. The dominating feature of this massive and compact scheme (the new building was nearly square and lacked the extended kitchen wing of the first design) was a monumental tower. Its curved spire loomed above the dwelling at the back, where it stood out majestically against the distant hills. From its high balconies and arcaded loggias, Vassar would have enjoyed panoramic views of the Hudson and surrounding countryside. But Vassar constructed neither this nor Vaux's earlier building.

While Vassar preferred to live his bachelor existence in the homey board-and-batten cottage that had first been intended for his gardener, he did erect a most original structure on the grounds of Springside that I believe Vaux designed. Referred to as "Uncle Tom's Cabin," this log house was the residence for Vassar's teamster. In my view, Vassar built it around the time that he had Vaux prepare the second mansion design.[49] In his 1855 article "Hints for Country House Builders," Vaux featured a log house that closely resembled Vassar's cabin (Fig. 3.13). And although Vaux did not tell his readers the location of the building, he published an illustration that showed a forest setting like that of the Springside cabin. Perhaps Vassar himself, who thought of his farm as a model of modern agricultural practices, encouraged Vaux to apply his architect's mind to

FIGURE 3.13.
Design for
a log house,
1854–1855.
From *Harper's
New Monthly
Magazine*,
November 1855.

NO. II.—LOG-HOUSE.*

the problem of improving the primitive accommodation that this vernacular form of shelter normally provided.

Vaux proposed his log house as an example of frontier accommodation for a family who wanted more than one all-purpose room in which to live. A door sheltered behind a recessed porch led to a large central room intended to serve as the family's living, cooking, and eating space. (In winter, the occupants could store firewood under the porch and use a more protected side entrance.) A separate sink room near the fireplace isolated more odious chores from daily life in the main room. On the opposite side of the living room, two small chambers, each with windows, provided sleeping quarters suitable for children. The parents, presumably, slept in the window-lit loft that they reached by a ladder in the sink room. By these simple means, Vaux sought to preserve, even under frontier conditions, the virtues of utility, order, and privacy in family life. Vaux may have come to concern himself with the primitive log cabin in answer to a challenge laid down by his associate Clarence Cook. Shortly after Downing's death, Cook had lamented the fact that "none of our architects has . . . worked up into a more refined and graceful form. . . the Western log-hut, which even in its rudest shape has enough of beauty to redeem it from the charge of total vulgarity."[50] Vaux found this building tradition much to his liking. "The study has been made on a small, simple scale," he wrote, "so as to be more generally available, but the mode of construction proposed to be adopted admits of considerable artistic treatment in a rural way; and if a log-house were required on a more extensive plan altogether, the style might be raised in character accordingly, without sacrificing in any way its primitive expression." Moreover, he wished that settlers who built such houses would appreciate their potential for homelike beauty and instead of cutting down all the nearby trees—as was the common practice of pioneers—would with "a little judicious forethought . . . preserve a few fine specimens round the family home for shade and enjoyment." Perhaps, to Vaux, nothing could be more expressive of architecture's origins in nature than a log house watched over by benevolent survivors of the primeval forest from which it was fashioned. Such imagery perfectly suited the wilder portions of a park like that at Springside. There Vaux had forged a rare marriage between vernacular architecture and the romantic landscape tradition.

IN THE MIDDLE OF the 1850s, Vaux had many clients with projects for large and small properties in the Newburgh area. At Limestone Hill, J. Walker Fowler, a lawyer from New York City with family ties to Newburgh, proposed to erect a moderate-sized brick villa that Vaux said was to stand on "an elevated space of table land" that commanded views "in which undulating hills intercept the river."[51] Like the Vassar and Rogers houses, the Fowler villa was to have had a four-story tower with an open observatory on top. However, Fowler seems never to have undertaken anything more than paying Vaux for a set of plans. For Nathan Reeve, a member of the Newburgh business community, Vaux also drew plans for a villa that his client never built. The house demonstrated Vaux's general principle of interior planning, whereby the best living spaces were to be located on the south and east sides of the house and the least desirable functions relegated to the north and northwest portions. In the Reeve house, the service wing, housing the kitchen and pantries, stood on the north; the drawing room, which enjoyed fine views of the river, occupied the southeast corner of the plan.

By this arrangement, said Vaux, the principal rooms courted "the pleasant southerly breezes in summer, and the southerly and easterly sun in winter."[52] In addition, Vaux's plans included a large 28' × 14' staircase hall at the entrance, an early instance of a feature that became popular in late-nineteenth-century domestic architecture. Halsey Stevens, a Newburgh man with multiple careers as a teacher, politician, and merchant, commissioned and built a house that Vaux designed for a suburban lot on Grand Street. In his discussion of the house in *Villas and Cottages*, Vaux drew special attention to the exterior design. Houses in towns, Vaux stated, should have symmetrical fronts facing the street so as to harmonize with other nearby buildings as well as to fit "with the regular and unavoidably formal line of the paved avenue, or street" on which it stood.[53] Such contextualism had governed the facade of the Warren house, which stands a few blocks away.

Vaux planned more modest dwellings for two other Newburgh residents, the Reverend Edward J. O'Reilly and a plumber named Daniel Ryan. Father O'Reilly was the new pastor of St. Patrick's Roman Catholic Church, duties he assumed in the fall of 1853. One of his first undertakings was to purchase land on Grand Street to erect a pastoral residence. This three-story brick structure cost $3,500 and went up in 1854.[54] The interior plan was unremarkable—two 16' × 15' parlors on the first floor, two like-sized bedrooms above, and two small bedrooms and storage space under the roof—but the exterior presented a new solution to the design of the urban townhouse on a 25-foot lot. The steeply pitched roof projected two feet beyond the walls and, together with a strongly marked stringcourse at the second-floor level, relieved the "high-shouldered and stilted appearance" that Vaux found objectionable in buildings of this type. He must have had in mind so many New York City "brownstones," which generally had flat roofs behind heavy cornices. And by setting the windows into recessed panels that were to be painted somewhat darker than the rest of the surface, he inexpensively imparted a pleasing sense of relief to the facade.

Mr. Ryan's more modest clapboard house (Fig. 3.14) shared with the parsonage a steep roof projected beyond the walls on brackets and a central chimney stack to conserve heat in winter. Concerned with meeting the needs of family life, Vaux brought the kitchen out of the basement (where it had been located in the O'Reilly house) to the first floor and planned adjacent to it a small living room that could double as a dining room. It was, however, the parlor, demurely screened from the street by the veranda, that concerned Vaux the most. Thinking that this modest house might be an example that other working-class families could imitate, he included it in *Villas and Cottages*, where he offered unusually detailed suggestions for decorating the parlor in a tasteful and cheerful manner.[55] The carpet, he advised, should be a quiet color with a small pattern; the woodwork might be stained or painted in light tints; the walls would look best covered with "a pretty, fanciful paper, harmonizing with the woodwork, and not large in pattern"; and the mantel could just as well be of wood rather than a "cold, costly white marble affair."

Perhaps thinking that readers of this class were more in need of instruction than others, Vaux continued with ideas for furnishing the parlor. The center of family leisure, this room, he said, should have something in it to please each member of the household. His inventory included a substantial table in the center of the room at which three or four people might sit and read; a sturdy chintz-covered lounge; several small tables "of fanciful design and trifling

NO. III.—SIMPLE SUBURBAN COTTAGE.*

FIGURE 3.14.
Daniel Ryan
house, New-
burgh, N.Y.,
1853–1855.
From *Harper's
New Monthly
Magazine*,
November
1855.

expense" that could be moved around at will; and half a dozen chairs as well as "an easy-chair or two for tired visitors." Neatly framed engravings and an inexpensive oil painting or two should hang on the walls. For the mantelpiece, Vaux suggested low-cost plaster casts, which might also be placed on brackets around the room—for 25 cents he had recently purchased a figure that he said was "full of grace, beauty, and artistic thought." Finally, a birdcage, fishbowl, or flowers in a hanging basket would help animate the room and give special pleasure to any young girls of the family. One could never know how many people of modest circumstances might have acted upon these simple recommendations, but they reflect an earnest wish, expressed earlier by Downing, that the not-so-rich be brought to the table of culture. Middle-class and conservative, as this attitude has been characterized, it was motivated nonetheless by an idealistic belief that art and architecture, traditionally the property of the prosperous, could improve the lives of all families.

IN *VILLAS AND COTTAGES*, Vaux mentioned four houses that he designed for patrons in Worcester, Massachusetts. Two of these were for individuals whose names are unknown. Design 23, which Vaux described as a brick and brownstone "suburban house with curvilinear roof," was, like the Stevens and Warren houses, compact in plan and symmetrical in elevation. Its round-headed windows, Classical details, and static composition both place it in the category of Vaux's more monumental designs, epitomized by the Parish house, and suggest emulation of the contemporary French suburban *maison particulière*. The ogee profile of the mansard roof, Vaux intimated, was chosen by the client because he had seen it on another house by Vaux in the neighborhood.

Henry H. Chamberlain, a wool dealer in Worcester, engaged Vaux to build a rambling wooden house near the city, where, Vaux said, nature had "suggested the exact position to be selected."[56] The ample wooden Gothic house capped with a turret and graced with a large veranda took its place at the edge of a pine wood, where it also enjoyed the protection of fine deciduous trees. "A country house built under such favorable circumstances as this," said Vaux, "may at once take its appropriate place in the landscape; and if it is agreeable in color, and designed with even an approximation to good proportion and picturesque arrangement of light and shade in its outlines, it will appear an old resident directly it is occupied."

The plan of the dwelling, Vaux was pleased to admit, owed its invention to Mrs. Chamberlain, a fact that led Vaux to reflect on the suitability of women for the profession of architecture. "There is no doubt," he said, "but that the study of domestic architecture is well suited to a feminine taste, and it has, moreover, so many ramifications, that it affords frequent opportunities for turning good abilities to profitable account." While he might concede the point that women would have difficulty in supervising construction because of the rigors of climbing ladders and the unseemliness of mingling with workmen on the construction site, he saw no impediments to women taking up careers in architectural drawing and the design of furniture, interior decoration, and ornaments. "I do not, it will be perceived, include in the difficulties to be overcome," he asserted, "want of natural ability, for this certainly does not exist."

The largest and most expensive commission the firm received in Worcester was from Thomas Earle, a local political figure who was noted for his promotion of public improvements. His $16,000 brick and brownstone house on Elm Street was the largest picturesque Gothic villa that Vaux had yet designed. To the approaching visitor, the dwelling loomed especially large because it lacked any veranda; instead, an uncovered terrace stood at the side, where a paneled polygonal plant cabinet extended out from the house between the library and drawing room. The massing of roofs, gables, dormers, and chimney stacks was especially lively seen from the rear, a fact to which Vaux called attention in a small view included in *Villas and Cottages*. Unfortunately for Earle, the promise of happy Victorian domestic life embodied in Vaux's design was to prove fugitive. After a divorce, Earle ended his days in a lunatic asylum, where he had been confined in an exhausted mental condition as a result of his unsuccessful attempt to gain custody of his children.

IT WAS IN New York City that Vaux received the most important commissions of this period, a fact that eventually led him to relocate his practice there. For Jeremiah Robins, whose house Vaux had built at Yonkers, Vaux designed a building on Washington Street in lower Manhattan for his client's meatpacking business. The only surviving visual record of the structure, which Vaux said he designed several years after Robins's villa, is the small illustration that Vaux published in *Villas and Cottages*.[57] On the exterior, the four-story building (which presumably was made of brick) rose in three levels, each of which was sharply defined by stringcourse moldings. Other than a corbeled cornice and rooftop lunettes, the design remained free of historical references. All the architect tells us about the interior was that, as in the case of the Commercial Block in Boston, the floors of the packing plant rested on internal stone corbels.

Other well-to-do New Yorkers also commissioned Vaux to plan houses for them. John W. Burt, the owner of a boot business on Broadway, approached Vaux for a house that he wished to build at Mountain Park (also known as Llewelyn Park), New Jersey. The brainchild of Llewelyn Haskell, Mountain Park was a new 500-acre residential community laid out by Eugene Baumann and Howard Daniels in the naturalistic style championed by Downing. As Vaux explained in *Villas and Cottages*, Haskell set aside 50 acres as a public pleasure ground and devoted the rest to spacious building lots he hoped would attract well-to-do New York families seeking a nearby location for a country house. Calling the philosophy behind Mountain Park an "excellent and truly republican one in principle," Vaux saw great advantages accruing to the residents, who would derive benefit from their collective investment in the beautifully laid out and well-maintained landscape.

Vaux's most important New York client, however, was John A. C. Gray. In 1852, Gray, who had been born in 1815 near Newburgh but spent his life in New York, retired from the dry goods business, in which he had earned a considerable fortune, to devote himself to various bank and railroad director-ships and to promoting the liberal movement in the Republican Party. Together with his wife, Susan Zabriskie, whom he had married in 1837, Gray also enjoyed the fruits of his wealth by traveling abroad. Probably in 1856, he and his wife made the decision to move from Staten Island to a new house that Gray asked Vaux to design for him at 40 Fifth Avenue, a prime lot immediately north of the grounds of Ascension Church (Fig. 3.15). Although the three-story brick and brownstone dwelling was not ready for occupancy until 1858 or 1859, it appeared as one of the "V&W" designs in *Villas and Cottages*. The association between architect and client blossomed into a lifelong friendship. Gray as well as Vaux must have been delighted when the *Builder* chose to bring his house to the attention of British readers as an outstanding example of American town-house design.[58]

The three-story, red brick dwelling seemed a splendid answer to the com-plaint of the *Crayon*, America's new art journal, that "a lack of roofs and a uniform brown color is the cause of Fifth Avenue monotony."[59] Its tall roof most distinguished the Gray house from its conventional "brownstone" neighbors. Sheltering servants' quarters behind segmental-arched dormers, the elegantly curved mansard was bordered below with paneled ornament and trimmed above with iron filigree railing. It rose in proud defiance of the flat roofs, invis-ible from the street behind heavy cornices, that were the norm in midcentury New York domestic architecture. Vaux made special note of this in *Villas and Cottages*. There he spoke of mitigating "the stiffness and formality that are characteristic of most town houses" by aiming "at some picturesqueness of effect in the arrangement of the roof lines," which because this house was exposed to observation on the south would "come prominently into view from the other side of the street."[60] To the *Crayon* critic, Vaux's Gray house gave heartening evidence of an advance "beyond the toy box standard of taste."

The Gray house also declared its independence from the usual brownstone row house by its unusual materials. The principal floor, which stood above the street on a high basement, was embellished by a series of horizontal red brick and brownstone bands. Such polychromatic layering was to become especially popular after the Civil War and may have been suggested to Vaux by the example of Wrey Mould's recent All Souls Unitarian Church (1853–1855), the first acknowledged masterpiece of "Ruskinian Gothic" in America. Above the ground level, the walls of the Gray house were composed of red Philadel-phia face brick relieved by brownstone window trim, hoods, and stringcourses. The soft, warm color contrast born of brick, brownstone, and brown woodwork

FIGURE 3.15. *(above)*
John A. C. Gray house, New
York City, 1856–1857. From
Builder 15 (December 12, 1857).

FIGURE 3.16. *(at right)*
Gray house, plan. From C. Vaux,
Villas and Cottages (1857).
Courtesy of Buffalo and Erie
County Public Library.

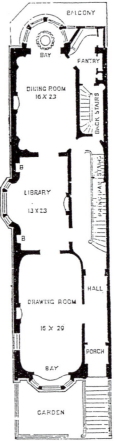

PLAN OF PRINCIPAL FLOOR

were a favorite of Vaux, who decried the tendency of many homeowners to hide the natural beauty of these materials beneath coats of paint. Vaux contended that while red brick, "unrelieved by any other material, is altogether too vivid in color to please in an American climate," when it was used in conjunction with a brownstone, "the effect is altogether too harmonious and satisfactory to need any attempt at improvement."[61]

The desire for brightness and openness guided Vaux in the design of the interior (Fig. 3.16). Because the south wall overlooked the perpetually open space of the churchyard, he augmented the library on this side with a projecting window from which occupants could enjoy an oblique view of the street. Likewise, Vaux expanded the drawing room into a bay window that directly overlooked Fifth Avenue and enlarged the dining room with a polygonal conservatory that allowed diners to glance through plate glass windows into the back garden. (The kitchen was in the basement.) Vaux also took steps to impart a gracious, easy feeling to the spaces in this first-floor suite of rooms. Corners in the 16' × 29' drawing room were curved, while those of the 16' × 23' dining room held semicircular niches, presumably for sculpture. Wide doorways allowed each room, which could also be entered from the stairhall, to be opened into the next. On the two upper floors, each of which held three bedrooms, Vaux made every effort to do away with space-consuming passages and dark entrances. Curving back the walls at the head and foot of the staircase, he created unusually ample landings and allowed the bedrooms to be entered directly from the skylighted hall. Furthermore, each bedroom benefited from hooded or round-headed windows in the south wall, where smaller oval openings lit adjacent dressing rooms. In general, one imagines that to a remarkable degree the inside of the Gray house eluded the unpleasant darkness and monotonous boxiness that afflicted the typical New York row house interior.

From the *Crayon*, we learn that Gray's rooms were also splendidly decorated. This work, we are told, Vaux entrusted to J. Wrey Mould (1824–1886), a fellow Englishman who had emigrated to New York City in 1853 to erect All Souls' Unitarian Church. (By the time that Mould became involved with Gray's new townhouse, he was already assisting Vaux and Olmsted on Central Park.) An associate of the great ornamentalist Owen Jones, Mould helped on the publication of Jones's monumental illustrated study of the Alhambra (1848) as well as that of his influential *Grammar of Ornament*. Described by George Templeton Strong as a "universal genius" and by Clarence Cook as a "more original artist than Richardson," Mould distinguished himself as America's archmaster of High Victorian ornamentalism.[62] The decoration of the Gray house, which Mould must have commenced in 1858 with a free hand and a liberal budget, was one of his first significant undertakings. "We have seen nothing in the way of painting in this modern Gotham which can compare with the detail of the painting in Mr. Gray's house," stated the editor of the *Crayon*, John Durand, in February 1859.[63] Having visited the house while painting was in progress, Durand came away with the impression that every "line and every leaf betrays the spirit and life of a master hand, and reminds us of the best works of the Alhambra and Gartner's modern production in Munich." Saluting Mould as a true disciple of the voluptuous doctrines of Jones, whom Mould helped to adorn London's Crystal Palace, Durand characterized Mould as "bold as a lion in the selection of his colors, and grave as a judge in their combination[;] he dazzles with brightness, without offending the most fastidious taste." Unfortunately, Durand recorded few particulars of what he saw inside the Gray house, although he did mention that Gustave Herter crafted some of the furnishings. In the absence of further evidence, we can form some idea of the decor from the way Mould arrayed the rooms of his own dwelling on East 26th Street. "It is small but the interior most exquisitely finished in polychromatic frescoing of his own design and superintending," Alfred Janson Bloor, an architectural assistant in Vaux's New York office, confided to his diary in March 1859. The dining room ceiling bore a design of gilded tracery, into which Mould had woven the inscription "Give Us This Day Our Daily Bread" in Old English lettering, and the word "Salve" in large white Roman characters greeted guests in the lapis lazuli–colored vestibule.[64] John Gray's house must have radiated a similar spectrum and spirit. Durand took pains to congratulate Gray for his "boldness in initiating poly-chromatic painting, from which most men are apt to shrink." He could think of no precedents in America for this accomplishment (he especially labeled as a glaring failure the interior colors of the Capitol in Washington), which he hoped "will prove the initiation of an era in the history of polychromatic decoration in this country." Considering that Mould had few opportunities to exercise his genius as a decorator ("The truth is," said Clarence Cook, "that people of only moderate wealth feared to put themselves in his hands"),[65] it is truly sad that John Gray's innovative house is gone without a trace.

John Gray expressed his pleasure with his elegant residence by promoting Vaux as architect for the new building of the Bank of New York, on whose board he served as a director. On January 10, 1856, the building committee, which included Gray as a member, invited Vaux and several other New York architects to submit plans for the new building, which was to stand at the corner of Wall and Williams Streets.[66] Some six weeks later, the committee approved the plans that the firm of Vaux and Withers had prepared for a $175,000, four-story brick and brownstone structure (Fig. 3.17). The corner-stone of this, the largest commercial building that Vaux had yet planned, was laid on September 10, 1856. At Gray's urging, Vaux left Withers in Newburgh to be near the job in New York, where he set up an office under the firm name at 358 Broadway.[67] A cloud hung over construction during the fall of 1857, when the financial panic that gripped Wall Street forced the directors to suspend specie payments for a month. However, Vaux had little reason to fear for the security of the bank, for as a biographer of a former director, Gardiner G. How-land, stated, it was "one of the best managed and most honorable institutions in America."[68] On March 29, 1858, the new banking room opened its doors to its first customers.

"The banks of New York are becoming every day more important in an architectural point of view," declared Clarence Cook in 1853. Like a number of banks that went up in the Wall Street area around the middle of the century, Vaux's Bank of New York was in the Italian style. "In architecture, as in history, Greece has fallen victim to Italy," commented Cook, who regarded Wall Street's ancien régime of Greek Revival banks as "grim temples, consecrated to Plutus . . . with their bulky and ungraceful leg-like columns, out of place, out of proportion, like a crowd of briefly-petticoated ballet dancers, who stand shiver-ing and unregarded after the play and its applauses are over, waiting for their carriages to carry them home."[69] Neither was Cook particularly impressed by most of the more recent buildings, which he found generally ill-proportioned, ugly in their decoration, and lacking in projections sufficiently bold to impart a

sense of vigor and richness to the facades. The *Crayon* also criticized contemporary New York bank architecture. In a review that appeared the very month that the cornerstone of the Bank of New York was laid, the magazine chose to make an example of the new Bank for Savings in the City of New York in Bleecker Street. It especially condemned the structure, whose architect went unidentified, for its lack of clear expression of purpose. A person standing in front of it, said the critic, "would range its uses somewhere between a synagogue and a State prison."[70] Furthermore, proportions were ungainly, materials were poorly used, ornamentation was "profanely redundant," and the interior, like that of so many banking institutions, was badly lit. "This building," concluded the *Crayon*, "is an admirable illustration of the ignorance of the moral significance of an architectural work." Architects were put on notice that only "a strict conformity of structure to the thought its purpose excites" would keep them from falling into such disturbing "architectural errors."

Against this background of dissatisfaction, Vaux must have thought long and hard about the bank of his that was to stand in the heart of the commercial capital of the New World. From a professional point of view, Vaux could have asked for no better introduction to the New York architectural scene than this imposing building, which occupied the site of the original 1797 banking house. Vaux's Bank of New York somewhat resembled an Italian palazzo because it had a flat roof hidden behind a heavy cornice; however, Vaux must have planned the building from the beginning to have the two upper floors and the curved roof that he added in the late 1870s. Evocative of the Florentine origins of modern-day banking, the Italian townhouse was a popular model for financial institutions on both sides of the Atlantic. For the building's exterior, which had a 38-foot facade on Wall Street and extended 126 feet down Williams Street, Vaux employed the same brick and brownstone materials he had proposed for John Gray's townhouse. The lower two floors displayed arcades of vermiculated brownstone, behind which were set large sash windows in a field of dark red brick. The two-story banking hall overlooking Williams Street, where the name of the bank was inscribed, received abundant light from floor-to-ceiling windows with circular centers. On the upper floors, pilaster-like strips of brownstone—ornamented with carved rosettes—projected from the field of red brick that surrounded round-headed windows. The strips created a consistent rhythm of verticals across the front and down the side of the building. The pattern of light and shade created by the projecting stone strips and window labels would have furnished that "pictorial effect" Cook found lacking in so many New York facades. Although Cook and the *Crayon* remained silent about Vaux's building, an anonymous critic in the *Times* called it "one of the most remarkable bank facades" he had seen. "The style shows great invention latent in the architect," he said, "and though it is elaborately ugly in its details . . . it has the great merit of being perfectly harmonious."[71]

One would like to know if in the gridlike articulation of the exterior Vaux intended to remind the viewer of the building's internal, structural iron elements. By 1856, iron had been used for beams in a number of New York bank buildings as a means of fireproof construction, and Vaux's Bank of New York employed wrought iron beams and an iron roof manufactured by the nascent architectural ironwork firm of John B. and William W. Cornell. In addition to these iron structural elements—Leopold Eidlitz's contemporary American Exchange and Continental Bank shared this technology—Vaux employed corrugated iron and iron laths for all interior partitions. He also built heavy iron shutters into the stone walls so that guards could seal off the windows of the banking room, the cashier's room, and the offices of the president and directors "simultaneously by a process that is too simple to get out of order at all readily."[72] Referring to Alexander Saeltzer's Duncan and Sherman Bank, in July 1856 the *Crayon* applauded the new use of iron construction, which it hoped would be adopted for important structures all over the country. However, the *Crayon* strenuously objected to the fact that on the inside Saeltzer tried to make metal columns look like stone by coating them with scagliola. "A true architect," asserted the critic, "would have worked nights in decorating them with gilding and color, before he would have allowed it."[73] Vaux avoided any sham on the interior of his bank.

The major public space of the Bank of New York was the 58' × 35' first-floor banking room. This was a "beautiful apartment," reported the *Times*. Eschewing the gaudiness of the Duncan and Sherman Bank, Vaux lined the walls of his room with fine-grained Caen stone, the warm creamy color of which he subtly highlighted with dark oak woodwork, which continued into the ceiling. The banking screen, counter, and desks were manufactured by Gustave Herter, who also took charge of ornamenting the ceiling. Ample light brightened the commodious room from the tall arcaded windows on the Williams Street side and from clear glass panels set in the 26-foot-high ceiling on the interior side of the room. Above this area, a lightwell reached to a rooftop skylight that, like the ceiling itself, was glazed with thick cast glass panels set in a burglar-proof iron frame. This handsome space must have seemed, to those who noticed such things, an answer to both the *Crayon*'s complaint of the want of light in bank-ing rooms and Cook's criticism of the prevailing ugliness of their decoration.

The remainder of the building served various purposes. The directors rented rooms on the front of the first floor and in the upper two stories to other busi-nesses, including the local clearinghouse. Behind the banking room, on the first and second floors, were located the cashier's room, the president's office, and the board of directors' room. The partially above-ground basement contained a lunchroom for employees and the vaults. The sub-basement held a coal furnace designed to heat the entire building according to specifications developed by Lewis W. Leeds, a pioneering expert on central heating and ventilation and a man with whom Vaux formed a long-term association.[74] The *Times* writer, who visited the new bank three days before it opened its doors to the public, expressed the opinion that "in its interior arrangement, in its solidity of construction, in the economy of space, in lighting, heating, and ventilation, the building seems to be absolutely perfect and a great triumph of mechanical skill in arrangement and execution." The directors were so pleased with the new $150,000 edifice that they voted Vaux a $1,500 bonus. Vaux had every reason to be thankful to his friend John Gray for his faith in him, for the board acknowledged in its resolution that it had "been most fortunate in the selection of a comparative stranger to do the work."

While the Bank of New York drew the attention of the New York business community to Vaux's talents, the publication of *Villas and Cottages* in February 1857 advanced his reputation before a national audience. Certainly inspired by the example of Downing, to whom Vaux dedicated the book, *Villas and Cottages* had been in the planning stages since 1854. By January 24, 1855, when Vaux wrote to Fletcher Harper to propose a contract with his publishing company,[75] Vaux had already paid to have some of the drawings engraved on wood blocks. (Most of the perspective views were drawn by Withers and engraved by Alexander Anderson, J. Pinckney, or J. W. Orr.) In his letter, Vaux also suggested that a portion of the volume should appear as an illustrated article in *Harper's Monthly*, an idea that materialized as "Hints" in November 1855. Although Vaux made some designs expressly for the book, the great majority of the 39 buildings represented actual commissions. In effect, the book chronicled most of the work for which Vaux had contracted between his arrival in Newburgh in 1850 and his move to New York City in 1856. Emulating the example of Down-ing's popular works, *Villas and Cottages* began with a general introductory essay that prepared the reader to examine the specific house designs that followed.

These Vaux arranged from smallest to largest residence, and he included perspective views and explanations of each dwelling. In order to avoid what Vaux considered a shortcoming of many architectural books, he included only one elevation drawing, for he believed that the general reader could form only an "incomplete" idea of a building solely from elevations. Elevations, plans, and sections were all necessary tools of the trade, but, asserted Vaux, "if the study is submitted with a view to show what sort of artistic effect may be produced, in execution, from a certain arrangement of ground plan, nothing but a perspective view will convey an accurate idea to the mind." Nonetheless, Vaux emphasized the importance of architectural fundamentals by including a set of ground plans for each dwelling. These and the written descriptions that explained them instructed the thoughtful reader in the disciplined manipulation of spaces that in the architect's mind preceded picturesque expression. "The plans are the best part of the book, and constitute its real value," stated Clarence Cook—an opinion that late-twentieth-century readers might also share.[76] Indeed, as *Villas and Cottages* makes clear, for Vaux style in architecture was a secondary consideration to larger esthetic and practical issues such as proportion, balance, planning, comfort, convenience, and compatibility with the setting. "Vaux sees architecture as primarily functional," observes the German architectural historian Hanno-Walter Kruft, "and this functionalism has its own aesthetic quality."[77] In this way, Vaux differs from many of his contemporaries, notably Philadelphia architect Samuel Sloan, whose *Model Architect* (1852) dealt with country houses primarily as embodiments of various historical styles. Kruft is correct in regarding Vaux's philosophy as related to the advanced architectural theories expounded by Horatio Greenough and Ralph Waldo Emerson. "Why need we copy the Doric or the Gothic model?" Emerson had asked and Vaux had repeated in *Villas and Cottages*. "Beauty, convenience, grandeur of thought, and quaint expression are as near to us as to any," wrote the poet-philosopher, "and if the American artist will study with hope and love the precise thing to be done by him, considering the climate, the soil, the length of day, the wants of the people, the habit and form of government, he will create a home in which all these will find themselves fitted, and taste and sentiment will be satisfied also."[78] Didactic in tone and intention, *Villas and Cottages* was a serious book that had much to say about the union of art and life that its author earnestly, if somewhat naively, hoped would reform the way Americans built and lived in their houses.

Unlike Downing's books, *Villas and Cottages* contained only works with which its author was directly associated, a fact that left Vaux open to the charge of self-promotion. Perhaps irked by what he saw as Vaux's attempt to fill Downing's shoes, Clarence Cook wrote in *Putnam's Monthly* that "Mr. Vaux's book—and we wish to do him no injustice—is too full of egotism." This, said Cook, put Vaux in opposition to Downing's modesty, "which never allowed him to speak an unnecessary word about himself, and which touched even his satire with good nature." Cook also complained that "the charming simplicity of Downing's style, and the evident sincerity of singleness of his purpose," were lacking in Vaux's otherwise fine book. In an age as yet unused to seeing architects publish collections of their own designs, a British reviewer also expressed the opinion that "Mr. Vaux's book is not free from suspicion of being a kind of advertisement of its author."[79] The reviewer's misgivings were confirmed by Vaux's display of his schedule of fees on the last page (2.5% for plans and specifications, 1% for detail drawings, and 1.5% for superintendence, for a total of 5%, the "usual commission of architects"). But to this same writer, Vaux's bravura scarcely compared to the loathsome pretentiousness of one of his clients, N. P. Willis. Taking the opportunity provided by Vaux's discussion of Idlewild, the reviewer blasted its owner as a "conceited, empty-headed snob" who in his 1850 book *People I Have Met* portrayed himself during a visit to England as "hail fellow-well-met with dukes, earls, duchesses, and ladies without number." Thanks to Vaux, the English public could see "the man at home" in his "unpretending" cottage, "the striking things of which had to be omitted because Mr. N. P. Willis could not afford them." Turning to the ground plan, the essayist pointed out with evident satisfaction that Willis, who was "courted, caressed, worshipped (according to his own silly and false account) in every baronal hall and princely palace in England, has actually got a dining-room sixteen feet by twenty!" Such were the perils of being persuaded by a rising young architect to illustrate one's house in his handsome new book.

For his part, Vaux was troubled by the accusation of self-promotion. He felt his critics misunderstood that in printing his schedule of charges he had intended not to advertise his practice but to confirm in the public's mind the right of architects to reasonable compensation for their services. "It touched me," he confessed, "and I asked myself, if this really was so and if I was shoving myself into notice under the impression that I was strengthening the best interest of the profession."[80] The issue of compensation had concerned Vaux as an aspiring architect in London and as a member of the fledgling profession in the States. When he had started his own practice in Newburgh, he had "found the system of remuneration defective and unsettled" and had set out to correct it. "I refused all business not in the plan I determined on," he later told his friend Frederick Law Olmsted, "and established a set of precedents quietly (quietly enough)." When he came to publish *Villas and Cottages*, he decided to quote these precedents "not so quietly and with considerable prominence presented my terms on the end of the volume—so as to attract attention," including the assertion that 5 percent was "the usual commission of architects." Indeed, Vaux believed that if architects (as well as artists) did not "extend themselves to protect the strictly legitimate pecuniary interests" of their profession, the future of their discipline would be in jeopardy. For if architecture were not a profitable pursuit, he reasoned, "young men of ability will be deterred from venturing into it." Yet in retrospect Vaux recognized that his bold action on behalf of his profession had misfired; in later printings of the book he deleted his fee scale.[81]

Of all the reviews of *Villas and Cottages*, Vaux must have been most surprised by the exceptionally negative remarks his book occasioned from the pen of Clarence Cook, who discussed it in his long essay entitled "House Building in America." After admitting that "there has been no book published in America, on the subject of architecture, which is more thorough than this one," Cook went on to link Vaux with Ruskin in their earnest desire to elevate public taste in architecture. But Vaux could take little solace from Cook's comparison, for Cook saw this mission as doomed to failure. It was even pernicious. "Of course, no people who need such advice will ever do anything good," said Cook, "and people who do not need it are hardly subjects for Mr. Ruskin's denunciation or counsel." The reason that the nineteenth century had little good architecture, he said, was that the study of architecture had taken over the art of building. Modern buildings were designed by professional architects who adhered to rules and theories and worked for money. Instead, every great building of the past was "the child of enthusiasm and rapture." This radical denunciation of the power of education, in which Vaux placed so much faith to improve American architecture, led Cook to denounce books like *Villas and Cottages* because they "set patterns for men to follow, and seek to induce a fashion which has no root in our instincts and relations." He went on to add: "We not only think they do very little good, but we think they do positive harm." Cook was especially critical of "meaningless" ornament that architects like Vaux induced people to apply to their dwellings. Instead, Cook extolled the virtues of American vernacular buildings. And although he did not name the Powell house before Vaux remodeled it, he could have used it as an example of "the old farm-houses of Dutch and English type, scattered here and there over the land, testifying to the worth of simplicity, and the beauty of common-sense, in the midst of pretense and gingerbread work." Perhaps Cook's sentiments were generalized enough for Vaux not to have taken them personally, for the two men remained on friendly terms, and in future years Cook championed Vaux's career.

Other reviewers found *Villas and Cottages* more to their liking than Cook did. The British essayist in *Frazer's Magazine*, despite his misgivings about Vaux's self-promotion, thought Vaux was "thoroughly up in the practice of pleasant rural architecture, as he is in the philosophy of it." He especially agreed with Vaux's assertion that the home was a formative influence on the child, and he quoted a lengthy passage from Vaux on the subject. He likewise admired many of the house designs, even those of wood, a building material scarcely used in England. In addition, the writer expressed pleasure with "some good designs for rustic gateways and fences, and some pretty plans for laying out and planting the piece of shrubbery and lawn which surrounds the abode." Vaux also must have been especially pleased with the positive reviews his book received in the serious American press. For the writer in the *Crayon* who waded through the introduction's "matter political, moral, physical, and financial in which the Pandora box of American character is peeped into," the most rewarding part of the book was Vaux's advice on color. Letting Vaux speak for himself, he reprinted a passage in which Vaux talked about the color of country houses in relation to their natural settings, advising the use of light cheerful tones, "sometimes neutral, seldom dark, and never black or white."[82] The *North American Review* gave high marks to the comprehensive introductory chapter. "The desiderata of the dwelling-house as to light, heat, ventilation, drainage, health, comfort, and beauty are carefully considered" and modes of decoration are discussed in a way that both "interests and satisfies us," remarked the anonymous reviewer, who advised readers that "the entire chapter is full of suggestions, which might make every owner of a house a quarter of a century old sorry that his house is not yet to be built."[83] The *Horticulturist* was so pleased with the book that it ran excerpts in both its August and September 1857 issues. To the editor of Downing's former journal, the illustrations, several of which appeared in the magazine, were particularly attractive and, in his view, unequaled by any previous book of its kind.

Periodicals catering to a more general readership also reviewed *Villas and Cottages* favorably. Directing its comments to the businessman contemplating building a rural residence, the *Merchant's Magazine* recommended it for the author's simple style, "free from all professional technicalities." Presumably with readers in mind who had little time to spare for such matters, the reviewer observed that the illustrations were arranged "in a condensed, regular manner, so that they may be examined with little trouble and with but slight reference to the descriptions."[84] William Cullen Bryant's *Evening Post* thought Vaux had put forward "suggestions from which the whole nation will profit," and *Spirit of the Times* referred to his book as "the best and handsomest work of the kind ever published." Indeed, many reviewers commended the book's well-dressed appearance, which set a new standard for architectural publications. "It is one of the handsomest specimens of book-making—beautiful paper, splendid typography, handsome cuts and drawings (three hundred engravings)—and is therefore an ornamental as well as useful volume," the *New York Observer* told its readers, advising them that it was well worth the two-dollar price.[85] But surely for Vaux the most satisfying notice of *Villas and Cottages* was the one that appeared in the *Builder*. "Mr. Vaux, who will be remembered by many of our London readers, when he went to America became the partner of Mr. Downing," stated the reviewer, who was probably George Godwin. *Villas and Cottages* demonstrated to his former countrymen that Vaux had "evidently built for himself a good reputation" in the New World. Perspectives and plans of the Dodge, Vassar, Earle, and Parish houses represented to English readers the range of styles of masonry buildings to be found in Vaux' book, which the journal asserted "deserves a sale as well in this country as in America."[86] Furthermore, the reviewer made favorable note of the schedule of fees that Vaux published, for the issue of remuneration for services was of deep concern to British architects at the time.

Coinciding with what Vaux called the "inexhaustible demand for rural residences that is perceptible in every part of these Northern States,"[87] the publication of *Villas and Cottages* brought its author much favorable attention. Vaux had reason to be optimistic about the reception his book had received. And although it never enjoyed the universal popularity of Downing's writings, *Villas and Cottages* commanded a wide and sustained readership. A revised edition came out in 1864, and subsequent printings appeared nearly every other year between 1867 and 1874. The modestly priced volume of thoughtful commentary and well-illustrated designs for all classes of dwellings earned Vaux the national recognition that he sought as philosopher and designer to the advancing ranks of home builders.

ALL THAT HUMAN INTELLIGENCE CAN ACHIEVE IN ADORNING AND BEAUTIFYING THE EARTH

4

1857–1858

As his career developed and the memory of Downing receded, Vaux must have come more and more to realize that the true path to future success lay not in Newburgh but in New York City. To be sure, Newburgh by the mid–nineteenth century ranked almost as a far suburb of the metropolis; yet it was enough removed to pose a handicap for an architect who might wish to attain a more central place in the profession. And probably for Vaux, who had grown up in the heart of London, the Hudson River town of 15,000 inhabitants, no matter how agreeable, would have seemed provincial and unexciting. His frequent trips to New York would have opened his eyes to the wide possibility for business that existed there, as well as to the opportunity for him and his family to live in company with other men and women of culture. By the end of 1856, the year in which Vaux became an American citizen,[1] he had taken up residence in New York City, where he was to remain until his death in 1895.

An early endeavor to which he devoted his energies in New York was the movement to place American architecture on a sound professional foundation. In early December 1857, Richard Upjohn, a distinguished Gothic Revival architect, invited several of his New York colleagues to meet with him at his office in the Trinity Building to discuss the formation of some sort of architectural organization. On that occasion, a plan of action was proposed and invitations to join in the endeavor were issued to Vaux, Withers, and several others. On February 22, 1857, what could be considered the first formal meeting of the group took place. Perhaps with Vaux in attendance, the group took steps to create an association that would be both a forum for the discussion of ideas and a sounding board for the profession. With Upjohn at the helm, the group worked over the next three months to regularize its existence. On the evening of April 15, 1857, the nascent body convened in the chapel of New York University to constitute itself as the American Institute of Architects (AIA). A constitution and bylaws were approved, and what must have been a lively debate on various matters ensued. "The object of this Institute," read the second article of the constitution adopted that night, "is to promote the scientific and practical perfection of its members, and to elevate the standing of the profession." Among those present were Vaux, Joseph C. Wells, Frederick Diaper, Henry Dudley, and Downing's former associate, A. J. Davis. And although we do not know what opinions Vaux expressed on this historic occasion, we can assume, given his experience with the Architectural Association in London, that he had much to contribute to the discussions, which the secretary, Richard Morris Hunt, reported centered on plans for the presentation of papers at future meetings, rules governing the finances of the organization, and suggestions as to where the institute could be housed.[2]

The issues that architects in New York confronted were generally different from those Vaux's young colleagues in the Architectural Association faced; nonetheless, there were a number of parallels. While institute members did not have to buck a tyrannical elder generation of architects, they did have to contend with public ignorance of and indifference to their skills. Like the members of the Architectural Association vis-à-vis the Royal Academy, New York architects felt shut out of the National Academy of Design, which, as A. J. Davis complained, gave scant attention to architectural drawings in its annual exhibitions. Improvement was to come gradually in both these areas, although it would not be until 1866 that the AIA organized an exhibition of its members' drawings. Of more purely technical interest was the matter of determining professional qualifications for architects. Eager to eschew the image of frivolousness, the organizers of the AIA sought to bring architecture out of its shadowland existence into the light of American mainstream life. As the son of a doctor, Vaux must have personally felt the need to attain for himself solid respectability as a member of a full-fledged discipline. All around him he could see, despite the reign of Jacksonian populism, men in many other areas of endeavor reaching for the same goal. Among those present on April 15, perhaps only Vaux and Richard Morris Hunt, who had recently returned to America after studying in Paris at the Ecole des Beaux-Arts and working under Victor Lefuel at the Louvre, could lay claim to long and thorough study and apprenticeship under professional guidance. Upjohn, Davis, Walter, and others of the older generation all had been largely self-taught. As of yet there were no schools of architecture existing in America, and no form of licensing prevailed, difficulties the founders of the institute got around by making approval by the board of trustees the only requirement for membership. In the absence of any other standards, the evidence of one's work would serve as proof of professional competence. Despite its valiant beginnings, the institute remained small and local until after the Civil War; yet even in its early years it offered men like Vaux a new means to advance the cause of their profession and provided a much needed forum for the serious exchange of views.

On the evening of June 2, Vaux delivered one of the first lectures, a paper extolling the virtues of multiple dwellings in New York and other American cities. Although shortly before his death Downing had talked informally about the desirability of communal pied-à-terre lodgings in cities, Vaux's address was the first thoughtful discussion in America of the true apartment building. (At the time, he and others referred to this quintessential urban building type as "Parisian flats"; by the end of the nineteenth century they were commonly called "apartment houses.") So interesting and novel was Vaux's idea that his paper attracted the attention of the popular press. In December 1857, the new

Harper's Weekly reprinted Vaux's remarks, together with the model elevation and ground plan that he had prepared for the edification of his colleagues (Figs. 4.1 and 4.2).[3] Vaux's interest in the subject may have been stirred by his own recent search for a suitable home for his family in New York, where, as Elizabeth Cromley has pointed out, middle-class residents in the 1850s had limited opportunities for setting up normal family life.[4] Many families lodged in boardinghouses or in hotels, where they took their meals in common with other lodgers, a mode of living that Vaux condemned for "the ceaseless publicity that ensues, the constant change, and the entire absence of all individuality in the every day domestic arrangements." Others, like Vaux himself, rented a house or part of a house and took in boarders to help defray expenses.[5]

The remedy Vaux proposed for these social ills came from abroad. Pointing to the superior example of European cities, Vaux asserted that New York, with its limited surface area and subsequent high cost of property, would do well to erect "extensive buildings, several stories high . . . with all the rooms required for a family grouped together on one level, or nearly so, and these approached through one hall from a public staircase."[6] The only buildings representative of this system in America were the so-called tenement houses. For this reason, Vaux perceived, polite society disfavored the notion of dwelling in such proximity to others. Even upscale European models would have to be modified, he conceded, to fit American prejudices. He could not foresee, for example, the 10-story-high apartments of Edinburgh being imitated here, because middle-class Americans would not tolerate living below the poorer residents who trudged up to the less desirable flats, those above the fourth level. The courtyard system so often encountered in Continental cities also would not work in New York, where residents wished to have a view on the street. (Vaux thought this especially important for women in comfortable circumstances, for in America, he observed, they were accustomed to spend most of their lives indoors.) Finally, Vaux questioned the common European practice of placing the shared staircase in the middle of the building, where it suffered from lack of light and want of architectural distinction. Although he personally acknowledged that "the agreeable effect of the rooms themselves, when arrived at, is possibly enhanced thereby," he said New Yorkers would think otherwise. A careful observer of society, Vaux knew that tenement houses had given multifamily dwellings a bad reputation; therefore, he advised his fellow architects that "the public staircase, which is the unusual feature to which we have to be accustomed, must be made light, airy and elegant; and if possible, lighter, airier, and more elegant than any other part of the house, or a prejudice will be likely to be excited on entering the premises against the whole effect; and this it is all important to avoid."

Putting into practice what he preached, Vaux made the vertical strip of tall windows lighting the central staircase the dominant element of the facade in the drawing for the "Parisian Buildings" that accompanied his text (Fig. 4.1). Indeed, the quest for light governed the entire facade design, which, other than the curved gable (perhaps introduced here to recall New York's Dutch origins), bore little resemblance to the picturesque designs in *Villas and Cottages*. Large tripartite windows stacked on either side of the staircase bay cheered the parlors of the eight 25-foot-wide flats and gave a sparkling appearance to the front of the building (which presumably was to be built of brick and brownstone.) Nor was there much that conformed to French architectural tradition, unless one sees in the "rationalism" of the three-part elevation and the recessed paneling that

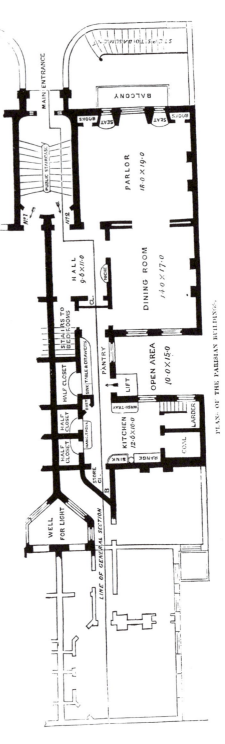

FIGURE 4.1. *(above)*
Design for "Parisian Buildings"
apartments, 1857. From *Harper's
Weekly*, December 1857. Courtesy
of Buffalo and Erie County Public
Library.

FIGURE 4.2. *(at right)*
"Parisian Buildings," plan of typical
apartment. From *Harper's Weekly*,
December 1857. Courtesy of Buffalo
and Erie County Public Library.

articulated it a repeat of Richard Morris Hunt's Néo-Grec-style Tenth Street Studio Building, which was then under construction. To most New Yorkers of Vaux's day, however, the large plate glass windows probably would have brought to mind the commercial "loft" buildings that were going up in the area today known as SoHo. Undoubtedly, Vaux expected that the promise of bright, cheerful rooms would dispel any misgivings that prospective residents might have about the external appearance of the building.

On his interior plan, Vaux addressed the same matters of convenience, comfort, and privacy that had occupied him in the design of houses for middle-class families. The basement accommodated a concierge and a bachelor apartment, as well as coal cellars for each tenant. A hydraulic lift allowed servants to transport fuel easily to the upper kitchens and to take laundry to an attic drying room. Above the basement level, each flat conformed to the same layout, which followed a careful division of the long rectangular space into three separate living areas (Fig. 4.2). First in line on the front of the building were the formal living spaces. From the entrance hall (9.6' × 11'), one entered either the large parlor (18' × 19'), which overlooked the street, or the smaller dining room (14' × 17'), which could be thrown open to the front room by wide sliding doors. The middle range of the plan held the kitchen, servants' room, air shaft, dustbin, lift, and closets. In the rear section, farthest from the noise of the street and the view of guests, three bedrooms were grouped with a bathroom. Vaux increased the isolation of the bedrooms by placing them on a level three feet higher than that of the parlor. By this arrangement, he said, "several advantages are obtained; for the bedroom passage and the kitchen being nine feet high, while the parlors and bedrooms are twelve feet high, the additional three feet can, by a difference of level, be so placed that it may be arranged for closet room, at a convenient height for use from both the bedroom and kitchen floor, and it also allows of a passage to the bedrooms that does not pass the kitchen door at all, which is desirable for the sake of privacy."[7] Furthermore, a triangular light vented the bathroom well and expanded into the bedroom passage, which, Vaux said, was "purposely diverted from a straight line, so as to avoid the uninviting appearance of a long, narrow corridor." Thus, with care and cleverness, Vaux sought to provide middle-class urban families with the same essential features of domestic life that he had extolled in *Villas and Cottages*. All who took time to examine his proposal would have realized that the commodious "Parisian Building" was no ordinary tenement house.

Despite Vaux's persuasive arguments in favor of French flats, initial reaction to his scheme seems to have been negative. Richard Upjohn reflected the majority sentiments of those in the audience who stayed to discuss Vaux's prophetic ideas. "Many of his colleagues felt that the form might be well enough for European cities," wrote Everard M. Upjohn of his grandfather's impressions, "but that it would never take root here, where land was so available and where people preferred to sit on their front porches and watch their neighbors!"[8] Another architect who was present but whose thoughts are not recorded was Richard Morris Hunt. Having lived in Paris, Hunt was in a position to know the truth of Vaux's remarks, and he may have remembered them when at the end of the following decade he designed the Stuyvesant, the building generally considered New York City's first true apartment house. As Sarah Landau has discovered, Hunt indeed experimented with a courtyard plan. He rejected it, however, in favor of the type of arrangement that Vaux had proposed, which allowed all the parlors to overlook the street.[9] The Stuyvesant also had spacious public stairs and only four floors of flats (artists' studios occupied the fifth level). As an early Stuyvesant tenant, Vaux surely took secret pride in the success of that fashionable building and those that followed its example in the 1870s and 1880s, for truly, he had planted the seed of their existence at that AIA meeting that took place in the spring of 1857.

BY THE TIME THAT Henry Dudley and Edward Gardiner debated the issue of architectural competitions at the AIA's September 1 meeting, Vaux had already been hard at work behind the scenes promoting the notion of a competition for the design of Central Park. The site for the park, a 750-acre rectangle bounded by 59th Street on the south, 106th Street on the north, Fifth Avenue on the east, and Eighth Avenue (present Central Park West) on the west, had been fixed in 1853, after several years of public debate on the subject.[10] In June 1856, Mayor Fernando Wood approved a plan for the park devised by Egbert Viele, the engineer who had made the topographical map of the site. "Being thoroughly disgusted with the manifest defects of Viele's plan," said Vaux, "I pointed out whenever I had a chance, that it would be a disgrace to the City and to the memory of Mr. Downing (who had first proposed the location of a large park in New York) to have this plan carried out."[11] Among those he must have buttonholed was surely J. J. Smith, the influential editor of the *Horticulturist*, who had just concluded a successful drive to erect on the Smithsonian grounds the monument Vaux had designed to honor Downing.[12] When the state legislature appointed a board of park commissioners in 1857, Vaux lobbied its members "and any other interested persons who cared to listen to my remarks" on the virtues of a competition. Two of the thirteen commissioners were especially sympathetic to Vaux and apparently advocated his idea. One of them was Charles Wyllys Elliott, a man who had worked with Downing for a time in the 1840s and who had written a clever article on barns for *Putnam's Monthly Magazine* that Vaux had reprinted in *Villas and Cottages*. The other was John A. C. Gray, the house client who the year before had secured for Vaux the prestigious job of designing the Bank of New York, the construction of which Vaux was supervising when Gray was named a park commissioner.

Well before October 13, 1857, the date on which the board announced a public competition for the plan of the park, Vaux probably knew of its decision, and he may have already contacted Frederick Law Olmsted to enlist his aid as a partner in developing an entry. "I first met Mr. Olmsted at the house of Mr. Downing at Newburgh," remembered Vaux, "and was led to ask him to cooperate with preparation of a competition design for Central Park because I was interested in Mr. Olmsted's book [*Walks and Talks of an American Farmer in England*], but mainly because at that particular time his days were spent on the park territory."[13] In early September, Olmsted, who had recently suffered a serious reversal of fortune with the collapse of *Putnam's Monthly Magazine*, a journal he had financed and edited, had been appointed superintendent of labor under Viele. "In this way," said Vaux, "Mr. Olmsted, without expense to himself or to me, was so situated that he could bring . . . accurate observations in regard to the actual topography which was not clearly defined on the survey furnished to competitors by the Board." Moreover, Vaux so strongly felt the need of special help in this huge undertaking that he might have foregone the competition altogether on his own. "I had no idea of competing because I felt my incapacity," he later confided to Olmsted, who initially resisted Vaux's invitation to join him.[14] Probably remembering Downing's troubles with Washington politicians, Vaux, who regarded himself primarily as an artist, thought that he lacked the ability and will to supervise single-handedly the construction of the park. In Olmsted, however, he discovered a rare individual who not only shared his esthetic and social ideals but who also, Vaux foresaw, possessed the strength of temperament that would enable them to successfully translate those ideals into reality. For his part, Olmsted felt honored to have been sought out by the man he saw as Downing's "chosen disciple." There was no one, thought Olmsted, "to whom it came more naturally, properly, and in due sequence of a strictly professional career," to undertake the design of the new park than Vaux. During the fall and winter of 1857–1858, Vaux and Olmsted worked hard at night, in Vaux's home on East 18th Street, developing the plan that they submitted on March 31 as Portfolio 33, under the name Greensward.[15] In this historic endeavor, Vaux and Olmsted had the assistance of Mould, who, despite his initial reluctance, came along in the evenings to help, and Jervis McEntee, who contributed oil sketches to accompany the pencil and watercolor drawings that Vaux prepared to show how the present landscape would be transformed by their ideas.

On April 28, the commissioners announced their decision to award the first prize to the Greensward plan. Several days later, in his office in the Appleton Building, Vaux divided the $2,000 premium with Olmsted. Turning to his new friend, Vaux instructed Olmsted that he was "at liberty to proceed to carry out the design without my taking further part in it, provided that our joint names were duly recognized in the plan as it then stood."[16] Yet Olmsted felt unable to attempt the task that lay ahead without Vaux at his side, and he asked that they continue to work together. Vaux gladly acceded to Olmsted's request. "New York at length has its crowning triumph," wrote Downing's friend George William Curtis in *Harper's Monthly* once work at the park had begun. "It is a garden in the largest and most generous sense—not a series of flower-beds, but a system of avenues, drives, walks, paths, terraces, lawns, streams, falls, bridges, grottoes, tunnels, shrubberies, groves, hedges, flowers, and all that human intelligence can achieve in adorning and beautifying the earth."[17] At the time, both men thought the job would last five years; neither of them foresaw that the park would be with them in one way or another for the rest of their careers. Yet unlike Olmsted, Vaux perceived that winning the Central Park competition placed its designers in the forefront of the evolving American park movement and would bring them other profitable commissions. He told Olmsted that the park "would some day be done and we could take the principal men that had helped us carry on the business that it would inevitably lead to. . . . This is what I always anticipated would be the outcome of the Park."[18]

Because Vaux and Olmsted insisted that the Greensward plan was a joint effort, it is difficult to identify the contributions that each man made to the project. However, Olmsted, who had no architectural training, credited Vaux with all structures called for in the park; "architectural design and superintendence, in which I have no appreciable property . . . is wholly yours," he affirmed to his partner.[19] Olmsted, whose life before the autumn of 1857 was a mixed bag of pursuits that included farming, writing, and publishing, had never designed a landscape plan. Vaux, on the other hand, had worked with Downing on the

Washington park and had laid out the grounds of numerous private houses. And in "Hints" and *Villas and Cottages* he had articulated a philosophy of domestic architecture predicated on the subordination of the house to its natural setting and on the acquisition of prospects for the pleasure of the inhabitants. He had also demonstrated over and over in his work the ability to conceive comprehensive schemes involving buildings, grounds, and distant views. Indeed, the equation of the Mall or Promenade with the position of a house in a private estate suggests a way of thinking that would have been natural to Vaux as a designer of country houses. In fact, a parallel to the sequence of elements that Olmsted and Vaux described as beginning at the 59th Street gate and culminating in the view of the lake and Vista Rock from the "missing mansion" site at the Terrace can be found in Vaux's layout of the Hoyt property at Staatsburg. There, as in the park, a curving road led to the elevated site of the house; from its terrace one enjoyed views northward over the waters of the Hudson to the distant Catskill mountains. With such experience behind him, one might expect Vaux to have taken the lead in the project, guiding Olmsted in unifying and articulating the design of so extensive a landscape plan as was called for at Central Park. He must also have given Olmsted much practical advice. In December 1857, for example, he referred Olmsted to Thomas Barton, the proprietor of Montgomery Place, for detailed information about the road system on that Hudson Valley estate that Downing had so loved.[20] Moreover, one can guess that because Vaux had agitated for the overthrow of Viele's plan and even claimed credit for "arranging the terms of the competition," he must have formed distinct ideas of his own concerning the park's design before he approached Olmsted with the offer of collaboration.[21] Until then Olmsted had taken no part in the competition campaign, and he even politely sought Viele's permission to compete once Vaux had approached him. I believe Vaux must have gone to Olmsted bearing in his mind the fundamental artistic outlines of the Greensward plan, as well as the philosophical foundation on which it rested.

The jointly written report that accompanied Olmsted and Vaux's competition entry succinctly explained the major features of the 750-acre pastoral

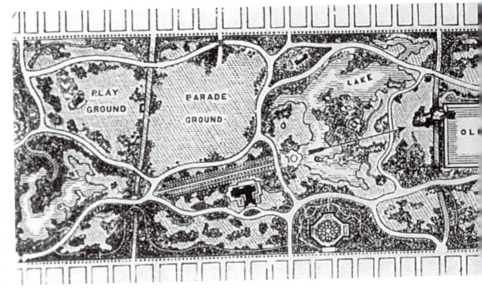

FIGURE 4.3.
Plan of Central
Park, 1857.
From C. Cook,
*Description of the
New York Central
Park*. Courtesy
of Buffalo and
Erie County
Public Library.

landscape that the designers intended to create (Fig. 4.3).[22] The terrain of the site, said the authors, naturally divided itself into two parts. The northern section, roughly between 79th and 106th Streets, possessed "bold and sweeping" lines that constituted "the highest ideal that can be aimed at for a park under any circumstances." For this reason, they proposed to alter only slightly the face of the ground here. Unfortunately, much of this northern area was taken up by two reservoirs, the smaller, rectangular old reservoir, and the much larger, irregularly shaped new reservoir, which nearly covered the width of the park between 86th and 96th Streets. Drives on either side of the reservoirs conducted visitors to and from the more open northern landscape, where in the northeast section they might enjoy an arboretum of American plants and, on Bogardus Hill, mount an observation tower. By contrast, the lower portion of the park had a far more mixed character and possessed only Vista Rock, a "long rocky and wooded hill-side" immediately south of the old reservoir (the rock formed part of the reservoir wall), as a feature of any scenic consequence. In the lower park, there-fore, the designers proposed many improvements to nature's unprepossessing physiognomy.

Regarding the primary park entrance to be at Fifth Avenue and 59th Street, Olmsted and Vaux directed the jurors through their plan from this point. The drive, which started at this gate, led visitors diagonally into the landscape so as to remove them as quickly as possible from urban surroundings. In a series of gentle curves, the carriageway arrived at the Avenue (the present Mall), a 2,000-foot-long pedestrian promenade shaded beneath straight rows of trees. "This avenue may be considered the central feature in our plan for laying out the lower park," explained Olmsted and Vaux. It was to be the place where large numbers of people could meet as in an "open air hall of reception." For this reason, the designers looked upon the area as "an artificial structure on a scale of magnitude commensurate with the size of the park." In their minds, it occu-pied the same position of relative importance in the general arrangement of the plan "that a mansion should occupy in a park prepared for private occupation." At its northern end, Olmsted and Vaux located a terrace, a feature one might

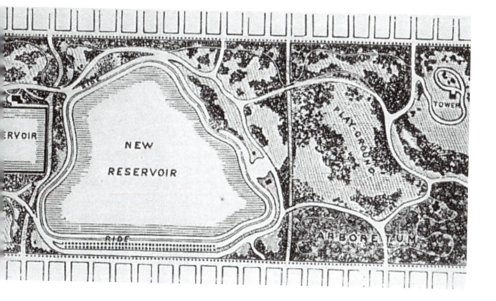

expect on the garden side of a large house. This terrace afforded visitors their first real view of parkscape, a prospect toward Vista Rock and over the 20-acre skating lake that they proposed to create at the foot of the terrace. Across the lake from the terrace, in the rugged area that later became known as the Ramble, the partners proposed to supplement the existing trees with hardy ever-green shrubs and other bushes. Thus, in a manner analogous to the way Vaux sited his houses, the partners organized this naturally elevated area to offer park users the pleasure of viewing picturesque scenery.

Other distinctive elements also figured in the plan. On the east side of the Mall was to be located a large music hall, a feature called for in the competition rules. A bit north of that, adjacent to Fifth Avenue, Olmsted and Vaux placed an elaborate flower garden, another feature stipulated by the commissioners. The colored design that Olmsted and Vaux submitted showed a large octagonal bed with intricate interlacing patterns. A wall fountain in the manner of the eighteenth-century Trevi fountain in Rome overlooked the flower garden on one side, while a three-tiered loggia that recalled the Villa Borghese stood on another side. The general Italian appearance of the flower garden, which was never constructed, may have been inspired in part by Olmsted's recent memories of Italy, for he had traveled there in 1856. Aside from the flower-garden loggia and the music hall (to which a conservatory would be attached), Olmsted and Vaux made limited provision for buildings within the park. A small tower for Vista Rock, a summerhouse east of the Mall, a shelter for spectators watching games on the playing field near the Eighth Avenue and 59th Street entrance, and a casino on the west side of the park comprised most of the struc-tures they envisioned erecting. The arsenal that already existed on the site near Fifth Avenue and 64th Street would be converted into a museum. In addition, one stone bridge was proposed for the northern part of the park, and seven wooden crossings were called for in the lower park. These modest structures were to accommodate carriage riders along seven miles of 60-foot-wide, terrain-hugging roadway that threaded its way around the entire park site.

The most innovative feature of the Greensward plan concerned the creation of four crosstown roadways. To prevent the heavy urban traffic on these routes from disturbing park visitors and disrupting the seamless pastoral landscape, Olmsted and Vaux proposed that these thoroughfares be depressed several feet below grade and that their borders be fenced and heavily planted so as to hide them from the view of people in the park. Park paths and drives would span the sunken roads by means of bridges, which themselves would carry provision for planting trees and shrubs. In this novel and expensive way, the partners sought to avoid the fragmentation of the park surface that had dogged Downing's plan for the Washington park, where city streets crossed at grade. Undoubtedly, Vaux's association with that earlier project would have made him especially sensitive to the similar problem he and Olmsted confronted in New York. It is entirely likely that Central Park's transverse roadways came about as a result of Olmsted and Vaux's reexamination of Downing's Washington plan and their desire to improve on the solution to the problem of crosstown traffic it embodied. They also may have been influenced by a scheme proposed by painter John Martin to link London's Bayswater and Kensington neighborhoods by means of a sunken road across Hyde Park and Kensington Gardens. Although Martin's scheme was not published until 1860, Vaux may have heard about it in the architectural circles that he frequented before leaving England.[23]

By June 1, 1858, construction of Central Park had begun. Olmsted was in charge of directing 200 men and bore the misleading title of "architect in chief." For this work as construction superintendent, he received an annual salary of $2,500. Vaux, who with Olmsted continued to refine the Greensward plan, was employed as his assistant to prepare architectural plans and working drawings at a salary of five dollars per day. Vaux was hurt as much by the unfairness of these arrangements as by Olmsted's failure to speak up in his defense. "I felt that was not what I should have done to you," he later told Olmsted. At the time, however, he held his tongue because he trusted in his friend's "purity of aim and intention." Personal feelings aside, Vaux found the situation particularly distressing because at the very moment when he and his fellows in the AIA had taken up the struggle to have their talents publicly recognized, title and authority for this historic project were extended to an amateur. "Knowing the state of the art and the position of artists and the needs of every strength being brought to bear, it was of course somewhat difficult to countenance the idea of an established architect serving as clerk . . . to a new man who chose to call himself or be called architect," said Vaux.[24] Nonetheless, in the interests of a greater good, he decided to accept the circumstances. "I made then as I considered it a sacrifice of my professional rights," he told Olmsted, "for the good of the common cause, not our common cause but the common cause of the park and all it meant in the best sense."[25] The situation improved in January 1859, when Vaux became "consulting architect" at an annual salary of $2,000. (A few months later, Olmsted's title changed to "architect in chief and superintendent.") During this early period, construction of the park proceeded at a remarkably fast pace. In the throes of a crisis of widespread unemployment brought about by the financial panic of 1857, local politicians were eager to provide jobs for the city's large population of laborers. The lower park was substantially finished by the summer of 1861; after that, park building proceeded at a more modest pace.

One of the first areas of the park to be worked on was the Mall. Also called the Promenade (in the Greensward plan, Olmsted and Vaux had referred to it as the Avenue), this area was a wide, straight pedestrian passage lined with rows of American elms. Beneath the 23-year-old specimens that workmen planted in 1859, walks and lawns extended a quarter of a mile from near the 65th Street transverse road to the Terrace at the level of 72nd Street. A similar feature had been a prominent element of Viele's earlier plan for Central Park. Viele's promenade, however, followed the central axis of the property, while Olmsted and Vaux positioned the Mall on a diagonal. Vaux maintained the superiority of this arrangement over Viele's more conventional approach, saying that "the ground of the park is such that if divided through the center, as shown upon the plan of General Viele, there would be no effect of breadth on either side." By way of the Mall, Olmsted and Vaux led the visitor from the major park entrance at Fifth Avenue and 59th Street to the heart of the park by the most direct means possible. "Excepting a necessary straight line along the eastern margin of the Croton Lake, which the designers had no control over," wrote a correspondent of the *Horticulturist* in 1859, "there is only one such in the park, and this is the Mall or Promenade ground." As Vaux would undoubtedly have done, the writer defended the introduction of this formal element into the otherwise informal landscape of the park by stating that "as we look at the plan upon paper, it certainly appears as the spoilation of a principle; on the ground, however, . . .

the disparity is not noticed unless by the prejudiced critic." To mitigate the incongruity of the Mall's regimented elms standing in the midst of the naturalistic landscape, the architects disguised its borders with diverse plantings to mask its formality from the eyes of visitors in other parts of the park.

Above all, the designers conceived the Mall as a place for democratic socializing. As such, it stood apart from the prevailing pastoral spirit that informed the park landscape. The Mall's wide, bench-lined gravel walks were intended to fulfill the city's desire to have an elegant public meeting place, a gracious promenade like those that existed in the metropolises of Europe. A stroll along the Mall in Central Park was to be the American equivalent of a walk through the gardens of the Tuileries in Paris, beneath Les Bastions in Geneva, along Unterdenlinden in Berlin, or in the Wasserglacis and the Prater in Vienna. In New York, it fell to the new park to provide for this popular form of urban entertainment. "It is reasonable to suppose that we must have, in a public establishment of this nature, a part for promenade and display of person," stated the *Horticulturist* writer quoted earlier. "We should think of the unrestricted freedom," he mused, "that a straight line one-fourth of a mile long, two hundred feet wide, composed of belts of grass turf and gravel, overtopped with our National Elm, will give to the elastic trip of the rising generation."

The Mall was an enduring success with the public. It was, testified Vaux's friend and assistant Samuel Parsons, the area of the park that attracted the most visitors. Writing in the 1890s, by which time the trees had assumed maturity, Parsons called it an "open air cathedral of elms, showing long vistas of natural Gothic arches" (Fig. 4.4). In its delicious shade, he said, people might "linger to enjoy the cool of morning or evening [or] gather on bright afternoons in thousands" to enjoy the music of a band occupying a stand (designed by Mould) near the north end.[26] A verdant boulevard crowded with pedestrians of all classes, the Mall fulfilled the esthetic and social promise that Olmsted and Vaux had envisioned.

As a thoroughfare, the Mall, which had all-weather walkways separated by rows of trees and lawns, can be viewed as the genesis of the parkway idea that Olmsted and Vaux introduced into American city planning in the mid-1860s. The architects even took the concept of the Mall a step further toward the parkway within Central Park itself when they laid out the 200-foot-wide strip of land along the eastern edge of the new reservoir. There, walkers, horseback riders, and carriages proceeded in streetlike fashion along separate parallel lanes beneath the shade of enfilade elms. Beyond the boundaries of the park, Olmsted and Vaux applied this scheme to the invention of special urban residential streets that they called parkways. These 200-foot-wide residential avenues provided discrete lanes for vehicles, horseback riders, and pedestrians. All of these usages were kept separate from each other by means of strips of turf and rows of native elms, a tree chosen perhaps as much for its association with the ideals of New England town life as for its overarching beauty. Parkways were first constructed on a comprehensive scale as part of the municipal park system that Olmsted and Vaux created for Buffalo in 1868–1870. They also proposed to use their new type of street in Chicago to link the city to the new suburb of Riverside and in Brooklyn to connect Prospect Park to the Atlantic Ocean. Inspired by similar roadways in Paris, Olmsted and Vaux's parkways assumed a more sheltered and parklike ambiance than French examples, an effect that resulted largely from the practice of lining these boulevards with American elms and allowing the trees to

assume their characteristic wineglass shape. Olmsted and Vaux's early experience with designing the Mall in Central Park clearly conditioned their thinking on the form that these revolutionary thoroughfares took.

EVEN AS WORK ON THE Mall went forward, the park design continued to evolve. During the summer of 1858, Olmsted and Vaux mapped a system of footpaths, drives, and bridle paths that would be totally separate from each other. This so-called separation of ways was as original an idea as the transverse roads and served the same purpose for traffic within the park. Thus, strollers on foot would never need to cross the carriage drives or bridle paths at grade. Where paths met the drives, bridges or underpasses conveyed walkers either over or under them.[27] This arrangement insured, in particular, that pedestrians' use of the park would be carefree. Olmsted and Vaux must have also realized that this system better allowed them to guide visitors through the various sequences of rural scenery and to increase for them the apparent extent of the park. They may have had in mind the advice of John Claudius Loudon, the great English gardener, who in his *Suburban Gardener and Villa Companion* of 1838 had talked about the advantages of "bridging and tunneling." In a large park, Loudon had written, "there must be a series of views . . . and, consequently, to see all the beauties of such a place, a stranger would require . . . after he had been once over it, to turn around and retrace his steps; but by the system of bridging and tunneling, the eye of the spectator is carried twice over the same ground without his knowing it, and without his passing over the same walks."[28] As a result of Central Park's complex circulation pattern, the simple pleasure of walking was greatly enhanced. It became necessary, however, to erect many more bridges than the seven originally called for in the Greensward plan. And as it turned out, these arches were to be far more expensive than those modest wooden structures the planners had first envisioned. Indeed, as a group, the Central Park bridges and viaducts, nearly all of which still exist, form Vaux's greatest architectural legacy.

"For the most part," stated Clarence Cook, "our bridges are as ugly as engineers, with their dryasdust brains, can devise." But in Central Park, he said, "the effort was made to have the bridges not only solidly built, but as elegantly, and in as great variety of designs, as could be contrived."[29] These highly varied bridge designs, which rightfully earned their creator an international reputation, put to the test Vaux's powers of design ingenuity. Vaux planned over 40 bridges for Central Park, including large and highly finished stone arches and cast iron bridges as well as many smaller, rustic crossings of stone and wood. Vaux and others justified the expense of these new bridges by claiming that they were "only introduced for actual convenience" and that variety in their design was demanded to prevent monotony from dulling the pleasing effect that the landscape was to have on the spectator's imagination.[30] The eye is "quickly sated and wearied with uniformity," admonished the British landscape architect Charles H. J. Smith, who believed, like Vaux, that it was necessary for landscape painters and landscape architects to provide viewers with a stimulating variety of impressions.[31] In this spirit, Vaux conceived his bridges as serving the eye as well as the foot and adapted their designs to the character and topography of the various areas of the park. But in all instances, Vaux insisted that his primary concern was to nestle these constructions quietly into the pastoral landscape. No single span was to be visible from another, he asserted, "except in the most subordinate way."[32]

The 20-some bridges that Vaux designed between 1858 and 1861 are distinguished by high standards of construction and ingenious diversity in appearance. Indeed, as Cook stated, America had not before seen bridges of such fine and sometimes daring design. Central Park's pleasurable purpose and the healthy construction budget at the commissioners' disposal presented Vaux with the unprecedented opportunity to experiment with design, materials, and structure while indulging his taste for picturesque architecture wedded to nature. The catalogue of designs includes arched openings of elliptical, segmental, and circular profile and facings of ashlar and rusticated masonry and various types of brick. Nearly every structure assumed a quaint name, in addition to the term "arch" for those that spanned paths or drives and "bridge" for those that crossed over water. Each span also bore an official number by which it was identified in park documents.[33]

The Balcony Bridge (Fig. 4.5) is one of the earliest bridges in the park; drawings for it bear the date of 1858. Located at the western end of the skating lake that Olmsted and Vaux created in the southern part of the park, it is faced with ashlar sandstone and bears a sandstone railing detailed with circular balusters. The 65-foot-long bridge, its roadway raised no higher than the adjoining banks, carries the western drive and a pedestrian path across a narrow channel that once led to a small bay. In addition to being kept low in order to be inconspicuous from a distance, Balcony Bridge responds to the landscape scenario in which it is placed. On the east side, two corbeled stone banquettes invite strollers to sit and enjoy the view over the broad waters of the lake. Between these wineglass-shaped balconies, the water flowed beneath the roadway through a 27-foot-wide elliptical barrel vault. Cook rightly singled this bridge out as "one of the handsomest" in the park landscape.[34]

Other bridges of formal design embellished the southern portion of the park. These structures, built of finely detailed ashlar masonry, stemmed from a British tradition of garden architecture stretching back to the eighteenth century. The lovely bridge that James Paine built at Chatsworth in the 1760s, when Capability Brown redesigned the landscape there, epitomized the type. In Central Park, Vaux brought this Classical heritage into a public setting where it served to facilitate the movement of large numbers of pedestrians and carriages. Driprock Arch, designed in 1858, carried the drive that originated at the Sixth Avenue gate across the bridle path that ran east and west at this point in the park. Vaux faced the exterior and lined the tunnel with red brick trimmed with New Brunswick sandstone, a material he came to favor for its fine texture and soft cream color. Riders passed easily through the wide, "muscular"-looking segmental arch, which stretched 27 feet over the path. Strollers approaching the broad Denesmouth Arch (1859; Bridge 7; Fig. 4.6) near the Arsenal were greeted by the most elegant archway in the park. Faced with ashlar New Brunswick sandstone, the Denesmouth Arch formed the gateway to the Dene, an area of irregular terrain on the east side of the park north of the Arsenal. Vaux accentuated the apparent breadth of the monumental 37-foot elliptical arch by laying the stones in the spandrels between the flanking buttresses in a sunburst pattern (in contrast to the horizontal courses of the abutments) and by framing the opening with alternating long and short voussoirs. In Mannerist fashion, these are abruptly cut across by the heavy horizontal coping of the balustrade. For all its elegance and fine detail, the bridge remains firmly tied to the undulating landscape by the low, ground-hugging profile of the elliptical arch. And as with all the arches designed for pedestrians, the tunnel of the Denesmouth Arch provided sheltered seating for walkers. Because the upper deck bore crosstown traffic, it was equipped with lamp standards, whereas bridges elsewhere in the park, which closed at dark, were unlighted. Another unusual feature of the Denesmouth Arch was tall iron fencing visible in the watercolor to either side of the structure. These barriers prevented people on the transverse road (which elsewhere is sunken) from entering the grounds, a method of control that recalled Downing's plans for the cross streets in his Washington park.

For pedestrians going to the Mall from 59th Street, Marble Arch (1858; Bridge 9) provided a delightful way to avoid crossing the busy carriage drive. The ingenious design of this demolished structure, which was built of limestone from nearby Westchester County, revealed Vaux's fondness for surprise. Entering Marble Arch's long underground corridor (which conducted pedestrians beneath the roadway), visitors glimpsed at the end of the passage a large niche lit by daylight from a source invisible to them (Fig. 4.7). Only when they reached the ribbed vaulted alcove was the mystery solved. There they would have discovered that the light came from a stairway, heretofore out of view, leading to the upper level. The subterranean niche, as well as the stone seats that lined the walls of the tunnel, proved popular resting places with park visitors. "The interior of this archway is peculiarly light and attractive," remarked Clarence Cook. Here, on a warm day, he said, "the children and their nurses gather with their luncheon-baskets, or the reader comes with his book and a sandwich, and whiles away a sultry hour at noon." Marble Arch underscored how much Vaux looked beyond utility when he conceived the designs of his bridges. They were intended to enhance the visitor's visual and emotional, as well as physical, enjoyment of the park.

A number of other stone arches and bridges went up before 1862 and still exist to lend an air of graciousness to the landscape of the lower park, including the lovely Glade Arch (1859; Bridge 8). Like the Denesmouth Arch which it resembles, the Glade Arch is faced with a reticulated pattern of tooled ashlar New Brunswick sandstone. Its wide elliptical opening carried a now discontinued branch of the drive over a pedestrian path near Fifth Avenue in the area north of the flower garden. The more vigorous-looking Dalehead Arch (1859; Bridge 6) on the western side of the park carried the carriage drive over the bridle path just south of the 65th Street transverse road. Its ashlar blocks, also of sandstone, received a herringbone pattern. Vaux extended the two large buttresses that flanked the high segmental arch opening as low spur walls to guide riders' mounts to the tunnel. By contrast, the Green Gap Arch (1859; Bridge 11) is more sedate in design. Horizontal courses of ashlar set off the projecting voussoirs of the tall segmental arch that permitted horseback riders to pass beneath the east drive near the 65th Street transverse road. The posts that divided the balustrade into three equal segments were apparently drawn by Mould and bear a resemblance to similar elements on the Terrace. More simple is the recently restored Winterdale Arch (1859–1860; Bridge 17; Fig. 4.8), whose low 45-foot-wide elliptical arch is the longest of all the masonry spans in the park.[35] Faced with granite brought to New York by boat from Maine, the arch sheltered a footpath and bridle path beneath the drive in the area northwest of the Ramble where, for the pleasure of wintertime riders, Olmsted and Vaux planted many evergreens. A wide molding drawn across the top of the arch merged with the thick copings that swerved down along the top of angled wing walls. Instead of a stone balustrade, a filigree iron railing crossed the top of the bridge, allowing those below a good view of the passing carriages. The gneiss and sandstone Greyshot Arch (Bridge 13), the drawings for which Vaux prepared in 1860, serves as a sort of gateway to the park for pedestrians who enter from 59th Street and Eighth Avenue. The first structure they encounter, the bridge

FIGURE 4.6. *(above)* Central Park, Denesmouth Arch, 1859. Courtesy of Collections of the Municipal Archives of the City of New York.

FIGURE 4.7. *(below)* Central Park, Marble Arch, 1858. Courtesy of Herbert Mitchell.

conducts visitors beneath the west drive by way of a barrel vault. Once strollers have passed through it, they find themselves immediately in the pastoral surroundings of the park. Vaux effectively used this arch to dramatize the point of transition from cityscape to parkscape, thereby enhancing our feeling of being far from town once we enter the park.

Several smaller masonry arches Vaux endowed with a less monumental appearance than those already described. The red brick and brownstone Willowdell Arch (1859; Bridge 3) serves as a gateway to the Dene for pedestrians approaching from the west. Stone seats occupy the blind arcades that line the segmental vault under the drive, where a drinking fountain formerly provided refreshment on summer days. The modest Dipway Arch (1860; Bridge 16), located just north of the Seventh Avenue entrance to the park, doubles as a portal to the grounds for visitors entering from Seventh Avenue, just as the Greyshot Arch does at Eighth Avenue. Alternate courses of softly rusticated stone and curving wing walls seem intended to give a warm, embracing welcome to incoming strollers. A more exuberant spirit animates the Greywacke Arch (1861; Bridge 23; Fig. 4.9),[36] a little jewel of Victorian park architecture tucked away in the gently undulating ground northeast of the Ramble, where it permits pedestrians to walk beneath the east drive. Its curious "bisegmental" pointed arch is composed of alternating voussoirs of brownstone and greywacke, a type of local grayish sandstone, and is inscribed beneath a molded brownstone gable that effectively sets it off from the banded spandrel walls. The polychromatic theme carries into the vault, which Vaux lined with red and white brick. Early park visitors could not have helped noticing the general similarity between this arch and that other pioneering example of "Ruskinian" taste in New York, Mould's All Souls Church. As Vaux's close assistant on the Central Park work, Mould may have exerted a significant influence on the design of this delightful bridge, which is the most ornamental of Vaux's stone constructions in the park after the Terrace. (In 1871, Mould designed an iron railing for the top of Greywacke Arch that in its diagonal lines and "bobbing" circles nicely complemented the vivacity of the stonework.) A close rival in this regard is the Playmates' Arch (Fig. 4.10), another colorful bridge on which Mould assisted Vaux in drawing the details. (The arch acquired its popular name from its location in the area of the park reserved for children's amusements.) The rusticated granite voussoirs of its earthbound elliptical arch seem to project forward from the merry yellow and red brick bands that face the spandrel walls and focus the stroller on the barrel-vaulted tunnel underneath the center drive. The feeling of lightness is increased by the iron railing that traverses the 66-foot-long archway. And like all its counterparts elsewhere in the park, the archway's unique design lent a special character to the section of the park in which it was located.

In addition to the many masonry bridges, a number of iron spans carry pedestrians over bridle path, drive, and water. To these Vaux imparted an especially festive mood. The longest and most famous is the Bow Bridge, which spans the 60 feet of lake separating Cherry Hill on the south from the Ramble on the north (Fig. 4.11). On the Greensward plan, no bridge was envisioned at this point, but in May 1858 Olmsted, arguing against an ill-conceived proposal by Commissioner Robert J. Dillon to raise a suspension bridge across the skating lake from the Mall to Vista Rock, conceded that a bridge might be placed in this less obtrusive location to achieve "more direct and rapid communication

FIGURE 4.8. *(above)* Central Park, Winterdale Arch, 1858.
Photograph by the author.

FIGURE 4.9. *(below)* Central Park, Greywacke Arch, 1861.
Photograph by the author.

FIGURE 4.10.
Central Park,
Playmates' Arch,
1858–1861.
Photograph by
the author.

with Vista Rock."[37] Olmsted cautioned, however, that any bridge erected at this point must be light and at "as low a level as possible," for he and Vaux would not have wanted it to dominate the view of the lake. In December 1858, six months after the Ramble had been opened to the public, the board approved Vaux's design for Bow Bridge and authorized the executive committee to sign a contract for its construction.[38] Knowing that this bridge would occupy the most conspicuous location of any span in the park, Vaux rose to the challenge and created a daring but unobtrusive design. The gracefully curved silhouette of the Bow Bridge has precedents in Rococo garden bridges in the Chinese taste. One wonders, however, if in its distinctive profile Vaux was not expressing his appreciation of engineer Thomas Pope's early-nineteenth-century proposal for a "Rainbow" or "Flying Pendant Lever Bridge" to join Manhattan to Brooklyn across the East River.[39] Even more lightsome and delicate than Pope's wooden truss design, Bow Bridge exploits the potential of cast and wrought iron to traverse, seemingly without effort, the considerable distance between the shores. The wide, clear span must have appeared even more breathtaking to mid-nineteenth-century eyes than it does to ours. But the way its fleeting and graceful lines ferry the eye from bank to bank—an effect accentuated by the optically reversing guilloche pattern of the balustrade and the undulating lines of foliage in the pierced spandrels (all the contributions of Mould)—still holds our admiration. Speaking for its admirers in Vaux's day, writer Frederick Beecher Perkins praised the Bow Bridge's curves and proportions as "extremely subtle and refined in trace and combination; their elements being conic and not circular curves." To Perkins, who was one of the first to photograph the park's structures, the arch seemed "to leap out with a lithe forward spring, like a leopard's, instead of the upward bound which higher arches take; and thus its long low move gives an impression as it were of sinewy active vigor, purposeful

and progressive, in place of the burdened massiveness of a flat bridge with piers and arches, or the upward spring of higher single arches."[40] One might add that the lovely Bow Bridge, which was restored in the late 1960s, was carefully conceived in relation to its place. In summer, when flowers and vines overflow from large vases at either end, it frames scenes of boaters on the water; in winter, when in Vaux's lifetime the water level was lowered from seven feet to four feet, it allowed skaters to pass with equal ease between the two sections of the lake. By lifting the bridge's deck in a gentle arch, Vaux suggested an inviting entrance through which one could paddle or glide to a distant shore and thus preserved the sense of continuity between the two portions of the lake. Recognized from the first as a masterpiece, Vaux's Bow Bridge has rightly remained one of the most popular emblems of the Central Park landscape.

The Pine Bank Arch (1860; Bridge 15), crossing the bridle path in the southeast corner of the park, and the Spur Rock Arch (1859; Bridge 19, demolished), located farther east along the bridle path, were also light and graceful expressions of cast iron construction. The long, undulating silhouette of the restored Pine Bank Arch resembled that of the Bow Bridge, but the original gossamer-thin iron railings and the open interlaced tracery beneath the roadway made it appear even lighter than the more conspicuous bridge. And certain unsigned drawings for the ironwork of this bridge seem prophetic of the intricate, nature-based ornamentalism of Louis Sullivan. The Spur Rock Arch, which after years of neglect was demolished in the 1930s, was a tour-de-force of fanciful iron construction (Fig. 4.12). Vaux also used iron for the triangular abutments, which he pierced with large circles. A euphonic composition of floridly curving lines, the spunky design of Spur Rock Arch, on which Vaux was assisted by little-known architect Edward C. Miller, often framed the moving picture of well-dressed equestrians passing along the bridle path beneath it.

FIGURE 4.11. Central Park, Bow Bridge, 1858. Courtesy of Prints and Photographs Division, Library of Congress.

FIGURE 4.12.
Central Park,
Spur Rock
Arch, 1859.
Courtesy of
Herbert
Mitchell.

OLMSTED DESCRIBED Central Park as "chiefly remarkable as an effort to reconcile the necessities of a park which is to be the centre of a crowded metropolis with scenery, the predominating quality of which shall be rural and in some parts rudely picturesque."[41] These "rudely picturesque" areas, notably the Ramble in the southern section and the Loch in the northern part, demanded a different, more primitive form of architecture than was called for in more open areas. At least, this was the thinking that evolved after Olmsted and Vaux won the competition. Instead of bridges erected of ashlar masonry or cast iron, spans in these wilder, out-of-the-way places were often constructed of rusticated stone blocks, and even with boulders. The best-known of these bridges is the Ramble Arch (1859; Bridge 20; Fig. 4.13).[42] This stone viaduct carries a footpath over a small ravine and is wholly reserved for pedestrians. Beneath the tall narrow round arch, a path winds along the floor of the hollow. This lower path, Cook tells us, was made by filling in the cleft between the large rocks that form the ravine's enclosing walls. The arch itself is composed of rusticated blocks of local stone chosen for their worn surfaces and seemingly held together without mortar. Draped with vines, as Vaux intended it to be, and framed by dense vegetation, the Ramble Arch presented walkers, as they rounded the bend in the path, with a classic scene of picturesque composition.

Such structures had a venerable place in the history of landscape architecture. Edouard André, the French landscape architect who praised Vaux for his bridge designs, generally thought that "les ponts de rochers sont du plus grand intérêt dans le paysage."[43] Grottos of rockwork had been built in Renaissance

FIGURE 4.13. Central Park, Ramble Arch, 1859. From Samuel Parsons Jr., *The Art of Landscape Architecture* (New York, 1915). Courtesy of Buffalo and Erie County Public Library.

gardens, and when the English discovered Chinese royal parks in the early eighteenth century they were fascinated by the artful compositions of rocks they found there. Illustrations of rusticated bridges and other structures were a standard part of the literature of British landscape architecture. In his *Encyclopedia of Gardening*, for example, Loudon had been pleased to illustrate Stonehenge, the observatory built in the 1820s out of crude blocks of stone by the Earl of Shrewsbury on the grounds of Alton Towers. In his *Suburban Gardener*, Loudon offered advice on rustic construction, recommending that the architect choose facing material that appeared old. Loudon even explained how to impart a weathered appearance to newly cut stone, for, he said, "whatever is very old, and at the same time very strong and secure, commands so much respect on account of these qualities."[44] His remarks call to mind the injunction written on drawings for the Ramble Arch to utilize worn stone in its construction. In 1856, the English landscape architect Shirley Hibberd published in his popular book *Rustic Adornments for Homes of Taste* a discussion of what constituted good design when building with rocks and boulders. The illustration that Hibberd provided of a rusticated stone arch in the Fernery at the Abbey Gardens, Ramsey, has many points of resemblance with the Ramble Arch. And Vaux himself, devising an imaginary plan for constructing a suitable vantage point for seeing the picturesque Catskill Falls, had proposed the creation there of "a rough stone wall built up in great blocks, and without mortar, to the requisite height in a bold, irregular manner" to support a viewing platform.[45] In Central Park, he received the opportunity to put into practice his theoretical knowledge of this rarified branch of architecture.

Even more elemental in appearance than the Ramble Arch is the Riftstone Arch (1860; Bridge 18). It was designed to carry vehicular traffic and two walks (in this regard it was more like the ornamental bridges) over the bridle path at the 72nd Street entrance on the west side of the park. Dark and light blocks of local gneiss "with their natural faces, or such faces as were formed in blasting them out of the ordinary rock excavations," are laid up without mortar to form a wide segmental arch that springs from boulders piled at either side.[46] Heavy plantings across the top of the structure and among the boulders thoroughly assimilated this cavernish passage to the landscape; to William Grant, the park engineer, it evoked the "appearance somewhat of a rock tunnel." Referring to the use of rocks in scenery as well as in architecture, Hibberd had cautioned that the builder of such things "must aim at the construction of large masses, and must pile them, however irregularly, on some definite plan of stratification, and must moreover take care at certain points to introduce large masses of earth, to afford root hold for sufficient vegetation." The Riftstone Arch displayed all of these features and especially delighted Olmsted, who during its construction suggested modifications to the tunnel to reduce the cost of construction.

Although none of the miscellaneous surviving drawings for boulder bridges in Central Park bear any architect's signature, there is no reason to assume that Vaux was not the author of these imaginative and powerful designs. Vaux made these evocative structures appear natural to their setting and even monumental in character. In his hands, rockwork architecture became an elemental language of design, distinguished by simplicity, breadth of scale, and direct expression of materials. This achievement was even more remarkable for having evolved in the 1860s and 1870s, when American architecture—including that of Vaux—generally pursued a very different course. The rustic stone bridges of Central Park, which were the first important examples of this type of construction in the United States, bore abundant fruit in a later season. Their legacy extended not only to H. H. Richardson—who as a resident of New York City in the late 1860s and early 1870s must have known these bridges and appreciated their strong expression of masonry—but beyond his time to twentieth-century park designers, especially those of the Works Progress Administration during the 1930s and 1940s.

The most striking example of rockwork in the park was the Cave, a partially man-made addition to the craggy scenery of the Ramble. "The Cave is remarkable as a work of art," noted J. K. Larke, an early chronicler of the park, "the heavy blocks of irregularly shaped stone, of which it is constructed, almost defying the imagination to picture the means by which they were placed in the positions they now occupy. Nature seems to have been completely outdone."[47] Approached by way of a steep path along an embankment thickly planted with rhododendrons and azaleas, the Cave appeared suddenly to the left as a dark, mysterious opening in the rock. For those fearless enough to enter this now vanished park feature, Clarence Cook tells us, a few steps brought them to the light and a delightful view of the lake. For those who continued along the path, a flight of roughly hewn steps led to an elevated spot where one could look down on the cave mouth and out over the lake.

The naturally rugged area known as the Ramble represented the most drastic reshuffling of nature in the park. Olmsted and Vaux directed especially heavy
planting in this barren terrain in order to achieve the sense of picturesque
remoteness that they had prescribed for this territory in the Greensward plan.
"Nowhere in the Park, as it seems to us," wrote Cook, "has the result been more
worthy of the money, labor, and thought expended to produce it, than in the
Ramble. . . . For the Ramble is, in almost every square foot of it, a purely artificial piece of landscape gardening."[48] Much of its charm derived from the clever
rearranging of rocks in such features as the Cascade, the Gill, and especially the
Nook. Here, wrote Perkins, after "turning aside through a sort of gateway in the
rocks that line the path," one found oneself "walled round with shelving gray
rocks." A "log formed into a rustic seat" invited the stroller to linger awhile in
this pleasant cul-de-sac, which Perkins found "a very silent place, oddly hidden;
where . . . one might sit and meditate and fancy and write all some long
summer day."[49] Such an artfully negligent byway epitomized the possibilities
for the intimate enjoyment of nature that attracted many nineteenth-century
visitors to the Ramble. The withdrawn mood that prevailed there found a
parallel in the work of contemporary American landscape painters, many of
whom in the 1850s were turning away from a preoccupation with grand and
panoramic scenery to more personal encounters with nature. This phenomenon,
which art historian Angela Miller refers to as "domesticating the sublime,"[50] was
especially marked in the pictures of Jervis McEntee, with whom Vaux so enjoyed
sketching in the Catskills. Indeed, I believe that the desire to create such intimate
effects in landscape architecture as once existed in the Ramble appealed more
to Vaux than it did to Olmsted.

CLOSELY ALLIED IN spirit to rustic stone bridges and rockwork features were
the many log constructions that Vaux built in the park. Nineteenth-century
visitors to Central Park might have chanced upon bridges, seats, summerhouses,
arbors, and other embellishments erected in this manner. (Unfortunately, most
of them are now gone.) Like Vaux's park bridges, these timber structures were
widely appreciated in their day. William Robinson, an influential British writer
on landscape architecture who generally disliked seeing architecture in parks,
found much to admire in these works. As Vaux intended, Robinson found them
"very suggestive of rural life." Impressed by their picturesque yet sturdy appearance, Robinson explained to readers of the *Garden*, the journal he edited, how
these objects were made. "The material employed in . . . construction," he wrote,
"is common American cedar, which abounds in the vicinity of New York. The
limbs and trunks are stripped of their bark and they are then put together in a
solid and workman-like fashion."[51] Robinson also liked seeing the liberal way
vegetation conspired to enhance the charm of these fabrications. "Nearly all of
them," he wrote, "are now covered with vines, which, in many cases almost conceal the framework, giving us instead of artificial decoration a profuse tracery
of the most graceful creepers." More than any other type of park structure, these
rustic work accessories most fully embodied the spirit of romantic naturalism
that informed the design of the entire park landscape.

Rustic log buildings had been erected in English and French private parks
since the seventeenth century. In Vaux's younger days in London, T. J. Ricautti's
Sketches for Rustic Work, published in 1848, had responded to the increased

demand that had arisen for such designs by midcentury. Ricautti's portfolio of symmetrical designs for various types of outdoor structures and furniture may have been rather overstudied for Vaux's taste, but it nonetheless indicated the seriousness with which architects and patrons regarded the appearance of these garden ornaments. Historian Paul Edwards is undoubtedly correct in saying that the publication in 1856 of Shirley Hibberd's *Rustic Adornments* marked the height of the fashion for rustic work in England. Hibberd's lengthy and wordy book abounded in illustrations of curious and elaborate pieces of furniture made from undressed parts of trees. His audience was the new English middle class, which felt that good taste demanded that they have examples of rustic design in their homes and gardens.

In the United States, Downing had furnished model designs for rustic work in his books and in the pages of the *Horticulturist*. His *Treatise*, for example, contained a discourse on rustic architecture and provided examples of recommended designs. On the grounds of Downing's own home in Newburgh there stood at least three such embellishments: a wisteria arbor, an outbuilding, and a summerhouse called the Hermitage. Vaux fondly remembered the Hermitage as ideal for sitting out the heat of a summer day while gazing at the river and mountains beyond. Downing's design for a cottage for a country clergyman which appeared in the July 1851 issue of the *Horticulturist*, and which Vaux probably helped design, displayed rustic work around the windows and on the veranda, which was to have been constructed of cedar logs. Two years later, the same periodical printed an article on rustic garden structures and furniture, the ideas and designs for which were drawn from McIntosh's *Book of the Garden*. In all of these instances, the reader learned that rustic work was appropriate only to picturesque locations and looked best when rendered less conspicuous by clinging vines and sheltering trees and shrubs.

Among American architects, Vaux enjoyed a special reputation for the artistry of his rustic work designs. As Robinson appreciated, Vaux expressed himself in these designs in a language of substantial forms. A particularly popular example of his work was the little rustic bridge that crossed the stream in the Ramble (Fig. 4.14). Sometimes referred to as the Gill Bridge, it was often reproduced as a model of its type and class of work. In 1866, John Arthur Hughes, an English landscape architect who had competed for the Central Park job, published a view of this bridge in his *Garden Architect and Landscape Gardening*, where he praised Vaux for having "a special talent for rustic buildings of all kinds." To Hughes's mind, Vaux's rustic designs displayed that "irregularity without wildness or contortion that is the skill of the rustic designer."[52] And when the *Gardener's Monthly* responded to a reader's inquiry on the subject of rustic bridges, the editor furnished a picture of the Gill Bridge, which he also commended for its lack of the "frippery" that so often disfigured such creations. In place of this, he said, the bridge displayed "durability and strength marked in every trace."[53]

In addition to the Gill Bridge, Vaux drew plans for many rustic-work resting places in Central Park. "The grounds abound in pleasant places of halt and rest in the form of seats and benches by the roadside," read an 1866 guidebook.[54] Edouard André selected the covered seat that once stood on an eminence overlooking the Bow Bridge for inclusion in his *L'art des jardins*, where it represented the most simple kind of park shelter (Fig. 4.15). André termed it a *kiosque-champignon* and praised it for its sturdy construction. A cedar log

FIGURE 4.14. *(above)* Central Park, rustic bridge in the Ramble, 1858–1861. From *Dunne and Co. Catalogue for Rustic Shelters and Furniture* (New York, 1902). Courtesy of Buffalo and Erie County Public Library.

FIGURE 4.15. *(below)* Central Park, "mushroom" rustic seat, 1858–1861. From *Dunne and Co. Catalogue for Rustic Shelters and Furniture* (New York, 1902). Courtesy of Buffalo and Erie County Public Library.

supported a circular roof that protected a seat built around the base of the trunk. Clarence Cook pointed out that the umbrella design was especially suited to high places, for it provided unobstructed views in all directions. He also stated that several of these types of seats had been constructed in the park but that no two were exactly alike. A grander type of covered seat appeared in the second edition (1864) of Vaux's book *Villas and Cottages*. In this example, three tree trunks supported a broad overhanging roof, beneath which a double settee offered ample seating for several persons. With its network of branches springing from the trunks to sustain the roof, the rustic bench vividly represented the Victorian notion of architecture's primitive origins.

The rustic shelter near the Artist's Gate was probably one of the first of several summerhouses to go up in Central Park. According to Cook, who admired this now restored structure as the finest summerhouse in the park, it was built by a "certain Hungarian who showed a great aptitude for this kind of architecture." Cook failed to identify the man about whom he spoke, but it is possible that he referred to Alexander Asboth, a Hungarian engineer whom Vaux and Olmsted later employed as a surveyor. Park records also indicate that in 1859 the board of commissioners authorized "payment of the men employed by Anton Gerster in the construction of rustic work." Gerster, about whom little is known, enjoyed a long association with Olmsted and Vaux as a builder of wooden structures. One of those on which Gerster would have worked was the delightful summerhouse near Fifth Avenue between 66th and 68th Streets. It came into view only as one approached along the pathway, which then passed through the building.

By the end of the nineteenth century, replicas of Central Park's log architecture would have been found in many other places, for several of Vaux's rustic designs were available for purchase. Dunne and Company of New York manufactured and sold rustic-work structures based on Central Park prototypes ready for assembly on the purchaser's site. The company's 1902 catalogue illustrated a number of Central Park summerhouses and covered seats, including the early summerhouse which Cook admired (and which the catalogue exaggeratedly stated had been standing for 50 years). Also available were copies of the cruciform shelter in the Ramble and Vaux's much admired Gill Bridge. In their catalogue, the proprietors made no mention of Vaux, leaving unknown the answer to the question of whether or not he had entered into any sort of business arrangement with the firm, whose workshops were located in Kingston, New York. But apart from any connection that may have existed with the architect, the Dunne catalogue attests to the enduring popularity of the splendid designs for rustic architecture that Vaux created for Central Park, for it was there that rustic architecture was widely employed for the first time in the United States. Sadly, little remains of those many log structures with which Vaux graced Central Park, though it was the park that introduced the American public to the charm and diversity of rustic architecture. Without these fanciful accessories, the present-day park landscape lacks one of its most picturesque and inviting aspects. Happily, in recent years, several of them have been sympathetically replicated.

THE ONLY THING THAT GIVES ME MUCH ENCOURAGEMENT THAT I HAVE IN ME THE GERM OF AN ARCHITECT

The Terrace

Located at the north end of the Mall, where it overlooks the lake and the Ramble, the Terrace is the architectural centerpiece of the Central Park landscape and Vaux's most important work (Fig. 5.1). Its cascading staircases carry visitors from the formal ambience of the Mall down to the lakeside, where winding footpaths wait to lead them off into the picturesque byways of the park. An abundance of carved ornament evocative of nature and country life decorate the Terrace's railings, posts, and walls, offering strollers a fictive sampling of the innocent beauties of flora and fauna that the park holds to delight them. Contemporary observers held all of the park masonry in high esteem, but they regarded the handsomely molded and carved stonework of the Terrace as demonstrating the highest standards of craftsmanship yet achieved in America.[1] Although it was never completed as Vaux wished it would be, the Terrace, begun in 1859, is the masterpiece of his park architecture.

Traversed by the carriage drive that runs east and west through this portion of Central Park, the Terrace is divided into two sections. North of the roadway, Vaux placed a rectangular concourse from which one gains an extensive view of the lake and the Ramble in the distance (Fig. 5.2). On either side of this central viewing area, two broad staircases descend to the lower terrace or esplanade at the level of the lake. This waterside terrace, which has a large circular fountain in the center, also can be reached by way of wide paths that curve in gentle arcs down the hillside; low walls of pierced stonework punctuated by large square piers guide us to them from the left and right of the main stairways. On the south side of the park road, a wall of elaborately carved stonework screens the end of the Mall from passing traffic. Beyond this parapet, a long flight of steps, entered at the termination of the Mall, passes beneath the roadway to a hall-like space under the viewing concourse (Fig. 5.3). From this covered area, one sees the lower terrace through the arcade of seven round arches that stands between the two north staircases.

Such lavish architectural display seemingly contradicted Vaux's dictum that in the park architecture must remain incidental to nature. The Terrace, Vaux maintained, represented a special case. It was needed, he said, because the miserable plot of ground with which he and Olmsted were forced to work offered no existing natural feature capable of serving as a center of interest. Feeling the need to clarify this position, Vaux wrote the following explanation to his friend, art critic Clarence Cook:

> Nature first and 2nd and 3rd—Architecture after a while. When the centre is reached, architecture [is] not inappropriate under the circumstances. If our area were boundless—no centre would be necessary perhaps, but if we don't provide a centre people would go in and out the other side looking for a resting place—a halt. . . . Size expressed in Nature to suggest magnificence [is] only measurable when [an] artificial attempt is made. [The] Terrace is big—for a terrace—rich for a terrace—liberal for a terrace—and in the absence of a mountain or a rock—will do. What else could be done[?] . . . If we had had a chance we would have preferred a natural center, although as it is we made the prospect, the Ramble and the water, a main feature.[2]

This view, in fact, was the chief pleasure that the Terrace was designed to convey. Having turned his back on the city at the Fifth Avenue entrance and passed through the straight tree-shaded walks of the Mall, at the Terrace the visitor encountered a wide prospect of the Ramble, the area of the most picturesque scenery in the lower park. From this elevated vantage point, Vaux invited one to observe the "great art work of the Republic," as he considered Central Park to be. Here the landscape architects spread their artistic shaping of nature before viewers and invited them to linger and appreciate its beauty. "The view on an autumn day from the drive across the Plaza and fountain and across the Lake to the Ramble, where the woods are flushed with crimson and gold," wrote Samuel Parsons, "is something to be treasured in the memory above all

FIGURE 5.2. *(above)* Central Park, view from the upper level of the Terrace toward the lake and the Ramble. Photograph by the author.

FIGURE 5.3. *(below)* Central Park, the Terrace stairs leading from the Mall to the level of the lake. Courtesy of Herbert Mitchell.

other scenes of the park."[3] Contriving to impart the maximum feeling of breadth in the view from the Terrace, Vaux and Olmsted laid out the Terrace and the adjoining Mall on an axis diagonal to the park site, so as to give the viewer the widest possible uninterrupted prospect over the park landscape. Likewise, the lake which Olmsted and Vaux created at the edge of the Terrace and which separated the Terrace from the Ramble also enhanced the feeling of spaciousness. "We determined that the Ramble should be the picture that people would come to see," wrote Vaux, who added: "Before the introduction of water it was a perfectly easy matter to go over there and there was consequently no artistic effect . . . for 50 feet of water will give an idea of distance and of difficulty in passing it greater than 500 feet of ground will."[4]

Vaux called attention to the Terrace as a prominent attribute that distinguished the Greensward plan from General Viele's earlier Central Park design. "His plan," stated Vaux, "is divided into six equal or nearly equal spaces and there is no central feature, each part is a good deal like each other." Viele's scheme also made no provision for a lake where Olmsted and Vaux planned one, and it foreswore any "artistic treatment" of the Ramble area. Undoubtedly, these criticisms, registered in the mid-1860s, reflected reasons why in 1856–1857, before he sought out Olmsted, Vaux had encouraged the commissioners to dismiss Viele and hold a competition for the park design.

IN ENGLAND AND ON THE Continent, terraces had traditionally been an element in the design of large houses. According to garden historian Brent Elliott, terraces were an essential part of country house architecture in England in the 1850s and 1860s.[5] In addition to providing a dignified setting for large dwellings, terraces usually formed a transitional space between the formality of the building and the informality of the surrounding landscape. Major British examples familiar to nineteenth-century educated taste were at Elvaston, Alton Towers, Chatsworth, and especially Shrublands. This last house, designed by Sir Charles Barry in 1848–1853, had an impressive series of stairs and landings descending to a circular fountain. An area of formally arranged bedding plants separated the lower end of the staircase from the heavily wooded park beyond. The view from the top of Shrublands's terrace, with its stairs, fountain, lower-level area, and distant woods, generally calls to mind the sequence of elements that make up the prospect from the Central Park Terrace, with the lake substituted for the flat area of formal plantings. It is possible that Barry's great work influenced Olmsted and Vaux's plan for this area of the park. It was Joseph Paxton, however, who first built a terrace in a public park. In the 1850s, he planned a capacious terrace between the Crystal Palace and grounds behind it at Sydenham, a park with which Olmsted and Vaux were familiar.

But the tradition of terrace architecture had its origins in Italy, and it was from there that Barry, Paxton, and other English architects had learned their lessons. This fact was acknowledged in March 1851 in an article on architectural terraces written by H. N. Humphreys and printed in the *Horticulturist*. Humphreys mentioned English terraces, especially Lord Shrewsbury's at Alton Towers, but he reserved most of his remarks for the beauties of Italian Baroque examples. Foremost among these were the Villa Doria Pamfilia and the Villa Borghese near Rome, which Humphreys praised for their "chaste" style and splendid views of distant scenery. To these might be added the Villa Torlonia, famous for its great garden stairways. Whether or not Vaux had a specific Baroque example in mind when he designed the Terrace is a matter of conjecture, but he was clearly aware of the Mediterranean origin of terraces, for on the Greensward plan he and Olmsted identified the feature as the "Italian terrace."

Vaux himself had planned terraces in conjunction with houses he had designed while in Newburgh. In *Villas and Cottages* he illustrated several examples, including the Rogers house at Ravenswood and Design 32, "Villa on a Large Scale." The most significant instance was that of the Hoyt house at Staatsburgh, New York, where a broad terrace around three sides of the house capitalized on splendid prospects of the Hudson. However, America had not yet seen an architectural terrace of such scale and magnificence as the one Vaux designed for Central Park. Its closest predecessor was the marble terrace that William Thornton had designed so that visitors could enjoy the view from the west side of the Capitol at Washington. The central feature of Thornton's terrace, twin flights of steps linked by an arcade, anticipated the form of the Central Park terrace. Vaux, who would have been familiar with the Capitol and its grounds from the time he spent in Washington as Downing's assistant, may have been influenced by that prominent earlier example. Vaux's claim that the Terrace in Central Park was unique at the time for existing by itself, however, without the dominating presence of an imposing building, appears to be valid. Vaux had boldly elevated an architectural form habitually conceived as an appendage to a larger structure to independent status, making it the primary architectural element within the grand design of the park landscape. As Vaux took pains to stress, this idea, which did not win universal acclaim, was "an original conception of my own."[6]

Vaux's notion of the Terrace had been only tentatively developed at the time of the Central Park competition. Not until after he and Olmsted began to implement their plan did they upgrade the Terrace to its central importance in the landscape. In fact, the structure barely received mention in the explanatory text that accompanied their plan. There they simply enumerated it together with a music hall, flower garden, and conservatory as one of the few "minor features" that should be erected on the park grounds. These improvements were "accessories of a composition in which the triple promenade avenue [the present Mall] is the central and only important point." All of them together were to have cost only $20,000. The Terrace alone would eventually far exceed this amount.

A proposition generated by one of the commissioners shortly after Olmsted and Vaux were engaged to carry out their plan would have erased the Terrace from the park altogether. At the end of May 1858, Olmsted had to defend their original design for the area against the desire of Commissioner Robert Dillon to erect a suspension bridge across the lake to link the north end of the Mall with the Ramble. Olmsted, however, did not mention the Terrace, the space of which would have been occupied by one end of the bridge, in his rebuttal of the commissioner's proposal. This omission suggests that the Terrace had not as yet achieved the significance that Vaux would eventually ascribe to it. In fact, Olmsted told the commissioners that the "simple, unartificial treatment" of the landscape was preferable to "stately architecture," which belongs "not to parks for the people, but to palatial gardens."[7]

The Terrace appeared on the Greensward plan as a rectangular open space at the north end of the Mall, on an axis with it and Vista Rock. A sketch view that accompanied the Greensward plan showed the jurors how the Terrace would look from the lake, a tall spray rising from a large circular basin near the shoreline. The plan and the drawing indicate that in Vaux's first conception, the Terrace was a far simpler affair than what he eventually built. In its original version, strollers approaching from the Mall would have crossed the park roadway and descended to the lake down a wide central flight of steps. A broad landing or parterre with flower beds formed an intermediate stage in the descent to the lakeside fountain. All of this must have changed shortly after Olmsted defended the Greensward plan to the commissioners in May 1858. Probably in June, he and Vaux came to realize the true potential of the Terrace as the primary element of the landscape design. The revised scheme must have been worked out during the busy summer of 1858, when Olmsted, Vaux, and their associates strove feverishly to develop the working drawings for the park's construction, which already occupied many workers. On September 16, the board of commissioners approved the final design of the Terrace, which was described as "the bridge, corridor and water-terrace at the north end of the Promenade."[8] The executive committee instructed Olmsted to proceed with the purchase of materials, a gray sandstone from Nova Scotia that was thought to contrast nicely with the greens of the park foliage. Three months later, a full view of the Terrace, drawn by Mould, appeared as the frontispiece of the commissioners' *Second Annual Report*.

In its revised form, the Terrace changed considerably from its appearance on the Greensward plan. The most significant modification was the addition of the central staircase and arcade beneath the roadway and viewing concourse. This arrangement permitted strollers from the Mall to reach the lake without having to contend with carriage traffic on the road. In this way, the Terrace became an element in the system of separation of ways, which emerged as the most innovative and farsighted feature of Olmsted and Vaux's park plan. The partners had formulated this system in the summer of 1858, after they had won the competition. As we have seen, in order to implement their new idea, Olmsted and Vaux had added many bridges to their first scheme in order to avoid grade intersections where paths and roads crossed. Vaux's decision to redesign the Terrace at the same time was clearly tied to the evolution of this program of distinct traffic patterns. Often referred to as Bridge 1, the Terrace embodied the most richly developed expression of that concept.

In its new, enlarged form, the Terrace replaced the Mall as the premier attraction in the park landscape. "Being the central and main architectural structure of the Park, to which all others were intended to be subordinate," proclaimed the commissioners, "and being, with its connections, the principal place for pedestrians, it seemed fitting that an expenditure should here be made commensurate in some degree with the important relative position that this structure was to hold."[9] Seconding the commissioners, Vaux proclaimed: "The Landscape is everything, the architecture nothing—til you get to the Terrace. Here I would let the New Yorker feel that the richest man in New York or elsewhere cannot spend as freely . . . just for his lounge."[10] At the time, Vaux felt that the Terrace was under attack from Richard Morris Hunt and his friends, who desired to erect elaborate gates at the 59th Street entrances to the park. These, Vaux feared, would both detract from the prominence of the Terrace and divert funds from its completion.[11] It was important, insisted Vaux, that the visitor leave behind at the park entrances all architectural display so that, "his Eye all purified," he would be better able to enjoy the riches the Terrace spread before him.

"It was judged that for this great democratic pleasure ground," wrote F. B. Perkins, probably reflecting Vaux's sentiments, "such a scene, open to the sky, was far more appropriate than the close exclusiveness of a house. In this place, would have been put the mansion of a gentleman or the castle of the baron, had such owned the Park."[12] Vaux insisted that his great Terrace was "essentially Republican in its inspiration and general conception."

THE TERRACE, which was largely completed by 1864,[13] constituted the most lavish piece of civic art that New York City had yet seen. Carved scenes of nature (now in varying states of preservation) decorate its stone posts and embellish the steps leading down to the water terrace. Art reinforces the great theme into which the viewer is about to immerse himself. These decorations, most of which were conceived by the teeming imagination of Wrey Mould, assistant to Olmsted and Vaux, take on the function of didactic images in the manner of medieval historiated capitals or scenes in late medieval manuscripts, which they resemble in style and expression. This clear reference to Gothic art in Mould's work carries with it religious implications, imbuing the theme of nature with the spiritual force commonly ascribed to it in nineteenth-century art and metaphysics. The nature alluded to in the reliefs, and present in the landscape itself, is a Christianized nature. In sharp contrast to the way so many of the country's natural resources were being treated in the mid–nineteenth century, nature here stood exempt from exploitation by man for material progress. Vaux and Mould conjured up the notion of paradise, a land where art had sanctified nature for the spiritual rather than the material well-being of modern men and women.

In addition to the delightful reliefs, the Terrace was to have been ornamented with an array of freestanding statues. All of these figures, which were to surmount the stone posts, partook of an elaborate iconographic program that Vaux described and illustrated in the *Sixth Annual Report*, published in January 1863. The visitor approaching the Terrace from the Mall was to have been met at the head of the descending steps (going beneath the roadway) by bronze images of Day and Night. Atop the four piers at either side of these steps, more statues evocative of the passage of time were planned. These were Sunlight, Moonlight, Starlight, and Twilight. Across the roadway, the piers at the heads of the east and west staircases were to have supported bronze images of Childhood, Youth, Maturity, and Old Age, while stone vases on the parapets behind them were to hold living flowers.[14] On the two landings below, pedestals were provided for figures of Spring, Summer, Autumn, and Winter. Natural personifications were also planned for the pedestals at the head of the lateral rampways. These were: The Mountain, The Valley, The River, and The Lake. Bronze groups representative of Science and Art were envisioned for pedestals positioned on the lower level opposite the bottom of the two main staircases. But the most intricate piece of sculpture was to have been enshrined beneath the arcade in the covered area between the two stairways. Vaux described this assemblage as "four figures, each arranged to occupy a separate niche, or shallow recess, in an architectural composition that will form a centre to the four and a background to each, and which will be terminated above with a vase or patera, filled with sculpted flowers, fruits, forest leaves, and grasses, the marble statues being intended to illustrate the ideas most readily expressed at this moment by the words 'Flora,' 'Pomona,' 'Sylva,' and 'Ceres.'" Light for this impressive group was to have come from a glazed opening in the pavement overhead, "so that without attracting attention to the real source from whence it comes, a tempered light will be shed directly over this group and appear to emanate from it." (In 1864, when the park commissioners gave permission for ice cream to be sold in this space, Vaux condemned the practice as "stupid.")[15] For the fountain at the end of the lower terrace, Vaux proposed a bronze figure that "should suggest both earnestly and playfully the idea of that central spirit of 'Love.'" This figure was to be the crowning attraction of the architectural composition of the Terrace and paramount within its iconography. The force of Love, Vaux explained, "is forever active, and forever bringing nature, science, and art, summer and winter, youth, age, day and night, into harmonious accord." Finally, Vaux drew references to the city and state, the political entities that had sponsored the park, and took the opportunity to stress their ties to the Union. New York City and New York State devices emblazoned on red pennants would hang from gilded flagstaffs (already in place by 1861) at either side of the esplanade, where landing steps accommodated boaters; the flag of the United States was to fly above the Ramble on the tower that was proposed for Vista Rock. Waving there, the national banner, Vaux said, would be "on the direct vista line from the central walk of the Mall, and thus situated, it will also be the culminating point of interest in the view both from the upper and the lower terrace."[16]

Vaux's iconographic program, which he presumably had worked out in the summer of 1858, concurrently with the architectural design, seems to bear the strong impress of Ralph Waldo Emerson's thought, especially his 1836 essay "Nature." It is highly likely that this American classic inspired Vaux, who harbored fond memories of evenings spent at Highland Garden listening to Downing read from Emerson. The universal, abstract imagery that Vaux employs in his sculptural program for the Terrace finds its match in Emerson's lofty and comprehensive point of view. "Idealism sees the world in God," wrote Emerson. "It beholds the whole circle of persons and things, of actions and events, of country and religion, not as painfully accumulated, atom after atom, act after act, in an aged creeping Past, but as one vast picture." Likewise, the overarching message of the Terrace statuary, the harmony of man's life with nature beneath the guiding hand of love, is also a thought expressed in "Nature." "The reason why the world lacks unity, and lies broken and in heaps," wrote Emerson, "is, because man is disunited with himself. He cannot be a naturalist, until he satisfies all the demands of the spirit. Love is as much its demand, as perception." Many of the nature personifications, such as stars, moon, sun, mountains, and rivers, that Vaux proposes for subjects of bronze statues are likewise encountered in Emerson's essay. "But if a man would be alone, let him look at the stars," Emerson instructs his readers: "The rays that come from those heavenly worlds will separate between him and vulgar things." Likewise, he declared that "not the sun or the summer alone, but every hour and season yields its tribute of delight."

Emerson establishes sympathy between these natural elements and the seasons and the course of human history, as Vaux does with the representations of the four ages of man placed in close proximity to nature images. "'The winds and waves,'" wrote Emerson, quoting Gibbon, "'are always on the side of the navigators.' So are the sun and moon and all the stars of heaven. . . . Ever does natural beauty steal in like air, and envelope great actions." And elsewhere he states that the "world is emblematic. . . . The whole of nature is a metaphor of the human will." In this regard, time is another theme common to both the Terrace and "Nature." "The motion of the earth round its axis," stated Emerson, "and round the sun, makes the day, and the year. These are certain amounts of brute light and heat. But is there no intent of an analogy between man's life and the seasons? And do not the seasons give us grandeur or pathos from that analogy?" And when Emerson wrote, "Nature stretcheth out her arms to embrace man, only let his thoughts be of equal greatness. Willingly does she follow his steps with the rose and the violet, and bend her lines of grandeur and grace to the decoration of her darling child," he could have been expressing the fundamental spirit that animated the complex amalgam of art and ideas that made up Vaux's plan for the Terrace.

In Vaux's scheme, art and science were placed in a triangular relationship with nature by means of the three statues proposed for the lower terrace and arcade. In "Nature," Emerson makes frequent references to art, which he calls "a nature passed through the alembic of man," as well as to science, which he saw as a new means, if properly interpreted, by which man could be led to moral and spiritual truth. "All the factors in natural history taken by themselves," he wrote in an often quoted passage, "have no value, but are barren like a single sex. But marry it to human history, and it is full of life." As suggested by Vaux's imagery and Emerson's writings, art and science are the means by which nature is joined to human history.

Vaux, who maintained a keen interest in sculpture, must have hoped that one day the Terrace would be populated by outstanding representations of that nascent American art form. But given the commissioners' increasing concern with economy, Vaux realized that the ambitious sculptural program that he envisioned for the Terrace would not be completed quickly. The extraordinary expense of the works of art, he admitted, was too high to be borne by public funds. Instead, he proposed that they be paid for by "the liberality of individuals, or in some other way." Meanwhile, the Terrace pedestals would be capped with carved terminations that could be removed when the time came to mount the statues. The only visual record of how Vaux intended the Terrace to look with its full complement of sculpture is the lithograph published in 1862 by Sarony, Majors and Knapp as the frontispiece to the *Sixth Annual Report*. The Nature group beneath the arcade is concealed from view, but the gesticulating figures representing Science and Art at the foot of the staircases are clearly visible, as are the various freestanding allegorical statues at the landing and roadway levels. Until the figures were in place, Clarence Cook pointed out, critics would be "half-justified in saying it [the Terrace] looks squat."[17] But he cautioned the public, as Vaux had done, not to be in a hurry to procure the bronze figures. Reflecting that the art of sculpture was poorly advanced in America of his day, Cook stated that "if one statue is found fit to be placed upon the Terrace in a generation, we shall think we are getting on very well indeed." Only one was ever erected.

IN 1862, the commissioners approved drawings by sculptress Emma Stebbins for a monumental bronze figure for the Terrace fountain basin (Fig. 5.2). Whether or not Vaux felt that this work suggested "both earnestly and playfully the idea of that central spirit of 'Love'" is not recorded. The large bronze figure, which was inspired by St. John's Gospel story of the Bethesda pool in Jerusalem, where an angel stirred the water and cured the sick, could conceivably be seen as suggesting the power of love. The sculptress herself, however, offered this rationale for the golden figure:

> An angel descending to bless the water for healing seems not inappropriate in connection with a fountain, for although we have not sad groups of blind, halt and withered waiting to be healed by the miraculous advent of the angel [a contention Vaux's friend Charles Loring Brace would have disputed], we have no less healing, comfort and purification, freely sent to us through the blessed gift of pure, wholesome water, which to all the countless homes of this great city, comes like an angel visitant, not at stated occasions only, but day by day.[18]

The park commissioners voted $8,000 for drawings for the monumental figure but left the cost of producing the statue to be borne by private donations. Henry Stebbins, head of the New York Stock Exchange and the artist's brother, came forward to pay for casting the figure, which his sister modeled in her studio near the Spanish Steps in Rome. As a member of the Central Park Board of Commissioners, Stebbins was in a good position to promote his sister's career. After a long delay occasioned by the Franco-Prussian War, *The Angel of Waters*, which was cast in Munich, was unveiled on May 31, 1873.

The artistic conception of the statue apparently owed itself entirely to Emma Stebbins, who may have shown her initial sketches to Mould, thinking he could help her obtain the commission. With the celebrated Nike of Samothrace undoubtedly in mind, the artist portrayed the angel with outstretched wings and fluttering robes at the moment it alights on a rock. Water gushes from the rock into a basin at the angel's feet and spills down into a polygonal stone basin raised on stubby colonnettes. The falling water veils four bronze relief figures representing temperance, purity, health, and peace. In one hand the heavily draped angel holds a lily, symbol of purity, while the other arm extends in a gesture of benediction. Having conceived her figure during the most disheartening days of the Civil War, it is not surprising that Stebbins either consciously or unconsciously evoked the image of a divine messenger of victory bringing the blessings of peace.

Despite the lofty sentiments and the evident expense of the gilded bronze figure, Emma Stebbins's glittering angel failed to stir the enthusiasm of all critics. "There was a positive thrill of disappointment," remarked the *Times*, at the moment the wrappings were pulled away.[19] "From the front it looks like a nautch girl jumping over stepping stones," wrote the *Times* critic, but more disturbing was the figure's puzzling gender. "The head is distinctly a male head of a classical commonplace, meaningless beauty, the breasts are feminine, the rest of the body is in part male and in part female." The only positive remarks the *Times* dispensed were bestowed on the granite-columned support—the work of Mould, who probably took his inspiration from the Lion Fountain at the Alhambra.

Other viewers, however, were favorably impressed by Stebbins's figure. Olmsted's friend Parke Godwin, writing in the *Evening Post*, praised its beauty as well as its "peculiar fitness to the locality." Calling the angel "a being all light and love," he compared it auspiciously with Giovanni da Bologna's *Mercury* for the way in which the figure gently alights on Earth. Godwin concluded, "The more we look at it, the more we are impressed with the profound significance of the design (more truthful than any truth that science has yet attained)."[20] Clarence Cook, who at the time was art critic with the *Tribune*, shared Godwin's positive opinion. Noting that the figure reminded him of Raphael and "two or three early Italian pictures of the Annunciation," Cook identified the angel with Gabriel, "who brings the message of rejoicing and causes the water of healing to flow."[21] He also found the new basin very handsome and gave the readers of the *Tribune* a detailed description of it. If the opinions of Cook and Godwin are any guide, we may assume that their friends Olmsted and Vaux also found the monumental angel pleasing, although neither of them left any written account of their reaction to it. In the popular mind, the angel was the most striking feature of the Terrace. Its popularity with the general public soon led people to refer to the Terrace as the Bethesda Terrace, the name by which it is still commonly known.

Modern opinion, however, tends to be less complimentary to *The Angel of Waters* than Godwin and Cook were. Both William Gerdts and Charlotte Rubenstein, in their studies of American women artists, give it faint praise while conceding its popularity as a gathering place for park users.[22] And as far as its relationship to the park landscape is concerned, the oversized, onrushing angel, one might argue, distracts attention from the lovely view of the Ramble and the Belvedere behind it. Ironically, it turns its back on the very "picture" that Olmsted and Vaux had wanted the viewer to enjoy from the Terrace. Nonetheless, it appears that neither of them raised any objection to the figure's direction when, two weeks before the unveiling, they gave their advice on "the best way of managing the flow of the water so as to produce as perfect a harmony as possible between the fountain itself and the landscape in which it is set."[23] In the 1862 Sarony, Majors and Knapp lithograph, however, the angel is shown facing the lake and Ramble, an orientation, one assumes, that Olmsted and Vaux would have preferred to the present one.

WHILE VAUX MAY have had reason to be disappointed with Emma Stebbins's angel, he was undoubtedly pleased with the decorative reliefs that were carved on the Terrace's posts and railings. This work, which was carried on throughout the 1860s, was the responsibility of Wrey Mould. Mould was a truly remarkable ornamentalist. "It was a fortunate day for the public," wrote Clarence Cook, "when Mr. Vaux made his acquaintance, and with that quick appreciation of excellence which distinguishes him, called him to his assistance" (as he had earlier called Olmsted).[24] Initially, Mould had declined to help with the Greensward plan, believing that the commissioners would ignore artistic excellence and make their decision on political grounds. When, to his astonishment, the board accepted Olmsted and Vaux's design, he determined to join the historic venture.

Mould was brilliant, but he was also a bohemian in a society dominated by a conservative moral code. The fact that Vaux and Olmsted continued their professional association with Mould throughout the 1860s is indicative of their broad-mindedness as well as their respect for his work. In 1861, when it was discovered that Mould was living with a woman who was not his wife, he fell into irretrievable disgrace in the eyes of many of his friends and colleagues. "Mould and his lady I saw in the dress circle and watched her a good deal through my glass," wrote the punctilious A. J. Bloor, when he had encountered the couple at a "lively French play."[25] Bloor later took Mould's mother to see her "outrageous" son and "talked with him and his mistress till near 10 o'clock in very plain language."[26] George Templeton Strong, who had gotten to know Mould through the architect's work for Trinity parish, confided to his diary that when "some rather disreputable proceedings of his came to light, and as I wished him to avoid the house for the future, I proceeded to cut him, mildly but firmly."[27] Yet everyone who knew his work conceded that Mould possessed great talent; Strong called him a "universal genius." It was truly a fortunate coincidence for American architecture that Mould was in New York City when Central Park was being constructed. In 1886, hearing from his sister, Mary Vaux, that Mould had died, Jervis McEntee reflected, as many who had been close to Mould must have done, that

> he was a man of talent and had many genial traits, but was without moral sense. . . . We were very intimate at one time, but his behavior has been such that I could not recognize him and have had the pain of passing him in the street as a stranger, which seems a cruel thing to do. He died almost friendless I learn, although the woman he called his wife stuck to him to the last.[28]

At the Terrace, Mould provided designs for reliefs that decorate the stone posts and took charge of ornamenting the covered area behind the arcade. His charming reliefs embroider the theme of the seasons with many vignettes of country life. On one pier on the upper level, Autumn is represented by a sheaf of wheat standing beside a thatched shed as well as by a figure draped in a long robe and resting on a pumpkin. Inspiration for these engaging scenes lay in medieval art, especially depictions of the Labors of the Months. (Andrea Pisano's fourteenth-century reliefs on the Campanile in Florence—Mould was a devoted Italophile—especially come to mind when viewing Mould's work.) In addition, Mould designed numerous details and border decorations for Terrace elements. Several of his drawings survive in New York's Municipal Archives. One sheet dated 1861 contains rows of fruit and flower friezes for piers at the foot of the western staircase. Elsewhere, birds and wildlife evoke life beyond the city.

"'Why there's a rooster!'" exclaimed Patsy, one of the children in Daniel Wise's 1873 novel *Little Peach Blossom*, a story that communicates the sense of wonderment that many Victorian children must have felt in the new Central Park. The youngster had just come upon the Terrace and was pointing out to her friends "a crowing cock carved in a niche on the front face of a large brownstone [*sic*] post at the head of the stairs." Further on, she found a farmhouse, some wheat sheaves, a shovel, and a scythe, while her companions Amy and Oswald marveled at a setting sun, a Bible, a lamp, and an hourglass.[29] Adult visitors as well as children derived pleasure from the Terrace reliefs. "A part of the beautiful designs which are carved in stone I have enjoyed over and over," Daniel Coit Gilman, president of Yale College, told Vaux. "These decorations," Gilman asserted, "seem to me as appropriate and charming as they are fresh and original. I think their introduction in the open air is likely to lead to a much purer style of decoration in architecture than the country at any rate has ever seen."[30]

Yet not all of Mould's contemporaries expressed enthusiasm for his work on the Terrace. In 1863, Peter B. Wight, architectural critic for the *New Path*, the mouthpiece of the radical Society for the Advancement of Truth in Art, reviewed the Terrace and its sculpture. It was "a dangerous place," he warned, "to display bad carvings which assume to be based on natural forms."[31] Wight, who had high praise for the architecture of the Terrace, objected to having the decorations drawn by an artist and executed by workmen. Separation of creation from execution, he maintained, was a pernicious practice. This was criticism Ruskin, whose philosophy inspired the society, had already leveled at modern sculpture; it was one of the reasons why Ruskin believed that contemporary work lacked the spontaneity and vitality of medieval carving. "What we see," stated Wight, "are merely clever copies of office drawings, by men who are degraded by being made the machines to carve other men's designs. . . . Moreover, all the architect's work is not only very conventional but much of it borders upon the grotesque; in some of it the conventional is mixed with natural ornament and the result is simply ridiculous." He also implied that the demands of the commission had overtaxed Mould's imagination, for he said that Mould had run out of ideas. Mould's pedestals on either side of the roadway were, according to Wight, uninteresting and "ugly."

However, Wight extolled the floral carvings along the open balustrades flanking the east and west staircases (Fig. 5.4) as well as the reliefs on the four posts at the bottom of the steps (Fig. 5.5). These decorations, he informed his readers, were not drawn first by Mould but were carved directly on the stone by artisans who were given free rein in the work. "Here what was cold, contorted and conventional," Wight pointed out, "is now easy, graceful and natural. We have fruits and flowers and berries which we know at first sight. . . . We can fearlessly pronounce the carving on the pedestals at the foot of the stairs to be the best work that has ever been done in this country." Wight, an architect who was

FIGURE 5.4. Central Park, the Terrace, detail of the western balustrade. Photograph by the author.

FIGURE 5.5.
Central Park,
the Terrace, detail
of carving on pier
at the base of the
western stairs.
Photograph
by the author.

shortly to institute this same practice in the construction of his National
Academy of Design building, was in a position to know what he was talking
about, although drawings for borders of flowers and fruit that appear on the
posts he mentioned are in the Municipal Archives. Wight must have been referring only to the floral decorations, and possibly the trefoil rondels, for which no
drawings exist. The stag head and flying duck rondels on the Autumn pier (Fig.
5.5), for example, appear more stiff and symmetrical (that is, more "primitive")
than the richly composed scenes on posts elsewhere on the Terrace. The contrast
is even more striking between the plants and flora on the posts at the end of the
Mall and those beneath the rondels on these lower piers. Here, the sprays of
flowers, grapes, and evergreens are as straightforwardly naturalistic as Wight said
they were and reveal by comparison how much more stylized is the work on
the upper level. The same uncomplicated naturalism characterizes the cheery
flowers and evergreens centered in the small panels of the staircase openwork
balustrades (Fig. 5.4). (These reliefs are emblematic of the seasons, beginning
with Spring on the east flank of the east stairway.) One has no trouble accepting them as the original creations of ardent handicraftsmen. Yet this is disciplined
individualism, for each of the little plants echoes the diagonal, adapting itself
nicely to the sloping lines of the balustrade that Vaux cleverly designed to mimic
one's movement along the stairs.[32]

Probably Vaux, who believed that artisans should be invited to join the AIA, and Mould together deserve credit for allowing the carvers to work unaided by drawings, the first instance, noted Wight, of this practice in America. The experiment—which followed the example Ruskin had set a decade earlier at the Oxford Museum—was a success, proclaimed Wight, because the carvers had succeeded in creating truth in art. They had reproduced "natural forms in stone faithfully and earnestly," the way medieval craftsmen had done. "Now if anyone wants to know what we mean by Gothic carving," said Wight, "let him go to the Central Park and see for himself. Let him examine carefully the bosses in the balustrades on both sides of the stairs, and then the pedestals with their birds and flowers and insects—with trees, vines, birds' nests, fire, and water cut in solid stone, and he will see work done as only the medievalists did it."[33] Perhaps stung by this criticism, Mould may have sought to assure New Yorkers of the fertility of his imagination as well as his devotion to the Ruskinian principle of truth when he designed the large relief panels for the eastern and western stair landings. These four great arabesques symbolic of the seasons—Spring (Fig. 5.6) and Summer appear at either side of the eastern stairs, while Autumn and Winter enframe the western landing—teem with vines, flowers, and birds. Comparison of the actual carved work with Mould's drawings, which date from 1866 and 1867,[34] reveals how faithfully the sculptors translated Mould's ideas

FIGURE 5.6. Central Park, the Terrace, detail of the Springtime relief on the eastern stair-case. Courtesy of Herbert Mitchell.

into reality. Cook was correct when, in 1869, he said of these reliefs, which certainly drew their inspiration from Mould's beloved Alhambra, that "on no public building in America has there yet been placed any sculpture so rich in design as this, or so exquisitely delicate in execution."[35] In the shadow of their enticing sensualism, the lovely balustrade flowers seem shy and chaste. Mould's splendid panels, which Olmsted, the fancier of lush tropical scenery, must have especially liked, are true masterpieces of High Victorian naturalism and ornamentalism.

Mould was also responsible for the decoration of the hall located between the Terrace stairs, beneath the viewing concourse and carriage drive. Here he exercised the full measure of his genius as a decorator, filling this space, which was originally intended for the Nature statue group described earlier, with colorful tilework of his own design. Describing himself as a man who was "death on color," Mould surrounded the visitor with expensive tilework on the floor, walls, and even overhead. The walls were divided into shallow niches for which Mould drew designs for bright mosaics of small encaustic tiles set in arabesque patterns. (Not all of this work was carried out.) The glory of the hall, however, was the ceiling. Here Mould installed tiles specially designed not to come loose and fall, for, he claimed, this was the first time that tile had been used to cover a room. He hung the tiles in sections between gilded iron beams. In addition to elaborate tilework, the hall was graced with delicate and varied carving. The capitals of the columns of the arcade facing the lower terrace and interior pilasters were delicately sculpted. The richest area of carving, however, appears on the walls flanking the staircase descending from the Mall. Here panels of stylized floral patterns (now badly weathered) gave visitors a foretaste of the exotic splendor that awaited them in the softly lit hall below. It is a shame that this space never received the sculpture that Vaux planned for it, and even more unfortunate that Mould's wonderful colored decorations no longer exist to delight our eyes.

The Terrace, even in the incomplete form in which it exists today, is one of the unsung monuments of nineteenth-century American architecture. Vaux was right to be proud of his accomplishment, of which he said, "Of all I have ever done it is perhaps the only thing that gives me much encouragement that I have in me the germ of an architect that might with good chance and proper culture be developed."[36] To contemporary eyes, the Terrace is probably more pleasing without the population of bronze personifications that the architect intended for it. There is more than enough to appeal to the eye and refresh the spirit in the many engaging instances of nature carving. (Many of these were restored in the 1980s by the Central Park Conservancy.) The low, uncluttered outline of the Terrace gives it the appearance of resting comfortably in the hillside. Moreover, the way space descends the wide, flowing steps in a gentle current and spills out onto the broad lower terrace engulfing the Bethesda fountain is worthy of Bernini and the Baroque designers. With great skill, Vaux shaped the Terrace to its role as a place of beginning as well as of gathering. But above all, the sloping lines, the open-ended vista, and the curving wing walls are calculated to invite us into the natural scenery, the personal experience of which Olmsted and Vaux regarded as the highest purpose of the park's existence.[37]

Unfortunately, even in their lifetimes, this fact was often disregarded or misunderstood by commissioners and public groups zealous to erect artworks and other memorials wherever it pleased them in the park. Olmsted, Vaux, and their supporters at times had difficulty maintaining the principle that monumental sculpture should be primarily concentrated at the Terrace and along the Mall. "We make no objections to a richly adorned centre, such as is proposed in the Terrace, where ample room is provided for all the really worthy works of art that are likely to be produced here in a hundred years," stated Cook, an able spokesman for the designers, "but we plead for the preservation, as far as possible, of largeness and simplicity, for the greatest amount of unobstructed lawn, for trees, and shrubbery, and flowers; for lakes and streams; in short, for as much of nature as we can get for the money, and for a very little art, and that only of the choicest and best."[38]

POSISBLE
TOGETHER,
IMPOSSIBLE TO
EITHER ALONE
1859–1865

$\mathscr{6}$

By the time Vaux had reached his 34th birthday, in 1858, he could regard himself as well along the road to success. He had authored an important book on domestic architecture, designed a major bank building, and won the competition to design the nation's largest municipal park. Undoubtedly buoyed by these achievements, Vaux sought and obtained entry into New York club life. As an early member of the Down Town Association (founded in December 1859), he often dined at its Exchange Place clubhouse, a building he may have taken charge of remodeling in 1860.[1] As one of the original 300 members of the Athenaeum Club, Vaux must have attended the opening of the organization's quarters, a commodious building on Fifth Avenue near 16th Street, "fitted up with every convenience requisite for the comfort of its members."[2] In addition to dining and socializing, the Athenaeum, whose executive committee included art biographer Henry T. Tuckerman, endeavored to provide its members with high-caliber programs, such as the evening that Vaux and Jervis McEntee spent listening to a lecture by expatriate artist William Page.[3] But most of all, Vaux valued his membership in the prestigious Century Association, a select circle of artists and men of letters to which Vaux was admitted in 1859.[4] Over the course of his lifetime, he was to pass many stimulating and pleasurable hours there, including a gala Twelfth Night celebration when, lounging on a Turkish rug, he joined fellow Centurians in "smoking, drinking, laughing, or suddenly singing a note on a horn."[5] At the Century, Vaux could enjoy the company of such artist friends as Jervis McEntee, Frederic Edwin Church, R. Sanford Gifford, Eastman Johnson, and George Henry Hall, one of whose pictures hung in Vaux's home.[6] These men shared Vaux's Romantic esthetic philosophy, as well as his hope that someday America would come to value its painters, sculptors, and architects as it did its practical men of business and industry.[7] Other friends in his circle at the Century included Richard Henry Stoddard, the "Nestor of American literature"; Edmund Clarence Stedman, poet, critic, and editor; Edwin Lawrence Godkin, essayist and editor of the *Nation*; Parke Godwin, editor and part owner

137

of the *Evening Post*; George William Curtis, the editor of *Harper's New Monthly Magazine* (Curtis's brother worked as an assistant in Vaux's office before the Civil War); and Henry Whitney Bellows, editor of the *Christian Examiner* and the quixotic pastor of All Souls Unitarian Church, where the Vauxes attended services. Intelligent, idealistic, well-educated, and endowed with a sharp sense of humor, Vaux, who relished smart talk, tasty food, and good wine (muscatel and Moselle were particular favorites), greatly valued bonds of friendship with astute men and women. With such people he enjoyed reading Tennyson, acting in plays such as *Antigone*, listening to chamber music (a particular passion of Mould's, whose house was often the scene of brilliant musical gatherings), attending the theater, skating by winter moonlight in Central Park—where once Vaux threatened to summon the police to stop a party from using foul language—and playing battledore and shuttlecock.[8] A convivial host who liked staging many a *petit soupé*, as Bloor described them, Vaux possessed, according to William Stiles, a friend of his in later life, a "kindly and unselfish disposition [that] endeared him to every one with whom he was closely associated."[9] Vaux truly could have counted himself fortunate to have lived when and where he did, for with his particular circle of friends he personally experienced the first high tide of culture that New York City had known.

IN THE PROFESSIONAL sphere, Vaux found that the time from winning the Central Park competition in the spring of 1858 to resigning from the park in May of 1863 was a busy and eventful period. His initial alliance with Olmsted for the park competition turned out to be the bright beginning of a profitable business partnership as the two men assumed the leadership of America's nascent discipline of landscape architecture. At this time Vaux also began his life-long association with Andrew Haswell Green (1820–1903). The powerful and often feared comptroller of Central Park became Olmsted's bête noire, but Vaux managed to get along with him.[10] Green's appreciation of Vaux's talents lay behind many commissions that the reformist public servant sent Vaux's way, for in addition to working on the Central Park designs, Vaux continued to forward his architectural practice.

Blessed with success, Vaux came to need help in coping with the greatly increased workload. He especially relied on the assistance of A. J. Bloor, whose diary is a primary source of information on Vaux's activity between March 1859, when Bloor joined his office, and 1861, when he went off to work for the United States Sanitary Commission in Washington. The war also took Olmsted away. In June 1861, two months after the fighting had begun, he left Vaux in New York to manage their affairs while he assumed the responsibilities of secretary of the Sanitary Commission. The same month, Stephen C. Earle came to ask Vaux to take him into the office on an informal apprenticeship basis.[11] A native of Worcester, Massachusetts, Earle may have been referred to Vaux by his distant relative Thomas Earle, whose house Vaux had designed several years before. Intent on an architectural career, Earle, who was 22 years old at the time, signed an agreement with Vaux in September 1861, whereby in return for a fee of $100 Vaux pledged to admit Earle as "a student in his architectural office and to furnish him with such opportunities for obtaining knowledge of the business of architecture as his practice may offer."[12] Given that there were no schools of architecture at the time, Vaux must have thought that he had an obligation to the profession to provide the opportunity for a young man of talent to learn the rudiments of the discipline. For Stephen Earle, Vaux's guidance pointed the way to success; in later years, Earle designed many buildings in his native city and elsewhere. His apprenticeship was to have lasted for a year, yet despite his Quaker heritage, in 1862 Earle cut his time with Vaux short to volunteer for service in the Union Army.[13] Following Bloor and Earle's departures, Withers moved to New York to join Vaux again in partnership.

But of all the associations Vaux formed during his early years in his adopted city, that with Frederick Law Olmsted ranked as the most important. Professional partnership quickly blossomed into enduring friendship as the two men came to know and respect each other for the different qualities each possessed. For Vaux, Olmsted was the "representative man" who could deal well with politicians and practical matters, but he also had innate esthetic sense that Vaux recognized and helped to cultivate. Although Olmsted was unlike George Truefitt and Andrew Jackson Downing in training and experience, he must have appeared to Vaux to possess a capacity for public life on which he, a more introverted personality, could draw for strength. For his part, Olmsted found in Vaux someone who shared his social democratic philosophy, his abiding ardor for natural scenery, and his enthusiasm for challenging work. A perfectionist himself, Olmsted spoke of Vaux's "pertinacity in overcoming difficulties, in turning and turning and turning—never caring how much it costs him, until he gets something that entirely suits his own convictions of what is honorable architecture and his client's crude demands."[14]

After the time when Olmsted put in long hours at Vaux's house preparing the Greensward competition entry, he and his family often socialized with the Vauxes. Olmsted lived on Staten Island, where for a time in 1859–1860 Vaux, who after Highland Garden remained attached to country life, also owned a house.[15] The men became even closer when in the autumn of 1859 they both moved their families—the previous June, Olmsted had married his brother's widow, Mary Perkins Olmsted—into the former convent at Mount St. Vincent on the grounds of Central Park.[16] Actually, Mary Olmsted and her three children by her previous marriage moved to Central Park while Olmsted was on a three-month trip to England and the Continent. With the blessing of the Central Park commissioners, he had gone there to study public parks and private estates. As Vaux well knew, however, his friend was seeking respite from the Central Park work, which had worn him out mentally and physically. "It seems such an absolutely scandalous misappropriation of means and opportunities for so nice a sort of work to lead to so poor a result as you show," Vaux wrote to Olmsted while he was in England. "I will not forgive you if you do not make a better show," he told his friend; in a spirit of gentle-hearted mockery, he warned that Olmsted would prejudice others from entering their new profession of landscape architecture by the "lugubrious, sallow, bloodless figure" he cut. Advising Olmsted to lighten up, Vaux confessed that "the only thing to be regretted in our last two years' operations is the absence of jollity. Because you see there are so many aspects of comicality in the whole affair." Vaux's remedy for Olmsted's future well-being was simple: "Get flesh on your bones and forget that you ever had a puritanical marrow."[17] It proved to be advice that Olmsted never could bring himself to observe. Even on this trip in search of health, Olmsted kept to a busy schedule; his written report to his employers on his return detailed the remarkable number of places and people he had encountered.

In charting his course, Olmsted availed himself of his partner's personal contacts in England. With him, for example, Olmsted took a letter from Vaux to George Godwin. Vaux introduced Olmsted to his friend as the man with whom he shared the responsibility for Central Park, "a public work," wrote Vaux to Godwin, "with which you will heartily sympathize if I judge your antecedents rightly."[18] Undoubtedly, information Godwin gathered firsthand from Olmsted went into the excellent article on the park that he printed the following November in the *Builder*. Also at Vaux's suggestion, Olmsted stopped in to see George Truefitt, who promised "to do what I can for a friend of my old friend Calvert Vaux."[19] Perhaps Godwin and Truefitt, as well as Vaux himself, helped shape the itinerary that Olmsted followed in England, a tour that included the Royal Botanic Gardens at Kew, where Sir William Hooker received him; Elvaston Castle, where Olmsted saw the "finest plantations of evergreens in Europe"; and Biddulph Grange, where he inspected the extensive garden that was "remarkable for its rock-work."[20] These places, Olmsted said, he had been advised to visit "as exhibiting the art of landscape gardening in higher perfection than others in England."[21] When Olmsted returned to New York in late December of 1859, he came armed not only with fresh knowledge of these and other outstanding examples of English, French, and Belgian landscape architecture but also with many photographs of London's Regent's Park and a complete run of the *Garden Chronicle* magazine, which had begun publication in 1846. Surely Vaux would have been highly pleased with these acquisitions, and he undoubtedly found in the photographs of bridges in Regent's Park inspiration for his work in Central Park. Also in his luggage, Olmsted carried a silver spoon, the gift of Vaux's sister Julia to her American namesake, the Vauxes' third child.

In Olmsted's absence, Vaux looked after Mary—proposing "various jaunts for her consideration"—and advanced his and his partner's professional interests. One of the possible new jobs he explored was a park in St. Paul, Minnesota.[22] Another potential source of work came from August Belmont, "The King of Fifth Avenue," who served as the New York representative of the Rothschild international banking interests and who exercised important influence in national politics. Shortly after his return to New York late in 1857 from four years as minister to The Hague, the cosmopolitan German-born financier—he and his elegant wife, Caroline, cultivated a "flashy reputation"—had been named a Central Park commissioner. Vaux must have been surprised by Belmont's invitation to meet with him concerning "some ideas he has for building,"[23] for the powerful Democrat's tenure on the park board had been marked by repeated attempts to alter the Greensward plan. It is unclear whether anything came from the discussion the two men had at Newport, where Vaux "dined and wined" and "talked park gingerly" with his lavish host. Presumably Belmont, who had recently remodeled his residence at 109 Fifth Avenue, discussed with Vaux his plans to build a summer home at Newport. And while no drawings or documents have come to light linking Vaux to Belmont's By-the-Sea, which went up in 1860 on the shore at Newport, historic photographs of the mansard-roofed, clapboard house (which was demolished in the 1940s) reveal that it resembled other Vaux designs of the period.[24]

More important for the partners' future was the introduction Vaux received through John A. C. Gray to fellow Republican James S. T. Stranahan. An upstate New Yorker who had moved to Brooklyn in the 1840s, Stranahan had made a fortune in developing the Atlantic Basin and Docks in Brooklyn. Having served his city well as a Whig congressman, the farsighted businessman had become a civic-minded public figure who now, together with his duties as police commissioner, was heading a move to create a municipal park in Brooklyn. The idea, however, was not universally popular. Stranahan had his work cut out for him convincing the citizenry at large of the value to them of a municipal park and trying to dissuade backers of the project from prematurely choosing among several contending sites. At the time Stranahan seems to have favored a location in the flat Ridgewood section of the city. Certainly Vaux would have had no trouble plying Stranahan with arguments in favor of parks in cities; he wished, however, to reserve his opinion on the sites Stranahan and his supporters had in mind. Before a ride with Stranahan through the suburbs of Brooklyn, Vaux politely told his host that he was simply "prepared to devote some little time to a consideration of the various localities." Wishing to leave his options open concerning the best park site, Vaux confided to Olmsted that he did not care to tell Stranahan "too much as to what mode we should recommend."[25]

At the end of November 1860, Vaux himself went to England. Bloor, Leeds, Mould, and Julius Munckwitz, another assistant, went with him to the *Kangaroo* and ran along the pier waving their hats to their friend as his boat departed. Unfortunately, we know nothing of what Vaux did or saw on this trip, which probably marked his first return to England since he had left 10 years earlier. However, he claimed that his voyage, which he made without his family, was related to the work at Central Park, and he was paid his salary while abroad.[26] Surely he renewed old friendships with Godwin, Truefitt, and members of the Architectural Association. Perhaps Truefitt and Vaux compared notes on the bank projects each had recently worked on, although Truefitt's promising collaboration with Ruskin had apparently come to nothing.[27] (Like Truefitt, Vaux agreed with much that Ruskin said but could not be considered a "Ruskinian.") One also can expect that Vaux told Truefitt and Godwin of the terrible misfortunes that had befallen his friend Olmsted, whom they had met the previous year: in August Olmsted had nearly lost his life in a carriage accident, and a few days later the couple's newborn child, John Theodore, had died suddenly of infant cholera. Vaux would surely have recounted how in October he and Olmsted had been ignored during the grandiose ceremonies that had surrounded the visit of Albert Edward, Prince of Wales, to the new Central Park, an event that Vaux could have characterized as another defeat in the long battle for professional recognition that architects on both sides of the Atlantic were fighting.[28] By the end of January 1861, Vaux was back in New York. Bloor remarked that on January 30 he came to the office for the first time since his return a few days before, "looking about the same as ever."

ONE OF THE PROJECTS that Bloor had been looking after in Vaux's absence was a new house that journalist John Bigelow proposed to build on his property at Highland Falls, New York. Presumably Bigelow had discussed the project with Vaux before the architect had gone to England. Bloor visited Bigelow in December 1860 to survey the site and to talk over the client's requirements. In

February, after Vaux's return, Bloor was working on plans for Bigelow.[29] These may be the undated ground plans in the possession of the present owner of the property that show a compact, asymmetrical house with a large 16' × 27' library to the right of the small entrance hall. A rough sketch, probably by Vaux, shows the front elevation of the stone villa, which was distinguished by a four-story corner tower and a recessed entryway. The sketch, which contains an alternate version of the tower in the upper right corner, also reveals in simplified form how the architect stressed reposeful balance between the horizontal and vertical dimensions as the underlying principle of the design. Unfortunately, despite the time and effort put into this house, nothing came of the undertaking. Bigelow, who had recently sold his one-third interest in the *Evening Post* to Parke Godwin, probably abandoned the project because he had accepted President Lincoln's appointment as general consul in Paris. With war on the horizon, Bigelow must have felt uncertain about the future. When he left for France in the spring of 1861 (he did not return until 1867), he is not likely to have had erecting a new home on his mind. Instead, Bigelow chose to retain for the time being the farmhouse which, three years earlier, Vaux had remodeled for him into a country villa and which Bigelow fondly called the Squirrels.

Vaux had undertaken work on the Squirrels shortly before he and Olmsted won the Central Park competition. A friend and political ally of Samuel Tilden, Bigelow was an associate of William Cullen Bryant in the ownership of the *Evening Post*, where he served in an editorial capacity. According to Bigelow biographer Margaret Clapp, he engaged Vaux in the spring of 1857 to transform the farmhouse he had purchased the year before into a modern country residence where he and his family could enjoy fresh air (a son was sickly) and views of the river and mountains.[30] The house itself, as revealed in Vaux's plans (dated 1857), incorporated the simple, two-story farmhouse into an enlarged T-shaped building. The ample new wing contained on the principal floor an 18' × 12' reception room and a spacious 18' × 16' living room, the eastern end of which communicated with a small veranda by means of a floor-to-ceiling window framed by closets. The main entrance to the house remained in the unaltered older wing, which also contained stairs to the second-floor bedrooms. The new wing was a simple structure and did not take long to build; in May of 1857 Bigelow moved in. Having sold his New York City residence, he hired nine wagons to carry his possessions, notably his 1,500-volume library, to the house at Highland Falls.

The modesty of the Squirrels reflected the unaffected tastes of its owner. According to a granddaughter, Bigelow let the children run barefoot, shunned card playing, and believed in homeopathic medicine. Politically, Bigelow was a progressive advocate of free trade, independence for Panama, and the abolition of slavery. His real pleasure at the Squirrels was to engage in animated conversation with the many distinguished political and literary guests whom he invited to visit him there. Yet there were also periods of quiet reflection. Bigelow's granddaughter's most indelible memory of the Squirrels was "Grandpa in his light homespun and a light blue necktie, slowly walking up and down the garden path to the summer house at the end, that hung practically over the cliffs above the river."[31] The enjoyment of such moments of solitude was one of the chief blessings, Vaux believed, that a country house could bestow upon men of affairs such as Bigelow.

The Squirrels was only a short distance from the steamboat landing that would be Bigelow's link to the larger world he never intended to leave behind. Indeed, in less than a year, Bigelow was off to Europe, where in March 1859 he attended a party at Jasper Cropsey's London studio; there he must have viewed with a tinge of nostalgia the artist's magisterial painting *Autumn—On the Hudson*, which so dramatically depicted the landscape close by Bigelow's Hudson Valley residence. A few months later, in Paris, he met Olmsted, whom he may have come to know through Vaux. In his travels, Bigelow made it a practice to visit public and private gardens. His observations on the Bois de Boulogne, the great English-style public park that Napoleon III had established shortly after assuming power in 1850, were greatly appreciated by Olmsted, who toured the new park several times with Bigelow in the fall of 1859. Sensing a sympathetic ear, Olmsted felt able to bear his soul to his partner's erudite client over the problems he had endured at the hands of the Central Park commissioners. "He had been in the habit of pouring into my ears accounts of want of harmony and of apparent indifference to the duties with which the park commissioners had allowed themselves to be charged," said Bigelow of Olmsted's memorials.[32]

Olmsted's dissatisfaction, which Vaux also must have discussed with Bigelow, culminated in a long letter that Olmsted wrote to Bigelow in February 1861. In it Olmsted frankly enumerated his friends and foes among the Central Park Board of Commissioners. Richard Blatchford, the presiding officer and a future Vaux client, dispatched "routine business rapidly and well," said Olmsted. But of all the commissioners, Olmsted regarded banker Henry Stebbins as "the only man of strong taste"; unfortunately, the press of business kept him away from many meetings. Charles H. Russell, a New York merchant, had "done more for the park than anyone else," and Vaux's friend John A. C. Gray had "at times worked hard and effectually to carry important points for the park, both in & out of the Board." But unfortunately, said Olmsted, Gray was a man who "moves always impetuously, often erratically and inconsiderately." Moses Grinnell, a respected philanthropist and the man who had invited Mould to come to the States, was excellent but often absent. Waldo Hutchins rarely appeared at meetings. Arrayed on the adverse side were John H. Butterworth, a man Olmsted characterized as "fearfully crotchety and [who] has done more harm than good," and August Belmont and Thomas C. Fields, both of whom had "been doing all the harm they could from the adoption of the plan."[33]

But most of all, Olmsted disliked the obstinate park comptroller, Andrew Haswell Green. A member of an old New England family, Green had come to New York in 1842 at the age of 22 to seek his fortune. Hoping for a career in the law, he became a student in the office of Samuel Tilden, who had only recently gained admission to the bar. The two young men (Tilden was only six years older than Green) found that in philosophy, temperament, and tastes they were much alike, and a bond of friendship soon formed between them that endured until Tilden's death in 1886. As a leader of the Democratic Party in the city and state, Tilden probably urged Green to enter public life; in 1854, Green won election to the board of education, on which he continued to sit until 1860. As president of the board, Green, a self-educated man who read the Bible daily and was fond of quoting passages from favorite authors, earned the reputation of an honest, hard-nosed reformer, a distinction that he would proudly carry with him through 40 years of public service. In April 1857, probably as a result of Tilden's influence, Green became a commissioner of Central Park. The appointment must have been motivated by politics, but Green found his new situation much to his liking. Having grown up on a large family homestead, Green Hill, in Worcester, Massachusetts, Green cherished rural life and natural beauty. Over the years that he was associated with the park, and as his fortune grew, he enlarged the house and transformed the grounds at Green Hill (with the help of Vaux, one would like to think), into an idyllic pastoral landscape to which Green fondly attached such names as the Brows, the Lea, and Morning-field. Here, Green—who never married, avoided wine and spirits, and found no enjoyment in food—spent his summers, taking pleasure in planting and arranging his 500 acres. At his death, he willed it all to the city of Worcester for a public park.

As comptroller of Central Park, Green held a tight grip on the purse strings, using them to exercise strict control over all operations and personnel, includ-ing Olmsted and Vaux. His unwillingness to give Olmsted, whom he regarded as an untried manager of men and affairs, free reign in purchasing materials and managing the labor force became an increasing source of friction between the two men.[34] Indeed, by early 1861, Olmsted perceived Green as his archenemy. He told Bigelow that "not a dollar, not a cent, is got from under his paw that is not wet with his blood & sweat." To make matters worse, Olmsted acknowl-edged that Green was the real mover on the board: "No one but Green knows or will take the trouble to inform himself of the fact bearing on any question of policy sufficient to argue upon it effectively," lamented Olmsted, who com-plained that "actually nothing is done in the Board unless Green has prepared it. . . . The practical effect is that my hands are often tied where it is the highest importance that I should act with an artist's freedom and spirit—namely, in the last touches, the finish of the work." Bigelow, who was also associated with Tilden, knew Green and respected him and must have seen Olmsted's fury for what it was, the frustration of an enthusiastic, idealistic beginner up against an inflexibly honest public servant bent on keeping the park from becoming a political boondoggle. Indeed, Green enjoyed the respect of most educated New Yorkers for his courageous stand against corruption and waste in municipal affairs. "The only person I ever heard speak ill of him," wrote George Temple-ton Strong, who had known Green since 1844, "was F. L. Olmsted, who had relations with him in Central Park administration, and Olmsted has a rather *mauvaise langue*."[35] Bigelow, whose paper the *Evening Post* had long been an advocate of the park, knew well that the park board consisted primarily of busi-nessmen who "gave very little time to its affairs and rather begrudged what they did give." He also realized that when Olmsted, a man Bigelow regarded as "devoted to his profession and not in the least a politician," wrote his letter that "he had reached a point where he found himself so helpless that he was quite ready to give up in despair." Seeking to prevent this, Bigelow, who surely must have discussed the issue with Vaux as they consulted on Bigelow's plans for a new house, encouraged Olmsted to stay on and gave him "such aid as was in my power."[36] Bigelow was in Paris, however, when, in the spring of 1863, both Olmsted and Vaux had had enough and tendered their resignation from Central Park.

WHILE WORKING FOR clients like Bigelow, Vaux continued also to attract men of wealth to his growing architectural practice. For Peter Chardon Brooks Jr., regarded as the richest man in New England, Vaux designed in 1858 an imposing stone residence in the Palladian style of the Parish villa.[37] Sadly, neither the house nor the large stone stable that once stood on Brooks's extensive property—perhaps laid out by Vaux—in West Medford, Massachusetts, remains standing. We no longer know how Vaux came to work for Brooks or for Federico Barreda, a Peruvian merchant who controlled the import of guano. Barreda also served as his country's special agent in the United States at a time of considerable difficulty with Peru over that country's policies governing the export of its rich fertilizer deposits. Originally from Spain, Barreda had acquired wealth and position in Peru and America, where he had residences in New York and Newport. Beginning late in 1859, A. J. Bloor recorded many visits, sometimes in the company of Vaux, to the house Barreda owned at 2 West 31st Street. Apparently Vaux had been given the task of remodeling and expanding the residence, which Barreda had purchased in 1856.[38] One would very much like to know what this house looked like and whether or not the ingenious Mould, who in the 1870s would move to Lima, had a hand in its decoration.

For his Newport residence, Barreda asked Vaux to design and supervise the construction of a grand villa (Fig. 6.1) for a site overlooking the sea near the Parish house.[39] Known today as Beaulieu—a name given to it by subsequent owners who included such luminaries of Newport society as William Waldorf Astor and Grace Wilson Vanderbilt—the Barreda house is set amid five acres of grounds landscaped by Eugene A. Baumann, one of the unsuccessful contenders in the Central Park competition. In Barreda's day, a curving roadway led from the entrance on Bellevue Avenue to the semicircular gravel area that set off the towered entrance to the house. Footpaths also threaded their way along the borders of the grounds to a terrace at the back of the property. Here, behind the safety of a stone balustrade, on land that Baumann had raised 14 feet above the grade of the lawn, Barreda's guests could admire the cliffs and sea below. Some little way back from this viewing terrace stood Vaux's splendid house, which fully lived up to the expectations of the site.

Characterized as a "princely residence" by Olmsted and Vaux's associate Jacob Weidenmann, the brick and brownstone Barreda house, which cost $100,000 to construct, is indeed a monumental expression of its owner's considerable wealth and social position.[40] The sense of monumentality, for which Vincent Scully praised the house, is especially striking to the visitor approaching from Bellevue Avenue. Here, from behind an elevated terrace that one reaches by a broad flight of steps, the three-story dwelling majestically dominates the broad expanse of lawn. At the top of the stairs, a recessed porch shelters the entrance, above which rises a grand three-story tower. A large bay with twin round-headed windows projects over the entrance area and admits abundant light into a room that the Barredas used as a nursery. Touched by the influence of the Munich Rundbogen style in the recurring double-light round-headed windows of the second floor and dormers, the house chiefly evokes the fashionable French Second Empire style. Its flaring mansard was the first important example of this sort of roof in Vaux's architecture. Indeed, together with such buildings as Renwick's Corcoran Gallery in Washington, the Barreda house is one of the earliest manifestations of this popular roof form in mid-nineteenth-century American architecture. The Francophile elements and the aggressively vertical expression

FIGURE 6.1. *(above)*
Federico Barreda
house, Newport, R.I.,
1859–1860. Courtesy
of Sally Taylor.

FIGURE 6.2. *(at right)*
Barreda house, plan.
From C. Vaux, *Villas and
Cottages* (1857). Courtesy
of Buffalo and Erie
County Public Library.

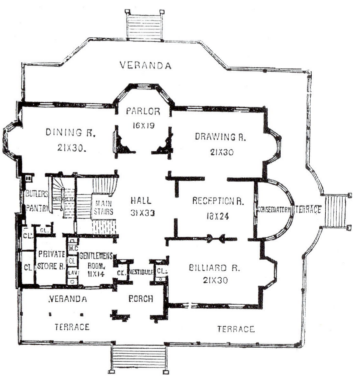

PLAN OF PRINCIPAL FLOOR.

of the Barreda house set it apart from the more reposeful-looking Newport dwelling Vaux had designed a few years earlier for Daniel Parish. On the exterior of the Barreda house, Vaux experimented with ideas that look forward to the architecture of the postwar period.

The compact plan of the Barreda house (Fig. 6.2) reflected a way of life that attached much importance to comfort and entertaining. The spacious ground floor centered around a 31' × 33' hall, onto which opened a suite of five rooms that in turn communicated with verandas, terraces, and a conservatory. (Barreda must have swelled with pride when he looked across his hall from the foot of the stairs toward the reception room at the right and the drawing room at the left.) On the seaward (western) side of the house, Vaux placed the 21' × 30' dining room and a drawing room of equal dimensions, joining the two spaces by means of a 16' × 19' parlor of polygonal shape. All three rooms overlooked the grounds from behind a deep veranda (Fig. 6.3). On the south side of the house, a reception room (18' × 24') occupied the space adjacent to the drawing room and allowed guests to enter a large semicircular conservatory that extended out into the area of the terrace. A billiard room and, across the hall, a "gentlemen's room" with water closet completed the program of major ground-floor spaces. Overnight guests stayed in bedrooms on the third floor, where quarters were also provided for a staff of six servants. (Servants had additional accommodations in the stable and gatehouse, buildings that Vaux also designed.) Bedrooms and a nursery for the Barreda children occupied the second floor. And one would like to think that all members of the household were invited to climb the small staircase leading from the third floor to the square room at the top of the tower. From there one could either contemplate what Weidenmann described as the "very happy combinations of the natural and the artificial style of landscape gardening"[41] that Baumann had created around the house or look far out to sea. Reflecting its owners' cosmopolitan taste and international position, the interiors of the commodious villa were splendidly arrayed. Barreda paid $30,000 to Gustave Herter to insure that the decorations and furnishings of the principal

FIGURE 6.3. Barreda house, view showing the southern and rear elevations. Courtesy of Sally Taylor.

rooms were thoroughly up-to-date. The grand dining room, we are told, possessed festive "Italian frescoes," a gleaming marble floor, and luxurious salmon-colored satin wall coverings. The more sedate drawing room was hung with crimson fabric.[42] Surely Barreda intended that his lavish summer home should not only express his own successful life but also, by implication, assert the wealth and stature of Peru, a country that Yankee interests often treated with little more than contempt.

FOR WEALTHY MISSISSIPPI plantation owner Thomas Evans Bedgegood Pegues, Vaux designed in 1859 a dwelling that is more closely related to the sober Palladianism of the Brooks and Parish houses than to the extravagance of the Peruvian consul's mansion. In 1856, Pegues had moved from North Carolina to Oxford, where he became a director of the Mississippi Central Railroad and a trustee of the University of Mississippi. Local tradition recounts the unlikely tale of how Pegues went on a tour of the Hudson Valley with Vaux before settling on a plan for his new house, which later generations called Ammadelle.[43] In addition to (and more likely than) the tour, Vaux must have presented the southerner with a copy of *Villas and Cottages*, for Pegues chose to build a residence that, as numerous commentators have pointed out, resembles in plan and elevation the designs for the villa that E. S. Hall had ordered from Vaux but never erected on his property at Middletown, Connecticut.[44] Like the Hall design, the well-preserved Pegues residence has an asymmetrical facade focused on a projecting entrance bay with a triple-arched entrance and a bracketed gable. One of the more significant deviations from the Hall plan, which Vaux described as "an irregular villa without wing," is the isolation of the kitchen in a separate wing at the back of the house. This alteration undoubtedly reflected a consideration for Mississippi's warm climate. Also in response to the environment, Vaux added a large veranda across the back of the Pegues house. It discreetly supplemented the single veranda that had been present on the side of the Hall house, which Vaux had described as "a principal feature in the design, and one, it is thought, that would add much to its desirability as a summer residence." Commonly regarded as one of the outstanding examples of mid-nineteenth-century architecture in the South, the Pegues house barely escaped destruction at the hands of Union troops in 1864.

SCANTY DOCUMENTATION exists for other commissions from wealthy clients who sought Vaux's services before the war. In October 1860, Bloor visited two clients on Vaux's behalf to discuss possible work. One was Major Rawlins Lowndes, husband of Gertrude Laura Livingston, the sister of Blanche Livingston, who with her husband, Lydig Hoyt, had commissioned Vaux several years before to design their house at Staatsburgh, New York. With the advice of Hoyt, Lowndes, who lived on Washington Square in New York City, contemplated building a country house on the Livingston property at Staatsburgh.[45] A few days before Vaux left for England, he took the train up the Hudson with Bloor and Mr. and Mrs. Lowndes to survey the site of the proposed house, the specifications for which Bloor already had in hand. Nonetheless, on the day of Vaux's departure word came from Lowndes that he had reconsidered his intentions and would not build "just now."[46] The major may have taken up the project somewhat later, however, for in the second edition of *Villas and Cottages* (1864), Vaux illustrated a roomy mansard-roofed square house that he said had been constructed at Staatsburgh.[47] Unfortunately, Vaux did not indicate the name of the patron in his text, and no record has been found of the building, which, like the Hoyt house, made liberal use of terraces and verandas. The other project that Bloor recorded apparently involved a commission to remodel the interior of the New York City residence of James Couper Lord. After an initial visit in mid-October to take measurements, Bloor returned numerous times to Lord's house on Gramercy Park. Unfortunately, no documents have turned up to explain the nature or extent of the work for this influential client, who was described as belonging "to that comparatively small circle of men of fortune, taste, and organizing power . . . who feel the conscious obligations of their position and give their best efforts to further the interests of the whole community."[48]

The greater demand on Vaux's attention in the early 1860s was for houses of more modest scale. The comfortable wooden dwelling that Vaux built in 1860 on East Putnam Avenue in Greenwich, Connecticut, for Francis Tomes Jr., Vaux felt represented "an amount of accommodation that is in very general request." He therefore illustrated it in the second edition of *Villas and Cottages*.[49] The principal floor of the square building contains a small reception room to the left of the entrance hall, with the drawing room, library, and dining room comprising the suite of living rooms. A separate wing provided space for the kitchen on the ground floor and rooms for three servants on the second floor. The upper two floors of the main part of the dwelling were ample for a large family: in addition to the four bedrooms on the second floor, four additional sleeping rooms occupied the full attic beneath the mansard roof, another early instance of this form in American architecture. Indeed, the tall, double-hipped roof, with a slightly curved lower profile and a balustrade at the second level, counted as a leading feature of the Tomes house. Fully aware of the practical advantages that tall roofs provided in terms of increased living space, Vaux also appreciated the expressive potential they possessed. He felt that the roof was especially important to the success of the Tomes house. In *Villas and Cottages*, he departed from his usual practice of illustrating buildings with perspective views and included an elevation drawing to better show his readers "the true pitch that should be given to a roof of this sort." When viewed in perspective, said Vaux, this roof appeared "irregular and picturesque" on the otherwise symmetrical dwelling.

In addition to the steady flow of commissions for new houses, Vaux, in association with Olmsted, undertook important landscape projects. The success of Central Park placed their names before the growing number of people who were concerning themselves with civic improvement. In April of 1860, the two men were appointed as design consultants to a commission set up by the State of New York to lay out the as yet uncharted area of Manhattan Island north of 155th Street. Apparently this event marked the first time that they used the professional title of landscape architects. Their charge, said Olmsted, in whose correspondence resides the only substantive evidence associated with the undertaking, was to deal with 1,800 acres of "very rugged & beautiful ground— impracticable to be brought into the square street & avenue system of the rest of the island."[50] In a long letter to commission member Henry H. Elliott, Olmsted outlined his (and undoubtedly Vaux's) ideas for preserving the area's picturesque topography. The land, said Olmsted, offered "the essential requirements for villa residences," while providing homeowners with "metropolitan advantages."[51] Regarded as Olmsted's "first systematic exposition of the way in which permanently attractive residential neighborhoods can be secured by the proper designing of streets,"[52] the letter to Elliott contains ideas that would later turn up in the firm's designs for new residential communities. Nothing tangible resulted from the deliberations of the Manhattan commission, however, and the group disbanded in 1865.

In July of 1860, Edward Knight Collins engaged Olmsted and Vaux to prepare a development plan for his 300-acre estate in the Larchmont section of New Rochelle, New York.[53] The "Yankee Lord of the Atlantic Ocean," Collins had made a fortune as steamship magnate. However, after a series of disasters that beset the Collins Line—including the wreck of the *Arctic*, in which Nockalls Cottingham as well as Collins's wife Ann had lost their lives—Collins had gone to live in semi-retirement at Larchmont. He now proposed to divide his holdings into saleable building lots, retaining 50 acres for himself. Olmsted and Vaux submitted an estimate of $1,389 for the work and commenced a topographic survey. The result of their labors, however, is unclear. A map drawn by Archibald MacDonald, which was reproduced on a notice advertising the auction sale of house lots in 1865, may partially reflect their ideas. From the announcement of the sale that appeared in the *Herald*, we learn that the undulating land extended well into Long Island Sound and that all of the building lots, most of which fronted on the water, commanded views of the sound and the East River. "Those wishing to locate a first class watering place," proclaimed the prospectus, "will, on inspection, find a combination of advantages probably not to be found elsewhere in the country."[54]

More successful was the commission to lay out Hillside Cemetery in Middletown, New York, a thriving manufacturing town located in Orange County on the rail line between New York and Buffalo. James N. Pronk, a successful attorney who desired to improve civic life in the town, was the prime mover behind the creation of the new cemetery. He must have spoken with Vaux about the job before Vaux left for England in November 1860. Perhaps Pronk contacted Vaux after the cemetery association was officially formed in October 1860. On February 13, 1861, a few days after Vaux's return, a local newspaper reported that much progress had already been made. In the spring, roads and lots would be staked out, and 2,000 trees and shrubs would be planted. The association optimistically looked forward to consecrating the ground in May. Guiding all of this work, the newspaper was proud to say, was "the eminent Rural Architect" Calvert Vaux, who would see the project through to completion under his personal supervision.[55] Acting as Vaux's agent, Bloor reported spending the day of February 19 in Middletown with Pronk, who took him on a sleigh ride to inspect the cemetery site. At the end of April, Bloor wrote that certain unspecified details of the plan remained to be worked out, a fact that foretold a delay in the completion date. One assumes that loose ends were tied up a couple of weeks later when Bloor spent the day with Vaux at Central Park working on the cemetery plan. Olmsted was also there giving advice on the project.[56] Construction must have gone on during this period, however, for by July a local newspaper reported that the grounds were nearing completion and would be ready for consecration in August.[57]

The reason for the delay in working out the design, in fact, may not have concerned the cemetery itself. In July, a local paper reported that "long pending negotiations have resulted in securing the most desirable entrance possible." The reporter was referring to a new street, which he called "The Avenue" (the present Mulberry Street), that was to lead from the center of town to the new burial ground. The roadway was to be "forty feet wide, curved slightly but regularly throughout," explained the writer, who predicted that when it was paved and bordered "with shade trees and finished with sidewalks and railing, as contemplated, [it] will be a specimen of tasteful and durable road making not often excelled."[58] If, as I strongly suspect, this new thoroughfare owed its creation to Vaux and Olmsted, it can be regarded as the earliest example of their intention to link one of their designed landscapes with an existing city plan by means of a special, parklike street.

Fifteen years after the completion of Hillside Cemetery, a New York City newspaper described its beauty as unsurpassed by that of "any place of sepulture in the country."[59] It contained several miles of all-weather paths, walks, and avenues, as well as two lakes and a large number of trees and shrubs, features that for the most part today must be retraced with the mind's eye. Fortunately, a plan made in 1861 by Otis Chickering, a civil engineer, survives to give us a clear idea of Vaux and Olmsted's intentions for the design of the 2,500-lot burial ground (Fig. 6.4). In this plan, the controlling feature is Circuit Drive. Entered at the southeast corner of the grounds, this easily negotiated carriageway follows a winding course that generally stays close to the perimeter of the nearly rectangular site. On the north and south ends it skirts two narrow lakes that were created with water from existing streams and springs. Clustered near the center of the grounds, a sinuous network of roads and footpaths climbs the hill from which the cemetery derived its name. Visitors following any of these primary roadways would eventually reach Observatory Hill. Here, in the middle of a grassy rond-point, Vaux hoped to erect a 40-foot-tall stone tower. Such structures were common to nineteenth-century rural cemeteries, and Olmsted and

FIGURE 6.4. Hillside Cemetery, Middletown, N.Y., 1861. Courtesy of Hillside Cemetery.

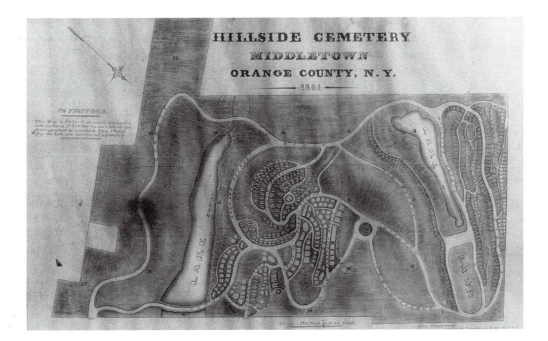

Vaux had even proposed that a similar one be placed on Bogardus Hill in the northern part of Central Park.[60] Vaux's design featured an arched base, above which a chamfered staircase shaft rose to a polygonal cupola and railed viewing platform. From this vantage point above the trees, one would have been able to contemplate a thought-provoking panorama of earthly life in town and country, perhaps while bearing in mind the mystery of resurrection proclaimed by the rooster atop the tower's tapering spire. Unfortunately, the Hillside Cemetery Association chose not to erect Vaux's observatory. Yet even without the tower, nineteenth-century visitors enjoyed prospects of the surrounding countryside from the elevated cemetery grounds, and many other than the bereaved resorted to the place for quiet recreation.

MANY NINETEENTH-CENTURY thinkers also saw nature as a therapeutic force in the treatment of mental illness. In the winter of 1860, Dr. John S. Butler, an outspoken advocate for the humane treatment of the insane and a man who also possessed an exceptional sensitivity to natural beauty, engaged Vaux and Olmsted to prepare plans for the grounds around the Hartford Retreat, of which he was superintendent.[61] Butler believed that mental institutions should create a restful, homelike environment that together with outdoor recreation in beautiful surroundings would promote the patient's return to mental health. Perhaps it was the example of Central Park, a work Butler greatly admired, or some personal association with Olmsted's father in Hartford that drew him to the partners. The superintendent did not regret his decision; in fact, he cherished the memory of ranging across the institution's property with Olmsted during his first professional visit to the site. The ideas that Olmsted had expressed on that occasion, said Butler, "were the 'punctum saliens,' the starting point of the advancement of the Retreat."[62] He was forever grateful to Olmsted and Vaux for the help and encouragement they gave him in his efforts to revitalize the retreat.

The work to be done was extensive. According to the Swiss-born landscape architect Jacob Weidenmann, whom Butler hired at Olmsted and Vaux's suggestion to carry out their plan,[63] their scheme involved draining a low-lying section of the 39-acre meadowland, thinning trees that crowded each other and interfered with views, laying out a perimeter drive that would be accessible to the public along two sides of the property, constructing a system of separate drives for the use of the retreat's 200 patients, and creating a new main gate that resembled the unpretentious entrances to Central Park. Weidenmann began working in June 1861 and completed construction by 1863, much to Butler's liking. "As the genius of the sculptor brings out the graceful statue from the shapeless block," he remarked, "so here has the same artistic power produced from the small meadow a combination of beautiful effects, whose existence was unknown, and of which we may well be proud." Butler was especially pleased by how popular the place had become with the citizens of Hartford, who were granted access to the grounds every afternoon. The pleasure people found here, Butler thought, represented a significant step toward reducing the general fear and ignorance that prevailed in the community concerning the mentally ill. In this way, the informal recreational landscape became a catalyst that encouraged in the public mind the enlightened attitude toward insanity that Butler and other reformers espoused.

In addition to working out the plan for the Retreat grounds with Olmsted, Vaux prepared plans for several architectural features as well. These included a new wing to the existing building to contain a bakery on the ground floor and quarters for employees on the second floor. More important was the "museum" building that Vaux designed for a pleasantly secluded site near the main building. Vaux sent Butler preliminary plans for the single-story structure before his departure for England in November 1860 and forwarded the final designs to him by March of the following year.[64] Now used by golfers, it was designed to house a reading room and a billiard room. Representing the superintendent's belief that "fun of all kinds is an essential element of moral treatment" of insanity, the little building, said Butler, was "in excellent taste and admirably adapted to its intended purpose."[65]

IN 1853, a new mental asylum was established at Towson, Maryland, from the bequest of Quaker merchant Moses Sheppard. In June 1859, the trustees of the Sheppard Asylum (the present Sheppard and Enoch Pratt Hospital) announced a competition for the design of a central administration building and two flanking wings to accommodate 200 patients on a 375-acre rural site north of Baltimore.[66] And although the trustees awarded prizes in December to James and Thomas Dixon, Samuel Sloan, and Richard Upjohn, no single plan fully satisfied the trustees' expectations. The following October, the board hired Howard Daniels, an unsuccessful Central Park competitor who had since secured the position of landscape architect of Druid Hill Park in Baltimore, to lay out the asylum grounds. Also in October 1860, a new committee of the board entered into discussions with D. Tilden Brown, the medical superintendent of the Bloomingdale Asylum in New York City (and the man who had assisted Upjohn in the preparation of his asylum competition entry) about the future of the institution's physical plant. Seeking to benefit from the most advanced information on asylum planning and management, the trustees sent Brown to inspect mental institutions in the United Kingdom and on the Continent. By March 1861, Brown had prepared for the board a plan for an up-to-date facility that incorporated ideas that he had gleaned from his European travels. Thanks to Olmsted's glowing recommendation of his friend's talents, Brown also contacted Vaux to make drawings to accompany his proposal. Vaux had these ready for presentation in May 1860, but the outbreak of war delayed his showing them to the board until the following November.[67] Shortly after the committee had reviewed Brown's report and Vaux's drawings, the full board voted to engage Vaux as architect to the institution. For the remainder of the war years, Vaux prepared working drawings and specifications for two similar red brick and white marble structures that he had designed in accordance with Moses Sheppard's humane injunction that they resemble domestic architecture (Fig. 6.5). Construction began in May 1862, but because of a provision in Sheppard's will that limited yearly expenditures to the interest on his donation, the structures, one for men and another for women, were completed only in 1891.[68]

While the picturesque exteriors of his buildings resembled the houses that Vaux had designed, their interior arrangements followed the dictates of Dr. Brown. The doctor based his ideas on the theories of Thomas Story Kirkbride, the renowned director of Philadelphia's Pennsylvania Hospital, who had written extensively about asylum design. Brown developed for each building a

FIGURE 6.5. *(above)* Moses Sheppard Asylum, male wing, Towson, Md.,
1861. Courtesy of Sheppard and Enoch Pratt Hospital.

FIGURE 6.6. *(below)* Sheppard Asylum, plan. Courtesy of Sheppard and
Enoch Pratt Hospital.

nearly identical linear plan that provided for the efficient management of patients and for their classification by type and degree of disturbance. Brown also sought to provide for the physical comfort of patients by means of modern central heating and a complete system of internal ventilation. (The picturesque turrets on each building served as collection points for an elaborate system of fresh-air flues connected to each room.) Brown departed from the usual pattern of Kirkbride-inspired asylums, however, in having two distinct buildings. This, in fact, represented the most significant divergence from the terms of the original competition, which had called for the usual central administration building with flanking pavilions. The change may have come about in response to the trustees' judgment that the three 1859 competition entries were, indeed, too institutional in appearance. The decision to erect two unconnected buildings also may have been influenced by Brown's high opinion of Scotland's Smith and Lowe asylum at Edinburgh. This private retreat for affluent patients, reported Brown, had two separate buildings, the more recent of which "combined more perfectly the agreeable exterior of a modern villa and the internal arrangements of a well-devised asylum, than any building with which I am acquainted."[69] The twin elevations devised by Vaux likewise expressed the notion of sheltering domesticity. These exceptionally well-built structures—the largest and best-preserved works by Vaux still left to us—display forms and shapes that the architect had used on his many Rural Gothic house designs and had catalogued in *Villas and Cottages*. Verandas, balconies, overhanging eaves, molded chimney stacks, ventilators, double-story bay windows, and hooded dormers impress us with their rich variety. Windows especially abound, for the trustees demanded bright, cheerful interiors. The leading exterior features of each of the two buildings, however, are twin stair towers. These five-story shafts terminate in spacious balconies and triple round-headed windows lighting observatory rooms. Against the sky, the tapering sides of the tall spires curve boldly, recalling the "Rhenish" tower of the Headley house. In addition, Vaux sought to tame the forbidding totality of the extended buildings by reducing their bulk to a series of projecting and receding masses. Imitating the features and rooflines of his most picturesque domestic architecture, Vaux brilliantly met the trustees' wish for buildings that instead of fear and impersonality would convey a message of humanity and intimacy. They still address us with that enlightened message.

The floor plans of each building reflected a carefully thought-out disposition of patients' rooms and services (Fig. 6.6). The plan of the second floor of the male building (Building A) especially demonstrates how Vaux adapted Brown's theories to his architecture. The central section of the building contains a series of patients' rooms on the north side, where they enjoy views of the spacious grounds. On the south side, a sitting area with a large curved bay window and two covered outdoor spaces labeled "ombras" promoted the healing power of socializing. Other amenities included a dining room, a billiard room, and a reading room. The large meeting room at the farther end of the second floor reminds us that originally the institution, which had no chapel, primarily served the needs of Quakers. (Others were accepted for treatment on a space-available basis.) A wing extending to the south off the main block fundamentally repeated the arrangement of the other ward but had rooms for more troublesome patients. Finally, the fourth story of the west or entrance section held servants' rooms as well as quarters for patients' family and friends to use when they came to visit. Remarkably, the asylum proved appropriate to treatment practices in place when, nearly three decades after its conception, it finally opened its doors to its first patients. It is perhaps even more of a testimony to Brown's foresight and to Vaux's talents that these well-maintained buildings still advance the benevolent purpose for which they were first designed.

ON THE EVENING OF April 14, 1861, Vaux and his wife Mary invited a number of friends to their home at Mount St. Vincent in Central Park. Probably many present that night thought it was one of the last occasions that they would be together for a long while. Two days before, the anticipated conflict between North and South had begun. The struggle was soon to claim the services of many of those friends and associates that formed Vaux's social and professional circle. Within less than a month, Jervis McEntee had enlisted, together with his brother Maurice and two of Gertrude McEntee's brothers, actions that may have made Vaux feel pressured to volunteer as well.[70] By June, Olmsted had left New York for Washington to assume the position of secretary of the Sanitary Commission, an organization formed by Henry W. Bellows, minister of All Souls Unitarian Church, to furnish medical supplies to volunteer troops. And on Vaux's advice, Bloor soon followed to work as Olmsted's assistant. Before the summer of 1861 was over, Vaux's former partner Frederick Withers, as well as office assistants Stephen Earle and the younger brother of George W. Curtis, had gone to the front. Indeed, the war quickly cast a shadow over the architectural profession in New York. The AIA frequently canceled meetings for lack of a quorum.

On his own in New York, despite the deepening war, Vaux carried on existing projects and acquired new clients. One of these was A. W. Langdon of Geneva, New York. In April 1862, Vaux contracted with him to remodel and enlarge Langdon's existing house, which stood on several acres in the prosperous Finger Lakes town (Fig. 6.7).[71] The resulting new dwelling is a seamless structure that ranks as one of the most characteristic Gothic villas of Vaux's career. The Langdon house, which received the name Ashcroft from a later owner, epitomizes the fully evolved picturesque dwelling represented in *Villas and Cottages*. One can only wonder why Vaux failed to include it in the second edition of his book.

From the second edition of *Villas and Cottages*, we learn of other houses that Vaux designed before March 1863, when he wrote his preface. For sites near the High Bridge Aqueduct, which carried the Croton Aqueduct from the Bronx to Manhattan, Vaux refers to two dwellings, but he does not name their owners.[72] One of these buildings was a rambling, picturesque house that Vaux described as an "irregular stone villa" (Fig. 6.8). Later in the 1860s, this imposing dwelling became the property of William B. Ogden, who called it Boscobel. Vaux described the walls of this house as constructed of a "cool gray" stone from the site, with quoins and other details fashioned from New Brunswick sandstone. This latter material, the architect said, had a "soft olive tint" that led him to choose a paint of similar color for the exterior woodwork. Roofed with dark gray slate, the dwelling overall possessed a subdued harmony of tones that Vaux said was pleasantly varied. The 160-foot-long facade resembled Vaux's designs for the Sheppard Asylum buildings and might serve to convince us of the homelike appearance that contemporaries would have seen in those institutional buildings. Like the Towson structures, the extended design reveled in

FIGURE 6.7. *(above)* A. W. Langdon house, Geneva, N.Y., 1862.
Courtesy of Mrs. Janet B. St. Louis.

FIGURE 6.8. *(below)* House in Fordham, Bronx, N.Y. (later W. B. Ogden
house), c. 1862. Courtesy of British Architectural Library,
Royal Institute of British Architects.

projecting and receding units, double-story bay windows, large vergeboarded dormers, numerous gabled roofs, and a fanciful ventilation turret crowning the entrance bay. The lower eastern portion of the house held the kitchen, adjacent to which was a small room (located behind a shallow porch) that served as a children's dining room. A small schoolroom stood next to it. The main portion of the principal floor comprised four large rooms arranged en suite. On the south side, in a manner analogous to the Barreda house, a polygonal parlor linked the dining room and library into a unit that allowed guests in any one of these spaces to step out onto a terrace or veranda. The house, of which Vaux sent a photograph to the Royal Institute of British Architects in 1867, was one of his most important commissions.

For another unnamed family Vaux designed a mountain vacation home that featured a powerfully expressive roof (Fig. 6.9). Vaux played up the precipitous surfaces and tall proportions of this exceptional roof by incorporating two rows of dormers that looked like so many chalets clinging to alpine slopes and by having twin chimney stacks pierce its high summit. Using this emotive design as an example, Vaux told the readers of the new edition of *Villas and Cottages* (the house was the frontispiece) that the roofs of houses in mountain areas ought to have "an overshadowing, sheltering effect." He also maintained that such dwellings should be simple in massing so as to convey an impression of breadth and strength. And in the present instance, materials were kept simple, even primitive, with walls laid up with irregular stone courses, and posts, railings, and balconies constructed of logs and sticks. "Self-reliance, liberality, simplicity, and humility must be prominent characteristics in any family that spends a few months successfully in a mountain home," asserted Vaux, "and if such a residence is to be specially adapted to its surroundings, it must in some way or other be suggestive of these ideas." This rugged, vernacular-looking stone lodge certainly embodied these sentiments. It had little of the refinement of Vaux's Rural Gothic suburban houses. Perhaps intended for Henry Bellows, who spent his summers at his family's homestead in Walpole, New Hampshire, the house was a truly original design.

FIGURE 6.9. "Family Cottage in the Mountains," c. 1862. From C. Vaux, *Villas and Cottages* (rev. ed., 1864). Courtesy of Buffalo and Erie County Public Library.

Other dwellings about which Vaux tells us in the revised text of his book suggest that he was able to maintain a steady practice during the early years of the war. Design 11, which Vaux said cost an unidentified gentleman $10,000 to erect in 1862 at Rondout, New York, was a two-story brick dwelling that in later years belonged to Charles M. Preston, a local judge. (The house has been demolished.) Compared to the earlier Halsey Stevens house in Newburgh, which had about the same amount of interior space within a square ground plan, the Rondout dwelling, said Vaux, possessed an "exterior outline" that was more "picturesquely broken."[73] Other new houses which are known to me solely from the revised *Villas and Cottages* were erected in Shrewsbury, Long Island, New York; in New Haven, Connecticut; near Springfield, Massachusetts, where Vaux said he had several commissions; in Llewellyn Park, New Jersey; and at West Point, New York. The latter building was an impressive Palladian design distinguished by a wide veranda with an overhead balcony. The two-story outdoor corridor of space extended around the four sides of the house. On the south, Vaux developed this remarkable feature into a large polygonal projection that jutted into the landscape, where it afforded persons lounging there an especially fine prospect of the Hudson.

IN ADDITION TO these numerous commissions for houses, Vaux also continued to prepare designs for work at Central Park. When the war broke out, the city had pressured the commissioners to abandon construction at the park as a needless extravagance in a time of crisis. In response, Vaux "plied Green with the arguments" why this was untrue, and Green succeeded in making the city supervisors back down from their position. One assumes that Vaux and Green argued that closing off park work would exacerbate unemployment as well as make the city look weak in the eyes of the world. The happy result of Green's victory for Vaux was that he continued to prepare designs for park structures.[74]

In 1862, Vaux drew plans for a building in which light refreshments would be served.[75] Popularly known as the Casino, and now unfortunately destroyed, the charming two-room stone cottage stood just east of the Mall and a short distance from the Terrace. The locale was intended as the special province of women. Olmsted and Vaux took pains to enhance the impression of snug comfort by enframing the building with leafy trees and bushy shrubs. The total picture nicely conveyed the Wordsworthian sentiments that the architect sought to express in this haven of Victorian middle-class feminine idleness. From the Casino (also called the Ladies' Refreshment House), a short walk took the visitor to the Vinery, a long wooden pergola covered with wisteria, honeysuckle, and climbing roses. Regarded as one of the most pleasant resting places in the park, it too was a favorite haunt of women visitors.

The Casino, Vaux explained, was one of three eating places that he and Olmsted had envisioned within Central Park. On the "plateau on the top of the hill on the west side, which overlooks the lake shore road, the lake, and the Ramble," Vaux said that he hoped to construct "a restaurant on an extensive scale."[76] Made convenient to Eighth Avenue by means of a footbridge over the carriage drive, the restaurant would offer hearty, full-course meals to individuals and families. The third establishment, said Vaux, was to have served "fresh milk, curds and whey, cakes, and other refreshments suitable for children." This building he intended to be named the Dairy. It was to be located near the south end of the

Mall, where a playground was to be created, as well as a shelter where youngsters might escape the sun and the rain. These three elements for the pleasure of younger park users were brought into being after the war; the full-scale restaurant, which Vaux hoped would command a view of some of the finest scenery in the park and at the same time be no threat to the peace and quiet of park visitors, never got beyond his sketch that appeared in the annual report for 1863.

The conservatory for the display of flowers and ornamental flora that Vaux planned at this period fared little better than his restaurant project. On January 6, 1862, the board approved his plans for a two-story iron and glass structure measuring 200' × 75' to be located near Fifth Avenue and 74th Street.[77] The construction of the greenhouse was contingent on an agreement with Long Island nurseryman Samuel Parsons, who had pledged to pay the cost of construction and maintenance in return for the right to sell flowers there. But Parsons dragged his feet in upholding his end of the bargain, and the conservatory project languished. Eventually Vaux's drawings for it were lost.

VAUX'S DECISION TO remain behind while so many of his friends and colleagues were volunteering for service in the Union Army may have been guided by his concern for his young family. Another reason may have been his physical condition. In August 1862, when he seriously considered volunteering, Olmsted discouraged him, saying that his friend's health was not "so much improved" as Vaux thought it was.[78] We do not know, however, the nature of his trouble. And any plans Vaux may have had for serving became irrelevant the following month, when he succumbed to a serious illness that affected his mind as well as his body. Described as remittent or brain fever, the typhoidlike attack left him incapacitated for days. Delirious and "incessantly philosophizing about glass and colors and drapery," he appeared in a bad way to Olmsted when he came from Washington to visit him.[79] Well-meaning friends like Olmsted and Clarence Cook were kept away by Dr. Brown, who now took personal charge of Vaux's case. Another visitor turned away was Andrew Green: when Vaux heard Green's name, he cried out to his wife, "Keep him away from me—and dear, it is not best that man's name should be mentioned in my hearing." Learning of this episode, Olmsted reflected that his unfortunate friend had nonetheless uttered "some very clever and sensible things." When the situation became desperate, Brown took Vaux to the Bloomingdale Asylum, a turn of events that prompted Olmsted to seriously consider returning to New York permanently to take up the park work again and to look after Vaux's affairs. "Poor fellow," Olmsted remarked, "how it will annoy and depress and perplex him that he has been liable to go crazy and may be again." But Vaux avoided the worst and steadily responded to Brown's brotherly treatment. It is not clear when he returned to full health, but the "infernal typhoid typhoon," as Vaux later called his illness, passed, and by the end of the year he was back at work. For his cure, Vaux was ever grateful to Brown. Some years later, when a state commission questioned the management of the Bloomingdale Asylum, Vaux told Whitelaw Reid, publisher of the *New York Tribune*, that "as a citizen, a Drs son, an insane asylum architect, and a patient, I believe in the Dr."[80]

Once back on his feet, Vaux laid blame for his crisis on the work at Central Park. The unrelenting struggle to maintain the ideals of the Greensward plan, he confessed to Olmsted, was not "healthy or practicable for so long a time without demoralization in some form."[81] Regretfully, Vaux proposed to Olmsted that they consider resigning from Central Park, where, in Olmsted's absence, Vaux had taken responsibility for the work. In February 1863, Olmsted, whose authority over the Central Park workforce had been severely limited by the board shortly before he had left for the Sanitary Commission, agreed to go along with whatever decision his partner made. Through the winter, Vaux consulted weekly with Ignaz Pilat, the Austrian-born gardener who was Olmsted and Vaux's right-hand man at the park, about the progress of the work, but by spring he had decided to quit. On May 12, 1863, Vaux forwarded to Olmsted a copy of the brief letter of resignation that he had handed to Green. "I look forward with satisfaction to the time when I shall again be a free agent," he told Olmsted. "This has been a dead weight to me ever since you left and for some time before." Nonetheless, Vaux had agreed to maintain an informal association with the park board. If nothing else, he thought that might keep the extension of the park between 106th and 110th Streets, an area for which Olmsted and Vaux had recently submitted a plan, "out of the hands of other professionals."[82] (Already in January 1863, Green had opened the door to Richard Morris Hunt to design gates for the 59th Street entrances to the park.) With Pilat, whom Vaux hailed as "a brother artist" and "a gentleman and a trump," left on the scene as guardian of the Greensward plan—a role he loyally performed—Vaux and Olmsted temporarily severed their ties with Central Park.[83]

Perhaps buoyed by his recovery from a terrible illness and anticipating his resignation from Central Park, Vaux had undertaken in the winter of 1863 to prepare a revised edition of *Villas and Cottages*, which appeared early in the following year. In the preface, which he dated March 23, 1863, Vaux briefly surveyed the progress of American art and architecture since the first edition of his book had appeared, six years earlier. Despite the depression that had followed the 1857 financial crash and the present state of civil war, Vaux perceived a notable increase in the "demand for works of art of a superior class" during this period. Likewise, the establishment of the AIA, the creation of public parks in New York City, Baltimore, and elsewhere, and the appearance of serious art criticism, such as that written by Russell Sturgis under the title "Greek Lines," were heartening signs of a growing national art sense. Vaux singled out for special praise the recently formed Society for the Advancement of Truth in Art. Its members espoused Ruskin's belief, as did Vaux, that "in all times of great art, there has been a close connection between Architecture, Sculpture, and Painting" and that "this union of the arts is necessary for the full development of each." Although he regretted the great sums of money "lavished with careless indifference on ugly, ill-planned buildings in every part of the country," Vaux remained optimistic about the future of his profession. He must also have been optimistic about his own prospects. What better way to call himself to the attention of the building public than with a new edition of his popular book, updated with several new house designs and numerous vignettes of Central Park?[84]

The latter part of 1863 brought further changes to the lives of both Vaux and Olmsted. By October, the Vauxes had moved out of their lodgings at Mount St. Vincent to a house at 16 West 24th Street. His wife Mary was especially glad, said Vaux, "to be in a civilized region again" and to have Gertrude and Jervis McEntee, now safely returned from the war, living with them.[85] And even with the war on, "my business is in good shape," Vaux wrote to Olmsted in California a few months after they had resigned from Central Park. By then, Withers had returned from the conflict and late in the summer of 1863 had entered into a three-year partnership with Vaux. In Bloor's absence, Julius Munckwitz lent his assistance on certain projects, and Pilat helped with "laying out several country places of small size."[86] Vaux also saw the prospect of further business. For his part, Olmsted was experiencing problems at the Sanitary Commission and in his personal life that must have made the park seem remote. By the spring of 1863, he was well on his way to resigning his post with the Sanitary Commission as well as his job at Central Park. Difficulties over the control of finances within the organization had led to a serious rift between Olmsted and members of the commission's executive committee. The failing war effort had also added to his sense of hopelessness. By the time that Vaux tendered his and Olmsted's resignation from Central Park, "chronic overwork and anxiety," notes historian Jane Censer,[87] had greatly weakened Olmsted in mind and body. When offered the position of manager of the promising Mariposa Mining estate in California, Olmsted, who also needed money, accepted. In September 1863, he left for the West. Just as Vaux felt that he was turning over a new leaf in his own career, Olmsted must have gone to California in the expectation of succeeding where twice he had failed to shape an organization according to his high standards. And even though he had recently confessed to Vaux that he "would sacrifice anything but honor and a fair reputation to maintain a position of considerable influence upon the management of the park," at this time Olmsted seems to have given no serious thought to returning to the profession of landscape architecture.[88]

Olmsted's departure was a personal loss for Vaux, who also felt the hurt of being publicly overlooked as Central Park's codesigner. Articles that appeared in the *Evening Post* and the *Times* praised the departing Olmsted for the historic design at Vaux's expense. In a letter to Olmsted he aired his irritation. Vaux complained that Olmsted's more public visibility as architect in chief as well as "partial statements that have appeared from time to time in the public prints" had led people to forget his place in the park's creation.[89] Vaux felt that he had grounds for true concern, especially since one of the recent articles had been written by their mutual friend E. L. Godkin. Confessing to a nagging impression that Olmsted himself regarded his role as superior to his own, Vaux asked his friend to "frankly communicate your personal feelings in this matter so that I may be able in the future to do your views the fullest justice, and at the same time be at liberty—as I never yet have been—to express my own." It must have been especially difficult for Vaux to watch Olmsted, who now seemed negligent of interest in the profession of landscape architecture, walk away with accolades that he had every reason to expect would have greatly fostered his own career.

SHORTLY AFTER ARRIVING in Bear Valley, California, Olmsted himself determined to become one of Vaux's clients. On October 15, 1863, Olmsted wrote to his wife Mary, who was still in New York, to "bring or send a plan for a house" for a hilltop site that he had already chosen. He went on to enumerate his requirements: "It should secure coolness and ventilation to the last degree. It should have deep piazzas or galleries with low shades. It should have a bold, rough-hewn character in outline as well as detail." In the latter regard, he had in mind the "Anglo-Swiss" cottage of his friend Frederick Knapp at Walpole, New Hampshire. Olmsted especially admired the dark brown house for the "roughness of its cottage carpentry—unplanned boards, etc.—which is agreeably congruous with the style."[90] Olmsted's sketch of a plan for his own house indicated a courtyard between the main house and the kitchen and roofs overhanging the walls on all sides. Generally, he told Mary, he dreamed of a living in a dwelling that looked as if it had been "knocked up by some mountaineer with a genius, and axe & steam saw mill."[91] Vaux first got wind of Olmsted's desire to build on December 1, when Mary Olmsted told him that she wanted to see him about a plan. By mid-January, Vaux was hard at work on "Marion House," the name Mary gave the new dwelling in honor of her youngest daughter.[92] (The name surely also pleased Vaux, who had dissuaded Olmsted from calling the child Content.) On January 30, 1864, Vaux put a study in the mail to California. Mary had apparently so well conveyed her husband's ideas to his friend that Vaux was able to say to Olmsted, "I feel that you are the Architect in Chief of this mansion." He only lamented that before finishing the plans he had not had time to see his friend Albert Bierstadt, who had just returned to New York from the West, where he had visited Olmsted. The great painter's personal description of the scenery around Bear Valley, Vaux felt, would have helped him develop the exterior design.

Unfortunately, the drawings which Vaux sent and for which he eventually charged Olmsted $50 have been lost. All we know about the plans comes from Vaux's written comments. From these remarks, we learn that the building readily admitted of being enlarged "in the three most important directions" and that Vaux thought the "large overhanging hood" Olmsted wanted instead of a veranda would be difficult to build. "I have introduced it," he said, "therefore only over [the] dining room, etc., supposing it to be of less projection like the terrace indicated." Nonetheless, he told his friend that "in execution, I think the general result would not be much unlike what you have in your mind." But Vaux took more into consideration than practicality. Turning to esthetics, he raised the discussion of his design to a higher plane of significance. "It is you may think too symmetrical," he wrote to Olmsted. "Perhaps so, but I have the idea that while irregularity is what we want here to contrast with our formal routine life and help to establish a natural balance of impressions, you need where you are a different suggestion, and it will not be objectionable if precision, decision, order, and regularity are allowed to preponderate a little in the general effect of your home."[93] Vaux had apparently taken to heart the description Olmsted had sent him of the Mariposa estate: "The majority of population Chinamen & Diggers. Nine-tenths of the rest floating adventurers, very reckless & rough. The climate is fearfully gloomy in winter, intensely hot in summer and delightful, spring and fall."[94] As he must have often explained to Olmsted, Vaux believed that if derived from right principles, design would promote moral health. Devotion to general principles—rather than adherence to a single style—formed the cornerstone of Vaux's theory of architecture. Yet in the end, Olmsted never erected the symmetrical house that Vaux helped him design. Throughout his stay at Mariposa, he and his family lived in quarters over the company store.

VAUX AND OLMSTED's resignation from Central Park in May 1863 may have severed Vaux's formal professional ties with the commissioners, but he by no means turned his back on the park. Pilat continued to consult Vaux informally on work that under Pilat's guidance progressed in accordance with the letter and spirit of the Greensward plan. But with Olmsted, the park's "representative man," far off in California and Vaux more and more occupied with his private practice, the way lay open for others to stake a claim to park design work. The first major attempt to alter the design came in June 1863, when the Committee on Statuary, Fountains and Architectural Structures won authorization to hold a competition for designs for the four southern entrances along 59th Street. Already by this time, Richard Morris Hunt had shared with his brother-in-law, Charles H. Russell, one of the board members, ideas he had on the subject. Hunt sought to replace the simple, unobtrusive openings that Vaux and Olmsted favored in the boundary wall with grandiose Neoclassical gateways.

In September 1863, the board rejected all the competition entries and came out in favor of Hunt's schemes. With the war on, however, the commissioners were in no position to take immediate action on their implementation. A year later, Vaux wrote to Olmsted expressing his strong disapproval of Hunt's designs, which he characterized as antithetical in spirit to the idealized pastoral landscape that he and Olmsted had worked so hard to create. To Vaux, Hunt's gates reeked of the despotism of Napoleon III and flew in the face of the enlightened republican spirit that he believed had produced the park. Vaux especially disliked Hunt's urbanistic scheme for the main entrance at Fifth Avenue and 59th Street. "His idea," he explained to Olmsted, "is to have a semicircular seat projecting over the western slope with a fountain in the centre running down right and left over stone steps with lines to the pool below." This scheme (which also included a central column) sought to connect "what we have carefully separated," said Vaux, and would destroy "the serenity of the rural district so successfully advanced to the very outer line of the park boundary on 59th Street."[95] Over the next two years, Vaux waged a behind-the-scenes campaign to discredit Hunt's proposals, which Vaux had the displeasure of seeing prominently displayed in the National Academy of Design building, where he, Mary, and the McEntees went often after it opened in the spring of 1864. Winning allies in his friends Clarence Cook and Russell Sturgis, who wrote architectural criticism for the newly formed *Nation* magazine, Vaux succeeded in turning the offending gateway designs, which Hunt published in a handsome book, into a matter of public controversy. Yet during this period, Vaux sought to maintain cordial relations with Hunt, assuring his colleague that "the fault of secrecy and official slight or neglect rested with the Commissioners" and not with Hunt.[96] Victory was assured in July 1865, when Vaux and Olmsted were reappointed as landscape architects to the Central Park commission, with authority to review all architectural plans submitted to the board "with reference to their effect" on the Greensward design.[97]

While the problem of the gates was stewing, the originality of the Greensward plan itself, as well as the integrity of its creators, came under attack. The accusation of plagiarism was hurled at Olmsted and Vaux by an embittered Egbert Viele, the engineer under whom Olmsted had first been employed at Central Park and whose plan had been thrown over in favor of the Greensward design. Already in 1858, Viele had sued John A. C. Gray for remarks Gray had made blaming Viele for a nasty caricature of the board. In January 1860, Viele filed a suit against the city for payment of compensation he never received for the topographical survey, map, and plan of Central Park that he had made before the commissioners announced the competition. During the trial that took place in February 1864, Viele accused Olmsted and Vaux of having merely copied his plan; in private, Viele fulminated that Vaux and Olmsted "might as well have painted a pair of whiskers on a copy of the Greek Slave and called the design of the statue" their own.[98]

With Olmsted in California, it fell to Vaux to defend their honor. Authorized to speak for both of them, Vaux prepared a lengthy testimony and eventually took the stand at the trial to refute Viele's pernicious charge.[99] Asked how his and Olmsted's plan differed from Viele's, Vaux replied, "In every respect." Specifically, he called attention to their own development of Fifth Avenue as the principal carriage entrance and to the way their drive was laid out diagonally from that point so that visitors would "reach the centre of the Park as soon as possible, . . . thus taking people out of the city into the Park with the least possible delay." (Viele had proposed a winding central drive entered from 59th Street.) Vaux also pointed to his and Olmsted's decision "to make the Ramble . . . a point of importance, and so place the water [the man-made skating lake at the foot of the Terrace] as to give a peculiar effect of distance; that is, in itself, the key of the Park." (Viele had planned several small ponds in various locations.) The sunken transverse roads were another major feature absent in Viele's plan, which had cross-park traffic mingling with park users. Vaux readily acknowledged that he and Olmsted and all the other competitors had had knowledge of Viele's plan, which featured curving roads and paths, manmade lakes, and other features generally common to both schemes. Vaux insisted, however, that the Greensward plan "was entirely original in us." And in response to Viele's lawyer's question whether he considered the $2,000 premium he had received for the Greensward design just compensation for his efforts, Vaux answered, "I do not." He underscored his assertion by adding that he would not do it again for the same amount.

Ironically, his reply may have been one of the factors that the court considered when it awarded Viele an $8,000 settlement for his uncompensated labors![100] The verdict rested solely on the issue of payment for Viele's services to the city in the early stages of the park's history; the court did not support his claim of plagiarism. Nonetheless, Vaux and Olmsted worried that the public would miss the legal nuance and think that their plan was a copy. Reacting to current reports in the *Independent* and the *Herald* that intimated this, Green came to visit Vaux to ask if there was anything the board, which strictly speaking was untouched by the verdict, might do to dispel this impression. "I appreciated the tender regard for our reputation," Vaux wrote to Olmsted.[101] Shortly thereafter, Vaux told Olmsted about his plans to prepare an illustrated pamphlet that would explain how their and Viele's plans differed. In the absence of a strong AIA (which essentially had gone out of existence during the war), Vaux proposed to raise the issues of "artistic veracity and social status" at the Century, where Viele was also a member. Vaux hoped a trial of sorts could be held that would lead to the expulsion of Viele from the club. To this end, Vaux approached Hunt, also a Centurian, telling him that he "desired the advice of a professional friend of acknowledged position." He also discussed the matter with Owen Dwight, editor of the *Times*, who agreed with Vaux that "somebody ought to be whopped for this," and Henry Bellows, who "approved the general idea and perceived that there might be something unclubbish (as he expressed it) in impugning the veracity of a member directly." For his part, Olmsted agreed that "Viele should be thrown upon his defense for making a claim to the present design of the Park before a body of gentlemen," for he feared that otherwise the matter would never be put to rest. He especially worried about what would happen "if Viele should become a candidate for an important office and the interest of a large party and its newspaper organs should become associated with him in this matter."[102] Despite Vaux's attempts to organize a campaign over the issue of artistic integrity, he apparently got little more than moral support from those he approached for assistance. Hunt doubted that such action as Vaux proposed would be in the best interests of the Century. A nasty confrontation, he feared, might only draw more attention to the slander than it had already received. As for Bellows, he too discouraged precipitous action and declined to bring the matter before the Century, as Vaux had hoped he would.[103] Perhaps he felt that the publication in 1864 of Frederick Perkins's book on the park— the first photographic survey of the new landscape and its architectural features—suitably restored the partners to their rightful place in the public's eye. As his temper cooled, Vaux watched the trial and its verdict recede from public consciousness. In the long term, Viele's false accusations failed to tarnish Vaux and Olmsted's reputation. Few ever questioned their role as the creators of the much loved and imaginative plan for the nation's greatest public park.

Inside the park, Pilat and others who remained on the job were steadily carrying out the improvements that Vaux had designed before his resignation. In September 1864, Vaux visited the grounds and was generally pleased with what he saw. To Olmsted, he wrote of seeing the iron bridges over the approaches to the reservoir and made special note of the rockwork laid up at either side of the bridge southwest of the reservoir (Bridge 27). Of the black walnut boat landing on the skating lake, he remarked that it was "so situated as to make a good photograph, some say." Vaux also paid his first visit to the Casino, which had been completed by Vaux's former assistant, E. C. Miller. "The building and the irregular arrangement of rooms is about as I expected," he said, "but Miller has put on vergeboards and details that are contrary to my taste and look weeping and udder like." His stroll through the park also occasioned remarks about Andrew Green, whom Vaux saw infrequently now. "He never affected me as he does you," Vaux told Olmsted, "being shallow and so evidently selfish—but he is a consistent specimen of the genus and deserves fully the lack of respect that he gets from our side of the house." Yet Vaux tempered his harsh appraisal with the realization that Green's continued presence on the board worked to protect the integrity of the Greensward plan. "His narrowness is, however, better even now than what would probably take its place," Vaux conceded. "He has some traditions to guide him," acknowledged Vaux, "and no power of invention and no ambition beyond the status quo." Vaux implied, for example, that due to Green's vigilance, the "absurd suggestions of Russell" for the new northern end of the park had been abandoned and Olmsted and Vaux's plan was being carried out.[104] But Vaux's efforts to explain Green to Olmsted never succeeded in reconciling Olmsted to the man whom he would ever regard as his enemy.

THE MANY LETTERS that Vaux wrote to Olmsted in California between the end of 1863 and the late fall of 1865 (when Olmsted returned to New York) reveal much about Vaux's professional life that would otherwise be lost to us.[105] We learn, for example, that at the invitation of a group of park advocates he traveled in November 1863 to New Haven, Connecticut, where he examined a site for a park. "I made the acquaintance of several of the college professors and other of like stamp," he reported to Olmsted, but he doubted anything in the way of work would come of it.[106] Nothing did. In March 1864, Vaux invited Samuel Bowles, the provocative editor of the weekly *Springfield Republican*, to his home to meet E. L. Godkin, who was soon to launch the *Nation*. It must have been a lively evening, for one contemporary said of Bowles that he "never knew a man who knew him who wouldn't rather have him at his table than any other man in the world."[107] Certainly, the three men discussed politics—despite serious criticism of Lincoln, Bowles supported the president for reelection—and if the subject turned to religion, Bowles may have conveyed his new enthusiasm for Octavius B. Frothingham, a rising young Unitarian preacher who was to become an important influence in the Vauxes' spiritual life. Bowles also talked with Vaux of his plans to build a house. The following year, Vaux was still referring to Bowles as "a client of mine,"[108] although by then the journalist had purchased in Springfield a residence that had been built in 1855. It is possible that instead of building anew, Bowles chose to have Vaux remodel this commodious dwelling. It might have been these plans that Bloor records having worked on for Bowles late in 1865 and early in 1866.[109] (After having been dismissed from the Sanitary Commission for his presumptuous behavior toward its directors, in May 1865 Bloor had returned to assisting Vaux and Withers.) Indeed, old photographs give evidence of a resemblance between the Bowles house and other symmetrical Palladian dwellings that Vaux had designed. E. L. Godkin also had ideas of having Vaux design a house for him. He waited several years, however, to build the townhouse for which Vaux and Withers made preliminary plans early in 1865.[110] Vaux also wrote Olmsted of being approached in the early spring of 1865 by William Cullen Bryant to give the poet and elder statesman of American journalism advice about improvements to Cedarmere, his house and grounds at Roslyn Harbor, Long Island. Accepting Julia Bryant's cordial invitation to "cultivate acquaintance generally," Vaux took along Pilat to look over the waterside property, which Vaux found "more picturesque than I supposed."[111] From the fact that the same year Bryant commissioned artist Frederick S. Copley to erect a picturesque board-and-batten cottage on the grounds of Cedarmere, one assumes that nothing came of Vaux and Pilat's visit. Four years later, however, Bryant's daughter Fanny and her husband Parke Godwin turned to Vaux and Withers to remodel the Federal-period house that Bryant had bought for them across from Cedarmere.[112] In addition to trips to Springfield and Long Island, Vaux told Olmsted of other excursions in search of work. In November 1864, he traveled to Hartford, Olmsted's hometown, to see a Mr. Chamberlain, who contemplated building a house there.[113] It would be interesting to know whether Olmsted played any role in connecting the two men, but his correspondence with Vaux yields no further information other than the fact of the architect's visit.

More clear is the meaning of the news that Vaux wrote to Olmsted late in the summer of 1865: "I have a private matter for Mr. Bartlett. 160 acres to lay out next to Barton's Hudson River you remember and a large house etc. to build."[114] The Bartlett referred to was Edwin Bartlett, a wealthy New York merchant who in 1865 sold Rockwood, the house Gervase Wheeler had designed for him at Tarrytown in the 1840s, and purchased Miramonte, an eighteenth-century homestead and large estate at Annandale, New York. Bartlett must have soon wished to change the living accommodations and grounds, putting Vaux in charge of the work. (The Barton in Vaux's statement was Dr. Thomas P. Barton, the owner of Montgomery Place—which was nearby but not directly adjacent to Miramonte—and the man to whom Vaux had given Olmsted an introduction when they were preparing the Greensward plan.) In August 1865, Vaux sent Bloor to Annandale to settle the site of the stable. Thereafter, Bloor visited the Bartletts several times in the fall to check on the progress of the commission and to oversee construction of the large stable with living quarters attached.[115] During one of these visits, Mrs. Bartlett, perhaps nostalgic for her former palatial home, showed Bloor a picture of Rockwood, which her husband had sold to his business partner, W. H. Aspinwall. Mrs. Bartlett may have had a premonition that a new house would never brighten her future; no record exists of a dwelling being built on the Annandale property, which now comprises part of the Bard College campus.[116]

In addition to relating his current projects, Vaux also wrote to Olmsted about the progress of the architectural profession in New York. One of the few positive developments during the war years was the increased attention that the discipline received in the art world. In the winter of 1863, several young artists and critics whom Vaux knew had founded the Society for the Advancement of Truth in Art. In the preface to the second edition of *Villas and Cottages*, Vaux wholeheartedly endorsed the society's belief that "all great art results from an earnest love of the beauty and perfectness of God's creation, and is the attempt to tell the truth about it." To Olmsted, he wrote that he took heart from the fact that this coterie of artists gave "architecture its true place among the arts," for they shared his belief that in all periods of great art there existed a brotherly alliance between painting, sculpture, and architecture.[117] "Architecture derives its greatest glory from such association," asserted Vaux in his preface. Through its publication, the *New Path*, the society sought to promulgate its ideals and to promote the spirit of reform among the arts. Yet although Vaux associated with many of the society's members, read the *New Path* regularly (and forwarded copies to Olmsted), and even took drawing lessons from Thomas Farrar, one of the group's most devoted Pre-Raphaelite painters, Vaux failed the test of membership. "I am anathema marantha," he jokingly confessed to Olmsted, "but kiss the rod and am really glad that a thoughtful little paper has been started."[118] Surely Olmsted scholars Charles Beveridge and David Schuyler are correct when they assume that the reason the society kept its distance from Vaux was that he did not share its members' exclusive devotion to Gothic architecture as the style from which modern designers should solely draw inspiration.[119] Perhaps some of them remembered how at the AIA meeting of June 1, 1858, Vaux had listened politely to Charles Babcock discuss the merits of the Gothic style for public buildings but later voiced the opinion that a true revival of Gothic could not be seriously undertaken in America because the people were "entirely unprepared for it."[120] Vaux himself, as the projects already discussed in this book illustrate, took a tolerant attitude toward style, choosing and modifying Gothic, Tuscan, Renaissance, or Baroque forms as the occasion commanded. Contending that all the different styles "belong to the history, not the art, of architecture,"[121] Vaux held the liberal view that "the past should always be looked on as a servant, not a master."[122]

In addition to business and professional matters, Vaux also kept Olmsted informed about his personal life. The outstanding news was the birth in February 1864 of his last child, Marion. Mary was apparently much weakened by the pregnancy and took a long time to regain her strength, but both parents were immensely proud of the new arrival. She was a "pattern baby," Vaux proudly wrote to his friend.[123] The following September, with Mary's health improved, Vaux took his sons Bowyer and Downing on a Catskills hiking trip. With Ignaz Pilat along, they made "an accommodating quartette and slept in the hay with commendable equanimity in the Clove, no other accommodation being available."[124] The following winter, Vaux spent two memorable days at the Catskill Falls. Not only did he see the falls frozen solid, but he and his party also experienced "a slice of all sorts of weather, ending after bright sunshine at the start and during our explorations with a heavy rain storm."[125] Among those joining him on this excursion were Sanford Gifford and Jervis McEntee.

The latter painter was enjoying more and more success with his pensive views of rural scenery. Vaux was particularly pleased that a sale of his brother-in-law's pictures in the spring of 1864 had gone well. However, Vaux took strong exception to the harsh remarks that Clarence Cook had leveled at the work in the *Tribune*, where Cook reigned as one of American journalism's first art critics. Given "full swing" by the paper to say what he thought, Cook, complained Vaux, "has been damning and blatching at a great rate." Vaux lamented Cook's "trenchant and rather shallow attempts at art analysis," which had disgusted people like himself, "whose sympathies were on the side of fair unbiased and even severe criticism provided it had point and was impartial." In his opinion, Vaux told Olmsted, their friend had simply found the opportunity offered by the position with the paper "too much for him and he has certainly made hay while his sun shone, and has strutted his hour with industrious pertinacity."[126]

Vaux also related his view of events in the ongoing war. In January 1864, Vaux attended a lecture by Edward Gantt. He was so impressed by this Arkansas Confederate general, who had taken the oath of Union loyalty, that he forwarded a copy of the speaker's remarks to Olmsted. In the spring of the same year, he donated several copies of *Villas and Cottages* to the "fair" staged by the Sanitary Commission to raise money for its efforts. And as a member of the newly formed Union League, a club of high-minded business and professional men dedicated to promoting national unity and political reform, Vaux was in frequent attendance at its functions.[127] "I met Hooker and other military celebrities at the Union League last evening," he informed Olmsted in September 1864. Vaux stayed on to listen to a rousing after-dinner speech that was followed by a call for contributions to Lincoln's reelection campaign. Deferring to "the well filled pockets of (some of) the members present," Vaux left "before they came to the Vs."[128] Two months later, he spent a tense evening at the league awaiting news of the outcome of the presidential election. He did not leave until four the next morning. "Lincoln is surely safe for the next four years," he wrote Olmsted, "and we are relieved somewhat from the mental pressure of the last few weeks." And as the end of the war approached in the early part of 1865, Vaux and Jervis McEntee took advantage of the invitation of the artist's cousin to spend a week at the front in Petersburg, Virginia. "Events are crowding on us now," Vaux thought, and the opportunity to see history in the making was too good to be missed.[129] Olmsted, who had seen his fill of the horrors of war, must have been distressed to read of his naive friend's holiday mood.

Much of what Vaux wrote to Olmsted was of a personal nature. Worried about the effect of frontier life on Mary Olmsted, Vaux confided to his friend that she "deserves to have some fun in life. . . . You must make the mines turn out luckily as you call it and bring her home in a year or two with plenty of cash and a silk dress for every day in the year."[130] Health was also a topic of concern to both men. Olmsted, who had endured a number of physical setbacks in his lifetime, often wrote of days when he felt bad. He grew especially depressed when someone predicted his approaching invalidism. "I never mean to allow such statements in regard to myself," Vaux told him, advising Olmsted to adopt the same brave attitude. For his part, Vaux had "the firmest belief in the wonderful recuperative power of the system," provided that one were placed in favorable circumstances. Indeed, one could see Vaux's belief that parks promoted the general health of urban society as an extension of this philosophy of personal well-being.

In his correspondence with Olmsted, Vaux reflected on the partners' collaboration at Central Park and tendered recurring pleas for Olmsted to return to the profession that Vaux believed he had mistakenly abandoned. Unburdening himself of a range of discontented feelings over Olmsted's conduct, Vaux brought up the fact that Olmsted had apparently come to regard himself, as others did, as the chief creator of Central Park. In a series of exchanges that historian Melvin Kalfus has thoughtfully analyzed, the two men candidly revealed their thoughts and feelings on this vexing subject.[131] But Vaux also objected to Olmsted's preoccupation with administration and management. Often, he felt, Olmsted had let these concerns take precedent over the art of landscape architecture. Vaux had likewise been annoyed with Olmsted's authoritarian manner, calling him "Frederick the Great" for the way he dealt with park police and workmen. But at heart, Vaux respected Olmsted's talents as an organizer of men and an insightful thinker on social issues. Yet most of all, he hoped that Olmsted would see a higher calling in the realm of art. The attachment that Olmsted had formed for the scenery of the Yosemite Valley as well as the interest he showed in developing plans for Mountain View Cemetery in San Francisco and the new campus of the College of California at Berkeley must have encouraged Vaux to believe that his friend's interest in landscape architecture still lived. Deeply appreciative of Olmsted's natural esthetic gifts and his personal integrity, Vaux reiterated to him that his true calling lay in this nascent profession, not in managing frontier mining towns or even in writing for the *Nation*, another occupation that attracted Olmsted around this time. Vaux strove hard to convince Olmsted that the creation of public parks was a lofty task in its own right. "I am quite as much a lover of the People as you or any man can be," Vaux told Olmsted. "I show it in my way, You in Yours. . . . [But] for us to be the means of elevating an unaccredited but important pursuit seems to me a direct contribution to the best interests of humanity."[132] Yet in light of their trials and tribulations with politicians and commissioners, Vaux stood convinced that he needed the strength of alliance with Olmsted to achieve his vision of future success. "I am perhaps deficient in personal ambition," he admitted, "but I can feel for it in others." But Vaux insisted that if Olmsted did decide to return, it must be "for the art of landscape architecture and the art of administration combined." Throwing down the gauntlet to his friend, Vaux taunted Olmsted with this challenge: "If you do not see that you are honored by developing this fitness for art work, of course—don't come." Hoping that Olmsted would see the wisdom of his argument, Vaux reminded him that "we are neither of us old you know" and reiterated his belief that Central Park "seems to me and always has seemed a magnificent opening." The opportunity to lead the American park movement, he asserted, was "possible together, impossible alone."[133]

BY MAY 1865, Vaux felt a particular urgency for Olmsted's return, for he could see another great municipal park commission taking form in connection with Brooklyn's Prospect Park. In 1860, the city had decided against locating a park in the Ridgewood district and purchased a 300-acre tract of undeveloped land, including Mount Prospect, approximately two miles southeast of the Manhattan ferryboat landing. The following year, Egbert Viele had been engaged to make a plan for the site. But dissatisfaction with Viele's ideas prompted James Stranahan, now president of the park commission, to approach Vaux again. Vaux had visited the area in the summer of 1864, but it was not until January of the following year that he informed Olmsted of "the Brooklyn affair." At that time, Stranahan had formally invited Vaux to look over the ground and to give his opinion on its potential as parkland. Vaux found that the tract suffered from one serious drawback. It was cut into unequal northern and southern portions by Flatbush Avenue, a street destined to become a major city thoroughfare.

In letters he sent to Stranahan and Olmsted, Vaux outlined his recommendations. Instead of accepting the existing divided condition of the property, as Viele had done, Vaux argued that the site should be augmented with the purchase of additional land. On the south, he recommended that the area around an old Quaker cemetery, which held mature forest trees, should be acquired. On the east, Vaux said that the hilly, low-lying land that Stranahan had considered worthless was nicely suited to being turned into a skating lake. The roughly triangular area north of Flatbush Avenue, which included the city reservoir, could be sold, said Vaux, to pay for the new lands. His scheme, he also pointed out, would alleviate the need for constructing either bridges or sunken transverse roads across Flatbush Avenue to connect the two disparate portions of the park. (He did, however, propose that park visitors be given access to the splendid views from the high banks of the reservoir by means of a suspension bridge.) To Olmsted, Vaux sent a letter with a sketch that summarized his ideas.[134]

Stressing that it was too early to talk about the "artistic arrangement" of the landscape, Vaux emphasized to Stranahan and his colleagues the need to settle pressing issues of "location, natural and artificial boundaries, approaches, and the regulation of surrounding property."[135] Vaux urged the commissioners to dispose of the area north of Flatbush Avenue and acquire the lands to the south and east of the site. He stressed the potential that this land offered for easily creating a skating pond that he saw "as a gymnasium needed for the healthy development of the young citizens of Brooklyn in winter." The lake would be much larger than the one in Central Park, where the surrounding terrain had greatly limited the water surface. Vaux also considered the important question of approaches to the park, urging Stranahan to deal with this matter now rather than later. He cited the example of London, Paris, and other European cities where failure to consider this issue at the time of park construction had led to the expenditure of great sums later. He even offered Stranahan a sketch of how he thought the main park entrance, at the northwest angle of the site, should be handled.[136] (He proposed to create an oval crescent at the intersection of

Flatbush, Ninth, and Vanderbilt Avenues and to widen the latter two streets to the same 100-foot width as Flatbush Avenue.) Overflowing with ideas, Vaux said that for $500 he would prepare a formal preliminary report. Convinced of the correctness of Vaux's views, Stranahan and his fellow commissioners agreed. Vaux's report appeared as an appendix to their *Fifth Annual Report*, which was dated February 1865.

Vaux must have entered into the work with some trepidation because of Viele's earlier presence on the scene. Yet Vaux surely would have agreed with author M. M. Graff that Viele was a man who lacked an original mind.[137] Given the job of laying out the awkward site the commissioners had purchased, he unblinkingly proceeded with the task, giving no thought to other possibilities. Vaux, on the other hand, had seized the initiative and boldly proposed to his host that he and his well-meaning colleagues had missed a splendid opportunity near at hand to create a truly great park. Inspired by the potential of what he saw, he conveyed his enthusiasm to others. This started the process toward the design and construction of what is generally acknowledged as America's finest romantic park landscape.

When Stranahan asked how much Vaux would want for preparing a complete new plan for the park, Vaux reflected on his recent troubles with the truculent Viele. Approaching the business "with a feeling akin to dislike, fearing to be annoyed" as he and Olmsted had been at Central Park, Vaux named the sum of $10,000. Vaux reported this to Olmsted and asked him to return to the East to work with him on this momentous project.[138] "My heart really bounds . . . to your suggestion," replied Olmsted in March, by which time it was clear that the Mariposa mining venture was a failure. Nonetheless, Olmsted held back, fearing that there would not be enough money in the park work to maintain his family; moreover, he dreaded the inevitable "squabbles with the Commission and politicians." Yet the chance to collaborate again with Vaux on work that he now realized that he truly loved was very real. "I think a good deal how I should like to show you what I really am and could do with a perfectly free & fair understanding from the start, and with moderate degree of freedom from the necessity of accommodating myself to infernal scoundrels," Olmsted wrote to Vaux. Confessing to "a perfect craving for the park," Olmsted revealed that Vaux's heartfelt attempts to rekindle his interest in landscape architecture had not fallen on deaf ears.[139]

During the winter and spring of 1865, the Brooklyn commissioners quietly negotiated with Vaux to take charge of the park, trying to reach terms he would accept. After the commissioners turned down Vaux's request for a trip to study European parks, he reacted irritably to an offer of $5,000. He informed Olmsted that he "gave them to understand that they did not stand between Brooklyn and myself as protectors of Brooklyn but that we were going in together to serve Brooklyn in a spirit of mutual confidence and that if we were not, the sooner the matter closed the better."[140] Vaux's prediction that in the end things would turn out well proved true; on June 13, 1865, a little over a month after the war had ended, the Prospect Park commissioners formally engaged him to make a plan for the park based on the boundaries he had suggested. Having assured Olmsted that the Prospect Park commissioners were "quiet inoffensive people" and that he believed Stranahan's "excuses for not carrying out Viele's plan," Vaux took the opportunity to send Olmsted a copy of the terms and to solicit his participation in the project.[141] "We may have some fun together yet," Vaux had written his friend, whom Vaux believed God had destined to devote himself to landscape architecture: "He cannot have anything nobler in store for you," Vaux declared.[142]

Olmsted's continued hesitation to commit himself, however, brought Vaux to the end of his rope. In two letters written in early July 1865, Vaux assumed a remarkably candid tone. Olmsted objected to joining with him, Vaux asserted, because partnership "involves the idea of a common fraternal effort. It is too republican an idea for you, you must have a thick line drawn all round your sixpen' worth of individuality. Of course you will grow out of this like you did out of your porcupine arrangement of Foremen's reports 70 to each pocket and one in your mouth so that you never had a word to say to a friend—but you are a damned long while about it."[143] Scolding Olmsted further for "an insatiable egoism," Vaux opened old Central Park wounds. He accused Olmsted of having taken the position "'all theirs is ours,' all ours is mine—and all mine is my own, or something like it. To the commission it was, I will work for the Park, but I must have the reputation—and I must have it all—and I must have it immediately and I must have it always." Olmsted had left in failure, Vaux said again, because his desire for control had misled him into putting aside his role as artistic creator, to which the commissioners and politicians had no claim, and becoming an administrator, which brought him into direct conflict with the board. In subordinating "the general design to the general management" of the park, Olmsted had fallen into a trap of his own making. "By assuming the position you did," said Vaux, "you assumed the responsibility of protecting others & You could not even protect yourself. I wonder that you did not see this. A scheme that can be upset by a Green is sure to be upset, for men of his caliber are to be found everywhere."[144] Vaux was reminding Olmsted that above all, Central Park was "the great art work of the Republic," a thing of beauty beyond the capacities of grasping politicians and arid businessmen to create, a sylvan antidote to the pervasive philistinism of the age.

In Vaux's idealistic view, the chief role of the landscape architect was to bring into being, in a way accessible to all, a wonderful enrichment of the spirit. Indeed, over Olmsted's objection he insisted on using the term "landscape architecture" to describe the new discipline which they had virtually formed with Central Park. "I think it is the art title we want to set out ahead," he argued, "and may it command its position—administration, management, funds, commission, popularity and everything else—then we had a tangible something to stand on. As administration with art attached as a makeweight the thing is in wrong shape."[145] Reissuing his call to return, Vaux pressed Olmsted to acknowledge a responsibility that they both owed to the future of landscape architecture as a profession. Especially by virtue of winning the Central Park competition, Vaux believed himself obligated to defend the interests of this field, which lacked any long-established authority. "I must try and do for it at least as well as I felt it my duty" to do for the architectural profession, he confessed to Olmsted, adding: "I feel that it will be a burning shame and a reprehensible mistake on our part if the Central Park slips up as a confused jumble of which there is nothing quotable as precedent, that will help our successors." And pointedly addressing his friend's conscience, he urged Olmsted: "Think of this—with me it is almost a matter of religion and I speak of it more distinctly because hitherto you seemed to me too much of a Bedouin, in your views of such matters. You have refused to accept such responsibility and have preferred to accept other responsibilities."[146] Vaux felt passionately about the need to correct society's indifference to artists of all types, whom it relegated to second-class status behind money-making occupations. He hoped to fire the same spirit in Olmsted. "The Gold mine people and the oil people get rich," Vaux reflected, while

> most of the artists remain poor, except they prostitute their abilities. In a properly civilized republic this should not be, in our republic it need not be if representative men were only true to their (implied) oaths of office. The designers of Parks if successful in one way should be successful in the other. In the present state of art development in the country, it is very necessary to protect the strictly legitimate pecuniary interests connected with the pursuits they follow for each in turn must be proved to be profitable or young men of ability will be deterred from venturing into it. . . . You have allowed yourself to stand before the Public as A[rchitect] in C[hief] of the C[entral] P[ark] and it is useless to argue that no responsibility attaches to you. Of course you can repudiate it and walk off and do the other thing, arguing all the while that you are badly used and injured innocent.
>
>   As a friend I wish you every success, but I cannot fail to see that you leave the cause in the lurch and that the bearing of the whole proceeding is unsatisfactory.[147]

These were harsh words, Vaux admitted, but they needed saying. It is a testimony to the strength of Vaux and Olmsted's friendship that Vaux could express these things so forthrightly. A short time later, he wrote again to tell Olmsted the important news that once more they had been offered the position of landscape architects to the Central Park board. (Vaux, remarks Laura Roper, "had with patient craftiness maneuvered Green into returning Central Park" to the partners' control.)[148] "You are, and I am, and several other people are, necessary to this work, and it can be successfully carried through in an artistic spirit to a real end," affirmed Vaux. Success, he challenged Olmsted, "depends on you—and the spirit in which you approach" the task. "I am willing to contribute all I can," pledged Vaux. "Are you content to do the same?"[149] We have lost Olmsted's reply to Vaux's trenchant analysis of his character and his summons to resume the career he dearly loved. Nonetheless, Vaux's severe but earnest words had their desired effect. By August 1865, Olmsted had accepted the Central Park and Prospect Park posts with Vaux. He was back in New York before the end of November. Years later, Olmsted admitted that had it not been for Vaux, he would have had nothing to do with the designs of Central Park and Prospect Park. "But for his invitation," said Olmsted, "I should have not been a landscape architect. I should have been a farmer."[150] Olmsted and Vaux were now firmly set on the course that Vaux had envisioned for their future, guiding the American park movement and promoting the new profession of landscape architecture.

COUNTRY LIFE IN COMPARISON WITH CITY LIFE ... A QUESTION OF DELICATE ADJUSTMENT
1866–1872

With the Central Park and Prospect Park positions secured, and content in the knowledge of Olmsted's eminent return, Vaux set off for a month's vacation with his family in the Adirondacks. While there, he must have been putting together in his mind details of the report that was due to the Prospect Park commissioners in December. Left behind to work on various office projects was Bloor, who also minded the Vauxes' house in their absence. Meanwhile, Olmsted made preparations in California for tying up his affairs and returning to New York, a process that included finishing plans for Mountain View Cemetery in San Francisco. On November 22, 1865, Vaux, together with Withers, Bloor, and Godkin, with whom Olmsted had agreed to coedit the newly established political weekly the *Nation*, went down to the pier to give Olmsted and his family a hearty welcome. When they disembarked from the steamer *Ericson*, the weary travelers must have felt glad to feel firm ground under their feet and to see familiar faces, for after three weeks of travel, bad weather had prevented their boat from docking the previous day. Unable to enter New York Harbor, they had spent the night beyond Hell's Gate riding out one of the fierce gales of the century. During the next few days, there was much socializing at Vaux's house, but Olmsted also surely applied himself to the task of adding his ideas to the drawings and written explanation that Vaux had commenced for the Prospect Park plan. In fact, the partners did not meet the December deadline; on January 14, Bloor was still assisting them on the work, staying until midnight with the two men at Vaux's residence and continuing the task all the next day in the office. Eventually completed on January 24, 1866, the historic report went to the printer in early February. On February 20, Bloor dropped off the first copies at Vaux's house and somewhat later distributed others to the Century and Athenaeum club libraries.[1] One can assume that the big party that Vaux staged at his home on the evening of March 2 celebrated the completion of the Prospect Park report. Over glasses of claret and orange juice punch, artist friends and many other guests must have been treated to animated descriptions of the new park from their host and Olmsted.[2]

The partners' lengthy text, which formed the major part of the Prospect Park commissioners' *Sixth Annual Report* (1866), is a landmark in the literature of the American park movement. For in addition to explaining the graphic plan for the new pleasure ground (Fig. 7.1), Vaux and Olmsted set forth for the first time in detail their philosophy of public park design. Acknowledging that few had written about "the purposes which town parks in general should be intended and prepared to fulfil," they proceeded in the manner of *Villas and Cottages* to lay out broad principles and then to apply these concepts to the specific example before them.[3] The purpose of a public park, they asserted, is to provide a place where townspeople can regain the energy they had expended in labor, for "without the recuperation of force, the power of each individual to add to the wealth of the community is, as a necessary consequence, also soon lost." Thus, a public park should be a place where one can "unbend" the "faculties" that have been exerted in daily life in the city. This could best be achieved, they maintained, by diverting the imagination with "a class of objects to the perceptive organs, which shall be as agreeable as possible to the taste, and at the same time entirely different from the objects connected with those occupations by which the faculties have been tasked." In order to fulfill its aim, therefore, a park must offer the visitor strongly contrasting impressions to those of the city, a notion, it should be observed, that neatly echoed the logic of employing "a natural balance of impressions" to restore psychological equilibrium that Vaux had used to defend to Olmsted his symmetrical design for Marion House. The universal pleasure people found in parks, Vaux and Olmsted maintained, "results from the feeling of relief experienced by those entering them on escaping from the cramped, confined and controlling circumstances of the streets of the town." In their eyes, this sense of freedom was best stimulated by the sort of pastoral

FIGURE 7.1. Design for Prospect Park, 1866. From the Board of Commissioners of Prospect Park, *Sixth Annual Report* (1866). Private collection.

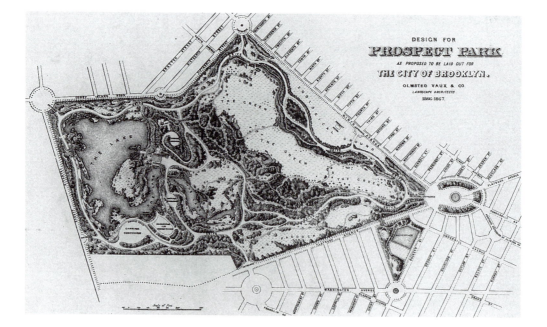

scenery that earlier ages had sought in royal parks and hunting grounds, where the term "park" had originated. "It consists," declared Vaux and Olmsted, "of combinations of trees, standing singly or in groups, and casting their shadows over broad stretches of turf, or repeating their beauty by reflection upon the calm surface of pools, and the predominant associations are in the highest degree tranquilizing and grateful, as expressed by the Hebrew poet: 'He maketh me to lie down in green pastures; He leadeth me beside the still waters.'"

But public parks must also offer their users occasion to enjoy human intercourse in a variety of pleasurable circumstances. "Men must come together, and must be seen coming together, in carriages, or horseback and on foot," Olmsted and Vaux maintained, "and the concourse of animated life which will thus be formed, must in itself be made, if possible, an attractive and diverting spectacle." The park should invite people to gather "for the single purpose of enjoyment, unembarrassed by the limitations with which they are surrounded at home, or in pursuit of their daily avocations, or of such amusements as are elsewhere offered." In this regard, architecture had a special role to play within the park. Since the late Middle Ages, when hunting parks began to be enjoyed for "gay parties of pleasure," Vaux and Olmsted noted, buildings had been designed to give such places an especially "festive character." Declaring the delights of scenery and the pleasures of socializing to be chief purposes for which parks are created, Vaux and Olmsted identified the task that lay before them. They recognized that providing for such pursuits as driving, walking, skating, sailing, picnicking, playing, and listening to music while maintaining a "rural, natural, tranquilizing and poetic character in the scenery" was the greatest challenge confronting the park designer. They attempted to meet this challenge by subordinating all the manmade elements of the park's design to the site's "natural circumstances."

But the mere preservation of nature or the simple imitation of her appearances was not enough. Reasoning like painters, Vaux and Olmsted stated that one rarely comes across perfectly composed scenes in the wild. As artists, landscape architects must artificially create satisfying scenery by discovering "laws of harmonious relation between multitudinous details." And within the limited space of an urban park they must put these laws into practice to evoke an idealized view of nature. "The result would be a work of art," they asserted, "and the combination of the art thus defined, with the art of architecture in the production of landscape compositions, is what we denominate landscape architecture."

Most of their report explained how the partners intended to carry out this program at Prospect Park. As Vaux had long before recommended, they began by calling for the enlargement of the boundaries of the property on the south and east sides and for the creation of a skating lake in the lowland thus acquired. They even admitted that "stony ravines shaded with trees and made picturesque with shrubs" might be introduced in an incidental way to suggest "wild mountain defiles." Furthermore, they felt that an attempt might be made to "secure some slight approach to the mystery, variety and richness of tropical scenery" that Olmsted had so much admired on his trips across the Isthmus of Panama. But most of all, they asserted that the development of the site, like that of most public parks, leant itself chiefly to the pastoral style. It was to this end that they directed the force of their creative efforts with results that neither of them ever surpassed.

Within Prospect Park's polygonal site, Olmsted and Vaux carefully defined the 526-acre terrain in terms of areas. These included meadowland, mature woods, a large lake, and broad highlands. The principal unencumbered space was a strip of undulating ground labeled the Green on early park maps and running roughly parallel to the Ninth Avenue border of the park. Fulfilling the need for a sense of "enlarged freedom," this extensive area of turf, advised the designers, should "upon special occasions at least, if not at all times, . . . be open to all persons on foot, as a common." All that was required to create a pleasing tree-studded greensward here, observed Vaux and Olmsted, was to fill up a few sinkholes, level several "graceless hillocks," improve drainage and soil conditions to encourage a finer crop of grass, and to expand the edges here and there by thinning out trees in the bordering woods. After annexing the additional land called for in their report, the Prospect Park commissioners carried out Olmsted and Vaux's scheme. The enduring result is that masterpiece of pastoral scenery, the incomparable Long Meadow, as the Green is known today.

Asserting that "next to groves and greensward, a sheet of water is the most important element" in pastoral scenery, Olmsted and Vaux implemented their plan to form a lake (the present Prospect Lake) in the southwest section of the park. In connection with this major water feature, they also proposed to create an elaborate pumping system to insure a constant supply of pure water in the artificial basin. By means of a large steam-powered device, water from a deep, unfailing spring would be fed to the lake. It also would circulate through the park in a system of pools, streams, and cascades that "would give opportunity for every variety of water scenery which is practicable within the space of the park." The architects also foresaw that a nearby hill would be nicely reflected in the lake water and would afford a vantage point from which visitors could watch summer rowers and winter skaters. From on high, they also could enjoy an extensive view southward over the ocean, the Highlands of Navesink, Sandy Hook, and the outer harbor. Lookout Hill, as this elevated area came to be called, would likewise allow visitors to watch military drills and sporting events that Vaux and Olmsted anticipated would be performed on the parade ground that they proposed to lay out adjacent to the southern boundary of the park. Indeed, the partners regarded Lookout Hill as the chief point of congregation within Prospect Park. To this location all walks of the park would tend, an arrangement that recalled the system of paths leading to Observatory Hill in Middletown's Hillside Cemetery. They foresaw the erection here of a refreshment pavilion as well as a "terraced platform one hundred feet in length, with seats and awnings" that would accommodate large numbers of visitors. In addition, a "broad terrace walk and staircase" would connect this area with a large oval concourse for the convenience of those arriving by carriage.

But the most imaginative aspect of the lake area was to be the special provision made there for open-air concerts. "The orchestra," explained Vaux and Olmsted, "will be situated upon an island in a bay of the lake, so that it can be seen from three sides." Directly across the water on the mainland, an audience of 10,000 would be accommodated beneath the shade of many tall trees. To the south of this fan-shaped seating area, a 500-foot circular concourse was to provide additional space for people to listen to the music. To the north, on slightly higher ground, a 300-foot-long oval concourse would be created for the convenience of spectators on horseback or in carriages. In conjunction with the music island and the facilities on Lookout Hill, Olmsted and Vaux nominated a site midway between these two areas for a "series of terraces and arcades . . . within which there will be room for a large restaurant." These arcades, which, like the restaurant, were never built, were projected as the chief architectural feature of the park.

Another important idea in the design for the new park was the establishment of four major zones of trees and shrubs. On the Green or Long Meadow and along the uppermost slopes of the lake, Vaux and Olmsted foresaw "a display of the finest American forest trees, standing singly and in open groups, so as to admit of the amplest development of individuals." Elsewhere around the lake, evergreens and deciduous trees and shrubs would be disposed in picturesque groups. In the central portions of the landscape (an area today known as the Ravine), a grove cleared of underbrush would afford visitors the possibility of rambling freely beneath the shade of fine old forest trees. And in the protected areas of the interior slopes of Lookout Hill and in the valley between it and another small hill, more delicate plantings, such as rhododendrons, kalmias, and azaleas, would be established in natural-looking groupings.

All of these sylvan pleasures were to be made available to visitors by means of a comprehensive system of drives and paths. Starting near the oval plaza at the Flatbush Avenue entrance, a perimeter carriage drive proceeded southeasterly in a meandering path to the heart of the park. First, riders would enjoy the prospect of the broad meadow to the west before entering woodland as they headed toward the lake area. Near the southeast corner of the site, they had easy access to the wide concourse, where they might stop to gather or listen to music on the lake. Continuing along on the western border, the main drive passed northward along the lakeshore. From here, one could enjoy views of the northeast shoreline of the lake, an area that Vaux and Olmsted regarded as the most picturesque section of the park. At this point, the unusually wide drive came alongside the bridle path and pedestrian walk to form the main "promenade" of the park. The designers viewed this area as comparable in function to the Mall in Central Park, a place where "the social or gregarious disposition" would be most completely satisfied. Farther along the drive, the rider experienced a change of scenery. Skirting the Long Meadow and continuing in a westerly direction, one passed the Friends' Hill area, beyond which one encountered "the most purely rural, and at the same time the most expanded and extended, view within the park." Reserving the best for last, Vaux and Olmsted carried the final portion of the drive around Long Meadow, following the Ninth Avenue park border. Here, according to the designers' description, the sinuous roadway "enters the western woods, divides again into two branches, and, after reuniting, passes on for some distance, still in the midst of groves, until, after passing along side of the meadow stretch that was viewed in the direction of its length, at the commencement of the drive, it reaches the starting point near the main entrance."

For those on foot, Vaux and Olmsted provided a series of paths that largely avoided crossing the circuit drive and bridle path. (Some paths, they lamented, would have to cross the carriage road at surface level.) The major and minor paths tended toward two chief points of interest: the summit of Lookout Hill, with its views toward the ocean, and the open air "hall of reception," where visitors might listen to lakeside concerts. Other walks encircled the lake as well as the Long Meadow and connected the music island and Lookout Hill areas with the site of the proposed refectory. The philosophy guiding the design of the entire path system, said the planners, was to give pedestrians the impression that "they should be able to ramble over the whole extent of the property with as much apparent freedom as if the whole park had been intended solely for their enjoyment."

Vaux and Olmsted's report likewise contained remarks regarding areas outside the park that they viewed as having a direct bearing on its success. Taking up a theme Vaux had struck in *Villas and Cottages*, the partners asserted that it was "generally conceded that a system of popular education is an essential part of a republican government." Because of this, they advised the commissioners to think ahead to the time when Brooklyn would wish to establish museums and art galleries. The land already acquired on the other side of Flatbush Avenue, they thought, was eminently suited for such purposes.[4] "If this suggestion is accepted," they prophesied, "the lots fronting towards the park on this part of Flatbush avenue, will probably, in the course of time, be occupied by handsome buildings, the objects of which will in some way be connected with the educational system of the city, but which will not be erected or owned by it, the terms on which the different sites would be given being such as to secure a share of control in the management of each institution, sufficient to ensure to the city an adequate return for the value of the land it parts with."

Vaux and Olmsted also made a novel proposal for special roads that would make travel to the park through the city romantic and fun. From the park's southern entrance they suggested that a pleasure drive be created leading to the beach area on the Atlantic, several miles away. This new carriage road would be "neither very straight nor very level," said the partners, who stipulated that it "should be bordered by a small belt of trees and shrubbery." Such a road anticipated the desire that they foresaw developing among Brooklyn's wealthier citizens for "a trotting course for fast horses." But this was not all. Seeing the new park in the wider context of the entire metropolitan area, they outlined a visionary system of regional recreational roads. They thought that if the opportunity were seized now, the city might lay out pleasure drives that not only connected the park with the ocean but also could link it with Manhattan. They suggested that at Ravenswood, ferries or high bridges could convey carriages across the East River to "one of the broad streets leading into the Central Park." From there, one might someday direct his carriage northward along similar "sylvan roads" that the Central Park commissioners were contemplating. Such a magnificent network of greenways would join Brooklyn to New York by way of their "most attractive and characteristic suburbs and through both their great parks." It was their dream that in the future a leisurely traveler might begin his drive in upper Manhattan with a view of "a long stretch of the noble Hudson, with the Palisades in the middle distance and the Shawangunk range of mountains in the back-ground," and finish with the sight of "the broad Atlantic with its foaming breakers rolling on the beach." One can only second the partners' assertion that had their optimistic scheme been realized, New York City would today possess "a grand municipal promenade, hardly surpassed in the world either for extent or continuity of interest." Their dream went unrealized, but in their 1866 Prospect Park report Vaux and Olmsted had articulated for the first time in America the notion of comprehensively linking park development to urban planning.

Two years later, Olmsted and Vaux devoted almost their entire report to the Brooklyn park commissioners to developing their progressive concept of urban pleasure roads. It began with a long, erudite discussion of the history of streets. Included was the admonition that had London heeded the advice of Sir Christopher Wren after the Great Fire of 1666 and laid out the three-sized street system that he had proposed, the city would have saved "an incalcuable expenditure which has since been required to mend its street arrangements."[5] The message for Brooklyn was clear: much of its land was not yet built upon, so now was the hour to seize the initiative and implement a forward-looking street system that would make the city a model for all nations. Already the world's cities had made great strides in improving the living conditions of their residents. This progress was largely due, said Olmsted and Vaux, to the "abandonment of the old-fashioned compact way of building towns, and the gradual adoption of a custom of laying them out with much larger spaces open to the sun-light and fresh-air." Seeing the two great divisions of town life as domestic and commercial, the partners asserted that in the future the separation of business from home life would become more and more marked. Increasingly, the rapidly expanding middle class would want to reside in pleasant surroundings apart from where it earned its living, while still holding onto the social and cultural benefits of town life. Brooklyn was in a position to become the special quarter of well-to-do family life within greater New York, for it lay closer to the Wall Street business district than most of the potential new residential areas in the upper part of Manhattan Island. Brooklyn, asserted Vaux and Olmsted, "seems set apart and guarded by nature as a place for the tranquil habitation of those whom the business of the world requires should reside within convenient access of the waters of New York harbor."

In order to capitalize on this advantage, however, Olmsted and Vaux advised the city that it must construct in conjunction with its new park a system of special streets that would foster middle-class residential development and discourage the spread of commerce and industry. These streets, which would be unusually wide and tree-shaded and have separate provisions for light vehicular traffic, horseback riding, and walking, would make it easy and pleasant for residents to reach Prospect Park from several directions. Furthermore, they said, such "parkways," as Vaux and Olmsted now called these corridors of well-mannered woods running through the city, would be attractive in themselves solely for the sites of individual family homes. But just to be sure that hardnosed businessmen like Stranahan would be convinced of the wisdom of their utopian-sounding scheme, the partners pointed to the promise of high returns on the city's investment. In extending the advantages of the park to the farther neighborhoods, they reasoned that Brooklyn, generally, would become especially desirable as a place of residence, with the result that "the higher will be the valuation of land . . . and the lighter will be the burden of the Corporation." Home buyers would be drawn to the new boulevard neighborhoods, Olmsted and Vaux asserted, because in them the sylvan attractions found in a large park— driving, riding, and walking—could be conveniently pursued in association with pleasant people, and without "the liability of encountering the unpleasant sights and sounds which must generally accompany those who seek rest, recreation or pleasure in the common streets." Here was one of the first rosy portraits of the American dream of suburban life.

Drawing inspiration from Paris and Berlin, Vaux and Olmsted laid before the commissioners their specific plan to create a series of parkways. Their original idea of building a driving road from the southern end of Prospect Park to

Coney Island now became a parkway that might develop branches "to any points which it should appear that large dwelling quarters were likely to be formed." Another parkway was to run from the main entrance of the park eastward to the Williamsburg section of the city. (This was the genesis of the present Eastern Parkway.) Yet another would go from Prospect Park in a southwest direction toward Fort Hamilton, "where ground for a small Marine Promenade should be secured, overlooking the Narrows and the Bay." Finally, already fashionable Ravenswood would be joined to Prospect Park by another parkway running through the western section of town. Pointing out that the average distance from Wall Street of a residence along one of these parkways was about half the distance from Lower Manhattan to Central Park, Olmsted and Vaux maintained that residents here could partake equally of the pleasures of city and country life. Vaux and Olmsted confidently envisioned their system becoming home to a population of 500,000 prosperous citizens, all of whose dwellings could stand on lots at least 100 feet wide.

The actual plan of the parkway, the partners explained, evolved from their understanding of historic and contemporary advances in street planning. In particular, they pointed to the example of Haussmann's 400-foot-wide Avenue of the Empress leading to the Bois de Boulogne in Paris and the spacious Linden Avenue leading to the Tiergarten in Berlin. Both of these fashionable residential boulevards differed from ordinary business streets in being lined with rows of trees and planted with areas of grass. They also had separate corridors for walking, horseback riding, and vehicular driving. Olmsted and Vaux's plan, however, advanced this concept a step further. Like the Mall in Central Park, their parkways were to be lined with six rows of trees. Between these, separate passageways served various types of movement. The central and widest lane provided for the pleasure of driving one's own "light, elegant, easy" carriage. These relatively new types of vehicles were "quite unfit to be used in streets adapted to the heavy wagons employed in commercial traffic," the partners said, and could only "be fully enjoyed in roads expressly prepared for them." The lanes to either side of the central carriageway accommodated only pedestrians, while the two outermost lanes allowed ordinary vehicles to gain access to the houses that lined the parkway.

At a distance of 260 feet from its neighbor across the street, each parkway residence would be a "detached villa" enjoying a luxury of space unknown in neighborhoods of existing cities. Individual lots, in addition to having 100 feet of frontage, would extend 225 feet back to a lane that would provide access to stables located at the rear of each property. In order to avoid the construction of "houses of an inferior class" on the streets behind the parkway, Vaux and Olmsted proposed to extend their design over four blocks. "If the two outermost streets are widened to 100 feet and sidewalks shaded by double rows of trees introduced in connection with them," they reasoned, "the house lots on these streets will be little inferior to those immediately facing the Parkway, for they also will be of unusual depth and will be supplied with stable lots" that would face those of the parkway residences across the intervening alley. Because of the advent of modern methods of transportation, the "unwholesome fashion of packing dwelling-houses closely in blocks," they maintained, need no longer prevail, except in certain special geographic circumstances, such as in Manhattan. In this regard, Brooklyn enjoyed a distinct advantage over its island neighbor, for it had neither natural nor artificial boundaries that would confine its buildings to close quarters. Furthermore, Brooklyn need fear no competition from upper Manhattan Island in its bid to attract prosperous residents to its parkways. The plans formulated chiefly by Andrew Green for that area specifically rejected the idea of constructing such spacious streets there. It must have been with a sense of mischievousness that the partners, who were eager to point out that they had not been consulted on the matter, quoted poor dim Green to their Brooklyn friends. "We occasionally, in some country city, see a wide street ornamented with umbrageous trees," ruminated Green, "having spaces of green interposed in its area, the portion used for travel being very limited," but such "fanciful arrangements" would not do "in a commercial city, under our form of government." Green's shortsighted dismissal of this modern urban concept represented for New York City a missed opportunity on which Vaux and Olmsted hoped Brooklyn would capitalize. Unfortunately for the rising town, its elected officials took the partners' bold advice only partially to heart.

CONSTRUCTION OF Prospect Park began in the spring of 1866, and the grounds were officially opened to the public on October 21, 1867. At that time the park was far from finished; work on the landscape and structures continued until 1873, when the lake was finally completed. During this time, Vaux and Olmsted continued to refine their overall plan. With few exceptions, however, such as the addition of a special children's area, the park came into being as they had first outlined in the *Sixth Annual Report*. One of the first areas to be laid out was the great oval that Vaux had proposed at the main park entrance (the present Grand Army Plaza). Entered by Flatbush and Vanderbilt Avenues "at points equi-distant from the lower end of the axis of the ellipse," where the main gateway to the park was located, the space recalled Michelangelo's design for the Capitol Hill in Rome. The sixteenth-century piazza may well have inspired Vaux, for as in the great Italian example, he proposed that a monument be placed in the center of the oval. By the end of 1866, however, Vaux had modified his plan by substituting a large fountain with a 160-foot circular basin for the central monument. Statues of Lincoln and Washington were now proposed for positions flanking the park entrance. The most interesting features of the plan, however, were two long curved berms on the north and south sides of the ellipse. By means of these raised beds for trees and shrubs, Vaux sought to shield the surrounding cityscape from the view of people within the ellipse and to introduce abundant greenery into this sheltered forecourt to the park. By 1869, workmen had largely completed the area according to the revised scheme; however, the idea of figures flanking the park entrance had been abandoned in favor of a single statue of Lincoln (by Vaux's friend Henry Kirk Brown) on the park side of the fountain. The monumental urban character of the Prospect Park ellipse may come as a surprise when we consider how Vaux had so vigorously condemned the gateways that Hunt had recently proposed for the 59th Street entrance to Central Park. Indeed, when completed, the Brooklyn ellipse ranked as the most impressive formal space in New York or Brooklyn. A clue to Vaux's decision to evoke the Renaissance tradition of civic life may lie in the fact that he and Olmsted viewed the ellipse not so much as a park entrance but as a place for public meetings. According to their directions, the ellipse received special paving to accommodate crowds of up to 7,000 people. They did not wish to see such gatherings take place inside the grounds.

Within the park, Olmsted and Vaux made construction of the drives a first priority. "As we pass between the banks of earth yet unreduced," wrote a visitor to the construction site late in the building season of 1867, "the eye catches flashing from a score of points on the slopes, and against the shadowy autumn colors of the distant trees, spots of flaming red."[6] The spots of color were little flags that the designers had placed across the landscape to indicate the course of the main drive and of the footpaths. The same observer recalled seeing workmen "laying deep and broad foundations of blue stone" for one of several archways that were built in conjunction with the drives and walks. These structures were necessary to carry horseback riders and carriages over pedestrian paths, for in Prospect Park Vaux and Olmsted maintained the principle of separation of ways that they had first developed at Central Park.

Endale Arch (also known as Archway C) raised the drive over the main pedestrian entrance (hence the original name, Enterdale Arch) (Fig. 7.2).[7] Oversized rusticated voussoirs of greywacke frame its low-springing segmental opening and seem playfully to raise the coping stones to a gable. Having learned well in Central Park how to use archway openings to enhance the visitor's appreciation of the landscape, Vaux and Olmsted positioned Endale Arch at the crucial point in the walker's entry into the grounds from the city. Vaux's low, earth-hugging design heralds passage to the pastoral landscape that lies ahead. The shadowy tunnel, lined with polished cedar planks and fitted with inviting seats, forms a pleasantly mysterious prelude to the wonderfully expansive prospect of the Long Meadow on the other side. "The view on one side, as we approach the bridge," wrote a perceptive nineteenth-century visitor, "is like passing through a romantic dell, the banks quite high, while, on emerging on the other side, a lovely lawn is beheld, stretching far away to the forest, and skirted with paths and roadway."[8] Endale Arch is perhaps the most subtle and effective use of the archway form in relation to landscape to be found in all of Vaux's park architecture.

Two other archways contemporary with Endale Arch eased pedestrians' entry into the Prospect Park grounds by freeing them from the worry of encountering horseback riders and carriages. "A feeling of security and of freedom from the hurry, bustling and watchfulness necessary to safety while walking in the streets of the city" was essential, said the partners, to their intention in creating a recreational pastoral landscape. It was an idea original with them, for as they pointed out, the "lack of a provision of this kind in most of the popular parks abroad leads to many accidents and much inconvenience."[9] Furthermore, wherever an arch carried the drive over a footpath, the structure appeared closely tied to the landscape by being placed in a recessed or depressed location. Obscured by foliage, vines, and creepers, and by generally bearing dense plantings across the top, the overpasses were "so far from being obtrusive objects," said Vaux and Olmsted, that carriage riders seldom realized when they were crossing them.[10] This is especially true of Meadowport Arch (Fig. 7.3), which was begun in 1868 and completed two years later. Conceived in tandem with Endale Arch, it stands slightly to the west of the main park entrance to aid Vaux and Olmsted's desire to disperse people in different directions as they entered the grounds. From the archway's domical vault beneath the carriage drive, strollers might choose to proceed either east or west along the path that skirts the Long Meadow. Externally, three massive diagonal corner buttresses support the vault and sweep to the ground in graceful arcs that echo the great round

FIGURE 7.2.
(above) Prospect
Park, Endale Arch,
1867. Courtesy of
Herbert Mitchell.

FIGURE 7.3.
(at left) Prospect
Park, Meadowport
Arch, 1868. Courtesy
of Herbert Mitchell.

arches and bowing cornice. As Clay Lancaster has pointed out, the design has the feel of the Mogul architecture of India.[11] Perhaps the considerable publicity that had surrounded the pictures of Indian buildings that British photographer Samuel Bourne had shown at the 1865 Dublin International Exhibition and at the 1867 Paris Universal Exhibition had stimulated Vaux's interest in this exotic architecture.[12] Eastwood Arch, which is faced with light-colored Ohio and Belleville sandstone, more closely resembles the Endale Arch. Located at the Willinck Avenue entrance in the eastern border of the park, it carries the drive and bridle path over a walk that leads to the lake area. Across the top of the arch, Vaux built up embankments of "earth and rocks, covered by a loose hedge of shrubs," that completely hid from view of strollers the traffic passing above them.[13]

In the heart of the park, Vaux designed Nethermead Arch (Fig. 7.4), the largest of the park bridges. It carries a bridle path and the central carriage drive across Binnen Water, a rocky brook that descends from the Pool to the Nethermead area, where it joins Lullwater Lake. Choosing a "retired rather than conspicuous" spot, here Vaux erected a viaduct of three segmental arches.[14] The central span crosses the stream, while the arches to either side pass over the bridle path and footpath that follow each bank. Designed to be built with ashlar blocks of Ohio sandstone and with a long low parapet pierced by trefoils, Nethermead Arch is the most elegant crossing in the park. Yet Vaux and Olmsted were especially anxious that this considerable structure would not compete with the nearby scenery, which they regarded as the most picturesque in the park. Vaux promised that once the stone had weathered and the bridge had acquired its dressings of foliage, it too, like its humbler sisters, would be unobtrusive in the landscape. But Vaux was also aware that the upper level of the bridge commanded views of "two distinct districts, seen comprehensively from no other point." So that visitors could profit from this unique situation, Vaux dispensed with the usual plantation of shrubs along the sides of the roadway. Emerging from the wooded banks onto the deck of Nethermead Arch, riders discovered unimpeded views of the beautiful Ravine.

In addition to the several masonry arches, Prospect Park also possessed rustic wooden bridges and incidental structures. Long-vanished Falls Bridge was one of many sassafras and cedar log crossings. Located a short distance downstream from Nethermead Arch, it allowed pedestrians to view the Pool and its waterfall, which riders could see from the viaduct. The scene, wrote an observant contemporary, was the finest in the park.[15] Together with Nethermead Arch and the original oak and stone Lullwood Bridge (begun in 1868 and completed the following year), Falls Bridge demonstrated the care with which Vaux used bridges and arches of all sorts to provide visitors with access to the park's enchanting sights and sounds.

Several buildings that went up early in the park's history also ministered to the comfort of visitors. The most striking of these was the thatched shelter that reached completion while Vaux was in Europe in the late summer of 1868 (Fig. 7.5).[16] Situated near the Flatbush Avenue entrance, the thatched shelter (which, sadly, no longer exists) stood on high ground behind a broad terrace where, contemporary descriptions state, visitors might stand to survey all of the park as well as the more distant landscape, all the way to the Atlantic.[17] Providing seats for 100 people close to the main park entrance, the fanciful shelter quickly became one of the more animated locations within the park: "Elegant equipages are

FIGURE 7.4. *(above)* Prospect Park, Nethermead Arch, 1868.
Courtesy of Herbert Mitchell.

FIGURE 7.5. *(below)* Prospect Park, thatched shelter, 1867–1868.
Courtesy of Herbert Mitchell.

constantly passing to and fro," we are told a few years after its completion, "affording life and variety to a very pretty scene." People must have delighted in the hutlike pavilions, sturdy posts and beams fashioned from untrimmed cedar logs, and, most of all, in the foot-and-a-half-thick straw thatching. Whether the exotic appearance resulted from Vaux's reading of Viollet-le-Duc's writings on primitive habitations or his secondhand knowledge of thatched huts in India or some other out-of-the-way source, the building demonstrated his continued willingness to explore forms of vernacular architecture for incidental structures. Whatever its inspiration, the 100-foot-long shelter was one of the most picturesque and delightful rustic buildings ever to grace an American public park.

Charming rather than exotic was the stone Farmhouse or Dairy, which Vaux designed for a wooded site deep within the park (Fig. 7.6). In this secluded spot, refreshments were made available to those park users on foot who wished a more "thoroughly rural experience" than could be enjoyed where numbers of people gathered.[18] Vaux in particular saw the Dairy's seclusion as an essential part of its allure. When Stranahan expressed the wish to build a carriage road leading to it ("an idea," said Vaux, "that is in every way disagreeable to me"), he made a special trip to the park to dissuade him.[19] The Dairy (now demolished) had rough-textured walls made of small pieces of bluestone obtained by blasting apart boulders found on the site.[20] Otherwise, Vaux expressed picturesque sentiments by sheltering the building beneath two steep roofs and a hooded turret and grouping on the side of the building the wooden entry porch with a tapering external chimney. This prominent feature especially pleased a writer in the *Manufacturer and Builder*, who noted that it called to mind a tradition "usual in most districts of the Southern States" and added considerably to the building's "rural appearance."[21] The framed porch opened into a 45-foot-long room where one might enjoy light refreshments and admire a beautifully carved

FIGURE 7.6.
Prospect Park,
Dairy, 1869.
Courtesy of
Herbert
Mitchell.

mantelpiece. Beyond, in the smaller wing of the building, a rest room served women visitors. Between these two public spaces, a staircase led to second-floor quarters for the concessionaire. Once the Dairy acquired its complement of vines and shrubbery, it became the perfect embodiment of the ideal of pastoral life that Vaux and Olmsted sought to evoke for the pleasure of their fellow city dwellers.[22]

WHILE CONSTRUCTION proceeded apace in Brooklyn, Vaux and Olmsted were also hard at work in Central Park. Their reappointment as consulting landscape architects to the commissioners brought with it renewed design activity in the years immediately after the war. For Vaux, this meant that he had responsibility for the design of several new structures. One of the first of these resulted from Olmsted's 1866 suggestion that a shelter be created especially for mothers with small children. Olmsted proposed this idea out of his concern for the appalling conditions under which working-class children were forced to live. "At one time," he later wrote, "I prepared a circular which was sent to every physician and clergyman in New York, calling their attention to the ease with which the children of the poor could be taken to the park by several lines of street railway, and to the conveniences there provided for them, with special reference to the danger of cholera infantum."[23] It is a tribute to Olmsted's generous spirit that he felt such concern for other men's children when he himself had recently lost a son to this terrible disease. For this reason, he must have regarded the Central Park Children's Shelter with special fondness, perhaps even as a sort of memorial to his own child. The remarkable design for the airy rustic shelter that Vaux created in 1866 (Fig. 7.7) consisted of an octagonal platform 110 feet in diameter. Above this platform rose an elaborate framework of logs and branches. Vaux cleverly divided the space under this trellis construction into "compartments and corridors of divers shapes" by means of double-sided seats running between the upright posts and enclosing small tables where games might be played. The perimeter of the shelter remained clear of furniture to afford "a running stretch of several hundred feet."[24] Vaux and Olmsted placed this shelter on an elevated spot that they described as "an uninteresting mass of rock which otherwise would have been a bleak and sterile blot in the view."[25] Yet they took care, as always, that it did not stand out unduly. Indeed, Olmsted was pleased to think that despite the shelter's considerable size and its popularity with youngsters and mothers, probably not one in a hundred other visitors to the park knew of its existence. Historic photographs verify the extraordinary appearance of this enclosure, the most elaborate and successful example of rustic architecture of Vaux's career.[26] A forest of cedar logs and twisted branches, it must have seemed a magical place to children and adults.

The area near the Children's Shelter became the special preserve of the youngest visitors to the park. In 1869, Vaux designed the Dairy (Fig. 7.8), a picturesque stone building located on a secluded site just south of the 64th Street transverse road where mothers might take their children to drink fresh milk and to buy or borrow playthings that could be used on the lawn out front.[27] Together with a spacious interior room, Vaux equipped the building with an equally large wooden porch covered by a steep roof. Open to the south, this framed "broad gallery" wearing a whimsical belfry gave young summertime visitors a sheltered place to enjoy the breeze that Vaux and Olmsted found

FIGURE 7.7. *(above)*
Central Park, Chil-
dren's Shelter, 1866.
Courtesy of Herbert
Mitchell.

FIGURE 7.8. *(at right)*
Central Park, Dairy,
1869. Courtesy of
Herbert Mitchell.

favored this particular spot in the park. Restored as a visitor center, the Dairy continues to be one of the more frequented destinations in the park.

But although this area in the southeastern part of the park, including the original playground, was identified with the wants of childhood, it too was made to share in the overriding arcadian spirit of the park, for youthful hearts and minds were just as much in need of esthetic stimulation as those of older people. "Hill and dale, wood and water, grass and green leaves, are the natural food and refreshment of the human eye," asserted Vaux and Olmsted. As thoughtful fathers of growing families, they saw such stimulation lacking in the "dull colors and uninteresting forms" that generally surrounded domestic life, as well as business, in the city.[28]

In addition to providing fresh milk on the park grounds, the commissioners agreed in 1867 to establish the Springs, a privately run pavilion where mineral water would be dispensed (Fig. 7.9). The Spring House, as the building came to be called, was constructed according to designs that Vaux prepared for the concessionaire, who erected the $30,000 wooden building on a site near the southwestern corner of the lake.[29] Following a Greek cross plan, the single-story space of the Spring House contained a central round counter from which servers dispensed waters from around the world. On the exterior, the building consisted of open arcades of trefoil arches supporting a double-hipped roof of curved profile. Decorative ironwork and a tall central flagstaff enlivened the roofline and enhanced the festive mood of a multicolored structure that like the Portuguese pavilion at the 1867 Universal Exhibition in Paris, which it vaguely resembled, swore allegiance to the exotic Orient.

FIGURE 7.9. Central Park, Spring House, 1869. Courtesy of Herbert Mitchell.

FOREMOST AMONG THE park structures erected after Vaux and Olmsted reestablished their association with the park was the Belvedere, a fanciful stronghold that stands atop Vista Rock at the level of the 79th Street transverse road. Olmsted and Vaux long realized the need for some sort of structure at this location in order to focus the expansive view that visitors enjoyed of the lake and the Ramble from the upper level of the Terrace. In the airy distance, Olmsted and Vaux desired to place a man-made object that would call viewers' attention to "the highest and most remote part of the hill as seen from the terrace."[30] The partners also recognized that the summit of Vista Rock was the only place where one could obtain a comprehensive view of both the southern and northern sections of the park. Therefore, they affirmed, "every available opportunity should be taken advantage of to give facilities for the gathering and shelter of a number of visitors in an informal picturesque way at this attractive point."[31]

Vaux proposed to achieve both goals by replacing the meager wooden bell frame that originally stood on Vista Rock with a broad terrace that was to be flanked by two dissimilar Romanesque towered pavilions. Vaux had evolved his plan by March 1867, when he produced a handsome watercolor drawing of the proposed scheme (Fig. 7.10). Later that year, the foundations were laid.[32] In keeping with the notion that the rock provided the ideal place from which to view the entire park, the pavilion on the western side of the terrace faced the upper park, while the pavilion on the eastern edge of the terrace overlooked the southern park landscape. Only the eastern of these was built (it was begun in 1869 and completed in 1871), but it was the more important of the two, for its slender tower was meant to complete the view from the Terrace and to promise a rewarding end to a journey through the Ramble. Rising from the natural foundations of the rock itself, it ranks as one of the most powerful designs of Vaux's career (Fig. 7.11).

Imposing in its proportions and picturesque with balconies and terraces, the Belvedere traces its descent from the many stone prospect towers—often distinguished by the Italian name—that since the eighteenth century had graced elevated sites of gardens in England and on the Continent. Repton himself had recommend that "there are some wild and romantic situations whose rocks, and dashing mountain-streams or deep umbrageous dells, would seem to harmonize with the grand baronal tower." And only the year before Vaux designed the Belvedere high above the now vanished 1840s reservoir, the waters of which lapped against Vista Rock, English landscape architect John Arthur Hughes had published an example of a "Norman" prospect tower overlooking the sea from a rocky cliff.[33] As historian Paul Edwards has pointed out, many of these fictive medieval keeps were meant to bring to mind historical associations. Sanderson Miller erected such a tower at Edgehill on the spot where King Charles supposedly raised his army's banner before the great battle.[34] Vaux was undoubtedly aware of this commemorative tradition and perhaps wished that his tower would stir memories of events in the history of the Republic. The park contains sites associated with the Revolution and the War of 1812 (a small defense post or blockhouse from this time still survives), and with the Civil War so recently concluded, the Belvedere, its resolute tower crowned with a tall staff from which an American flag waved proudly overhead, could easily have been taken as a symbol for the triumphant Union.[35]

Patriotic sentiments aside, the Belvedere admirably embodies the idea of a far-off outpost occupying a high and picturesque site. From atop its lower

STUDY FOR BELVEDERE — SOUTH ELEVATION

FIGURE 7.10. *(above)* Study for the Belvedere in Central Park, 1867. Courtesy of Collections of the Municipal Archives of the City of New York.

FIGURE 7.11. *(at left)* Central Park, the Belvedere, 1867–1871. Courtesy of Herbert Mitchell.

arcaded level, one might cast his glance beyond the parapet or out from corner balconies toward the upper park. From the rooftop platform of the taller portion, with its charming covered balcony, as well as from the upper stage of the tower, one can gaze down on the entire park landscape. At the same time, the Belvedere's three-part composition of staggered elemental masses culminating in the spire of the flattened oval tower celebrates the rugged promontory. And the simple medieval style deliberately offered no competition to the rich baroque architecture of the Terrace. Instead of fine stone and delicate reliefs, the Belvedere manifests rusticated Manhattan schist, the very material of Vista Rock itself. As he had done with the Commercial Block, Vaux called on the rugged power of the material—which he set off with smoothly dressed pink granite trim—to give esthetic pleasure to those who came to see the Belvedere. The walls, he said, were "executed with special care and accuracy, so as to attract some attention as a piece of stone-work."[36] The building displays no carved flowers, birds, or beasts to excite the imagination of the visitor; instead, it imparts a romantic sense of solitude and remoteness to its lofty spot.

In casting his design for the Belvedere in such simplified architectural language, Vaux ignored the ornate High Victorian Gothic or Second Empire styles of his time. Rather, the Belvedere, restrained and clearheaded, looks forward to developments in American architecture in the later nineteenth century. It is entirely possible that young H.H. Richardson, who was living in New York at the time of the Belvedere's construction, found much to admire in its robust massing, simple detailing, harmonious balance between horizontal and vertical dimensions, and impeccable stone craft. (Particularly in the way that the building incorporates natural rock into its foundations and is approached by a path winding among boulders, it anticipates Richardson and Olmsted's designs of the late 1870s for the Ames Memorial Building at North Easton, Massachusetts.) One would like to think that it was recognition of the Belvedere's prophetic design that led *Building* to publish a view of Vaux's structure, which he conceived in the 1860s, in the journal's issue for May 1886, the month of Richardson's untimely death.[37]

In addition to enhancing Central Park's attraction for children and to providing access to the park's splendid scenery, Olmsted and Vaux concerned themselves with developing plans for a zoological garden. Their first utterance on the subject was a letter to the commissioners written in January 1867 and published in the annual report for that year.[38] They proposed to turn so-called Manhattan Square, a tract of land bounded by Central Park West and Amsterdam Avenue and 78th and 81st Streets (the present site of the American Museum of Natural History) that the commissioners had recently acquired, into a series of buildings and sheltered areas for the exhibition of various types of animals. (Hardy grazing species, such as deer and sheep, were given pasturage within the grounds of the park, where they formed part of the pastoral scenery.) For various reasons, the commissioners showed only mild enthusiasm for implementing this proposal. The issue of creating a public zoo, however, continued to engage Olmsted and Vaux over the next few years and was one of the chief objects of study for Vaux when he visited Europe in 1868.

TOGETHER WITH THEIR work at Central Park and Prospect Park, the newly reestablished partnership embarked on other plans. In Brooklyn, Vaux and

Olmsted prepared designs for several new public spaces before Vaux left for Europe in the summer of 1868. The most important of these was Fort Greene or Washington Park, plans for which were submitted to the Brooklyn park commissioners on September 9, 1867 (Fig. 7.12).[39] The 35-acre site overlooking Wallabout Bay had held a fort during the Revolution and for many years had served the citizens of Brooklyn as a place for "patriotic demonstrations." The city had now destined the hillside to receive the remains of hundreds of Revolutionary patriots who had died on British prison ships anchored below, in the harbor. The memorial character of the spot as well as the limited extent of the property presented different challenges than those that Olmsted and Vaux had dealt with at Central and Prospect Parks.

Seeking to meet the needs of an already densely populated neighborhood, Olmsted and Vaux coordinated opportunities for passive and active recreation with an area for public meetings and military drills and the precinct of the Prison-Ship Martyr's memorial. The centerpiece of the design was the Revolutionary soldiers' monument that stood on elevated ground near the center of the property. Here Vaux and Olmsted proposed to erect a multi-corridored "Vine-Covered Walk." One arm of its cross-shaped plan extended toward an observatory tower at one end and toward a commanding view over the city at the other end. A large refreshment house terminated a third arm and culminated the rising axis that extended from the park entrance through the monument site (Vaux did not prepare a design for the memorial until 1873)[40] and an open area designated for firing military salutes. At street level, most

FIGURE 7.12. Design for Fort Greene (Washington) Park, Brooklyn, 1867. Courtesy of National Park Service, Frederick Law Olmsted National Historic Site.

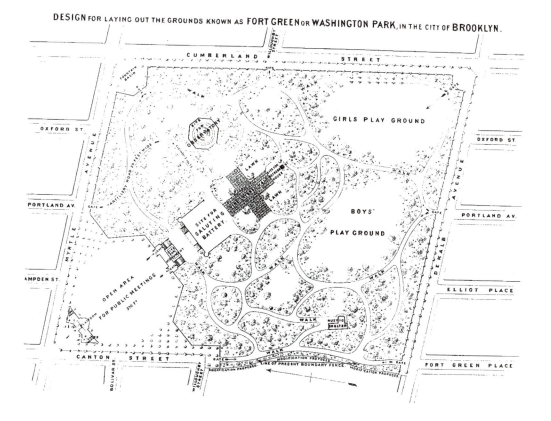

DESIGN FOR LAYING OUT THE GROUNDS KNOWN AS FORT GREEN OR WASHINGTON PARK, IN THE CITY OF BROOKLYN.

visitors were expected to enter this pedestrian park at the northwest corner, where the designers created a large octagonal open space capable of accommodating 30,000 people. Olmsted and Vaux believed that citizens gathering here for meetings (a covered rostrum was planned) would be reminded by the soldiers' memorial of "the real solemnity of the duty which meetings ostensibly held for political and patriotic purposes should always have in view." So that crowds might enter and leave the meeting ground with complete freedom, no fence or wall would bound the area, which, unlike the rest of the park, would be lighted at night. This space also could be used by the regimental soldiers (an armory stood nearby) for parades or whenever a staging area for a body of troops would be required. (Following New York's Draft Riots of 1863, city fathers continually worried about urban unrest.) Olmsted and Vaux laid out the remainder of the site with curving walks that threaded around and through the undulating terrain, encircling in the more distant area separate playing fields for boys and girls. A 30-foot-wide tree-shaded walk around the perimeter of the site completed the program they proposed. The promenade allowed citizens to enjoy a nighttime stroll after the gates to the park footpaths were closed, for Vaux and Olmsted believed that it was "undesirable, with reference to public morals and the general police of the city," to allow people onto the grounds of their parks after dark.[41] Fort Greene Park represented a remarkable example of the adaptation of urban public space to promote recreation (paths and playing fields), democracy (public meetings), and patriotism (Revolutionary monument and parades). One can understand why their contemporary, Jacob Weidenmann, hailed the Fort Greene plan as "a masterpiece of landscape architecture" worthy, given its ingenuity, to be ranked with Central and Prospect Parks.[42]

THE INVITATION THAT Olmsted and Vaux received in October 1867 to advise the city of Newark, New Jersey, on a park plan provided them with another opportunity to develop their ideas about the role of public parks in urban planning. One of the matters that they addressed in the report that they prepared for their hosts was the vexing problem of terminology. The word "park," they said, "in its simplest usage means merely an enclosure, and is applied to enclosures of widely different character."[43] But a true park should be a property of large extent and should provide the sort of pastoral scenery and opportunities for extensive walking and riding that such places as Central Park, Hyde Park, and the Bois de Boulogne afforded. "These and others of the same class," they said, "all offer certain advantages for the recreation and the conservation of health of the people of the towns which respectively possess them, that are not found in some other enclosures, also called Parks, that have been set apart for public use" and were much smaller in area. As a description of a true park, they quoted the definition of pastoral landscape they had published in the 1866 report to the Brooklyn park commissioners. "The first thing we ask for, then," remarked Vaux and Olmsted in a statement that revealed what they looked for in a potential park site, "is opportunity for economically establishing upon it scenery of this character, and for so arranging this scenery that it may be brought under the eye of a large number of observers continuously, for a considerable period of time, during which they are able, by moderate and agreeable exercise, to enjoy in succession a series of views, and thus have their interest constantly stimulated by a pleasant variety." But even most of the large parks that existed in this country and abroad, they noted, usually included structures. The usual museums, water-works, arsenals, and even private residences had nothing to do with the true purpose of a park: to furnish citizens with a place to enjoy outdoor recreation. Henceforth, Olmsted and Vaux told the city fathers of Newark, municipal parks must be considered as distinct works of art "entirely freed from extraneous considerations." Vaux had anticipated this view when he had told the sponsors of Prospect Park to reserve the area outside of the main grounds on the north side of Flatbush Avenue for museums; their statement in the Newark report now assumed the force of doctrine for their future work.

Vaux and Olmsted also took the opportunity afforded by their invitation to Newark to expound on their evolving theory of how to marry the park landscape to the city by means of new parklike streets. In addition to recommending that Newark create a park of the 400 acres that the city had already eyed for recreational development, Olmsted and Vaux suggested that it "would be desirable for your city, at the same time that it acquires a park, to secure possession of strips of land of from two to four hundred feet in width, reaching from the park site in different directions, and running through pleasant neighborhoods where land is cheap; these strips being secured with reference to the future construction thereon of pleasure drives and walks." One of these residential boulevards, they proposed, should connect the park with Llewellyn Park, the early residential suburb in nearby West Orange. If Newark had heeded Vaux and Olmsted's advice, residents could have traveled from town to the park and to suburban homes entirely via parkways. Olmsted and Vaux believed that the way lay open for Newark to acquire a network of greenspace that would be the envy of the world's great metropolises.

The partners reiterated ideas from their Newark report in similar documents that they prepared for Philadelphia and Albany. In November 1867, they formulated their lengthy proposal for Philadelphia's park commissioners.[44] In it they outlined their recommendations for a rural park containing a "series of beautiful landscape pictures" as well as provisions for "public gatherings of a lively and festive character." And as they had told their Newark clients, Vaux and Olmsted warned against avoiding "serious conflict with other municipal interests" in choosing a site and advocated laying out "agreeable approaches and liberal extensions" to and from the park. Regarding the latter consideration, they added the observation that construction costs would soon be returned to the city in the form of property tax revenues from the new parkway residences. The notion of threading parkland like a ribbon through the cityscape was also central to the proposal that the partners made the following year to the city of Albany, New York.[45] Here a band of greenspace was to extend in a U-shaped arc around the town. Starting on the south, near the house and grounds that Vaux and Downing had designed for James Hall, the corridor followed Beaver Creek westward away from the city's waterfront to a proposed park site. At the head of Beaver Creek, it crossed northward to Patroon Creek, where it turned eastward back toward the river, terminating near the Dudley Observatory, another property with which Vaux was familiar from his days with Downing. This linear parkland, which was to have been reserved for footpaths rather than vehicular traffic, would have been within easy reach of most residents. The manner in which it embraced the space of the future city revealed that by the end of 1868 Olmsted and Vaux habitually thought about parks in terms of their larger urban context.

WHILE THE PARTNERS occupied themselves with these many park undertakings, they also received commissions for landscaping the grounds of various institutions. Early in 1866, Vaux traveled to Worcester to advise the trustees of the new Free Institute of Industrial Science (the present Worcester Polytechnic Institute) on laying out the grounds of the campus that they were about to build. Trustee D. Waldo Lincoln, a lawyer and railroad director who in 1864 had worked with Vaux and Boston architect Joseph P. Richards on plans for the Massachusetts Agricultural College (the present University of Massachusetts) at Amherst, took responsibility for the arrangements that the board made with Vaux.[46] After inspecting the elevated site, Vaux planned a curving approach road leading to one corner of the property, where he indicated the location of two future edifices. Set on a natural pedestal, these buildings presented an imposing aspect to visitors mounting the drive or walking the footpaths that Vaux also laid out. From the buildings that Stephen Earle, Vaux's former apprentice, designed a short time later, students were able to enjoy splendid views of the grounds, city, and surrounding countryside. In contrast to the way he ordered his park schemes, here Vaux gave architecture top billing. In Washington, D.C., Vaux and Olmsted performed the same service for Edward Minor Gallaudet, the president of the Columbia Institution for the Deaf and Dumb (the present Gallaudet University). Gallaudet first spoke with Vaux in November 1865 concerning a plan for his unique institution. But with Olmsted recently back from California, Vaux wrote to Gallaudet that the press of business prevented either of them from visiting Washington for several weeks. (He also politely informed the young president that they expected to receive $100 for their preliminary visit.)[47] A friend of Olmsted's from Hartford, Gallaudet had charge of creating a campus in the northeast section of the capital for the first institution of higher education for the deaf. Following the plan that Olmsted and Vaux prepared for him by July 1866, Gallaudet employed Vaux and Olmsted's partner Frederick Withers to erect a number of admirable High Victorian Gothic buildings, including the president's house and several dwellings for faculty.[48] Withers was also the architect for the huge buildings of the Hudson River State Hospital (present Hudson River Psychiatric Center) at Poughkeepsie, New York, for which Olmsted and Vaux in 1867 furnished plans for the 500-acre grounds.[49] Set atop a hill commanding views of the Hudson and distant Catskills, the rambling polychrome brick buildings, which were built according to the Kirkbride system of asylum planning, look across an expanse of turf that rivals Prospect Park's Long Meadow in breadth and extent.

IN AUGUST 1868, Vaux finally fulfilled his long-standing wish to revisit Europe. The little we know of what he did during this three-month stay (he returned on November 18) suggests that he made the most of his time to catch up on the latest developments in architecture and landscape architecture. From a remark of Olmsted's, we get the impression that one of Vaux's purposes was to gather information for a new publication. "Vaux has made at least six visits to the Crystal Palace and is doing London in detail," Olmsted told his sister, drawing his information from a now lost letter from Vaux. "At the rate he is moving," Olmsted reflected, "he will make a very big book." With him was his wife Mary. After supervising the move of her family to a house on elegant, tree-lined Lafayette Place, she apparently was making her first trip abroad.[50] To a friend she wrote that she was having "a good time all the time."[51] Also along was George K. Radford, an engineer who assisted Vaux and Olmsted on much of their work. By the end of October, Vaux had inspected parks and buildings in London—where he rode the new underground and enjoyed the popular Turkish bath—Liverpool, Manchester, and Birmingham and had made a "hurried and fatiguing" visit to the Continent. There he had spent time in Paris, where he had especially enjoyed "the perfection of artistic arrangement" in the city's many small parks and squares. "The most desirable combination of the natural with the artificial being invariably reached," he wrote of these spaces, "each is like a freely arranged bouquet, which is not exactly natural, but is still a harmony produced out of exactly natural materials."[52] Yet in the Bois de Boulogne and Bois de Vincennes, Vaux became critical of the same "French arti-ficiality" that he found even in the most pastoral sections of these extensive parks. Especially interested in zoos, Vaux visited the Jardin d'acclimatation, where he thought that "the true ideal of what a zoological garden should be is in many parts nearly reached." The bamboo buildings that he saw there he believed perfectly suited their purpose. He also praised the modern aquarium. In a dark room, the fish tanks were illuminated so that the living displays alone held the visitor's attention. Vaux also visited zoos in several Netherlands cities. The "perfectly-arranged, rambling, picturesque" zoo in Brussels pleased him, but there were too few animals; Antwerp's semicircular deer house with an interior court for exercising the animals was exceptionally well designed, but "the elephant and the rhinoceros were housed in princely style, the building being an absurdly grandiose Egyptian affair that was very disagreeable to look at"; and the small size of the Amsterdam zoo caused the various departments to be very close together, but the layout, which consisted of low structures facing courts, struck Vaux as nearly perfect. Most of all, Vaux admired the zoological gardens at Cologne. "There a general effect of openness and picturesqueness," he said, "impresses the observer on first entering, but there is no confusion of the mind, either then or afterward." The clarity of the zoo's organization resulted from the way the grounds were thoughtfully divided by plantings into a series of discrete spaces. Each of these contained separate animal displays. "Everything of interest comes into view in regular sequence," remarked Vaux, who had found the "bareness and openness" of the grounds of the zoo in Regent's Park in London especially wanting in this regard. The example of Cologne confirmed Vaux's opinion that the creation of intimate spaces in which the visitor could concen-trate on observing the wildlife before him was "the key-note of any successful design for a zoological garden." In the previous year, he and Olmsted had applied this principle to the "rural and park-like general effect" of their design for a zoo in New York's Manhattan Square.[53]

Also while in London, Vaux met Thomas Wisedell (1846–1884), a 22-year-old assistant in the architectural office of Robert J. Withers (Frederick's brother).[54] Like Wrey Mould, young Wisedell had a genius for creating orna-ment. He and Vaux hit it off, and Vaux asked Wisedell to make drawings of Regent's Park and Chiswick, presumably in connection with Vaux's projected book. The previous December, Vaux and Olmsted had lost the services of the volatile Bloor, who had accused Vaux of dishonesty in his dealings with him. At first Vaux had apparently dismissed Bloor's allegations, but when Bloor denounced him in front of fellow architect Peter B. Wight, an ugly scene ensued. Incensed, Vaux threw Bloor's letter into the office fire and "rushed off, white with extreme ire, and poking vindictively at his spectacles." Thus ended a beneficial alliance.[55] The firm must have suffered from the lack of Bloor's aid, and it is possible that Vaux had the intention while abroad of looking for someone to fill his place. Finding Wisedell talented, hardworking, and personable, Vaux proposed that he come to America to work in the office. The young Englishman readily accepted the offer and joined the Vauxes and Radford on their return voyage. Travel and study abroad had exhilarated Vaux, and when he and Mary arrived in New York on November 16, he was "ready to take hold of anything."[56]

Thanks to Olmsted, much new challenging work awaited Vaux on his return. In his absence, Olmsted had opened discussions with several important new clients. One of these was Dr. Brown of the Bloomingdale Asylum. In September 1868, Brown had urged Olmsted to accept an appointment as adviser to his board, which was preparing to move the institution to a new home in White Plains, New York. The idealistic Brown intended that "our future Asylum will be the 'Chatsworth' of Lunatic palaces and domains."[57] Other undertakings at Riverside, Illinois, and Buffalo, New York, would become milestones in the history of American urbanism. In August 1868, Olmsted had traveled to Riverside, where a group of investors hoped to create a large residential community. By the first of September, Olmsted had prepared a preliminary report for the 1,600-acre site on the Des Plaines River, nine miles west of Chicago. The prairie land was to be laid out in series of curving roadways on which individual house lots would be located. The partners' plan gave much attention to planting trees and to preserving the area along the river as a public park. In addition, other common spaces dotted the grounds, and a parkway linked the new town to Chicago. Enthusiastic at the prospect for implementing ideas about suburban living which he had formulated while in California and which Vaux surely shared, Olmsted wrote to Vaux that the Riverside project promised to bring them fame and fortune. For his architect partners, Olmsted also foresaw many commissions for houses.[58]

Shortly after he returned from Europe, Vaux visited the site, and over the next year he and Olmsted worked out the details of the proposal. Their definitive map was ready in 1869, by which time lots had already begun to sell. But as Riverside proved less and less promising financially, relations between the firm and the promoters soured. "The Company looks a rather Kiteflying affair," Vaux confessed to Olmsted in June 1869, even after construction had begun on the parkway. To make matters worse, the board members themselves showed little sympathy with Olmsted and Vaux's high ideals. When one of the directors proposed building his house on the Long Common, Vaux fumed to Olmsted that he "objected utterly, wholly and without any qualification" to this affront to "the keynote of the whole design." Placing principle above profit, Vaux declared, "I certainly will be no party to it," and he told Olmsted, who was at Riverside at the time, to adopt the same position. "I trust you will present our resignation without fail if this preposterous arrangement is persevered in," he wrote.[59] Unfortunately, the firm had unwisely agreed to take payment for their services largely in stock, the price of which the developers had misrepresented to them. They had to sue the developers twice before negotiating their way out of the disadvantageous contract in the fall of 1870.[60] Nonetheless, in later years, the growth of Riverside generally followed what Olmsted and Vaux had laid down on their 1869 map.

OLMSTED AND VAUX'S experience in Buffalo was much more positive. At the invitation of William Dorsheimer, a local lawyer and politician who headed a group of park advocates, Olmsted stopped in the city in August 1868 on his way to and from Riverside. After surveying the city for possible park sites, Olmsted attended a meeting of civic leaders chaired by Millard Fillmore, who was living in retirement in the city. Although no record survives of Fillmore's opening remarks, one assumes that he reminisced about his experiences 17 years earlier, when, as president, he had brought Downing to Washington to lay out the governmental grounds there. Through Fillmore, Olmsted must have felt the distant presence of the lamented master of Highland Garden as he outlined his far-reaching ideas for bringing the country into the city. In the undeveloped northern section of town, Olmsted proposed to create one large and two small parks that would be joined to each other and to the central city by a system of parkways and boulevards. When Vaux returned to America in November, the Buffalo proposal was waiting to be developed. Early in the following year, the partners submitted their formal report, which included the addition of a residential neighborhood modeled on Riverside.[61]

In their Buffalo report, Vaux and Olmsted perfected ideas that they had stated earlier. Conceiving their plan as a citywide recreational system, they ascribed certain discrete functions to the three public grounds, each of which now received a specific name (Fig. 7.13). The 230-acre park (the present Delaware Park) was the largest of the three areas and represented the classic naturalistic or pastoral landscape; the Front (32 acres), overlooking Lake Erie and the beginning of the Niagara River, featured a viewing terrace and playing fields; the Parade (56 acres), on the eastern side of town, held space for military drills and active sports as well as children's games and picnicking. Distinguishing different functions with different names, the partners reserved the term "park" solely for the large pastoral landscape. All activities incompatible with the relaxed enjoyment of rural scenery by means of walking, riding, or boating were moved to the other two localities. These three grounds were to be linked to each other by six miles of new parkways that would curve around the city in an arc of green. In addition, several existing city streets were to be upgraded to boulevards (notably Delaware Avenue) to carry residents directly from the center of the city to the new parks. All of these thoroughfares were to be planted with rows of American elms, a tree that Olmsted and Vaux had first used in this way on the Mall in Central Park. Apart from its beauty and poetic associations, the elm enjoyed special favor with Olmsted and Vaux for street planting because, they said, "the natural angle of its branches adapts it to a situation where abundant clear space is wanted below the foliage."[62] At major parkway intersections, the partners also planted elms around broad circles, a street feature that they had first used at the entrances to Prospect Park. To be sure, elements of the Buffalo plan benefited from Olmsted and Vaux's earlier park designs. More important is the fact that the overall scheme embodied their fully evolved ideal of a modern urban park system. And this time, the city fathers took their brilliant consultants' advice to heart.

In 1869, the state legislature gave its approval to this forward-looking plan, which in effect laid the foundation for the future growth of the city. By September 1870, construction was under way. Over the next six years, under the able supervision of Radford and Olmsted's friend William MacMillan, Buffalo became the first city to implement the advanced ideas that Vaux and Olmsted

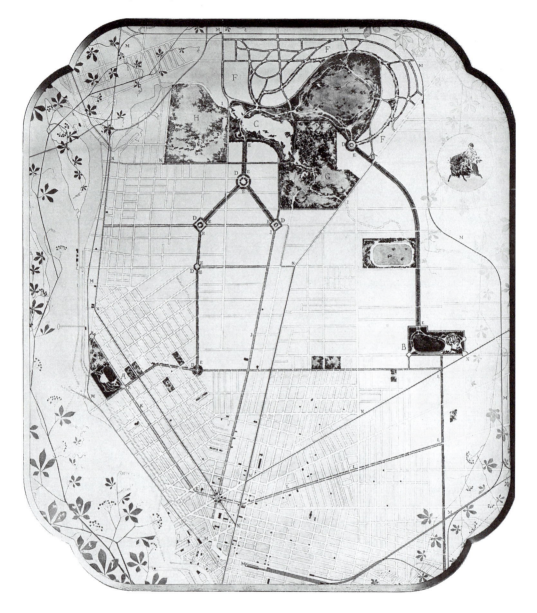

had written about in their proposals for such places as Brooklyn, Newark, and Albany. At the Centennial Exhibition in Philadelphia (by which time Vaux and Olmsted had dissolved their association) and, two years later, at the Paris Exhibition of 1878, Olmsted called the world's attention to the plan of Buffalo with a large map display. Buffalo, Olmsted told the world, was "the best planned city, as to its streets, public places and grounds in the United States, if not the world."[63]

For the new Buffalo parks, Vaux designed a number of structures. Outstanding among them was the Parade House (Fig. 7.14), a spectacular timber building that Vaux proposed in 1871.[64] The building stood near the entrance to the Parade, where from the comfort of long verandas visitors could watch activities on the parade field. From the observation tower attached to the rear of

the structure, they might also contemplate the city and Lake Erie. But most of
all, the Parade House was the primary place within the Buffalo park system for
festive socializing. Containing a large restaurant and smaller rooms for private
parties, it became the scene in summer of public amusements that members of
the large German community that lived nearby especially favored. On a special
wooden floor set up outside, dancers twirled to the music of an orchestra seated
overhead on a balcony while loungers on the extensive verandas enjoyed watching the gay proceedings. Instantly popular when it opened in 1876, the Parade
House, noted a reporter for a local newspaper, became a place where "nightly
congregates the young and tall and short and thick and thin, and a glance at
many faces gathered there opens to view many sides of life." It fulfilled Olmsted
and Vaux's intention that their parks foster the democratic spirit.[65] The Parade
House itself offered visitors a breathtaking display of turned, carved, and drilled
wooden architecture. And as Thomas Wisedell prepared the working drawings
and supervised construction, it may be that he was chiefly responsible for the
building's ornate detailing. Painted in shades of red, green, and black, Buffalo's
Parade House (which was demolished in the early twentieth century) ranked as
one of the most lavish and fanciful park structures ever to grace an American
municipal park.[66]

FIGURE 7.14.
Parade House,
Buffalo,
1871–1874.
Courtesy of
Buffalo and
Erie County
Historical
Society.

In addition to guiding the development of the parks in Buffalo, Vaux joined
Olmsted in advising Dr. James P. White and the directors of the Buffalo State
Hospital (present Buffalo Psychiatric Center) on the building they were to erect
according to plans of young H. H. Richardson. In 1870, the year after the state
legislature had authorized the construction of the huge facility, the directors, for
reasons now lost to us, had chosen the little-known New York architect for the
huge project. But it was to Olmsted and Vaux that Dr. White turned for advice
on siting the mammoth structure, which, like Withers's Hudson River State
Hospital, followed the Kirkbride system of organization. "Mr Vaux and I being
first consulted as to the position of the buildings," Olmsted said, "we proposed
to set them out in a line diagonally to the line of the street." Richardson and
White may have initially puzzled over this unusual alignment. They and the
directors endorsed the novel idea when they understood that by turning the

long facade toward the southeast, Olmsted and Vaux were insuring that as much sunlight as possible would reach the interior during the winter months.[67]

White also sought Olmsted and Vaux's help in planning the 200-acre grounds. Consulting with Radford on drainage and with Richardson on the location of outbuildings, Olmsted and Vaux created a plan for the site before construction of the main building began. From the start, they must surely have realized that their task involved more than providing a therapeutic landscape and farm land for the hospital's troubled residents. Because the hospital grounds were adjacent to the Park and close to the parkway system, they would play a role in the growth and development of the residential quarter of the city. For this reason, undoubtedly, Olmsted said that he and Vaux labored for a long time over the plan. Unfortunately, work on the grounds waited until 1877, when the hospital buildings were half completed. By that time, the partners' drawings had been lost. White then engaged Olmsted, who was no longer associated with Vaux, to prepare a new plan.

At the beginning of the 1870s, a number of other cities requested Olmsted and Vaux's services. In March 1870, the partners submitted their design for Walnut Hill Park in New Britain, Connecticut. This 40-acre park included a "fountain close." This area, which was immediately adjacent to a public street, would have equaled Buffalo's Parade as a place of public rendezvous. Here, a large pavilion "of timber construction with decorations in wood of the chalet style painted in bright colors" and with an "orchestral balcony" was planned (but never built) to overlook a broad esplanade. In the middle of this space, three jets of water would rise from a large, shallow basin and would shoot higher than those in any other fountain on the continent.[68] Although the citizens of New Britain never got the opportunity to dance or watch gala waters in Walnut Hill Park, they did see the creation there of a large meadow or common, a feature that Olmsted and Vaux considered the most important in any naturalistic park. "There is nothing which people desire more in a park than to walk upon the turf," they told the New Britain city fathers. Meadowland was also an important element in the park plan that Olmsted and Vaux prepared around this time for Bridgeport, Connecticut. And in June 1870, they visited Fall River, Massachusetts, to urge the city to construct "a circuit of pleasure travel" and to acquire land that while not extensive would provide citizens with broad views of Mount Hope Bay and the Taunton River.[69]

Scenery was also a primary consideration for Olmsted and Vaux in the plan they outlined in March 1871 for Chicago's 1,000-acre South Park.[70] In Buffalo, they had laid out a terrace on high ground at the Front where promenaders might view the broad waters of Lake Erie and the beginning of the Niagara River. At Chicago, they sought to establish an even more intimate relationship between South Park and Lake Michigan. "Aside from the actual advantages of access which it offers," stated the partners, "it is most desirable that whatever sources of interest there may be in the lake should be as closely as possible associated with those of the Park and be made to appear, as much as possible, part and parcel of the Park." Chief among these features was a lagoon for pleasure boating that would be formed as an arm of the lake. Moreover, in connection with the creation of the lagoon, Olmsted and Vaux foresaw the erection of a 200-foot-long pier projecting into the channel leading from the lake to the lagoon. But this mighty wall was, in their view, to be more than a work of engineering, for it would also offer all the citizens of Chicago an exceptional opportunity to enjoy their lake. Citing the example of British and French seaside resorts, where piers were popular attractions, and sounding like it might have been a passage from a draft of Vaux's European book, Olmsted and Vaux observed that "experience shows that where an offset into the water from a tame coast has been thus formed people are strongly drawn to gather upon or near it." Unfortunately, this marvelous idea, born of both the experience of travel and the perception of nature's poetry by two extraordinary men, was not to be. Its spirit, nonetheless, lived on. When Olmsted returned to Chicago in 1892 to lay out the grounds of the World's Columbian Exposition on the site of South Park, he took inspiration from the report that he and Vaux had authored 20 years earlier.[71]

FROM THE EARLIEST DAYS of Central Park, Andrew Green had envisioned placing a museum and an art gallery within its grounds. In addition to championing public grammar schools as a member of the board of education, Green, like Vaux, believed that America stood in need of educational institutions devoted to the advancement of knowledge among the general public. Early in May 1869, the state legislature gave its blessing to Green's idea and authorized the establishment in Central Park of an art gallery, natural history museum, and meteorological station. A short time after Vaux's return from Europe, he found himself hard at work on a plan (that he may even have conceived prior to his trip abroad) for a large building to display objects of art. For though the city as yet owned no works of art, it contemplated construction of a museum at the eastern edge of the park near Fifth Avenue and 82nd Street. (This site had been proposed for a zoo in 1860 and was the current location of a deer paddock.) "I worked at the drawings in the top room of the Bank of Commerce building in Nassau-street over the Park Commissioners' office," remembered Mould, who collaborated with Vaux on the work, "and many were the quiet hours passed there with Mr. Andrew H. Green, Mr. Vaux, and myself in the discussion and elaboration of the plan—in fact, Mr. Green used to come upstairs every half-hour he could spare and take interest in the results on my drawing board."[72]

Meanwhile, the art committee of the Union League met in October 1869 to discuss the suggestion of the club's new president, John Jay, that "a permanent national gallery of art and museum of historical relics" be established in New York. The committee, which included Vaux's friends George H. Putnam, a publisher, and Worthington Whittredge, a landscape painter, gave enthusiastic support to the idea and called a general meeting for November 23, 1869. Invited to attend were all members of the league, as well as the membership of the Century, the AIA, and other interested groups. On that occasion, Green, Mould, Vaux, and Olmsted heard a stirring address by William Cullen Bryant, who said it was time for New York, the "third great city of the civilized world," to have a suitable place for the permanent display of works of art from all periods. Others seconded his remarks, including Richard Morris Hunt, who, citing the AIA's attempt over a decade ago to establish a national museum, pledged the institute's assistance in the erection of a suitable building. Architect Russell Sturgis admonished those present that now was the hour to act to acquire works of art before valuable opportunities were lost to others. Henry Bellows, who spoke of "the redundant wealth with which our prosperity threatens to possess us," echoed this sentiment. He asked why the city could not be expected to "outbid the world in any market for those great recondite works of Art which are so necessary to the cultivation of every people."[73] By the end of the evening of rousing speeches, a provisional committee had formed to apply for a charter and generally to carry the project forward. Green, Vaux, and Olmsted were among its 50 members. After the meeting, Vaux and 11 others stayed on for supper at the club. "Much good humor prevailed," recalled A. J. Bloor, who sat at the table that night and engaged in the "free exchange of opinion as to the prospects of the new-born institution." And despite the antipathy he must have felt toward his former employer, Bloor raised his glass in toasts to Vaux and his fellow committee members for the success of their endeavors.[74]

When the group convened for the first time in early December, chairman Henry Stebbins named Vaux, Olmsted, and Green to a 13-member subcommittee charged with formulating a "plan of organization for a Metropolitan Art Museum Association."[75] By the end of January 1870, the subcommittee had submitted a plan for acquiring a collection of works of art. It had also put together a slate of permanent officers for a Metropolitan Museum of Art. In addition to its president, John Taylor Johnston, the new board included Green and Olmsted as well as Vaux's artist friends Frederic Church and Eastman Johnson. Meanwhile, Vaux and Mould continued to develop their plans for the museum building that the state legislature had authorized the park commissioners to erect. This project was destined to become merged with the nascent Metropolitan Museum of Art.

THE NEW ART MUSEUM must often have been a topic of conversation between Vaux and Church, who saw each other frequently during this period. In 1869, the illustrious landscape painter turned to Vaux for help in building his new home at Hudson, New York (Fig. 7.15). Two years before, Church had purchased his site, a promontory adjacent to the farmstead where he lived when not at the Tenth Street Studio Building. Known as Long Hill, the wooded bluff commanded far-reaching views of the Hudson River and the Catskill Mountains. At the time, Church had consulted Richard Morris Hunt about a design for a dwelling. Although Church apparently had received from Hunt two Francophile elevation drawings for houses—one reveled in polychromatic brickwork and featured a rooftop belvedere, the other was a picturesque stone villa—the artist hesitated to proceed with the commission.[76]

Instead, he took his wife, her mother, and his one-year-old son on an extended trip abroad. From November 1867 until late June 1869, the family toured Europe and the Middle East. It was there, especially in lovely Beirut and historic Damascus, that the receptive artist fell in love with the decorative tradition of Islamic art and architecture. Travel also rekindled Church's desire for a new house. Not long after he had left, he wrote to a friend back in the States that he had "new and excellent ideas about building."[77] There is reason to believe that this desire received its first impulse from the "aesthetic" homes of artists that Church presumably met in London. Among the colleagues Church is known to have visited there was George Boughton, a popular history painter who had lived in Albany in the 1850s. Church and his wife attended at least one of the Boughtons' famous dinner parties.[78] Church also may have had knowledge of the architectural displays of several Islamic nations that captivated

FIGURE 7.15.
Olana, Frederic
E. Church house,
Hudson, N.Y.,
1870. Courtesy
of New York
Office of Parks,
Recreation and
Historic Preser-
vation, Olana
State Historic
Site.

visitors to the 1867 Universal Exhibition in Paris, where the Churches first dis-embarked in Europe. Eventually, Church decided that his new dwelling would have stone walls, possess a central court or hall (he admired this feature espe-cially in Lebanese dwellings), and be decorated in the Near Eastern style. Church also concluded that the best architect for his purpose would be one "good at contriving" and "good at effect," talents that he may have come to feel Hunt lacked.[79]

After his return to New York at the end of June 1869, Church engaged Vaux as his architect. No correspondence survives to indicate conclusively why Church abandoned Hunt for Vaux, but surely the fact that Vaux was well-known to a number of Church's friends played a role in the artist's decision. If asked, Olmsted could have given his distant cousin the same praise of Vaux that he had written his father a few years earlier.[80] And if Church had disclosed his intentions to Jervis McEntee while they sketched the Arch of Titus together in Rome in the winter of 1869, McEntee, who also was living abroad at the time, would surely have put a good word in for his beloved brother-in-law.[81] But in addition to having good references, Vaux possessed the same Romantic attachment to natural scenery that inspired the painter's greatest pictures. Vaux's assertion in *Villas and Cottages* that the design of country houses must be "adapted to the location, and not the location to the design" would have struck a sympathetic chord with Church. And having already begun planting and grading to enhance the secluded rural character of his extensive property, Church also would have found congenial with his thinking Vaux's statement that woods, "fields, mountains, and rivers will be more important than the houses that are built among them."[82] By 1869, Vaux had demonstrated his words in Central Park and Prospect Park, places where Church could have observed Vaux's genius for enfolding architecture in nature's bosom, the way a painter might have done. He had shown himself "good at effect." Furthermore, the evidence in *Villas and Cottages* attested to Vaux's ability to "contrive" efficient and original ground plans. And if it is true that Church wished to emulate the homes of fellow artists he had seen in England, he may have felt that Hunt's Second Empire leanings were alien to this fresh affection.[83] What is puzzling, however, given Church's newly acquired preoccupation with Middle Eastern architecture, is that he did not call upon Mould, that supreme Orientalist who in 1866 had designed Malkastan, the residence at Irvington-on-Hudson of painter Albert Bierstadt. Perhaps Church's New England upbringing discouraged contact with so profligate a character as Mould, or maybe Church wished to choose someone who had not worked for a rival to his claim to be America's preeminent landscape painter. But above all, Church determined to be guided chiefly by his own lights in the design of his new home. Olana, as his house came to be called (meaning an ancient fortress treasure house), would be predominantly the master's own creation.

Many tentative ground plans preserved at Olana attest to the evolution of the plan of the house until late May 1870, when Vaux prepared a series of professionally delineated floor plans.[84] It appears that most of the earlier items (none of which, unfortunately, are signed or dated) were by Church. They show how client and architect moved from thinking about the interior in fairly conventional terms to conceiving the cross-axial articulation of space that exists today. And in the process, the position and importance of the staircase, which in earlier schemes occupied a secondary position at one side of the entrance hall, emerged as a major feature of the plan. By May 28, 1870, Church considered the floor plan near enough to his requirements for Vaux to furnish him with a carefully drawn perspective view of the proposed dwelling (Fig. 7.16). Presumably showing the eastern elevation as the entrance facade (the present entrance is on the east), Vaux's proposal included a broad circular terrace in front and a high basement over the sloping ground of the hillside. From the terrace, one entered the house through an arcaded porch set between dissimilar two-story wings. The section to the right—nearly windowless on the ground floor—held a picture gallery that doubled as a dining room and had bedrooms above.[85] To the left of the main doorway, two ground-floor sitting rooms flanked a recessed porch framed by a pointed arch, over which a balcony projected from a second-floor dressing room. Under the arch, another pointed opening pierced the stone walls of the basement to allow a drive—depicted in the drawing lined with boulders—to pass mysteriously beneath the building. The dominating feature of the design, however, was a rectangular tower surmounted by an arcaded balcony and a pointed dome. This dome, and some patterns in the stonework, was the only non-Western reference visible in the design, a fact that may have perturbed Church. Located at the southwest angle of the house, this exotic observatory, together with the veranda beneath it on the west, promised magnificent views. From its height, one might have surveyed the surrounding countryside in all directions. The most engaging prospects, however, were southward down the Hudson and westward across the valley to the Catskills. Rising above the treetops on its hilltop site, the tower, to my mind, bears analogy with Vaux's Belvedere in Central Park. Indeed, the proposed dwelling generally displayed the asymmetrical balance, sturdy stone construction, and round-arched openings that one sees in the unbuilt second structure that Vaux projected for the northwest corner of the Belvedere terrace.[86] Church undoubtedly saw the

Belvedere drawing that Vaux had exhibited at the National Academy of Design the year before Church left on his travels abroad.[87] And one would like to think that his knowledge of that fictive stronghold that so splendidly expressed its lofty site influenced Church to enlist Vaux rather than Hunt as his ally in realizing his aerial dream house.

Yet Church remained hesitant to give his approval to this plan of May 28, 1870. Three weeks later, Vaux sent a revised ground plan that contained elements that advanced the scheme further toward the house that Church eventually constructed. The plan was somewhat larger than the previous scheme and showed a landing at the foot of the staircase toward the court hall.[88] (However, a double fireplace that occupied the location of the doorway leading from the court hall into the boudoir and two columns that screened the entrance to the court hall from the vestibule, as well as certain changes in arrangements in the service wing, did not survive in the final version of the house.) Moreover, artist and architect took pains to locate windows so that the most important rooms took full advantage of the extraordinary visual drama that the elevated site possessed. For ultimately, Olana truly became a belvedere from which the artist might gaze out upon incidents of magnificent Hudson River scenery. "The house will be a curiosity in Architecture," Church confessed, "but it will be convenient and the picture from each window will be really marvellous." In the end, Church determined to lay out his house in a way that combined elements of the May 28 and June 23 plans (Fig. 7.17).[89]

As built, the spaces of the principal floor develop around a cross-axial plan that has as its center the large hall called the court hall (Fig. 7.18). The two axes intersect here and continue to the west and south toward scenic vistas. From the vestibule, one axis runs east and west through the court and library (this room had originally been called the boudoir), where in the west wall, tall French doors extend one's line of vision to the Catskills. (This doorway originally opened onto a veranda; it now gives access to the spacious hall that Church added in 1888 to connect the house to a new studio.) The second axis extends from north to south through the stair hall, court hall, and recessed south porch or "ombra," which, glazed on the court hall side, commands a panoramic view down the Hudson. (This recessed porch, reminiscent of the "ombras" on the rear of the Sheppard Asylum building, took the place of the earlier veranda. It is flanked by two sitting rooms that open onto it.) On its north side, the court hall merges with the stair hall. As the wide flights of steps draw our attention upward to the landing and beyond to the second story, they too contribute to the interior's sense of freedom and openness. The dining room–picture gallery occupies the northeast corner of the building and is centered on another north-south axis that passes through the vestibule and east parlor. And as Vaux had recommended in *Villas and Cottages*, the kitchen, which is connected to the dining room by a passage beneath the stair landing, stands on the north side of the house.

The court hall, defined as a square space by four wide pointed arches (and possibly originally planned with the ceiling opening into the second-floor hall), holds the heart and soul of Olana. The large window on the south side lets occupants of the court contemplate beyond the shadowed foreground of the recessed porch a breathtaking composition of river, mountains, and sky (Fig. 7.19). Enshrined within a Gothic arch, this view is one of the most potent instances of prospect and connectedness in all of nineteenth-century American architecture. It must have been truly an experience of renewal each morning

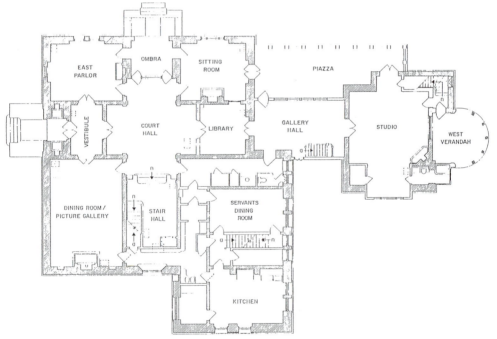

FIGURE 7.16. *(above)* "Study of a House for F. E. Church, Esq.,
at Hudson, N.Y.," 1870. Courtesy of New York Office of Parks,
Recreation and Historic Preservation, Olana State Historic Site.

FIGURE 7.17. *(below)* Olana, plan as built. Courtesy of New York
Office of Parks, Recreation and Historic Preservation, Olana State
Historic Site.

FIGURE 7.18. *(above)* Olana, court hall. Courtesy of New York Office of Parks, Recreation and Historic Preservation, Olana State Historic Site.

FIGURE 7.19. *(at left)* Olana, view from court hall toward the south. Courtesy of New York Office of Parks, Recreation and Historic Preservation, Olana State Historic Site.

for Church to descend the steps into the court hall and face that compelling image of the wide river flowing toward the sea. As it does to modern visitors, it must have seemed to Church that the space of his house was following the river's lead and moving with it. Standing at the south end of the court hall and turning one's back on this memorable vista, one sees another picture. The elaborately carved staircase, elevated from the level of the court by a flight of several steps, becomes the focus of a luxurious composition of carved wood, sumptuous carpets, and exotic bric-a-brac, all bathed in mellow, Old Master light from the yellow-tinted glass of the landing window. Here, then, is an image to pair with the landscape panorama framed by the south porch arch. Taken together, these two "pictures" represent what historian Roger Stein has termed the dual "manifestations of spirituality in the worlds of nature and art" that inspired Olana. Fortunately, the purple-tinted court hall and its magnificent vista, as well as its unique furnishings, survive to stir in us that same sense of long ago and far away that captivated Church. With modest effort, we can imagine the pensive artist sitting here on a quiet autumn afternoon reading Alexander von Humboldt's *Cosmos*, while perhaps on a nearby table a book of Thoreau's essays lies open to the passage, "The deepest thinker is the farthest traveled." In the court hall, the artist achieved perfect union with his romantic vision of art and nature.

For all his genius as a painter, Church, I believe, was not up to orchestrating architectural space and outdoor vistas as finely as they are orchestrated here; this was the enduring contribution of Vaux to Olana. Focusing on the central hall, the interior of Olana, while certainly reflecting the requirements of Church, bears the impress of the compact yet open plans for large houses that one finds in the pages of *Villas and Cottages*. The notion of configuring space, doorways, and openings along axes that intersect in a central hall and extend the visitor's view beyond the interior of the dwelling occurred earlier in the Barreda house. An even closer analogy exists between Olana and the Findlay house in Newburgh (Fig. 2.8). There, the drawing room and dining room on either side of the hall have bay windows at each end. Thus, explained Vaux, when the owner opened the hall doors to these rooms he and his guests enjoyed "an agreeable vista effect" through the width of the house and beyond to the out-of-doors.[90] Lengthwise, the central axis of the Findlay house bisected the library, hall, and a recessed entrance porch, the arched opening of which faced the Hudson. "Thus another extensive vista is obtained in summer evenings through the house in this direction," remarked Vaux, "and when the doors are open, any one sitting in the library bay can see the river view framed, as it were, in the outer arch of the porch." And if Vaux had taken Church to Newburgh to see the Findlay house, he would have pointed out to him, as he did to the readers of *Villas and Cottages*, that "standing in the hall when the rooms are thrown open, one can see clear through the house, north, south, east, and west; and the porch, hall vestibule, library, dining-room, drawing-room, and veranda, are converted, as it were, into one connected apartment." The south porch at Olana, sandwiched between two sitting rooms, also has precedents in Vaux's earlier architecture. Similar suites of three spaces face the sea in the Barreda and Parish houses (Figs. 2.13 and 6.2). And surely in his mind, Vaux compared the staircase and Hudson view at Olana to the Terrace and Ramble view in Central Park and saw the ombra arch as a repeat of the scenery-filled openings of his park underpasses. Thus, in my opinion, Olana is an amalgam of Vaux's consummate ability to devise structures with reference to the surrounding landscape and Church's own transcendent vision of creation and his newly discovered genius for decoration.

The exterior appearance of Olana also underwent modification after Vaux's perspective sketch of May 28, 1870. As constructed, the house sits at grade rather than on a high basement. The tower dome and bifurcated arched windows disappeared, and the tower itself was shifted from the southwest corner to the southeast corner of the house. Here it is grouped with an arched and recessed entrance porch that replaced the original triple-arched entrance. And in place of cut stone for the walls, Church substituted less costly fieldstone and brick. The choice may have been recommended to him by Vaux, who had advised the readers of *Villas and Cottages* that "a very sound and picturesque-looking wall may be constructed by using small, rough stones for the body of the work, and red brick for the angles and window-dressings."[91] Having lamented that it was "uncommon, however, in this country to find a taste suited to this bold, unconventional treatment," Vaux would have been especially pleased with Church's decision. The artist, who had spent several weeks in an architect's office in 1867, took personal charge of developing the decorative details of the elevations. In a series of his own drawings, Church showed how the exterior could be made to embody the Persian style. Having never visited Persia, Church told a friend that he had had to "imagine Persian architecture." Perhaps an even greater challenge for Church was the need to explain his flights of fancy "to a lot of mechanics whose ideal of architecture is wrapped up in felicitous recollections of a successful brick school house or meeting house or jail."[92] Fueled by inspiration from books on architectural ornament and by his memories of travels in Arab lands and Sicily, the artist prepared hundreds of watercolor and pencil sketches for details ranging from tilework around doors and windows to teapot finials on the tower. One wonders, however, if Vaux did not find the bright colors and bold patterns a bit too showy for his taste and if he did not miss the vines that he thought should grow on the rough stone walls.

On July 22, 1872, Church invited Vaux, his wife Mary, and the McEntees to noontime dinner. During the meal, which took place in the house where the Churches lived elsewhere on the Olana property, the talk must surely have turned to the artist's relations with the other reform commissioners of Vaux's new employer, the Department of Public Parks. In the previous November, Church had been named to the park board. Vaux also may have mentioned the recent dissolution of his partnership with Frederick Withers and his contemplated parting with Olmsted.[93] But most of all, the subject of conversation must have been the new house, which, McEntee said, consumed most of Church's time. Later in the day, the party walked over to see the building that stood almost ready to receive its occupants. The great artist had begun constructing Olana in the summer of 1870, and since that time, Vaux had made many trips to the site.[94] Church, however, had personally superintended the progress of the extraordinary dwelling, which he rightly regarded as a work of art. "It is certainly a beautiful house," thought McEntee, "and commands one of the finest views of river and mountain in the country."[95] Perhaps the sensitive McEntee was the first guest to note how the enframed bird's-eye views seemed calculated to call forth a mood of meditation, a phenomenon that one also experiences in the front of the paintings of Church and his Luminist contemporaries. Indeed, like these pictures, Olana itself is the embodiment of what art historian John Wilmerding has called a "construct for reverie."[96] And perchance while looking downriver toward Rondout, where his own modest dwelling stood unfinished for lack of money, McEntee reflected that Olana "looks like an artist's work."

Before the summer ended, Church had moved his family into the building's second floor, where they lived for the next two years while stenciling and carpentry work continued downstairs. (The grand staircase was completed in 1876.) The splendid house truly enthralled Church, and he spent the rest of his life furnishing its colorful rooms with a catholic assortment of objects emblematic of East and West. He could have chosen no one better equipped by imagination, philosophy, and experience than Vaux to manage this wedlock of his sensuous Oriental fantasies with his high-minded belief in the holiness of nature. For his part, Vaux had found the perfect client, an artist of sufficient wealth who could understand his elevated ideas about architecture, art, and nature and with whom he could work sympathetically toward a noble goal.

Perhaps there was even something of a shared worldview that bound Vaux to Church. Church's eclectic display of old and new objects from all over the world alongside his paintings of scenery from South America, the United States, Europe, and the Middle East, taken together, bespeak a universalism with which Vaux would have sympathized. That Vaux shared a comparable point of view can be surmised from the fact that by 1870 he and his wife Mary had attached themselves to the "church for the unchurched" of Octavius Brooks Frothingham. In 1859, after having made a reputation in Jersey City for his radical views and eloquent sermons, the Boston-born Frothingham moved to New York City. At the request of Henry Bellows, he started the Third Congregational Unitarian Society, where, dressed in an elegant silk gown and standing in a pulpit surrounded by flowers, Frothingham preached to a congregation composed of many well-educated New Yorkers. A decade later, Frothingham broke with Bellows and mainstream Unitarianism and formed his own Independent Liberal Church. Here, in the tradition of Theodore Parker, he preached his new "religion of humanity." Each Sunday, while Vaux's ecclesiastical architect partner Frederick Withers worshiped in strict accordance with the revived medieval liturgy of high-church Episcopalianism, Vaux joined the 500 to 600 people who filled Lyric Hall theater on Sixth Avenue at 42nd Street to listen to stirring sermons in which Frothingham quoted non-Christian writings as frequently as he did the Bible. (Even though he admired Gothic architecture, Frothingham repudiated architectural and liturgical display in modern religion.) His voice suggested "Beacon Hill and Harvard College—clear, deep, earnest, but not musical," said a reporter who expressed an admiration that Vaux also must have felt for Frothingham's way of elucidating a theme. He did so without "driving platitudes like nails into the individual conscience and heart" but by drawing examples from "history, literature, philosophy, science, and art."[97] Often these homilies advocated unpopular social reforms, but they always heralded "a day when Science and Religion should work together in the service of man."

We do not know precisely when Vaux became a member of Frothingham's congregation, but one can see why this unusual man would have attracted the idealistic Vaux. By 1869 he and Mary were members of the clergyman's inner circle, a group of people who constituted the Fraternity Club. The club met weekly throughout the 1870s to hear papers read by its members on a variety of subjects. As an early Frothingham biographer states, the Transcendentalist churchman "hoped to make every form of intellectual conviction conduce to the building up of character as well as to the sustaining of a high spiritual faith." Calvert and Mary Vaux's names appear often in the Fraternity Papers, a collection of stories, poems, papers, and illustrations that the group compiled as a record of its activities from 1869 until 1879, when Frothingham resigned his ministry because of failing health. Other Fraternity members included Vaux's educator friend James Herbert Morse; the historian Bayard Taylor; the spirited writer of children's stories Mary Mapes Dodge; the publisher George Haven Putnam; writer Edmund C. Stedman; and poet Christopher Cranch. Jervis McEntee also attended from time to time—he was particularly impressed by a paper that Vaux read on the history of dress. Vaux found these gatherings stimulating and congenial affairs. "But a toy with a turn for reflection," he once said of his cherished club, comparing it brightly to a kaleidoscope.[98]

IN MID-APRIL 1870, Vaux wrote to warn Olmsted, who was in Chicago at the time looking after Riverside and South Park, that matters at Central Park were about to take a bad turn. A new city charter approved earlier in the month by the legislature had put control of the park, as well as all other public greenspaces, under a new Department of Public Parks that was responsible to the mayor, who named its commissioners. (Formerly, the governor had appointed the Central Park commissioners, effectively exempting them from local control.) The new Parks Department board, headed by William Marcy Tweed's right-hand man, Peter B. Sweeny, was to take office on April 20. Referring to the five-member board, which still included Green, Vaux told Olmsted that "this is not a quintette that we should have selected but probably that was not taken into account."[99] Yet he confessed to his partner that he had no reason to feel sentimental about the previous board, calling his friend's "affection for the personnel of the old Commission so suddenly shot in the head" one of Olmsted's "idiosyncrasies."[100] Maybe, Vaux quipped, "it is the office that wins your respect and the new Board will have a sanctity still in your mind's eye." Whatever group of men were in power, Vaux said, it was always up to him and Olmsted to defend the ideals of the park, even if it cost them employment. "I hold that we are the final guardians of this interest as long as we live," asserted Vaux, "and as you know [I] always argued that the commission element must from the nature of the case be a transitory one." Hoping to steel Olmsted for future conflict, he added: "I wish you felt as disposed for active hostilities as I do, but you don't and I am not going to be caught again on the war path alone, so shall follow your lead and resign gracefully if such a course seems called for."

Vaux's expectation "that every one now engaged will be thrown out" proved a bit premature, but rather than hire either one of them for the newly created position of landscape architect, the new board voted to keep both Vaux and Olmsted on in an advisory capacity. This soon revealed itself as nothing more than window dressing, for the board proceeded to ignore the partners' advice. Instead it gave orders directly to Pilat, who was kept on at a much improved salary. Finally, the following December, the board formally relieved Vaux and Olmsted of their titles. In effect, from April 1870 until late November 1871, when Olmsted and Vaux were reinstated as advisers to a new board, the two men were forced to watch from the sidelines as President Sweeny, after making a hasty trip to Europe to inspect parks there, spent lavishly on projects that often did violence to the letter and spirit of the original Greensward plan. (For example, Sweeny relentlessly pursued a policy of clearing away plantings that had been carefully arranged to frame and soften natural and architectural features and even had workers scrape lichen off rocks in the Ramble.) One wonders what Pilat must have thought about all of this, and whether the stress of seeing so much of his earlier effort destroyed might have contributed to his early death in September 1870.[101] Responsible for much of what occurred, however, was another associate of Olmsted and Vaux, Wrey Mould. In May 1870, Sweeny had him named the new Department of Public Parks' architect in chief.

Whatever his friends Vaux, Olmsted, and Green may have thought about the Tweed-dominated board, Mould praised the new body and took to his duties with enthusiasm. Never a member of the Century, Mould may have preferred the company of audacious Tammany men like Sweeny and Henry Hilton and their allies, such as real estate developer William R. Martin, for whom Mould had designed a house on Fifth Avenue, to the circle of earnest genteel thinkers and lovers of arts and letters frequented by Olmsted and Vaux. Mould may also have seen the higher wages that Sweeny instituted for all park workers not as a corrupt waste of public funds for political ends but as enlightened and humane policy that redressed long-standing exploitation, for Mould had felt undervalued for his previous work on the park.[102] In September 1870, Mould wrote to Whitelaw Reid of the *Tribune* to condemn the "repressive un-American policy" of the old board. "I can assure you on my honor," he asserted, "that the question of politics is entirely ignored by our new board," which included Robert Dillon, a longtime enemy of the Greensward plan. Mould also told Reid that with the able assistance of William Grant, an engineer who had worked with Olmsted and Vaux, "more work and of the best kind, has been done every month, in this office since our appointment in May than in any previous year under the old thick-in-the-mind regime; sic transit jerias mundi."[103] Now Mould was enjoying what must have seemed to him the long-denied chance to exercise fully his extraordinary talents as well as to receive appropriate remuneration for his efforts. In a gesture indicative of his expansive mood, he repaid with interest a debt years overdue to his former friend George Templeton Strong, who had "forgotten that the tender tie of debtor and creditor bound us to each other."[104]

Chief among the projects Mould supervised were the completion of Vaux's Dairy and Belvedere and the construction of Mould's own designs for the Sheepfold (the present Tavern on the Green restaurant). In addition, he drew plans for a conservatory (begun but never finished on the site of the present Conservatory Water),[105] the offices of administration (a stable, repair shop, and keeper's dwelling adjacent to the 79th Street transverse road near Vista Rock), a lovely "ladies cottage," and a zoological garden. Mould also took charge of renovating the Arsenal museum and paving the surface of the lower Terrace. Now visitors would no longer trail gravel across the beautiful Minton tiles that he had designed for the area behind the arcade.[106]

DURING THE PERIOD of the Sweeny board, while Olmsted and Vaux were cut off from the work at Central Park, progress at Prospect Park in Brooklyn continued smoothly. In 1870, the partners formulated their plans for the Concert Grove. This was the area of the park that they had dedicated to providing large numbers of people with the summertime pleasure of outdoor music (Fig.

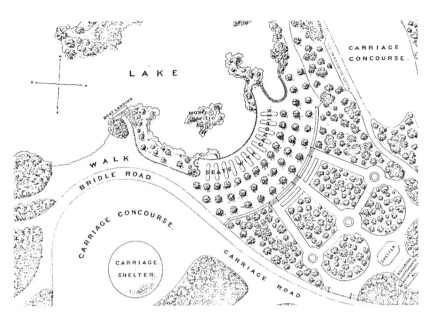

FIGURE 7.20.
Prospect Park,
"Design for the
Arrangement
of the Pedestrian
Concourse,"
1870. From
Brooklyn Park
Commission,
*Eleventh Annual
Report* (1871).
Private
collection.

7.20).[107] Accommodating both pedestrians and carriage riders, their plan focused on the bandstand situated on a small island in the lake. On the nearby mainland, Olmsted and Vaux planned a large concourse where visitors in carriages and on horseback might stop to hear the concert. The pedestrian area was adjacent to this concourse. Reasoning that the music of "a proper promenade band does not require close attention," Olmsted and Vaux designed this commodious space as much for strolling as for listening. It was common in Europe, they observed, "for at least the central part of the audience to rest during the performance of each piece, and for the greater part of it to stroll or drive off, and return between the pieces." With perambulating auditors in mind, Olmsted and Vaux laid out the Concert Grove according to a symmetrical plan: its axes radiated from the center point of the island music pavilion. On the shore about 100 feet from the island, they formed an esplanade consisting, at lakeside, of a fan of seats covered by awnings. Behind the seats, less attentive listeners could stroll beneath the shade of three rows of equidistant plane trees arranged in a radiating pattern. The slightly elevated area to the rear of the esplanade was planted as a grove "pierced by three alleys on the lines of vistas opening toward the music island." Terminating the central axis of this grove, an "open pavilion, with tables and seats," would accommodate many visitors. Nearby, a less conspicuous building, to be known as the Concert Grove House, would provide refreshments and lavatory facilities. The partners designed the whole area in the expectation that "the larger part of the audience . . . will be moving during the interval of the music, and will stand among the planes, or continue walking in the alleys of the upper grove during its performance." In addition, people in small boats could moor them in front of the esplanade during concerts, when the "music will float across the lake."

Construction of the Concert Grove area began in 1871 and was substantially complete three years later. Yet at one point during the work, Olmsted had to reassure an anxious Stranahan that the audacious plan would be a success. "The Court Grove," he advised his friend, "with its masonry and fuss will seem an anomaly and great waste of capital until the boats crowd the water in its front and the music pavilion is built." In its unfinished state, Olmsted admitted that it was "more like a richly furnished room without a fire place or chairs."[108] In addition to stone walls ornamented with beautiful carved designs drawn by Wisedell and emblematic of music, the area received several structures by Vaux. Chief among them was the graceful Concert Grove Pavilion (at the right in Fig. 7.21).[109] Its 40' × 80' curved roof, hovering on eight slender iron columns, provided sheltered, open-air seating space for a large number of visitors. Perhaps the writings of Viollet-le-Duc in praise of modern materials had persuaded Vaux to use iron columns in this bold way, for the striking roof possessed an almost magical air of suspension. Bearing ornamental patterns designed by Wisedell, its light-hearted mood suited perfectly "the pervading gayety of a great company coming together simply for pleasure." Behind the Concert Grove Pavilion stood the now demolished Concert Grove House (at the left in Fig. 7.21), a wooden building that Vaux designed in 1871.[110] Its gridwork of wood braces and boarding and elaborately framed entrance porch suggest contemporary European park buildings more than did the structures in Central Park, and its style may have been a souvenir of Vaux's 1868 trip. For equestrian concertgoers, Vaux specified a freestanding canopy to shelter horses at the carriage concourse (dating probably from 1871; Fig. 7.22). Disappointed by Olmsted's continuing reservations about the whole idea of erecting such a fanciful structure, Vaux tried to persuade his partner to relax his "confoundly ill-timed opposition" to it. "We want a sensation," exclaimed Vaux.[111] If this $30,000 progeny of engineering and whimsy had been erected (the commissioners seemed to have shared Olmsted's skepticism), it would have provided Prospect

FIGURE 7.21.
Prospect Park,
Concert Grove
House (*left*) and
Concert Grove
Pavilion (*right*),
1870. Courtesy
of Prints and
Photographs
Division, Library
of Congress.

Park with an even more remarkable structure than the Concert Grove Pavilion. Spreading outward from an axial base, wood and iron beams supported an immense circular roof that seemed to hover above the ground and central water troughs like a spinning child's top. If he saw the drawing, spendthrift Mould must have smiled.

When the construction of a new pedestrian path to the Concert Grove area necessitated a fifth arch in the park, Vaux took the occasion to experiment with a new industrial material. To permit visitors to reach the concert ground and lake along a gentle incline, Olmsted and Vaux proposed cutting a gap in Breeze Hill, a low ridge that blocked direct access to the area from the main entrance.[112] The Cleftridge Span, erected in 1871–1872, allowed pedestrians easy passage through the hill while it carried the drive out of sight over their heads (Fig. 7.23). It also came at a point in the landscape where, at some times of the year, Olmsted told Stranahan, the view toward the head of the Lullwater was "one of the most superb and refined park scenes I ever saw."[113] Hence, the partners aligned the tunnel of the new arch so as to enframe this view. But once Vaux had designed the Cleftridge Span, he set aside his plans for building it of granite and brick and decided to employ the recently patented stonelike concrete called Beton Coignet. This material, which had been invented in France and brought to America in the late 1860s, rivaled stone in hardness. Poured into wooden molds, the fine-grained mixture could be formed into blocks of any shape and impressed with remarkably detailed ornament. It could even be colored a variety of shades. The material especially pleased Vaux because with it he could inexpensively face the interior of the tunnel with patterned blocks. Cut stone in this situation would have been prohibitively costly. Working with the assistance of Bassett Jones, who developed the working drawings for the shapes and patterns of the blocks used in the arch ("The object to be reached," said Vaux, "was to reduce the number of moulds or separate castings to a mini-

FIGURE 7.22. Prospect Park, design for the Carriage Concourse Shelter, c. 1871. From Brooklyn Park Commission, *Thirteenth Annual Report* (1873).

mum"), Vaux created a tapestry of embossed blocks using only three molds. If the new material lived up to its reputation for strength and durability, Vaux proclaimed, it would provide architects with a valuable new decorative resource.[114]

Vaux doubtless intended to use the advanced concrete for the tower that he and Olmsted proposed to erect on Lookout Hill. Conceived in the picturesque spirit of William Burgess's 1866 competition entry for the London Law Courts, the cruciform tower rose from a base level in a series of banded piers that expanded into a massive, arched cornice. The crowning feature of this extraordinary design (working drawings were prepared by Bassett Jones) was to have been a lacy canopy of wood or iron. And when the young trees on Lookout Hill reached maturity, Olmsted and Vaux believed that the monumental structure— the most dramatic design for an observatory of Vaux's career—would not be "unduly prominent" in the landscape. From the open treetop balcony, visitors would have enjoyed a panorama superior to that seen from the reservoir walls. Vaux's design for the tower first appeared in the park report for 1870; but four years later he illustrated it in a subsequent report with its surface resplendent with ornament (Fig. 7.24).[115] Although Vaux did not mention the material that he intended to use in the second proposal, he knew that such an abundance of decoration would have been impossibly expensive in either stone or brick. Pleased with the success of Cleftridge Span, Vaux obviously wished to investigate more fully the decorative potential of Beton Coignet. Yet neither the tower nor the nearby refectory, which the partners conceived of as together adding "much to the accommodation of visitors and the comfort with which the scenery of the Park would be enjoyed," was ever erected.

FIGURE 7.24.
Prospect Park,
design for a tower
on Lookout Hill,
1874. From Brooklyn
Park Commission,
*Fourteenth Annual
Report* (1874).
Private collection.

THE TWEED RING's power over Central Park was relatively short-lived. By the
end of the summer of 1871, Sweeny, Dillon, and Hilton were gone from the park
board, their places taken by men who were sympathetic to the Greensward ideals. Among the new commissioners were Frederic Church and Henry Stebbins,
who assumed the presidency.[116] At the end of November 1871, Olmsted and
Vaux officially received joint appointments as landscape architect and general
superintendent of the Department of Public Parks. Yet even though he
undoubtedly thought badly of Mould, as well as Julius Munckwitz, who had
served as Mould's assistant, for accepting a position with those whom he considered the enemies of the park, Vaux kept his high standards for the battlefield
of public opinion. Vaux must have found the ebullient Mould, a free spirit who
devoted far more of his time to music, art, and yachting than to advancing himself in business, a man hard to stay angry with for long. Despite their differences,
Mould, Vaux, and Olmsted remained on good terms after the fall of Sweeny.
Mould remained on the payroll, assisting Vaux (until Vaux resigned in June 1873)
as if nothing had ever happened.

Olmsted and Vaux immediately set about to modify or undo much of the transgressions that Mould had committed.[117] Even though he had finished the Dairy "in accordance with the plans of those who conceived it," he had transformed it into a general restaurant. Mould had also redesigned the area around the Dairy to make the building easily accessible to large numbers of visitors. This work disregarded the lovely secluded character of this part of the park and its special purpose as a place for mothers and their young children. Mould and his associates, said Olmsted and Vaux, had demonstrated "a willing ignorance of the real elements of value in all the work of the neighborhood, and a blind disdain of the study which had been given to the harmonious and equitable adjustment of its several motives."[118] They set about to correct the matter. Much the same had happened at the Spring House. Mould had constructed a road directly to the building so that the carriage class could go there without leaving their vehicles. Thus, an element of "individual interest" gained its way at the expense of the "public interest," and as a result of the board's decision, the sale of waters ceased at other locations in the park. To Vaux, the lesson was clear: "Individual interest is a sleepless, while public interest is a sleeping force," he observed.[119] As for the Belvedere, the portion that Mould had completed (and which stands today) had followed Vaux's drawings. In an effort, however, "to eliminate from the plan every item of extravagance that could be avoided consistent with the then condition of the building," Mould had determined to forgo construction of the second structure at the northwest corner of the Belvedere terrace. In its place, Mould substituted a large, gaily colored canopy. "This conspicuous wooden structure . . . will be removed," announced the *Times* in November 1872. From the Terrace, this "gaudily painted contrivance" attracted more attention than the Belvedere's stone tower, which Olmsted and Vaux had intended as the subtle focal point of the view. Furthermore, the heavy canopy shook so much in the wind that the wall beneath it was already in need of rebuilding.[120]

Fortunately for posterity, Olmsted and Vaux did not call for the removal of the building called the Sheepfold. Erected on the west side of the park near the 68th Street transverse road, it served as nighttime quarters for 200 sheep that pastured on the nearby meadow. The principal structure that Mould designed in the park, it is his best surviving work. Even Olmsted and Vaux must have admired it. Yet they could not resist launching criticism at this intrusion into their landscape. After enumerating the flamboyant building's "high pitched, slate roof, decorated with turrets and gilded iron work," and its walls "of pressed brick, with trimmings of cut blue stone and polished granite," they dryly observed that "its general aspect suggests a large English parochial school." And in the view of Olmsted, Vaux, and many others, the $70,000 structure served a nearly nonexistent purpose. Moreover, Vaux surely must have suspected that it existed at the expense of his second Belvedere tower, which the wily Mould had suggested that the commissioners delete because of its estimated $50,000 price tag.

In any event, what offended Olmsted and Vaux most about the Sheepfold was its inappropriateness to its place in the park landscape. Designed in a way to call attention to itself, it occupied elevated ground at the end of the meadow just where, in the Greensward plan, the visitor's view in that direction from the Mall was to have "become dim under large trees" that screened the park boundary. Furthermore, in order for pedestrians to reach the building—where in either wing they were to have been edified by portraits of sheep and samples of wool—they were forced to traverse the bridle path at a point where a galloping rider might not see them until it was too late to slow his mount. A much safer and less conspicuous location could have been found nearby for this building, noted Olmsted and Vaux.

But the most flagrant violation of the Greensward plan resulted from the Sweeny board's decision to transfer the zoo from the Manhattan Square site to the park itself. As part of his work at the Arsenal, Mould took charge of erecting behind the building a menagerie for the display of several species of animals. This attraction proved popular with the public, and even Olmsted praised Mould's buildings as "the best of the class on the continent."[121] Yet the board's intention to erect a large deer paddock on the North Meadow in the upper park infuriated Vaux and Olmsted. In December 1870, the partners had gone public with their protest against the board's decision. To the *Times*, they sent copies of the letter they addressed to Sweeny, together with his curt reply and a defense of their position. All of this, the paper saw fit to print.[122] When Vaux and Olmsted regained their position of influence with the subsequent board, construction of Mould's design for a paddock in a "series of small yards, of walks between them, and of lines of trees following these walks" was well advanced. By the fall of 1872, workmen had removed this work and stockpiled the materials for future use. Vaux and Olmsted did not object to zoos because, as historians Rosenzweig and Blackmar have suggested, they threatened "bourgeois (and primarily adult) decorum and order" in the park.[123] In fact, as we have seen, they had prepared a design for a zoo in Manhattan Square that, if built, would have housed the largest animal display in the country. But by 1870, Olmsted and Vaux had professed the notion of providing discrete spaces in cities for various forms of recreation. This was an essential feature of their Buffalo park system. In New York, their proposal that the zoo be housed in Manhattan Square conformed with this thinking. Their plan would have preserved the park for passive recreation and would also have given the public a far superior attraction than the compromise scheme adopted by the Sweeny board.

During this period, Vaux also took charge of a number of new architectural projects for Central Park. Among them were the beautiful new Merchant's Gate at the Eighth Avenue entrance to the park (the present Columbus Circle entrance) and three new bridges called for by modifications to the path and drive system in the southeast area of the park.[124] Inscope Arch, construction of which began in the spring of 1873, carries the east drive over a pedestrian path at a point that had been a particular nuisance to walkers and riders alike.[125] The banded Florentine arch and the expensive pink and gray granite materials reflect Vaux and Mould's thinking about their contemporary design for the American Museum of Natural History building, which featured like arches and materials.[126] Nearby stood the now demolished Outset Arch, a lovely cast iron span bridging the bridle path near the Arsenal. Its attenuated segmental arch seemed all the more slender because of delicate floral ornament in the spandrels and a lacy iron railing across the top.[127]

The most important park structure from this time was the boathouse that became necessary due to the remarkable popularity of boating on the lake (Fig. 7.25). Wanting an inconspicuous location for this structure, Olmsted and Vaux placed it on the lake's eastern shore, where it did not figure prominently in the view one had from the Terrace. (Before the boathouse was erected,

passengers embarked from the end of the Terrace.) Designed by Vaux in 1873 but not completed until at least two years later, the long wooden boathouse, which rivaled Buffalo's Parade House in its ornamented structure and surfaces, provided covered space for docking and storing boats. Vaux said that he deliberately designed the building on "a liberal scale" to forestall any future commissioners from taking the excuse of its inadequacy to place a boat dock at the foot of the Terrace. Any such structure would both interfere with the view toward the Ramble and mar the prospect of the Terrace from the Ramble.[128] Vaux's boathouse, likewise, conformed to his desire to preserve for nonboaters the pleasure of viewing the lake. Vaux explained that he arranged the roof "in the form of a terrace, with two flights of steps to it, so that the ordinary visitor, on arriving at this structure, instead of being shut out from a close view of the Lake, is provided with an elevated promenade, from which a view of the water can be obtained, with a special charm of its own." From this raised vantage point, visitors might stand either in the open air or beneath the shelter of two canopies to watch activities on the water. The building (now demolished) was yet another example of the comprehensive approach Vaux took to designing park structures.

In their positions with the new Department of Public Parks, Vaux and Olmsted also acquired responsibility for all other public greenspaces. In the fall of 1872, the *Times* reported that the department was busy implementing improvements in Union, Madison, and Washington Squares.[129] The most important of these projects was the modification of Union Square according to plans that Olmsted and Vaux prepared in July 1872. They concentrated their attention on the north side of the square, where they enlarged the cross street by reducing the northern boundary of the park. This area became a place for public events involving as many as 20,000 people. A Swiss-style cottage designed by Vaux and Mould on the edge of the square served as a comfort station for women and children who might also enjoy its pleasant, vine-covered veranda in summer and a heated waiting room in winter. On the rear of this charming pavilion, a rostrum overlooked the street. Here speakers could address the assembled crowds at public meetings and dignitaries could review passing troops during holiday parades. Surviving drawings for the delicately ornate wooden cottage (now demolished) suggest the predominance of Mould's hand in the design.[130] Another small city park that Olmsted and Vaux worked on was the design for Mt. Morris Square. Their plans for this area, which extended from 120th to 124th Street between Fifth and Madison Avenues, date from October 23, 1872. The rectangular square included some rocky outcroppings that Vaux and Olmsted preserved within an elaborate network of winding pedestrian paths. Surviving drawings indicate how the partners intended to integrate an existing iron fire watchtower that had stood on the site since 1856, but they fail to reveal exactly where in the square they intended to reerect Mould's wooden canopy from the Belvedere terrace. However, virtually nothing from the time of Olmsted and Vaux (other than the fire tower) survived the drastic rebuilding of the park (the present Marcus Garvey Park) that the city carried out in the 1960s.[131]

WHILE VAUX ALWAYS remained opposed to erecting large zoological buildings within Central Park, he would have acknowledged that the Sweeny board's decision to abandon Manhattan Square as the site for the zoo had been directly related to the progress of the American Museum of Natural History and the Metropolitan Museum of Art. Johnston, the art museum president, and his board had been quietly but effectively raising money for the new institution among New York's wealthiest citizens. In March 1871, the officers reported their success in a pamphlet addressed to the general public.[132] The board of the American Museum of Natural History, on which Green also served, had likewise been working to good purpose since its formation in 1867. Beginning in that year, a committee of financiers advised by scientist Albert Bickmore had begun to promote the creation of the American Museum along the same lines followed by the founders of the Metropolitan Museum of Art. Armed with a petition signed by men prominent in business and real estate, representatives of the boards of both the natural history and art museums paid a call on William Tweed and Peter Sweeny, hoping to forge an alliance between the city and the two educational institutions. "Please inform these gentlemen that we are the servants of the people," Sweeny is reputed to have said, adding: "This is just in our line, in line with our ideas of progress in New York City." By early April 1871, the state legislature had given its blessing to an enlightened agreement whereby the Central Park commissioners would undertake to construct a building or buildings in Manhattan Square for the two institutions (the organizations' boards jointly proposed this site); in return, the directors were responsible for amassing and administering the collections, which would remain their property. When the commissioners eventually returned the art museum to the site originally proposed for it at Fifth Avenue and 82nd Street, they gave Manhattan Square entirely to the American Museum. (The decision on location was strongly influenced by West Side developers who had donated the land for Manhattan Square to the city with the understanding that it would be improved as a park. When plans for the zoo on the site were aired, adjacent property owners had raised loud objections, not wishing to endure the sounds and smells of wild animals outside their windows.)

I cannot help but think that shrewd Green, who served as a Central Park commissioner as well as a member of the boards of the Metropolitan Museum of Art and the American Museum, had manipulated this entire scenario, for in the end, the two admirable institutions that he had envisioned in 1857 were brought into being exactly along the lines he had proposed. Green had talked about establishing educational institutions in the city long before John Jay, John Taylor Johnston, or the other public-spirited men of wealth who served on the Metropolitan and American Museum boards had come to the cause. In 1865, Olmsted and Vaux themselves, in their Prospect Park report, had questioned why "the City, without absolutely assuming the whole expense and the whole control of undertakings for this end, may not wisely offer some encouragement to associations voluntarily formed by citizens for the purpose."[133] By 1868, Green had championed a law under which the city would erect and maintain museums within Central Park that private boards of leading citizens would administer. Behind the scenes, could not Green have advised his fellow board members when and how to approach Tweed and Sweeny, men whom he despised but who he knew would take the bait dangled in front of them by such influential and well-heeled petitioners? In the post-Tweed era, when Green assumed the role of city comptroller and crusaded long and hard to right abuses of the Ring, he never sought to overturn the agreements that Tweed influence had forged between the two institutions and the municipal government. Furthermore, one senses Green's hand in the reform park board's refusal to go along with the suggestion of the art museum board that a competition be held for the design of their new building. Having two years before directed Vaux and Mould to devise plans for a gallery building, Green and his fellow commissioners politely vetoed the idea and insisted on constructing Vaux and Mould's design.[134] Budgetary considerations aside, those many "quiet hours" that Green had spent in the company of Vaux and Mould at their drawing boards must have made him feel a deep personal attachment to that 1869 plan, which may even have incorporated some of his own suggestions. During the early 1870s, Vaux worked closely with the Metropolitan's executive committee to perfect the plan, which in its essentials remained true to Vaux and Mould's 1869 scheme.

THE DAY THAT VAUX signed the plans for Mt. Morris Square, he resigned his $6,000 per year position as landscape architect and superintendent with the Department of Public Parks. Only a few days before, on October 18, 1872, he and Olmsted had agreed to dissolve their partnership of seven years. Vaux continued to work for the next several months as consulting landscape architect to the department, but more and more he must have come to see that his time would be taken up with major new architectural projects. As for Olmsted, he was becoming impatient at being tied to Vaux and Withers, men whose careers as architects offered them opportunities for commissions in which Olmsted could not share. He was also feeling the stress of overwork. To Samuel Bowles, Olmsted complained as early as June 1871 of his desire to escape from the pressure of so much labor, of finding "some way of living in the country and escaping this drive."[135] Yet he felt that this was impossible because of ties of "sentiment and obligation" to Vaux and because of his lack of courage "to dispense with Vaux's cooperation." Differences had also developed between the two men. "Mr. Vaux's ways are not my ways and I could not fit mine to his," he later confessed to A. J. Bloor.[136] And even though he never severed his friendship with Vaux, by the fall of 1872 Olmsted realized that it was best that they separate. It was "a relief to me to part company with him," he told Bloor.

From several of Vaux's letters to Olmsted during this period one can surmise what Olmsted meant when he talked of the two men having different ways of doing things. Writing to Olmsted in Chicago, Vaux chided him for not being firm enough in his dealings with the local park board, of letting himself be drawn into unrealistic agreements. "I do not see that we can wisely encourage the Commissioners in the idea that they can make a great single demonstration with the sum they propose to expend," he advised Olmsted about negotiations over South Park. Rather, he hoped to hear of "a sure beginning, cautious and not too full of attractive promises. . . . It is not really advantageous to them and certainly it is not for us, that they should get you to Chicago for the purpose of inventing cheap processes gratis."[137] And concerning Riverside, Vaux had told Olmsted at one point, "I do not think we argue to the same ends and a business cannot be properly managed except on some one theory of beginning, middle and end."[138] For Vaux, the business side of their fledgling profession was a serious matter, one that, it seems, he felt Olmsted took too casually at times. The discussion Vaux had in April 1871 with his friend James Morse reveals the nature of his attitude. Vaux thought that men of letters "would be better if they kept themselves in pretty close relation with the busiest business life—that their literature would be healthier."[139]

Nonetheless, Vaux and Olmsted's divergent views on how business should be conducted never impeded the design work they did together, and neither of them ever lost respect or friendship for the other. In the months immediately after the dissolution of the partnership, the two men continued to work together on New York's Riverside and Morningside Parks, the initial plans for which they presented to the board in 1873. On several later occasions, too, they joined forces on important projects. I agree with the view of the late Dennis Francis that Vaux terminated the partnership in the belief that architecture rather than landscape architecture would be his source of future success. By 1872, Vaux had received the commissions to design the American Museum of Natural History, a building touted as the largest structure yet to be erected in America, and the Metropolitan Museum of Art. Initial portions of both of these immense buildings were being staked out on the ground in August 1872.

Vaux also must have recognized that the faith he had had in Olmsted's abilities had been well-founded. By 1872, Olmsted had become recognized as a man of genius in park design. Vaux knew that his partner could now count on a brilliant future in their new profession. But as Olmsted's national reputation grew, he began to feel less and less at home in New York City. Before the 1870s were over, Olmsted had accustomed himself to life in suburban Boston (where he spent his summers). Eventually, in 1881, he moved permanently to Brookline, where his home and office assumed the central position in the American park movement. Vaux, however, never contemplated leaving New York.

ALWAYS LIGHT-ARMED, CHEERFUL, AND READY FOR A RUN TO THE NEAREST SUMMIT

1873–1880

After June 4, 1873, when Vaux resigned his position as consulting landscape architect to the Department of Public Parks, he had no official association with New York's parks until the following decade. Olmsted, however, served as the landscape architect from 1873 until January 1878, when the department abolished his position, and Mould retained his post until May 1875. With the dissolution of Olmsted, Vaux & Company, Olmsted moved his office from 110 Broadway to a room in his house at 209 West 46th Street, where he tended to his personal clients. Vaux must have been touched to see his own picture, together with those of Ruskin and other notables, on Olmsted's office mantelpiece. When Vaux and others came to visit, they were often greeted by the sight of their workaholic friend tending to business in this downstairs room. Only later would he abandon his desk for conversation upstairs in the living room. Vaux retained his office at the old address until 1877, when he moved to 71 Broadway, and later, in 1884, to Bible House on Astor Place. Wisedell continued to assist both men, helping Olmsted especially with the design of ornamental walls around the grounds of the U.S. Capitol. And throughout the 1870s and 1880s, Vaux relied on the services of George K. Radford, the able engineer with whom he and Olmsted had worked on many projects.[1]

Not long after they had ended their formal partnership, Olmsted and Vaux collaborated once again on the design of two new pleasure grounds for New York City. Morningside and Riverside Parks were planned for sites in the northern portion of Manhattan Island, an area that would soon become a desirable residential quarter. Riverside Park, a long strip of land overlooking the Hudson River between 72nd and 129th Streets, was first proposed as the site for a park in 1865 by park commissioner William R. Martin, a land speculator who promoted residential development of the city's Upper West Side. In 1872, the city completed the acquisition of land for the park and Riverside Drive, the avenue that would define its eastern edge. At the time, the board authorized Vaux, then the department's landscape architect, to outline a plan for the area.

It seems, however, that Vaux submitted nothing to the board before October of that year, when he became consulting landscape architect and Olmsted assumed the position of landscape architect. Then, and apparently with Vaux's assistance, Olmsted composed a preliminary report that he presented to the board at the end of March 1873.[2] For the next several years, Olmsted refined this plan and worked toward its realization on the ground.

In July 1870, the Tweed-dominated park board, which had jurisdiction, through legislation passed in 1866, for laying out the entire northern area of Manhattan Island, instructed engineer William Kellogg to make a topographic map of the site then designated as Morningside Park. A 31-acre eastward-facing hillside, Morningside Park is bounded by Ninth Avenue on the east, Tenth Avenue on the west, 110th Street on the south, and 125th Street on the north. Although Kellogg finished his survey of the rocky landscape in the fall of 1871, the city did nothing more until after the reform board took office in the following May. At that time, Martin urged his fellow commissioners to press forward with a plan for the park. In September 1873, when Olmsted finally received definitive direction to prepare a plan for Morningside Park, he turned to Vaux for help. They filed their preliminary plan with the park board in the following October.[3] From Olmsted and Vaux's introductory remarks, one gathers that neither of them was pleased that the city fathers had selected the site mainly because they recognized that the steep ledge here made the land difficult to adapt to a grid of new streets. This traditional street system, despite Olmsted and Vaux's suggestions for a more thoughtful plan, was being extended over the northern part of the island. Having planned a modern, city-wide recreational system for Buffalo, Olmsted and Vaux now more than ever realized how seriously deficient New York City was "in many provisions which unquestionably will soon be urged upon it by advancing civilization."[4] New York, they pointed out, had no athletic fields, no truly grand promenade, no adequate marketplaces, no suitable settings for civic ceremonies, no places for exhibitions or fireworks displays, and no proper zoological or botanical gardens. "Unfortunately," they observed, "Morningside Park adds but another public ground chosen without the slightest reference to any of these special requirements of the city, and happens to be singularly incapable of being adapted to them."

Resigned to developing the limited potential of the site as best they could, Olmsted and Vaux drafted a plan that advocated the creation of a number of enjoyable features within the boot-shaped space. Special consideration went into exploiting the views to be obtained from the elevated western side. Here, along the uppermost portion of the 30-foot-wide tree-lined pedestrian mall that was to surround the entire park, Olmsted and Vaux planned semicircular balconies where strollers could stop to enjoy the fine prospect that extended over Harlem to the East River and Long Island Sound. In the southeast corner of the grounds, which the topography protected from western winds, the designers suggested that either "tamer tropical animals" be allowed to roam freely or that a garden of subtropical flora be planted. Along the base of the cliff running from the level of 116th to 120th Streets, the architects envisioned a walk that would "present a greater continuity of picturesque rocky border than an equal distance of walk on any other park possessed by the city." Other proposals included the construction of a 500-foot-long upper esplanade where a low structure might be erected and the formation of an Alpine garden in the rocky terrain in the northwest area of the site. Finally, the dramatic rise and fall of surface called for retaining walls and staircases, all of which, said Olmsted and Vaux, should be suitably decorated to accentuate, by contrast, the naturally rugged character of the site. At the time, the board took no action to construct the park, but Olmsted and Vaux's 1873 draft laid the basis for the future development of Morningside Park.

THE AMERICAN MUSEUM of Natural History had been brought into being in 1869 by the same act that Tweed had ushered through the state legislature to establish the Metropolitan Museum of Art. Green had also played a key role in its formation. As a member of both the natural history museum's executive committee (created in May 1869) and the parks department board, he occupied a powerful position from which to further his goal of creating "an establishment that shall afford opportunity for popular instruction and amusement, and for the advancement of the Natural Sciences." At first, the institution's collection consisted of stuffed animals that the trustees had purchased in France and Germany. These they set on display in the Arsenal building in Central Park, which Mould had fitted up for the purpose in 1871. However, in 1870 the legislature had already authorized $500,000 for the construction of a new permanent building. Like the art museum, it would be owned by the city and managed by the institution's trustees. With the parks department board's decision in March 1872 to locate the art museum on the east side of the park, the American Museum became the sole tenant of Manhattan Square.[5] During the summer of 1872, Olmsted and Vaux made plans for the improvement of the area in anticipation of the construction of a large building there. They also proposed modifying the 79th Street transverse road to have it exit Central Park at 81st Street. This diversion of the former line of the cross-park route apparently resulted from the shrewd foresight of Albert Bickmore, the museum's first director, who wanted "to prevent anyone from ever making the suggestion that our square should be cut in two by an easterly extension of Seventy-ninth street."[6]

With the site question settled, the trustees turned immediately to the matter of a new building. Meeting at the 20th Street home of board member Theodore Roosevelt, the group voted to request Richard Morris Hunt, Russell Sturgis, and the firm of James Renwick Jr. and Joseph Sands to submit plans for the proposed museum. By May 16, these plans were in the hands of a special committee that was charged with selecting "the best ideas in each" for presentation to park department representatives at a meeting on May 28. We do not know which ideas contained in the architects' plans pleased the committee, and the plans themselves have not survived, but apparently none of them engaged the interest of the park board. A terse entry in the trustees' minutes for May 28 simply records that the board decided to accept "the plan presented by Mr. Vaux and to proceed with construction of its initial section." I suspect that the park board felt that as the representative of the city it had sole responsibility for the new building; it did not wish to see the museum trustees overstep their authority in the public-private contract that had been crafted to create the institution. In any event, if there were any hard feelings on the part of the trustees over the dismissal of the architects' plans, they had evaporated by the following November 11, when they seconded the park board's approval of Vaux and Mould's plans for the initial wing of the museum.

The choice of Vaux as the museum's architect enraged the editors of the *Sunday Mercury*, the mouthpiece of Tammany Hall Democrats. Since the fall of William Tweed, the *Mercury* had focused its venom on Andrew Green. The paper characterized Green as a mean-spirited hypocrite bent on enriching himself from the public treasury, which as comptroller and a park commissioner he claimed to defend against corruption. According to the *Mercury*, Vaux and Olmsted were in the pocket of Green, who saw to it that they received lucrative treatment from the city. In return for his favors, the weekly intimated, Green asked for kickbacks from the two men. Over the next few years, Vaux in particular would be reviled by the paper for a variety of reasons, all linked to Green.

The *Mercury*'s opening salvo against Vaux came in January 1873, when the paper published the minutes of a park commissioners' meeting that had taken place the previous September.[7] On that day, commissioners Church, Green, and Olmsted (who while still the department's landscape architect had filled in for Henry Stebbins while Stebbins was abroad) voted to have Vaux receive 2.5 percent for his preliminary studies and for all future working drawings for both the natural history and the art museum buildings. At Green's insistence, Vaux's commission would be paid out as the work progressed over the next several years. "Now let it be remembered," said the *Mercury*, "that at the time this resolution was passed Olmsted and Vaux were partners," an accusation that was technically true, for the men had not as yet formally dissolved their firm. Vaux, the department's consulting landscape architect, and Olmsted, the proxy board member, the editorial charged, had made a "raid on the Treasury" by placing themselves in a position to split $25,000 (2.5 percent of the projected $1 million cost of construction for both buildings). The paper pointed out that the 1870 city charter prohibited municipal employees from having "any interest in any contract for work done on behalf of the city." Calling Olmsted a "veritable old coon who was interested in the job" and Green an old man "with duplicity in his heart and a constructive lie on his lips," the *Mercury* charged that nothing "more outrageous than the barefaced and shameless act embodied in these official minutes has ever been perpetuated on the tax-payers of this city." The paper's animosity toward Green stemmed from his position as Tilden's zealous lieutenant in the reform Democrats' victory over the Ring. As comptroller, Green had refused to pay the claims of many workers and suppliers of goods and services contracted for by the previous administration. Nonetheless, according to the *Mercury*, he had endorsed raising the city debt to pay for grand projects in the park like the two new museums. In its attack on Olmsted and Vaux over the commission, however, the paper failed to realize that Olmsted would not be receiving any of the timed payments because he had already seen the end of his partnership with Vaux. Moreover, from his fee, Vaux would have to pay Mould, Radford, and other assistants. Nonetheless, the allegation of impropriety must have disturbed Vaux. It may have been the reason why six months later he abruptly resigned even his consulting position with the park department and did not seek to rejoin public service until after 1880, when he finished his work for the Metropolitan Museum of Art.

Vaux and Mould's ground plan for the monumental American Museum of Natural History comprised a vast rectangle 850 feet long (along the Eighth and Ninth Avenue sides) by 650 feet wide (along the 79th and 81st Street sides) and covered nearly all of Manhattan Square's 15 acres (Fig. 8.1). Each of four interior sections were defined by wings in the form of a Greek cross. The entire complex held 12 exhibition halls, each approximately 200 feet long and five stories high. A central octagonal rotunda dominated the vast building, with eight lofty towers punctuating the intersections of the other wings. Entrances in the middle of the Eighth and Ninth Avenue facades admitted pedestrians, while visitors arriving by carriage proceeded to 79th or 81st Street, where curved drives conducted them from the street to portals beneath grand staircases.

According to Bickmore, the plan for the museum evolved under his direction. "Cordially invited" by Vaux and Mould to meet with them, he showed the architects a plan that he had been pondering for several years. Resembling the United States Capitol, Bickmore's ideal museum consisted of a rotunda joining two 60-foot-wide, double-story wings. Open galleries surrounded the tall interior space of each of the two floors, which contained an office for a curator as well as a staircase at one end. Certain elements of Bickmore's scheme appear in Vaux and Mould's plan; however, the architects increased the number of floors to five and arranged only the main exhibition halls of each wing with a mezzanine level. But more than from Bickmore's advice and the British Museum, which Bickmore said had influenced his scheme, Vaux and Mould's plan derived from French example. As early as 1778, Jean-François Delannoy had won the Prix de Rome at the Academie d'Architecture in Paris with a plan for a natural history museum that employed a series of wings arranged as a Greek cross within a square. Delannoy also included a central rotunda and smaller rotundas at the intersections of the exhibition units. The influential architectural theorist

FIGURE 8.1. American Museum of Natural History, plan. From *American Architect and Building News* 1 (August 12, 1876). Courtesy of Buffalo and Erie County Public Library.

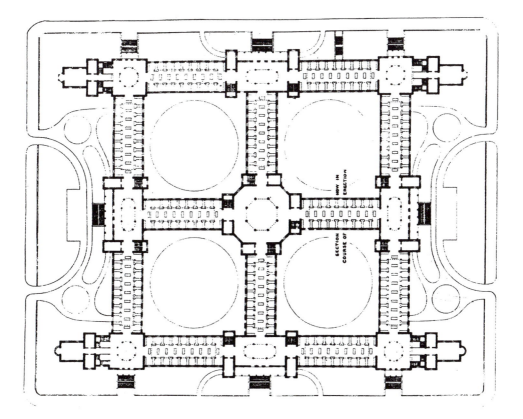

Jean-Nicolas-Louis Durand had developed a similar plan for a grand museum. As Durand had published his scheme in his *Précis des leçons* of 1809, it would have been more readily accessible to Vaux and Mould than Delannoy's exercise. And like the grandiose schemes of the visionary Neoclassicists of the previous era, Vaux and Mould's design looked more to the future than to the present. All concerned with its creation regarded the immense structure, which the designers proudly estimated to exceed by three times the size of the British Museum, as a project for the ages. "The museum as planned," remarked the *New York Times*, "is intended for America when the population of the United States shall be 400,000,000, instead of 40,000,000, as it is now."[8]

From the beginning, the city intended to erect the building in stages. Early in August 1872, the park board approved Vaux and Mould's preliminary plans for the first section, for which the state legislature had appropriated $500,000.[9] This initial wing comprised the southern arm of the central Greek cross unit and included the stair tower block that would abut the future octagonal rotunda. (This wing now stands amid later additions by other architects.) The board chose to erect this portion of the building near the center of the property, said Bickmore, to "show from the first that our future edifice was ultimately to occupy the entire area" of Manhattan Square. Unfortunately, this wise decision added considerable cost to construction because a rock ledge here had to be cut down to prepare the building's foundations. Ground-breaking ceremonies for this 200' × 60' exhibition unit took place early in 1873, and in June 1874, President Grant came to New York to lay the cornerstone. By that time, Vaux and Mould had finished all of the working drawings, but it would take three years for the wing to be completed.

Vaux and Mould's freestanding wing presented an imposing if truncated appearance to early museum goers (Fig. 8.2). Tall arcades of banded pointed arches dominated the identical east and west elevations and distinguished the two chief exhibition levels. Smaller banded arches in three large dormers animated the roofline and emphasized the symmetry of the design. Early drawings reveal that the walls of the main floors were to have been faced with rusticated panels of reddish granite trimmed with a light-colored, smoothly finished stone that also formed the basement course. Concern over the high cost of leveling the site, however, led the board in the early summer of 1873 to rescind its earlier approval of these costly materials and to ask the architects to substitute red brick for the rusticated granite. In July 1873, one year after the board had approved the first plans, Vaux went before the commissioners again to assure them that the modified design could be built for the sum appropriated. Because in the future this section of the museum would face an inner court rather than the street, the decision to use brick instead of stone must have seemed to Vaux unessential to the success of the building. Yet for the general public of the so-called Gilded Age, the plainness of his edifice became the subject of derision. Moreover, the widespread if ill-informed negative reception that the new museum building received eventually had serious consequences for Vaux. Responding to criticism of the building's factory-like appearance, a later board denied Vaux the opportunity to design additional portions of the museum.

The question of materials aside, an observant viewer can still see how the original interior arrangements were reflected in Vaux and Mould's elevations. Above the ground story, the two-level principal floor stands out clearly between stringcourses; the upper stringcourse serves as the base for the arches of the

fourth floor. The 40-foot-tall principal floor is composed of a 25-foot lower section—lit by tall rectangular windows divided by a central colonnette—and a 15-foot gallery space above. Light entered this area through square windows set into stone panels directly above the columned openings.

Indeed, the chief feature of the elevations is the number of windows they contain. Vaux regarded natural light as essential to the success of the exhibition spaces. At each level below the attic story, the large windows lighted glass display cases that stood between them. In addition to these normal windows, on the second and fourth levels Vaux introduced small, slit-like openings that admitted light through ground glass directly into the backs of the cases. Louis Pope Gratacap, scientist and writer, singled out Vaux's idea as a simple and clever way to eliminate the inevitable shadow that formed at the wall end of the cases.[10]

Construction of the initial wing of the American Museum proceeded at a slow pace, and the building opened to the public only at the end of 1877. By the middle of December, Bickmore had installed most of the collections in the new structure. On December 17, he must have been deeply impressed to see the building "lighted from top to bottom for the first time." It was a brilliant spectacle that enthralled residents as far away as New Jersey. A few days later, Rutherford B. Hayes came from Washington to dedicate the building. It was Hayes's first visit to New York since he had questionably gained the presidency over Samuel Tilden, who declined to attend the ceremonies.

Hayes and his party were the first to view the interior of the museum. In order to make the building fireproof, Vaux and Mould had supported each floor on cast iron columns and metal beams, between which sprung arches formed of concrete blocks. As a further precaution, the architects made the floors of cement and covered them with Minton tiles rather than wood. In addition to

FIGURE 8.2. American Museum of Natural History, original wing. Courtesy of American Museum of Natural History.

fire protection, the method of construction provided a great deal of open space, which, together with the many windows, made for bright and airy interiors. (Unfortunately, no documentation survives concerning the color scheme.) Between the mammal exhibition on the first floor and the fossil and geology cases on the fourth floor, the two-level main floor contained a popular exhibit of birds, with anthropology displays arranged in the surrounding galleries (Fig. 8.3). (The attic floor held work rooms and offices.) Each exhibition space consisted of rows of glass cases ranged on either side of a central aisle. The iron and plate glass cases themselves, remarked Gratacap, were of an unusual, T-shaped design, with the wider end placed along the center aisle and the narrow end positioned against the wall. This design, which Gratacop credited to Vaux but others gave to Radford, afforded better viewing conditions than straight-sided display cases. They also had the esthetic advantage of imparting a roomlike effect to the alcoves between them and of creating an impressive vista down the central corridor. Bickmore took advantage of the cases' expanded terminations to feature larger curiosities.

Far from the late-twentieth-century concept of the natural history museum, Vaux and Mould's original wing of the American Museum laid before its visitors an edifying display of objects that reflected nineteenth-century scholars' faith in the compartmentalization of knowledge. Speaking for his age, Gratacap, who had arranged the paleontology and mineralogy exhibits, thought the proportions of this first section of the American Museum were "almost ideal," and he recommended it as a model for other institutions to follow. The building, he said, "might make a museum unit, and every museum be a juxtaposition of such units, or a multiple combination of them." To Gratacap's well-ordered Victorian mind, the long, narrow plan and repetitive elevations represented the

FIGURE 8.3. American Museum of Natural History, main floor. Courtesy of American Museum of Natural History.

perfect way to house collections of objects. All such structures, he reasoned, must be "essentially rectangular," for the "box" was the "ultimate museum cell element." Viewed in this way, the "building, the cases, the trays, the labels— one dimension reduced to zero—are boxes, and their multitudinous sizes and ornamentation and positions do not conceal the uniform and necessary form underlying all." Thus, what appeared factory-like to some represented efficiency and logic to professionals like Gratacap.

WHILE WORK PROCEEDED ON the American Museum, Vaux kept his eye on the preparations for the international exhibition to be held in Philadelphia in 1876 to celebrate the 100th anniversary of the American Revolution. In March 1871, President Grant signed a bill creating the Centennial Commission, a body of distinguished citizens chosen to oversee the management of the great event. Congress, however, declined to appropriate any funds for the exhibition. Instead, it created a separate board of finance with authority to issue shares of stock in the venture. When the members of the board were appointed in April 1873, most of them turned out to be businessmen from Philadelphia. Indeed, the city and the state of Pennsylvania adopted the exhibition as their own and together pledged significant sums of money to insure its success. On July 4, 1873, the city donated a portion of Fairmont Park for the exhibition grounds. "So far, this grand project has, to some extent at least, appeared local," noted Governor John F. Hartranft on that occasion, "but henceforth it will be purely national. If a failure, it will be a national failure. If a success, a national success."[11]

Already on April 1, 1873, the Committee on Plans and Architecture, chaired by Alfred T. Goshorn, a Cincinnati businessman who was also director-general of the Centennial Commission, had issued the terms of a nationwide competition to choose the design for the main building. Vaux read the prospectus in New York and decided to compete. Having created the extensive plans for the Metropolitan Museum of Art and the American Museum of Natural History— as well as having prepared with Downing a design for the 1853 New York exhibition—Vaux stood ready to tackle the design of a monumental exhibition hall. With the assistance of Radford to help with technical matters, Vaux spent much of his time during the next three months preparing his entry. By the July 15 deadline, he had ready handsome perspective drawings that together with a written description and a cardboard model he sent to Philadelphia under the name Pavilion plan (Fig. 8.4).

Vaux's plan called for a vast covered space under a single roof. Over 1,500 feet long by nearly 700 feet wide, the hall enclosed 20 acres under arched iron trusses that formed a series of 21 cruciform spaces or pavilions. Pointed arches 150 feet wide defined these areas, which were spanned by round transverse arches. Each square unit of these great pointed and round arches rose from polygonal footings that themselves defined smaller enclosed spaces that Vaux designated as garden courts. Despite its mammoth size, the constructive system was economical to build because each self-sufficient pavilion could be raised with the same scaffolding. All together, the 21 pavilions sheltered a continuous space that Vaux divided at ground level into six concentric zones or "departments" for the display of the myriad products of the world's leading manufacturers. (This system of arrangement, which allowed the visitor to locate any item easily and to compare it with like items made in various countries, had

FIGURE 8.4.
Competition
model for
main building,
Centennial
Exhibition,
Philadelphia,
1873. Courtesy
of Pennsylvania
Historical
Society.

been devised by William Phipps Blake, a geologist at Yale University.) One of the chief advantages of Vaux's entry, wrote Clarence Cook before the jurors had made their decision, was that internally its 120-foot-tall arches treated visitors to views of the exhibition in several directions. For whether "we look across the building or up and down its length or diagonally," stated Cook (probably with Vaux's prompting), there "is always stretching before us an attractive vista, saved from wearisome monotony by its wide openings on either hand."[12] Galleries around the sides of the vast enclosure also provided vantage points from which visitors could survey the exhibition. To demonstrate to the jurors the mighty extent of this space, Vaux had Wisedell translate the prose of his proposal into a spectacular perspective drawing (Fig. 8.5). The lofty interior depicted there counted as one of the most breathtaking constructions envisioned by a nineteenth-century architect.

To many observers, even before the committee announced its decision, Vaux and Radford's scheme stood out as the most original design among the 43 entries. Seconding Cook's opinion of its superiority, the *Times* published a long description of the Pavilion plan on its front page. Only this entry, the paper declared, satisfactorily met the demands of the competition.[13] Surely, the *Times* said, most people who took the time to review the renderings on display in Philadelphia knew the identity of its authors. By championing the Pavilion plan, the New York press sought to warn the jurors that this was a national, not a local competition. Fearing that the commissioners would be unduly influenced to choose a Philadelphia architect, Cook admonished in the *Tribune* that if the celebration of the 100th anniversary of the Republic was to be truly representative of the country at large, then "the nation has an interest in the Temple, as a matter of architectural taste and beauty, in which it is to be held."[14] Unfortunately, observed Cook, the city of Philadelphia had rarely erected a building of note in the nearly 200 years of its existence: "The unesthetic spirit of the Founder and his sect," he noted, referring to William Penn and the Quakers, "still rests upon their city." One of the city's few good buildings, Latrobe's Bank of Pennsylvania, had been "sacrificed by a discreditable sale to the Federal Government" and foolishly demolished. "Certainly neither Vitruvius, nor Palladio, nor Sir Christopher, nor even Inigo has yet made his appearance in the City of

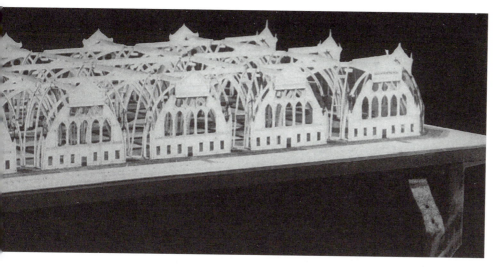

Penn," quipped Cook, who reasoned: "Are we wrong then in asking the administrators of this great trust, even the Philadelphians, to rise above the local influence?" Let not the magnificent exhibition site on the banks of the beautiful Schuylkill, pleaded Cook, "be disfigured by some quadrangular monstrosity." One of those who read the papers and shared the New York press's opinion was Jervis McEntee, who confided to his diary that he was "all anxiety; but I feel most hopeful for Vaux's success."[15]

On the afternoon of August 8, 1873, when the committee announced its decision on the 10 finalists who would be allowed to compete among themselves in a second competition, Vaux was one of them.[16] The fact, however, that seven of the other competitors came from Philadelphia only served to fuel the flames of discontent in New York. "I happened to see all the designs on exhibition," said Alexander F. Oakey, an architect who for a while had a partnership with Bloor, "and thought the display of talent so poor that there were only eight designs that deserved any consideration, and in this opinion I am supported by many professional gentlemen who have studied the question." An anonymous correspondent to the *Times* blamed the committee for handling the entire competition badly; he said that few architects of standing even bothered to submit. Moreover, of the 43 entries, at least 30 "were either lead pencil sketches or drawings of novices without any merit whatever"; in his opinion, not even five were worthy of a premium.[17] Oakey spoke for many when he said that Vaux's plan was clearly the best one and that "the managers of the Centennial Exhibition cannot expect much sympathy from other cities, if they are determined to conduct their affairs solely for the benefit of Philadelphians without regard to justice."

The 10 finalists had until September 30 to submit their revised schemes. The committee gave each architect photographs and written descriptions of the 10 selected designs to help him improve his second submission. This time, competitors were also instructed to provide an estimated cost of construction and to show how their building would link up with a special railroad being constructed to bring visitors to the grounds. They also had to agree to have working drawings ready by October 1 so that construction could begin in November, a deadline that proved overly optimistic.

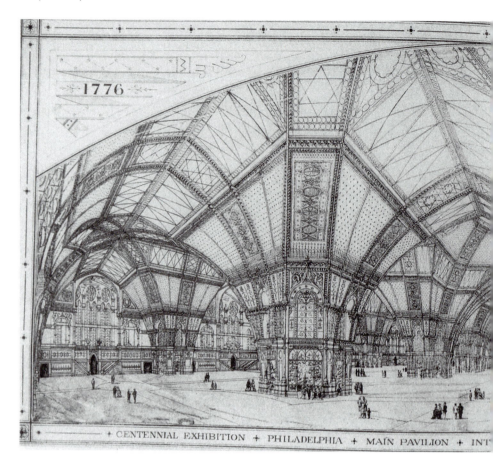

On October 25, while the committee debated the issue of choosing a winner of the competition, the *Times* showed its readers Vaux's revised entry (Fig. 8.6). The ground plan remained fundamentally the same as in the first proposal, with the addition of an arcaded promenade ringing the entire building at ground level. The greatest change had taken place in the external appearance of the building. It seems that Vaux had taken to heart the remarks of one critic who had noted that while his first scheme was "designed to show the lines of construction and not to hide them" and that it nobly depended on "size and proportion for effect," to some it might appear "tame and without relief."[18] After seeing the designs of the other nine semifinalists, most of which were highly symmetrical compositions with domes and towers, Vaux undertook to ensure that his design would not suffer by comparison in the judges' eyes. Abandoning the clean lines and simple repetitive arched shapes of his first elevations, Vaux added grandiose features. Monumental triumphal archlike pavilions marked the larger of the 20 entrances, triple-tiered Gothic screens with circular windows of plate tracery beneath steep roofs (curved and double-level over corner pavilions) replaced the simple gable ends of the smaller pavilions, and bold lettering over each pavilion proclaimed the international exhibitors. The most striking additions, however, were five domed towers, the central of which was the largest. Their daggerlike spires transformed the onetime simple horizontal roofline into an elaborate and picturesque skyline. Pulling out all the stops, Vaux revised his

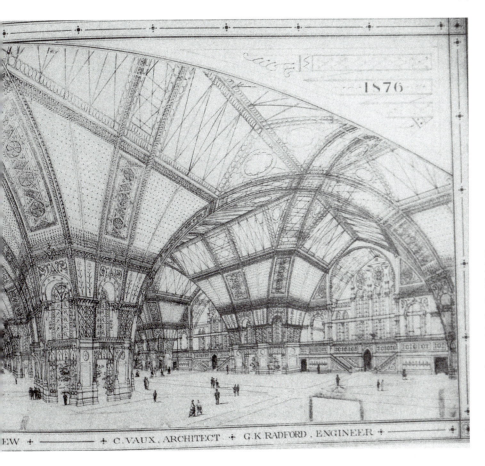

FIGURE 8.5.
Design for main
building, Cen-
tennial Exhibi-
tion, interior.
From *New York
Sketchbook of
Architecture* 1
(September
1874). Courtesy
of Buffalo and
Erie County
Public Library.

straightforward, no-frills elevations upward into the realm of grand opera. Gaug-
ing the taste of the jurors from the example of their finalist choices, Vaux must
have calculated that such changes as these would favorably impress the committee members. These nonprofessional men had already been instructed by the
press on the merits of his plan; they were now counting on a hefty appropriation from Congress to help fund construction of the main building.

Vaux stated that in developing his design, he had taken into account recent
developments in exhibition building design in Europe. Specifically, he had
looked at the structures erected for expositions in Paris in 1867 and in Vienna
in 1873. The Paris hall had been regarded as an improvement over the 1851
London Crystal Palace because its elliptical shape had allowed the exhibits to be
grouped in concentric zones. This system, Vaux acknowledged, afforded visitors
the possibility of "a consecutive examination, in each department, of the results
produced by different nationalities."[19] Yet critics had complained of the
monotony of the Paris building, as well as its lack of architectural distinction.
"No special emphasis was possible anywhere," said Vaux (who may have had
occasion to see the building while he was in Paris in 1868), "so that the impressions of the visitor in regard to position were easily confused, and the inter-
minable circular line prevented vista effects of any greater length than about
one-third of the short diameter." By contrast, the Vienna building returned to
the nave and transepts arrangement pioneered by Paxton's Crystal Palace, but

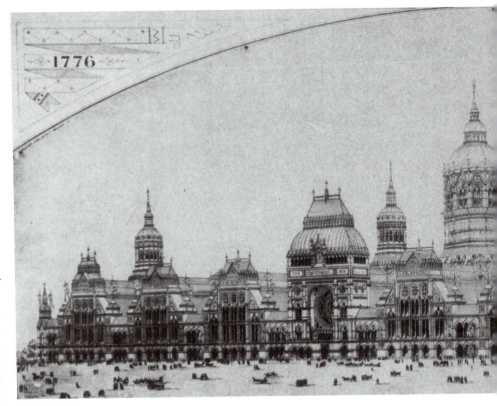

with a 300-foot-wide central rotunda that created a grand impression. It also had several open courts. Among the advantages of this system, acknowledged Vaux, was that it provided for much better side lighting of the interior than did the elliptical shape. Clearly, Vaux saw his design for Philadelphia as incorporating the best features of the Paris and Vienna structures. From French example, he took the zone arrangement, adapting it to a rectangular ground plan rather than the less practical circular plan; from Vienna he borrowed the idea of interior courts, which in his design became "essential features in reference to the light and air of the building, and the discharge of water from the roof." But in Vaux's scheme a rotunda would have been gratuitous, for his aim was to make the interior of the building itself a breathtaking space. "The various parts of the building are thus included in one grand whole," Vaux proudly asserted, "and the result becomes a spacious hall . . . with long vistas, central and intermediate points of emphasis, direct lines of transit throughout its length and breadth, diagonal lines of communication where really needed, and an entire relief from any appearance of contraction anywhere, for the visitor is always in an apartment over 200 feet wide, that opens without any intermediate corridor into the other apartments, also over 200 feet wide." His words less perfectly conveyed his intention than did Wisedell's vivid drawing of the all-embracing space.

When Goshorn announced the final recommendation of the Committee on Plans and Architecture in early November, he made it clear that the process had been a troubling one. Instead of awarding the $10,000 prize to a single competitor, as the committee had stated it would do in its prospectus, the jurors decided to divide the money unevenly among four Philadelphia firms. Yet in

announcing its decision, the committee cautioned that it was issuing the awards because it believed that these architects had best complied with the original terms of the competition. But because none of them fully met the new requirements, the committee did not feel itself bound to recommend any of the designs for adoption.[20] Instead, the committee gave its approval to Vaux and Radford's plan, which had ignored the stipulation that an art gallery and a memorial hall be included in the main building. Since it had published the terms of the competition, the committee had changed its mind about the exhibition's architecture. By October 1873, its members had become convinced of the need to combine the art gallery and memorial building into a separate structure. Furthermore, they now recognized the wisdom of choosing a design that, if necessary, could be easily extended. Seeing Vaux and Radford's solution as fully commensurate with these new ideas, the committee voted to recommend it, without a premium, to the Centennial Commission for adoption.

Yet when the executive committee of the commission met the next day, it balked at ratifying the recommendation of Goshorn and his colleagues. Instead, wrote McEntee, they gave "the whole thing into the hands of a Philadelphia firm, alleging that Vaux's [plan] was too costly and could not be built in time."[21] The executive committee asked Collins and Autenreith (the building committee's choice for the first-prize award) to come up with a new plan and appointed a former mayor of Philadelphia and a governor of Pennsylvania to take part in the deliberations. A short time later, however, the executive committee retreated from this decision and adopted Vaux and Radford's plan. Triumphant, Vaux conveyed the news to McEntee that he had the centennial building "to build, superintend and make contracts for, but involving grave responsibilities."[22] The change of heart may have come as a result of the commissioners' renewed hope that they could convince Congress to fund the exhibition. Pleased with their success, Vaux and Radford happily signed their contract with the board of finance and began working in earnest on their plans.

But the story did not end there, for eventually Philadelphia triumphed over New York. During the winter of 1873–1874, the commission lobbied hard in Washington for its cause. Vaux himself seems to have joined the effort to secure a $3 million appropriation, for on March 15 McEntee noted that his brother-in-law had departed for Washington "on Centennial business." Vaux also wrote to Whitelaw Reid to ask that the *Tribune* publish a letter that William P. Blake, the world-traveled scientist, had drafted outlining the tangible and intangible benefits that the nation would derive from a successful exposition. "The international comparative element is vital in any attempt to show our progress," Vaux declared to Reid. And especially in light of the "inadequate representation" of the nation's industry that private interests had assembled at the recent Vienna Exhibition, "a success at home," said Vaux, "would justify the trouble and cost of it." Condemning the shortsightedness of such men as Senator Charles Sumner of Massachusetts, who opposed any federal involvement in the Centennial Exhibition, Vaux reasoned that "there is an ascending scale in lines of responsibility: the individual, the corporation, the city, the state, the U.S., and this is a U.S. matter." It all reminded him of the early days of the debate over Central Park, when, Vaux noted, "the same kind of criticism I meet with now was very flourishing."[23] Yet with the country locked in a deep depression following the Black Friday financial crash of May 9, 1873, the House was in no mood to spend such money. The appropriation bill went down to defeat, largely at the hands of western congressmen.

With the hope for federal revenue gone, the board of finance asked Vaux to modify his grand design, estimated at $2,871,500. But while Vaux and Radford were at work on scaling back their scheme, they learned troubling news. The board had asked Henry Pettit, a young engineer associated with the Pennsylvania Railroad who had visited the Vienna Exhibition in the service of the commission, to prepare an alternate design. Pettit developed a plan that Vaux said combined "the distinguishing features of our pavilion plan, and the cheapest form of shed construction."[24] In June 1874, Vaux and Radford submitted plans and specifications to the board for two buildings, each of which they estimated would cost no more than $100,000 per acre to erect. One of these designs preserved the main features of their innovative pavilion plan, while the other "was for a building in iron, of twenty acres, composed of three parallel sheds, with curved roofs of 150 feet span, connected by covered spaces of 50 feet wide, with open courts." This more simple design, Vaux maintained, represented "the minimum as a building which we considered it advisable for the commission to erect." The board accepted both of Vaux and Radford's plans but decided that together with them it also would send Pettit's design out for bid. From Philadelphia builder R. J. Dobbins, the board received an estimate for Pettit's building of $59,777 per acre, while several other contractors projected a cost of slightly over $58,000 per acre to construct Vaux's second plan. In a remarkable turn of events, the board endorsed Dobbins's bid and Pettit's plan and instructed Vaux and Radford that their contractual obligations compelled them to prepare working drawings for it as well as to superintend its construction! "We naturally objected to this," said Vaux, "and remonstrated against being placed in such a position." But short of taking legal action, which Vaux and Radford were wont to do, they had no recourse. Adding insult to injury was the fact that the New Yorkers had prepared detailed specifications for both of their designs, while Pettit had submitted none. In his winning bid, Dobbins had said nothing about how he would construct the building; he had not even specified the amount of iron he intended to use. Nonetheless, Vaux and Radford reluctantly accepted the distasteful situation. Expecting to be allowed "to exercise the rights and power of architects as to constructive and aesthetical details," they perhaps hoped to impress something of their own ideas on the final design of the mammoth structure.

Having gotten Dobbins to promise the board in writing that he would employ as much iron as was necessary to erect safely the main building, Vaux and Radford set about in the summer of 1874 to make working drawings for Pettit's plan. In the process, they attempted one more time to resurrect their honor by asserting their role as designers. "During the preparation of these [drawings]," said Vaux, "we found that we could modify the plan in such a manner as to produce a building which should be reasonably satisfactory to ourselves, and not more expensive for Mr. Dobbins to construct." For a moment, it appeared that the partners might succeed. According to Vaux, the new design pleased Director-General Goshorn, as well as "all who had any voice in the matter." Dobbins, however, despite his earlier written commitment, "when informed of the amount of iron that would be required, declined to accede to the change." In this showdown between out-of-town architects and a respected local builder, the board of finance sided with Dobbins. It declined to add any money to its contract with the builder and refused, in Vaux's words, to allow him and Radford "to make such changes in constructive or aesthetical details as we should consider necessary." Thus, Vaux maintained, the board had provoked an impasse. As a result, he and Radford "were prevented from carrying out our contract and at a later date we were notified that it was annulled." The main building went up under Pettit's supervision, with the assistance of Joseph M. Wilson, another Pennsylvania Railroad engineer. Vaux had little to show for one of the most promising commissions of his career.

At the beginning of 1875, a lengthy description of the main building (the foundations of which had recently been laid) appeared in the *Times* and reinforced the sense of injustice that Vaux felt over the way he and Radford had been treated.[25] Learning from the paper that Pettit was using over 7 million pounds of iron in his structure, that its final cost was nearly $1.5 million, and that Dobbins had actually carried out "alterations of constructive details, such as foundations, etc.," that he and Radford had suggested, Vaux felt compelled to lay his case before the public. In a long letter to the *Times*, Vaux recounted the history of the affair and asserted that "the annulling of our agreement on economical grounds" was not "justified by the facts." Vaux staunchly maintained that if in June 1874 the board had accepted one of the bids from a "first-class" builder for his and Radford's second design, "the commission would have obtained a building which, in our judgment, would have been better adapted for the purpose of the Exhibition than the one now being erected, and at a less cost." Indeed, when it was completed in December 1875, Pettit's main building attracted little attention as a piece of architecture. Some observers noted, however, that in its nave, aisle, and central transept plan it bore a general resemblance to the 1851 Crystal Palace. One would be glad to know what Vaux's thoughts were as he and Jervis McEntee toured the exhibition shortly after it opened in May 1876. We can be certain, however, that he would have been both dismayed and amused to read in James McCabe's popular *Illustrated History of the Centennial Exhibition* that the roof trusses of the main building "were similar in form to those in general use for depots and warehouses, and consisted of straight rafters with struts and tie bars."

DURING THE OPTIMISTIC early stages of the Philadelphia competition, Vaux received a request to prepare a plan for the grounds in front of the new Canadian government buildings in Ottawa. On June 6, 1873, Thomas S. Scott, chief architect of the Department of Public Works, called on Vaux in New York to discuss the project, which involved uniting Thomas S. Fuller's Parliament Building with two new departmental buildings going up on lower ground to either side. Scott may have sought out Vaux at the suggestion of Frederick Temple, Earl of Dufferin, whom Queen Victoria had recently appointed Governor General, the representative of British authority in Canada. Lord Dufferin and his accomplished wife were determined to raise the level of civilization in the New World. Immediately upon their arrival in Canada, they launched a round of elegant balls, festive dinners, and stirring concerts. Perhaps it was Lord Dufferin's first visit to Ottawa to address Parliament on March 5, 1873, that aroused his concern for the shabby physical appearance of the government grounds. Local citizens would surely have told him of their efforts to have something done, and they may even have shown him Canadian sculptor Marshall Wood's plan to fill the area with fountains, walks, urns, and statuary. We probably will never learn whether the sight of Wood's unsophisticated proposal prompted Lord Dufferin to politely suggest to Hector Langevin, the minister of public works, that he seek the advice of the British-born codesigner of Central Park. Yet we do know that the governor general took an interest in the project, for at least once he conferred with Prime Minister Sir John MacDonald and Langevin about it.

When Scott visited Vaux in his office in New York, the Canadian architect was warmly received. While the two men talked, Vaux even drew a rough plan of what he thought should be done at Ottawa. Generous with his time and knowledge, Vaux proceeded to spend most of the next two days guiding Scott around Central Park and Prospect Park, all the while explaining the nature of his ideas for the Parliament Building grounds. Scott returned to Canada with Vaux's promise to send him a developed drawing in the near future. For his preliminary study, Vaux requested a payment of $500. If engaged to carry it forward, he expected to receive 1 percent on the cost of the work. He also told Scott that he would like to visit Ottawa to inspect the site, for which he would ask another $500. On June 20, Vaux sent Scott his promised plan, and three days later he forwarded two tracings for modifications of the design. By July 2, Scott had the approval of the minister of public works to carry forward Vaux's plan (Fig. 8.7). Yet the following May, the minister abruptly informed Vaux that he had laid aside his design in favor of Wood's 1872 scheme. Thanking the New Yorker for his help, the minister enclosed a draft for the $500 fee that Vaux had asked for his preliminary study. In his letter of acknowledgment, Vaux indicated that he bore no hard feelings. Surely with the Philadelphia dealings in mind, Vaux acknowledged that such projects often took unexpected changes of direction.

Nonetheless, he added politely that "if the decision should be reversed at some future time and my design should be adopted, the original understanding with Mr. Scott would I trust be carried out."[26]

In trying to knit together into a unified group the picturesque Parliament Building and the two similar but smaller governmental buildings that flanked the open space in front of it, Vaux faced a number of difficulties. The major obstacle to overcome was the difference in level between the elevated position of the Parliament Building and the lower departmental buildings. Rather than try to mask this fact of topography, as Wood had attempted to do, Vaux exploited it. "As the Parliament House stands at a conspicuously higher level than the Departmental Buildings," he said, "it seems very desirable to make the whole arrangement of the ground seem to grow out of this controlling and somewhat peculiar circumstance."[27] Vaux must have realized that in following this course, he could make the spirited skyline of Fuller's High Victorian Gothic building capture the attention of approaching visitors, the majority of whom entered the grounds from the lower street. Across the front of the Parliament Building, Vaux suggested running a terrace that would come forward in the center to ease carriage access to the main entrance, located in the base of the tower. Vehicles reached this area along approach drives that entered the grounds at the street and passed up to the Parliament Building in front of each of the departmental buildings. At either end of the eight-foot-high terrace wall, Vaux introduced projecting bays and steps so that, he said, "the appearance of steepness may be still further increased." Here, too, he placed lofty flagstaffs to frame one's general view of the Parliament Building. Indeed, the treatment of these "salient angles," said Vaux, held the key to "the successful solution of the problem." Also important was a flight of steps positioned in the center of the terrace retaining walls. This broad staircase descended to a large circular fountain standing in the middle of the sloping lawn. From the fountain, two diagonal paths extended to gates near the carriage entrances, and a wide central walk continued straight ahead to the street. Vaux calculated that all of these elements would direct the attention of visitors approaching either on foot or in vehicles toward the tower in the

FIGURE 8.7.
Parliament
Square, Ottawa,
1873. Courtesy
of John Stewart.

center of the Parliament Building. In this way, Vaux united the three picturesque buildings and the sloping ground between them into a harmonious and dramatic architectural composition.

Vaux felt confident of the general effectiveness of his simple, symmetrical scheme. Yet because he had not visited the site, he advised Scott to test his assumptions by staking out the design on the ground with cords before letting any contracts for the work. As for the fine points of the design, Vaux relied on Scott's having absorbed enough valuable information on their tour of New York's parks to develop them properly. Vaux must have lingered a long time with Scott at the Terrace in Central Park, for elements of his Ottawa plan echo that great formal design. Coordination of one's movement along central and flanking ways, the gracious sweep of space from the upper terrace—from which one got a comprehensive view of the entire area—to the lower lawn, the placement of flagstaffs at the edge of the composition, and the location of the fountain basin at the base of the central flight of steps all look back to the Central Park example.

Despite the minister of public works's statement to Vaux that he had rejected his plan, in the summer of 1874 the government instructed Scott to proceed with laying out the grounds according to the American's scheme. This work proceeded under the supervision of Scott, who made the designs for the terrace walls, staircases, and other architectural elements that Vaux had indicated on his plan. By the end of 1878, when construction had been completed, Vaux became aware that without his knowledge or assistance Scott had landscaped the grounds following the outlines of his design. Angered by this shabby treatment, Vaux published a pamphlet recounting the history of his involvement with and exclusion from the momentous project.[28] He also applied to the Canadian government for redress. Acknowledging the justice of his claim, in 1882 and 1883 the Dominion paid Vaux additional compensation. Looking back over the 10-year history of this humiliating episode in his career as a landscape architect, Vaux must have reflected on how his fate stood in sharp contrast to the success and recognition that Olmsted had obtained during the same period for his design of the grounds of the United States Capitol.

THE SUMMER OF 1873 was for Vaux a busy and promising time. For together with preparing the Centennial competition entry and advising on the Ottawa grounds, he became involved with the efforts of Andrew Green and others to erect a new courthouse and prison in New York City. Late in August, after Vaux had cut all ties with the parks department, he was named architect to the newly formed City Prison Commission. The commission included Samuel Vance, president of the board of aldermen, and William Havermeyer, the recently elected Democratic mayor. Havermeyer, a wealthy businessman who helped found the New York City Council of Reform, had been instrumental in ousting the Tweed Ring from power. Vowing to rebuild city and county government after the depredations of the Ring, Havermeyer initially focused public attention on the unfinished county courthouse. That "sink of political corruption" was commonly known as the Tweed Courthouse. One of his early actions as mayor had been to call in Vaux to prepare an estimate of how much it would cost the city to complete the infamous building without the expensive dome that its architect, John Kellum, had originally designed for it. Undoubtedly Green, the city comptroller, had been responsible for hiring Vaux to consult about the Tweed courthouse, a job that must have paved the way for Vaux to become involved with the city prison commission.

The act passed by the state legislature creating the commission instructed that the city would erect a modern court and prison facility to replace John Haviland's "Tombs." Constructed in the 1830s on Centre Street, the Egyptian Revival landmark was in dilapidated condition, suffering from cracked walls, inadequate sanitation, and overcrowding. During the spring of 1873, before Vaux became associated with the project, the commissioners had set out to determine a suitable location for the new penitentiary. After much discussion, Green, who led the group, announced on August 12 that the commission had selected the block bounded by Canal, Elizabeth, Bayard, and Mott Streets. This land, Green pointed out, was conveniently located, suitably elevated, modestly assessed (most of the buildings here were tenements), and partially owned by the city.[29] By the end of the month, the commissioners instructed Vaux to prepare as soon as possible a plan for a building at this location.

Opposition to the choice, however, surfaced almost immediately. In September, a group of neighborhood property owners objected that the designated site possessed too much value for business and commerce to be given over to use as a prison and courthouse. Furthermore, they suggested that there was really no need for the city to erect a costly new structure when the old Tombs could be repaired and enlarged. A few days later, a delegation called on Green to persuade him to give up the idea of building a new prison. Green demurely replied that he and his fellow commissioners were simply carrying out the provisions of the law. In any event, he remarked, protest from property owners could be expected no matter where the commissioners had decided to put the new building. But in an apparent effort to placate objectors, the commission asked Vaux and R. G. Hatfield, the architect of several institutional buildings in the city and an acknowledged expert on building construction, to take another look at the Tombs. On January 23, 1874, the two men completed their investigation, the results of which they reported a short time later to the commissioners. The architects concluded that because of problems with the foundations, additional stories could be added to the old prison only at unknown expense. Even then, the cells would be very small, and the lowest floors around the courtyard would be cast in perpetual shadow. Furthermore, they pointed out that it would be very difficult to fit a large new courthouse on land adjacent to the Tombs. Together with his and Hatfield's report, Vaux presented his own plans for a prison and courthouse at the Canal Street site. Because of the complexity of the work and the commissioners' early deadline, Vaux said that he had asked his former partner, Frederick Withers, to help him with the design, which they had been working on since the previous August.[30]

Vaux's plans are lost, but fortunately, the local press published the perspective drawing (Fig. 8.8), the two ground plans, and the written description that he forwarded to the prison commission.[31] The building consisted of two large units: the nearly square courthouse building facing Canal Street and a prison of two freestanding cell blocks behind it. Because the courthouse would become one of the principal edifices of the city, Vaux maintained that it "should present an attractive and somewhat picturesque appearance."[32] Following the example of recent public buildings in England, especially Alfred Waterhouse's Manchester Town Hall of 1868, Vaux's design expressed the notion of justice in Victorian

Gothic terms. The 200-foot symmetrical facade on Canal Street bore a hand-some central tower—not unlike that in H. F. Lockwood's 1866 competition entry for the London Law Courts—and two smaller towers at the corners. Inside, on each of the two main floors, three large hearing rooms opened off a central hall. In contrast to the courthouse, which was to have been built of superior face brick trimmed with stone, Vaux designed the prison wing to be constructed of brick "in the plainest way." Nonetheless, he and Withers took care to make all of the cells in the two seven-story blocks bright and airy. Furthermore, their new building, which could support additional floors, allowed authorities to separate hardened criminals from juvenile and first offenders, a highly desirable policy that the overcrowded conditions at the Tombs made impossible to implement. Basing his estimate on recent bids for the American Museum, Vaux calculated that the price for the entire structure would come to $3 million, a sum far below what naysayers had warned the project would cost.

Despite Vaux's claim, opponents of the new prison continued to throw the argument of economy in Green's face. Why, complained the *Mercury*, could the city spend millions for "a palace such as Vaux has designed" to house murderers and thieves when so many honest working men and their families lived nearby in miserable tenements?[33] This issue was one of many that a resurgent Tammany Hall used to embarrass Havermeyer, who through a series of events had by the early part of 1874 lost most of the Democratic and Republican support he had once enjoyed. Green noted ironically that two years before, some of the men now campaigning against the much needed facility had memorialized the state legislature for the erection of the new prison. Adversaries succeeded in petitioning Albany to repeal the prison act, and by the time the local press published Vaux's drawings, the project was dead.

THE SETBACKS VAUX suffered in Philadelphia, Ottawa, and New York must have come as no surprise to his friend Mould. One can imagine Vaux confiding his troubles to him when, in the evenings, he would stop by Mould's house to consult about the drawings that, after his hours at the parks department, Mould was making for the Metropolitan Museum of Art. Having seen his own star rise and fall at the hands of New York politicians, Mould, who always felt he was underpaid and underappreciated, was in a position to commiserate with Vaux. And in the spring of 1874, Mould found himself again badly treated by the commissioners of the Department of Public Parks. Citing the need to economize operations, Henry Stebbins, then president of the board, dismissed Mould from his position with the department. The action ended Mould's association with the city's parks, which had begun back in 1858. "The removal of Mr. J. Wrey Mould is a shame and a disgrace to the Park Commissioners which the public will expect them at once to redress," declared Manton Marble in the pages of the *World*.[34] "The removal of such a man from a post for which he is so eminently fit and to which he has given some of the best years of his life, and where the best work of his best remaining years is still requisite, is a public scandal and indecency," said Marble, who had employed Mould to do architectural work for him. The *Tribune* also expressed dismay at his firing. "If he is now thrown out in a spirit of mistaken economy, he will at least have the double satisfaction of knowing that every penny of his meager pay for unthanked services has been earned by faithful work," remarked an editorial, probably written by Whitelaw Reid.[35] Eventually, the department relented and kept Mould on the payroll for a few more months. Mould saw the handwriting on the wall, however, and began to look for greener pastures.

Within a year, Mould had accepted an offer from Henry Meiggs to join the enterprising railroad builder in Peru. In 1854, the flamboyant entrepreneur had fled California for South America to escape huge financial obligations and charges of forgery. Possessed of great energy, sharp business acumen, and an indomitable spirit, Meiggs had rebounded and gone on to create the extraordinary trans-Andean railroad. He now proposed to undertake the modernization of Lima. At the time, the city, according to one nineteenth-century commentator, was "surrounded by a rampart of filth and rubbish, the accumulated refuse of many generations."[36] Riding the crest of his wave of influence, Meiggs had convinced the city administration to replace the squalor with a great park some seven miles in length. Having acquired title to much of the worthless land in the area, Meiggs hoped to realize a fortune from its sale for building lots adjacent to the new park. Beyond securing personal gain, Meiggs, who had come to love Lima, hoped to transform the place, said Mould, "from a collection of adobe structures into a modern city fit to be the capital of a progressive State."[37] By December 1875, Meiggs had arranged Mould's appointment as the engineer and architect in chief to Lima's Board of Public Works.

When Mould left New York in March 1875 for his new post, he took with him the good wishes of Green and the other park commissioners, who recognized his special contributions to the decoration of the Terrace. The *Tribune* took the occasion to note that the city was losing one of its most talented public servants "only because he has been insufficiently paid."[38] In private, however, Clarence Cook expressed the opinion to Whitelaw Reid, the paper's publisher, that "Mould owes a great deal of the ill-treatment he complains of to himself." Unable to manage money, he constantly turned to friends for loans. In financial matters, Cook admitted, "Mould has a ravenous maw, and could borrow ad libitum" with no thought of ever repaying. And Cook, who like Vaux greatly admired Mould's talent and capacity for labor, felt that his character displayed even deeper flaws. Not only was he "excessively egotistical," but his unconventional personal life isolated him from the respectable people with whom he worked. "On the social and moral side it must have been hard for Mr. Green to have Mould about him at all," said Cook, "and it certainly was hard for some of the others." Most friends and colleagues, confessed Cook, "could not ask him to their homes, and their families could never visit his."[39] For all his professional support of Mould, Vaux was presumably among this group. After a certain date, he seems never to have included Mould in any social gatherings. One supposes that the adventurous Meiggs, whom one biographer described as "an incurable prodigal," had no such scruples.[40]

Mould himself may have had mixed feelings about leaving New York, but his early impressions of his new situation were highly positive. "Remember me to Vaux, Radford, Withers and all at 110 [Broadway]," he wrote buoyantly to Olmsted shortly after he had arrived in Lima in April 1875. Despite the fact that it seemed to him that he and his life's companion, Mary Elizabeth Daly, had "come to the Antipodes!, everything is so utterly and totally unlike all I have been accustomed to all my life," Mould expressed satisfaction with his new arrangements. The weather was splendid, his living quarters were fine, and when he had been on the job for only a day, Meiggs's people had paid him nearly $1,000 and reimbursed all his travel expenses. "Rather a contrast to the two penny, halfpenny way in which the DPP is being managed," he told Olmsted.[41] Mould stayed in Lima for four years, during which time he both designed important private houses and laid out Parca de Recerva. One also gets the impression from his letters that during this time in Lima he enjoyed the most contented years of his life.

WHILE MOULD MADE ready to depart for Peru, Vaux and his family prepared to leave their residence at 331 East 15th Street (where they had lived since 1871) for a suburban dwelling at Alpine, New Jersey. Vaux had taken a three-year lease on the house as part of a scheme with which he was involved to create a residential community on land adjacent to the Palisades, the high rock cliffs that form the western shore of the Hudson above Manhattan Island. (This land today forms part of the Palisades Inter-State Park.) Details of this venture are unclear, but it must have been connected with the plans of Crammond Kennedy, editor with Henry Ward Beecher of the *Christian Union* magazine, and the Palisades Land Company to develop the area as a fashionable suburb. After the war, a line opened by the Northern Railroad to Demarest had brought the long-isolated locality within a 30-minute ride from New York. In 1868, Lewis Leeds, the ventilation expert with whom Vaux sometimes consulted and who lived at Englewood Cliffs, New Jersey, noted that "probably not one in a thousand, if one in ten thousand, of the intelligent citizens of New York has any idea of the peculiar characteristics of the beautiful plateau" that lay behind the Palisades. He extolled the forests, fine views, and fresh air and looked forward to the day when "the salaried clerk, the teacher, and most professional men, who under the present extravagant rates of rent and living cannot afford to have a home of their own" in town, would come to live there.[42] In 1875, the railroad published a brochure touting the virtues of the area and calling attention to a "stone boulevard and public park on the cliffs" that promised to transform the Palisades into "one of the most inviting residences in the suburbs of New York."[43] Apparently Vaux had charge of constructing the boulevard and park and laying out lots for houses.

On Sunday, May 30, 1875, the day after the Vauxes moved into their new house, Jervis McEntee went to see them. Young Downing, now a lad of nineteen who was especially close to his artist uncle, met McEntee at the station and conducted him to the house. There the painter found his sister and her family "getting comfortably settled and happy in the idea of a country life." Vaux now lived in the manner he had extolled to others in *Villas and Cottages*. On his first walk with Vaux to explore the area, McEntee was impressed with what he saw. "It is certainly very striking," he thought. He believed there was every reason to hope that the locale would soon be regarded "as by far the finest suburb of New York."[44] McEntee was especially pleased to see how much his sister Mary loved the area. "Mary enjoys her new home in the Palisades," he happily observed, "and has no desire to go away."[45]

But it is from James Morse, Vaux's young friend from the Fraternity Club, that we get the most intimate glimpse into this period of Vaux's home life. In the fall of 1875, Morse took the train to Yonkers and then crossed the river by ferry to visit the Vauxes at their home on the Palisades. Climbing the winding road to the top of the cliffs, Morse, who directed a boys' classical school in Manhattan, took special delight in observing asters, goldenrod, and other wildflowers bathed in the mellow light of an Indian summer afternoon. "At the summit which is wooded to a considerable distance back," he remarked, "the sumac become abundant." Confirming Leeds's report, Morse observed that progress had skirted this lovely place that lay within view of the great metropolis. Morse found the area "wild pasture, and swamp, and forest" with here and there a small farmstead where the very door encroaches on the untamed forest. The wilderness, he observed, "creeps up behind the house, and presses to the very edge of the pathway."[46] Then, making his way along a wood road through a thick grove of walnuts and oaks, Morse came upon "an opening delightfully sloping down to the edge of the Palisades where a magnificent scene lay under and before me—the river, the hills beyond, and, if it had not been twilight, a glimpse of the Sound and far-away Long Island." Sighting Vaux's 11-year-old daughter Marion, Morse realized that here "in the midst of the opening, in a semi-wild region, was the house which Mr. Vaux has hired for three years, repaired, renewed, almost made over." Inside, Morse admired his friend's fine taste. Here were "delicate vases, rich hangings, quaint wood work and bronze furniture, landscapes by our dearest American artists, books, and all the objects of taste and refinement which made the country the city and the city the suburb of Heaven." It is a pity that no photographs exist to reveal more clearly the personal treasures with which Vaux and his wife surrounded their life. From Morse's description, one can picture their home interior as having that rarified "aesthetic" quality which Vaux, who especially delighted in Japanese bronzes, admired at Olana and which distinguished the rooms about which his friend Clarence Cook wrote in *Scribner's Monthly*. Expressive of his deep love for art and nature, Vaux's Alpine home surely represented his complete ideal of cultivated home life.

The next morning, Vaux conducted a tour of the area. He led his family and their visitor through the woods and along the cliffs, where the enthusiastic architect admonished his followers to note "every unusually beautiful opening." Vaux also showed Morse the now vanished boulevard then in construction, under his supervision, 1,000 feet back from the edge of the cliff. In the future, Vaux explained, the parkway would "radiate walks and horse-back paths toward the finer points of the river." Once these improvements were made and the land was drained, building lots would be surveyed. From the sale of these sites for country houses, the company for whom Vaux worked hoped to eventually realize a handsome profit. But schemes for making money were far from Vaux's mind that delightful Sunday morning. "We spent the entire forenoon in rambling about," remembered Morse, "picking autumn leaves and fringed gentian which grew in abundance; and arrived at the house only in time for dinner— loaded with gorgeous things."

A year later, Morse paid a Christmastime visit to his friend's suburban home. After making his way through the snow-covered landscape from the station at Closter, he reached Vaux's house to find a cordial welcome awaiting him. A fire burned in the Franklin stove and cast its glow over pretty Christmas ornaments that decorated the room. The next morning, the family sleigh appeared at the front door, and with Vaux's daughters Julia and Marion, Morse drove across the snowy landscape to see the progress of the place. "The few houses along the road were half buried," he remarked. Morse appreciated the lonesome atmosphere of snow-covered gates, urns, and arbors on properties embraced by "wintry woods, rugged and undisturbed."[47] Later in the morning, Morse went with Bowyer to cut ice from a pond. One of the family dogs joined on this excursion. "There are four dogs in the house," reported Morse, "all trained to do some feat of dog-gymnastics. One will jump to a height of six feet, seize hold of a rope and hang by the jaws several minutes." The dogs also served, he realized, as the companions for the girls on their wanderings through the woods. He especially remembered how charming Marion looked, brightly dressed and frolicking in the springtime forest, with three of the agile guardians by her side.[48] It led him to muse on how women especially seemed to love the country life. Surely he must have shared Jervis McEntee's observation that Mary flourished in her Palisades home. "It is charming to see how quickly the ladies of our party put themselves into harmony externally with the flowery loveliness of the woods," he wrote, "transferring a bit of wild nature to hair or dress so as to become at once a part of the handiwork of the Great Artist." This made the earnest headmaster wonder if women were not "nearer to Nature than men; or is it an innate, unconscious coquetry grown into the sex from the necessities of their lives? It is a delicious coquetry, at any rate, one worthy of being interwoven among the soberer traits of their life."

These thoughts occurred to Morse after he and his wife had enjoyed a picnic lunch with Calvert and Mary in the rustic summerhouse which Vaux had constructed in the spring of 1877 and which he seems to have called Restawhile. Located about a mile from the Vauxes' house, Restawhile projected over the edge of the Palisades and commanded, said Morse, "a wonderfully beautiful river scene."[49] Vaux himself may have taken the opportunity that afternoon to air his own opinions about the special beauty of the Palisades. In 1879, Vaux made a splendid drawing of this rustic aerial observatory (Fig. 8.9), the view from which must have always held for him the tragic memory of that terrible day in July 1852 when Downing had met his death across the river at Yonkers.

Residence at Alpine did not curtail the pleasure that Vaux took in the social and intellectual life of the city, including his customary New Year's Day visits to friends. In February 1876, he took a room in the Tenth Street Studio Building, perhaps as a pied-à-terre to be near Gifford, Whittredge, and other artist friends with whom he enjoyed socializing. He also often frequented the Century. And at the Union League in the winter of 1877 Vaux played the role of Caleb Plumer in a performance of Dickens's *The Cricket on the Hearth*. He and Mary were also sure to be present at meetings of the Fraternity Club. Perhaps encouraged by Morse, who was a classical scholar, in 1877 Vaux published the paper on Marcus Aurelius that he had read to the little group.[50] This inquisitive, cosmopolitan Roman, Vaux maintained, "would be at home in any century; but none so completely, it seems to me, as in the nineteenth." Vaux thought it would have been especially interesting to converse with him on the new scientific theories of Darwin and Spencer that were so changing humankind's view of itself. From reading Marcus Aurelius's writings, Vaux felt that the meditative emperor would be in sympathy with the "recognition of a process of development in all things—or as it is well termed, 'evolution.'" Moreover, one cannot help but think that Vaux was expressing his personal philosophy when he wrote

FIGURE 8.9. *Restawhile on the Palisades*. From A. F. Oakey, *Home Grounds*. Courtesy of Buffalo and Erie County Public Library.

that although his ancient hero was "habitually thoughtful and theoretical, his main desire is to be equal to the work of the day, whatever it may be." And when one recalls Vaux's conduct in the struggles over Central Park, the Centennial building, Hunt's Central Park gates, and even the manner in which he confronted Olmsted's reluctance to return to New York from Mariposa, it takes little effort to see autobiography in the following sentence: "He expects to meet with opposition, as a matter of course, and tries to be always light-armed, cheerful, and ready for a run to the nearest summit, from which a new view may be obtained."

Vaux and his family continued to live at Alpine until the end of 1878, after which they returned to the city and took up residence in Richard Morris Hunt's Stuyvesant Apartments at 142 East 18th Street. Apparently, like Riverside, the residential development on the Palisades had run into financial problems. Once again, McEntee's house at Rondout became the Vauxes' frequent home away from town. It was there on May 5, 1879, that they marked their silver wedding anniversary, the happiness of which was shaded by the death a few months earlier of Jervis McEntee's wife, Gertrude.[51] Springtime only sharpened the family's nostalgia for the charms of suburban life at Alpine. "I tell you I had a sort of home-sick feeling," wrote Downing Vaux to his mother after the move, "and would like to have sailed back to Palisades and gone for a walk or [for a] sail in the canoes." He thought especially that his mother must miss spring days in the country and that his little sister Marion would look "for the first hepaticas in vain."[52] I suspect that the three years that Calvert and Mary spent at Alpine were the happiest time of their life together.

DURING THE MID-1870S, wealthy men of affairs still called on Vaux to provide them with houses signifying their elevated social status. One of these Gilded Age magnates was William B. Ogden, an elderly upstate New Yorker who had made a fortune in land speculation and railroads in Chicago; in 1837 he had become that city's first mayor. By the end of the war, Ogden's interests focused more and more on New York City, where the astute entrepreneur promoted the construction of an underground urban rail system. In 1866, Ogden purchased the large stone villa that Vaux had designed a few years before for a now unknown client at Fordham Heights, New York (Fig. 6.8). Following the disastrous Chicago fire of 1871, Ogden relocated permanently to his new home. The move to New York seems to have given the 70-year-old bachelor a renewed zest for life as well as for business, for four years later he married Mariana Arnot, the 53-year-old daughter of a prominent Elmira, New York, family. Just when he engaged Vaux to remodel the interior of the Fordham Heights dwelling and to improve the grounds around it is not known; most likely he did so at the time of the marriage.[53] Indeed, it may have been the bride who took charge of this matter, for Vaux continued to work for Mrs. Ogden after William's death in the summer of 1877. As a wealthy widow, Mariana looked for advice and assistance to her husband's attorney, Andrew Green, the man who undoubtedly brought Vaux and the Ogdens together. To Green, the executor of William Ogden's will, Mrs. Ogden turned over the management of the luxurious house and parklike grounds that constituted her beloved Villa Boscobel. By this name, her resplendent residence was featured in George Sheldon's 1886 book, *Artistic Country Seats*. There the author discreetly noted that in the house "many negotiations involving enterprises destined to leave deep foot-prints in the progress of the settlement of the western portion of the continent" had been made during the last years of William Ogden's long and prosperous life.[54]

From Sheldon's pretentious volume, we learn the most we know about Boscobel, for the house has long since disappeared. It went down before the force of urban expansion, along with many neighboring villas dating from the 1840s and 1850s that once graced the elevated ground between the High Bridge Aqueduct and the Washington Bridge. Constructed in 1888, the bridge joined the area to Manhattan and opened the way to the development of the Fordham section of the Bronx. In the days before the bridges, Boscobel's impeccable lawns sloped down to the shore of the lovely Harlem River, the name given to the estuary between northern Manhattan Island and the Bronx. From their broad veranda, which summer draped with wisteria, clematis, and woodbine, the Ogdens could watch the many boaters who found this protected sheet of water a favorite spot for sailing small pleasure craft. Across the river, they could see the cliffs of Manhattan Island and the picturesque water tower that still marks the southern end of the great High Bridge Aqueduct.

William Ogden, who had gradually acquired half a mile of river frontage, sought to make the grounds around his house as green and lovely as a park. Planting walls of evergreens, he carefully screened the greenhouses and stables, as well as the neighboring property, from view. Yet it seems that it was the former mayor's cultivated wife who most of all loved sylvan nature. After William's death, Sheldon tells us, Mariana bestowed considerable care upon the landscape, extending and renewing the original plantings until the broad lawns bore an impressive array of fine deciduous and evergreen trees. Undoubtedly she engaged Vaux to help in this endeavor, supplementing her own good judgment and "memories of observations of much travel" with his expert knowledge. Inside, Mariana Ogden's Boscobel displayed the devotion to opulence that distinguished upper-class taste after the war. As pictured in *Artistic Country Seats*, the library and drawing room had heavy woodwork of oak and ebony and high ceilings elaborately ornamented with vaguely Japanese designs. The house, reported Sheldon, was "liberally furnished with the richest materials of silk and satin" and hung with works by now forgotten European masters such as Schreyer, De Haas, Ziermann, and Bela. We do not know what role, if any, Vaux played in the choice of furnishings, hangings, and frescoes, but one cannot help but think that he would have preferred Olana's more heartfelt "artistic" surroundings to Boscobel's conservative eclecticism.

An even more exalted client than William Ogden was Henry B. Hyde, the founder in 1859 of the Equitable Life Assurance Society. By 1874, Hyde's company enjoyed overwhelming financial success—although some questioned its method of managing assets—and he was a quintessential Gilded Age self-made millionaire. In July of that year, Hyde approached Olmsted with a request for his services in creating a landscape plan for property that he was acquiring at West Islip, Long Island.[55] Although Olmsted seems to have visited the site, he soon turned the work over to Weidenmann, who since Vaux and Olmsted had gone their separate ways had been assisting Olmsted on a part-time basis with ongoing parks in Buffalo and elsewhere. On August 21, Weidenmann made the first of many visits to Masquetux, the name Hyde gave his 29-acre country estate. A few days later, Weidenmann went there with Vaux, whom Hyde had engaged as the architect for his new dwelling.[56]

After many revisions, Weidenmann produced a splendid landscape plan that satisfied Olmsted's demanding client, who spent until 1877 acquiring the property necessary to implement it. Actually, the experience with Hyde, who on numerous occasions had summoned Weidenmann to his Equitable office to discuss the project, was irksome and costly for Weidenmann. One wonders if he did not confide to Vaux his sense of frustration with Olmsted's loose business arrangements, which made no allowance for travel expenses or extra time consumed in accommodating repeated alterations to the plans. Provoked by the situation, he complained to Olmsted that he knew that his "object in the agreement is simply to keep an office staff ready to your disposition at any time you please without expense." In the future, however, Weidenmann informed Olmsted that he intended "to divide the Receipts after the cash outlays and office expenses are deducted." Despite his discontent with his payment, Weidenmann took pride in the outcome of his labors and planned to include Masquetux in his projected book, *American Garden Architecture*.[57]

In Weidenmann's scheme, the impressively scaled dwelling by Vaux enjoyed a secluded wooded location facing a wide expanse of open lawn. The house must have been finished by 1880, for in that year Vaux exhibited a drawing of the rambling, half-timber dwelling at the National Academy of Design. Like the much smaller Farmstead that Vaux designed in 1874 for the Park in Buffalo, the Hyde house represented a turning away from the Rural Gothic style of his earlier country houses. The medieval English vernacular design of the Hyde house resonated with developments in British domestic architecture identified most closely with Norman Shaw. Yet despite the importance of its owner and the obvious expense of the commission, the Hyde house attracted little attention. The indifference of the architectural community was a sign of things to come.

A great fortune also lay behind the design that Vaux drew in 1874 or 1875 for the townhouse of Dr. George J. Bull of Worcester, Masssachusetts (Fig. 8.10).[58] The gift of the doctor's father-in-law, the gun manufacturer Daniel B. Wesson, the house rests on mighty walls of rusticated reddish granite trimmed with smooth gray granite, a combination of materials reminiscent of Vaux and Mould's original design for the American Museum of Natural History. The most inventive feature of the design, however, is the way Vaux orchestrated the street and side elevations in reference to the steeply rising site, which held a garden on the southern side. The three-bay main facade overlooking the street forms a nearly symmetrical composition of twin gables projecting forward from an asymmetrical skyline of chimney stack and corner tower. The four-story tower is also the dominant component of the more loosely arranged side elevation. For the observer coming up the hill, its rising mass punctuates the significant angle of the dwelling. By means of beveled and chamfered corners, Vaux subtly diminished its scale toward the ground level, where a hooded entrance discreetly welcomed the doctor's patients to his office. Unfortunately, the young physician found little happiness in the dignified house that his wife's wealthy father had presented to him; within two years, he had obtained a divorce and headed west to seek his fortune on the frontier.

FIGURE 8.10.
Design for George J. Bull
house, Worcester, Mass.,
1874–1875. From *American
Architect and Building News* 1
(April 18, 1876). Courtesy
of Buffalo and Erie County
Public Library.

AT THE END OF THE 1870s, two of Vaux's friends turned to him for designs for houses: the artist Worthington Whittredge and the geographer-explorer Raphael Pumpelly. Whittredge, whom the National Academy of Design had recently chosen for its president, was enjoying considerable renown for his placid, luminous landscape paintings. He and McEntee were especially close friends. United by their mutual affinity for nature's intimate moods, they often spent time together sketching out-of-the-way scenery in the Catskills. At times Vaux joined them on their excursions. Frequently the three men enjoyed each other's conversation over dinner at the Tenth Street Studio Building. A longtime resident of the Stuyvesant Apartments, Whittredge informed McEntee in February 1879 that he had asked Vaux to design a house for his growing family on property he had purchased at Summit, New Jersey.[59] The work went quickly, and early in December 1880, McEntee received an invitation from his friend to spend the night in his commodious new dwelling.

As is all too often the case with Vaux's architecture, images of the Whittredge house have outlived the actual building. Historic photographs show an asymmetrical frame dwelling set on a wooded hilltop site (Fig. 8.11). The exterior bore a grid pattern that called attention to the planarity of the walls, which in this instance were covered with clapboard. The design also imparted an orderly and elegant sense of proportion to the elevations. Two wide horizontal bands indicated the three floor levels, while thinner strips defined an odd number of

FIGURE 8.11.
Worthington
Whittredge
house, Sum-
mit, N.J., 1879.
Courtesy of
Summit
Historical
Society.

vertical sections that corresponded to the width of the windows. The design had a logic reminiscent of H. H. Richardson's own house of 1868 on Staten Island and, in general, of French rationalist design principles. But in the massing of the entrance facade, with its doorway sheltered behind a two-story porch between a tower at one side and a broader unit at the other, one could see echoes of Church's Olana. Like his friend Church, Whittredge could enjoy panoramic views from the open platform that crowned the tower of his house.

Even more ample provision for viewing the surroundings informed the design for the house at Newport that Vaux designed in 1880 for Raphael Pumpelly. Vaux had been friends with this extraordinary man for a long time. An indefatigable traveler and explorer, Pumpelly had received a degree in geology from the Royal School of Mines in Freiberg, Germany. In the late 1850s, he had gone to Arizona to manage silver mines, but his inveterate spirit of wanderlust led him on to California and then across the Pacific, where he studied the geology of Japan, China, Mongolia, and Siberia. Back in the States in 1869, he married and settled briefly in Cambridge, Massachusetts, before going off in the summer of 1870 to investigate ore deposits in the Upper Peninsula of Michigan. Equipped with tents, a bark canoe, a sailboat, and two guides, Pumpelly and his party, which included Mary Vaux and her daughter Julia, set out from Marquette to have a good time while the astute geologist eyed land purchases for powerful mining interests. During the next ten years, Pumpelly busied himself compiling a list of the mineral resources of the United States, examining the effects of water pollution on human health (he was one of the first to be aware of the problem), and preparing a geological survey along the projected route of a railroad that Henry Villard proposed to build in the Northwest. When in New York, Pumpelly frequented the Century, whose members remembered him as always "just back from Japan or Tibet or the turquoise Southwest, a great blue-eyed giant with a long flowing beard, a vivacious tongue, and a courtly manner."[60]

What did the notion of home signify to a man like this? Certainly it would have been fascinating to have overheard the discussions he had with Vaux as they planned his large two-and-a-half-story frame house (Fig. 8.12). According to Pumpelly's own testimony, he dictated that "the building should embody my ideas of sanitation," a subject that had also interested Vaux since his days in London.[61] It was, in fact, a matter to which he was devoting renewed attention as he tackled the problem of designing modern low-cost urban housing. Pumpelly also wished to make his dwelling (which is gone) free "from decaying organic matter." This led the health-conscious scientist to devise a new formula for plaster that dispensed with the usual mixture of sand and hair. Unaware of worse consequences, however, he chose to import asbestos from Italy to serve as a binder. From the evidence of a contemporary illustration, the spirit of experiment did not extend to the ground plan, although the cross-shaped plan would have provided an abundance of light and air in each area of the house. An unexceptional arrangement of rooms on the principal floor centered around a commodious hall and located the staircase in a wide passage leading to the kitchen wing. Historic photographs of the exterior, which was framed in a manner analogous to the Whittredge house, suggest that Pumpelly must have placed as much emphasis on the enjoyment of the outdoors as he did on interior

FIGURE 8.12. Raphael Pumpelly house, Newport, R.I., 1880. From R. Pumpelly, *My Reminiscences.* Courtesy of Buffalo and Erie County Public Library.

living. A broad terrace extended around three sides of the house, and the walls of both the first and second floors had spacious verandas facing the water. The way the upper of these two spectacular stories of pierced brackets and delicate supports merged with the body of the house and the tall hipped roof (a form repeated three times in the design) implies the influence of Shingle-style houses by Richardson and by McKim, Mead and White. The Venetian reference and the tall proportions of Vaux's design, however, were at odds with that emerging esthetic. Other provisions for enjoying the fresh air included a balcony over the entrance porch and curious outdoor alcoves recessed in large Flemish-style dormers above the second-floor bay windows. These seating areas must have been delightfully protected belvederes from which family members could enjoy the pleasure of seeing without being seen. Perhaps the widely traveled Pumpelly, whose interests also extended to the study of primitive man, had sensed the pleasure that modern-day geographers tell us all human beings take in viewing landscape in this way.

GIVEN PUMPELLY'S WIDE-RANGING interests and enthusiasms, it would be surprising indeed if Vaux had not told him about his momentous dream of establishing in New York a Metropolitan Museum of Scientific Industry. By the mid-1870s, the city no longer needed the large distributing reservoir that since 1843 had been contained behind massive, Egyptian-style stone walls on Fifth Avenue at 42nd Street. New potential uses for this valuable site soon became a matter of public discussion. Sending a letter and drawings to Mayor Smith Ely Jr. on June 29, 1877, Vaux and his partner Radford entered this debate.[62] Vaux proposed to construct a permanent exhibition facility that would cover the entire area of the reservoir and would be joined to Reservoir Square (present Bryant Park), a public park behind the reservoir on Sixth Avenue where in 1853 the Crystal Palace had stood. Arguing that "at present there is no permanent educational institution of a polytechnic character in this country," Vaux predicted that the time would soon come when an "active movement in this direction" would develop in New York City. Pointing to the example of the art and natural history museums, he raised the expectation that if the board of such an educational institution were wisely organized, it could surely count on aid from the state to construct its building. The city required a place, contended Vaux, where men who labored in the industrial arts could come to study the latest products of American and foreign manufacturers. The museums of art and natural history were fine additions to the cultural life of the city, he said, but the exposition hall he envisaged would appeal especially to "the hard working man" and could be considered "an outgrowth of the common school system" that would enrich polytechnic instruction. Thus, the museum that he proposed grew out of Vaux's lifelong desire to raise the level of skill and knowledge among mechanics and craftspeople. The idea surely took its immediate inspiration from the example of the Centennial Exhibition in Philadelphia, but as long ago as 1849 Vaux had told the members of the Architectural Association that London stood in need of "a central and permanent exposition of inventions connected with practical architecture."[63]

The building Vaux and Radford designed to house their Metropolitan Museum of Scientific Industry was related to their competition entry for the main building at the Centennial Exhibition (Fig. 8.13). Arched iron trusses

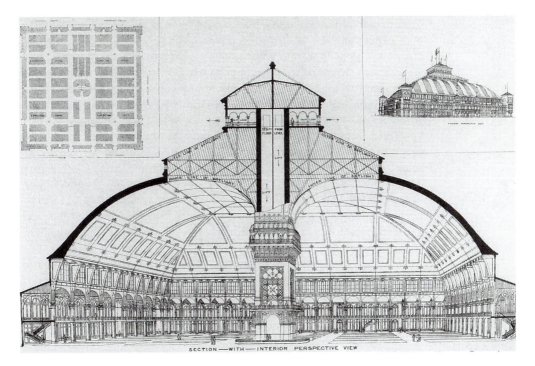

SECTION—WITH—INTERIOR PERSPECTIVE VIEW

rising to a height of 135 feet sprang from the outer walls to converge on a central shaft. This shaft would contain an elevator to carry visitors to a balcony just beneath the glass ceiling. Above that, the car continued to a rooftop viewing platform some 175 feet above the ground. Although this outside area had little to do with the function of the building as an exhibition hall, it was undoubtedly included in Vaux's design because he knew that the walk along the top of the 40-foot-high reservoir walls had long been popular with New Yorkers as a promenade that afforded a splendid prospect of their entire island. On the inside, Vaux preserved this perimeter walk around the 300-foot-square space in the form of continuous, second-level gallery. Also with recreation in mind, he reserved the area in front of the central shaft as a place for audiences to listen to orchestral music. And so that the public could enjoy the glassed-in space year-round, Vaux paid special attention to the problem of heat buildup in summer. By reason of various design features, he promised that "the inconveniences arising from the glare and heat of the sun will be much less than is usually experienced in buildings" of this type.[64] Finally, Vaux thought that his magnificent six-acre exhibit hall building could be erected for only $850,000.

If Vaux was counting on the goodwill that the local press had generated in support of his entry in the Philadelphia competition to advance his current proposal, he was sadly mistaken. Of course, he would not have been surprised by negative remarks in the *Mercury*. Ignoring the high-minded aim of Vaux's proposition, the weekly called Vaux "one of the most successful leeches on our City Treasury for the past thirty years." The paper must have spoken for John Kelly, the Tammany chief who had replaced Green as city comptroller and who enjoyed considerable power under Mayor Ely. The *Mercury* characterized the museum proposal as just another ploy by Vaux to enrich himself. Instead, the weekly backed a suggestion put forth by Ely himself, who had made limiting

FIGURE 8.13. Design for Metropolitan Museum of Scientific Industry, New York City, 1877. From *American Architect and Building News* 2 (August 11, 1877). Courtesy of Buffalo and Erie County Public Library.

expenditures for public construction a cornerstone of his mayoral policy. In the spirit of economy, Ely wished to retain the reservoir walls and to use them to construct a vast central armory that would save the city the rent it currently paid for drill space. Even the mainstream press, which usually supported Vaux in his constant vigilance on behalf of the parks, found little merit in his suggestion for an exposition hall. "The Central Park Museum experiments have not been encouraging," wrote the *Herald*, "and we do not believe that the people will care to see them repeated elsewhere." Instead, the paper endorsed the creation of a park on the reservoir site, an idea favored by well-to-do homeowners in the neighborhood.[65] Mariana Van Rensselaer, who admired Vaux's Central Park bridges, likewise criticized the industrial arts museum. In the pages of the *American Architect and Building News*, she observed that it would be better "to allow the present black elephant to rest on our municipal hands than spend time and money in substituting for it a white elephant, about equally useful or useless." Nonetheless, the new architectural journal laid Vaux and Radford's scheme before its readers, together with the letter of explanation that they had sent to the mayor.[66] Mrs. Van Rensselaer summed up the reaction that generally greeted Vaux's scheme when she wrote that his "great museum of scientific industry has received several severe newspaper kicks, and finds nobody anxious enough for its establishment to get up any enthusiasm."[67]

Far more interesting to most followers of the New York architectural scene were the deliberations of architects Joseph M. Wilson, George B. Post, and Napoleon Le Brun—"these budding Barons Haussmann," Mrs. Van Rensselaer called them—who were charged with guiding the designs for the Manhattan and Brooklyn approaches to the Roeblings' new East River Bridge. In the hot summer of 1877, that epoch-making piece of architectural engineering overshadowed any attempt by Vaux to reclaim by means of his metal and glass exposition hall the place in the history of American architecture that had been lost to him with the defeat of his innovative plans for the Centennial building. Indeed, one wonders why Vaux, with no organization behind him, thought that in the charged atmosphere of New York politics anyone would have championed his idea, no matter how forward-looking it might have been." Of course, it is unpopular at this time to propose anything with appropriation in its belly," he admitted to Olmsted, "but I venture to plant the standard a little ahead of our lines trusting that defenders will rally round it in season."[68] They never did. As historians Rosenzweig and Blackmar have pointed out, the late 1870s saw the weakening of support among New York City property owners and reformers for financing public parks and educational institutions. The optimistic belief that Vaux had expressed in *Villas and Cottages* that a "true and intelligent republicanism" would lead to the formation of parks and museums so that the ordinary man might enjoy life "almost on the same footing as the millionaire" was less likely to become reality in the new era of class politics. Despite the brief controversy that engulfed it, the reservoir remained in place until the early twentieth century, when the city cleared the site to make way for Carrère and Hastings's New York Public Library.

THE RISE OF JOHN KELLY to the position of comptroller put Tammany Hall enemies of Vaux and Olmsted in a position to do mischief. Having seen the two men denounced in the pages of the *Mercury* and the *Evening Express*, Kelly now took it upon himself to have Olmsted fired from his post with the Department of Public Parks. In December 1877, Kelly informed the park commissioners (most of whom at the time were his allies) that since Central Park was completed, Olmsted, who was often away on private business, was no longer needed. The order coincided with and probably propelled Olmsted's failing health. During the winter of 1878, Olmsted went to Europe with his son John to regain his lost stamina and to visit park sites. In his absence, Vaux joined with Henry Bellows, Whitelaw Reid, William Cullen Bryant, E. L. Godkin, and many others in mounting a newspaper campaign to have their friend reinstated with the parks department. On January 11, 1878, Godkin published a long letter in the *Tribune* passionately defending Olmsted's 20-year association with Central Park. Eleven days later a petition addressed to the park commissioners and signed by many prominent New Yorkers appeared in the *World*. The park board, however, did not budge from its position.

Conspicuously absent from the *World* petition was Vaux's name. I believe that this did not signal any weakening in Vaux's support of Olmsted but instead reflected protest of statements that Godkin had made earlier in the *Tribune*. Vaux had been deeply hurt and offended to find his name totally absent in Godkin's long discussion of Central Park, which he repeatedly credited solely to Olmsted's genius. Furthermore, Godkin had disregarded Vaux's claim to a foremost place in the profession of landscape architecture. "No other American has worked in the same field with equal success" as Olmsted, Godkin had asserted, pushing aside without a mention all that Vaux had done to promote the new discipline. Motivated by the demands of the moment to make the strongest possible case for his friend, Godkin had consciously intended no slight to Vaux. Nonetheless, the omission opened old wounds. Vaux held his tongue while he waited for Olmsted to speak up on his behalf by sending a correction to the papers, for in a discussion with Mary Olmsted, Vaux had been led to believe that Godkin's letter had been forwarded to her husband. But Olmsted had deliberately wished to stay out of touch with troubling events in New York while he was recuperating in Europe and did not know what was transpiring in defense of his job. Eventually, hearing nothing, Vaux took matters into his own hands. Without airing his grievance to either Godkin or Mary Olmsted, Vaux vented his feelings in a bitter letter that appeared in the *Tribune* on February 19. Pointing out that he was "the author in every respect, equally with Mr. Olmsted," of Central and Prospect Parks, Vaux said that because Olmsted's name stood first in the partnership title, he was under a special obligation as the "trustee of our joint property, the Central Park plan," to see always that Vaux's role was remembered. Calling Godkin Olmsted's representative, Vaux claimed that he too was under the same charge. But, said Vaux, Godkin had maliciously ignored him. "To F. L. Olmsted, everything; to C. Vaux, the cut direct," Vaux fumed.

Vaux had every right to feel anger at being denied credit for the creation of Central Park, a historic work to which, he said, he had "devoted the very heart of my life." Vaux's letter, however, shocked McEntee by its harsh tone, and as the days passed, McEntee became concerned over the intensity of Vaux's feelings in the matter.[69] "Calvert is in a fearful state over this Park discussion," he wrote on February 21, "[and] all his eccentricities are exaggerated." The next day, when Vaux and his son Downing came to breakfast, McEntee found him even more agitated: "Calvert is nearly crazy with this Central Park business," he noted in his diary. Exasperated by this extreme behavior, McEntee told Vaux "to let it drop now and go home and forget it," strong words that seem to have had the desired sobering effect. Nonetheless, the painter could not help feeling that his brother-in-law "does act so strangely when he gets into these moods."[70] Mary Olmsted would have shared this opinion, for when Vaux had finally broached the subject with her, he had displayed, she said, the worst of his "chivying English disposition." The whole affair had greatly troubled her (she confessed to having cried all day after Vaux's visit) and severely tried their friendship.[71]

For his part, Godkin replied with a letter to the *Tribune* in which he apologized to Vaux for unintentionally disregarding him. His concern at the time, he explained, had been only to see Olmsted restored to his position at the parks department. To that end, he had thought it best not to have entered "on a detailed distribution of the honors of the design" because it "would have confused the issue before the public mind." Godkin, who had the reputation for being right-thinking but insensitive, also noted that if Vaux had come to him, he would have understood his grievance and taken steps to correct it. Unfortunately, as matters now stood, said Godkin—none too graciously, considering that he was penning an apology—"the language of Mr. Vaux's letter seems to indicate that in his present state of mind explanation or discussion would be wasted on him." Nonetheless, the following day, Godkin forwarded to the *Tribune* a note from Owen Olmsted, stating that his father and Vaux were equally responsible for the design of Central Park. "I hardly say that the acknowledgment it contains would have been cheerfully made at any time during the past month," affirmed Godkin, "if Mr. Vaux had requested it."[72]

Reading these memorials, Vaux wrote to the *Tribune* that he accepted Godkin's explanation and apology and was grateful for Owen Olmsted's acknowledgment. Having won his ground, Vaux now gave his unequivocal public endorsement to the reinstatement of his former partner in his post at Central Park. "We have worked and played together in the art of it for twenty years," said Vaux in a letter to the *Tribune*, "and have only half succeeded." Much work still remained to be done in order "to develop the poetry" of the park landscape, Vaux said, and he lauded the hard-working Olmsted as the man capable of taking "the few steps intervening between the dream and the reality."[73]

Always sensitive to being forgotten as Olmsted's equal in the design of Central Park, Vaux nonetheless disturbed his friends by laying his grievance before the public in this way. Surely it would have been better if he had taken Mary Olmsted's advice and waited for Olmsted to return to settle the matter. One can be certain that if Olmsted had been in town, he would have insisted that Vaux's name be linked with his own in any discussion of the park's design. Only a few months before, he had sent a letter to the *American Architect and Building News* correcting the omission of Vaux from remarks on the history of Central Park that Vaux's disgruntled former assistant, A. J. Bloor, had made before the AIA in 1876. No one, said Olmsted, "has more claim than Mr. Vaux to the design of the Park or to what in the address is termed 'the aesthetic arrangement of the grounds.'" Concerning architectural works, Olmsted attested that "during twelve years he made the original studies for them; and his superintendence of their details was personal, direct, and controlling."[74]

Perhaps the serious illness of Vaux's daughter Julia had contributed to his unreasonable outburst, but it is also likely, as Mary Olmsted rather callously remarked at the time, that Vaux was also on edge because of failing business.[75] By the beginning of 1878, not only was New York City in the throes of a depression, but Vaux personally had watched several opportunities for important commissions slip away from him. When Mould returned to New York from Peru in November 1879, Vaux "chanted" to him a "Jeremiad" of professional decline during his absence.[76] And Vaux also must have reflected that the same people who had advocated for Olmsted had failed to utter a word in support of the industrial arts museum that he had proposed a short time before. Under the circumstances, Vaux not only saw fortune abandoning him but felt that he stood in danger as well of losing his reputation for past achievements. "How nearly I was engulfed in oblivion," he confessed to Godkin (with whom he quickly reestablished amicable relations), a remark that sadly foreshadowed the fate of Vaux's reputation in coming years.[77]

BY THE BEGINNING of the 1880s, Vaux had found a new field for his talents. For the next decade and a half, he would serve as the architect to reformers dedicated to alleviating the living conditions of New York's enormous population of poor. According to Vaux's friend Charles Loring Brace, there existed on the East Side of Manhattan from Houston Street up to 40th Street "an overcrowding of human beings in comparison with the space covered, beyond what has thus far ever been known in any civilized country."[78] Even though Vaux did not participate in the landmark 1879 competition for a model tenement chaired by R. G. Hatfield and sponsored by the new journal *Plumber and Sanitary Engineer*, he followed the progress of the high-minded exercise. The announcement of the competition in December 1878 presaged a series of events that for the first time stirred serious concern for the plight of the city's poor. One assumes that Vaux attended services on "tenement Sunday," February 23, 1879, and heard a sermon on the evils of overcrowding and nonexistent sanitation that typified buildings in the impoverished quarters of the city. He may even have been present at the historic meeting at Cooper Union a few days later, when Mayor Edward Cooper appointed a Committee of Nine to come up with solutions to the vexing social problem. Early in March, Vaux went to see the best of the 190 plans that the *Plumber and Sanitary Engineer* had received from architects all over the country. Reflecting that "the poor we have always with us, and the tenement-house problem so nearly always," Vaux expressed his disappointment with the plans, all of which were for buildings on the standard 25' × 100' New York City lot. In particular, he faulted his colleagues for failing to pay close enough attention to the crucial issue of providing adequate light and ventilation to the individual apartments. But here he acknowledged that the terms of the competition had also been flawed, for they had not specified, as Vaux thought they should have, that each room must have a window. "The result shows," he remarked, "that a dark bedroom has been no bar to success, and that direct lighting from street or court has not been valued as of pre-eminent importance."[79]

Stimulated by what he saw to offer better, Vaux prepared a plan of his own that paid special attention to the problems of light and air. His solution prescribed a window in every room. A few days after the so-called dumbbell plan of James E. Ware had been awarded first prize, the *Graphic* gave more space to Vaux's scheme than it did to the designs of Ware and other premium winners.[80] Vaux's four-story brick building, which was influenced by Alfred T. White's pioneering 1876 model tenements in Brooklyn, featured large windows aligned for cross ventilation and a ground-floor passage running from the front of the building to an interior stair court, from which a second similar hall extended to a light court at the rear of the building. This continuous open-air corridor Vaux considered as important for the year-round flow of air as for the movement of people. The upper floors of Vaux's building each had small recessed balconies where a tenant might step out from his living room to overlook the street. A small pavilion centered above the facade imparted a festive touch to the architectural composition and was "especially intended for infants in care of older children who may need fresh air," thus formalizing the rooftop as a community space.[81] At street level, Vaux placed two small shop fronts on either side of an enlarged entrance to the central passageway, an arrangement that the *Graphic* praised for imparting a cheerful, welcoming aspect to the front door through which all residents passed.

Yet not all of the city's architects were impressed with the efforts of Vaux and others to raise the level of public discourse on the problem of low-income housing. John B. Snook, architect of Cornelius Vanderbilt's $3 million Grand Central Depot and a man whose practice included the construction of many tenements, felt that all "these fanciful arrangements are worse than useless; they might be conveniences to some persons, but to a tenement-house population" they meant nothing. What this class of people needed, thought Snook's son, "was a janitor to each family."[82]

Despite the prevalence of such attitudes, reformers greatly advanced their cause on March 22, 1879, when the mayor's Committee of Nine made its report. Out of this historic document came plans for legislation to license tenement-house owners and to create building regulations for all multiple dwellings. Also resulting from the committee's work was the decision by a number of businessmen to form the Improved Dwellings Association. Headed by W. Bayard Cutting, a young, civic-minded lawyer and railroad executive, the association proposed to build hygienic tenements that could be leased to working-class families for $8 to $17 per month. These rents were no higher than those that slumlords took. Seeking to disprove the contention of cynics like Snook that the new-style tenements would never "return a fair income on the cost," the company expected to realize a 5 or 6 percent annual profit. Their model was the example of White's Home Buildings in Brooklyn and Sir Sydney Waterlow's Industrial Dwellings Company in London. Once the association started its work, it made swift progress toward its goal. By the late summer of 1879, Cutting had put together $300,000 in capital. The backers had also hired little-known Brazilian-born architect George Washington da Cunha.

Early in the following year, the association purchased 21 vacant lots—almost an acre of ground—near the East River on First Avenue between 71st and 72nd Streets, an address made convenient to downtown by the newly completed elevated railroad on Third Avenue. By March, da Cunha had filed plans for two groups of three five-story brick dumbbell buildings on 71st Street and 72nd Street.[83] But soon after announcing its plans, the association replaced da Cunha with Vaux and Radford and expanded the undertaking to include 13 dwelling units for 1,000 people. What precipitated the switch of architects is not known. It may be that Vaux was playing an advisory role all along. In any event, Vaux's new plan envisioned multiple dwelling units around three sides of a T-shaped courtyard in the center of the square lot (Fig. 8.14). This open space would be used for both recreation and laundry by residents in the three blocks of buildings, all of which would be entered from the courtyard rather than from the street. With some modification, Vaux retained da Cunha's series of buildings along the two side streets, although these structures now rose to six stories in height and varied in the number of apartments that each contained.

But more important than these alterations to the existing plan was the new building that Vaux designed for the First Avenue side of the property. This six-story brick building possessed a frontage of 200 feet between 71st and 72nd Streets (Fig. 8.15) and incorporated ideas that Vaux had demonstrated in the model tenement that he had published the year before in the *Graphic*. Like that paper scheme, his building had shops on the ground floor, windows in all rooms, and communal recreation space on the roof. Vaux's development of the roof as a useful area (an especially welcome refuge from summer's nighttime heat) was "one indication of the intelligence of the design," commented the *Times*.[84] At ground level, tenants entered the courtyard through pointed arch gateways immediately behind the building on the two side streets; the openings also secured a north-south draft through the court. This common area was to have been shaded by trees and kept safe and clean by a custodian employed to watch over it. (Old photographs indicate no trees, and one doubts that anyone ever called the yard Linden Court, as Vaux suggested.) Internally, Vaux's First Avenue building dispensed with the dumbbell plan of da Cunha's tenements. Harking back to earlier British example, Vaux arranged the plan so that each three-room apartment ran lengthwise through the width of the structure, thus enjoying exposure on both the street side and the court side. In addition to the natural light and fresh air, each family enjoyed the convenience of a kitchen with running water as well as an ash chute, clothes closets, and a dumbwaiter for lifting coal from the basement storage area. For the hardworking men and women who came to live there, the new address, which was "open to breezes from the East River and the south," offered many advantages over life in the crowded slums of Lower Manhattan. Here they could pass their daily life in a bright 12' × 18' room for living and eating and also enjoy the privacy of two separate bedrooms and a water closet. In addition, they shared the use of such facilities as a steam-injection laundry, a reading room, a club room, and a bath. And following the example of Octavia Hill in London and Mrs. Miles in New York, the association instructed tenants in the methods of good housekeeping and personal hygiene. In return, the management expected all residents to conduct themselves for the common good.

When the apartments were finished in 1881, they won high praise for the association and its architect. The long block on First Avenue drew special attention when the *Times* reported that on a visit to the site Sir Sydney Waterlow himself had pronounced the building a success. For less than $300 per apartment, the association had erected a substantial, comfortable building that promised to yield the anticipated revenues for its investors, thus assuring its long-term future. According to the *Times*, Cutting and his philanthropic associates had done everything right: they had "had the good fortune to secure an architect (MR. VAUX) who unites to a remarkable degree practical contrivance and economy with a sense of the picturesque," they had made "contracts and purchases in cheap times," and they had wisely acquired a piece of land "fronting on an avenue which will always be favorite place for mechanics and laborers."[85] As historian Elizabeth Cromley has pointed out, buildings of this scale for housing multiple families were new to New York at this time.[86] Their only architectural precedents were hotels and commercial buildings. Avoiding any-

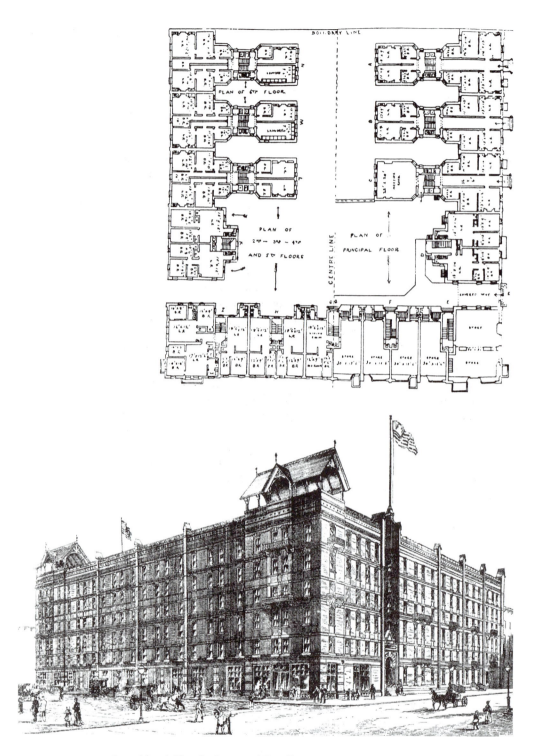

FIGURE 8.14. *(above)* Plan for Improved Dwellings Association buildings, New York City, 1880. From J. Ford, *Slums and Housing*. Courtesy of Buffalo and Erie County Public Library.

FIGURE 8.15. *(below)* Improved Dwellings Association building, First Avenue, 1880. From J. Ford, *Slums and Housing*. Courtesy of Buffalo and Erie County Public Library.

thing that would have suggested the traditional 25-foot-wide tenement building of the East Side slums, Vaux's First Avenue Improved Dwelling emulated the appearance of such newly fashionable middle-class apartment houses as the Albany. This five-story, block-long residence had been designed by John C. Babcock in 1876 for a site on Broadway between 51st and 52nd Streets. Perhaps the general resemblance that Vaux's building bore to such grander cousins as the Albany was the reason why the city's building department called the association's residences "French flats." Inspectors generally reserved this term for the better class of multiple dwellings, rather than tenements. In addition to ground-floor shops and discreet side entrances, Vaux's building shared with the Albany a sense of imposing scale worthy of a fancy hotel. Like Babcock, Vaux took pains to emphasize the oneness of the commanding facade of his building. He did this by means of bluestone stringcourses and a wide cornice, as well as by projecting the end units slightly forward from the middle four, which were marked by slender buttresses. These measures, together with the repetition of single and paired bedroom windows, also gave the facade a sense of architectural logic that recalled Vaux's Commercial Block in Boston.

But the once-upon-a-time author of *Villas and Cottages* would not have been content to leave any human habitation appearing bare and uninviting. With limited means at his disposal, Vaux sought to enliven the brick exterior with such agreeable details as patterned brickwork in the cornice, banded segmental arches over the third-, fifth-, and sixth-floor windows, and several decorative iron balconies. (Vaux kept the facade free of unsightly fire escapes by placing them in the rear courtyard.) The most striking features of the design, however, were large rooftop shelters that Vaux proposed to erect at either corner of the building. These picturesque wooden hoods, which resembled the porch of the Dairy in Central Park, added an unexpected element of whimsy to the building and promised, said the *Times*, to be of "incredible enjoyment to the tenants and their families." Standing under them, proud residents might have appreciated most fully the admirable views that their building commanded. (Unfortunately, the porches were never constructed.) Optimistic that in the realm of work "only the opportunity to improve was needed" to elevate the quality of mechanics' labor, Vaux must have regarded the association's new dwellings as offering a similar chance to the working man to better his private life. And few residents or their more well-to-do neighbors would have missed the implied reference to solidarity between rich and poor symbolized by the American flags flying from tall poles above either courtyard entrance. The Improved Dwellings were an immediate success. They continued to benefit both tenants and investors into the 1930s, when they came down.

Yet as fine as it was, the association's high-minded project constituted a small, isolated step toward improving the notoriously bad housing situation among the poor in New York. Vaux and others realized that broader measures were needed if true social reform were to progress. On the evening of November 18, 1880, Vaux joined many prominent New Yorkers at the first annual meeting of the New York Sanitary Reform Society, the brainchild of the Committee of Nine. At that time, Vaux lent his voice to the society's plans to secure passage of a law putting the supervision of plumbing in all houses under the jurisdiction of the board of health. He also supported its campaigns to license vendors of milk, to change the method of cleaning streets, and generally to improve the physical conditions of the city. After addresses by C. F. Chandler, the respected head of the board of health, on the progress that had been made since new tenement-house laws had taken effect, and Eldridge T. Gerry, president of the Society for the Prevention of Cruelty to Children, on the dreadful effects of tenement-house life on youngsters, Vaux heard Henry C. Potter, whose parish of Grace Episcopal Church included many tenements, lecture on the moral obligations of sanitary reform. In order to overcome the evils of drunkenness and promiscuity that "the enforced herding together in tenement houses of men, women, and children like animals" brought about, the socially conscious minister called for further improvements in tenement-house conditions. One would like to think that after his talk, the speaker discussed with Vaux the progress of his buildings then under construction uptown on First Avenue. Potter, who had been one of the judges in the *Plumber and Sanitary Engineer's* competition, regarded them as Manhattan's first "model" tenements.

ALTHOUGH THE MOVEMENT to improve tenement houses lost momentum between the mid-1880s and 1896, when another group of citizens created the City and Suburban Homes Company, Vaux's personal commitment to the architecture of social reform remained strong. By the late 1870s, Vaux became architect to the Children's Aid Society, a philanthropic organization formed in the 1850s to aid the children of immigrant families, who were concentrated on the city's East Side. One of the founders of the society was Vaux's friend Charles Loring Brace. Brace, who had joined Olmsted on his travels in England in 1850, lived at Hastings, New York, in a house that Vaux designed for him. A deeply religious man who gave up a promising career in the Episcopal Church to devote himself to serving the disadvantaged, Brace built the Children's Aid Society into a well-organized force for good that enjoyed financial support from some of the city's wealthiest citizens. By the late 1870s, Brace was in a position to undertake an ambitious campaign to erect lodging houses for homeless children, many of whom eked out livings on the streets by selling newspapers and shining shoes. In addition to providing safe, clean resting places for the night, these buildings also included classrooms, for Brace and the society believed that the way to conquer poverty was to teach children to be self-sufficient tradespeople.

Early in 1879, Vaux designed the first of the society's shelters, the East Side Boys' Lodging House and Industrial School (Fig. 8.16). The $45,000 cost of constructing the building, which before being demolished in the twentieth century stood at the corner of East Broadway and Gouveneur Street, was underwritten by Catherine Lorillard Wolfe, a woman who used much of her considerable wealth to alleviate the conditions of New York's poor. Guided by a building committee that included Bayard Cutting, construction of the three-story building of "deep red Trenton bricks" trimmed with brownstone began in June 1879.[87] After a delay caused by a shortage of iron due to an upsurge of construction activity following the long depression of the 1870s, the building received its first lodgers in May of the following year. In the basement, the boys had use of a gymnasium and bath, as well as a special room where their rain-soaked clothing could be dried quickly in temperatures approaching 250 degrees. In the upper two floors, one of which was in the steep roof, a homeless child could rent an iron bunk in a dormitory or pay ten cents for a bed in a private alcove. (Brace believed that charging a modest fee gave the young lodgers a claim to dignity that out-and-out charity deprived them.) On the ground floor, volunteers served healthy meals in a room that during the day doubled as a classroom for neighborhood children. This floor also had a sickroom and a dispensary. The largest space inside the building was a room 60 feet long by 40 feet wide on the third floor. In the daytime, this high-ceilinged space, which was well-lit by tall round-arched windows, served as a classroom; at night, the desks were folded away and the hall became a living room. Here, under supervision, the youngsters might talk or read books from a well-stocked library. The waifs could also take pleasure in the sight of green plants growing in an adjacent plant cabinet. "This green-house in which plants are disposed in a pyramidal form, eight or ten feet high," reads a contemporary description, "seems to fill the east end of the room, and is in full view of the boys as they sit facing in that direction."[88] Like the children of middle-class suburban families, the homeless boys of New York's streets were to experience the refining influence of floraculture. In addition to this touching amenity, propagating rooms existed elsewhere in the building. Flowers raised there filled boxes that in summer brightened the lodging-house windows.

Amid the depressing scenery and numbing poverty of its tenement-house neighborhood, the picturesque exterior of the East Side Boys' Lodging House,

FIGURE 8.16.
East Side Boys' Lodging House and Industrial School, 1879. Courtesy of Children's Aid Society.

historic photographs reveal, conveyed the optimistic, humane purpose of Miss Wolfe and the society. And while Brace allowed no overt religious symbols to be present, he and Miss Wolfe (who was a communicant at Henry Potter's church) must have been pleased to see their new building referred to in the press as "Christianity solidified in brick and mortar." Avoiding anything that suggested the standard urban tenement, Vaux wished this proudly freestanding structure to evoke the image of a snug country inn or small hotel. To that end, he introduced such picturesque elements as towers and dormers and carried chimney stacks—those potent symbols of haven—from ground level to the sky. While remaining faithful to the spirit of the picturesque, Vaux clearly derived the major part of the building's design from the so-called Queen Anne style then sweeping England and beginning to exert influence on the American architectural scene. Like many urban buildings in London, the facade of Vaux's modest but attractive building gained a sense of life from the off-center placement of the entrance bay, the variety of window shapes, sizes, and spacing, and the simple ornamental features in the brickwork such as the stringcourses and the recessed panels beneath certain windows. The rising and falling roofline was the aspect of the building that Vaux probably took the most care and pleasure in developing. "In any architectural design," he said, perhaps with this building in mind, "the separate groups of forms may be, in themselves, attractive, or the building may be splendid in its general conception of masses, or rich in its varied and charming detail, but it will be defective as an architectural composition if it fails in its sky-line."[89] Vaux knitted these gestures together into an architectural composition that struck a quiet, reassuring balance between horizontal and vertical expression. To its destitute young transients, the commodious building must have indeed seemed a welcoming refuge in a bleak and inhospitable world.

But not only in terms of architectural distinction did the East Side Boys' Lodging House and Industrial School stand apart from its overcrowded surroundings. On either side of it, two small open areas offered lodgers and neighborhood residents a bit of protected greenspace. This modest gift of nature to the esthetically deprived anticipated the call that Vaux issued a few years later to the members of the Architectural League that our cities should have, "every few blocks, some reservation kept open that will tempt a man, woman or child to sit down and rest, and look about for a while." One surmises that in this forward-looking idea, Vaux enjoyed the full support of Brace, who regarded the lack of access to fresh air and light as one of the greatest evils of tenement neighborhoods.

BRACE HIMSELF WAS doubtless present on March 30, 1880, when Vaux attended the opening in Central Park of the new Metropolitan Museum of Art. During the ceremonies, however, the architect's presence went unacknowledged. Yet McEntee and other artists and friends present that day knew that as the principal in his collaboration with Mould and Radford, Vaux had labored for over a decade on the design and construction of the historic building. Before Mould's departure for Peru in the spring of 1875, all working drawings had been prepared; since 1874, Vaux had watched the structure go up on land that he and Olmsted had designated as a deer paddock on the Greensward plan. Located between the eastern drive and Fifth Avenue and the 79th and 86th Street transverse roads, this space of about 25 acres lay east of the old receiving reservoir and south of the much larger new receiving reservoir. (In the 1930s, the city drained the old reservoir to create the present Great Meadow.) As long ago as 1869, the park commissioners and the museum's board of trustees had approved Vaux and Mould's ambitious plan for a huge museum of galleries and courts arranged in a grid similar to that of their plan for the American Museum (Fig. 8.17). The art museum, however, was not to have had a central tower, although domes were to have risen over large octagonal exhibition halls that formed the junctures of the two-story gallery wings. And following the example of the American Museum's board, the Metropolitan's trustees planned to proceed with building their monumental edifice, which the architects projected would eventually cover 18 acres, in sections. As the first step toward what everyone saw as a decades-long building project, the trustees planned to use the $500,000 appropriation that they had received from the state legislature to erect the westernmost section of the central area of the plan. This structure would comprise a gallery wing and the octagonal pavilions at either end.[90]

In June 1870, Vaux and Mould prepared a beautiful drawing that has survived to show us their original idea for this and future gallery segments (Fig. 8.18). Vaux and Mould envisioned their exterior as a robustly ornamented surface. Tall and graceful Florentine arches were set into walls of rusticated pink granite with disks of polished granite adorning the spandrels between the arches and reliefs of cherubs crowning each window. Above the arcade, Vaux and Mould laid a cornice of multicolored tiles that signaled the transition to the windowless second-floor picture galleries. Over these spacious rooms hovered a continuous metal and glass skylight, the roofline of which bristled with spiky iron cresting.

But this festive repository for art was to exist only on paper. By late July 1872, John Taylor Johnston, the railroad executive who chaired the museum's board, and his fellow trustees had decided to begin their new building by constructing a space that did not appear on the 1869 master plan. Instead of erecting a two-story gallery wing, they wished to commit their resources to building a lofty hall for the display of statuary and large objects. This rectangular structure would be placed on axis with 82nd Street, running east and west at a right angle to the original gallery wing and spanning one of the two middle courtyards indicated on the master plan. In order that the museum's nascent collection of paintings also could be displayed in the new structure, two picture galleries would be located on the upper level of two-story sections at either end of the main hall. Subsequently labeled Wing A on plans (the space, marked in black in Fig. 8.17, was remodeled in 1939 as the present Medieval Court), the new wing was designed to connect with galleries that would surround it when the museum building was eventually completed. Cognizant of its future secluded position and aware of the present need for economy, Vaux and Mould treated the exterior walls of Wing A much less elaborately than they had proposed for their original outer gallery extension. They substituted red brick for pink granite and renounced colorful tiles and carved reliefs. They relied primarily on Florentine arches of gray and white stone to impart a sense of grace and strength to the frugal exterior. This powerful arcade crowned the tall windows that, separated by buttresses, lighted the north and south sides of the main hall. Conceding that it is "perhaps wiser to have a solid, unadorned casket in which the jewels should be preserved" than an ornate and costly container, one contemporary critic reflected the generally less-than-enthusiastic reception that the facadeless exterior of the new building received when it opened in 1880.[91]

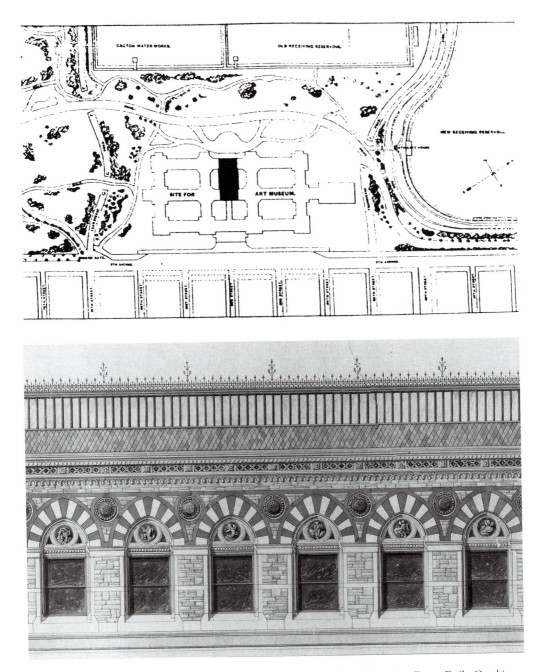

FIGURE 8.17. *(above)* Metropolitan Museum of Art, plan, 1869–1874. From *Daily Graphic* (New York), February 19, 1879. Courtesy of Buffalo and Erie County Public Library.

FIGURE 8.18. *(below)* Metropolitan Museum of Art, elevation drawing, c. 1870. Courtesy of Collections of the Municipal Archives of the City of New York.

But others also shared the same writer's opinion that inside the building was impressive. "We have yet to hear the first word of cavil as to the interior," seconded the *Times*.[92]

When the museum opened its doors to the public, its 199' × 66' main hall ranked as one of the most impressive interior spaces in the city (Fig. 8.19). Great semicircular metal arches suggestive of Viollet-le-Duc's architecture rose from sturdy iron columns stationed between the windows and swept overhead to a height of 95 feet to support a sloping glass roof and central clerestory. Those who came to look at the collection displayed there, much of which consisted of ancient Greek statuary and pottery excavated on Cyprus by Luigi Palma di Cesnola, expressed special pleasure with the abundant light that filled the hall. "You can pick up a pin in any portion of the room," remarked one early eyewitness.[93] Vaux also took pains to insure the viewers' physical comfort. In summer, shades could be drawn over the inside southern surface of the roof glass to shield the hall from the heat of the sun; in winter, even warmth permeated the hall by means of an unusual system of steam pipes located beneath the black and white marble floor. At the sides, radiators warmed fresh air that continually entered the room through perforations in the walls. The threat of ice and snow building up on the roof Vaux dealt with by carrying steam pipes into the rafters.

Despite the sense of spaciousness and comfort that the main hall embodied, its appearance must have been a bit of a disappointment to Mould, who had returned to New York from Peru in time for the opening of the building. In his absence, Vaux and the trustees had decided to erect iron balconies across the north and south sides of the hall to provide visitors with a means of direct communication between the upper-floor picture galleries. Even though Radford had designed these 20-foot-high balconies to rest on the slenderest of columns,

FIGURE 8.19.
Metropolitan Museum of Art, Main Hall, 1880. From *Art Journal* 6 (June 1880). Private collection.

they compromised the general impression of breadth that the interior was designed to convey. They also obscured from view the springing of the great semicircular arches. (Seeing this, Mould must have felt especially pleased that the members of the First Presbyterian Church in Bath, New York, had faithfully carried out his plans for a similar space in their church.) Vaux could have encouraged Mould to take solace from the fact that these utilitarian intrusions into their splendid hall were only temporary. Once the surrounding gallery wings were built, the spatial configuration of the upper floors would be much changed, and the balconies could be removed. Most visitors probably did not even notice that they were out of place here.

People were more likely to have appreciated the admirable color scheme, which one expects came from Mould. Tones of maroon contrasted with light blue, and touches of white unobtrusively highlighted capitals and cornices.[94] The now vanished transverse arches, one observer tells us, were "painted of an approved colour." The large lunettes at either end of the hall were intended eventually to receive murals, but in the meantime they were merely painted some light color. Visitors generally found the whole effect pleasing and harmonious and suitably complementary to the art displayed there. "Attention is purposely directed toward the objects exhibited," wrote one satisfied reviewer, "and not to the building itself."[95]

Calling attention to the building itself, however, did figure in Vaux's plans for the four corner staircases. These led to the upper-level picture galleries located on the east and west sides of the main hall.[96] At each of the broad landings that interrupted the two-story journey, Vaux cut a large round opening into the inner wall, enticing visitors to gaze down upon the main hall from these bird's-eye vantage points (Fig. 8.20). "The circular windows, which are at the intermediate landings," remarked an enthusiastic critic in the *Times*, "are so alluring, giving such pleasant glimpses of the rooms, that one must fain linger for a moment to look within, and an unconscious rest is gained."[97] Making the building and its contents an object of contemplation in this way was a novel idea. We can see Vaux's fanciful invention as evolving from the many park structures that he had designed for viewing landscape. It also recalled his wish to give visitors to the Centennial Exhibition a prospect of his main building from galleries surrounding its grand interior space. The museum's inward-turning fenestration, which James Morse observed allowed "the eye [to] barely guess at remoter spaces," directed one to marvel at the extensive assemblage of treasures that the trustees had gathered within the walls of the museum.[98] The oculi were the architectural embodiment of that sense of wonderment that must have stirred in the breasts of many of America's early museum goers.

Perhaps most visitors to the museum derived the greatest pleasure from viewing the Old Master and modern paintings that hung close together on fabric-covered walls in the four picture galleries. Warmed in winter by freestanding radiators (so as not to damage the paintings on the walls), these long rooms were lit by means of central skylights running the length of high coved ceilings. A discreet note of color was present in the dark blue and cream tints of the pierced metalwork that trimmed the inside base of the skylights, which had large attics above them into which daylight entered through metal and glass panels in the roof. This arrangement, which Vaux had also used in his proposed design for the Metropolitan Museum of Scientific Industry, tempered the inside light and also mitigated against summer heat. At night, a softer radiance filtered

FIGURE 8.20.
Metropolitan
Museum of Art,
view through cir-
cular opening on
stair landing.
From *Art Journal* 6
(July 1880).
Private collection.

through the clerestory from gas jets located in the attic space. Critics praised the quality of light in these galleries. "Light comes in floods from the ceiling," remarked a writer in the *Art Journal*,[99] while the *Times* reported that a deputa-tion of artists were of the opinion "that they knew of no galleries in the United States where pictures were shown to such great advantage." In the all-important matter of illumination, the picture galleries were a great success.

Although Vaux, who himself loved painting and sculpture, must have felt pride in the completed building, he had every reason to be uneasy about the fact that before one stone of the museum had been laid the trustees had aban-doned the 1869 master plan. Surely he must have sensed the threat that this decision held for the ultimate realization of the building that he and Mould had laid out. The trustees' change of heart may have come about, as one author said, because of their sudden desire to have a space emulating European museums, where especially large objects could be displayed. At a time when the new museum was seeking to win public as well as private support for its goal to become a world-famous art institution, the trustees might have believed that a striking architectural statement would have furthered their cause.

Some, however, must have noticed the essential modesty of the new build-ing. Indeed, no one was in a better position than Vaux to understand how much had been done to conceal the fundamental economy of construction. In espous-ing the ambitious plan for Wing A, the trustees were probably building beyond their means, and the architects had been forced to compromise wherever possi-ble. Not only were the murals lacking and the ornamental stone exterior that

Vaux and Mould originally proposed for the gallery wing trimmed back to brick, but even the great semicircular arches of the main hall were not the high-priced expression of metal construction that most visitors thought them to be. "What appears to be iron wrought into a pierced pattern . . . is in reality a cheap affair of iron rods covered with zinc," complained Clarence Cook, who saw Radford's ruse as "that last sweet thing out in architectural sham."[100]

Knowledgeable individuals knew that the odd-looking structure with temporary wooden stairs and porches (one could step out of the eastern picture gallery for a breath of fresh air) represented only a small portion of a much grander scheme. Yet the unfinished, makeshift appearance of the building's exterior prejudiced Vaux, who soon found his work being criticized for its drab and truncated appearance. And as was to happen in the case of the American Museum, he would be passed over a few years later when further additions to the art museum were undertaken. On May 3, 1887, Vaux and McEntee visited the museum again together. McEntee reflected to himself that Vaux's "plan of the Museum has been set aside and they are at work on a new design." To the painter, the decision to replace Vaux with Theodore Weston showed "how little integrity and conscientiousness go in this country." One wonders if Vaux's fate would have been different if instead of erecting Wing A, he and Mould had been allowed to proceed with the construction of the first wing of their 1869 master plan. Vaux's exclusion from later construction at the museum, however, was symptomatic of a general decline in the demand for his services. Throughout the 1880s, he found success recede more and more from his grasp.

A SCHOOL OF ROMANTICISTS EVEN THEN FAST VANISHING 1881–1895

By 1881, Vaux could look back on 30 years of success and near success. While much work and many challenges lay ahead, over the next decade and a half he would see his name eclipsed by others, especially as America became enamored of modern Neoclassicism. But a taste for Roman monumentality was not in Vaux's makeup, and until his death in 1895, he remained true to the ideals of naturalism in landscape design and to picturesque expression in building. When Olmsted moved to Brookline, Massachusetts, in 1881 (he told Vaux that it "would be Hell" for him to stay living in New York), Vaux must have felt that indeed an era had ended in his life. Vaux was to continue to concern himself with the parks that he and Olmsted had designed together, and from time to time he would prepare plans for significant new pleasure grounds with his old partner. Especially after 1888, when Vaux became landscape architect with the Department of Public Parks, a post that he held until his death in November 1895, he had the opportunity to fulfill his desire to plan for the city he loved many new small parks and squares. Much of this work was done with his devoted protégé, Samuel Parsons Jr., who became Vaux's professional partner in 1880. The son of a well-known Flushing, Long Island, nurseryman, Parsons came to study landscape architecture with Vaux after graduating from Yale in 1862 and having worked for a time in his father's business. Assisting Parsons, Radford, and Vaux was the architect's son Downing, who by the beginning of the 1880s, after completing his degree at Columbia, had determined on a career in architecture and landscape architecture under his father's tutelage.

A rare glimpse into Vaux's office life at this time comes from the reminiscences of H. Van Buren Magonigle, a New York architect who got his start under Vaux in the summer of 1881.[1] Looking back from the perspective of the 1930s, Magonigle remembered how in the days before large architectural establishments, he and Downing were usually the sole assistants to the firms of Vaux and Radford, Architects, and Vaux & Co., Landscape Architects. Together with Vaux, "Samuel Parsons, Jr., was one Co.," said Magonigle, "Mr. Radford the other."

Magonigle characterized Radford as "an old dear and as kind as they come," who spoke with a heavy British accent and gladly gave up the arduous task of copying out specifications to the young student with good handwriting.[2] From Downing, Magonigle learned how to grind India ink, which he used to make both original drawings on cloth-backed paper and contractors' copies on tracing paper. Blueprints, he said, were too new for Downing's father to trust. In addition to tutoring Magonigle, on hot summer days Downing would take him down to the Battery to the "public swimming baths" attached to the seawall there. The swimming became a thing of the past, however, in 1884, when Vaux moved his office from 71 Broadway, which was near Trinity Church, to Bible House on Fourth Avenue south of Astor Place. Erected in 1852, the building was well-known as the center of the American Bible Society's effort to print and distribute Holy Scriptures free of charge to all the world. Vaux's new quarters overlooking the inner court, Magonigle tells us, were far from ideal: "All day long the thump and rumble of the presses printing Bibles filled our ears," he recalled, "and the evil odors of paste glue from the bindery assailed our noses."

Of Vaux himself, Magonigle had fond memories. To a young man of the early 1880s, his mentor, who was then in his late fifties, represented one of "a school of romanticists even then fast vanishing." A devoted heir of the noble "Byronic tradition," Vaux, in Magonigle's eyes, was "all for 'originality' and the world well lost." Surely Vaux must have strengthened this impression when he recounted to his receptive student stories of his arguments with Olmsted about the superiority of art over administration and of his many battles to safeguard the ideals of the Greensward plan against attacks by philistine park commissioners and politicians. Magonigle also cherished personal memories of his early teacher, who often responded to questions by pushing his spectacles up on his forehead and answering in a "cultivated, abstracted way." As a man always "immensely absorbed" in some thought, Vaux appeared to Magonigle as "one of the most absent-minded men I have ever known." Such concentration offered opportunities for amusement for those around him. One winter day in Central Park, Magonigle recounted, "I saw Mr. Vaux skating on the lake with his hands behind him and his eyes on the ice, perhaps thinking of how he had helped to make the lake and establish those shores; and just to test him out I skated backward in front of him for at least a quarter of a mile; he looked up once or twice in a dim way but I doubt if he saw me, and if he saw me he didn't know who I was." And while Vaux's architecture seemed hopelessly old-fashioned to Magonigle's mature sensibilities, he could still admire the "really lovely and graceful bridges" that Vaux had designed for Central Park. Likewise, Magonigle conceded that Vaux "had a real feeling for stonework." Central Park, he said, abounded in "splendid retaining walls, fine in structure, in texture, in everything that gives a wall meaning and quality and reveals the fine mind and taste behind it."

ONE OF THE FIRST projects on which Magonigle might have assisted would have been the landscaping of the churchyard of New York's Grace Church (Fig. 9.1). It was to be the finest small urban space that Vaux had the opportunity to lay out. Undoubtedly, the commission came to him as a result of his association in the model tenement movement with Henry C. Potter, the rector, and his acquaintance with the benefactress of the Children Aid Society's boys' lodging house, Catherine Lorillard Wolfe, a devoted parishioner. In 1881, Potter asked

FIGURE 9.1.
Grace Church,
grounds, New
York City,
1881. Courtesy
of Grace
Church.

Vaux to prepare a plan for the 100' × 66' close on the north side of the church in front of the rectory and Grace House, the parish hall paid for by Miss Wolfe and erected the year before according to designs by James Renwick Jr. In the mid-1840s, Renwick had also designed the Gothic Revival rectory and more famous church, a building that Vaux found "agreeable in line and proportion."[3] As for the grounds of this, the most fashionable parish in the metropolis, Vaux realized that they were "under the control of a liberal corporation which could afford not only to do what was right in the first instance, but to keep everything in good order afterward."[4]

Here was an exceptional opportunity for Vaux to set an example of how a diminutive space could be given "its correct landscape treatment." The architect began by arranging the walks from the street to the parish house, rectory, and church. By replacing the existing path that led straight from the sidewalk to the rectory porch with a diagonal one some distance to the south, he created a new, indirect approach to the minister's house that allowed the larger part of the space in front of the building to be given over to lawn. Visitors entering the church-yard from Broadway enjoyed a pleasing, angled view of the rectory, which now seemed appropriately secluded from the busy city street. Vaux also laid a curved path alongside the church to the new parish house. From there, a flagstone walk led to the rectory and linked the two footpaths. Thus, Vaux's system of walks permitted visitors and churchgoers to proceed directly to Grace House without passing in front of the rectory. He also took care to isolate the comings and goings of servants and tradesmen from the movements of parishioners by providing a discreet service entrance on the north side of the property, where a walkway from the street led directly to the basement stairs. Certainly, the accumulated experience of designing walks and drives for different sorts of uses in Central Park and elsewhere went into Vaux's creation of this simple but thoughtful plan.

A desire for uncomplicated expression also guided Vaux in his choice of plants. After removing all of the existing earth to a depth of 18 inches and replacing it with rich topsoil, Vaux brought in weed-free sod to form a thick lawn. "The greensward," said Vaux, "should appear at a glance to be the prepondering color fact." Indeed, Vaux saw no appropriate place within these limited grounds for the introduction of flowers, except in front of the rectory door. There, he conceded, a bed of bright color "had a definite value, because it accentuated the line of separation between the close cut green grass of the lawn and the bluish gray pavement selected for the approach to the house." The larger area of lawn in front of the rectory was bordered on the north by a wall of dense shrubbery, while inside the existing iron fence that separated the grounds from the public sidewalk Vaux introduced California privet, a plant that he said thrived "under the peculiar stress of the city." Vaux retained a box tree growing near the southwest angle of the rectory and a magnolia that stood near the middle of the grounds. Otherwise, he built up the areas of low bedding plants that bordered the small sea of grass with a harmonious variety of shrubs. Azalea took its place, together with taller species of rhododendrons; the "neat attractive leaves" of japonica "served to make an agreeable contrast with the variegated and dwarf leafed and dwarf Japan Quince"; purple barberry appeared here and there among the green foliage; spirea mingled with privet; several species of mock orange filled out larger groupings of shrubbery; and feathery "masses of tamarix Indica and Africana were disposed at intervals among the other shrubs to lighten their general effect and to accentuate their skyline." And wishing to create a year-round oasis of green (as well as to cope with the site's westerly exposure), Vaux introduced many sorts of evergreens among the deciduous shrubs.

From the walks, the plantings were disposed so as to direct the eye of the passerby toward certain pleasing, if circumscribed, views. Approaching the rectory on the main path, for example, one saw to the right "a bay of turf extending almost to the angle formed by a transept of the church." This was followed soon after by a diagonal glimpse of bordered lawn reaching to the corner formed by the meeting of Grace House with the rear of the church. On these buildings, as well as on the rectory, Vaux trained Japanese ivy, which, he noted, "grew freely and rapidly" and, by means of tiny rootlets, clung close to the walls to create a luxuriant mantle of delicate foliage.

Today the walls of the church and rectory are bare of the ivy that Vaux so admired, and we search in vain for many of the plants of which Vaux spoke. Yet the grounds of Grace Church preserve to a remarkable degree the look and feel that Vaux gave to them.[5] Passing through the old iron gate, we still walk the curving pathways that led Vaux and his contemporaries to the rectory door and to the parish house entrance. Most of all, we can still enjoy amid the bustle of an active city the spirit of informal intimacy and serenity that Vaux created here. "The planting of Grace Church yard," remarked the *Tribune* in 1881, "bears witness to the thousands who pass it every day that a few square rods beside the city's great thoroughfare can be transformed into a marvel of quiet beauty." In the late twentieth century, Grace Church is perhaps the best place left to us to experience a piece of landscape architecture for which Vaux himself was primarily responsible.[6]

THE GROUNDS OF prestigious Grace Church certainly aided the fortunes of Vaux & Co., and in the 1880s, numerous other organizations sought out the firm for landscape design work. Since his days with Withers and Olmsted, Vaux had worked for the trustees of New York's Trinity Cemetery, located at 155th Street and Broadway in Upper Manhattan. In 1870, when Broadway was extended through the cemetery grounds, dividing the property into eastern and western portions, Withers had designed a suspension bridge over the street to link the two sections. The origins of this handsome Gothic structure, which critic Montgomery Schuyler praised as one of Withers's finest works, lay in Downing's idea to join parts of his Washington park with a suspension bridge across Tiber Creek.[7] In the mid-1870s, Vaux had designed the stone walls that surround the cemetery. Now, in 1881, he prepared a plan for part of the steep landscape of the extension west of Broadway. The bucolic resting place that Vaux created there, which included a picturesque gatehouse, won the special admiration of Olmsted.[8] The following year, Vaux was asked by the Spanish-Portuguese Synagogue, Congregation Shearith Israel, to lay out their Fourth Cemetery in the Cyprus Hills area of Brooklyn. Vaux also designed the cemetery chapel there. This simple but picturesque red brick structure with sturdy round arches forming a gateway-like porch is the only religious building that Vaux is known to have built. It was surely through the good graces of Andrew Green, who had many friends among the Jewish community and was a frequent visitor to this congregation's old synagogue on Crosby Street, that this unusual opportunity came Vaux's way. Farther afield were commissions for new cemeteries in Macon, Georgia, and Trenton, New Jersey. In July 1887, when a group of prominent Macon citizens became dismayed over the lack of maintenance in Rose Hill, the city's rural cemetery, which had been laid out in the 1840s, they determined to form their own association. For them, Vaux provided a plan for Riverside Cemetery. His design for the new 23-acre burial ground echoed the curving system of roadways in adjacent Rose Hill and took care to preserve a Civil War redoubt overlooking the Ocmulgee River, a memorial to the death of the Old South. In addition, the local newspaper reported that Vaux's plan incorporated "extensive drives and walks, pleasant surprises, striking views, chapel, receiving vault, Sexton's office, and pagoda."[9] In June 1888, the trustees of Riverview Cemetery in Trenton paid Vaux & Co. $280 for a plan for a large burial ground along the banks of the Delaware River. Educational institutions also became Vaux's clients during these years. In addition to the plans he made in 1882 for the grounds of Bryn Mawr College near Philadelphia, Vaux claimed to have designed the campus of the Wesleyan Female Seminary (present Wesleyan College) in Macon, Georgia. Somewhat later, in 1894, Vaux was consulted on the plan for the new Bronx campus of New York University.[10]

Private individuals who would not hire Vaux to design their house did, however, turn to him for advice on landscaping their grounds. In 1889, when wealthy businessman John Wisner had Babb, Cook and Willard build him a large Colonial-style house at Summit, New Jersey, he hired Vaux & Co. to prepare a plan for the wooded grounds. It appears that only part of the plan that Vaux and Parsons prepared was carried out. One assumes that they determined that the house, which Wisner called the Clearing, would be placed, as Parsons said, on "a small level platform of made earth extending out to a sharp declivity and just allowing enough space for the house and drive and a turn around beyond it."[11] From the house and the entrance drive, the owners and their guests could enjoy attractive views of the hollow, which Vaux and Parsons merely cleared of some of its trees in order to open the view to the bottom. They also laid a path winding around the perimeter of the property (about seven acres). This walk, Parsons remarked, "revealed many beautiful spots" among the native groves of oaks that nature had interspersed with pine. In 1888, when Robert Bowne Suckley inherited Wilderstein at Rhinebeck, New York, he turned to Poughkeepsie architect Arnout Cannon Jr. to enlarge the house. Two years later, Suckley, whose relative R. S. Bowne had commissioned a house from Vaux in 1885 at Flushing,[12] asked Vaux to landscape his extensive grounds, which overlooked the Hudson. For the next three years, Vaux, Downing, and Parsons (who was related to the Bowne family) laid out roads, planted tress and shrubs, and erected structures on the property.[13] Identifying the opportunity that nature offered, Vaux laid out a path to the one spot from which a person might gaze out on a serene panorama of river scenery, with the earlier Hoyt property in the distance. Furthermore, Vaux realized that this unique vantage point (now called Umbrella Point) also offered the spectator, when he or she turned around, a picturelike perspective view of the towered house on its hilltop site. Wilderstein, which is currently the object of a preservation campaign, was Vaux's last chance to create a domestic landscape expressive of the Romantic principles that he had first articulated in *Villas and Cottages*.

W. M. Burr, a lawyer at Cazenovia, New York, gave Vaux one of his last opportunities to lay out a residential community. In March 1889, the local newspaper of the pretty little upstate town on the shores of Lake Owaghena announced that Vaux & Co. were subdividing waterfront property that Burr owned along Lake Shore Road in preparation for its sale as building lots for summer homes. The plan that Vaux drew, which was never implemented, employed a circuit road to connect a number of home sites, each several acres in size. Because of the sloping topography, each owner might have enjoyed views of the lake. Vaux's plan also made provision for a community park so that everyone could have access to the water. In New York City, the Convent of the Sacred Heart also engaged Vaux around this time to prepare a street plan for property it owned and wished to sell in Manhattanville. Speaking to the members of the Architectural League in March 1889, Vaux explained how this elevated tableland lying between 126th and 135th Streets, with Convent Avenue on the west and St. Nicholas Avenue on the east, could offer residents here a view of Long Island Sound. "In the residence quarter open for occupation in the city of New York such an opportunity for overlook is of rare occurrence," Vaux told his listeners. His scheme, which he presented that night in a map that is now lost, involved the creation of a street "partly straight and partly serpentine" running north to south along the edge of the bluff above St. Nicholas Avenue.[14] The present St. Nicholas Terrace suggests that the sisters won the city's approval to lay out the street of which Vaux spoke. However, instead of developing into an area of detached or semidetached residences, as Vaux envisioned, in 1903 the land became the site of City College (the present City College of the City University of New York).

ALTHOUGH VAUX WAS TO become less and less in demand as an architect of private houses, he received a number of commissions for dwellings in the early 1880s. The most important client of these years was the former governor of New

York and presidential candidate Samuel Tilden. Since coming to New York as a lad in the early 1830s, Tilden had amassed one of the largest fortunes in America from his work as a lawyer to large corporations, especially railroads. Always a champion of the principles of good government in local politics, Tilden earned wide acclaim for his successful attack on William Tweed and his "ring" of associates. In 1874, Tilden and Olmsted's friend from Buffalo, William Dorsheimer, were elected on a reform ticket as governor and lieutenant governor of New York. In the national election of the centennial year, Tilden won the Democratic nomination for president but lost the office to Rutherford B. Hayes under circumstances that many regarded as fraudulent. Following his defeat, Tilden turned the greater part of his attention to his private affairs and to building up the finest private library in the country. In 1879, he purchased Greystone, a large stone villa built in the early 1860s in Yonkers, and employed Vaux to redesign its 113-acre grounds. Here Tilden, who throughout his life suffered from delicate health, spent much of his time walking, riding, and breathing the fresh Hudson Valley air.[15] But after a distinguished and active career in business and politics, Tilden was unwilling to abandon completely city life. Two years after buying his suburban home, he determined to remodel the adjacent townhouses on the south side of Gramercy Park in New York that had long been his primary residence. This work he also entrusted to Vaux, who must have been first introduced to Tilden by Green, his client's longtime friend and associate. From 1881 to 1884 Vaux worked on transforming 14 and 15 Gramercy Park South (the present home of the National Arts Club) into a single palatial dwelling that featured a magnificent library for Tilden's impressive collection of books (Fig. 9.2).[16]

Under Vaux's direction, the unexceptional exteriors of the two traditional brownstone houses gave way to a single picturesque facade. An asymmetrically balanced arrangement of pointed arches and multistory bay windows imparted a lively rhythm and cheerful openness to the four-story elevation, which Vaux carried well above the levels of its neighbors. And as one might have expected of Vaux, instead of the usual horizontal cornice line, he endowed Samuel Tilden's house with an exuberant roofline. Perched on a false pediment that stood above the west party wall, a tall pole raised an American flag high above the surrounding buildings. It seemed designed especially to proclaim to passersby on nearby Park Avenue that here was the home of a president. On the front of the house, two finial-crowned gables with slitlike windows carried the vertical lines of the facade beyond the level of the tall upper floor. Between these gables, a low parapet wall topped with a brass railing presumably defined a place from which the melancholic bachelor could gaze out over the city to which he had given so much of his life's energy. But to the late-nineteenth-century architectural critic Montgomery Schuyler, the most striking feature of the north-facing facade was its subtle combination of stone materials. "An unusually large variety of colors, and those of the most positive tints that natural stones supply," wrote Schuyler, "has here been employed and harmonized; and, what is even rarer, they have all been used with architectural propriety to accentuate the construction and to heighten its effect."[17] Within a field of salmon-colored masonry composed of sandstone from quarries in Belleville, New Jersey, Vaux set bands of polished charcoal granite that continued into the banded arches above various windows. The combination of tones was enhanced by the introduction of a reddish stone imported from Carlisle, Scotland, for use around

FIGURE 9.2.
Samuel Tilden house,
New York City,
1881–1884. From
*L'Architecture
américaine*, 1886.
Private collection.

the windows. Many of these had pink granite colonettes supporting their carved stone lintels.

Vaux reserved the most ornamental treatment of the facade for the first floor above the basement. Here, within easy view of people on the street, he arranged a panel of decorative carving that resembled a book cover with carved heads of Tilden's favorite authors in three bands. Franklin, whom Tilden regarded as the ideal American man of letters, occupied the central band, with Shakespeare and Milton above Goethe and Dante. Reliefs of the four seasons decorated the stone portico (now demolished) that greeted visitors at the main entrance on the east side of the facade, while a bust of Michelangelo looked down upon the governor's business clients who climbed the steps to enter through the west doorway. Despite the gaiety of this facade, the most ornamental piece of design in Vaux's career after the Terrace, the overall impression one receives from it is one of restraint, for as Schuyler pointed out, Vaux made decoration keep its place within a predominantly architectural scheme of things. Especially to modern eyes, the true beauty of the Tilden house facade derives from the subtle abstract balance that Vaux maintained between planarity and projection, horizontality and verticality.

In the winter of 1882, Jervis McEntee, who disliked Tilden because he procrastinated in paying Vaux for his work, went with his brother-in-law to inspect the progress of the house. "The details of the carving," McEntee remarked, "are charming and I think Calvert has shown unusual ability in it."[18] A year later, however, when the scaffolding had come down, a writer in the *Art Amateur* was not pleased by what he saw. He especially faulted Vaux for having cast his design in the fading Victorian Gothic style. "Mr. Vaux is a very good landscape architect," said the journal, "but he has apparently not been awake to what has been going on in domestic architecture in New York during the last few years."[19] Indeed, the facade harked back to Ruskin's notion of a wall veil of natural materials and decorative sculpture. Perhaps Vaux had in mind John P. Seddon's 1858 renovation of Eatington Park in Warwickshire, a building that Charles Eastlake himself used in his *History of the Gothic Revival* (1872) as an example of a successful remodeling of a former nondescript building. In comparison with the new taste for French Renaissance elegance and display, represented by such works as George B. Post's Cornelius Vanderbilt residence of 1879 and William Morris Hunt's William K. Vanderbilt house of the same year, the facade of the Tilden house, despite the excellence of its proportion and detail, appeared old-fashioned. "I know by a recent comparison of dates," remembered Van Buren Magonigle, who must have worked on the Tilden house drawings, that in Vaux's office little attention was paid to the facts that at the time the great Richardson was creating "some of his best work," that McKim, Mead and White were "rising to the primacy they later achieved," or that Richard Morris Hunt occupied the august position of "dean of the profession."

More up-to-date taste appeared on the interior. Here the wealthy lawyer seems to have spared no expense in converting the main rooms of his house into marvels of what has come to be called the Aesthetic Movement. In the vestibule, John La Farge created pearly opalescent glass panels for the doors, and in the dining room, Ellin and Kitson carved and gilded beautiful satinwood wall panels depicting birds fluttering among vines. In this extraordinary apartment (which, sadly, is remodeled) Tilden and his guests dined beneath a ceiling of turquoise blue tiles, which reflected light in shifting patterns from a massive chandelier that hung from a central octagon panel carved with fruits and berries. A diaper pattern formed of blocks of satinwood enriched the upper space of the walls, and a band of delicate lotus leaves brightened the cove of the ceiling. "This beautiful room," wrote Sheldon in *Artistic Houses*, "indeed, abounds in such subtleties of design, and becomes, through them, a banqueting-chamber where the imagination and the eyes alike may feast." But even more impressive was the library. Here Tilden spent many hours reading and admiring his wonderful collection of books, which were destined in his will to form the nucleus of a municipal library. And perhaps if Vaux were kindly disposed, he would have ascribed Tilden's frequent tardiness in paying him his fee to his client's absorption in higher thoughts. ("Rich and too mean and selfish to pay for work finished satisfactorily long ago," was McEntee's view of the matter.)[20] Raising his gaze from a page of Shakespeare or Goethe, Tilden might feast his eyes on the many-faceted surface of the glass dome that formed the high ceiling of this chamber. Fortunately, this jewel-like creation (made by Donald MacDonald of Boston) of small pieces of clear glass held together by a web of thin lead lines still exists for us to admire. And though the library is presently put to less erudite purposes than Tilden and Vaux intended, it remains one of the most enchanting nineteenth-century interiors in all of New York.

IN THE SPRING OF 1882, the great actor Edwin Booth, a close friend of Jervis McEntee, asked Vaux to design a summer home for him at Newport. By this time, Vaux and his wife, who had followed the actor's career in New York since the 1860s, were also in his circle of friends. (It had been Booth who had arranged for Vaux to take his nephew, Van Buren Magonigle, into the office.) By the early 1880s, Booth had achieved international fame for his portrayal of Hamlet and other Shakespearean characters, but he had also suffered many personal tragedies, including the disgrace of having for a brother the assassin of Abraham Lincoln. Booth's home at Newport, which he came to call Boothden, was to be a retreat from the world, a place where the famous actor and his pretty daughter Edwina might enjoy life far from the public eye (Fig. 9.3). The large two-and-a-half-story dwelling on Indian Avenue was well under way by September 1882, when Vaux paid a visit to the site. Construction proceeded to completion while Booth was away on an acting tour of Europe. On June 28, McEntee joined Vaux in Newport to show the recently returned celebrity his new house. "It is a very interesting place," said McEntee, who thought it would "entirely suit" his famous actor friend.[21]

Generally resembling large wooden country houses in *Villas and Cottages*, Boothden also displayed the taste of the 1880s in its simple, broad roofline and wood shingle covering. For Booth, its prized feature was the veranda that extended across the side of the house facing the broad lawn that sloped down to the Sakonnet River. On this porch, wrote one biographer, the wearied actor would doze for hours in a hammock, pulling up canvas panels when necessary

to protect himself from chill breezes. And like pensive James Morse, who around this time had Vaux add a similar porch to his summer house at Cotuit, Massachusetts,[22] Booth enjoyed sharing his leisure with close friends. Guests such as McEntee, we are told, would "stretch in chairs and hammocks and talk idly, and idly watch smoke drift away, blue in the air."[23] Undoubtedly the stoical Booth also spent many hours on his veranda reflecting on how misfortune had dogged his personal life and seemed to threaten the future of his beloved Edwina. In 1863, after three years of marriage, his wife, actress Mary Devlin, had died suddenly, leaving him alone with their two-year-old daughter. At age 20, Edwina had become engaged to Downing Vaux. Vaux was quite fond of his son's fiancée and happy that Booth warmly approved of his daughter's choice. He also perceived that motherless Edwina especially appreciated "the home aspect of our family circle."[24] But during the period when Booth's house was going up, sad events overshadowed the romance.

On October 13, 1882, Vaux found his 26-year-old son in his room near death from gas asphyxiation.[25] Two days passed before Downing regained consciousness. Despite the fact that he was a strong athlete—Magonigle remembered that he "was like a seal in the water"—Downing endured a long and uncertain convalescence. At the beginning of November, McEntee received a letter from Mary Vaux, who lamented that her son was getting on "very slowly."[26] In December, Booth generously suggested that the Vauxes let him take Downing and his sister Julia with him and Edwina on his European tour. Booth hoped that the change of scenery would do the young man good, and in England, he thought, they might find doctors who could help him. A letter that McEntee received from Booth at the beginning of February, however, gave discouraging news. Downing had only gotten worse since their arrival in England, and it was clear that he must be sent home. "Calvert and Mary are greatly distressed," reported McEntee, "as Downing went entirely against the better judgment of both of them."[27] After 17 days on the ocean, Downing and Julia returned to New York in mid-February. Downing immediately went to stay with McEntee at Rondout. One wonders, however, how gay the atmosphere could have been there, for in his diary, McEntee continually mourned his departed wife and lamented the lack of demand for his pictures. Nonetheless, by spring, Downing appeared well enough to take a room in New York and, presumably, resume assisting in his father's office. It was, however, a false dawn, for on May 7, after breakfasting with his father, Downing disappeared. At the end of two days of searching, Vaux, who had been relieved to find Downing's revolver still in his room, went to the police; one can imagine with what dismay he and his friends read in the *Tribune*, "Son of a Prominent Architect Missing."[28] Fortunately, Downing, who had been upset over a letter he had received from Edwina, turned up at a friend's house.

Life seems to have returned to normal after that, and Downing probably went along with his father and McEntee to the opening of the Brooklyn Bridge on May 24. That night, the whole family watched from the roof of the Vauxes' house as the city put on a great display of fireworks to celebrate the historic event. Edwina and her father got their first glimpse of the completed bridge on June 19, when their boat arrived from Europe. Downing was at the pier to greet them, and a few days later he joined his father and McEntee on their trip to Newport to introduce Booth to his new house. But it is clear from entries in McEntee's diary that things were not right between the reunited couple. Booth saw it and remarked to McEntee that he was "somewhat discouraged about Downing." Edwina found him "abstracted." A trip in July to the Mountain House in the company of her father and future in-laws apparently did nothing to reassure her of Downing's ardor. Two weeks later, just before dinner at Rondout, Downing received a letter from Edwina with the news that she was breaking off the engagement. Not long after, her father went to the post office in Newport to return Downing's letters to him. "He is reasonable and manly," remarked McEntee of Downing a month after their visit to Boothden, "and shows himself capable of bearing a severe strain."[29] In 1885, Edwina married a stockbroker; Downing remained a bachelor until much later in his life, which he ended in 1926 by committing suicide.

DESPITE HIS ASSOCIATION with public figures like Tilden and Booth, Vaux attracted fewer well-to-do architectural patrons after the early 1880s. One who did seek him out was New York City mayor William Russell Grace. He asked Vaux & Co. to landscape the grounds of his Long Island estate, Graceland, and to add a large conservatory to his city residence.[30] In Rondout, which could be considered Vaux's second home, several individuals commissioned designs for houses from him. In the summer of 1883, McEntee reported that Vaux was planning a home for a Mrs. Columbus van Denson, although whether or not the dwelling was built is unknown. Two years later, McEntee mentioned that Vaux was erecting a residence for a Mr. Terry, but the painter gave no further details.[31] In 1886, Vaux designed at Rondout a large house for F. H. Griffiths, a feed and grain dealer in Kingston. The rectangular clapboard and shingle dwelling with four broad gables resembles an enlarged and simplified version of the chalet-style house that Vaux is said to have designed in 1871 for John C. Dore in Riverside, Illinois. The Griffiths house stands on Chestnut Street, where it commands much the same lofty vista of Hudson Valley scenery as McEntee's vanished studio, which was located a short distance to the north.[32] Also on Chestnut Street was the house of Samuel D. Coykendall, a man whom Vaux had known for several years. A wealthy owner of Hudson River steamboats, Coykendall purchased a piece of McEntee's property in July 1890 and commissioned Vaux to design a house and lay out the grounds.[33] The large brick dwelling was probably one of the first projects that Vaux took up in September after he and Mary returned from a two-month trip to Europe.[34] And although we do not know their itinerary for this last trip abroad, one assumes from the design of the Coykendall mansion that Vaux saw in England examples of the sober brick architecture of James Brooks. Unfortunately, this last house known to have been constructed from Vaux's designs no longer stands to command the magnificent vistas that must have filled its many large windows. There may be other houses by Vaux from this period of which I am unaware, but clearly the time when the architect was regarded as a foremost thinker on the design of country houses had passed.

Fortunately for Vaux, other areas of activity filled the void left by the loss of private commissions. For a number of years beginning in the mid-1880s, the Children's Aid Society employed Vaux to design more than a dozen buildings for its use. In 1879, Vaux had furnished plans for the first lodging house that the society had erected. He had won the confidence of Brace and the society's president, banker William A. Booth, when the charitable organization with ties to the city's upper class was expanding its work among New York's population of homeless children. Most of the commodious and picturesque buildings that Vaux designed for the society have gone down, but their story forms an interesting and unstudied chapter in the history of architecture and philanthropy in New York. As a group, they constitute the most important architectural work of Vaux's later life.

In 1883, Vaux prepared plans for the West Side Lodging House (Fig. 9.4), which the society erected at the southeast corner of Seventh Avenue and West 32nd Street with donations from Catherine Wolfe and John Jacob Astor. The long-since-demolished building aided waifs of the city's notorious Tenderloin district, many of whom earned their pittance on Sixth and Eighth Avenues selling papers and shining shoes. The new structure held accommodations similar to Vaux's earlier lodging house. In place of a conservatory, however, the large main room—which in winter could be ventilated with little loss of heat by tilting open the glass transoms—provided the boys with the homey pleasure of a fireplace.[35] But like the earlier structure, the society's lodging house distinguished itself from its surroundings by reason of its picturesque character, which found special expression in the gay roofline of dormers, gables, and chimneys. Vaux took pains to develop the corner angle into a polygonal tower that featured a large bay window that opened off the main room.

To Vaux's picturesque sensibility, end lots in New York possessed special potential for architectural display. "In a street system laid out on the rectangular plan, the chief points of interest are the corners of the blocks, because, from

FIGURE 9.4. West Side Lodging House, New York City, 1883. From *American Architect and Building News* 16 (November 29, 1884). Courtesy of Buffalo and Erie County Public Library.

each, by a half turn of the head, a view can be obtained of the opposite corner," Vaux stated in an 1889 address to the Architectural League.[36] Vaux even thought that the city should relax the building code so that bay windows and other projections might encroach more on the street at corners. "As the avenues are 100 feet wide, and the streets 60 feet wide," he said, "the open space of 6000 square feet at every crossing is certainly large, and it would add greatly to the opportunity for picturesque composition if even a foot of extra projection was permitted for, say, ten feet, each way." Looking diagonally across an intersection at a building, he pointed out, we see "a perspective effect of lines" in even a simple building. Likewise, the "variety of light given by the cross street" enhanced by the "chiaroscuro of the atmosphere" produces a pleasing contrast of light and shade. Vaux might have brought forth the perspective view of the West Side Lodging House, one side of which is cast in shadow and the other in bright light, that he published in the *American Architect and Building News* (Fig. 9.4) to illustrate these points.[37] "We thus secure some of the elements that are needed to make a picturesque composition, in accordance with the landscape painter's idea of it," Vaux maintained. Reasoning that everyone enjoys "agreeable architectural compositions to look at," Vaux believed that "property owners of corner lots should be tempted to emphasize their salient angles." It is an argument that he made successfully to donors of the society's lodging houses.

The sole survivor of the four lodging houses that Vaux designed is at the northeast corner of 8th Street and Avenue B (Fig. 9.5). Converted to cooperative apartments in the 1980s, the red brick structure was originally designed by Vaux and Radford in 1885 and built with money donated to the society by Mrs. Robert L. Stuart. The donor's husband, a wealthy candy manufacturer, had been an early president of the American Museum and a benefactor of the Metropolitan Museum of Art.[38] Similar in plan and accommodation to the East Side Lodging House, the 87' × 47' building, which opened in 1887, stands directly across Avenue B from Tompkins Square. From the arched windows on the western end of the high-ceilinged main room, the boys, many of whom were of German extraction, could look out at the square, for which Olmsted had made a plan in the mid-1870s. In 1886, perhaps encouraged by the society's taking up residence on the square, the parks department undertook an ambitious beautification campaign in the square. Sod was laid down, and 110 trees some 30 feet in height were planted. (One would like to know if Vaux ever discussed with Mrs. Stuart her misguided efforts to have trees cut down along the border of Central Park so that she could see into the park from her Fifth Avenue mansion.) On the facade of his building that faced the square, Vaux developed the corner into a rectangular tower that lifted a steep pyramidal roof into the skyline. A taller tower section on 8th Street projected above the building's main entrance, although youngsters coming for the night generally entered by way of a side gate, where steps took them to basement washrooms. Here they cleaned themselves before climbing to the first-floor dining room, second-floor main room, or third- and fourth-floor dormitories. On March 28, 1887, Vaux and McEntee attended the building's dedication and heard Judge Hooper Van Vorst praise Vaux and Radford for the fine building that they had erected with a limited budget. "Mr. Vaux . . . has done nothing better than this," proclaimed the enthusiastic judge.[39]

A second type of building that the society erected was the industrial school. Here children of the poor were taught skills that would enable them to earn

FIGURE 9.5.
Tompkins
Square Lodg-
ing House and
Industrial
School, New
York City,
1885. From
Harper's Weekly
30 (March 6,
1886). Private
collection.

their living at a trade. The well-preserved example at 256–258 Mott Street (Fig.
9.6), which Vaux designed in 1888 as a memorial to the recently deceased wife
of John Jacob Astor III, is representative of the five other brick schoolhouses that
Vaux is known to have planned for the society in the late 1880s and early
1890s.[40] A two-story oriole window projects from the center of the five-story,
red brick and terra-cotta facade that, like its sisters, terminates in a precipitous
stepped gable. Vaux first introduced this elevation formula on the side elevation
of the 44th Street Lodging House for Boys, which millionaire Morris K. Jessup
funded in 1887 (Fig. 9.7).[41] While Vaux was well aware that the stepped gable
was a common feature of the British Queen Anne style, he and the society also
may have wished to recall the city's roots in thrifty Dutch mercantilism with
an architecture that approximated the seventeenth-century houses of New
Amsterdam. The society's trade schools, however, were freestanding structures
in which classrooms received light and air from the sides as well as from the front
and back of the building. Indeed, on the south elevation of the Sullivan Street
School, which Vaux designed in 1892, the outer walls of the three main floors
consist entirely of windows. The Mott Street School was typical in its interior
arrangements, with each floor providing open classroom space (the kindergarten
met on the second floor, while industrial courses were given in the third and
fourth stories) that could be subdivided by means of rolling partitions.

In addition to lodging and educating poor children, the society also took a
special interest in the welfare of mothers and young women. In the summer of

FIGURE 9.6.
Mott Street Industrial
School, New York City,
1888. Courtesy of
Children's Aid Society.

1882, the society opened a health home or sanitarium that Vaux had designed to accommodate 120 women and children. Intended as a place to which mothers from the tenement districts might bring sickly sons or daughters in summer, the home was located at the west end of Coney Island "in a quiet nook, away from the rush of summer visitors, where the strong ocean breezes sweep across the sands."[42] Vaux greatly pleased the trustees by creating a simple and inexpensive building. Here the debilitating effects of cholera infantum and other intestinal disorders were reversed with a healthy diet. Staff members also instructed mothers in the proper care of infants and themselves. Every summer, several hundred women from the city's crowded slums brought their children to the society's sanitarium. From ample porches of this large clapboard building, the gift of D. Willis James, guests might take the fresh air and enjoy a lovely view of the open sea, Gravesend Bay, and the Narrows. During the cool evenings, residents would gather in common rooms where fireplaces warmed body and spirit. For most who came to this tranquil corner of New York's oceanfront, the experience must have been the nearest thing to a seaside vacation that they ever had.[43] Surely their memories of a Coney Island summer were far more poignant than those of the carefree middle-class families who vacationed there.

FIGURE 9.7. Forty-Fourth Street Lodging House for Boys, New York City, 1887. Courtesy of Children's Aid Society.

Perhaps as a result of its experience with mothers at its summer facility, the society became aware of the special problems that the daughters of poor families faced. In order to improve their lot, in 1892 the society erected the Elizabeth Home for Girls at 307–309 East 12th Street. The four-story brick building, the gift of Elizabeth Davenport Wheeler, went up according to designs by Vaux, who developed its roofline with the stepped gables that were characteristic of the society's other buildings. The Elizabeth Home provided shelter and schooling for homeless girls, "not a few of which," sadly noted the matron, "had been turned out by relatives and even by parents, because they could not find employment."[44]

Few well-known architects strayed into New York's tenement districts to leave their mark. But Vaux, it may be assumed, like author Brander Matthews, had an affinity for these working-class areas of town as well as for more fashionable quarters. Always a generous-minded idealist, he had had his social consciousness quickened by contact with such men as Frothingham, Brace, and Potter. He must have felt that in league with some of New York's wealthiest families he was offering hope to a class of people far more in need of help in improving the circumstances of their lives than his antebellum readers of

Villas and Cottages had been.[45] And Vaux surely found considerable satisfaction in knowing that in parts of the metropolis beyond the pale of his earlier clientele there existed buildings of his design that represented the few instances of architectural art. Most people who read the new architectural magazines or followed the rising tide of lavish and monumental Neoclassicism in the careers of McKim, Mead and White or Carrère and Hastings were unaware of the existence of these modest buildings. Nonetheless, their substantial and picturesque appearance—which demonstrated how enduring were lessons that Vaux had learned long ago from such buildings by his genial mentor, L. N. Cottingham, as the Bury St. Edmunds Savings Bank—gave a human face to a heroic effort to break the advance of poverty in America's largest city.

ALTHOUGH VAUX HAD severed his ties with the parks department in 1873, he seldom put Central Park out of his thoughts after that date. Especially following Olmsted's dismissal in 1878, Vaux kept a close watch on the doings of the commissioners. He often used his influence with the press to rouse public opinion against their most egregious decisions affecting the integrity of the Greensward plan. In 1879, for example, Vaux wrote a long letter to the *Times* condemning the addition of a "sprawling, vulgar" boat rental booth at the foot of the Terrace, where it spoiled the view of the Lake and Ramble. Reaffirming the Terrace's central place in the park design, Vaux took the opportunity to remind people that its decoration was incomplete and to express the hope that "the time will surely come for an expansion of the whole idea on the liberal scale originally contemplated."[46] Vaux was also undoubtedly behind the movement to have Cleopatra's Needle erected at Fifth Avenue and 59th Street rather than behind the Metropolitan Museum of Art on Greywacke Knoll, one of the highest points in the park. Editorials in the *American Architect and Building News* and the *Tribune* seconded the urban location as the place to display the ancient Egyptian obelisk to its best advantage. Here, proponents pointed out, the open, level ground would accentuate the verticality of the tall sandstone monolith and allow it to be viewed from different distances and from various points of view. Yet even a petition from prominent painters and sculptors circulated while the ancient stone was making its slow progress from the dock to the park could not dissuade the commissioners from abandoning the original site, which had the backing of the art museum trustees and the donor, William Henry Vanderbilt. Despite setbacks, Vaux kept up his defense of the founding vision of the park, and he surely welcomed the publication in 1881 of Olmsted's *Spoils of the Park*. With this impassioned polemic, Olmsted, who now lived in Brookline, intended to stir renewed public awareness of the original intent of the park. Vaux believed that "the permanent safety of the Park could be found only in having the general public thoroughly informed upon the subject of its original design." In addition to such publications as *Spoils*, he felt that the press was one of the best means for accomplishing this end: Vaux foresaw that if knowledge of the true purpose of the park as a place for passive recreation in an idealized pastoral setting were confined only to a few professionals and their close associates, the park would surely be "pulled to pieces and utterly spoiled when these men had died off."[47] A backer of Cleveland and civil service reform, Vaux hoped, furthermore, that Central Park could eventually come under the management of a professional superintendent. Such a person would safeguard the spirit of the Greensward plan while making changes that the times might dictate. "It is a magnificent pleasure ground," reflected Jervis McEntee, "and will always remain a monument to its designers, Vaux and Olmsted, and to Vaux's faithfulness and persistence in defending and protecting it at critical periods in its management."[48]

Green's reappointment to the park board in 1880, during the administration of Mayor Edward Cooper, eventually paved the way for Vaux's return to service as landscape architect in November 1881.[49] During his uneasy 13-month tenure, Vaux managed to have Parsons given the responsibility (without pay) of supervising planting in Central Park. Vaux's plan, he explained to Olmsted, was to train his young assistant, to whom he gave half his salary, to be their successor. When Vaux resigned from the department in December 1882, angered at being ignored by the commissioners when they contemplated the erection of a skating house on the Harlem Meer—they had also refused to act upon his plan for a new path "with views of a truly park-like character on either side" leading to the Loch in the northern part of the park—Parsons went with him.[50] But two years later, under Mayor William R. Grace, Parsons became superintendent of parks. The appointment represented a significant victory for Parsons and for Vaux. Parsons held the post with distinction for more than 20 years.

THROUGHOUT THIS PERIOD when Vaux and Olmsted were expressing their concern for preserving the park, not all threats to its integrity came from incompetent administrators. Others were eyeing Central Park as a site for an international exhibition to mark the centennial of the end, in 1783, of the American Revolution. The proponents for locating the exposition in the park included former president Grant. Yet opposition to this proposed misuse of the park emerged as soon as the Committee on Sites had made its first report, which identified 12 possible locations, in the summer of 1880. The *Times* remarked that the suggestion to use Central Park "may as well be dismissed at once."[51] Olmsted, who advised the Citizens' Committee of the New York World's Fair, favored the plan that Vaux put forward to locate the fair at Port Morris, a peninsula that juts into the East River from the south Bronx just north of Manhattan Island. This piece of flat land was already accessible by road and rail and, because of its deepwater frontage, could easily be made to accommodate boat traffic as well. This would be a great advantage to overseas exhibitors in transporting their wares to and from the fair. Furthermore, explained the *Tribune*, it seemed most appropriate for New York, "the chief maritime city of the continent," to stage this exposition "in sight of blue water and with the tide rushing by."[52]

By January 1881, Vaux had come up with an architectural design to house the display of the world's arts and industry. To Olmsted, he described the plan that he and Radford had devised to cover 65 acres in a series of rectangular iron and glass exhibition halls placed adjacent to each other (Fig. 9.8).[53] The main building on the south end would cover 23 acres, with the 24-acre machinery hall jutting out toward the water behind it and the 10-acre agriculture hall appended on the north. Each of these halls would be composed of tall units of 100 feet in width, with lower, smaller units running transversely between them. Most visitors were to have entered the fair buildings on the inland side of the site through the arm that joined the main building to the small, four- and five-acre art and horticulture buildings. Trains would have let passengers out under the

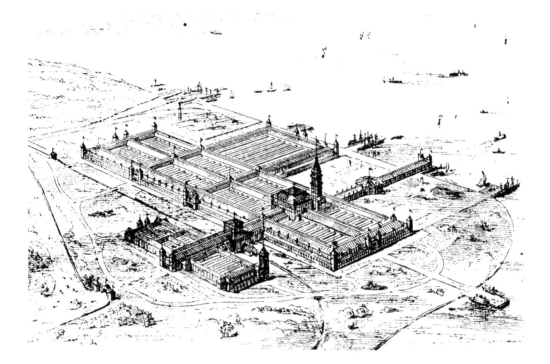

FIGURE 9.8.
Design for
World's Fair
buildings, Port
Morris, N.Y.,
1880–1881.
Courtesy of
Library of
Congress.

shelter of this freestanding entrance hall, the axis of which Vaux extended toward the water by means of a long "promenade pier." Yet despite its large scale, one looks in vain for signs of the grandeur of Vaux's conception for the ill-fated Philadelphia Centennial building design. Perhaps all this much more utilitarian scheme owed to that earlier masterpiece was the architect's intention to include all of the major exhibits under one continuous, covered space. But once again, Vaux's scheme for a vast exhibition hall was never to leave the paper stage. Olmsted confidentially told his friend that despite the strong merits of the Port Morris site, the organizers were dead set against any location that was not on Manhattan Island.[54] In the end, the fair movement itself lost momentum and eventually petered out. After a postponement to 1885, the promoters laid their idea aside until the end of the decade, when local enthusiasm revived for commemorating the 500th anniversary of Columbus's historic voyage.[55]

Another of President Grant's wishes also posed a momentary threat to Central Park. Before the great hero died in the summer of 1885, he expressed the desire to be buried in New York. To some local citizens, Central Park seemed the obvious place to erect his tomb. Objections from Olmsted and many others quickly ended such talk. Vaux favored the site overlooking the Hudson in Riverside Park where Mould had built a vault to temporarily hold Grant's remains. When Olmsted heard of this idea, however, he wrote to Mayor Grace to express his reservations about placing a mortuary monument in a public pleasure ground. Explaining his position to his friend, Vaux, who together with Parsons had been charged by the parks department with recommending the best site for the tomb, assured Olmsted that the location near the northern end of the park drive would stand entirely within the roadway and not on actual parkland. With the purchase of some additional land to the east between 122nd and 127th Streets, this elevated area could be made even more separate from the park, as well as more retired from the life of the city.[56] By the summer of 1885, Vaux's views had carried the day and he had prepared a ground plan for the tomb site that included pathways leading to it from the park itself. In the meantime, an association formed to raise money for the permanent monument.

Riverside Park consisted of a narrow strip of land about 400 feet wide running between the river and Riverside Drive from 72nd to 130th Street. The long, sinuous drive had been planned by Olmsted in the 1875, but it and the park had been slow to materialize. By 1885, the three-mile roadway was laid, but paths and other features within the often steep and rugged park terrain were yet to be completed. During Vaux's 1881–1882 tenure as landscape architect to the Department of Public Parks, he had prepared plans for finishing the park, which writer Martha Lamb called "a tract of land of the rarest beauty." Vaux would continue to do work here after rejoining the department in 1888.[57] The site that Vaux wished designated for Grant's tomb lay within the last, most picturesque section of the drive, the so-called Bloomingdale Mile, which extended from 104th Street to the Loop in front of the Claremont Hotel restaurant at 130th Street. This 200-foot-wide tree-lined parkway with separate lanes for vehicles, pedestrians, and horseback riders followed the top of a bluff high above the forested riverbank and commanded splendid views of New Jersey and the Palisades. Rather than terminate the drive at the tomb itself, as some had proposed, Vaux diverted the roadway around it and continued the boulevard another 200 feet to the end. Visitors would view the monument both going to and coming from the Claremont Hotel. The scheme preserved this popular gathering place as the culmination of the drive that many considered the finest pleasure road in the world.[58]

Despite the efforts on the part of the city to secure a suitable tomb site, the Grant Monument Association seemed in no hurry to make a decision on its design. When the *North American Review* published, in September 1885, the opinions of several prominent New Yorkers on what should be built, Vaux was among those persons offering advice. Speaking in general terms, Vaux expressed the opinion that the monument should include a statue of Grant and an interior that could be decorated with murals and stained glass windows. Always a champion of the sculptor's art, he also expressed his hope that there would be ample opportunity "for the use of bronze and other metals admitting of artistic treatment." Vaux hoped that neither a triumphal arch nor a freestanding column would be erected; instead, he praised the example of the Tower of St. Jacques in Paris, a medieval church tower that Haussmann had rededicated as a monument to the philosopher Pascal. Most of all, Vaux urged the organizers to secure a good design by staging a competition managed by America's leading architects. The association chose to ignore this sound counsel and went about the business of raising money without making any move toward sponsoring an architectural competition. This led numerous individuals, including sculptor William Wetmore Story, to take it upon themselves to prepare plans that they submitted privately to the association in the hope of being chosen as the monument's designer. Surely Mould would have been among them, but on June 14, 1886, heart disease claimed his life.

In the winter of 1886, Vaux himself prepared a large model demonstrating his notion of what Grant's tomb should be. He undertook this project in collaboration with the sculptor Samuel J. Kitson, who had carved the author heads on the exterior of the Tilden house. Unfortunately, Vaux's model, which

McEntee painted for him, has not survived. We know what it was like, however, from a lengthy description by a *Times* reporter who saw it in Vaux's office in the summer of 1886.[59] In addition to a vaulted tomb chamber, the red granite monument was to contain a chapel with stained glass windows and a memorial illuminated by skylights and large round-arched windows. The most important feature, however, was to have been a 270-foot Gothic tower, from whose top visitors might obtain a panoramic view of the region. Inside, the tower would hold a presidential library and a multilevel hall, 100 feet in height, for government records. To commemorate Grant's greatness, Vaux outlined a program of sculpture that in its use of allegorical imagery recalled his scheme for the Terrace of 20 years earlier. The memorial hall was to have housed large bronze statues representing the Soldier and the President; the tower buttresses would be terminated by kneeling figures representing Warring, Watching, and Praying; the staircase roof would hold a standing Angel of Benediction; elsewhere were to be figures representing North, South, East, and West and, surrounding the exterior of the mortuary chapel, eight statues of "heroic size" symbolizing the Infantryman, the Cavalryman, and other military figures. In addition, three over-life-size bronze friezes were to have encircled the tower, illustrating Peace, the Suffering of War, and the Fury of War. What reaction the members of the memorial association had to this grandiose scheme is not known; however, when they finally held a competition for the monument design, in the autumn of 1890, they chose the Classicizing submission of John H. Duncan, who based his design on reconstructions of the Mausoleum at Halicarnassus. Surely Vaux and Kitson had had little hope that their grandiose conception would ever have been built. Vaux's landscape scheme for the site, however, was implemented and partially survives.[60]

IN 1887, AS DISCUSSIONS were going on concerning the site of Grant's tomb, the park commissioners tried to entice Olmsted to resume his old relationship with the department. In particular, they wished him to take charge of the renewed efforts to finish Riverside and Morningside Parks. Informing Vaux on June 30, 1887, of a meeting he had had with the commissioners two days before, Olmsted assured his old friend that he had refused the offer that had been made to him to work without Vaux on the New York parks. A short time later, Olmsted wrote to J. D. Crimmins, the president of the board, reiterating his intention never to become involved with the city's parks without Vaux's collaboration. Vaux, he told Crimmins, "had never ceased to be a citizen of New York, never lost his hold of New York life nor allowed his attention to be withdrawn for a moment from the park system of New York."[61] A few days later, the board, some of whose members had been stung by Vaux's criticism of their ignorance of the true principles of landscape architecture, acceded to Olmsted's wishes and extended an offer to both men. This marked a renewal of professional relations between Vaux and Olmsted that before the decade was out would be extended to include important new work at Niagara Falls and at Newburgh.

By the end of 1887, Olmsted and Vaux had filed a report outlining their intentions for Morningside Park.[62] The partners had originally laid out this boot-shaped strip of steep terrain lying between 110th and 123rd Streets in 1873. Since then, construction had proceeded intermittently, and changes had taken place at the site. A section of elevated railway crossed one corner of the grounds, and walls, parapets, and stairways erected according to designs by Mould along the high western border of the park were much more elaborate than the rusticated masonry that Olmsted and Vaux had envisioned. These and other circumstances now compelled Olmsted and Vaux to revise their first plan. Retaining the essential features of the original scheme, the partners simplified their earlier intentions. They deleted the former exhibition building and the entrance structure proposed at the southwest corner. Having before them a concrete example of how disregard of "leading motives in the direction of the required operations" had derailed the progress of their carefully conceived design, they took pains to admonish the commissioners that the preservation of the "life and soul" of any park required sympathetic management. Vigilance was needed "not simply for two or three years, but constantly and permanently thereafter."[63]

NOWHERE WAS THIS admonishing instructive more necessary than in the case of Niagara Falls. Beginning in the late 1860s, Olmsted had led an international campaign to have the State of New York acquire and preserve the land around the famous cataract, including the incomparable rapids above the falls and primeval Goat Island in their midst. Vaux had helped in this effort, as had their friend William Dorsheimer, the original promoter of the Buffalo park system who later, as Tilden's lieutenant governor, had been responsible for turning over the job of completing the capitol at Albany to Olmsted, Richardson, and Eidlitz. When Grover Cleveland, former mayor of Buffalo and a Dorsheimer political ally, became governor, the prospects for success brightened considerably. "Governor Cleveland strongly in favor of Niagara," Richardson ebulliently informed Olmsted the day after he and Dorsheimer had dined with the new governor in February 1883.[64] In April, Cleveland signed a bill creating a commission (of which Dorsheimer and A. H. Green were members) charged with identifying the land needed to be acquired by the state in order to protect the falls. On April 30, 1885, Cleveland's successor, David B. Hill, signed into law the bill creating the Niagara Reservation. In June 1886, the commission hired Olmsted and Vaux to prepare a plan that would restore and preserve the scenery around this natural wonder while making its beauty easily accessible to large numbers of visitors. It was, said Olmsted, "the most difficult problem in landscape architecture to do justice to, it is the most serious—the furthest above shop work—that the world has yet had."[65] Vaux felt equally awed by the challenge. The problem of creating a park at Niagara had led him to reflect that the landscape architect must always remember to approach his task in a spirit of humility and to let nature be his guide. "In every difficult work," he had said specifically with the falls in mind, "the keynote of success of course lies in this idea of thorough subordination, but it must be an intelligent, penetrative subordination, an industrious, ardently artistic and sleeplessly active ministry that is constantly seeking for an opportunity to do some little thing to help forward the great result on which nature is lavishing its powers of creation."[66]

Carrying out this philosophy at the falls proved to be a formidable undertaking. "It was much more of a job (the study on the ground) than he apparently supposed it would be," Olmsted wrote of Vaux to his son John in December 1886.[67] By that time the two men had conceived the general outlines of their plan. "We have got it in our heads I think at all points, and in several pieces of linen and paper, memoranda and data for the whole," Olmsted informed John. It must have been with a sense of turning to more fruitful endeavors that Vaux, after a discouraging interview with Tilden's executors over his outstanding fees for the Gramercy Park house, traveled to Brookline on February 11, 1887, to join Olmsted in putting the final touches on the Niagara plan.[68] For his part, Olmsted too felt daunted by the task. As the chief author of the written report that he and Vaux were to submit with their plan, Olmsted found himself at a loss for words to express adequately what was in his mind. He worked on the historic document right up until the time that the partners presented it to the commissioners on March 2. Olmsted and Vaux's plan won speedy approval, and later that year the commissioners hired a superintendent, Thomas Welch, to begin implementing it. Olmsted, whose practice was flourishing, let Vaux take charge of supervising construction, work that involved the erection of several bridges and other small structures. Together with Parsons and Downing, who was responsible for most of the architectural work, Vaux remained occupied at the falls until his death in 1895. After that, Downing stayed with the project until its completion in 1902.

Olmsted and Vaux's plan for the Niagara Reservation comprised two parts: the mainland, the shore along the American side of the river, and Goat Island, the triangular island around which the waters of the Niagara parted before descending into the cataract as the American and Canadian (or Horseshoe) Falls. Along a narrow strip of the shoreline, Olmsted and Vaux proposed to lay out paths and a carriage drive leading to Prospect Point. From this spot, one might obtain a comprehensive view of the great U-shaped, 180-foot-deep gorge. Over the years, a motley collection of factory buildings and hotels had grown up along this riverbank. These were now to be removed and the land graded and planted in a manner that would recall its original appearance. But the most important part of the reservation was Goat Island (Fig. 9.9). Connected to the mainland by a bridge that had been built across the American Rapids in the early nineteenth century, Goat Island possessed not only a spectacular location but also a primeval forest. Here grew vegetation that botanist Asa Gray declared more varied than any to be found in such a small area anywhere in the Old World and rarely in the New. Olmsted valued the "rare beauty of the old woods, and the exceeding loveliness of the rock foliage," as much as the falls themselves. For Vaux, too, Goat Island represented "a beautiful example of natural landscape design."[69]

In the plan of walks and drives that he and Olmsted drew up for the island, they intended to preserve this unique sylvan setting and to make it an intimate part of the visitor's experience of the falls. A woodland carriage drive starting from the bridge followed a winding circuit around the perimeter of the island. It conveyed riders to five principal viewing points: the eastern tip of the island, where one could look upstream at the broad, placid river; Three Sister Islands, a series of islets in the Canadian Rapids linked by footbridges; a point on the bluff where one might observe the Canadian Rapids immediately above the falls; Porter's Point, the best location for obtaining a panoramic outlook toward the Canadian Falls; and Stedman's Bluff, high ground in the northwest corner of the island where one could both survey the American Falls and make the descent to the Cave of the Winds at their base. Below Stedman's Bluff, Vaux designed a low bridge across to tiny Luna Island on the brink of the gorge. It

must have seemed to Vaux that nature had placed the island there to be a safe platform for close-up viewing of the raging waters plunging into the cataract. In building the bridge over to it, he must have felt that he was doing nothing more than taking the "opportunity to do some little thing to help forward the great result on which nature is lavishing its powers of creation."[70] Most of all, Olmsted and Vaux hoped that visitors would traverse Goat Island on foot. They wished to lead them through the dense forest along a network of footpaths. As tourists walked the fragrant trails, they would hear the roar of the surrounding waters mingled with the chirping of the many birds who made the sheltered spot their home. Eventually pedestrians would emerge to view the raging rapids and the sublime falls, their experience of these wonders heightened by the contrast with the quiet woodland scenery. Olmsted and Vaux also reserved for the pedestrian the privilege of getting closer than those in carriages to the dramatic shoreline. Here and there, stone benches were to have been provided so that visitors might sit and contemplate some particularly beautiful water view. The product of the accumulated professional experience and the mature artistic vision of America's two greatest landscape architects, the layout of the Niagara Reservation was a masterpiece of clear-headed planning, respect for the natural environment, and extraordinary sensitivity to natural scenery.

Unfortunately, Olmsted and Vaux's scheme found only partial realization on the ground. Today one drives around the island essentially along the route that Olmsted and Vaux proposed for the carriage drive. However, even Vaux himself could not prevent the carriage road from being modified during construction by Welch and others who objected to its distance from the shoreline at certain points. Many fewer footpaths were laid out through the woods than projected on the plan; nonetheless, historic photographs reveal that this once lovely area was a favorite spot with tourists. More unfortunate is the fact that later generations of management at the reservation lost sight of Olmsted and Vaux's

FIGURE 9.9. Plan for the Niagara Reservation, 1887. Courtesy of National Park Service, Frederick Law Olmsted National Historic Site.

high-minded ideals. Parking lots, restaurants, monumental statuary, and other intrusions, together with disregard for the island's extraordinary fauna, have reduced Goat Island in the late twentieth century to a shadow of the place that Olmsted and Vaux knew. Addressing himself to such a tragedy, Vaux wrote of Goat Island: "An analysis of its sources of effect, will, however, show that if it was all burned over . . . (if a record had been kept) [it] could be reproduced with comparative rapidity, if the resources of the art of the landscape gardener were consecrated to the work."

As splendid as it was for Vaux's spirits to undertake the great work at Niagara with his old friend, he also welcomed the opportunity for financial reasons. "Calvert I can see is worried as I am and life seems a struggle," confided McEntee to his diary shortly before Vaux got the Niagara job. A few months earlier, McEntee, himself in tight circumstances from the lack of interest that the buying public showed in his paintings, had loaned his brother-in-law money to pay his taxes.[71] And shortly after Olmsted and Vaux had presented their report in March 1887, when Vaux wrote to Olmsted to ask if there had been any indication of the state's willingness to pay them their fee, Olmsted offered to advance Vaux "four or five hundred dollars."[72] It is possible that Olmsted, who told Vaux that he was "well windward of expenses," declined to work for the Niagara commissioners after 1887 so that his friend might obtain a much needed source of income. Olmsted biographer Elizabeth Stevenson is surely correct when she blames "difficulties of temperament" as a reason for Vaux's troubles.[73] His diminishing practice as both architect and landscape architect was probably the chief reason why late in 1887 he agreed to rejoin the Department of Public Parks as landscape architect. Presumably this post, which he began in January 1888 during the tenure of Mayor Abram Hewitt, an old Tilden political ally, and held until his death seven years later, kept Vaux's money troubles at bay.

In addition to working again in Central Park, Vaux spent much of his time as the city's landscape architect designing new small parks. The Small Parks Act of 1887 (of which Hewitt was a chief promoter) called for the creation of many airing places, especially in the densely populated tenement districts of the Lower East Side, where Hewitt had long had his political base. For his part, Vaux believed the city should provide "every few blocks, some reservation kept open that will tempt a man, woman, or child to sit down and rest, and look about for a while." New York was fortunate to have many places scattered throughout its street system that might be easily developed for this purpose; "any triangle or small irregular figure that grows out of it in what appears to be a natural way is sufficient for the purpose of invitation and detention," Vaux explained.[74] Working with Parsons as parks superintendent, Vaux prepared plans for many odd-shaped parcels of city-owned property at the irregular junctures of streets in the older part of town below 14th Street. Canal Street Park (Fig. 9.10), a triangular plot of land at the western end of the street which was opened to the public in 1889, was representative of these charmingly simple verdant oases that Vaux created. A wide gravel path bisected the ornamental lawn in a lazy curve that widened at one point to afford young children an area in which to play under parental supervision. Benches with footrests lined the pathways but were set on the grass to save space. The fenced-in borders of the square bore a rich variety of shrubs, small trees, and flower beds, while a row of shade trees lined the surrounding pavement. (Vaux was careful not to plant trees at the angles where they might be easily damaged by turning carriages.) The same "jewel-

FIGURE 9.10.
Canal Street Park,
1887–1888. From
Scribner's Magazine
12 (August 1892).
Courtesy of Buf-
falo and Erie
County Public
Library.

like effect of bedding and the same charm of trees and shrubs," testified Parsons,
who said that he often took charge of "filling in of shrubs and plants" in
order to get the effect that Vaux desired,[75] characterized the now vanished land-
scaping of Jackson Square (Greenwich and Eighth Avenues at West 13th Street),
Abingdon Square (Jane and Hudson Streets at Eighth Avenue), Duane Street
Park (Hudson, Jane and Staple Streets), Christopher Street Park, East River
Park (between 84th and 89th Streets; present Carl Schurz Park), Lincoln Square
Park (Broadway, Ninth Avenue, and 66th Street), Rutgers Slip Park, Corlear's
Hook Park (overlooking the East River on South Street between Jackson,
Cherry, and Corlear's Streets, land that forms the south end of the present
East River Park), and other similar small parks.[76] In Greeley Square, the trian-
gle of land bordered by Broadway, 34th Street and Sixth Avenue, Vaux, who
remained devoted to promoting the cause of public sculpture (in 1893, he would
be one of the founding members of the National Sculpture Society), had an
opportunity to create the setting for Alexander Doyle's bronze statue of Horace
Greeley, the founder of the *Tribune*. Vaux harbored the memory of Greeley as
the curmudgeon who had found the scenery in Central Park so convincing that
he thought it had always been that way. Vaux took pleasure and amusement in
quoting the remark that Greeley had made after his first visit there: "Well, they
have left it alone better than I thought they would." Surely, if Vaux had had
his way, carvers would have inscribed this guileless testimony to the true artistry
of Central Park on the pedestal of Doyle's figure.[77]

The small urban park that mattered most to Vaux was Mulberry Bend Park (the present Columbus Park; Fig. 9.11). Social reformers intent on doing away with the notorious Mulberry Bend slum had legislated the park into existence in 1887 under the Small Parks Act. It took the city another seven years, however, to appease the demands of the landlords and to acquire legal title to the tenements that filled nearly every square foot of the area bounded by Mulberry, Baxter, Park, and Bayard Streets. During this period, proponents of the project had to face political apathy as well as slumlord resistance. Often it appeared to them that the promise of sunlight and greenspace that Richard Watson Gilder and others of the Tenement-house Investigating Committee had made to the residents of this benighted neighborhood would remain just that. But by June 1895, the city had become the owner of those dreadful rookeries of poverty. "It seems little less than a revolution to see them go down," remarked Jacob Riis, the newspaper reporter who became a leader in the fight to demolish the unsanitary tenement district.[78] "In its place," said Riis, "will come trees and grass and flowers; for its dark hovels light and sunshine and air." Certainly Vaux shared the journalist's optimism. "I feel that I have put the best work I have to give," he told his daughter when, in the spring of 1895, he signed the final plans for the new park.[79] By June 19, the park commissioners had approved Vaux's design, and a short time later the city authorized a bond sale to cover its construction.

Vaux's scheme called for 18-foot-wide, bench-lined walkways sweeping in broad curves through the bend-shaped parcel of land. Areas of greensward were to be planted with elms and lindens. While the grass was off-limits to visitors (a rule that irritated Riis), children could use the wide intersections of the paths as play space. A large pavilion in the north part of the park afforded sheltered recre-

ation as well as a location for concerts. The park welcomed visitors from the surrounding neighborhood through entrances on all sides, which also took into account the movements of people traversing the park. By the time of his death in November 1895, Vaux would probably have seen the rudiments of his design taking shape on the ground. By the following summer, the park was already in use, although the official dedication had to wait until June 1897, when the summerhouse was finished. From the perspective of nearly 40 years later, Riis hailed the park as a key factor in civilizing the lives of the many disadvantaged city dwellers who resided within sight of it. "The Bend had become decent and orderly," he said, "because the sunlight was let in, and shone upon children who had at last the right to play, even if the sign 'keep off the grass' was still there." And certainly Vaux, who had often devoted his professional energies to the service of social reform, would have seconded his assertion that this was "what the Mulberry Bend park meant."[80]

IN ADDITION TO planning the many small parks, Vaux's official duties as landscape architect to the Department of Public Parks brought him back to Central Park. One of the first things he did there was to draw plans in 1888 for a greenhouse. The following year, he planned an elephant house.[81] But in the summer of 1889, Vaux saw the park landscape again put in jeopardy. With the backing of many prominent citizens, Mayor Grant had launched a campaign to have Congress designate the city as the location for a world's fair to celebrate the 500th anniversary of the discovery of America by Columbus. The mayor and promoters were eyeing the northern section of the park as the site for exhibition buildings, claiming that little if any permanent damage would be done to the landscape. Vaux took heart that the commissioners supported his efforts to complete the upper park and voted against allowing the area to be used in this way. Also siding with Vaux were Andrew Green and the new journal of landscape architecture, *Garden and Forest*, whose editor was Vaux's friend William Stiles. "Nothing more distinctively or characteristically American can be imagined than the upper portion of the park," stated *Garden and Forest*, calling the scenery there "a picture of pastoral rest and peace which has no rival in the heart of a great city."[82] To place a great exposition there would place the park's very existence as a place of passive recreation in a pastoral landscape setting in jeopardy.

As he had done earlier in the decade, when the city had hoped to stage a world's fair to celebrate the end of the Revolution, Olmsted became involved with the controversy. He hoped that land near Grant's Tomb would be chosen for the site of the 1892 fair. To H. R. Towne, one of the chief members of the Committee on Sites, he wrote in October 1889 that "the Fair must go on Bloomingdale Heights or nowhere." (Olmsted was apparently referring to the site of the Bloomingdale Asylum, on Broadway between 117th and 199th Streets and Amsterdam Avenue. The institution was abandoning that land for a new home in White Plains. In February 1892, it sold the property to Columbia University for its new campus.) In his letter, Olmsted also candidly revealed that his feelings toward Green had not changed in all these years. Green, he warned Towne, "will fight you malignantly and with the most industrious and painstaking, underhanded if not open, labor." Towne would be wise, however, to win Vaux as an ally, which he surely could do if his group would choose a location outside the park. "Don't be deceived by what you hear to Vaux's disadvantage," Olmsted told Towne. For in solving "problems of planning for convenience—he is unsurpassed," declared Olmsted. Unfortunately, Olmsted observed, undoubtedly remembering many a long and passionate debate with his former partner, that he was "apt to greatly misrepresent his own mind in talking; a nervous defect."[83] Writing these lines, Olmsted may have reflected that it was chiefly this shortcoming that had robbed Vaux of the success that his own ability to deal effectively with men in public life had won for him. "He is unfortunate in attempting to present his ideas verbally," Olmsted once told a friend, "although if you have patience and faith, you will find under appearance of incoherence and even of a wandering mind, he generally has a singular command of the problem he is dealing with." Fortunately for the future of Central Park, the storm blew over when opposition to using it as the fair site became so strong that even several members of the Committee on Sites resigned in protest. Proclaiming victory, *Garden and Forest* pointed out that if Central Park had been compromised in this way it would have had serious repercussions throughout the country. If this great park had been misappropriated for nonpark purposes, said the journal, "there would be little hope that parks in other cities would be able to withstand the pressure for admission constantly brought to bear upon them by all sorts of enterprises foreign to the purpose for which they were created."[84] In any event, the New York fair movement received its death blow on April 25, 1890, when Congress voted Chicago rather than New York the honor of hosting the World's Columbian Exposition.

Hand in hand with the threat posed by the world's fair, the park became the object of an effort to construct a new road within its borders for drivers who wished to race their carriages. The brainchild of an unusual alliance between Tammany Hall, Mayor Hugh Grant, and wealthy New Yorkers, the "speed-road," as the road came to be called, was to be located along the western border of the park. Since 1888, attempts had been made in the state legislature to create such a straight and level drive within the park, but in March 1892, proponents succeeded in getting a bill passed authorizing its construction. Reaction in the New York press against yet another threat to the tranquility of the park was immediate. This project was a particularly offensive one, argued *Garden and Forest*, because a few rich men asked that much of the park's fine scenery be destroyed so they might indulge their whim to ride fancy horses in the fall and spring. At other times of the year, they left town for more comfortable climates, observed the journal, leaving behind less affluent citizens who depended on the park as their major resort for recreation. In face of such arrogance, the journal stated, the park "should be preserved for the people, and the whole people, and not ruined in the interest of horses and their drivers, however aristocratic may be the breeding of either."[85] These words, undoubtedly, exactly represented Vaux's view of the matter, for, said Olmsted, "the denial of advantages to the rich man that the poor man cannot command—is, I remember, a point in which Vaux has a certain chivalric interest."[86] Olmsted himself agreed that the speedway did not belong in the park, but in a long letter to Paul Dana, he advised the park commissioner, who greatly respected his opinions, to seek a location outside the park where such a thoroughfare might be laid out. Otherwise, he feared, there would be continued pressure in the future to provide for this pastime.[87] Due to a concerted press campaign against the new roadway, in April 1892 the legislature repealed the act that had authorized it a few weeks earlier.

But Mayor Grant and his allies had put up a rancorous fight on behalf of the speedway. Vaux and Parsons had been particular targets of their anger. At the Century one evening, the two men admitted to James Morse that a majority of the park board "would gladly get rid of them if they dared."[88] And in mid-March, when the commissioner of accounts of New York City launched an investigation into the management of the park department, it soon became clear that its purpose was to discredit the two men. Parsons spent several hours being grilled on the witness stand but revealed no serious irregularities in his conduct of park business. Vaux, on the other hand, became flustered and did not acquit himself well. Asked the botanical name for the Rose of Sharon, he was at temporary loss for an answer. The lapse troubled him so, William Stiles later informed Olmsted, who was in England at the time, that "in his nervousness, he made such a display as you might expect." Furthermore, in answer to the question of how much time he spent in Central Park each day, Vaux had ingenuously replied, "Two or three hours," an answer that gave the unfair impression that he took a large salary for little effort. The humiliation had been so great, reported Stiles, that it put him "on the verge of insanity." Even worse was that the commission's call for his resignation on grounds of incompetence found its way into the newspapers.[89] Undoubtedly pleased with the turn of events, Mayor Grant, whom Stiles accused of being "enraged at Mr Vaux" for opposing him in the speedway fight, referred the matter to the park board for action. The board in turn delegated its president, Paul Dana, to deal with the matter. "Now if you could see your way to write a note to Paul," Stiles urged Olmsted, "saying that you are glad that Mr. Vaux has fallen into such good hands, it might help things on."[90] Deeply troubled by what he heard, Olmsted felt equally troubled because there was little that he could do at such a distance.

By May, however, Vaux seemed to have weathered the storm. Dropping by his house, Morse found him in good spirits. Insisting that Morse join them for "landscape gardening," as he called green salad, Vaux talked about the attack on him by the "Tammany hogs." He was confident that he would not be let go.[91] When Olmsted met Dana in London in the summer, he got a first-hand account of Vaux's troubles. He was reassured to learn that the *Times* and others had stood by him. Vaux had not thrown in the towel, as Olmsted had been led to believe during a visit from Radford, but was merely nursing his wounded ego at Rondout during an extended vacation. In the end, the board took no action against Vaux, and the young son of publisher Charles A. Dana came to regard him with considerable affection. He quickly grew to share Stiles's opinion that "so long as matters of design or construction are referred to Mr. Vaux the park is safe."[92] Although Vaux could take heart that by the end of 1893 Hugh Grant had been voted out of office chiefly as a result of the Central Park controversy, in the future he would find himself fighting similar battles.

But for Vaux, Rondout was no longer the place of solace that it formerly had been. In January 1891, Bright's disease had taken Jervis's life. Mary had been at his bedside. Her sister Sara now inhabited the little house and studio that had been the scene of so many happy times. During the period of all the agitation over the Central Park speed-road, Vaux had been helping to organize an executor's auction of 173 of his brother-in-law's paintings at the Fifth Avenue Galleries. Whittredge, Lockwood de Forest, and J. C. Nicoll chose the works from those that had been left in the artist's possession at the time of his death, taking care, they said, to present only paintings that he would have wished shown. Now more than ever, the absence of Jervis, Vaux's longtime companion and confidant, must have seemed an aching loss. But the summer of 1892 was to bring more tragedy. Early in August, the horse that had been pulling the carriage in which Mary and a friend were riding through the Palisades woods suddenly bolted. Both women were thrown to the ground. The friend perished instantly, but Mary survived with a fractured skull. She lingered for a week before dying on the morning of August 13 at Closter, New Jersey, near where she and her family had so loved living in the mid-1870s.[93] It must have seemed to Vaux, who was experiencing bouts of failing health (carbuncles were a troublesome problem), that both his personal and professional lives were collapsing at the same time.

IN SEPTEMBER 1892, architect Ernest Flagg, who had designed Tilden's tomb, published a design for a large municipal library that he and Vaux's old client John Bigelow proposed to erect on the site of the Croton Reservoir at Fifth Avenue and 42nd Street. With the settlement of heirs' claims against Tilden's will, the Tilden Trust, of which Bigelow was a trustee, was in a position to establish the great municipal library that the former governor had specified in his will. Flagg's huge cruciform building, which reflected his training at the Ecole des Beaux-Arts in Paris, was, in fact, the culmination of a dream that Bigelow had shared with other architects, including Vaux, for many years. The huge structure, which would have reached from Fifth to Sixth Avenues and from 42nd to 41st Streets, was probably seen as much too ambitious and was soon dropped in favor of the suggestion of Thomas F. Gilroy, the new mayor, that City Hall be used for this purpose. The building, which had been erected in 1804 to designs by Joseph F. Mangin and John McComb Jr., was too small for the modern-day city, and Gilroy and others were looking to erect a new building. Bigelow and Flagg came to support the plan to reuse the historic building, which they proposed to move to Reservoir Square. Yet all of this took place outside the purview of the Tilden Trust's Plan and Scope Committee, which had been charged with determining a site and plan for the new library. The three-man committee, which numbered Vaux, Paul Dana, and Green, the chair, took strong exception to the City Hall proposal. Their objection drew sharp criticism from Bigelow and other trustees. At the heated meeting of the trust in March 1893, Bigelow told Green that as his committee "could not act in harmony with a majority of the board, it might as well be discharged." By a majority vote of the board, it was.

The dismissal of the committee did not, however, end Green and Vaux's public opposition to moving City Hall. "Green will doubtless continue to obstruct, for it is his nature to," Bigelow thought to himself, "but if he has no more success in the future in putting obstacles in the way of the Tilden Trust than he has had . . . in passing his bills for the Greater New York and his North River Bridge we need not worry.[94] As for the other two men, Bigelow reflected: "Unhappily, his creature Vaux is still architect of the Park and Paul Dana of the *Sun* is President of the Park Board and a champion of Vaux. What complications are to be apprehended from that source time can only determine." When Dana was replaced as board president by William Tappan in late April, Bigelow felt that his chances for success had improved. Indeed they had, for shortly afterward the governor signed the bill authorizing the reuse of

City Hall as a free library. But the city was unprepared to engage the expense of draining the old reservoir and dismantling its monumental walls. Under the bill, City Hall was to be placed in Bryant Park, the public park behind the reservoir on Sixth Avenue.

Passage of the bill, however, did not deter Green. On January 21, 1894, at the first meeting of the trust in six months, he reiterated his objection to the use of City Hall for the library, applying "more or less offensive language" to its proponents, and nearly coming to blows with Bigelow.[95] Much of what he said that day about the unsuitability of the building for use as a library and the sacrilege of moving it from its present site must have formed the text of the pamphlet he published the following month.[96] Arguing like a modern-day preservationist, Green defended old city hall as "an example of fine architectural taste" that in its design was "as faultless as any structure in the City." (One would like to think that Vaux had coached him in this opinion.) It would be wrong, Green said, to compromise the integrity of the handsome building in order to fit it up for a library (Flagg was apparently already at work on the task), a purpose for which it was not well suited. Moreover, the building and its site had shared in events "of paramount interest to the Nation, State and City," many of which he went on to enumerate. Taking up the defense of the city's parks, Green also insisted that "no portion of Reservoir Square, or any other Park, Square or open ground on this Island provided for the use of the people, may hereafter be appropriated for buildings." (If, in the future, the reservoir were to be removed, the land, he said, should be used to increase the city's inadequate amount of park space.) Leave historic City Hall where it is, Green urged. If the city needs a new, larger building for its present needs, let it dedicate the old structure to the most important municipal offices and to the site of civic ceremonies and receptions. In the end, Green's enlightened views and hard campaigning carried the day, for by the end of April the legislature repealed the law. "This disposes of my scheme for the Tilden library in Bryant Park, I suppose," confided Bigelow to his diary, "and imposes upon us the duty of devising some new plan for carrying out the library provision of Tilden's will."[97]

During the city hall controversy, Vaux also became a thorn in Bigelow's side over a proposed statue to William Cullen Bryant. In October 1893, Bigelow and Flagg had chosen a site in Central Park, near the 59th Street entrance, for the large memorial to Bryant that the Century Association wished to commission. Learning of their intentions and possibly angered at not being consulted on the matter, Vaux, together with Parsons and Dana, raised a strong objection to placing so large a monument in the park. Only the year before, Vaux had recommended that the 59th Street border of the park be designated as the location for future statuary. Here, between trees bordering the wide sidewalk, he envisioned an impressive avenue of sculptural monuments, including works that had already been inappropriately placed in the naturally landscaped portions of the park.[98] Moreover, concerning the Bryant statue, Vaux, as a member of the Century, objected that the association had never approved the statue's design, a point seconded by John LaFarge. The artist paid a special visit to the park board to inform its members that the club's art committee, which he headed, had never reviewed the project. When Vaux made his formal report to the board on the matter in early November 1893, Bigelow was present to hear him speak against the proposal on the grounds that it took too much land. A few days later, the board approved Vaux's report. Vaux must have believed that Bryant himself would agree that the board's decision represented a little victory for the preservation of the Greensward ideals.[99]

A SIMILAR PROBLEM erupted when, in 1893, the trustees of the American Museum of Natural History came to the park board with a plan in hand for enlarging their building. Displeased with the outward appearance of Vaux and Mould's original wing, the trustees had already passed over Vaux once, in 1887, when they had added the south or 77th Street extension to the existing structure. Now they once again engaged the services of J. C. Cady to make a plan for a large lecture hall that they wished to erect where Vaux and Mould had destined the grand rotunda to stand. But as this was a park structure, its plan had to be approved by the park board, which, in turn, was obliged to hear the opinion of its landscape architect. Calling Vaux and Mould's structure an "abortion," Morris K. Jessup, the president of the museum board of trustees, vowed never to permit Vaux to review their plans. The park commissioners did solicit Vaux's opinion, but most members seemed not to care when he pointed out the discrepancy with the master plan. Taking Vaux's part, however, Paul Dana and Andrew Green objected to going ahead with the museum's proposal. It "stultifies totally without warrant" the existing plan for the museum that the board had adopted in 1872, claimed Dana, who pointed out that even though the 1887 elevations departed in style from the first section, their footprint respected the master plan.[100] Dana now wanted the chastened directors to return to the drawing board and come up with a scheme that would be compatible with the original plan. Eventually the museum trustees acquiesced to Dana's demands. Apologizing for their "oversight" in not technically obeying the law, the museum trustees returned to the park board in March 1893 with Cady and his portfolio of drawings for enlarging the museum according to the original ground plan. "The interests of the city have been restored to their proper place," declared the *Sun* (Dana's newspaper), while Vaux expressed the opinion that "having made my technical point with precision—The City can do as it pleases about the addition without breaking my work."[101] But one cannot help think that the process had been humiliating for Vaux, for even though he and Dana had won their argument, the affair had shown just how marginalized Vaux had become in the New York architectural scene.

The news from Brooklyn was equally discouraging. With the passing of Stranahan from the park scene there, new commissioners had come to power. Like their counterparts in Manhattan, they had less allegiance to the original pastoral ideals embodied in Prospect Park than their predecessors had had. After 1889, when Vaux designed the beautiful Terrace Bridge in Prospect Park, the Brooklyn commissioners steadfastly refused to employ him. Seeing no chance that they would change their mind and hire Vaux, Olmsted reluctantly agreed to work with them, breaking his rule of not wanting to compete with his former partner in the New York area. Yet Olmsted honestly hoped that he might be able, where Vaux had failed, to convince the new generation of managers to keep alive the original spirit of the park's design. It was not easy. "Really our principal duty there is to hinder, delay, and resist operations further upsetting the original design," Olmsted confessed to Vaux, "while we wait and seek opportunity to urge and advance restorations and recoveries."[102] Primarily, he focused his attention on getting trees and shrubs planted that Vaux and he had indicated long ago, on bringing into being the children's playground which the partners had designated on their plan but which had never been created, and on preventing the removal of the fountain from the main entrance oval and the leveling of the mounds that enframed that great space, which was undergoing John Duncan's Neoclassical transformation into Grand Army Plaza. Olmsted also tried to implement the original plan for the music island in the lake, "to get the soul into the concert grove," as he said. However, the commissioners considered the idea totally impractical and regarded Olmsted as slightly absurd for promoting it. But as if to advise Vaux on how best to operate under such trying circumstances, Olmsted confessed that he had been "cautious as yet, not wishing to be thought a crank."

FOLLOWING THE DEFEAT of the Central Park speed-track, promoters of the idea searched elsewhere in the city to create a roadway for fast driving and riding. In October 1893 park department officials announced plans to create the Harlem River Speedway, a fast and level trotting road along two and a half miles of the beautiful west bank of the Harlem River between 155th Street and Dyckman Street. But instead of adopting Vaux's plan, which "included designs for preserving and enhancing the natural beauties of the water-front and for making them available" to pedestrians as well as equestrians, the board turned the matter of planning the roadway over to an engineer.[103] Echoing Paul Dana's dissenting protest, *Garden and Forest* decried the result of the board's high-handed action. Instead of taking advantage of the picturesque scenery that this stretch of shoreline possessed, the journal observed, the engineer cut "his way along the river-bank as remorselessly as the builders of the West Shore Railroad have done along the Hudson, and with no more regard for the defacement of the scenery than was manifested by them."[104] Furthermore, the only provision for pedestrians that he allowed was a narrow sidewalk on the inland side of the carriageway, an arrangement that denied walkers access to what might "become one of the most interesting walks in the city, or, indeed, in any city of the world." Stung by loud criticism of its action from the press and the city's artistic community (including Augustus Saint-Gaudens, William Merritt Chase, and Stanford White, who sent letters of protest to the mayor) and irritated by Vaux's unwillingness to go along with its scheme, the board, under George Clausen, dug in its heels. Overruling Dana, who eventually resigned over the issue in March 1894, the board refused to compromise with its critics or to give Vaux a say in the design of the drive. A year later, however, after having given out contracts for the construction of the road, the board agreed to seek the advice of an outside landscape architect to enhance the plans and asked anyone who wished to apply to appear in person before the board with his credentials. At the end of October, the board followed this slap in Vaux's face with the decision to ask Olmsted, who was working at Biltmore at the time, to assume the role of consultant on the project. Olmsted replied that he would not work for the board knowing that they had refused to avail themselves of the services of Vaux, "the best-qualified man in the world for that sort of work."[105] Hailing Olmsted's action as "a conspicuous example of professional loyalty and honor," the *American Architect and Building News* observed that "the dislike which a majority of the Board seems to have conceived for Mr. Vaux is trivial and personal." The chief complaint leveled against him was that he "antagonized the Board." Noting that

Vaux was "a man of very great experience and skill," the journal said that it would be unlikely that he would oppose the board without good reason. It was sheer pettiness "to attribute publicly his firmness in maintaining his own convictions against those of people without a thousandth part of his knowledge, or sense of professional responsibility, to a mere desire to 'antagonize' the members of the Board," asserted the journal. The impasse ended early in the following year, when Clausen resigned his post. "So much for the artists and the 'landscape architect,' whatever that newly-coined term may mean," he said in his disparaging letter to newly elected Mayor William L. Strong.[106]

With a new park board that included Paul Dana in place by February 1895, the battle appeared to have turned in Vaux's favor. However, while the new board immediately directed him to examine and report on the Harlem River Drive plans, they added the stipulation that his work would be subject to review by a committee of architects and artists. This advisory committee was to include Olmsted and William Stiles as well as Stanford White, George B. Post, and Richard Morris Hunt. "I know that the resolution has almost broken Vaux's heart," Stiles told Olmsted. Fearing that Vaux would resign, Stiles observed that he was "old and poor and it is too bad to place him in a position where he has to swallow an indignity like this or be thrown out into want." For his part, Stiles could not bring himself to take a position looking over Vaux's shoulder, although he felt that the new board had acted out of ignorance rather than malice. Olmsted was equally disturbed by the idea of an advisory committee composed mainly of architects ruling on the work of the man whom he regarded as a great master of the discipline that he had fought so hard to establish as a profession. "It makes me grind my teeth to see how Vaux is treated," Olmsted told Stiles. To the board, he wrote warning them of the error of placing an advisory board, unaccountable to the public, between themselves and their own landscape architect. "One method of obtaining advice on matters of design has been consistently followed by almost every Park Board in the country," Olmsted said. "It is the employment of a paid, professional Landscape Architect, directly and solely responsible under the Board for the ultimate result obtained."[107]

In addition to being an affront to his and Vaux's professional integrity, the advisory committee, Olmsted saw, was "essentially packed against natural landscape," the Romantic esthetic that had guided him and Vaux from the very beginning. The new men, disciples of the Ecole des Beaux-Arts, saw the role of landscape design, said Olmsted, as "an intensification and aggrandizement of urban art rather than a means of recreation from the town; any broad rural effect being considered out of place and anachronistic." Olmsted chiefly singled out Stanford White, with whom he had worked on the World's Columbian Exhibition in Chicago and in Prospect Park, as the black beast of this position. White, he said, "has been trying to establish the rule of those motives that are at war with those that ruled in the original laying out of the Brooklyn Park." In Olmsted's view, White detested the older style and wished to see it replaced by "efforts approaching the ruling Versailles character." White's huge Doric-columned Battle Monument then nearing completion on the hilltop in Olmsted and Vaux's Fort Greene Park must have seemed to Olmsted a particularly egregious instance of the architectural assault on rural parks. Feeling himself severely tried by the same forces that had attacked Vaux, he pleaded with his editor friend Stiles that now was the time that "we, who are essentially of

one faith in this matter, however we may differ among ourselves, should be closing ranks and be moving more warily than we have been." The great master saw
"an organized enemy" that was "strong in its convictions, able, proud even to
superciliousness, confident and enthusiastic," taking the field before them. "They
have struck down Vaux," he lamented, "and are doing their best to kill him in the
name of the Lord of France."[108]

In the end, however, Vaux was not vanquished. Thanks to the efforts of Paul
Dana, the role of the advisory committee (which Stiles eventually agreed to
join) became virtually to rubber-stamp Vaux's plans. In mid-March, the board
told Vaux that it had accepted his designs and instructed him to go forward
with developing them. On April 10, the board gave its final approval to Vaux's
drawings. "The carrying out of the plan for the Harlem River Driveway so as
not to violate or sacrifice its picturesque advantages or capabilities" would now
be assured, the next day's edition of the *Times* told New Yorkers (Fig. 9.12).[109]

FIGURE 9.12.
The Harlem
River Speed-
way, looking
toward High
Bridge Aque-
duct. Courtesy
of Prints and
Photographs
Division,
Library of
Congress.

DURING THIS TRYING TIME, it was surely with a sense of relief that Vaux took
up work to which he and Olmsted had committed themselves in the late summer of 1889, when they had agreed to donate their services to the city of Newburgh to design a public park in memory of Andrew Jackson Downing. The
city council had delayed for two years before acting on the partners' offer, which
had been made through their mutual friend Mrs. John Monell, Downing's
widow. The land that the city purchased comprised a city block of high, sloping
ground. Both Olmsted and Vaux quickly realized, however, that even though the

site enjoyed a fine prospect of the Hudson and the surrounding countryside, it suffered from certain limitations. In the report that they had put together in December 1889, they devoted most of their attention to arguing for the need to add to the plot a parcel of low-lying land that the city owned immediately to the west of the site. In a park of this size, they said, it was greatly to be preferred if part of it could be elevated and part of it could be "of a sheltered, tranquil, meadow-like aspect."[110] Eventually the city conceded their point and annexed the second block of land to the park. Chiefly under Olmsted's expert guidance, it became the site of lovely Polly Pond.

As historian David Schuyler has pointed out, Vaux took responsibility for developing a plan for the original eastern hilltop section of Downing Park.[111] Indeed, in 1889, Vaux had already told Olmsted of his wish to create a carriage drive on the higher ground in the northwest area and to devote the rest of the park to pedestrian use. But because the city dragged its heels in funding the project, it appears that Vaux did not seriously concern himself with the design until April 1894, when he made a sketch for drives and walks.[112] The final plan that grew out of these preliminaries featured a carriage drive that terminated in a circular concourse in the elevated northwest corner of the property. Standing there and looking down at the mountain-framed river, Vaux must have been taken back to his earliest days at Highland Garden, which shared a similar prospect. The sight would have held a poignancy for Vaux that Olmsted could not have shared. Here, in the highest part of the park, Vaux wished to locate an observatory (eventually designed by Downing Vaux and now destroyed) so that visitors might fully enjoy the splendid panorama of Downing's beloved Newburgh Bay and the Highlands (Fig. 9.13). After all, the river that art and poetry had made a symbol of nature's power to uplift and refine the human spirit uniquely embodied the meaning of Downing's legacy. Vaux also could have reflected that he himself had devoted most of his creative energies to furthering that legacy. The celebrated river had run through Vaux's life as surely as it had flowed through Downing's. Contemplating it from this evocative vantage point may well have prompted Vaux to repeat to himself his own words: "Having studied carefully the works and the method of working of the Creator, the designer of a landscape can bring into successful play the great forces of Nature, and subordinating his own personality, can secure for his work an undying vitality which can only follow from such a direct reliance on the resources of the Infinite."[113]

Unfortunately, Vaux, for whom Downing Park must have represented more of a labor of love than it did for Olmsted, did not live to see his work completed. The grounds, which like Central Park included a system of footpaths distinct from the carriage drives, were only ready to be dedicated in the summer of 1897, nearly two years after his death. His son Downing saw the job through to the end, together with John C. Olmsted, who took up the reins of his father's business when, also in 1895, poor health forced Olmsted to retire.[114]

For Vaux, the victory over the Harlem River Speedway marked a rise in the tide of his professional fortunes. No longer at odds with the park board, Vaux took up his duties as landscape architect with renewed vigor. In addition to Mulberry Bend, Downing Park, and other park projects, Vaux was working in the early summer of 1895 on a plan for laying out the new Bronx Park, which a contemporary described as "one of the most picturesque spots to be found this side of the Adirondacks."[115] The new park was to include the New York

FIGURE 9.13.
Downing Park,
Newburgh,
N.Y., 1889.
Courtesy of
Downing Park
Planning
Committee.

Botanical Garden, a nascent institution sponsored by a number of prominent New Yorkers who were deeply impressed with the plans Vaux developed for their site.[116]

Despite the demands of this work, Vaux had time to enjoy visits with his son Bowyer in Bensonhurst. Three years before, Bowyer had built a house, probably to his father and Downing's design, at the seaside resort community in southern Brooklyn. There, Vaux loved to walk on the beach and to watch the sun go down over the water. By the middle of August, after toiling night and day on the Bronx plans, his work was complete. But he was now 70, and the physical strain of such labor had begun to take its toll on him. His family, seeing their father near collapse, insisted that he take an extended rest. During the month of October, he greatly curtailed his schedule. He moved to the Madison Avenue Hotel on 58th Street, where, under treatment for a troublesome hernia, he was looked after by his daughter Marion. In November, he went to stay with Bowyer. While he was there, Vaux must have been heartened to read that the park board had again been reorganized. Following the resignation of President King and his three colleagues, Mayor Strong had appointed a group of thoroughly anti-Tammany commissioners, men whom Vaux could count on to share his and Olmsted's vision of the parks. The appointment that would have pleased Vaux most was that of his close friend William Stiles, a man who, Bowyer said, had "perhaps a keener appreciation" of his father's genius than any other citizen.[117] Facing the bright prospect of sympathetic commissioners, Vaux must have been eager to pick up his responsibilities once again. He told his daughter that he hoped to live three more years to see completed his plans for Central Park, the work of art on which he had most devotedly bestowed his ideals of beauty.[118]

In the late afternoon of November 21, Vaux went for a walk to the ocean, as he often did, to view the setting sun. At the new Captain's Pier, he stopped to chat with the owner and to offer him some advice for improving the nearby beach. That evening, however, Vaux did not return home. Worried for his safety, family and friends, with the aid of the police, launched a search. At 9:30 the next morning, a workman spotted his body floating in Gravesend Bay, near the Captain's Pier. His son Bowyer speculated that he had fallen off the boardwalk, perhaps while bending down to inspect its understructure. Dispelling rumors of suicide, Bowyer confided to John C. Olmsted that his father had "no money anxieties nor family troubles, and except for his age, the hard work of the past five years which had told upon him and a local trouble with his hernia . . . he was pretty much in his usual health." Lack of sleep the past few nights and his nearsightedness—Vaux had forgotten to take his spectacles on his last walk—Bowyer felt, not despondency, were the causes of his fall to his death. Unhappily, John's own father had experienced a precipitous decline in his health since the previous spring, and Olmsted's mental condition was too poor at the time for him to be told of his old friend's passing.[119] Truly, an extraordinary chapter in the history of American art had ended. Only the family and Parsons were present at Calvert Vaux's funeral. The simple ceremony took place at Bowyer's cottage, which was filled with plants that the park commissioners had sent. "The idea of all the flowers and vines and leaves in profusion coming from Central Park," thought Bowyer, "seemed most appropriate."[120]

NOTES

ABBREVIATIONS

BCCP   Board of Commissioners of Central Park

BCPP   Board of Commissioners of Prospect Park

Bloor Diary   Manuscript diary of Alfred Janson Bloor, New-York Historical Society, New York

BPC   Brooklyn Park Commission

DAB   *Dictionary of American Biography* (New York, 1928–1936)

DPP   Department of Public Parks

McEntee Diary   Manuscript diary of Jervis McEntee, Archives of American Art, Smithsonian Institution, Washington, D.C.

"Memorandum"   Handwritten list of Vaux's works compiled in November 1894, Vaux Papers, Rare Books and Manuscripts Division of the Astor, Lenox, and Tilden Foundations, New York Public Library, New York

Morse Diary   Manuscript diary of James Herbert Morse, New-York Historical Society, New York

Municipal Archives   Collections of the Municipal Archives of the City of New York

PFLO   *The Papers of Frederick Law Olmsted*, ed. Charles MacLaughlin, 8 vols. to date (Baltimore, 1977–)

Reid Papers   Whitelaw Reid Papers, Manuscript Division, Library of Congress, Washington, D.C.

Vaux Papers   Calvert Vaux Papers, Rare Books and Manuscripts Division of the Astor, Lenox, and Tilden Foundations, New York Public Library, New York

INTRODUCTION

1. Samuel Parsons Jr., *Memoirs of Samuel Parsons*, ed. M. Parsons (New York, 1926), 4.

2. Melvin Kalfus, *Frederick Law Olmsted: The Passion of a Public Artist* (New York, 1990).

3. Vaux to Olmsted, January 18, 1864, Frederick Law Olmsted Papers, Manuscript Division, Library of Congress, Washington, D.C. Unless otherwise noted, all correspondence cited in the notes is from this collection.

4. Vaux to editor of the *New-York Daily Tribune*, February 18, 1878, 7.

5. F. L. Olmsted, "Mr. Vaux and the New York Parks," *American Architect and Building News* 22 (December 10, 1887): 295.

6. [C. Bowyer Vaux], "Calvert Vaux, Designer of Parks," *Parks International* 1 (September 1920): 139–140.

7. [Henry T. Williams], review of W. Robinson, *The Parks, Promenades and Gardens of Paris, Horticulturist* 25 (January 1870): 12.

8. Edward Kemp, *How to Lay Out a Garden: A General Guide in Choosing, Forming, or Improving an Estate*, 2d ed. (London, 1858), 178.

9. Charles H. J. Smith, *Landscape Gardening* (New York, 1853), 289.

10. Calvert Vaux, "Landscape Gardening," in *Encyclopedia Britannica*, supplement (New York, 1886), 564.

11. Parsons, *Memoirs*, 5

12. Downing Vaux, "Historical Notes," in *Transactions of the American Society of Landscape Architects* (Harrisburg, 1908), 82.

13. C. Vaux, "The Palisades" (1878), Fraternity Papers, New-York Historical Society, New York.

14. Parsons, *Memoirs*, 4.

15. DPP, *Second Annual Report* (1872), 83.

16. Parsons, *Memoirs*, 4.

17. Andrew Jackson Downing, *Cottage Residences*, 4th ed. (New York, 1852), 72.

18. Parsons, *Memoirs*, 5.

CHAPTER I

1. Vaux to Marshall P. Wilder, July 18, 1852, in the John Jay Smith Papers, Historical Society of Pennsylvania, Philadelphia.

2. [C. Bowyer Vaux], "Calvert Vaux, Designer of Parks," *Parks International* 1 (September 1920): 139–140. In this article, Vaux's son says that his father made this trip alone when he was 21, which would have placed it in 1845.

3. Vaux to Wilder, July 18, 1852, Smith Papers.

4. [M. P. Wilder], "Col. Wilder's Eulogy on Mr. Downing," *Horticulturist* 7 (November 1852): 496.

5. Vaux to Wilder, July 18, 1852, Smith Papers; David Schuyler, *Apostle of Taste: Andrew Jackson Downing, 1815–1852* (Baltimore, 1996).

6. [Clarence Cook], "A Corner Stone," *Galaxy* 5 (February 1868): 149.

7. "Architectural Association," *Builder* 5 (October 2, 1847): 472.

8. "Architectural Association," *Builder* 7 (December 15, 1849): 598.

9. Editorial in *Builder* 7 (March 10, 1849): 109.

10. "Architectural Exhibition, Pall-Mall," *Builder* 8 (August 17, 1850): 386. The design, which has not survived, received mixed reviews. The *Ecclesiologist*, in a notice that would have appeared after Vaux had left for America, rejected it out of hand, advising that it "had better not have been exhibited." See "Free Architectural Exhibition, 1850," *Ecclesiologist* n.s. 8 (1850): 172. Items in the exhibition were to have been "of works contemplated or in progress, designs submitted in competition during the year, studies and delineations of existing buildings, and antiquities and architectural models." This would imply that the baptistery design was more than a fanciful creation, although no record of its actual construction has come to light and no competitions for baptistery buildings were listed in the *Builder* for 1848–1850. The remarks by the *Builder* calling attention to the cleverly deigned groining of the octagonal lantern suggest that Vaux may have been influenced by the stone lantern that his mentor Cottingham restored over the crossing of Hereford Cathedral.

11. According to the parish records of St. Bennet Grace Church (where Vaux was baptized on February 9, 1825), Vaux's father, Calvert Bowyer Vaux, was buried on September 5, 1833. Records of the Society of Apothecaries of London indicate that after a five-year indentureship to George Vaux of Ipswich, Calvert Bowyer Vaux became a

licensed apothecary on May 2, 1816. His name also appeared as a member of the Royal College of Surgeons in London in 1822, 1825, and 1833. Unfortunately, nothing has come to light concerning Vaux's mother, Emily Brickwood Vaux, who probably died in 1882. Early in 1883, Vaux received a legacy of $3,000 from England, presumably the settlement of his mother's estate.

12. The entrance requirements were stated in *Merchant Taylors' School* (London, 1861), 69. Vaux entered the Third Form, in which he had to read Latin catechism, prayers, and psalms, Butler's *Ancient and Modern Geography* and *Ancient Atlas*, Liddell's *History of Rome*, and Church's *Prose Latin Lessons* and to master Latin prosody and commence verse making. A few years before his arrival, the school had introduced writing, arithmetic, and mathematics to the curriculum. Vaux's brother Alfred entered in 1835.

13. C. J. Robinson, *A Register of the Scholars Admitted into the Merchant Taylors' School*, 2 vols. (London, 1883), 1:xi–xii.

14. In this year, the school awarded him a copy of James Rennie's *Architecture of Birds* (1831). From Rennie's little book, which Vaux treasured all his life, he would have learned, through descriptions that were both scientific and moralizing, how most birds constructed their nests. Perhaps this prize stimulated Vaux to study human architecture.

15. A certificate issued at St. Mary's Newington, dated April 10, 1848 (and now in the Archives of American Art), names Vaux as a special constable and gives his address as Kennington Place.

16. [James H. Morse], "Calvert Vaux," in *Appleton's Annual Cyclopedia* (New York, 1895), 598. The Reynell Academy was first listed in the Post Office London directory in 1846 (p. 937). It is possible, however, that the school was in existence before this time.

17. T. Miller, "Picturesque Sketches in London" (London, 1852), quoted in E. Walford, *Old and New London* (London, 1877), 6:334.

18. Another project, one on which Vaux is known to have assisted, was an addition that Cottingham made in 1844 to St. Leonard's Church in Horringer in Cottingham's native Suffolk. A letter to the vicar dated April 1, 1845, was signed "Calvert Vaux, Clerk to L. N. Cottingham."

19. "L. N. Cottingham," *Gentleman's Magazine* 182 (December 1847): 649.

20. The fact that the men made the tour together is mentioned in "George Truefitt Retires." The date is deduced from the publication of Truefitt's "Gothic Staircase at Antwerp," which appeared in the January 30, 1847, issue of the *Builder*. The accompanying text, which was probably written by George Godwin, states that the illustration is "from a sketch made for us last summer."

21. Review in the *Ecclesiologist*, n.s., 5 (1848): 108.

22. David W. Matzdorf, "Calvert Vaux, 1824–1895" (General Studies thesis, Architectural Association, 1977), 11.

23. "The Designs for the Army and Navy Club," *Builder* 5 (May 5, 1847): 214.

24. George Truefitt, *Designs for Country Churches* (Manchester, 1850), vii, and review in *Ecclesiologist*, n.s., 8 (June 1850): 48.

25. [C. Bowyer Vaux], "Calvert Vaux," 139.

26. "Late George Godwin," *Builder* 44 (February 4, 1888): 76.

27. "Architectural Association: Opening Conversazione," *Builder* 8 (October 13, 1849): 485.

28. "Water Supply for London," *Builder* 8 (July 13, 1850): 331.

29. When Godwin published Truefitt's drawing of a staircase in Antwerp, he said that the sketch had been made at his request. This indicates that Godwin had told Truefitt where to find an otherwise out-of-the-way architectural detail.

30. [G. Godwin], untitled editorial, *Builder* 7 (July 28, 1849): 349.

31. "Memoir of the Late Mr. Cottingham, Architect, F.S.A.," *Builder* 5 (October 23, 1847): 502.

32. *Builder* 6 (May 6, 1848): 218.

33. "Architectural Room of the Royal Academy," *Ecclesiologist* 5 (1848): 371, and "Hereford Cathedral," *Ecclesiologist* 6 (1849): 345–347.

34. William Holman Hunt, *Pre-Raphaelitism and the Pre-Raphaelite Brotherhood* (New York, 1905), 1:178.

35. "Bankrupts," *Times* (London), May 10, 1854, 12.

36. The *Gentleman's Magazine*, which had printed a long obituary of L. N. Cottingham, noted without comment the death of his son. See 196 (1854): 639.

37. "Young Architects of England by Another of Themselves," *Builder* 5 (February 6, 1847): 65.

CHAPTER 2

1. [Leonora Cranch], *Life and Letters of Christopher Pearse Cranch* (Boston, 1917), 174.

2. Cook, "Late A. J. Downing," *New York Quarterly* 1 (October 1852): 369.

3. George William Curtis, "Memoir," in A. J. Downing, *Rural Essays* (New York, 1853), xlvi.

4. Vaux to Wilder, July 18, 1852, in the John Jay Smith Papers, Historical Society of Pennsylvania, Philadelphia.

5. Statement read to the Boston Society of Landscape Architects in 1916 by J. C. Olmsted and printed in Frederick Law Olmsted Jr. and Theodora Kimball, eds., *Frederick Law Olmsted, Landscape Architect, 1822–1903: Forty Years of Landscape Architecture*, 2 vols. (New York, 1922–1928; reprint, New York, 1970), 1:89.

6. Calvert Vaux, *Villas and Cottages* (New York, 1857), 41.

7. C. Cook, "Home of the Late Andrew Jackson Downing," *Horticulturist* 8 (January 1853): 21.

8. Vaux recommends the use of revolving bookcases as doors in *Villas and Cottages*, 78.

9. Walter Creese, *The Crowning of the American Landscape: Eight Great Spaces and Their Buildings* (Princeton, 1985), 84.

10. Fredrika Bremer, *The Homes of the New World: Impressions of America*, 2 vols, trans. Mary Howitt (New York, 1853), 1:13.

11. Bremer and Downing's opinions on England are taken from her letter to Downing of November 11, 1850, in A. B. Benson, "Fredrika Bremer's Unpublished Letters to the Downings," *Scandinavian Studies and Notes* 11 (May 1931): 195.

12. Vaux presented the portrait to the Century Association in 1864 on the occasion of the 70th birthday of William Cullen Bryant. Vaux drew the head from a daguerreotype that Downing had presented to Fredrika Bremer, who later returned it to Downing's widow. When Vaux showed the portrait to his friend Frederick Withers, who had also been in the Highland Garden office, Withers said that he found it far more true to Downing than the popular engraving that had been taken from the same daguerreotype (Vaux to Olmsted, November 9, 1864).

13. "Editor's Table," *Horticulturist* 8 (February 1853): 103.

14. Vaux, *Villas and Cottages*, iv.

15. For the history of Springside, see Robert M. Toole, "Springside: A. J. Downing's Only Extant Garden," *Journal of Garden History* 9 (1989): 20–39, and H. K. Flad, "Matthew Vassar's Springside: '. . . the hand of Art, when guided by Taste,'" in *Prophet with Honor: The Career of Andrew Jackson Downing, 1815–1852*, ed. George B. Tatum and Elizabeth B. MacDougall (Washington, 1989), 219–257.

16. Toole, "Springside," 25.

17. Vaux, *Villas and Cottages*, 277.

18. Drawings for the stable are preserved in the Vassar College Library, Special Collections Department.

19. The smaller drawing is signed in script, as are existing drawings Downing sent to Davis; the larger drawings are labeled with print lettering. The larger drawings are also colored to differentiate various materials.

20. It also appeared as Design 15 in the fourth edition of Downing's *Cottage Residences* (New York, 1852), 186–187.

21. The ventilator, which Vaux considered an important feature of the Robins house in Yonkers, resembled this one. See *Villas and Cottages*, 164.

22. Vaux to Wilder, July 18, 1852.

23. These drawings and the 29 pages of specifications are preserved in the Vassar College Library, Special Collections Division.

24. Vaux, *Villas and Cottages*, 279–280.

25. Among the few records documenting this commission is a small watercolor sketch of Algonac signed by Vaux and dated 1851. This drawing and the other Algonac materials are in the Delano Family Papers, Franklin D. Roosevelt Presidential Library, Hyde Park, New York. In a letter to F. H. Delano dated August 15, 1852, Warren Delano II states that the house was finished and that all of the rooms were furnished except for the drawing room and dining room. On March 21, 1852, Warren Delano had written to F. H. Delano that he would be plowing for roads and planting grass and trees in April.

26. Down below the hill on which Algonac stood there were several outbuildings that were undoubtedly designed by Downing and Vaux. One of these was a brick stable. In a letter to F. H. Delano dated March 21, 1852, Warren Delano II states that "the stable is nearly finished and has been occupied since early in January." The building duplicated the one which the partners built for Daniel Parish at Newport, Rhode Island, and which Vaux illustrated in *Villas and Cottages*, 313. Several photographs of the stable are filed with the estate inventory dated November 14, 1938. According to correspondence of Warren Delano, the gate lodge must have been erected after Downing's death. In a letter to F. H. Delano dated August 15, 1852, Warren Delano says that he is debating exactly where to locate the lodge. The lodge, which still stands, conforms in style to the other Downing and Vaux buildings at Algonac.

27. Clara Steeholm, *House at Hyde Park* (New York, 1950), 9.

28. Curtis, "Memoir," xlv.

29. Steeholm, *House at Hyde Park*, 23.

30. The additions to Algonac were closely related in style and arrangement to two Tuscan villas that the firm built in the Georgetown section of Washington, D.C. In 1850, the merchant brothers Robert P. and Francis Dodge Jr. commissioned nearly identical houses for each of them. (A description of the Francis Dodge house appears in "Local Matters, Modern Building," *Georgetown Advocate*, December 7, 1852, 3, quoted in Daniel D. Reiff, *Washington Architecture, 1791–1861: Problems in Development* [Washington, 1971], 122, n. 135, and 126–127.) The plans, however, were reversed in the two dwellings, and exterior details were different. The Francis Dodge house repeats the layout of the main section of Algonac. But Vaux took pains to isolate the routine of daily life from the formal space of the main hall. Thus, it was possible for someone coming from the second floor to enter any of the first-floor rooms without having to pass through the hall. "An arrangement of this sort," insisted Vaux, "is calculated to add much to the privacy of the inmates of any country house" (*Villas and Cottages*, 222). The Dodge brothers' brick and stone villas were finished by December 1852. Slightly earlier than Thomas U. Walter's Ingleside (designed in 1851), they seem to have introduced the imagery of the Italian villa to the capital area.

31. In the 1852 revised edition of *Cottage Residences*, Downing mentions (48n) that an unnamed resident of Staten Island had recently completed a house based on Design 2. Whether or not Downing and Vaux were directly involved with its construction is unknown.

32. Leila El-Wakil, *Batir La Campagne: Geneve, 1800–1860*, 2 vols. (Geneva, 1988), 1: 297.

33. Vaux, *Villas and Cottages*, 189.

34. C. Vaux, "Memorandum." This handwritten list of works was compiled by the architect in November 1894 and is preserved in the Vaux Papers.

35. Andrew Jackson Downing, *Architecture of Country Houses* (New York, 1850), Design 32, 343–352.

36. *DAB*, 8:480.

37. Vaux, *Villas and Cottages*, 213.

38. Ibid., 228. Hoping construction costs would drop, Betts initially hesitated to build; after the death of his friend Downing, he let his plans gather dust.

39. Vaux, *Villas and Cottages*, 242–243.

40. Fire and vandalism have left only the first story of the empty building standing. On the history of the building, see Hugh Goodman, "Calvert Vaux and Andrew Jackson Downing: The Newburgh City Club," *Journal of the Orange County Historical Society* (1994), 22–29.

41. Vaux, *Villas and Cottages*, 58. Two drawings for the house, surely by an assistant, bear the signature "Downing and Vaux, Architects, Newburgh, 1852," in the Hall Papers, New York State Library, Albany.

42. John M. Clarke, *James Hall of Albany, Geologist and Paleontologist, 1811–1898* (Albany, 1923), 236.

43. Joseph A. Scoville, *Old Merchants of New York City* (New York, 1885), 4:134–149.

44. Some distance from the house, Downing and Vaux erected a stable that is the subject of Arthur C. Downs Jr., *Downing and Vaux, Newburgh, NY, 1852, and the Architeck- tonishes Skizzen-Buch, Berlin, 1852* (Newton Square, PA, 1989).

45. Antoinette F. Downing and Vincent J. Scully Jr., *The Architectural Heritage of Newport, Rhode Island, 1640–1915*, 2d ed. (New York, 1967), 137–138.

46. Curtis, "Memoir," 1.

47. Quoted in May King Van Rensselaer, *Newport: Our Social Capital* (Philadelphia, 1935), 47.

48. The Parish family eventually sold this second house to William Waldorf Astor, who christened it Beechwood. In its later history, the house underwent alteration in the Neoclassical style, and the grand veranda was taken down and rebuilt in modified form across the back of the house.

49. Vaux reported in *Villas and Cottages*, 311, that Dakin's death put a stop to construction when only part of the foundations had been laid. My assumption that the house was located at Dobbs Ferry is based on the fact that Dakin's home address is listed there in Doggert's *New York City Directory* for 1851–1852. In the previous year, his residence was given as Bond Street in Manhattan.

50. A. K. H. B., "Concerning Villas and Cottages," *Frazer's Magazine* 29 (December 1858): 704.

51. Vaux, *Villas and Cottages*, 34.

52. Jill Franklin, *The Gentleman's Country House and Its Plan, 1835–1914* (London, 1981), 78.

53. For an obituary of Howland, who died suddenly on November 9, 1851, after learning of the death of a friend and who left an estate of $1 million, see "Mr. Gardiner G. Howland," *New York Herald*, November 13, 1951, 2, and *DAB*, 9:312–313.

54. For Withers's career see Francis R. Kowsky, *The Architecture of Frederick Clarke Withers and the Progress of the Gothic Revival in America after 1850* (Middletown, CT, 1980).

55. Vaux discussed this building briefly in *Villas and Cottages*, 63. The building must have been completed by 1853, for in the Boston city directory for that year Stone is listed at 130 Commercial Street for the first time. The building was renovated by Mintz Associates in 1978.

56. James M. Bryan, "Boston's Granite Architecture, c. 1810–1860" (Ph.D. dissertation, Boston University, 1972). Bryan misdates the Commercial Block to c. 1856–1857, viz., after Bryant's Mercantile Wharf and State Street Block. In fact, it preceded these buildings by at least two years.

57. Siegfried Giedion, *Space, Time, and Architecture*, 5th ed. (Cambridge, MA, 1967), 360–361.

58. Vaux to Wilder, July 18, 1852.

59. Therese O'Malley, "'A Public Museum of Trees': Mid-Nineteenth-Century Plans for the Mall," in *The Mall in Washington, 1791–1991*, ed. Richard Longstreth (Washington, 1991), 62–63.

60. Downing's introduction to Vaux's essay "Should a Republic Encourage the Arts?," *Horticulturist* 7 (February 1852): 73.

61. Anne C. Lynch, "A Sketch of Washington City," *Harper's New Monthly Magazine* 6 (December 1852): 6. The article was written before Downing's death.

62. The description of the plan for the Washington park is based on Downing's "Explanatory Notes," dated March 3, 1851, which accompanied the map that he sent to Fillmore. Both of these documents are reprinted in W. E. Washburn, "Vision of Life for the Mall," *Journal of the American Institute of Architects* (March 1967): 1–8.

63. Vaux to Wilder, July 18, 1852.

64. Downing to Lynch, February 26, 1852, Rare Book and Manuscript Room, Boston Public Library.

65. Benjamin Silliman and Charles R. Goodrich, *The World of Science, Art, and Industry Illustrated from Examples in the New-York Exhibition, 1853–1854* (New York, 1854), 13. The authors state that the drawings used in the publication were furnished by Vaux, who undoubtedly had also sent along a written explanation.

66. "Our Crystal Palace," *Putnam's Monthly* 2 (August 1853): 123.

67. Most of the information in this discussion of the observatory is drawn from the *Annals of the Dudley Observatory* (Albany, 1866).

68. Cook, "Late A. J. Downing," 381.

69. "Burning of the *Henry Clay*," *Albany Argus*, July 31, 1852, 2.

70. Downing to Lynch, February 26, 1852, Rare Book and Manuscript Room, Boston Public Library.

71. Curtis, "Memoir," lvii.

72. Olmsted and Kimball, *Frederick Law Olmsted*, 1:91–92.

73. Quoted in Clarke, *James Hall*, 236.

CHAPTER 3

1. Calvert Vaux, "American Architecture," *Horticulturist* 8 (April 1853): 168-172.

2. "The Hudson River, V," *Art Journal* 1 (1875): 171.

3. Calvert Vaux, *Villas and Cottages* (New York, 1857; rev. ed., 1864), 249.

4. T. Addison Richards, "Idlewild, the Home of N. P. Willis," *Harper's New Monthly Magazine* 16 (January 1858): 145–156.

5. *DAB*, 20:308.

6. Quoted in "The Hudson River, V," 171.

7. Vaux, *Villas and Cottages*, 248.

8. Walter Creese, *The Crowning of the American Landscape: Eight Great Spaces and Their Buildings* (Princeton, 1985), 66.

9. Willis to Vaux, August 8, 1855, in *Villas and Cottages*, 255. Leonard Lee, a neighbor of Willis at Cornwall, may have been one of those who came to Vaux after seeing Idlewild; in 1855–1856, Vaux designed a small wooden cottage for him. The date of the Lee house is suggested by the fact that it appeared in *Villas and Cottages*, where Vaux said that it was being erected as the book went to press, presumably late in 1856.

10. In a letter to Vaux dated December 24, 1855, Robins said he and his family had been living in the house for "two or three years." See Vaux, *Villas and Cottages*, 167.

11. Ibid., 166.

12. Andrew Jackson Downing, *A Treatise on the Practice of Landscape Gardening*, 4th ed. (New York, 1849), 34.

13. Vaux, *Villas and Cottages*, 28.

14. Plans in the possession of the Beacon Historical Society, Beacon, New York, for the remodeling of Wodenethe are signed by Vaux and dated 1853. On Wodenethe generally, see J. E. Spingarn, "Henry Winthrop Sargent and the Early History of Landscape Gardening and Ornamental Horticulture in Dutchess County, New York," *Yearbook of the Dutchess County Historical Society* (1937).

15. Vaux, *Villas and Cottages*, 54. Wodenethe is example D in the group of sketches that illustrate Vaux's remarks.

16. Sargent, "Supplement," in Downing, *Treatise*, 6th ed. (New York, 1859), 440.

17. Vaux, *Villas and Cottages*, 83.

18. Vaux, "Hints for Country House Builders," *Harper's New Monthly Magazine* 11 (November 1855): 766.

19. Vaux discussed and illustrated the cottage in *Villas and Cottages*, 287–288, where he noted that because it was in view from the road "it therefore seemed worth while to consider it as an accessory in the landscape as well as a convenient home for those who were to live in it." As Kenneth Lutter points out, Vaux's statement implies that the heavy growth of understory trees and shrubs that exists at the site today was not present in the 1850s. At that time, most of the Hoyt land was probably a working landscape of fields and pastures.

20. Vaux, "Hints," 766.

21. Vaux, *Villas and Cottages*, 284.

22. Ibid., 151.

23. At the end of the nineteenth century, the interior was remodeled in the Neo-classical style.

24. Strong's mention of Hoyt is found in Allan Nevins and Milton Thomas, eds., *The Diary of George Templeton Strong: Young Man in New York, 1835–1849*, 4 vols. (New York, 1952), 1:206.

25. The house and grounds were sold to the New York Office of Parks, Recreation, and Historic Preservation in 1963 by Mrs. Helen Hoyt. The property now forms part of Mills-Norrie State Park and is administered by the New York Office of Parks, Recreation, and Historic Preservation.

26. McEntee Diary, July 29, 1873, and November 1, 1883.

27. Vaux, *Villas and Cottages*, 153. McEntee's studio was located on Chestnut Street in Kingston.

28. In the New York city directory for 1853–1854, Warren's home address is already listed as Newburgh. (His office was on Wall Street.) In *Villas and Cottages*, where the Warren house is Design 14, Vaux did not list it as a Vaux and Withers commission. Hence, I believe the design was prepared before the early part of 1854, the most likely date for the formation of the partnership.

29. Vaux, *Villas and Cottages*, 55.

30. E. M. Ruttenber, *History of the Town of Newburgh* (Philadelphia, 1859), 286.

31. Vaux, *Villas and Cottages*, 125–126.

32. Ibid., 205–206.

33. Vaux, "Hints," 772.

34. Ramsdell to Vaux, September 24, 1855, in Vaux, *Villas and Cottages*, 209–210.

35. Vaux included the Case house in his 1855 article "Hints," 772, by which time the dwelling had been built, and later in *Villas and Cottages*, as Design 8.

36. Vaux, *Villas and Cottages*, 129–132.

37. Trow's *New York City Directory for the Year Ending May 1, 1856,* lists Rogers's address for the first time as Ravenswood, indicating that the house was completed during 1855. The dwelling is featured as Design 11 in Vaux's *Villas and Cottages*.

38. The boathouse, which also provided a changing room for bathers, was illustrated in ibid., 294. Vaux showed the gate on the Rogers property on page 196.

39. Ibid., 291.

40. Ibid., 303–304. The precise location of this house, which Vaux said was under construction at the time of writing, is not known.

41. The Hall house is Design 27 in *Villas and Cottages*.

42. Mary Vaux was born on January 26, 1830. The Vauxes had two other children: Julia, born in 1858, and Marion, born in 1864.

43. Vaux, *Villas and Cottages*, 115.

44. Ibid., 38–39.

45. Ibid., 38.

46. Ibid.

47. Likewise, "Hints" contained houses that in *Villas and Cottages* were indicated as having been started during Vaux's partnership with Downing. Yet Vaux did not mention Downing's association with those jobs in the article.

48. "Springside for Sale or Exchange," printed advertisement dated December 29, 1854, in the Vassar College Library, Special Collections Division, where drawings for the house are also preserved.

49. B. J. Lossing, *Vassar College and Its Founder* (New York, 1867), 72. Lossing lists the log cabin as one of the structures erected during Downing's lifetime; it is more likely, however, that the building was built after Downing's death and before November 1855, when Vaux published it in "Hints." He also included it in the 1857 edition of *Villas and Cottages,* where no mention is made of Downing's collaboration on the design. Cook, who was in the Downing and Vaux office, would surely have known of Uncle Tom's Cabin if it had been built by the time of his article.

50. C. Cook, "Late A. J. Downing," *New York Quarterly* 1 (October 1852): 372.

51. Fowler was the son of Gilbert O. Fowler, a prominent citizen of Newburgh and president of the Highland Bank there. See Ruttenber, *History of the Town of Newburgh,* 1276–1277. Vaux discussed the house in *Villas and Cottages,* 193–195. Plans for the house, dated 1854, are in the New-York Historical Society, New York. They are signed only by Vaux, even though in *Villas and Cottages* Vaux indicates that the house was a Vaux and Withers commission.

52. Vaux, *Villas and Cottages,* 194.

53. Ibid., 267.

54. John J. Nutt, comp., *Newburgh: Her Institutions, Industries and Leading Citizens* (Newburgh, NY, 1891), 133. The O'Reilly house is Design 5 in Vaux, *Villas and Cottages.*

55. Vaux, *Villas and Cottages,* 110. According to the Newburgh city directory for 1858-1859, Daniel Ryan's residence, which is no longer standing, was located at 33 Smith Street.

56. Ibid., 235.

57. Ibid., 63. In his text, Vaux stated that the building had already been built, which would mean that it was standing by the end of 1856.

58. Ibid., 300–302. The house, which is no longer standing, did not appear in Vaux's November 1855 article, "Hints," suggesting that Gray commissioned it after that date. Gray was first listed at this address in Trow's *New York City Directory* for the year ending May 1, 1860. However, the house was indicated as standing in "Sketchings," *Crayon* 5 (September 1858): 266. Construction probably did not begin until early in 1858, for English readers of the *Builder* were told in December 1857, when the journal published an illustration of the dwelling, that it was "about to be built." See "An American Town House," *Builder* 15 (December 12, 1857): 719.

59. "Sketchings."

60. Vaux, *Villas and Cottages,* 301.

61. Ibid., 243–244.

62. C. Cook, "Obituary—Jacob Wrey Mould," *Studio* 2 (July 1886): 15.

63. [J. Durand], "Street-Musings On Architecture: Decorative Painting in the House of J. A. C. Gray, Esq.," *Crayon* 6 (February 1859): 60.

64. Bloor Diary, March 21, 1859. Bloor entered Vaux's office on March 21, 1859.

65. Cook, "Mould."

66. The other architects invited to compete were John Warren Ritch, Thomas Thomas, Robert Griffin Hatfield, and Frederick Diaper. Unfortunately, none of the plans has survived. See Minutes of the Building Committee of the Bank of New York, January 10, 1956.

67. Trow's *New York City Directory for the Year Ending May 1, 1857,* 845. In the directory for the following year, Vaux was listed without Withers.

68. "Mr. Gardiner G. Howland," *New York Herald,* November 13, 1851, 2.

69. C. Cook, "New-York Daguerreotyped. Group First: Business Streets, Mercantile Blocks, Stores, and Banks," *Putnam's Monthly* 1 (February 1853): 132.

70. "The Savings' Bank in Bleecker Street," *Crayon* 3 (September 1856): 273.

71. "The New Banking House of the Bank of New-York," *New York Times*, March 26, 1858, 4.

72. "Bank of New York," *Builder* 16 (February 20, 1858): 126.

73. "Architecture," *Crayon* 3 (July 1856): 215. While willing to employ iron for structural elements in the Bank of New York, Vaux was reluctant to endorse its widespread use on the exterior of buildings. He told his AIA colleagues that the great defect of iron was its "destructibility by corrosion and otherwise" and that the need to paint it would "do away with our respect for it." If, however, a process could be developed whereby it could be "vitrified or otherwise prepared to guard against the influence of the elements," then Vaux saw a brighter future for its acceptance. Vaux's remarks are reported in "Architecture," *Crayon* 6 (January 1859): 24.

74. This may have been the first project on which Leeds collaborated with Vaux. Vaux and Leeds formed a brief partnership in 1863–1864.

75. This letter, as well as another of January 29, 1855, that Vaux sent to Harper with the final contract, is in the Pierpont Morgan Library.

76. C. Cook, "House Building in America," *Putnam's Monthly* 10 (July 1857): 108.

77. Hanno-Walter Kruft, *A History of Architectural Theory from Vitruvius to the Present*, trans. R. Taylor, E. Callander, and A. Wood (Princeton, 1994), 354.

78. Vaux (quoting Emerson), *Villas and Cottages*, 31 32.

79. A. K. H. B., "Concerning Villas and Cottages," *Frazer's Magazine* 29 (December 1858): 701.

80. Vaux to Olmsted, June 3, 1865, *PFLO*, 5:386–387.

81. Vaux to Olmsted, July 8, 1865, *PFLO*, 5:404.

82. Review of *Villas and Cottages*, *Crayon* 4 (May 1857): 160.

83. Review of *Villas and Cottages*, *North American Review* 98 (1857): 276–277.

84. Review of *Villas and Cottages*, *Merchant's Magazine* 36 (June 1857): 778.

85. Statement quoted in advertisement in *Harper's Weekly* 2 (May 29, 1858): 351.

86. "Designs for Residences in the United States," *Builder* 15 (November 14, 1857): 657-658. A British edition was printed by Sampson, Low and Company.

87. Vaux, *Villas and Cottages*, iii.

CHAPTER 4

1. Vaux received citizenship on October 24, 1856, according to John Donaldson, "Notes on Calvert Vaux by a Grandson," in John D. Sigle, "Calvert Vaux, an American Architect" (master's thesis, University of Virginia, 1967), 24.

2. "Architecture," *Crayon* 4 (May 1857): 151.

3. Calvert Vaux, "Parisian Buildings for City Residents," *Harper's Weekly* 1 (December 19, 1857): 809–810. Virtually the same article appeared under the same title in the *Architects' and Mechanics' Journal* 2 (July 21, 1860): 154–156.

4. Elizabeth Collins Cromley, *Alone Together: A History of New York's Early Apartments* (Ithaca, NY, 1990).

5. Vaux's first residential address in New York City was 225 West 31st Street, where he was listed as living in Trow's *New York City Directory for the Year Ending May 1, 1857*. The following year, the family moved to 136 East 18th Street. Vaux's office during this period was at 348 Broadway. Jervis and Gertrude McEntee rented a room in the Vaux house.

6. "Architecture," *Crayon* 4 (July 1857): 218.

7. Vaux, "Parisian Buildings," 810.

8. Everard M. Upjohn, *Richard Upjohn, Architect and Churchman* (New York, 1939), 164.

9. Sarah B. Landau, "Richard Morris Hunt: Architectural Innovator and Father of a

'Distinctive'American School," in *The Architecture of Richard Morris Hunt*, ed. Susan Stein (Chicago, 1986), 62–63.

10. For a detailed discussion of the creation of the park, see Roy Rosenzweig and Elizabeth Blackmar, *The Park and the People: A History of Central Park* (Ithaca, NY, 1992), Chapter 1, "Creating Central Park."

11. "Memorandum."

12. Vaux had forwarded the drawing for the monument, which was in the form of a large marble vase, to Smith in 1852. See Vaux to Smith, July 8, 1852, in John Jay Smith Papers, Historical Society of Pennsylvania, Philadelphia. Smith published the design, which Vaux said was "carefully modeled from a chaste but highly enriched antique example," in the November 1856 issue of the *Horticulturist*. (Vaux's description and an illustration appeared in his Preface to *Villas and Cottages* [New York, 1857; rev. ed., 1864], xii and xiv.) The following month, he told his readers that the memorial was nearly finished. See "Editor's Table," *Horticulturist* 11 (June 1856): 286; "The Downing Monument," *Horticulturist* 11 (November 1856): 32–33; and "Editor's Table," *Horticulturist* 11 (December 1856): 526.

13. "Memorandum."

14. Vaux to Olmsted, June 3, 1865, in *PFLO*, 5:387. Olmsted later remembered that once Vaux had "selected" and "invited" him to collaborate, it was "with some difficulty" that he was "persuaded to join him." "The Central Park," *American Architect and Building News* 11 (June 2, 1877): 175.

15. For a detailed account of the early years of Central Park, see Charles Beveridge's introduction in *PFLO*, 3:1–48.

16. Vaux to Olmsted, January 18, 1864, *PFLO*, 5:177.

17. G. W. Curtis, "Editor's Easy Chair," *Harper's New Monthly Magazine* 19 (December 1859): 841.

18. Specifically, Vaux had in mind employing Ignaz Pilat, Edward C. Miller, "and half a dozen others" who could be hired "in a proper professional way if we are lucky without engaging to pay them annual salaries" (Vaux to Olmsted, November 10, 1865). The earliest mention of the official formation of the Olmsted and Vaux partnership appears to be in a letter from Olmsted to his father dated July 22, 1860 (*PFLO*, 3:256–257).

19. Frederick L. Olmsted Jr. and Theodora Kimball, eds., *Frederick Law Olmsted, Landscape Architect, 1822–1903: Forty Years of Landscape Architecture*, 2 vols. (New York, 1922–1928; reprint, New York, 1970), 2:70.

20. Vaux to Barton, December 8, 1857, Rare Book and Manuscript Room, Boston Public Library.

21. Vaux to Olmsted, June 3, 1865, *PFLO*, 5:387. "I had a will—an ambition, or plan of life, in connection with the park," Olmsted confessed to Vaux, "by which my conduct had been greatly moved before I knew you. Under its influence, I had obtained the post of Superintendent of the Park—this before I knew you, before I entertained the idea of having anything to do with the design or with you." In this position, Olmsted clearly regarded himself as a manager of park affairs, but he was not concerned with the design matters. "It was normal, ordinary and naturally outgrowing from my previous life and history—the purpose I had in this position—and it occupied my whole heart," Olmsted stated. Referring to the "higher ambition, if you please, to which your comradeship afterwards brought me," Olmsted conceded that it was Vaux who roused him to set his sights above the level of merely implementing Viele's faulty plan (Olmsted to Vaux, November 26, 1863, *PFLO*, 5:146). Perhaps some of Vaux's thinking on the matter informed the article "Park Hints for 'The Manhattan,'" which appeared in the *Crayon* in August 1856. Signed "NI-DES," it contained a number of "hints" that later characterize the Greensward plan.

22. The full text, as well as the drawings Vaux and Olmsted submitted, are reprinted and annotated in *PFLO*, 3:119–187.

23. See "Design for Connecting the Populous Quarters of South Kensington and

Bayswater, and the Districts Adjacent, by Means of a Subway under the Middle Walk in Kensington Gardens," *Builder* 12 (November 17, 1860): 735–736. In a letter to Mariana Van Rensselaer, Olmsted made the following statement in reference to an article she had written on the origins of the Greensward plan. "There are one or two things in your article which I wish were not there," wrote Olmsted. "One is the statement about the transverse roads, which you made from a recollection of what I said to you of the manner in which the suggestion for these roads grew out of an experience of fire engines running across the park. There is nothing literally untrue in your statement, and yet it is hardly just to Vaux. He seized, I remember, upon my tentative suggestion with the greater eagerness because of his familiarity with some construction partially serving a similar purpose in the zoological garden in Regent's Park" (Olmsted to Van Rensselaer, September 23, 1893).

24. This and previous quotes are from Vaux to Olmsted, June 3, 1865, *PFLO*, 5:387.

25. Vaux to Olmsted, January 18, 1864, *PFLO*, 5:178.

26. Samuel Parsons Jr., *Landscape Gardening* (New York, 1895), 276.

27. "The chief classes of communication are so arranged," wrote Olmsted, "that, by a peculiar system of arched passages, it never becomes necessary for a person on foot to cross the surface of the carriage roads, or the horseman's track, or the horseman to cross the carriage roads, though he may ride upon them if he prefers" ("Parks," *New American Cyclopedia* [New York, 1861], 3:355).

28. John Claudius Loudon, *Suburban Gardener and Villa Companion* (London, 1836–1838), 158.

29. Clarence Cook, "Central Park," *Scribner's Monthly* 6 (September 1873): 538. Others also grouped the bridges that Vaux designed for Central Park among his most important achievements. "Parmis les ponts á citer dans les parcs publics," wrote the French landscape architect Edouard André, "se placent en premiere ligne ceux que M. C. Vaux a dessinés pour le Central-Park de New York" (Edouard André, *L'art des jardins: Traité général de la composition des parcs et jardins* [Paris, 1879], 858).

30. Vaux to Cook, June 6, 1865.

31. Charles H. J. Smith, *Landscape Gardening* (New York, 1853), 291.

32. Vaux to Cook, June 6, 1865.

33. Most of the bridge names were agreed on at least by 1873, when Olmsted prepared a list of the popular names of park bridges and places. See his memorandum dated February 6, 1873.

34. Clarence Cook, *A Description of the New York Central Park* (New York, 1869), 70.

35. The executive committee authorized the comptroller of the park, A. H. Green, to contract for Bridge 17 in June 1861. See "Report of the Executive Committee," BCCP, Minutes, September 30, 1861.

36. Construction of Bridge 23 was authorized by the executive committee on June 30, 1861. See "Report of the Executive Committee," BCCP, Minutes, September 30, 1861.

37. BCCP, "Document No. 5, May 31, 1858," in "Report to the Board of Commissioners of the Central Park from Frederick Law Olmsted, Architect-in-Chief," *PFLO*, 3:195.

38. BCCP, Minutes, December 23, 1858, 172. The cast and wrought iron components were manufactured by the Janes, Kirtland and Company Iron Works in the Bronx. The bridge, which has a span of 87 feet and carries a wooden floor, was contracted for in May 1860 and finished when the 140-foot railing was installed in 1862. Citing "a much larger amount of work having been done" on the Bow Bridge, the commissioners voted on June 6, 1861, to extend an extra payment of $1,000 to the J. B. and W. W. Cornell foundry. See BCCP, Minutes, June 6, 1861. The Bow Bridge was restored in 1974.

39. Pope illustrated and explained his unique design, which he intended to construct of wood, in *A Treatise on Bridge Architecture* (New York, 1811).

40. Frederick B. Perkins, *The Central Park* (New York, 1862), 59–60. Similar flower-

pots crowned the abutments of Digby Wyatt's recent St. James's Park bridge in London. See "St. James's-Park Bridge, London," *Builder* 15 (June 27, 1857): 17.

41. Olmsted, "Parks," 355.

42. In August 1859, Vaux's friend John A. C. Gray introduced the motion approving "the study for a rough stone archway in Ravine near to the head of the Pond" that had been presented to the board that day. See BCCP, Minutes, August 18, 1859, 108.

43. André, *L'art des jardins*, 510.

44. Loudon, *Suburban Gardener*, 464.

45. Vaux, *Villas and Cottages*, 155.

46. W. H. B. Grant, "Report of Superintending Engineer," in BCCP, *Fifth Annual Report* (1862), 95. Grant also reported that the arch was finished in 1860 and that the carriage road over it was opened the following year.

47. J. K. Larke, *Davege's Handbook of Central Park* (New York, c. 1868), 39.

48. Cook, *Central Park*, 115.

49. Perkins, *Central Park*, 61.

50. Angela Miller, *The Empire of the Eye: Landscape Representation and American Cultural Politics* (Ithaca, NY, 1993), 243–288.

51. William Robinson, "Public Gardens: The Central Park, New York," *Garden* 1 (May 11, 1872): 544–545.

52. John A. Hughes, *Garden Architecture and Landscape Gardening* (London, 1866), 163.

53. "Rustic Bridge," *Gardener's Monthly* 4 (March 1862): 88.

54. J. Miller, *Guide to Central Park* (New York, 1866), 21.

CHAPTER 5

1. Clarence Cook, *A Description of the New York Central Park* (New York, 1869), 54.

2. Vaux to Cook, June 6, 1865.

3. Samuel Parsons Jr., *Landscape Gardening* (New York, 1895), 276–277.

4. Handwritten document beginning "Calvert Vaux Duly Sworn" (1864), in the Olmsted Papers. Vaux prepared this document when Viele brought suit claiming his plan had been plagiarized.

5. Brent Elliott, *Victorian Gardens* (London, 1986), 115.

6. Vaux to Cook, June 6, 1865.

7. Olmsted to Board of Commissioners of the Central Park, May 31, 1858, *PFLO*, 3:195.

8. BCCP, Minutes, September 16, 1858, 120.

9. BCCP, *Sixth Annual Report* (1863), 33.

10. Vaux to Cook, June 6, 1865.

11. For a discussion of the controversy over the gates, see Francis R. Kowsky, "The Central Park Gateways: Harbingers of French Urbanism Confront the American Landscape Tradition," in *The Architecture of Richard Morris Hunt*, ed. Susan Stein (Chicago, 1986), 79–89.

12. Frederick B. Perkins, *The Central Park* (New York, 1862), 16. Perkins had interviewed Vaux before writing the text of his book.

13. BCCP, *Eighth Annual Report* (1865), 6. In the late summer of 1864, Vaux updated Olmsted in California on the Terrace: "The circular fountain basin is in," he reported, "and increases the water effect as I anticipated. The flag standards are up. The standards looked low but now the banners are added the proportion is satisfactory. This afternoon was fine and the effect was good from the Terrace balcony looking over the crowd below, the fountain basin enunciating the idea of the design significantly" (Vaux to Olmsted, September 17, 1864).

14. Of these vases, Vaux wrote to Olmsted in 1864 that they "are up and look tolerable. I modified the designs in the Spring and visited the park with Mould and Green for the purpose, but the effect is not all that could be hoped; however, they are intended to

be subordinate and I believe the loss of effect arises from their appearing permanent, central and focal, whereas the statues will ultimately make them of minor importance" (Vaux to Olmsted, September 17, 1864).

15. Vaux to Olmsted, September 17, 1864.

16. Calvert Vaux, "Description of the Terrace," BCCP, *Sixth Annual Report* (1863), 63–65.

17. Cook, *Central Park*, 48.

18. DPP, *Third Annual Report* (1874), 17.

19. "Bethesda Fountain," *New York Times*, June 1, 1873, 5.

20. [P. Godwin], "The Angel of the Waters," *New York Evening Post,* May 19, 1873, 2.

21. [C. Cook], "Angel of Waters," *New York Tribune*, May 19, 1873, 5.

22. William Gerdts, "Emma Stebbins," in *Notable American Women* (New York, 1973), 3:121; Charlotte Rubenstein, *American Women Artists from Early Indian Times to the Present* (New York, 1982), 85–86.

23. Cook, "Angel."

24. Cook, *Central Park*, 51. Mould apparently joined the Central Park work on December 3, 1858, and continued his association with the undertaking until March 10, 1875. During 1870–1871, he assumed the role of architect in chief.

25. Bloor Diary, March 30, 1861.

26. Ibid., April 11, 1861.

27. Allan Nevins and Milton Thomas, eds., *The Diary of George Templeton Strong: Young Man in New York, 1835–1849,* 4 vols. (New York, 1952), 4:52.

28. McEntee Diary, June 21, 1886.

29. Daniel Wise, *Little Peach Blossom* (New York, 1873), 37.

30. Gilman to Vaux, November 19, 1863, Archives of American Art, McEntee Papers.

31. [Peter B. Wight], "What Has Been Done and What Can Be Done," *New Path* (October 1863): 74. Vaux proudly sent a copy of Wight's article to Olmsted in California without making any remarks about errors of fact in the text.

32. "In this idea of a design," he had written in *Villas and Cottages* (New York, 1857; rev. ed., 1964) of a comparable scheme, "all the forms are made to adapt themselves to the general upward line of the staircase, and a more easy and graceful effect can be arrived at in this way than in any other" (87).

33. [Wight], "What Has Been Done," 74. For Vaux's remarks on artisans and the AIA, see "Architecture," *Crayon* 5 (July 1858): 200.

34. See BCCP, *Tenth Annual Report* (1867), and BCCP, *Eleventh Annual Report* (1868). According to statements in the *Twelfth Annual Report* (1869), 7–8, carving of the ornament continued into 1868.

35. Cook, *Central Park*, 55.

36. Vaux to Cook, June 6, 1865.

37. Statuary, Vaux had advised readers of *Villas and Cottages*, was best left out of grounds landscaped in the naturalistic manner, for in such locations it divided one's "attention between the beauties of art and the beauties of nature. . . . The true situation for statues is on an architectural terrace" (278).

38. Cook, *Central Park*, 81–82.

CHAPTER 6

1. Evidence of Vaux's membership comes from the Bloor Diary: Bloor frequently mentions dining there with Vaux. On March 7, 1860, Bloor went to the Down Town Association to "take measurements," and on October 16, 1860, he noted a meeting at the club with a Mr. Gordon to discuss unspecified changes.

2. "The New Club-House of the Athenaeum Club," *New York Times,* March 24, 1859, 5.

3. Bloor Diary, November 1, 1860.

4. Vaux was elected to membership in the Century Association on June 4, 1859. Olmsted became a member the same day. The architect Joseph C. Wells sponsored Vaux.

5. J. H. Morse diary quoted in *The Century, 1847–1946* (New York, 1946), 45.

6. Vaux owned Hall's *Flowers from Nature*, which the artist exhibited at the National Academy of Design in 1860.

7. In a letter to Thomas Webb Richards, a Philadelphia architect who apparently worked in Vaux's office during the war, Vaux told Richards, "I know Bierstadt, Church, Kensett, Leutz, Hall, McEntee, Gifford, Hays, Thompson, Danna, E. Johnson, Hennesey, H. K. Brown and, of course, the architects of most reputation" (Vaux to Richards, January 26, 1863, in University Archives, University of Pennsylvania).

8. Primary evidence of these activities comes from the diary of A. J. Bloor. The skating incident is reported in a letter Vaux wrote to Olmsted on January 30, 1864.

9. Obituary in *Garden and Forest* 8 (November 27, 1895): 480. Stiles was the journal's editor.

10. For the story of Olmsted's struggle with Green during the early years of the park's existence, see Laura Wood Roper, *FLO: A Biography of Frederick Law Olmsted* (Baltimore, 1973), 128 passim, and *PFLO*, 3:1–40.

11. See C. Dahl, *Stephen C. Earle, Architect: Shaping Worcester's Image* (Worcester, 1987), 8.

12. This "Memorandum of Agreement" is privately owned.

13. Earle spent 11 months in service before returning to New York. In the fall of 1863 he again worked briefly with Vaux before leaving for Worcester, where he established his practice in 1866.

14. Olmsted to John Olmsted, August 17, 1864.

15. Bloor mentions going with "Vaux to Staten Island to his house" on October 6, 1859. See also Mary Olmsted to F. L. Olmsted, October 18, 1859.

16. The Vauxes remained at Mount St. Vincent until 1863.

17. Vaux to Olmsted, letter dating from the fall of 1859.

18. Vaux to Godwin, September 29, 1859.

19. Truefitt to Olmsted, October 17, 1859.

20. F. L. Olmsted, "Document No. 4," from BCCP, *Third Annual Report* (1859), in *PFLO*, 3:234–239.

21. Olmsted to Sir William Hooker, c. November 29, 1859, in *PFLO*, 3:232–233.

22. Vaux to Olmsted, undated but written while Olmsted was abroad in 1859–1860.

23. Ibid.

24. A photograph of the house is reproduced in Irving Katz, *August Belmont: A Political Biography* (New York, 1968), 268.

25. Vaux to Olmsted, undated but written while Olmsted was abroad in 1859–1860. When the park site commission filed its report in 1860, its members recommended seven sites. See *PFLO*, 6:336, n. 7.

26. Actually, the board initially withheld Vaux's salary. Three years later, after his lawyer friend John Monell interceded for him, he was reimbursed. See Vaux to Olmsted, December 1, 1863, and February 5, 1864, *PFLO*, 4:183.

27. On Truefitt and Ruskin's 1856 bank design, see Michael W. Brooks, *John Ruskin and Victorian Architecture* (Brunswick, NJ, 1987), 135.

28. In a letter to his father, Olmsted remarked that during the prince's visit "neither Vaux or I were taken any notice of" (F. L. Olmsted to John Olmsted, October 21, 1860, *PFLO*, 3:274).

29. Bloor Diary, December 17, 18, and 31 and February 20, 1860.

30. Margaret Clapp, *Forgotten First Citizen: John Bigelow* (Boston, 1947), 108–109.

31. The recollections of Bigelow's granddaughter, Grace Tracy Cook, are found in Frances F. Dunwell, *The Hudson River Highlands* (New York, 1990), 120 and 199.

32. John Bigelow, *Retrospective of an Active Life*, 2 vols. (New York, 1913), 1:340.

33. Olmsted to Bigelow, February 9, 1861, in *PFLO*, 3:323–327.

34. On Green's management of Central Park, see Roy Rosenzweig and Elizabeth Blackmar, *The Park and the People: A History of Central Park* (Ithaca, NY, 1992),190–196.

35. Allan Nevins and Milton Thomas, eds., *The Diary of George Templeton Strong: Young Man in New York, 1835–1849*, 4 vols. (New York, 1952), 4: 385.

36. Bigelow, *Retrospective*, 1:340.

37. Eighteen sheets of drawings (mostly for details) for the Brooks house signed by Vaux and dated 1858 are in the Frances Loeb Library, Graduate School of Design, Harvard University.

38. Records in the Barreda Papers at Southern Illinois University indicate that Barreda made numerous payments to Vaux in 1860 for work at the "5th Avenue house." On December 7, 1860, Vaux was paid $778.78, 5 percent of $15,575.71 that had been spent on an addition to the house.

39. On November 5, 1860, Barreda settled Vaux's bill of $5,253.00, a fee that represented 5 percent of the $100,000 cost of the dwelling, plus traveling expenses for twenty-three visits at $11.00 per trip.

40. Jacob Weidenmann, *Beautifying Country Homes* (New York, 1870; reprint, Watkins Glen, NY, 1978), Plate 13. Weidenmann illustrates the plan of the grounds.

41. Ibid.

42. Frederick B. Sherman, *From the Guadalquivir to the Golden Gate* (Mill Valley, CA, 1977), 65.

43. M. W. Crocker, *Historic Architecture in Mississippi* (Jackson, MS, 1973), 150–151.

44. Calvert Vaux, *Villas and Cottages* (New York, 1857; rev. ed., 1864), Design 27, 291–294. Vaux signed several undated plans for the house that are now in the possession of the present property owner.

45. Hoyt's involvement in the project can be surmised from Bloor's statement in his diary for November 10, 1860, that he "met Major Lowndes and Mr. Hoyt and showed them the plans and had conversation with them."

46. Bloor Diary, November 14, October 31, and November 22, 1860.

47. Vaux, *Villas and Cottages*, rev. ed., 296.

48. "Death of James Couper Lord," *New York Times*, February 12, 1869, 11. Lord, who owned an ironworks, promoted the arts in New York City and devoted much of his time and money to improving the lot of the poor. Even less information is preserved in Bloor's diary concerning a commission for a Mr. Rogers. We simply know that Bloor stayed overnight at least once with Vaux at Mount St. Vincent to help "on Rogers' plans" (Bloor Diary, September 6, 1860).

49. The house is presently the rectory of Christ Church.

50. Olmsted to J. Olmsted, July 22, 1860, *PFLO*, 3:256.

51. Olmsted to H. H. Elliott, August 27, 1860, *PFLO*, 3:259–269.

52. Beveridge, *PFLO*, 3:244.

53. The Collins commission, as Charles Beveridge has pointed out, is the first instance of which we have knowledge confirming the existence of the Olmsted and Vaux partnership outside of Central Park. It is mentioned by Olmsted in a letter to his father dated July 22, 1860.

54. Judith D. Spikes, *Larchmont, New York: People and Places* (Larchmont, 1991), 56–60. MacDonald's map is in the Larchmont village hall. Two other maps from the early 1870s in the village hall show a system of curving and straight streets with a public park near the center. However, there is no reference on either of them to Vaux or Olmsted, leaving open to further investigation the intriguing question of what role the partners may have had in shaping the present landscape of the area.

55. "Hillside Cemetery," *Whig Press* (Middletown), February 13, 1861, 2.

56. Bloor Diary, April 30 and May 18, 1861.

57. "The New Cemetery," *Whig Press* (Middletown), July 10, 1861, 2.

58. Ibid.

59. "A Thriving Country Village," *Daily Graphic*, September 6, 1877, 461.

60. Bloor recorded finishing the specifications for the Middletown tower at the end of April 1860. See *PFLO*, 3:132.

61. A letter Butler wrote to "Messrs Vaux and Olmsted" on April 13, 1860, discusses preliminary plans (now lost) that the partners had already submitted.

62. Butler to Olmsted, December 3, 1872, in *PFLO*, 3:32.

63. Weidenmann had studied architecture in Geneva and Munich before coming to the United States in 1856. After working with landscape architect Eugene Baumann in New York, Weidenmann moved to Hartford in 1859.

64. Vaux had also prepared plans for a conservatory, which was not built. See Butler to Olmsted, January 19 and March 18, 1861.

65. Weidenmann, *Beautifying Country Homes*, Plate 18.

66. Unless otherwise noted, my information concerning the history of the Sheppard Asylum comes from the Minutes of the Board of Trustees.

67. Brown also sought out the partners for advice on laying out the grounds around the Bloomingdale Asylum buildings, which stood on the present site of Columbia University. However, it appears that the project did not get beyond informal conversations Brown had with Olmsted in the winter of 1861. See letters from Brown to Olmsted dated March 9 and 10, 1861. Lack of funds seems to have precluded anything being done on the Bloomingdale Asylum grounds.

68. According to the trustees' account book, Vaux received final payment on May 13, 1865. His total payment for the job was about $3,000.

69. D.T. Brown, "Report of an Examination of Certain European Institutions for the Insane," *American Journal of Insanity* 20 (October 1863): 203.

70. Bloor Diary, May 7, 1861. On May 17, 1861, Bloor recorded giving Vaux advice "about the brother-in-law trouble," which might refer to family urgings that he serve.

71. Vaux's detailed specifications as well as the client's contract with a local carpenter are in the possession of the present owner. Both documents specified a completion date of October 15, 1862; Smith and Gaylord, the builders, received final payment for their work on February 24, 1863.

72. Vaux, *Villas and Cottages*, rev. ed., 333–334. Another prospective client at this time was Richard Milford Blatchford, a wealthy New York City lawyer who served as a Central Park commissioner from 1859 to 1872. Part of this time, he was in Rome as Lincoln's ambassador to the Vatican. Perhaps in anticipation of his second marriage, which took place in November 1860, Blatchford contemplated building a new house. And although Vaux made some plans for Blatchford before the prominent Republican left for Rome in 1862, the house was never erected. (Blatchford's address in city directories did not change during the 1860s.) In a letter Vaux wrote to Olmsted in 1865, he implies that Blatchford's new wife may have discouraged her husband from building and talks about how "Blatchford treated me queerly about drawings for his house." But rather than sue Blatchford in Rome for his proper commission, Vaux let him "do me out of $100." This indicates that the drawings were done before Blatchford took up his post at the Vatican. See Vaux to Olmsted, May 30, 1865.

73. Vaux, *Villas and Cottages*, rev. ed., 187.

74. In a letter to Olmsted dated March 24, 1864, Vaux recalled this episode.

75. In a letter to the editor of the *New York Times*, July 10, 1863, 5, Vaux stated that the building, which was then nearing completion, was "measurably in accordance with a study I made for the purpose last year."

76. Ibid. Vaux referred to his "slight sketch" for this building, which was published in BCCP, *Sixth Annual Report* (1863). Already in 1860, Olmsted had told the commissioners of the need of a restaurant in the park. Citing European examples, especially the parks he had visited the year before in Germany, he called for the construction of a similar facility on the site west of the lake that he and Vaux had designated as the location of "a principal refectory" in the Greensward plan. The design (now lost) for a

wooden structure, which Olmsted attached to his report and which Vaux presumably prepared, included an outdoor dining veranda "unobstructed by posts or columns, but shielded from the sun and rain by a boldly projecting roof," as well as an indoor dining hall, a room where "substantial refreshments" might be obtained "at a moment's notice," a smoking room, and room for the sale of soda water. See F. L. Olmsted, "Report to the Board of Commissioners of Central Park, April 26, 1860, Document No. 6 for 1859–1860," BCCP, *Third Annual Report* (1859). In the winter of 1862, Olmsted had written from the Sanitary Commission to Green protesting the proposal that a restaurant be established in the convent building at Mount St. Vincent. Olmsted feared that opening a dining room there would postpone the construction of the much-needed facility in the lower park. Despite Olmsted's objections, the former convent building was remodeled for a restaurant. Clarence Cook (*A Description of the New York Central Park* [New York, 1869], 168–170) commented favorably on the conversion, which included a sculpture court displaying the works of Thomas Crawford.

77. From statements in the DPP, *First Annual Report* (1870–1871), 24, it appears that the foundations of this conservatory were laid prior to 1870.

78. Olmsted to Mary Olmsted, August 23, 1862.

79. Olmsted to Mary Olmsted, September 15, 1862.

80. Vaux to Reid, January 9, 1873, Reid Papers.

81. Vaux to Olmsted, December 1, 1863.

82. Vaux to Olmsted, May 12, 1863. On May 14, 1863, the commissioners adopted the partners' plan, which had featured a central road that Vaux had convinced Green should enter the park from 110th Street. See *PFLO*, 5:185, n. 8.

83. Vaux to Pilat, July 26, 1865, and Vaux to Olmsted, May 12, 1865. In a letter to Olmsted of February 5, 1864, *PFLO*, 5:183, Vaux implies that he had been advising Pilat. Two years after their resignation, Vaux told Olmsted that during the interim Pilat had seen to it that their plans had been faithfully carried out. See Vaux to Olmsted, May 12, 1865. To Pilat, Vaux wrote that "if our design has been virtually carried out, it is your persistent adhesion to its letter, and to its spirit . . . that has ensured the result under circumstances of peculiar embarrassment." Vaux backed up his appreciation of Pilat's work with a gift of $500. See Vaux to Pilat, July 31, 1865.

84. Vaux to Bellows, February 25, 1864, indicates that Vaux sent a copy to Bellows on that date. A review that linked Vaux with Loudon and Downing appeared in the *New York Times,* May 7, 1864, 2.

85. Vaux to Olmsted, December 1, 1863.

86. Ibid. Vaux had recently gone with Pilat to visit an unnamed client (or prospective client) in Oswego, New York.

87. *PFLO*, 4:59.

88. Olmsted to Vaux, February 16, 1863, *PFLO*, 4:515.

89. Vaux to Olmsted, October 19, 1863, *PFLO*, 5:115. In this same letter, Vaux also talks of a forthcoming payment from Robert B. Minturn, suggesting that the partners had done some sort of work for this wealthy New York merchant, who owned a house at Dobbs Ferry, New York.

90. Olmsted to Mary Olmsted, August 12, 1862, *PFLO*, 4:408.

91. Olmsted to Mary Olmsted, October 15, 1863, *PFLO*, 4:111.

92. Vaux to Olmsted, January 18, 1864.

93. Vaux to Olmsted, January 30, 1864.

94. Olmsted to Vaux, November 26, 1863, *PFLO*, 5:155.

95. Vaux to Olmsted, September 17, 1864.

96. Vaux to Olmsted, February 25, 1864.

97. See *PFLO*, 5:389, n. 9.

98. Vaux to Olmsted, January 30, 1864. On the trial, see "The Facts in the Viele Case," in *Frederick Law Olmsted, Landscape Architect, 1822–1903: Forty Years of Landscape Architecture,* 2 vols., ed. Frederick L. Olmsted Jr. and Theodora Kimball (New York, 1922–1928; reprint, New York, 1970), Appendix 3, 2:554–562.

99. Vaux forwarded a copy of his testimony to Olmsted on April 2, 1864.

100. Vaux realized that he had played into Viele's hands. After he had testified, he wrote to Olmsted, "I believe that I helped his financial case by saying in answer to enquiries that although we accepted $2000 as per bargain, I thought that $5000 would be a moderate charge for the labor etc. we bestowed on it" (Vaux to Olmsted, January 30, 1864).

101. Ibid.

102. Olmsted to Vaux, March 25, 1864, in Olmsted and Kimball, *Frederick Law Olmsted*, 2:561.

103. Vaux, who during the winter of 1864 must have been preoccupied with the birth of his daughter Marion, never published his pamphlet. He may, however, have furnished information that Cook used in his article "Central Park," *Scribner's Monthly* 6 (June 1873): 523–539, in which the author made a point of discussing the essential differences between the two plans.

104. Vaux to Olmsted, September 11, 1864. For an illustration of the boat landing, see *PFLO*, 3:386.

105. The diary of A. J. Bloor, who resumed working for Vaux in the spring of 1865, also provides information on Vaux's clients at this time. Bloor records working on projects for Vaux and Withers for several individuals not discussed here. Among them are: Mr. Stebbins at Springfield, Massachusetts (October 17, 1865); Mr. Shipp (November 15, 1865); Mr. Schifflin (November 20, 1865); Massachusetts Agricultural College report (December 8, 1865); and C. J. Pierson (December 11, 1865).

106. Vaux to Olmsted, December 1, 1863.

107. *DAB*, 2:517. Bowles would later make Olmsted's acquaintance as a member of a party of journalists who visited Yosemite in August 1865. Thereafter, he became a supporter of Olmsted's plan to have the Yosemite Valley declared a national reserve. See *PFLO*, 5:435–438.

108. Vaux to Olmsted, March 24, 1864, and Vaux to Olmsted, April 13, 1865.

109. In his diary, Bloor recorded that he was working on "Bowles' plans," which he ascribed to Vaux and Withers, on December 30, 1865, and January 8 and February 8, 1866. Vaux to Olmsted, April 13, 1865. The house is presently Main House on the grounds of the Mac Duffie School.

110. Vaux to Olmsted, mid-April 1865.

111. Vaux to Olmsted, fragment of letter dated one week before opening of the National Academy of Design building (April 27, 1865).

112. The firm's 1869 drawings for the Godwin house, which was known both as Montrose and as Clovertop, are in the Bryant Library in Roslyn.

113. Vaux to Mary Olmsted, November 10, 1864.

114. Vaux to Olmsted, August or September 1865.

115. See Bloor Diary for October 10 and 25 and November 27, 1865. The stable was demolished in the early 1970s.

116. Nor is it sure that Vaux got the opportunity to lay out the grounds before his client's death in 1868, for he complained to Olmsted of the lack of professional help available to prepare adequate topographic surveys. In 1869, Withers designed a mortuary chapel for Bartlett's remains.

117. Vaux to Olmsted, February 5, 1864.

118. Vaux to Olmsted, February 5, 1864, *PFLO*, 5:182. Vaux must have been especially pleased to see architectural criticism assume a place in American journalism. Several years earlier, as chair of the AIA Committee on Public Lectures, Vaux had stated that a "high standard of popular criticism has ever been an essential element in those eras of society when Art has achieved its greatest triumphs" ("Architecture," *Crayon* 6 [September 1859]): 278).

119. Vaux to Olmsted, February 5, 1864, *PFLO*, 5:182.

120. "Architecture," *Crayon* 5 (July 1858): 200.

121. Vaux, *Villas and Cottages*, 50.

122. Downing Vaux, "Historical Notes," in *Transactions of the American Society of Landscape Architects* (Harrisburg, 1908), 82.

123. Vaux to Olmsted, April 29, 1864.

124. Vaux to Olmsted, September 7, 1864.

125. Vaux to Olmsted, February 26, 1865.

126. Vaux to Olmsted, May 6, 1864.

127. Vaux became a member, according to Henry W. Bellows, one of the league's founders, at the March 6, 1863, meeting. See Henry W. Bellows, *Historical Sketch of the Union League Club of New York* (New York, 1879), 46.

128. Vaux to Olmsted, September 23, 1864.

129. Vaux to Olmsted, February 26, 1865.

130. Vaux to Olmsted, May 6, 1864.

131. Melvin Kalfus, *Frederick Law Olmsted: The Passion of a Public Artist* (New York, 1990), 232–255.

132. Vaux to Olmsted, July 6, 1865, *PFLO*, 5:402.

133. Vaux to Olmsted, May 10, 1865, *PFLO*, 5:364.

134. Vaux to Olmsted, January 9, 1865, *PFLO*, 5:294.

135. Vaux to Stranahan, January 10, 1865.

136. The sketch is in a letter from Vaux to Stranahan dated January 10, 1865.

137. M. M. Graff, *Central Park, Prospect Park: A New Perspective* (New York, 1985), 111.

138. Vaux to Olmsted, January 9, 1864, *PFLO*, 5:295.

139. Olmsted to Vaux, March 12, 1865, *PFLO*, 5:324.

140. Vaux to Olmsted, June 3, 1865, *PFLO*, 5:383.

141. Vaux to Olmsted, May 20, 1865, *PFLO*, 5:372. For the terms Vaux finally agreed to, see *PFLO*, 5:405, n. 1.

142. Vaux to Olmsted, May 10, 1865, *PFLO*, 5:359.

143. Vaux to Olmsted, July 8, 1865, *PFLO*, 5:404.

144. Vaux to Olmsted, July 6, 1865, *PFLO*, 5:402.

145. Vaux to Olmsted, May 20, 1865, *PFLO*, 5:374.

146. Vaux to Olmsted, June 3, 1865, *PFLO*, 5:387.

147. Vaux to Olmsted, July 8, 1865, *PFLO*, 5:404.

148. Roper, *FLO*, 291.

149. Vaux to Olmsted, July 21, 1865, *PFLO*, 5:406.

150. Olmsted to Mariana Griswold Van Rensselaer, May 22, 1893.

CHAPTER 7

1. Bloor Diary, February 20 and March 22, 1866.

2. Bloor Diary, March 2, 1866.

3. Olmsted, Vaux & Co., "Report of the Landscape Architects," BCPP, *Sixth Annual Report* (1866), 14. Olmsted and Vaux's report is dated January 24, 1866.

4. This area became the location of the Brooklyn Botanic Garden and the Brooklyn Museum.

5. Olmsted, Vaux & Co., "Report of the Landscape Architects and Superintendents," BCPP, *Eighth Annual Report* (1868), 37.

6. [E. Cary], "Prospect Park," *Brooklyn Daily Union*, October 18, 1867, 1.

7. Two drawings for this arch survive in the Vaux Papers. According to BCPP, *Eighth Annual Report* (1868), 59, construction of the arch started in 1867. On August 29, 1868, Olmsted noted, "Enterdale Arch complete and people using the road over it" (Olmsted to Vaux, *PFLO*, 6:270).

8. "Rustic Archway, Prospect Park, Brooklyn, N.Y.," *Horticulturist* 25 (January 1870): 18.

9. Olmsted, Vaux & Co., "Report of the Landscape Architects and Superintendents," BPC, *Eleventh Annual Report* (1871), 424.

10. Ibid., 425.

11. Clay Lancaster, *Prospect Park Handbook* (Brooklyn, 1988), 55.

12. On Western interest in the architecture of India, see R. Head, *The Indian Style* (Chicago, 1986).

13. BCPP, *Eighth Annual Report* (1868), 205.

14. BPC, *Eleventh Annual Report* (1871), 425.

15. "Bridge in Prospect Park, Brooklyn," *Horticulturist* 19 (January 1874): 21–22. The original Lullwood Bridge was replaced in the late nineteenth century by a metal bridge known as Lullwater Bridge.

16. Olmsted's letter to Vaux of August 29, 1868, *PFLO*, 6:269, contains the statement that the "Rustic Shelter is well advanced, nearly ready for the thatchers." A photograph of the completed building appeared in the BPC's *Tenth Annual Report* (1870), 18.

17. "Editorial Notes," *Horticulturist* 19 (February 1874): 53.

18. BCPP, *Eighth Annual Report* (1868), 357.

19. Vaux to Olmsted, June 18, 1869.

20. The structure was begun in 1868 (see BCPP, *Ninth Annual Report* [1869], 289) and opened to the public in 1871 (see BPC, *Twelfth Annual Report* [1872], 486).

21. "Sketches from Prospect Park, Brooklyn," *Manufacturer and Builder* 2 (May 1870): 137.

22. In addition to the construction of recreational buildings in the park, Vaux also designed a boiler house that was erected near the lake. It powered a huge pump that raised water from a deep well to a reservoir on Lookout Hill. From there, the water descended first to the Swan Boat Lake and then along the course of Binnen Stream to the Lullwater arm of the lake. "The boiler house attached to the well, is in a conspicuous position on the lake shore, and we have designed its exterior with special reference to this prominence of situation," Olmsted and Vaux informed the Brooklyn Park Commission in their year-end report for 1869, by which time the structure was nearly complete. The curious public had access to this engineering marvel, in which Vaux included an inside stairway. See Olmsted, Vaux & Co., "Report of the Landscape Architects and Superintendents," BPC *Tenth Annual Report* (1870), 366–367.

23. Olmsted to Charles Elliott, April 28, 1890.

24. BCCP, *Tenth Annual Report* (1870), 38.

25. Olmsted and Vaux, "A Consideration of Motives, Requirements and Restrictions Applicable to the General Scheme of the Park," DPP, *Second Annual Report* (1872), 71.

26. Also demolished is the Boys' Play House, which Vaux designed in 1867 as a place where youngsters might change and store clothing. See BCCP, *Eleventh Annual Report* (1868), 26–27.

27. On June 18, 1869, Vaux wrote to Olmsted, "Dairy is being started." See also BCCP, *Thirteenth Annual Report* (1870), 10.

28. BCCP, *Tenth Annual Report* (1867), 39.

29. According to the BCCP's *Twelfth Annual Report* (1869), 26, the Spring House opened in 1868. Though a drawing of the building was exhibited at the National Academy of Design in 1868 under the name of Olmsted & Vaux, Vaux later made it clear that he designed the structure. See his "A City Zoological Garden," *New York Times*, March 3, 1878, 10. The Spring House no longer exists.

30. BCCP, *Second Annual Report* (1859), 23.

31. Olmsted and Vaux, "Report from Olmsted and Vaux & Co. relative to works in progress on their Designs, June 7, 1870," in *Frederick Law Olmsted, Landscape Architect, 1822–1903: Forty Years of Landscape Architecture*, 2 vols., ed. Frederick L. Olmsted Jr. and Theodora Kimball (New York, 1922–1928; reprint, New York, 1970), 2:478.

32. The drawing, dated March 12, 1867, together with several other drawings for the structure, is in the Municipal Archives. In 1867, the Croton Reservoir board turned over control of Vista Rock to the Central Park commissioners. The BCCP's *Tenth Annual Report* (1867) noted that during the past building season, construction of the foundation walls of the Belvedere had been started.

33. John A. Hughes, *Garden Architecture and Landscape Gardening* (London, 1866), 136.

34. P. Edwards, *English Garden Ornaments* (London, 1965), 40–41.

35. Vaux had already alluded to this idea in his description of the iconographic program for the Terrace.

36. Olmsted and Kimball, *Frederick Law Olmsted*, 2:478.

37. "Belvedere, Central Park, New York City," *Building* 4 (May 22, 1886): 246.

38. Olmsted, Vaux & Co. to the President of the Board of Commissioners of Central Park, in BCCP, *Tenth Annual Report* (1867), reprinted in *PFLO*, 6:184–189.

39. Olmsted, Vaux & Co. "Report Accompanying a Design for Washington Park," in BCPP, *Eighth Annual Report* (1868), reprinted in *PFLO*, 6:202–208. The report is dated September 9, 1867.

40. Olmsted and Vaux, "Report of the Landscape Architects," in BPC, *Fourteenth Annual Report* (1874), reprinted in *PFLO*, 6:670. The report is dated January 1, 1874.

41. The description of the plan is drawn from Olmsted and Vaux's "Washington Park," in *PFLO*, 6:202–208.

42. Most of the grading and paving of Fort Greene Park was done in the building season of 1868. And although Vaux and Olmsted's plan was carried out—with the notable exception of the observatory and commemorative column over the tomb—the park was drastically altered in the late nineteenth century by McKim, Mead and White. In 1867, Olmsted and Vaux also laid out Carroll Park, a two-acre square near the commercial center of Brooklyn. Probably the first small urban square that the partners designed, it had two "lodges," presumably designed by Vaux, as well as 150 birdhouses installed in the trees to attract sparrows. See *PFLO*, 6:339, n. 31. Another park in Brooklyn was the Parade Ground, which was located adjacent to the southern border of Prospect Park. Laid out on paper in December 1867, the 40-acre space consisted of a large rectangular field for military drills that was overlooked at one end by sloping elevated ground. Here, a long wooden structure sheltered spectators in inclement weather.

43. See Olmsted, Vaux & Co., "Architect's Report," in *Documents of the Ninety-Second Legislature of the State of New Jersey, 1868*, reprinted in *PFLO*, 6:210–211. The report is dated October 5, 1867.

44. Olmsted, Vaux & Co., to the Chairman of the Committee on Plans of the Park Commission of Philadelphia, December 4, 1867, *PFLO*, 6:231–245.

45. Calvert Vaux and Frederick L. Olmsted, *Report on the Proposed City Park* (Albany, NY, 1868), in *PFLO*, 6:293–301. The report is dated December 1, 1868.

46. H. F. Taylor, *Seventy Years of the Worcester Polytechnic Institute* (Worcester, 1937), 39. Lincoln, who at the same time still served on the board of the Massachusetts Agricultural College, asked Olmsted to advise that body on ongoing discussions about the location of the main building there. By June 1866, however, Lincoln had had a falling-out with Olmsted and voted to have his recommendations rejected. At the Worcester school, he supported Vaux's proposals, which became the basis of the campus plan.

47. Vaux to Gallaudet, December 26, 1865, Gallaudet University Library.

48. See Olmsted and Vaux to Gallaudet, July 14, 1866, *PFLO*, 6:95–99, and the author's "Gallaudet College: A High Victorian Campus," in *Records of the Columbia Historical Society* (Charlottesville, 1973), 439–467. Other colleges also engaged the services of Olmsted and Vaux around this time. In 1870, Olmsted wrote that his firm "has been employed in consultation by the faculties of Yale, Amherst, Harvard and Cornell." (See Olmsted to W. W. Folwell, June 18, 1870, *PFLO*, 6:378.) The work at Yale included a design for grounds around Withers's memorial chapel, which was never constructed, and plans for a dormitory, presumably Farnum Hall, which was eventually erected in 1869–1870 according to plans by Russell Sturgis. Olmsted himself took sole or chief responsibility for plans sent to the other institutions as well as for a report prepared in January 1867 for the Maine College of Agriculture. On April 5, 1870, Olmsted forwarded to President W. A. Stearns a plan for expanding the campus of Amherst College. Recalling the Buffalo parkway system, the proposal called for large

circles to be laid out where city streets intersected at the entrances to the campus. (See *PFLO*, 6:369–374.)

49. *PFLO*, 6:16–17. This commission may have come to the firm as a result of Brown recommending Olmsted serve with him on the committee headed by Dorothea Dix to locate a site for the hospital. See Brown to Olmsted, April 1866.

50. Olmsted to Mary Olmsted, September 26, 1868. According to city directories, the Vauxes lived at 43 Lafayette Place from 1868 to 1871. After that they moved to 331 East 15th Street.

51. D. T. Brown to Olmsted, October 12, 1868.

52. Vaux, "Zoological Garden."

53. Olmsted and Vaux's plan for the New York zoo was published in the BCCP's *Tenth Annual Report* (1867), reprinted in *PFLO*, 6:184–189.

54. Vaux first talks of meeting Wisedell in his letter to Olmsted of October 29, 1868. This letter also contains information on Vaux's European itinerary.

55. Bloor Diary, December 6, 1867. Vaux's trouble with Bloor may have been responsible for Vaux's resignation from the AIA. Bloor had taken his grievance with Vaux to the institute for adjudication but had been denied satisfaction from a Committee of Conciliation. "Afterwards a new set of By-Laws was reported and printed in accordance with resolutions offered by me," Bloor explained to Olmsted, "with the exception of one, rejected thro' V's influence; but this (as well as the rest) was adopted on my representations, and against the violent opposition of V." Vaux and Withers resigned from the AIA in 1869.

56. Withers to Olmsted, November 16, 1868.

57. Brown to Olmsted, October 12, 1868. The hospital is the present New York Hospital and Cornell Medical Center.

58. Vaux must have contributed to the design of houses that Olmsted, Vaux & Co. planned at Riverside for G. M. Kimbark, E. T. Wright, and John C. Dore. See Walter Creese, *The Crowning of the American Landscape: Eight Great Spaces and Their Buildings* (Princeton, 1985), 229.

59. Vaux to Olmsted, October 3, 1869.

60. For the history of the Riverside project, see *PFLO*, 6:30–32, and Creese, *Crowning of the American Landscape*, 221–239. In October 1870, Olmsted and Vaux became involved with another suburban residential development on the Hudson at Tarrytown, New York. Undeterred by their experience at Riverside, they also accepted stock shares as payment. Largely Olmsted's project, the subdivision of Tarrytown Heights, for which Olmsted and Vaux prepared a map in October 1871 and a written report in February 1872, fell victim to the financial panic of 1873. The year before, however, Vaux had sold his shares to Olmsted. See the sales prospectus reprinted in *PFLO*, 6:503–522, and Olmsted, Vaux & Co. to Olmsted, March 4, 1872. Another subdivision project was Needham Hundred, a 1,000-acre tract near Boston for which Olmsted and Vaux prepared a report on October 3, 1870. Apparently nothing came of this proposal.

61. Calvert Vaux and Frederick L. Olmsted, *Preliminary Report Respecting a Public Park in Buffalo* (New York, 1869).

62. Olmsted, Vaux & Co., "Report Accompanying a Design for the Parade Ground," in BCPP, *Eighth Annual Report* (1868), reprinted in *PFLO*, 6:311.

63. Olmsted to George Waring Jr., April 13, 1876.

64. The design for the Brooklyn building was published in BCPP, *Ninth Annual Report* (1869), 270–271. According to the BCPP, *Tenth Annual Report* (1870), 356, the building, which no longer exists, was constructed in 1869.

65. "Parade," *Buffalo Morning News*, August 27, 1876, 1.

66. Even after his professional separation from Olmsted, Vaux continued to furnish plans for buildings (none of which survive) in the Buffalo parks. In 1874–1875, Vaux prepared designs for several structures in Delaware Park, including the farmstead, boathouse, Gala Water bridge, and Spire House. The latter was a wooden summerhouse in the style of the Parade House. See Francis R. Kowsky, "Calvert Vaux and the Archi-

tecture of Buffalo's Parks," in *The Best Planned City: The Olmsted Legacy in Buffalo* (Buffalo, 1992), 42–55.

67. Olmsted to J. P. White, March 9, 1877 (draft).

68. Olmsted and Vaux to the Board of Park Commissioners of the Borough of New Britain, Connecticut, March 23, 1870, *PFLO*, 6:360–368.

69. See Olmsted and Vaux, "Report to the Committee on Park Improvement of Fall River, Mass.," in *PFLO*, 6:374–378. The report is dated June 16, 1870.

70. Vaux joined Olmsted and Radford in Chicago to study the park site in mid-April 1870. See Vaux to Olmsted, April 8, 11, and 18, 1870. Presumably the large refectory pavilion and farmstead mentioned in the report were to be designed by Vaux.

71. For a thoughtful comparison of the 1871 and 1893 plans, see P. B. Wight, "Apotheosis of the Midway Plaisance," *Architectural Record* 28 (November 1910): 335–349.

72. "Mr. Mould and the Museum of Art," *New York Times*, May 1, 1880, 5. In this letter to the editor, Mould suggested that he and Vaux had been working on this plan as early as 1868.

73. Winifred E. Howe, *A History of the Metropolitan Museum of Art*, 2 vols. (New York, 1913), 2:113–114.

74. Ibid., 117.

75. Ibid., 119.

76. Both of these Hunt drawings survive, but they are undated. One assumes, however, that they were made for Church in 1867, shortly after Hunt had returned from a visit to Paris.

77. Church to Erastus Dow Palmer, March 10, 1868, quoted in J. A. Ryan, "Frederic Church's Olana: Architecture and Landscape as Art," in F. Kelly et al., *Frederic Edwin Church* (Washington, 1989), 134.

78. For the evidence of possible association between Church and artists in England, where he visited in December 1867 and again in May 1869, see ibid., 154, n. 72.

79. Writing in the fall of 1868 from Rome to his friend and patron William Osborn, a New York merchant and art collector, Church referred to a new country house Osborn was planning to build. "You have a high opinion of the architect you have heretofore employed," wrote Church, "and I have the boldness to say that I think him not a great man in his department—I don't think him good at contriving nor good at effect— both pretty important considerations in architecture—I would not say this (perhaps I am mistaken) were it not that I want you to be provided with the best." The architect in question was probably Hunt, for in 1869 Osborn had built a house in New York designed by Hunt. Perhaps Church is referring to this building, which could have been designed in 1868, and telling his friend to choose someone else for the country house he was contemplating. See Church to Osborn, November 9, 1868, in the Olana archives.

80. F. L. Olmsted to J. Olmsted, August 17, 1864.

81. Church, McEntee, and George Healy worked jointly on a painting (now in the Newark Museum) of the famous arch.

82. Calvert Vaux, *Villas and Cottages* (New York, 1857; rev. ed., 1864), 55.

83. On Olana and the Aesthetic Movement see R. B. Stein, "Artifact as Ideology: The Aesthetic Movement in Its American Cultural Context," in his *Pursuit of Beauty: Americans and the Aesthetic Movement* (New York, 1987), 24–25.

84. These items, most of which exist in the Olana archives, bear the Vaux, Withers & Co. stamp and are dated May 28, 1870.

85. A gallery had been a constant feature of the house plans developed for Church by both Hunt and Vaux. At one point, Church and Vaux contemplated putting the gallery on the north side of the court hall, where the present staircase is located. Exactly who conceived the idea of combining the art gallery with the dining room, or when the idea occurred, is not known. There is no precedent for such a clerestory-lit dining room in Vaux's earlier country houses.

86. Early elevation sketches for Olana were also in a Romanesque style. See items OL.1982.1066, OL.1982.1071, and OL.1982.1069 in the Olana archives.

87. The drawing was Item 43 in the 1867 exhibition. See the National Academy of Design Exhibition Record, 1861–1890, 96, in the Mary B. Cowdrey Files on the NAD Exhibits, Archives of American Art.

88. This is plan OL.1980.1621, dated June 23, 1870, in the Olana archives.

89. Church to Osborn, July 22, 1871, Princeton University Archives. Unfortunately, no plan survives that exactly matches the house as built. One assumes, however, that such a plan was made after June 23. By November, Church reported that "the house steadily grows. Its solid walls and perfect substructure are the astonishment and admiration of all." The walls had risen by then to four feet above the water table (Church to Osborn, November 7, 1870, Olana archives).

90. Vaux, *Villas and Cottages*, 188.

91. Ibid., 69.

92. Church to J. F. Weir, June 8, 1871, Weir Papers, Archives of American Art.

93. Vaux had informed Olmsted in a letter dated January 30, 1872, that Withers had concluded "not to carry on Vaux and Withers partnership." Withers may have assisted Vaux with the Olana work.

94. Church made payments to Vaux on September 8, 1870 ($300); September 21, 1871 ($300); and January 7, 1873 ($235). In February 1873, however, Church was apparently still consulting with Vaux. On February 13 he wrote jokingly to the architect to warn him not to commit a "Vaux pas" by coming to Olana during his absence. In 1888, Church undertook the construction of a studio on the west side of the house. There is no indication that he hired Vaux or any other architect for this work.

95. McEntee Diary, July 22, 1872.

96. John Wilmerding, *American Views* (Princeton, 1991), 72.

97. J. P. Quincy, "Memoir of Octavius Brooks Frothingham," *Proceedings of the Massachusetts Historical Society* 2 (1896): 526.

98. Vaux, "The Kaleidoscope," *Fraternity Papers* 3 (October 1871–March 1872).

99. Vaux to Olmsted, April 18, 1870.

100. Vaux to Olmsted, April 16, 1870.

101. Obituaries on September 20, 1878, in the *New York Times* and the *New-York Daily Tribune* stated that Pilat, who suffered from consumption, died after a short illness; the *New York Staats-Zeitung* said that a heart disease ended his life.

102. On the politics of the park during the Tweed era, see Roy Rosenzweig and Elizabeth Blackmar, *The Park and the People: A History of Central Park* (Ithaca, NY, 1992), Chapter 10, "The Spoils of the Park."

103. Mould to Reid, September 29, 1870, in Gordon L. Ford Collection, Rare Book and Manuscript Division of the Astor, Lenox, and Tilden Foundations, New York Public Library, New York.

104. George Templeton Strong, Manuscript Diary, March 28, 1870, New-York Historical Society, New York.

105. When the new board took office, work was already under way on the foundations for the conservatory that Vaux was designing. However, it was "soon discovered that, apart from a picture in the office of the Department, there was no plan existing for the superstructure." A perspective drawing of Mould's elevation design, which enlarged Vaux's building, appeared in the DPP's *First Annual Report of the Department of Public Parks for the Year Ending May 1871*, 13. In 1878, Vaux wrote of the still unfinished structure that originally it had been designed "in accordance with the views of Messrs. Parsons, who obtained the privilege from the Park authorities giving the right to sell flowers in the lower story of the building under the Conservatory proper, and the design of all that section of the Park was modified to suit the plan I prepared for them—the formal basin of water being introduced to secure a reflection of the bright glass building. They asked to be relieved from the engagement when the war broke out, and the present foundations

were put in during the Sweeny administration, with the expectation that the whole expense of the building and maintenance would be sustained by the City" (Vaux, "City Zoological Garden").

106. Drawings for the conservatory, ladies' cottage, and offices of administration are in the Municipal Archives, as well as Mould's encaustic tile designs, which were made the year before he became architect in chief.

107. Olmsted, Vaux & Co., "Report of the Landscape Architects and Superintendents," BPC, *Eleventh Annual Report* 1871, reprinted in *PFLO*, 6:417–422.

108. Olmsted to Stranahan, undated.

109. The Concert Grove Pavilion was probably designed in 1872, given that it appeared as the frontispiece to the BPC's *Thirteenth Annual Report* (1873). It was completed in 1874 and restored in 1988.

110. According to the BPC's *Twelfth Annual Report* (1872), 485, the building was nearly finished by the end of 1871.

111. Vaux to Olmsted, undated. Presumably the shelter was designed in 1872, the same year Vaux designed the Concert Grove House.

112. BPC, *Twelfth Annual Report* (1872), reprinted in *PFLO*, 6:497.

113. Olmsted to Stranahan, undated.

114. Olmsted, Vaux & Co., "Report of the Landscape Architects and Superintendents," BPC, *Twelfth Annual Report* (1872), reprinted in *PFLO*, 6:499. Vaux found disappointing, however, the materials color characteristics; the blue, red, and yellow tints he had experimented with turned out to be "much less decided than was originally proposed." See BPC, *Thirteenth Annual Report* (1873), 535. The arch was restored in 1988–1990.

115. BPC, *Tenth Annual Report* (1870), 391, and BPC, *Fourteenth Annual Report* (1874), reprinted in *PFLO*, 6:669.

116. In a letter that was probably written around this time, Vaux told Whitelaw Reid that Stebbins would make a good commissioner. Like Green, said Vaux, Stebbins understood and appreciated the Greensward plan. Hoping that the *Tribune* would come out in favor of Stebbins's nomination, Vaux also told Reid that Stebbins "is a Democrat, I believe, if Politics is to be the controlling point at this time" (Vaux to Reid, undated, Reid Papers).

117. On May 29, 1872, Olmsted assumed the presidency of the park board and Vaux became landscape architect and superintendent. He retained this post until October 24, 1872, when Olmsted, no longer president of the board, assumed the title of landscape architect and Vaux became consulting landscape architect. Vaux resigned this post on June 4, 1873. Olmsted continued on until January 1878, when his position was abolished.

118. Vaux and Olmsted, *Two Letters to the President on Recent Changes and Projected Changes in the Central Park* (New York, 1872), 9. The letters are dated January and February 1872. At this time Mould also modified Vaux's Greywacke Arch. For the screen of shrubbery across the top, Mould substituted an iron railing resting on an additional course of bluestone.

119. Vaux, "City Zoological Garden."

120. "Central Park," *New York Times*, November 28, 1872, 3. The writer indicated that the canopy would be moved to Mount Morris Park, a public square on upper Fifth Avenue for which Olmsted and Vaux had prepared a landscape plan. In the 1982 restoration of the Belvedere, Mould's canopy was rebuilt.

121. Quoted in Rosenzweig and Blackmar, *The Park and the People,* 344.

122. Their protest appeared in the *New York Times* for December 21, 1870. See Olmsted and Vaux, "The Central Park—Character of the Proposed Change—A Protest," in *PFLO*, 6:392–393. The letter also appeared in "Letters from the People," *New-York Daily Tribune*, December 21, 1870, 4. See also Vaux to Whitelaw Reid, December 16, 1870, Reid Papers.

123. Rosenzweig and Blackmar, *The Park and the People*, 344.

124. Drawings labeled "Calvert Vaux and Jacob Wrey Mould, Architects" for the

Merchant's Gate are preserved in the Municipal Archives. The plans were approved on July 30, 1872.

125. "Superintendent's Report," DPP, *Third General Report of the Department of Public Parks for 1872–1873*, 57–58. See also, in this same source, Olmsted's "Report of the Landscape Architect on the Proposed New System of Walks in the Southeast Quarter of the Central Park," 293–295.

126. Several drawings for the Inscope Arch in the Municipal Archives dating from the winter of 1873 are signed by Vaux and Mould. Many of the working drawings are signed only by Mould.

127. Drawings for the Outset Arch, labeled with Vaux as landscape architect and Mould as associate architect, are in the Municipal Archives. The Gapstow Arch, now replaced by a later structure, was the third new bridge erected in connection with the redesign of the path system in this part of the park. Drawings that survive for this wood and iron structure are signed by Mould and date from 1875, a period when Vaux was not officially associated with the park department. Therefore, I believe that Mould was solely responsible for its eccentric design.

128. Vaux, "A Plea for the Artistic Unity of Central Park," *New York Times*, August 27, 1879, 5.

129. "City Improvements," *New York Times*, October 8, 1872, 5.

130. The drawings are in the Vaux Papers.

131. Plans for Mt. Morris Square signed by Vaux as landscape architect and by Olmsted as president of the board of commissioners are preserved in the Municipal Archives. The date, October 23, was actually a few days after Olmsted and Vaux had dissolved their partnership, which they had agreed to do on October 18.

132. On the early history of this institution and its relation to Central Park, see Rosenzweig and Blackmar, *The People and the Park*, 349–357.

133. Quoted in Vaux, "City Zoological Garden."

134. "Fine Art Museum," *New York Times*, April 30, 1880, 2.

135. Olmsted to Bowles, June 2, 1871, in *PFLO*, 6:443.

136. Olmsted to Bloor, October 4, 1882.

137. Vaux to Olmsted, April 7, 1870.

138. Vaux to Olmsted, April 11, 1870.

139. Morse Diary, April 10, 1871.

CHAPTER 8

1. Vaux had a formal partnership with Radford in 1874 and again from 1878 to 1892.

2. See *PFLO*, 6:596–600.

3. Olmsted and Vaux, "Preliminary Report for the Design of Morningside Park," DPP, Minutes, Document No. 50, October 11, 1873, 2.

4. American Museum of Natural History, *Second Annual Report* (1871), 21.

5. According to their minutes, the trustees ratified this decision on March 26, 1872. Presumably it was shortly after this date that Vaux began planning the new building.

6. A. Bickmore, *Autobiography* (unpublished manuscript, American Museum of Natural History, undated), 29.

7. "Green's Unclean Skirts," *Sunday Mercury*, January 19, 1873, 4.

8. "Natural History Museum," *New York Times*, December 20, 1877, 2.

9. Several drawings dated August 7, 1872, are in the Municipal Archives.

10. Louis Pope Gratacap, "Making of a Museum," *Architectural Record* 9 (April 1900): 384.

11. Quoted in J. D. McCabe, *Illustrated History of the Centennial Exhibition* (Philadelphia, 1876), 205.

12. [C. Cook], "The Centennial Building," *New-York Daily Tribune*, July 24, 1873, 3.

13. "Centennial Building," *New York Times*, August 5, 1873, 1.

14. [C. Cook], "Architecture in Philadelphia for 1876," *New-York Daily Tribune,* August 8, 1873, 4.

15. McEntee Diary, August 6, 1873.

16. Vaux and Radford's Pavilion Plan is preserved in Scrapbook 3 of the Centennial Collection at the Pennsylvania Historical Society.

17. Alexander F. Oakey, "Centennial Building," *New York Times,* August 19, 1873, 5, and "Engineer," Letter to the Editor, *New York Times,* August 30, 1873, 5.

18. "Centennial Building," *New York Times,* August 5, 1873.

19. "Centennial Anniversary Building—Pavilion Plan," *New York Times,* October 25, 1873, 1.

20. "Centennial Building," *New York Times,* November 5, 1873, 3.

21. McEntee Diary, November 9, 1873.

22. Ibid., November 16, 1873.

23. Vaux and Radford, "Letters to the Editor," *New York Times,* January 21, 1875, 8. The letter is dated January 15.

24. Ibid.

25. "The Centennial: What They Are Doing in Philadelphia," *New York Times,* January 1, 1875, 8.

26. Vaux to F. Braun, May 9, 1874, in J. J. Stewart, "Notes on Calvert Vaux's 1873 Design for the Public Grounds of the Parliament Buildings in Ottawa," *Bulletin of the Association for Preservation Technology* 8 (1976): 6–7.

27. Vaux to Scott, June 20, 1873, in ibid., 3.

28. Vaux, *Official Correspondence, etc. in Reference to the Plan for the Arrangement of the Public Grounds in Front of the Parliament Buildings at Ottawa, Dominion of Canada* (New York, 1882).

29. "New City Prison," *New York Times,* August 13, 1873, 4.

30. "City Prison Commission," *New York Times,* February 11, 1874, 2. In his turn, Withers sought Vaux's assistance in February 1874, when he received the commission to design the Jefferson Market Courthouse at Sixth Avenue and West 10th Street.

31. "New City Prison," *Daily Graphic,* March 9, 1874, 57 and 60. The building also appeared in the *New York Sketchbook of Architecture* 1 (April 1874): 1–2 and Plate 14.

32. "New City Prison," *Daily Graphic,* March 9, 1874, 60.

33. "A New Job," *Sunday Mercury,* February 1, 1874, 4.

34. Editorial, *World,* May 28, 1874, 4.

35. *New-York Daily Tribune,* May 29, 1874, 5.

36. *Appleton's Cyclopedia of American Biography* (New York, 1899), 4:287.

37. "Situation in Peru," *New York Times,* July 21, 1879, 5.

38. "Personal," *New-York Daily Tribune,* March 10, 1875, 6.

39. Cook to Reid, March 10, 1875, Reid Papers.

40. *DAB,* 12:501.

41. Mould to Olmsted, April 18, 1875.

42. L. Leeds, "Report as to the Desirability of the Palisades as a Place of Residence" (1868), in *Summer in the Palisades: A Description of the Northern Railroad of New Jersey and the Palisades* (New York, 1875), 43 and 48.

43. *Summer in the Palisades,* 27.

44. McEntee Diary, May 31, 1875.

45. Ibid., June 26, 1975.

46. Morse Diary, October 31, 1875.

47. Ibid., December 29, 1876.

48. Ibid., May 13, 1877.

49. Ibid.

50. Calvert Vaux, "A Philosophical Emperor," *Popular Science Monthly* 11 (August 1877): 461–469.

51. Gertrude had died suddenly on October 24, 1878.

52. Downing Vaux to Mary Vaux, March 30, 1879, McEntee Papers, Archives of American Art, Smithsonian Institution, Washington, D.C.

53. A letter dated January 28, 1873, from Vaux to Olmsted implies that Weidenmann had done work on the Ogden grounds under Olmsted, Vaux & Co. auspices prior to the breakup of the firm.

54. George W. Sheldon, *Artistic Country Seats: Types of Recent American Villa and Cottage Architecture* (New York, 1885–1886), 175.

55. Hyde to Olmsted, July 28, 1874.

56. Weidenmann memorandum to Hyde, c. October 28, 1874.

57. Weidenmann to Olmsted, January 11, 1875. Materials relating to Masquetux are in the Weidenmann collection in the Print Room at the New York Public Library. The property is presently owned by the Southward Ho Country Club in the village of West Bay Shore. The dwelling survives but has been altered.

58. I base the date of the house on the fact that when it was illustrated in the *American Architect and Building News* for April 8, 1876, the accompanying text stated that the dwelling was nearing completion. (The drawing was by Vaux's assistant, J. M. Farnsworth.) Located at 55 Pearl Street, the building is presently owned by the city of Worcester. Around this time, Vaux also prepared a plan for the grounds of the house that his former partner F. C. Withers designed for Dr. G. Pierrepont Davis in Hartford, Connecticut. Vaux's planting plan, which dates c. 1880, is in the Vaux Papers.

59. McEntee Diary, February 20, 1879. The house, which stood at 166 Summit Avenue, has been demolished.

60. H. S. Commanger, "The Century 1887–1906," in *The Century*, 61.

61. Raphael Pumpelly, *My Reminiscences*, 2 vols. (New York, 1918), 2:623. The house, which stood at 284 Gibbs Avenue, has been demolished.

62. Vaux and Radford's letter was printed in "Reservoir Square," *New York Herald*, July 1, 1877, 6, which also contains an interview with Vaux about his proposal.

63. "Architectural Association," *Builder* 7 (December 15, 1849): 598.

64. "Polytechnic Museum," *Daily Graphic*, July 2, 1877, 5.

65. "Give Us a Park," *New York Herald*, July 1, 1877, 8.

66. [Marianna Van Rensselaer], "Correspondence," *American Architect and Building News* 2 (July 7, 1877): 218.

67. [Marianna Van Rensselaer], "Correspondence," *American Architect and Building News*, 2 (July 28, 1877): 242.

68. Vaux to Olmsted, July 3, 1877.

69. McEntee Diary, February 19, 1878.

70. Ibid., February 22, 1878.

71. Mary Olmsted's remarks were made in a letter to her son John dated October 24, 1878.

72. Godkin to the *New-York Daily Tribune*, February 20 and 21, 1878.

73. C. Vaux, "Central Park Plan," *New-York Daily Tribune*, February 21, 1878.

74. F. L. Olmsted, "Central Park, New York," *American Architect and Building News* 2 (April 14 1877): 120.

75. In her letter of February 24, 1878, to her son, John, Mary Olmsted said that "Mr. Cook and Mr. Wisedell say he [Vaux] is almost out of his head with worry that he has no business."

76. Mould to Olmsted, November 28, 1879.

77. Vaux to Godkin, March 1878 (no day is indicated).

78. Charles Loring Brace, "Model Tenement Houses," *Plumber and Sanitary Engineer* 1 (February 1878): 46.

79. C. Vaux, "The Model Tenement," *New York Times*, March 9, 1879, 5.

80. "The Proposed New Tenements," *Daily Graphic*, March 12, 1879, 80. Although the *Tribune* failed to print Vaux's design as he requested, the paper apparently did take his views into account in its editorial comment on the tenement house competition win-

ners. See Vaux to Whitelaw Reid, March 4 and 6, 1879, Reid Papers, and "Tenements without Light," *New-York Daily Tribune*, March 5, 1879, 4, and "Concerning Model Tenements," *New-York Daily Tribune*, March 7, 1879, 4.

81. "The Proposed New Tenements."

82. "Criticisms on the Prize Plans," *New-York Daily Tribune,* March 7, 1879, 1.

83. See "Improved Tenement-Houses," *American Architect and Building News* 7 (January 31, 1880): 40, and "Building Intelligence," *American Architect and Building News* 8 (March 1, 1880): 134.

84. "Improved Dwellings," *New York Times*, November 6, 1881, 8.

85. Ibid.

86. Elizabeth Collins Cromley, *Alone Together: A History of New York's Early Apartments* (Ithaca, NY, 1990), 76.

87. "A Newsboys' Lodging-House," *New-York Daily Tribune,* April 11, 1880, 2.

88. "New York," *Churchman* 42 (July 31, 1880): 122.

89. Calvert Vaux, "Street Planning in Relation to Architectural Design," *Proceedings of the Architectural League of New York* (1889): 136–137.

90. Photographs of drawings for this project survive at the Metropolitan Museum of Art. One of them showing an elevation and ground plans is reproduced in Winifred E. Howe, *A History of the Metropolitan Museum of Art*, 2 vols. (New York, 1913), 177.

91. "Metropolitan Museum of Art," *Art Journal* 6 (June 1880): 181.

92. "The Fine Art Museum," *New York Times*, April 30, 1880, 2.

93. Ibid.

94. "A Metropolitan Museum," *New York Times*, March 30, 1880, 10.

95. "The Fine Art Museum," *New York Times*, April 30, 1880, 2.

96. The two easternmost of these stairways have survived and have recently had their original colors restored.

97. "The Fine Art Museum," *New York Times*, April 30, 1880, 2.

98. Morse Diary, March 9, 1880.

99. "Metropolitan Museum of Art, III," *Art Journal* 6 (August 1880): 237.

100. [C. Cook], "Fine Arts, Metropolitan Museum," *New-York Daily Tribune,* March 20, 1880, 7.

CHAPTER 9

1. H. Van Buren Magonigle, "A Half Century of Architecture, 1: A Biographical Review," *Pencil Points* 14 (November 1933): 477–480.

2. Radford stayed with Vaux until 1892, when he moved to San Francisco.

3. Calvert Vaux, "Street Planning in Relation to Architectural Design," *Proceedings of the Architectural League of New York* (1989): 142.

4. C. Vaux, "Church Grounds," *Churchman* 55 (June 4, 1887): 641.

5. The process of planting the grounds apparently continued at least until the fall of 1882. See Samuel Parsons Jr., "Home and Society: Grace Church Lawn," *Century* 2 (October 1882): 954–955.

6. "Reservoir Square," *New-York Daily Tribune*, August 22, 1881, 4. Vaux may have been inspired in his work at Grace Church by the example of the small garden around the Tour St. Jacques in Paris, which he singled out as one of the best examples of a successful "street garden." See Calvert Vaux, "Parks and Gardens of Paris," in Calvert Vaux and Samuel Parsons Jr., *Concerning Lawn Planting* (New York, 1881), 16.

7. Montgomery Schuyler, "New York Bridges," *Architectural Record* 18 (October 1905): 252. See Allan Nevins and Milton Thomas, eds., *The Diary of George Templeton Strong: Young Man in New York, 1835–1849*, 4 vols. (New York, 1952), 4:277, 293, 368, 327, and 395. In "Memorandum," Vaux credits the bridge to "Vaux and Radford." However, his partnership with Radford did not begin until 1874, and it is clear from Strong's diary that the bridge was planned and erected in 1870–1871. I am therefore inclined to trust the

well-informed Schuyler's emphatic attribution of the bridge, which went down in 1911, to Withers.

8. The keeper's house was erected in 1883. A few years later, Olmsted informed Vaux that he had taken a park superintendent to Trinity Cemetery to show him what might be done with his piece of ground that had a similar topography. See Olmsted to Vaux, summer 1894.

9. *Macon Telegraph*, July 30, 1887. Vaux detailed his preliminary plan in a letter dated August 9, 1887, to P. E. Dennis, the superintendent of construction.

10. "Memorandum."

11. Samuel Parsons Jr., "Small Country Places," *Scribner's Magazine* 11 (March 1892): 308. The Wisner house and part of the original grounds are the present Reeves-Reed Arboretum.

12. A perspective drawing of the R. S. Bowne house, drawn by Downing Vaux, appeared in *Building* 4 (February 13, 1886): 78.

13. The earliest correspondence from Vaux to Suckley is dated June 4, 1890, by which time it is clear that Vaux had outlined the plan. The general plan is dated 1891. It appears from surviving correspondence that most of the work, including some alterations to the house, was carried out under the supervision of Downing Vaux. Drawings and documents are in the possession of Wilderstein Preservation, Rhinebeck, N.Y.

14. Vaux, "Street Planning," 144–145.

15. A portion of the grounds of Greystone are now part of Untermeyer Park in Yonkers; the house has been demolished.

16. Documents relating to Vaux's work for Tilden are preserved in the Prints and Photographs Collection, Astor, Lenox, and Tilden Foundations, New York Public Library, New York.

17. Montgomery Schuyler, "Concerning Queen Anne," in *American Architecture* (New York, 1892), 41.

18. McEntee Diary, February 1, 1882.

19. "New Houses—Indoors and Out," *Art Amateur* 8 (February 1883): 68.

20. McEntee Diary, February 17, 1885.

21. McEntee Diary, June 28, 1882. The house stands altered at 357 Indian Avenue. Booth engaged local architects to enlarge the house as early as 1883.

22. Morse Diary, July 11, 1881.

23. Richard Lockridge, *Darling of Misfortune: Edwin Booth, 1833–1893* (New York, 1932), 287.

24. Vaux to Olmsted, October 20, 1881.

25. McEntee Diary, October 23, 1883.

26. Ibid., November 1, 1882.

27. Ibid., February 9, 1883.

28. *New-York Daily Tribune*, May 9, 1883, 6.

29. McEntee Diary, July 1 and 25, 1883.

30. The conservatory is described in "Plant Cabinets," in Vaux and Parsons, *Concerning Lawn Planting*, 27–30.

31. McEntee Diary, August 27, 1883, and May 11 and June 21, 1885.

32. On April 1, 1886, McEntee mentioned that Vaux had made preliminary plans for the Griffiths house; by May 29, he had seen the completed plans. The house is located at 194 Chestnut Street.

33. McEntee Diary, July 20, 1890.

34. Evidence for the trip abroad comes from McEntee Diary, July 23, 1890, and DPP, Minutes, July 16, 1890, where Vaux's application for a two-month leave of absence "for the purpose of visiting Europe" was approved. The Coykendall house was enlarged after Vaux's death.

35. Vaux explained this innovative window design in "Our Lithographic Illustrations," *Building* 3 (January 1885): 43, pl. 64.

36. Vaux, "Street Planning," 137.

37. "Our Illustrations," *American Architect and Building News* 16 (November 29, 1884): 25, pl. 46. The drawing is signed by D. A. Greco as delineator.

38. The mason's agreement, preserved in the society's archives, is dated September 29, 1885. According to the society's *Thirty-Fifth Annual Report* (1887), the building opened on April 21, 1887.

39. *Opening of the Eleventh Ward Newsboys Lodging House* (New York, 1887), 6.

40. The Mott Street School, also known as the Fourteenth Ward Industrial School, is presently a cooperative apartment. A brief description of the new building appeared in "Memorial to Mrs. Astor," *New York Times*, February 5, 1888, 16. The New York City Landmarks Preservation Commission designated the Mott Street School as a historic site chiefly as a result of the efforts of the late Dennis Francis, a resident of the building who undertook the first serious research into Vaux's career. The other school buildings that Vaux and Radford built for the society were the Sixth Street School (1888), the gift of Mrs. William Douglas Sloan at 630–634 East 6th Street; the James H. Jones Memorial School (1888; demolished) at 407 East 73rd Street; the Henrietta School (1889; demolished) at 215–217 East 21st Street; the Rhinelander School (1890) at 350 East 88th Street; and the Sullivan Street School (1892) at 219–221 Sullivan Street.

41. This building, which went down in 1932, stood at 247 East 44th Street, near the corner of Second Avenue. The society's *Thirty-Sixth Annual Report* (1888), 6, states that in its design, which was "in harmony with the generous donor's well-known taste in artistic matters," Vaux took inspiration "from an old Nuremberg house, called the 'Petersen' building." As president and benefactor of the American Museum of Natural History, Jessup had opposed hiring Vaux in 1887 to design an additional wing on the south side of the museum. "I never could take Jessup quite seriously," Vaux later confided to Olmsted, "he is so inconsistent." Vaux "revenged himself" on Jessup for denying him the museum job (the work went to J. C. Cady) "by compelling him to employ me on his C. A. [Children's Aid] Building through C. L. Brace" (Vaux to Olmsted, January 29, 1893).

42. *Thirty-Second Annual Report of the Children's Aid Society* (1884), 56.

43. In order to provide more women and children the chance to escape the slums in summer, the society asked Vaux in 1888 and 1889 to draw plans for several cottages and a second, smaller sanitarium building. The archives of the society preserve a contract dated March 20, 1888, for two cottages and a contract of September 14, 1889, for a sanitarium.

44. *Forty-Second Annual Report of the Children's Aid Society* (1894), 24.

45. It may have been as a result of her knowledge of Vaux's work for the Children's Aid Society that in 1887 Mariana Arnot Ogden turned to him to design the Arnot-Ogden Memorial Hospital in Elmira, New York. Unfortunately, Vaux's three-wing brick structure for 25 patients was demolished in 1963. Another social institution that employed Vaux was the New York Juvenile Asylum. In 1890, while A. H. Green chaired the reform school's building committee, Vaux designed the House of Reception. Located at 106 West 27th Street, it served as a temporary detention center until it was demolished in 1909. Vaux and Radford had also remodeled the asylum's building at 30 West 24th Street. See the *Thirty-Eighth Annual Report of the New York Juvenile Asylum* (1890), 15, and the *Thirty-Ninth Annual Report of the New York Juvenile Asylum* (1891), 14.

46. Calvert Vaux, "A Plea for the Artistic Unity of Central Park," *New York Times*, August 27, 1879, 5.

47. "The Mismanagement of the Park: Mr. Calvert Vaux on Its Present Condition and Remedies," *New York Times*, September 8, 1879, 8.

48. McEntee Diary, May 7, 1886.

49. The board voted to hire Vaux as superintending landscape architect at a salary of $2,500 and to make Munckwitz his assistant at $1,500 on November 19, 1881 ("Park Department Affairs," *New York Times*, November 20, 1881).

50. See "Park Department Affairs," *New York Times*, December 28, 1882, 8. Vaux tendered his resignation on December 27.

51. "Site of the Fair," *New York Times*, August 15, 1880, 6.

52. "The Site of the Fair," *New-York Daily Tribune*, August 15, 1881, 6.

53. Vaux to Olmsted, January 1, 1881. Vaux further explained his plan to Olmsted in a letter of January 4, 1881.

54. Olmsted to Vaux, January 5, 1881, Vaux Papers. See also Olmsted to Vaux, January 3, 1881, in the same collection.

55. Another engineering project of the early 1880s for which Vaux and Radford prepared designs was the Harlem River Bridge, connecting Manhattan with the Bronx across the Harlem River near the High Bridge Aqueduct. In a controversial decision, however, the Bridge Commission awarded the contract to another firm. See "The New Harlem River Bridge," *Building* 5 (July 31, 1886): 49–50.

56. See Olmsted to Grace, August 6, 1885, and "Where Shall the Monument Be," an unlabeled newspaper clipping in the Olmsted Papers.

57. Martha Lamb, "Riverside Park: The Fashionable Drive of the Future," *The Manhattan* 4 (July 1884): 53. On Vaux's role in the later development of Riverside Park, see "Improving the Parks," *New York Times*, July 3, 1888, 8. On April 5, 1889, J. H. Morse visited Vaux in the Arsenal building in Central Park, where the architect showed him "rolls of drawings—'studies,' he called them, for the new Riverside Park, the principal being of a proposed projection into North River, near 80th Street, for a boat approach." (See Morse Diary, April 5, 1889.) Morse credits Vaux with "all details of Riverside Park west of the drive" in his obituary in *Appleton's Cyclopedia* (New York, 1895), 20:599. However, little of this work survives.

58. In the early twentieth century, the drive was continued to Dyckman Street. Later, the West Side Drive was laid out along the river, on former park land.

59. "Monument to Grant," *New York Times*, July 25, 1886, 3.

60. Drawings for the area are in the Municipal Archives.

61. Olmsted to Crimmins, July 2, 1887.

62. Calvert Vaux and Frederick L. Olmsted, *General Plan for the Improvement of Morningside Park* (New York, 1887).

63. For Vaux's ideas on how to plant rows of elms along the park border, see his letter to Olmsted, November 12, 1889.

64. Richardson to Olmsted, February 6, 1883.

65. Olmsted to J. T. Gardner, October 3, 1879, Gardner Papers, New York State Library, Albany, N.Y.

66. C. Vaux, "Letters from the People: A National Park at Niagara," *New-York Daily Tribune*, October 5, 1878, 4.

67. F. L. Olmsted to J. C. Olmsted, December 13, [1886].

68. On February 2, McEntee had gone with Vaux to the Jackson Ironworks in New York to see the railing that he had designed for Niagara Reservation.

69. Vaux, "Letters from the People."

70. The present Luna Island Bridge replaces Vaux's original structure.

71. McEntee Diary, January 7 and May 19, 1886. Vaux was also helping McEntee subdivide the property around his Rondout studio for sale as building lots.

72. Olmsted to Vaux, April 16, 1887. On other occasions, Olmsted had tried to bring Vaux in on his projects. In a letter from John C. Olmsted to Mary Vaux of October 11, 1889, Olmsted's son says that his father had sought in 1887 to have Vaux hired with him for work in Prospect Park, where he would have assigned "a larger share of the proposed compensation to Mr. Vaux," and in Rochester, where Olmsted was designing a park system.

73. Elizabeth Stevenson, *Park Maker: A Life of Frederick Law Olmsted* (New York, 1977), 372.

74. Vaux, "Street Planning," 141.

75. S. Parsons Jr., "The Evolution of a City Square," *Scribner's Magazine* 12 (August 1892): 112, and "Central Park Inquiry," *New-York Daily Tribune*, April 14, 1892, 4.

76. See "Opening Jackson Park," *New-York Daily Tribune*, August 27, 1888, 2; drawings dated December 15, 1891, and January 12, 1892, in the Municipal Archives for the exten-

sion of East River Park, which included the Archibald Gracie house (c. 1813) on Horn's Hook; "Design for Improvement of the Public Place at the Intersection of the Boulevard, Ninth Avenue and 66th St.," signed by Vaux (c. 1890), in the Municipal Archives; DPP, Minutes, August 12, 1891, where the landscape architect is instructed to make a plan for Rutger's Slip Park; and "Corlears Hook Park," *Garden and Forest* 7 (October 24, 1894): 422–423. Other items related to the latter park, for which a drawing exists in the Municipal Archives, are found in DPP, Minutes, January 24 and May 16, 1894, and January 11, 1895, and in "Notes," *Garden and Forest* 9 (July 1, 1896): 270. (Jeanette Park, which was created by filling in Coentis Slip, was apparently entirely the work of Parsons. See "Jeanette Park, New York," *Garden and Forest* 3 [October 15, 1890]: 498–499.) Much of what Vaux did as landscape architect in the Office of Design at the Department of Public Parks is probably lost to history. Miscellaneous references attest to his involvement with plans for laying out a plaza at Fifth Avenue and 110th Street ("New Central Park Plaza," *New York Times*, July 15, 1888, 7), for planting trees along 72nd Street between Ninth and Tenth Avenues (Vaux to J. H. Robb, September 20, 1888, Olmsted Papers, and Vaux, "Street Planning," 139–140); for designing the site in Washington Square for Stanford White's Centennial Arch (DPP, Minutes, March 6, April 18 and 30, 1890, and drawings dating from June 1890 in the Municipal Archives); for laying out small parks on Park Avenue between 56th and 67th Streets ("Department of Public Parks," *Appleton's Annual Cyclopedia* [New York, 1891], 586); for designing the location of the Columbus Monument at 59th Street and Eighth Avenue (DPP, Minutes, July 5, 1892); for erecting a shelter in Cedar Park in the Bronx (DPP, Minutes, February 15, 1893); for preparing a plan for Cathedral Parkway (DPP, Minutes, February 15, 1893; for Vaux's ideas about how to best to treat this street and the area around the Cathedral of St. John the Divine, see his essay "Street Planning," 145–146); for laying out a children's playground in East River Park (DPP, Minutes, April 20, 1893); and for designing the Fifth Avenue entrance to Richard Morris Hunt's addition to the Metropolitan Museum of Art ("Museum's New Wing," *Sun*, November 8, 1895, 7, and drawings in the Municipal Archives).

77. Vaux, "Letters from the People," 4. Drawings for the Greeley Square dating from 1890 and signed by Vaux are in the Municipal Archives.

78. Jacob A. Riis, "The Clearing of Mulberry Bend: The Story of the Rise and Fall of a Typical New York Slum," *Review of Reviews* 12 (August 1895): 172.

79. Morse, "Calvert Vaux," 599.

80. Jacob A. Riis, *The Making of an American* (New York, 1934), 183.

81. Drawings in the Municipal Archives for the greenhouse are dated October 31, 1888; those for the elephant house were prepared in March 1889.

82. "A Crisis in the History of Central Park," *Garden and Forest* 2 (October 2, 1889), 409. Vaux appears to have been less opposed to the idea of housing the exhibition in Manhattan Square, on land reserved for the as yet unbuilt portions of the American Museum of Natural History. Over lunch at the Cooper Hotel on Astor Place, he told Albert Bickmore that it would be difficult to deny the erection of temporary buildings there if the items to be exhibited "were to be of a natural history character and international in selection" and the landscape work in place were preserved (Vaux to Olmsted, November 12, [1889]).

83. Olmsted to Towne, October 2, 1889. Two years later, Olmsted made a similar statement to his friend Paul Dana. Vaux, Olmsted said, "is absolutely the most ingenious, industrious and indefatigable man in his profession of all that I have known for the study of plans to meet complicated requirement of convenience, and the most fertile in expedients for accomplishing difficult ends in this respect" (Olmsted to Dana, March 12, 1891, Olmsted Office Letterbook).

84. "Central Park and the Exposition," *Garden and Forest* 2 (November 27, 1889): 565.

85. Editorial in *Garden and Forest*, 3 (May 21, 1890): 246.

86. Olmsted to H. R. Towne, October 2, 1889.

87. Olmsted to Dana, February 24, 1891. In this same spirit, Vaux had recommended

the creation of a small playground in the park, west of the Kinderberg rustic shelter. He told Dana in the winter of 1891 that he considered the project "upon the ground of expediency and as a means of heading off something else which might be more undesirable." The leading idea of the scheme was a large playroom building that Vaux proposed to construct spanning the 65th Street transverse road. The building, which would have rested on metal arches resembling those of Vaux's 1889 Terrace Bridge in Prospect Park, never got beyond the drawings that Vaux made for it. Surely the playroom was a casualty of the speedway controversy of the following year. In 1894, Vaux was successful in having his plans for the path system in the northeast section of the park accepted and implemented (DPP, Minutes, January 10, 1894).

88. Morse Diary, March 1, 1891.

89. "Woolson Fails to Appear; Commissioners of Accounts Recommend Mr. Vaux's Removal," *New York Times*, April 13, 1892, 3, and "Park Management Censured," *New-York Daily Tribune*, June 10, 1892, 11.

90. W. Stiles to Olmsted, April 18, 1892.

91. Morse Diary, May 8 and 15, 1892.

92. After splitting from Vaux in the spring of 1892, Radford went on a trip to England before settling in San Francisco. His ungracious description of Vaux's behavior had amounted to an attack on Vaux's integrity and professional ability and had deeply troubled Olmsted.

93. "Death of Mrs. Calvert Vaux," *Kingston Weekly Leader*, August 13, 1892, 1.

94. J. Bigelow, Manuscript Diary, April 14, 1873, Rare Books and Manuscripts Division, New York Public Library, Astor, Lenox, and Tilden Foundations, New York. Bigelow was referring to the Greater New York Commission, which was created in 1890 to expedite the consolidation of the various municipalities into one city government. Green, whose dream it was to see the vast urban area thus joined, presided over the committee, with J. S. T. Stranahan of Brooklyn as vice president. Vaux was one of the nine other members of the commission. Green's vision for a bridge across the Hudson to match the Brooklyn Bridge had to wait until 1931, when the George Washington Bridge was constructed.

95. Ibid., January 21, 1894.

96. A. H. Green, *Preservation of the Historic City Hall of New York* (New York, 1894), quoted in Stokes, *Iconography of Manhattan Island*, 5:2016–2017.

97. Bigelow Diary, April 30, 1894.

98. Editorial in *Garden and Forest* 5 (October 5, 1892): 470.

99. The history of this episode can be traced in the Bigelow Diary, October 7, 24, and 28 and November 5 and 14, 1893.

100. DPP, Minutes, January 19, 1893.

101. Vaux to Olmsted, January 29, 1893.

102. Olmsted to Vaux, summer 1894. In this same letter, Olmsted tells Vaux of efforts to save the Palisades from destruction (some businessmen wanted to blast away the rock to make paving stone). Plans were under way, said Olmsted, to mount a campaign similar to the one that had saved Niagara. Olmsted told the promoter of the movement to have New Jersey take over the great cliffs for a park that Vaux "long since had seen the danger to the Palisades" to which his correspondent was "just waking up" and would be "better able than I should be even after considerable study" to advise him. The dream of saving the Palisades was greatly advanced by Andrew Green in 1895, when he founded the Trustees of Scenic and Historic Places and Objects, later known as the American Scenic and Historic Preservation Society. As a result of the efforts of this society and other groups, the Inter-State Palisades Park Commission came into being in 1901.

103. "Harlem River Speedway," *Garden and Forest* 7 (August 8, 1894): 311.

104. "New York's Proposed Speed-Road," *Garden and Forest* 6 (October 18, 1893): 431. Vaux and Parsons had designed nearby High Bridge Park in 1888.

105. *American Architect and Building News* 46 (December 8, 1894): 98.

106. "President Clausen Out," *New York Times*, January 2, 1895, 3.

107. Olmsted to C. D. F. Burns, Secretary of the Park Commission, March 9, 1895.

108. Olmsted to Stiles, March 10, 1895.

109. "Bridge for North Siders," *New York Times*, April 11, 1895, 16. The Harlem River Speedway was first opened for use on June 26, 1898.

110. Olmsted and Vaux to Benjamin Odell, Mayor of Newburgh, December 7, 1889.

111. David Schuyler, "Belated Honor to a Prophet: Newburgh's Downing Park," *Landscape* 31 (1991): 13. In his "Memorandum," Vaux also indicated 1894 as the year in which he undertook the design of St. John Park (present Rockwood Park) in St. Johns, New Brunswick. Downing, who frequently summered with relatives in New Brunswick, completed the park plan in 1899.

112. Vaux to Olmsted, November 12, [1889]. Vaux's sketch, labeled Plan 4, as well as several other plans for the park, is preserved at the Olmsted National Historic Site in Brookline, Massachusetts.

113. Vaux, "Letters from the People," 4.

114. The Downing Park Planning Committee is presently directing the restoration of this historic park.

115. A. M. Vail, "Bronx Park," *Garden and Forest* 4 (July 8, 1891): 314.

116. "More Funds Needed," *New-York Daily Tribune*, December 7, 1895, 5. See DPP, Minutes for August 21, 1895, for the park commissioners' approval of Vaux's plans, and October 22, 1895, for their acceptance by the board of managers of the New York Botanical Garden.

117. C. Bowyer Vaux to John C. Olmsted, November 22, 1895, Frances Loeb Library, Graduate School of Design, Harvard University.

118. "Calvert Vaux Drowned," *Sun*, November 22, 1895, 3.

119. Olmsted lived on until 1903 as a patient at the McLean Asylum in Waverly, Massachusetts.

120. C. Bowyer Vaux to John C. Olmsted, December 8, 1895, Loeb Library. Vaux is buried in the family plot in Montrepose Cemetery in Kingston, New York.

BIBLIOGRAPHY

MANUSCRIPT SOURCES

Brookline, Massachusetts
 Frederick Law Olmsted National Historic Site, National Park Service
  Olmsted firm records

Cambridge, Massachusetts
 Graduate School of Design, Harvard University, Frances Loeb Library
  Olmsted Collection

New York, New York
 American Museum of Natural History
  Albert Bickmore Autobiography

 Municipal Archives of the City of New York
  Drawings relating to Central Park and other projects

 New-York Historical Society
  Alfred J. Bloor Diary
  Fraternity Papers
   C. Vaux, "The Palisades" (1878)
  James Herbert Morse Diary
  George Templeton Strong Diary

 New York Public Library, Astor, Lenox, and Tilden Foundations, Rare Books and
  Manuscripts Division
  John Bigelow Papers
  Calvert Vaux Papers

Philadelphia, Pennsylvania
 Historical Society of Pennsylvania
  Centennial Exhibition Collection
  John Jay Smith Papers

Washington, D.C.
  Library of Congress, Manuscript Division
    Frederick Law Olmsted Papers
    Whitelaw Reid Papers

  Smithsonian Institution, Archives of American Art
    Jervis McEntee Diary
    Jervis McEntee Papers

BOOKS, ARTICLES, AND DISSERTATIONS

Alex, William, and George B. Tatum. *Calvert Vaux, Architect and Planner.* New York, 1994.

Allen, Oliver E. *The Tiger: The Rise and Fall of Tammany Hall.* Reading, MA, 1993.

André, Edouard. *L'art des jardins: Traité général de la composition des parcs et jardins.* Paris, 1879.

Andrews, Malcolm. *The Search for the Picturesque: Landscape Aesthetics and Tourism in Britain, 1760–1800.* Stanford, CA, 1989.

Armstrong, William M. *E. L. Godkin: A Biography.* Albany, NY, 1978.

Baker, Paul R. *Richard Morris Hunt.* Cambridge, MA, 1980.

Bellows, Henry W. *Historical Sketch of the Union League Club of New York.* New York, 1879.

Bernstein, Gerald S. "In Pursuit of the Exotic: Islamic Forms in Nineteenth-Century American Architecture." Ph.D. diss., University of Pennsylvania, 1968.

Beveridge, Charles. *Frederick Law Olmsted: Designing the American Landscape.* New York, 1995.

Beveridge, Charles, and Kowsky, Francis. *The Distinctive Charms of Niagara Scenery: Frederick Law Olmsted and the Niagara Reservation.* Niagara Falls, NY, 1985.

Bigelow, John. *Retrospective of an Active Life.* 2 vols. New York, 1913.

Book of the Fairs: Materials about World's Fairs, 1834–1916, in the Smithsonian Institution Libraries. Chicago, 1992.

Boyer, M. Christine. *Manhattan Manners, Architecture, and Style, 1850–1900.* New York, 1985.

Braceland, Francis J. *The Institute of Living: The Hartford Retreat, 1822–1972.* Hartford, 1972.

Bremer, Fredrika. *The Homes of the New World: Impressions of America.* 2 vols. Trans. Mary Howitt. New York, 1853.

Brooks, Michael W. *John Ruskin and Victorian Architecture.* Brunswick, NJ, 1987.

Brown, Charles H. *William Cullen Bryant.* New York, 1971.

Burns, Sarah. *Pastoral Inventions: Rural Life in Nineteenth-Century American Art and Culture.* Philadelphia, 1989.

Caruthers, J. Wade. *Octavius Brooks Frothingham, Gentle Radical.* Selma, AL, 1977.

Clapp, Margaret. *Forgotten First Citizen: John Bigelow.* Boston, 1947.

Commonwealth Historic Resource Management. *The Landscape of Parliament Hill: A History and Inventory.* Ottawa, 1991.

Conway, Hazel. *People's Parks: The Design and Development of Victorian Parks in Britain.* Cambridge, 1991.

Cook, Clarence. *A Description of the New York Central Park.* New York, 1869.

Creese, Walter. *The Crowning of the American Landscape: Eight Great Spaces and Their Buildings.* Princeton, 1985.

Dahl, C. *Stephen C. Earle, Architect: Shaping Worcester's Image.* Worcester, 1987.

Darby, Michael. *The Islamic Perspective: An Aspect of British Architecture and Design in the Nineteenth Century.* London, 1983.

Dermott, Henry W. *A History of the Bank of New York, 1784–1884.* New York, 1884.

Dickason, David H. *The Daring Young Men: The Story of the American Pre-Raphaelites.* Bloomington, IN, 1953.

Dixon, Roger, and Stefan Muthesius. *Victorian Architecture.* London, 1978.

Downing, Andrew Jackson. *Cottage Residences*. 4th ed. New York, 1852.

————. *A Treatise on the Practice of Landscape Gardening*. 6th ed. New York, 1859.

Downing, Antoinette F., and Vincent Scully Jr. *The Architectural Heritage of Newport, Rhode Island, 1640–1915*. 2d ed. New York, 1967.

Downs, Arthur C., Jr. "Downing's Newburgh Villa." *Bulletin of the Association for Preservation Technology* 4 (1972): 1–113.

————. *Downing and the American Home*. Newton Square, PA, 1988.

Dunwell, Frances F. *The Hudson River Highlands*. New York, 1990.

Edwards, Paul. *English Garden Ornaments*. London, 1965.

El-Wakil, Leila. *Batir La Campagne: Geneve, 1800–1860*. 2 vols. Geneva, 1988.

Emerson, Ralph Waldo. *Nature*. Boston, 1836.

Feldman, S. K. *A Selection of Drawings by Jervis McEntee from the Lockwood DeForest Collection*. New York, 1976.

Ferber, Linda, and William Gerdts. *The New Path: Ruskin and the American Pre-Raphaelites*. New York, 1985.

Flick, Alexander C. *Samuel J. Tilden: A Study in Political Sagacity*. New York, 1939.

Foord, John. *The Life and Public Service of Andrew Haswell Green*. New York, 1913.

Forbush, B. *The Sheppard and Enoch Pratt Hospital*. Philadelphia, 1972.

Ford, James. *Slums and Housing with Special Reference to New York City: History, Conditions, and Policy*. 2 vols. Cambridge, MA, 1936.

Francis, Dennis S. *Architects in Practice: New York City, 1840–1900*. New York, 1980.

Francis, Dennis S., and Joy Kestenbaum. "Calvert Vaux." In *The MacMillan Encyclopedia of Architects*, 4 vols. New York, 1981, 4:303–304.

Frothingham, Octavius Brooks. *Recollections and Impressions, 1822–1890*. New York, 1891.

Gratacap, L. P. "The Making of a Museum." *Architectural Record* 9 (1900): 376–402.

Hall, Edward H. "A Short Biography of Andrew Haswell Green." In *Ninth Annual Report of the American Scenic and Historic Preservation Society*. New York, 1904, 113–220.

Hamilton, J. Crawford. "Snap Shots in Central Park." *Munsey's Magazine* 6 (1891): 3–10.

Hammack, David. *Power and Society: Greater New York at the Turn of the Century*. New York, 1982.

Handbook for Prospect Park, Brooklyn, L.I. New York, 1874.

Hecksher, Morrison. "The Metropolitan Museum of Art: An Architectural History." *Metropolitan Museum of Art Bulletin* (Summer 1995): 3–80.

Hersey, George L. *High Victorian Gothic: A Study in Associationism*. Baltimore, 1972.

Hibbard, Shirley. *Rustic Adornments for Homes of Taste*. London, 1856.

Hiss, Tony. *The Experience of Place*. New York, 1990.

A History of Real Estate, Building and Architecture in New York City. New York, 1898: reprint, New York, 1967.

Hitchcock, Henry-Russell. *The Architecture of H. H. Richardson and His Times*. Cambridge, MA, 1961.

————. *Architecture, Nineteenth and Twentieth Centuries*. Baltimore, 1963.

Holli, M. G., and P. Jones. *Biographical Dictionary of American Mayors, 1820–1980: Big City Mayors*. Westport, CT, 1980.

Howe, Katherine S., and Alice C. Frelinghuysen. *Herter Brothers: Furniture and Interiors for a Gilded Age*. New York, 1994.

Howe, Winifred E. *A History of the Metropolitan Museum of Art*. 2 vols. New York, 1913.

Huehner, Leon. "Andrew H. Green: A Tribute to His Memory." *American Hebrew* (November 20, 1903): 12.

Hughes, John A. *Garden Architecture and Landscape Gardening*. London, 1866.

Hunt, John D. *Gardens and the Picturesque: Studies in the History of Landscape Architecture*. Cambridge, MA, 1992.

Jackson, Kenneth. *Crabgrass Frontier: The Suburbanization of the United States*. New York, 1985.

Kalfus, Melvin. *Frederick Law Olmsted: The Passion of a Public Artist*. New York, 1990.

Kelly, F., et al. *Frederic Edwin Church.* Washington, 1989.

Kemp, Edward. *How to Lay Out a Garden: A General Guide in Choosing, Forming, or Improving an Estate.* 2d ed. London, 1858.

Kennedy, John M. "Philanthropy and Science in New York City: The American Museum of Natural History, 1868–1968." Ph.D. diss., Yale University, 1968.

Kowsky, Francis R. "Gallaudet College: A High Victorian Campus." In *Records of the Columbia Historical Society.* Charlottesville, 1973, 439–467.

_____. *The Architecture of Frederick Clarke Withers and the Progress of the Gothic Revival in America after 1850.* Middletown, CT, 1980.

_____. "H. H. Richardson's Ames Gate Lodge and the Romantic Landscape Tradition." *Journal of the Society of Architectural Historians* 50 (1991): 181–182.

_____, ed. *The Best Planned City: The Olmsted Legacy in Buffalo.* Buffalo, 1992.

Kruft, Hanno-Walter. *A History of Architectural Theory from Vitruvius to the Present.* Trans. R. Taylor, E. Callander, and A. Wood. Princeton, 1994.

Lancaster, Clay. *Prospect Park Handbook.* Brooklyn, 1988.

Landau, Sarah Bradford. *Edward T. and William A. Potter: American Victorian Architects.* New York, 1979.

_____. *P. B. Wight: Architect, Contractor, and Critic, 1838–1925.* Chicago, 1981.

Landau, Sarah Bradford, and Carl W. Condit. *Rise of the New York Skyscraper, 1865–1913.* New Haven, 1996.

Lasdun, Susan. *The English Park: Royal, Private and Public.* London, 1991.

Lockridge, Richard. *Darling of Misfortune: Edwin Booth, 1833–1893.* New York, 1932.

Lynch, Anne C. "A Sketch of Washington City." *Harper's New Monthly Magazine* 6 (December 1852): 1–15.

McCoy, G. "Jervis McEntee's Diary." *Journal of the Archives of American Art* 8 (1968): 32–57.

Magonigle, H. Van Buren. "A Half Century of Architecture, 1: Biographical Review." *Pencil Points* 14 (1933): 474–480.

Major, Judith K. *To Live in the World: A. J. Downing and American Landscape Gardening.* Cambridge, MA, 1997.

Matzdorf, David W. "Calvert Vaux, 1824–1895." General Studies thesis, Architectural Association, 1977.

Meyer, Annie Nathan. *My Park Book.* New York, 1898.

Miller, Angela. *The Empire of the Eye: Landscape Representation and American Cultural Politics.* Ithaca, NY, 1993.

Mills, Louis Van Orden. *A History of Hillside Cemetery and the Community It Serves, 1861–1994.* Middletown, NY, 1994.

[Morse, James H.] "Calvert Vaux." In *Appleton's Annual Cyclopedia.* New York, 1895, 598.

Myers, Kenneth. *The Catskills: Painters, Writers, and Tourists in the Mountains, 1820–1895.* Yonkers, NY, 1988.

Myles, Janet. *L. N. Cottingham (1787–1847), Architect of the Gothic Revival.* London, 1996.

Nevins, Allan, and Milton Thomas, eds. *The Diary of George Templeton Strong: Young Man in New York, 1835–1849.* 4 vols. New York, 1952.

Nutt, Charles. *History of Worcester and Its People.* 2 vols. New York, 1919.

Nutt, John J., comp. *Newburgh: Her Institutions, Industries and Leading Citizens.* Newburgh, NY, 1891.

Oakey, Alexander F. *Home Grounds.* New York, 1881.

O'Donnell, Patricia, and David Schuyler. *Andrew Jackson Downing Memorial Park, Newburgh, New York: Comprehensive Master Plan Report.* Newburgh, 1989.

Olmsted, Frederick Law. *The Papers of Frederick Law Olmsted.* Ed. Charles MacLaughlin; Charles Beveridge, series editor. 8 vols. to date. Baltimore, 1977– .

Olmsted, Frederick L., Jr., and Theodora Kimball, eds. *Frederick Law Olmsted, Landscape Architect, 1822–1903: Forty Years of Landscape Architecture.* 2 vols. New York, 1922–1928; reprint, New York, 1970.

O'Malley, Therese. "'A Public Museum of Trees': Mid-Nineteenth-Century Plans for the Mall." In *The Mall in Washington, 1791–1991*, ed. Richard Longstreth. Washington, 1991, 61–78.

Parsons, Samuel, Jr. "Home and Society: Grace Church Lawn." *Century* 2 (October 1882): 954–955.

_____. "The Evolution of a City Square." *Scribner's Magazine* 12 (August 1892): 107–116.

_____. "Small Country Places." *Scribner's Magazine* 11 (March 1892): 302–315.

_____. *Landscape Gardening.* New York, 1895.

_____. *Landscape Gardening Studies.* New York, 1910.

_____. *The Art of Landscape Architecture.* New York, 1915.

_____, ed. *Hints on Landscape Gardening by Prince von Puckler-Muskau.* Trans. B. Sickert. Boston, 1917.

Peck, Amelia, ed. *Alexander Jackson Davis: American Architect, 1803–1892.* New York, 1992.

Perkins, Frederick B. *The Central Park.* New York, 1862.

Phillips, Sandra S., and Linda Weintraub, eds. *Charmed Places: Hudson River Artists and Their Houses, Studios, and Vistas.* New York, 1988.

Pumpelly, Raphael. *My Reminiscences.* 2 vols. New York, 1918.

Pursuit of Beauty: Americans and the Aesthetic Movement. New York, 1987.

Quincy, J. P. "Memoir of Octavius Brooks Frothingham." *Proceedings of the Massachusetts Historical Society* 2 (1896): 507–539.

Reed, Henry Hope, and Sophia Duckworth. *Central Park: A History and a Guide.* New York, 1967.

Reed, Henry Hope, R. M. McGee, and Esther Mipaas. *Bridges of Central Park.* New York, 1990.

Rhoads, William. "The Resurrection of Calvert Vaux." *Hudson Valley* 18 (1989): 102–104, 114–117.

Riis, Jacob. "The Clearing of Mulberry Bend: The Story of the Rise and Fall of a Typical New York Slum." *Review of Reviews* 12 (August 1895): 172–173.

_____. *The Peril and the Preservation of the Home.* Philadelphia, 1903.

Robinson, William. "Public Gardens: The Central Park, New York." *Garden* 1 (1872): 544–545.

Roper, Laura Wood. *FLO: A Biography of Frederick Law Olmsted.* Baltimore, 1973.

Rosenzweig, Roy, and Elizabeth Blackmar. *The Park and the People: A History of Central Park.* Ithaca, NY, 1992.

Saville, Jennifer. "Jervis McEntee (1828–1891), Artist of Melancholy." Master's thesis, University of Delaware, 1982.

Schuyler, David. *The New Urban Landscape: The Redefinition of City Form in Nineteenth-Century America.* Baltimore, 1986.

_____. *Apostle of Taste: Andrew Jackson Downing, 1815–1852.* Baltimore, 1996.

Schuyler, Montgomery. "Concerning Queen Anne." In *American Architecture and Other Writings by Montgomery Schuyler,* ed. W. H. Jordy and R. C. Coe. Cambridge, MA, 1961, 2:227–261.

Severini, Lois. *The Architecture of Finance: Early Wall Street.* Ann Arbor, 1981.

Sheldon, George W. *Artistic Houses.* 2 vols. New York, 1884.

_____. *Artistic Country Seats: Types of Recent American Villa and Cottage Architecture.* New York, 1885–1886.

Sherman, Frederick B. *From the Guadalquivir to the Golden Gate.* Mill Valley, CA, 1977.

Sigle, John D. "Calvert Vaux, an American Architect." Master's thesis, University of Virginia, 1967.

_____, comp. *Bibliography of the Life and Works of Calvert Vaux. Papers of the American Association of Architectural Biographers,* vol. 5. Charlottesville, 1968.

Simo, Melanie Louise. *Loudon and the Landscape: From County to Metropolis, 1783–1843.* New Haven, 1988.

Smith, Charles H. J. *Landscape Gardening.* New York, 1853.

Stein, Susan, ed. *The Architecture of Richard Morris Hunt*. Chicago, 1986.

Stephenson, Sue Honaker. *Rustic Furniture*. New York, 1979

Stevenson, Elizabeth. *Park Maker: A Life of Frederick Law Olmsted*. New York, 1977.

Stewart, John J. "Notes on Calvert Vaux's 1873 Design for the Public Grounds of the Parliament Buildings in Ottawa." *Bulletin of the Association for Preservation Technology* 8 (1976): 6–7.

Stokes, I. N. Phelps. *The Iconography of Manhattan Island, 1498–1909*. 6 vols. New York, 1926.

Sweeting, Adam. *Reading Houses and Building Books: Andrew Jackson Downing and the Architecture of Popular Antebellum Literature, 1835–1855*. Hanover, NH, 1996.

Tatum, George B. and Elizabeth B. MacDougall, eds. *Prophet with Honor: The Career of Andrew Jackson Downing, 1815–1852*. Washington, 1989.

Thornton, Tamara P. *Cultivating Gentlemen: The Meaning of Country Life among the Boston Elite, 1785–1860*. New Haven, 1989.

Truefitt, George. *Architectural Sketches on the Continent*. London, 1847.

_____. *Designs for Country Churches*. Manchester, 1850.

United States Centennial Commission. *International Exhibition, 1876: Report of the Director-General*. Washington, 1880.

Upjohn, Everard M. *Richard Upjohn, Architect and Churchman*. New York, 1939.

Van Zanten, David. "Jacob Wrey Mould: Echoes of Owen Jones and the High Victorian Styles in New York, 1853–1865." *Journal of the Society of Architectural Historians* 28 (1969): 41–57.

[Vaux, C. Bowyer.] "Calvert Vaux, Designer of Parks." *Parks International* 1 (September 1920): 139–140.

Vaux, Calvert. "Should a Republic Encourage the Arts?" *Horticulturist* 7 (February 1852): 73–77.

_____. "American Architecture." *Horticulturist* 8 (April 1853): 168–172.

_____. "Hints for Country House Builders." *Harper's New Monthly Magazine* 11 (November 1855): 763–778.

_____. "Parisian Buildings for City Residents." *Harper's Weekly* 1 (December 19, 1857): 809–810.

_____. *Villas and Cottages*. New York, 1857; rev. ed., 1864.

_____. "The Central Park of New York: Notes by Calvert Vaux." *New York Times*, July 10, 1864, 5.

_____. "A Philosophical Emperor." *Popular Science Monthly* 11 (1877): 461–469.

_____. "A City Zoological Garden." *New York Times*, March 3, 1878, 10.

_____. "A Plea for the Artistic Unity of Central Park." *New York Times*, August 27, 1879, 5.

_____. *Official Correspondence, etc. in Reference to the Plan for the Arrangement of the Public Grounds in Front of the Parliament Buildings at Ottawa, Dominion of Canada*. New York, 1882.

_____. "Landscape Gardening." In *Encyclopedia Britannica*, supplement. New York, 1886, 562–564.

_____. "Church Grounds." *Churchman* 55 (June 4, 1887): 641–642.

_____. "Street Planning in Relation to Architectural Design." *Proceedings of the Architectural League of New York* (1889): 135–146.

Vaux, Calvert, and Frederick L. Olmsted. *Description of a Plan for the Improvement of the Central Park*. New York, 1858.

_____. *Preliminary Report to the Commissioners for Laying Out a Park in Brooklyn: Being a Consideration of Circumstances of Site and Other Conditions Affecting the Design of Public Pleasure Grounds*. Brooklyn, 1866.

_____. "Architect's Report." In *Documents of the Ninety-Second Legislature of the State of New Jersey*. Jersey City, 1868, 891–897.

_____. "Report Accompanying a Design for Washington Park." In Board of Commissioners of Prospect Park, *Eighth Annual Report*. Brooklyn, 1868, 77–80.

_____. *Report on the Proposed City Park.* Albany, NY, 1868.

_____. *Preliminary Report Respecting a Public Park in Buffalo.* New York, 1869.

_____. *Two Letters to the President on Recent Changes and Projected Changes in the Central Park.* New York, 1872.

_____. *General Plan for the Improvement of Morningside Park.* New York, 1887.

_____. *General Plan for the Improvement of the Niagara Reservation.* Niagara Falls, NY, 1887.

Vaux, Calvert, and Samuel Parsons, Jr. *Concerning Lawn Planting.* New York, 1881.

Vaux, Downing. "Historical Notes." In *Transactions of the American Society of Landscape Architects* (Harrisburg, 1908), 81–83.

Veiller, Lawrence. *Tenement House Reform in New York, 1834–1900.* New York, 1900.

Weeks, L. *Prominent Families of New York.* New York, 1897.

Weidenmann, Jacob. *Beautifying Country Homes.* New York, 1870; reprint, Watkins Glen, NY, 1978.

Weiss, Jo Ann. "Clarence Cook: His Critical Writings." Ph.D. diss., Johns Hopkins University, 1977.

Wilmerding, John. *American Views.* Princeton, 1991.

Wise, Daniel. *Little Peach Blossom.* New York, 1873.

INDEX

Buildings and parks that Calvert Vaux designed, either alone or in collaboration with others, are listed by location.